D1521565

THE JEWS AND THE EXPANSION OF EUROPE TO THE WEST, 1450 TO 1800

EUROPEAN EXPANSION AND GLOBAL INTERACTION
_____

GENERAL EDITORS
Pieter Emmer, Institute for the History of European Expansion,
    Leiden University
Karen Ordahl Kupperman, New York University
H. G. Roeber, Penn State University

*Published in association with the Forum on European Expansion and
Global Interaction*

VOLUME 1
The Language Encounter in the Americas, 1492 to 1800
Edited by Edward G. Gray and Norman Fiering

VOLUME 2
The Jews and the Expansion of Europe to the West, 1450 to 1800
Edited by Paolo Bernardini and Norman Fiering

THE JEWS AND THE EXPANSION OF EUROPE TO THE WEST, 1450 TO 1800

Edited by
Paolo Bernardini
and
Norman Fiering

Berghahn Books
NEW YORK • OXFORD

Published in 2001 by

Berghahn Books

www.berghahnbooks.com

© 2001 The John Carter Brown Library

Library of Congress Cataloging-in-Publication Data

The Jews and the expansion of Europe to the west, 1450 to 1800 / edited by Paolo
Bernardini and Norman Fiering.
     p.   cm.
Includes bibliographical references (p.   ) and index.
ISBN 1-57181-153-2 (alk. paper)
    1. Jews—Latin America—History. 2. Jews—North America—History.
3. Jews—Migrations. 4. Europe—Emigration and immigration. 5. Latin
America—Emigration and immigration. 6. North America—Emigration and
immigration. I. Bernardini, Paolo. II. Fiering, Norman.

F1419.J4 J52   2000
980'.004924—dc21   99-044924

*This collection of essays derives, selectively, from a conference of the same name held at
the John Carter Brown Library, 15–18 June 1997. The John Carter Brown Library is an
independently funded and administered center for advanced research in history and the
humanities, located at Brown University since 1901. For 150 years the Library has been
collecting books relating to the Americas, North and South, printed before ca. 1825. In
order to facilitate and encourage use of the collection, the Library offers fellowships, sponsors lectures and conferences, regularly mounts exhibitions for the general public, and
publishes catalogues, bibliographies, and other works that interpret its holdings. For further information, write to: Director, John Carter Brown Library, Box 1894, Providence,
Rhode Island 02912, or visit www.JCBL.org.*

British Library Cataloguing in Publication Data

A catalogue record for this book is available from the British Library.

Printed in the United States on acid-free paper.

CONTENTS

LIST OF ILLUSTRATIONS

FIGURES

(Unless otherwise indicated in the figure captions, all of the figures are from the collection of the John Carter Brown Library.)

MAPS

PREFACE

THE PRECISE ORIGINS of the international conference held at the John Carter Brown Library from 15 to 18 June 1997, from which this collection of essays is derived, are impossible to specify. Over the course of six or seven years, various stray ideas, influences, and trends coalesced, until finally we knew what we wanted to do. I will sketch out here some of the elements that contributed to the concept of this book.

The basic idea of approaching the subject of "Jewish" history in the early modern period from an Atlantic and a hemispheric perspective was one that itself had diverse sources. The first Touro National Heritage Trust Research Fellow at the John Carter Brown Library, Judith Laikin Elkin, who arrived in 1990, was also the founder, as it happens, of a new scholarly group, the Latin American Jewish Studies Association. It was evident from talking to Dr. Elkin that the history of "Jews" in Latin America was relatively undeveloped territory, especially for the colonial period. The subsequent Touro Fellows in continuing succession, all concentrating in their research on some aspect of the history of the Jewish experience in the Americas, North or South, prior to ca. 1825, increased our awareness of the validity of a hemispheric approach.

In general, students of the discrete and bounded subject areas of Spanish America, Portuguese America, French America, Dutch America, and English America, which incorporate, as well, diverse populations of African Americans and American Indians, need encouragement and inducement to broaden their horizons. Some fifteen years ago, the Library established a Center for New World Comparative Studies, the purpose of which is to encourage specialists in the colonial period of the Americas to peek over the wall of their academic confinement and try to incorporate the findings of Americanists in geographic areas other than their own.

Jews were settlers throughout the Western Hemisphere and participants (often as *conversos*) in the Spanish, Portuguese, French, Dutch, and English empires. This breadth of involvement, which uniquely cut across the Protestant/Catholic divide, was accidental rather than by design, but the dispersion of the New Christians and Jews—sometimes tolerated, sometimes persecuted—offers unusual opportunities for comparative study.

From 1977 to 1997, a team at the Library—headed initially by John Alden and then for seventeen years by Dennis C. Landis—compiled and edited a massive chronological guide to European books about America printed before 1750. This work, *European Americana* (New Canaan, Conn.: Readex, 1980–1997), available in six hefty volumes, is by far the best bibliography of European commentary about America in the first 250 years following the great Encounter. The work includes books published in seventeen different languages, Hebrew among them, but the editors of the series know that its record of titles in Hebrew is far from complete. Rectifying this particular deficiency was another factor behind the "Jews and the Expansion of Europe" project at the John Carter Brown Library.

In 1991 the Library sponsored a conference, "America in European Consciousness, 1493–1750" (also subsequently published as a book, edited by Prof. Karen Ordahl Kupperman, University of North Carolina Press, 1995), which addressed the question of the development of European awareness of the New World in the three centuries after the Discovery. In that instance, no one formally asked, "What did the Jews of Europe, generally segregated in ghettos and everywhere marginalized, know about the New World, or think about it?" But it was a question that remained to be considered and one pregnant with implication, because, among other things, it was Jewish destiny to find freedom and fulfillment in America as nowhere else.

The John Carter Brown Library was instrumental in the founding in 1994 of the Forum on European Expansion and Global Interaction, as an American counterpart to the Institute for the History of European Expansion at Leiden University. The idea behind this new scholarly organization, FEEGI, is that the contention between so-called "multiculturalists" and "eurocentrists" in the historical profession misses the great point that the global European expansion beginning in ca. 1400 was the single most consequential fact of modern history and deserves close study as a comprehensive, coherent phenomenon, regardless of how that expansion may be morally judged and subdivided.

Giving early modern European expansion its due has the peculiar effect of considerably rearranging the standard European History curriculum in the United States, by compelling academic departments to pay far more attention to the history of Spain, Portugal, and the Netherlands and far less to Germany and Russia than is now customary. As it happens, one cannot study Portugal and the Netherlands without taking into account their significant populations of Jews and of Christians descended from Jews.

In both 1992 and 1993, the Library organized and sponsored four-week-long summer institutes on early modern maritime history, funded by the National Endowment for the Humanities. At the 1993 institute, Jonathan Israel of the University of London delivered a lecture on marginal "in-groups" that had an important impact on Atlantic trade in the colonial period, citing individual merchant networks of Portuguese New Christians, Jews, Huguenots, and Armenians (the last functioning mostly in the Portuguese empire in the east), which made possible trade that crossed conventional political boundaries. Professor Israel's work on this subject—because of its originality and high scholarly merit, and its linking of an aspect of Jewish history to the larger network of world commerce—has been something of an inspiration to the Library.

The problems posed by the conference on the Jews and expansion were not unlike those dealt with at another conference, "Scotland and the Americas, 1600 to 1800," which took place in June 1994 at the John Carter Brown Library. The goal of that conference was manifestly not to celebrate isolated Scottish contributions, as an exercise in "heritage," although the Scots were enormously involved in trade, empire, war, and education. But certain questions arose from the conference quite naturally, such as: Did it make any difference that Scots as a group were participants in any particular event or string of events? The practice of historical research and writing is in good part the development of precise tools for analyzing and describing the past. All of the participants in the conference on Scotland came away with a much more developed sense of who the Scots were and what they did and did not do. Our ambition in collecting essays on the Jews was similar.

The 1997 conference "The Jews and the Expansion of Europe to the West," then, and this resulting book were both founded on three principles that are not commonly applied to "Jewish" history and indeed go against current academic conventions: that when it comes to the study of Jews in the Americas in the early modern period, (1) European history and American history should not be separated; (2) one should also not separate North American history and South American history; and (3) "Jewish" history for this period and this place must include also the thousands of Christians who were descended from Jews (known as New Christians, *Cristãos novos*, in the Portuguese empire and *conversos* in the Spanish empire) for the precise reason that despite their conversion, however far back it occurred and regardless of their actual practices, these people continued to be commonly regarded as "Jewish."

In compiling and editing this book, Dr. Bernardini and I have striven to produce a work that not only contributes to Jewish history but also is illuminating about the New World in general in this period. By making every effort to transcend filiopietism and parochialism, we hope that these essays will be useful and suggestive to a wide range of historians of the Americas who have no particular interest in Jewish history per se.

As is evident from all of the above, this book has numerous origins. We did have, however, for the 1997 conference an informal planning committee whose advice and suggestions were essential to the organization of the program and hence to the contents of this volume. The committee consisted of Mordechai Arbell of the Ben Zvi Institute, Hebrew University; Seymour Drescher of the University of Pittsburgh; Judith Laikin Elkin of the University of Michigan; Jonathan D. Sarna of Brandeis University; and Paolo Bernardini, who has been affiliated with a number of institutions in Europe and the United States, including recently the Institute for Advanced Study in Princeton, New Jersey.

Dr. Bernardini's enthusiasm for this project, above all, was the key factor in our moving ahead. Moreover, the Library's alliance with him, I can say here with pleasure, is not yet over. Dr. Bernardini is compiling the data for an exhibition of books, drawn entirely from our distinguished collection, that will be illustrative of the central theme of this anthology, the Jews and the expansion of Europe to the west. This exhibition has been under consideration for some time, but from the beginning Dr. Bernardini and I believed that the publication of these essays was a necessary prerequisite, since only with this work behind us would it be possible to bring out in an exhibition all of the dimensions of this complicated and largely unrecorded subject.

Numerous agencies and individuals provided grant money and gifts that underwrote the conference and the later editing and production of this volume. We received major support from the Lisbon-based Fundação Luso-Americana para o Desenvolvimento, from InterAmericas/Society of Arts and Letters of the Americas/Sociedad de Artes y Letras de las Américas, from the Rhode Island Committee for the Humanities, and from the Lucius N. Littauer Foundation. In addition, we were helped substantially by the Touro National Heritage Trust, the Abramson Family Foundation, Dr. and Mrs. J. Allen Yager, Joseph F. Cullman III, the Joseph and Rosalyn Sinclair Foundation, the Charles and Donald Salmonson Foundation, and the Ira S. and Anna Galkin Charitable Trust. Mr. Bernard Bell, representing the Touro Trust, was the Library's ally beyond the call of duty in helping us to find the needed funding. Our fondest hope is that these generous supporters are gratified by the material accomplishment seen here, which is of course far outweighed by the intangible results and ramifications.

In the concrete editing of the manuscript and its preparation for the publisher, Dr. Jennifer Curtiss Gage was of indispensable help. In the final stages of formatting and proofreading this complex book, Ms. Shawn Kendrick played a stellar role.

Finally, it would be a mistake to leave the impression that this venture by the John Carter Brown Library into Jewish history in the Atlantic world of the early modern period is now over and done with. A forthcoming exhibition has been mentioned. The Touro National Heritage Trust Fellowship, also mentioned earlier, which was supported formerly by annual grants, has recently been fully endowed by a combination of matching gifts from the Dorot Foundation and the Touro Trust. Hence, Touro Fellows will be coming to the Library in perpetuity. Moreover, in the area of acquisitions, the Library's incentive to collect relevant Judaica has been much enhanced by the revelations in this book.

The John Carter Brown Library's mission is to collect and preserve books, maps, and manuscripts, and to promote research. The entire history of the Americas—from Hudson Bay to Patagonia, from the time of Columbus to the attainment of independence from European domination—falls within the Library's purview. No element of that history is beyond our interest, and the Library has been collecting Judaica-Americana for more than a century. But this field needed definition and consolidation within the larger enterprise of the Library's work, a definition which we feel has been achieved with this publication.

Norman Fiering

Editorial Note

The editors of this volume have attempted to bring as much stylistic and orthographic consistency to the book as a whole as has been practicable. There are some differences among the authors' contributions, however, that we have permitted to remain. For instance, there are numerous ways to transliterate Hebrew letters into English spelling, and we have allowed each author discretion in this matter. Also, systematic use of accents in Spanish names was not common in early manuscripts. In the seventeenth century, the name "Perez" might have appeared without an accent, whereas today it would be written as "Pérez." In these instances as well, we have simply let each author follow his or her preferred practice.

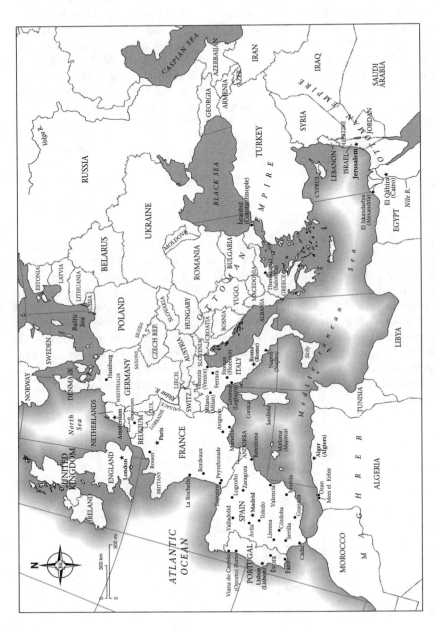

MAP 1 Europe and the Mediterranean

MAP 2   South America

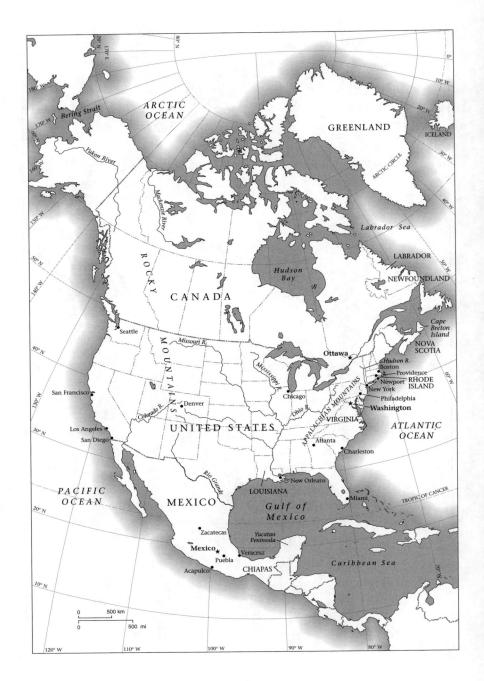

Map 3 North America

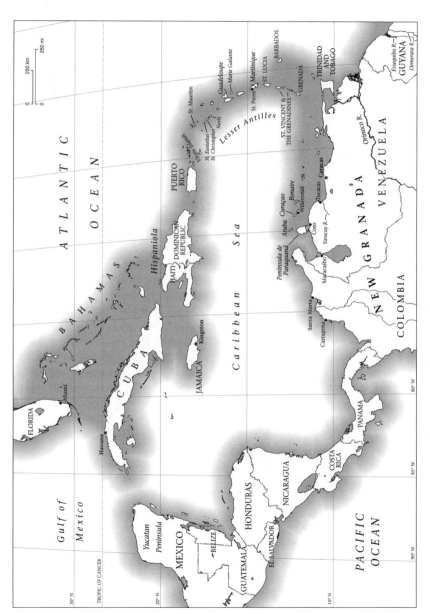

MAP 4 Caribbean Basin

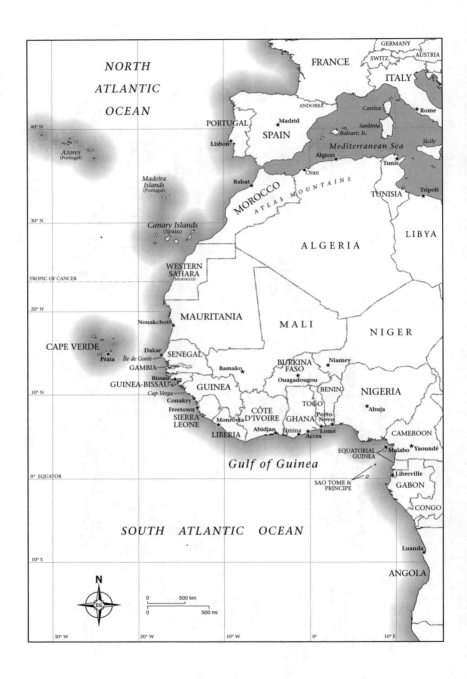

MAP 5 West Africa

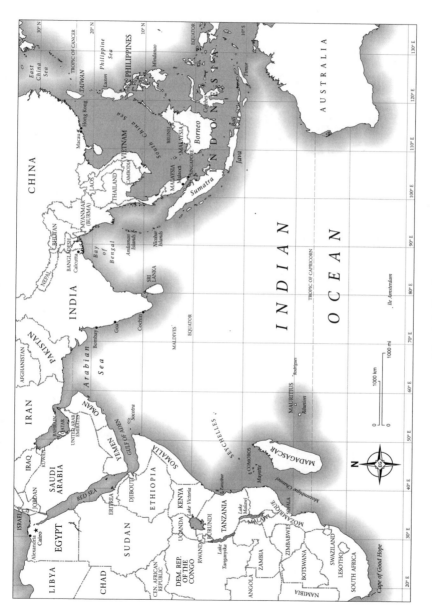

MAP 6 Indian Ocean

A MILDER COLONIZATION: JEWISH EXPANSION TO THE NEW WORLD, AND THE NEW WORLD IN THE JEWISH CONSCIOUSNESS OF THE EARLY MODERN ERA

Paolo Bernardini

I T IS BOTH AN HONOR AND A PLEASURE to write the introductory pages to a book that includes essays written by the major international specialists in the field.[1] In the following pages I attempt to offer the reader a frame of reference for entering the fascinating and complex worlds examined in these essays. Every one of them offers an uncommon perspective and is the result of a major scholarly effort. This volume provides not only a broad overview of the complex encounter(s) between a European ethnic and religious minority and an entire continent newly "discovered" and immediately colonized, but also enlightens us with single, seemingly minor episodes that took place in the shadow of this major encounter. These essays—written by specialists in economic, social, political, and Jewish history, as well as in anthropology and geography—tell a story that has been scarcely told thus far, at least in its entirety. Since the time of the conquest, the Jewish presence in the Americas—North, South, and the Caribbean, as dealt with extensively in this volume—has been extremely meaningful. It is not an exaggeration—as will become clear by reading these essays—to state that Jews, both real Jews and crypto-Jews, marranos and *conversos*, have contributed deeply to the shaping of the political, social, and economic patterns of the New World. The contrary will also prove to be true; the New World has deeply influenced the destiny, as well as the character, of the Jewish "Nation," especially in liberal North America, but also in Central and South America and in the Caribbean islands.

The *terminus ante quem* of the essays presented in this book is set by the revolutions for independence in South America, in the early decades of the nineteenth century. For this reason, the most important chapter in the socioeconomic and demographic history of the American diaspora—the migration flood in the last decades of the nineteenth and the early decades of the twentieth centuries—is not touched upon. The book deals with the very first encounters, the first "colonization" by European Jews in the New World. For the most part these were Jews who were free to profess their own faith in the British and Dutch Americas, to a certain degree also in French America, and crypto-Jews, marranos, and *Cristãos novos* in Spanish and Portuguese America.

The "Jew" Christopher Columbus

Jewish involvement in the discovery and "conquest" of America begins as early as Columbus's enterprise. His daring esprit, his constant uneasiness with the Catholic establishment, and his twofold if cunning dealings with the highest political authorities of his time has turned Cristoforo Colombo, in the eyes of historians and writers, into a quasi-archetypal embodiment of the Renaissance taste for free, individual inquiry, intellectual freedom, and skepticism. Notwithstanding his personal uncertainties, actual difficulties, and greed, he cherished for a long time a dream that was eventually to be realized, even though in the end it turned out to be a *felix error*, for he aimed at opening up a new route west to reach the East Indies.

In a certain sense, Columbus was the first American, long before any white person settled in the vast if untamed landscapes of the Western Hemisphere. Not surprisingly, his quite extensive if utilitarian knowledge of contemporary sciences, as far as they were relevant to his enterprise—astronomy, geography, navigation—combined with his taste for action and adventure, lead some historians today to identify him as a perfect Renaissance man. Moreover, he faced the destiny of being identified as a Jew, or, at least, as a descendant of an Italian Jewish family only recently converted to Christianity. Undoubtedly, the "Jewish" factor in Columbus's personality is almost one with his peculiar Renaissance character: individualism, skepticism, willingness to challenge the powers that be while at the same time pleasing them.

The historiographical assumption about the Jewishness of Columbus and his family—from Hermann Kellenbenz in the late nineteenth century to Sarah Leibovici in the 1980s, and including Salvador de Madariaga—has been fiercely attacked by historians, on the grounds of substantial, if incomplete, documentary evidence to the contrary. Columbus does incarnate, however, a kind of adventurous and learned man, who challenges the established authorities, both political and intellectual, to reach into the unknown. If not a Jew, he was certainly a man of the Renaissance, as much as Lorenzo de Medici, Leonardo da Vinci, and Michelangelo, all of whom dared to venture where others would or could not.

Although Columbus's "Jewishness" can be questioned and regarded as a myth, the very fact that the question is raised is worthy of reflection. The Renaissance, in its "spirit of initiative"—to paraphrase Felipe Fernández-Armesto—owes something to the Jewish spirit of inquiry and "skepticism." The most daring scientists and philosophers of the Renaissance, such as Marsilio Ficino and Pico, were decisively influenced by Jewish mysticism, and scholars are beginning just now to understand and reappraise the role of Kabbalah, prominent and so far neglected, in late Renaissance authors, such as Giordano Bruno. This is probably only the beginning of what is bound to become a major reassessment of Christian Renaissance thought.

An Old New World: Biblical Geography and the Impact of the New World on the Old

The idea of a "new world" was difficult to understand, even in the Renaissance. Time and space were somehow intertwined, leaving little or no room for novelty. The world was conceived of, according to a Classical paradigm, as getting older and older with the course of time. New beginnings in either space or time were not considered. According to the authority principle, to the unchallenged voice of the *auctoritates*—whether Jewish, Greek, or Latin—new lands had to be identified with those lands belonging to Classical geography. As is well known, Columbus himself set off to discover a new route to the Indies and never realized that he had in fact discovered a route to altogether new lands. The authority of the texts was rarely attacked, even in the intellectually daring context of the Renaissance, as Professor Anthony Grafton has brilliantly demonstrated. Thus, Columbus well epitomizes the spirit of his time. Daring, but not daring enough even to understand the full potential of his discoveries, the full meaning of the fruits of his spirit of initiative.

The first section of the present collection of essays deals with this set of problems. It offers the reader a prehistory of Jewish settlement in the New World. At the same time, this first part provides a wide intellectual framework, which will prove useful to better understand and assess the future role of the Jewish factor in the colonization of the New World, as well as the multiple relationships (social, economic, religious, intellectual) between Old and New World.

James Romm,[2] an expert on the geography of the "extremes," provides, in the opening essay, a learned and revealing reading of Columbus's and his contemporaries' geography, as it was related to biblical and Classical scholarship and sources. As was common in European biblical interpretation—at least until the time of Richard Simon, who began the tradition of critical and philological interpretation of the Scripture in the second half of the seventeenth century—Columbus and his contemporaries treated the Bible as a unique and unchallengeable source of knowledge. Biblical geography offered not only names but even "clear" coordinates to locate places. When he landed on Hispaniola's wild shores, Columbus thought he had landed on Ophir, the mythical shore of King Solomon's travels (Gen. 1: 29, but especially I Kings 9: 28). Unfortunately, deeper readings of the Bible demonstrated that those geographical coordinates were far from precise—they were even vague and contradictory. It was therefore empirical investigation, along with more accurate readings of the text, that helped establish a better identification and naming of the known and unknown worlds after Columbus's pathbreaking voyages.

Cosmography and the art of mapmaking acquired, slowly but definitively, the status of science. The process of undermining the ancient authorities had just begun, but the weight of those millennial authorities remained heavy nonetheless. Even the boldest freethinkers, anarchists of philosophy and philology such as Guillaume Postel and Isaac La Peyrère, had to come to terms with those *auctoritates*, and all their works seem entangled in this never-ending, potentially devastating confrontation. For even after the novelty of geography was eventually established and conventionally accepted, what about the ethnography? Where did those bizarre peoples come from? In what way did their existence confirm, or deny, the prophetic books of the Old Testament and the Second Coming announced by the prophet Daniel? Could we convert them all to Christianity, in order to fulfill the prophecies and make the Second Coming come faster?

James Romm's essay raises questions that are historically fundamental, the answers to some of which can be found in David S. Katz's and Benjamin Schmidt's essays, the first devoted to the "wandering of the lost ten tribes in America" from Menasseh ben Israel to present-day millennialism, and the second to "Menasseh ben Israel and the Dutch Idea of America." Here, biblical geography and ethnography—the myth of the Lost Ten Tribes—become matters of religious enthusiasm and political concern. In the seventeenth century, an era obsessed and fractured by religious fanaticism, millennialism, and judeophobia, Menasseh ben Israel made good use of the argument that the Lost Ten Tribes could be identified with the Native Americans—as support for the cause of the readmission of the Jews into England, a goal that he partially achieved.

Benjamin Schmidt[3] offers, in a highly informative essay, an original interpretation of America in Dutch history, politics, arts, and imagination during Menasseh ben Israel's time. Schmidt places Menasseh in the context of contemporary Dutch culture and Dutch proto-Americanism. The idea of applying a "Dutch republican dimension" to the "Sephardi profile" proves to be fertile and heuristically groundbreaking. In the early modern Jewish vision of the New World, the "republican," "freedom" factor plays a fundamental role, along with millennialism and other peculiar adaptations of the "revelation" of the New World to particular, politically oriented visions and aims. What Schmidt says about Menasseh could be applied to other outstanding figures of the contemporary Sephardi community of Amsterdam, including the fascinating baroque poet Miguel Levi de Barrios (1635–1701), who traveled to Tobago in his youth and constantly kept the image of the New World in his poetic mind while at the same time praising Dutch republicanism and independence.

David S. Katz, the major international authority on Anglo-Jewish history, and the author of a fundamental book about the "readmission" of the Jews into England under Cromwell[4]—where the role played by Menasseh ben Israel in this context is somewhat reduced—offers a daring perspective on the offspring of millennial thought, from Menasseh to the contemporary fanatical sects haunting the United States and, to a lesser degree, Europe. Menasseh's *Hope of Israel* (*Mikveigh Yisrael*), in which millennialism plays a positive role in presenting the Jews in the most favorable light, in the Old as well as the New World, turns into an ill-fated, ill-starred nightmare when the Bible undergoes misleading, distorted interpretations by fanatical sects, rabble-rousers, anti-Semitic groups, and pseudo-pagan cults, such as the notorious "Children of Satan." Katz carefully describes four centuries of evolution/involution of millennial thought, showing how biblical exegesis, especially the exegesis of the prophetic books, is far from being a dead letter or just a matter for academic disputes.

The other two essays in the first part of the volume are concerned with what we could label the "view from within." Patricia Seed's and Noah J. Efron's essays offer a view of Jewish "technical contributions" to the discovery of the New World and of Jewish views and interpretations of America in the early modern era, respectively.

Patricia Seed, the author of an acute volume on the symbolic European "conquest" of the Americas,[5] offers a brief overview of the "Jewish" cosmography and sailing technology behind Columbus's and Vasco da Gama's enterprises. Without the first mariner's astrolabe, assembled by the Jewish astronomer Abraham Zacuto, who presented it personally to Vasco da Gama in 1497, not only da Gama's voyages but also subsequent travels to America would have been much more problematic.

Noah Efron's essay illuminates an area fairly neglected by previous scholarship. He analyzes the ways in which Jewish scholars, writing mainly in Hebrew and thus aiming at a Jewish public, understood and interpreted the discovery of the New World. The overall picture we get is more shaded and differentiated than that we can draw from contemporary non-Jewish authors. Millennial and apocalyptic veins are present, as well as the identification of the New World with the biblical Ophir, especially in Azariah de' Rossi and David Gans, but there are other, peculiarly Jewish, aspects that are not to be found in Christian authors. Often Jewish geographers and scientists saw in the New World an unexpected resource for their hopes of a better life, more or less theologically or eschatologically founded. They perceived that the discoveries meant that the world was changing. For a people oppressed from time immemorial, a New World implied a new set of expectations, possibly a way out from disgrace and suffering. In this, the Jews were no less fascinated by the New World than other European minorities. In fact, they often anticipated and occasionally cherished an American, *the* American, dream. Like contemporary Christian scholars, Jewish geographers and historians tended toward a utilitarian, often parochial, vision of the New World. As Efron brilliantly demonstrates, Jewish understanding of the New World was closely related to Jews' understanding of their own biblical past as well as their dire contemporary plight. "Pure" science—interest in the natural world for its own sake—was hard to be found at that time, even in contemporary Christian thought. Erasmian *utilitas* and scriptural evidence were the keywords in humanist interpretation and in Renaissance thought in general. Efron's essay contributes in a special way to the long overdue rediscovery and reappraisal of Jewish science—in its positive, open-minded, and reciprocal relationships with gentile science—throughout the early modern period. This relationship has brilliantly emerged in recent scholarship, notably in the path-breaking works of André Neher, David B. Ruderman, and Raphael Patai, among others.

The Question of Identity: Marranos, New Christians, *Conversos* in Spanish and Portuguese America

While the first section of the volume addresses questions pertaining to intellectual history, the history of science, and theology, the second section approaches themes belonging more properly to socio-anthropological history. Whereas in British, Dutch, and to some extent French America the Jews could openly profess their faith, protected by toleration and, after the War of Independence, granted the full rights of citizens by the American constitution, the Jews in Spanish and Portuguese America had to conceal their identity. Their legal status and social condition mirrored exactly that present in the Iberian Peninsula after 1492 (for Spain) and 1497 (for Portugal). The Jewish migration to what we now call "Latin America" should be renamed, more precisely, the "New Christian migration." The fact that the New Christians in Latin America in the colonial era by far outnumbered the "daylight" Jews in North America makes the treatment of New Christian identity almost compulsory in this book. Before analyzing the prominent role that New Christians played in American society and economy, it is necessary to investigate who they in fact were, and how they represented themselves—or more often, *were* represented—by external sources (the Spanish civil and ecclesiastical authorities, the surrounding society).

Threatened by the Inquisition—"tribunal de los infiernos," according to a contemporary marrano poet, Antonio Enríquez Gómez (ca. 1600–63)—

and regularly surrounded by the hostility of the "pure blood" population, the New Christians in the New World often succeeded, nonetheless,
in securing for themselves a stable position and a sound income by
engaging in trade with Europe and North America, and by coming to
terms with the hostile social and natural environment.

Robert Rowland, an international expert in historical demography
and early modern social European history,[6] provides in his essay the
methodological coordinates needed to identify, as well as to further analyze, the phenomenon of "marranism" and the figure of the marrano in
the Iberian Peninsula before and after the expulsion of 1492. Rowland,
partially accepting I. S. Revah's seminal definition of marrano religion as
a "religion of will," describes the complex shape taken by Judaism in the
practices and self-understanding of the New Christians. Marrano
Judaism was primarily a religion constructed according to remembrance,
to recollection, even to the image and understanding of it held and prop-
agated by the Inquisition itself, occasionally labeled by historiography
and New Christian popular opinion alike as a *fábrica de judeus*.

Referring to the Iberian Peninsula, Rowland deals with the key problem of "dual identity" (Catholic in the external world, Jewish in the
secrecy of home and in familial networks) that characterized marranos
well before the expulsion of the Jews from Spain in 1492 or their forced,
even tragicomic, conversion in Portugal in 1497. Marrano identity thus
becomes a sort of schizophrenia, although neither Rowland nor Nathan
Wachtel in the following essay arrives at this extreme conclusion. The
social and intimate conflicts that shaped marrano identity and conscience
in the Old World were reproduced, with subtle differences, in the New
World when the Inquisition was reproduced there with all its power,
which was diminished only by the vastness of the territory. Marranism
has certainly been a developing rather than a static faith. Even well-
rounded faiths, such as Catholicism and Judaism, often unthreatened by
social forces and much easier to grasp and define, were far from being
frozen in the early modern era. Both were affected by reformatory
streams, Protestantism in the first case, and Karaitism, Sabbateanism,
Hassidism, Frankism, and other heresies in the other. Catholicism and
Judaism underwent, at a theological and a social-individual level, major
changes from 1400 onward.

Finally, Rowland correctly emphasizes the primary role played by
Portuguese New Christians, both in Spain—to which they emigrated
massively after 1580, the year of the union of the Spanish and Portuguese
crowns—and in the New World. Their impact was felt not only in Brazil,
of course, but also in the Spanish dominions, where they maintained for
a long time a key role in trade.

Nathan Wachtel's essay should be read in close conjunction with
Rowland's. Wachtel, whose most recent work, written together with
Lucette Valensi, has shed a new, keen light on Judaism, memory, and iden-
tity in modern and contemporary Europe,[7] widens Rowland's concept of

"dual identity" to encompass the cognate one of "dual sincerity." Wachtel's unsurpassed knowledge of Andean historical anthropology[8] guides his masterly reconstruction, on the basis of selected cases, of marrano religious practices and beliefs in the seventeenth century. He demonstrates the complex syncretism of marrano religiosity—well exemplified by the awkward cult of "Saint" Moses—and the ways in which contemporary identity mingled with memories of the past (original Judaism) and messianic and political expectations (as in the hopes that arose among Portuguese New Christians, at home and in Hispanic America, regarding the reconquered independence of Portugal in 1640). The way in which marranism slowly lost its religious meaning and helped to bring about, in a certain sense, through memory and recollection, the reconstruction of a Jewish national identity is particularly interesting. Both Rowland's and Wachtel's essays invite a closer, serial as well as analytical investigation of marrano religiosity using the huge and invaluable sources of Inquisitorial trials and other external records. It is in the spirit of this book not only to offer a vast amount of new historical evidence and interpretation, but also to stimulate new research in uncommon directions and from original perspectives.

Solange Alberro's essay is based on her previous, extensive research on the Inquisition in New Spain.[9] Alberro describes the complex and fascinating ways in which the New Christians reconstructed and changed their own social and religious identity in Mexico during the seventeenth century. Outwardly acting as Spanish Christians—even singing the poems of Lope de Vega, an author who was certainly not a philosemite—they practiced their own version of Judaism at home. Alberro's essay illuminates the twofold interaction between New Christians and the Inquisition in New Spain. Belonging to the same social elite, Inquisition officers and New Christians to a certain extent shared a range of values; they even had reciprocal social intercourse on a friendly basis. Crypto-Judaism often could be so cryptic as to escape even the keen eyes of the Inquisition. The New Christian community in New Spain proved hard to destroy, and the Inquisition was frequently too weak to destroy crypto-Judaism.

After 1640, however, the situation changed for the worse. The newly reacquired independence of Portugal, after sixty years of Spanish domination, helped to create a web of suspicion in the Spanish American empire against the New Christians, most of whom were of Portuguese descent (at a certain point "portuguese" became another name for Jew, along with marranos and *conversos*). The New Christians were accused of being part of the *complicidad granda* ("Great Plot") to subvert the Spanish crown. From the point of view of the history of political thought, this is one of the first appearances of the conspiracy theory on a vast scale, long before Augustin Barruel (1741–1820) assigned it a firm status in political thought. The persecutions of the 1640s accelerated the process of assimilation of the New Christians, at the same time enlarging the gap between New Christian social layers, and, paradoxically, bringing about the decline of the Inquisition itself, due to the dissolution of its major targets. Alberro's essay shows how the Inquisition followed a political formula, the creation of *Sozialdisziplinierung* (social discipline)—according to Otto Brunner's seminal definition—which was its main task in Europe (including Italy, as has been recently demonstrated by Adriano Prosperi).

Eva Alexandra Uchmany, the author of a lavishly illustrated and highly informative book on the New Christians in Spanish America,[10] offers in her essay a narrative description of the New Christians' and crypto-Jews' involvement in the colonization of Spanish America from the early sixteenth century until 1660. Uchmany's essay closes with an overview of the development of the New Christian community from 1660 to the late eighteenth century, almost on the eve of the Wars of Independence that freed Latin America from Iberian rule. Her approach, encompassing political, social, religious, and economic history, is most useful for understanding particular phases and aspects of New Christian history as they are dealt with in the essays that follow. Uchmany draws a distinction between the New Christians of Spanish and of Portuguese origins—to help us better identify the changes that affected the marrano presence in the New World—while analyzing in detail some peculiar, individual personalities. The profile and destiny of those New Christians belonging to economic and social elites is particularly striking. While they constituted an upwardly mobile social cluster, because of their (concealed) faith they were at the same time subject to constant fear, blackmail, and pressure exerted by authorities as well as by the surrounding community. Their future was often doomed, and their lives uneasy. Uchmany's views of the New Christian experience in Spanish America is less positive than that offered by Alberro. At the same time, the two perspectives can—if carefully read and understood—co-exist.

The last essay in this section of the book, by Günter Böhm, deals with the experience, in the long term, of the crypto-Jews and *conversos* in colonial Peru and Chile. Professor Böhm,[11] a leading authority on this subject and a follower of the masterly scholarly tradition inaugurated by José Toribio Medina, offers a brief account of the problem of historical sources for the study of the New Christians in Chile. At the same time, through some individual examples as well as a serial overview of the Inquisitorial trials, Böhm demonstrates how the evolution of marranism in Chile paralleled the trend throughout Spanish America, with an increased number of trials in the 1630s and 1640s during the time of the "Great Plot." That New Christians did not emigrate to Chile before a comparatively rich economy had emerged bears a certain typicality. New Christians and crypto-Jews tended to migrate where the economy was already flourishing, or where at least it showed promise of growth. New Christians and Jews alike were rarely pioneers in wastelands, where everything, including trade and markets, had to be built. This fact differentiates those minorities from other religious sects—such as Quakers, Mormons, and Hutterites in North America—endowed with a more "pioneering" spirit and more able to start in an undeveloped land the primary economic activity needed to make it grow: agriculture.

The Jews in Portuguese America

Anita Novinsky,[12] a well-known expert on Brazilian-Jewish history, discloses a new chapter in the history of the New Christian community in Brazil. Focusing on a relatively late time period, the first half of the eighteenth century—a time of decline for the New Christians in Spanish America—Novinsky offers a detailed view, based on extensive archival research, of the marranos in the vast Brazilian region of Minas Gerais. The results of this case study show interesting differences between the New Christian experience in Spanish America and that in Portuguese America. In the latter, for instance, a still vigorous New Christian community proved to be more daring in colonization and participated, along with some 300,000 Portuguese, in the rush for gold that exploded at the beginning of the eighteenth century. Novinsky's essay casts new light also upon the process of secularization undergone by the New Christians in the first half of the eighteenth century, which can be fruitfully compared with the same occurrence in Europe among professing Jews. Skepticism—not as a philosophy but as a way of life—and agnosticism became common among the Minas Gerais New Christians in this period.

Novinsky discerningly discusses both current and classical (Max Weber) interpretations of the social and economic meaning of religion. Of particular interest is the assumption, shared by some contemporary historians, including Novinsky herself, that the introduction of the Inquisition in Portugal was "a reaction to European economic growth, namely, the development of a competitive and upwardly mobile mercantile middle class, which inserted itself into the spheres of power, thereby threatening the aristocracy's political and financial hegemony." Can this theory be applied to Brazil as well? In her brilliant and massively documented essay, Novinsky addresses this fundamental question. The competition between New and Old Christians in Brazilian markets seems to have offered the latter a comparative advantage over the former, in that New Christians could be accused of crypto-Judaism, which had the effect of diminishing their economic power. Religion and economy play, in this context, a role even subtler than that conferred on them in Max Weber's or Werner Sombart's classical analyses. Finally, the process of secularization led the New Christians slowly to attach to Judaism not a religious but an ideological, "national" meaning. From this perspective, Novinsky's conclusions seem to coincide with the interpretation of marranism put forward by Nathan Wachtel in his essay.

Geraldo Pieroni's essay deals with the prehistory of New Christian settlement in Brazil, namely the banishment of New Christians from Portugal to Brazil, and is mainly derived from his in-depth analysis of the phenomenon presented initially in his doctoral dissertation.[13] Pieroni gives a substantial account of Portuguese trials and the subsequent exile to America. He shows how this form of punishment fit into the legal and theological schemes of the Inquisition and was conceived of as a kind of "purgatory" to prepare for full conversion to Christianity and the return home. It was a purgatory that turned into hell for many, but also into a paradise for quite a few, who decided not to return home and to settle in the bountiful New World. Pieroni's essay is in conformity with the most recent European historiography about the Inquisition, which includes such works as Francisco Bethencourt's pioneering research on European Inquisitions in comparative perspective.

The New Christians in French America

The fourth section of this book deals with a subject that has so far received very little scholarly attention: the history of the Jews and the New Christians in the French colonies in the Americas. Gérard Nahon,[14] a leading authority on Sephardi and French-Jewish history, offers a precise overview of the "American dimension" of the Jews in Bayonne. Contrary to Bordeaux, which has been studied in depth, Bayonne, a relatively minor harbor on the French Atlantic coast, has been generally neglected by scholars, at least with relation to its Portuguese Jewish community. The Portuguese Jews of Bayonne, whose religious identity (Jews? New Christians?) was socially and legally unclear until the French Revolution, played an important role in commerce with the Americas. As so often happens—and Fernand Braudel has once and for all demonstrated— trade at the same time implied and fostered cultural exchanges. This is true not only at the level of elite culture—and the case of Daniel Lopez Laguna, the author of a splendid translation of the Psalms into Spanish (1720), seems quite isolated—but especially at the level of cultural practices and imagination. Bayonne Jews cherished a certain kind of "American dream" which "pervaded conversations and thoughts"; as Nahon presents it, they "interiorized" American spaces in a peculiar way. Some of them once again brought credibility to the myth that the Lost Ten Tribes were located in America. Nahon, focusing mainly on the eighteenth century, solidly demonstrates how the American dimension was also instrumental in enabling Bayonne Jews to strengthen their own socioeconomic position in France. This fact can be confirmed by the substantial weight carried by the French Atlantic Jewish community during the French Revolution.

Silvia Marzagalli[15] brings a new and fresh perspective to one of the most studied among the Jewish communities in France: that of Bordeaux. Focusing once again on the eighteenth century—when Bordeaux rose to national prominence as a port of trade—Marzagalli analyzes the commercial and familial *réseaux* that gave to the Sephardi merchants of Bordeaux a comparative advantage in Atlantic colonial trade. By using Zvi Loker's argument to identify this advantage that the Jews possessed in comparison to non-Jewish merchants—namely, "family networks," "higher geographical mobility," and "knowledge of foreign languages" —Marzagalli sketches out a line of continuity and evolution in the economic history of the Bordeaux Jews. She demonstrates that the comparative advantage was to be found especially in the "tertiary" sectors of the economy: banking and insurance. She also most appropriately regards political and social history as deeply intertwined, while presenting some notable examples of Jewish mercantile families. Marzagalli takes into account both the direct and the indirect (investments, finance, insurance) participation of Jewish merchants in the Atlantic trade. Her conclusion goes against any typicality in the Bordeaux case. On the basis of the evidence, and for a variety of historical reasons, the case of Bordeaux appears to be unique. Only some comparisons can be made—though merely in quantitative terms—with the Jewish merchants of Bayonne, studied by Nahon.

Mordechai Arbell[16] provides, in his long and detailed study, a most useful mapping of the social, legal, and political conditions of the Jews in the French Caribbean colonies. Arbell shows how the conditions under which the Jews lived were altered by the passage from the overtly tolerant regime of the Dutch to French rule. The legal entitlements of the Jews became unclear and shifting, and the restrictive power of the Catholic Church often overwhelming. Arbell clearly describes the various economic activities practiced by the Jews in the Caribbean area, especially sugar production and trade. He also stresses the political weight of the coalition of Jesuits and French planters—how a mix of social envy and religious hatred blended and resulted in the expulsion of the Jews from Guadeloupe and Martinique. The relationship between the political events in France and those occurring in the colonies is of particular interest. Often, policy toward the Jews in the French Caribbean mirrored and followed developments at home; occasionally, it went its own way. The situation in Haiti is of particular interest, especially after the revolution, when a large number of Jews married freed slaves, gradually constituting the Haitian middle class—a phenomenon not easily found elsewhere.

A gem of scholarship, John Garrigus's[17] essay addresses the complex question of citizenship in Saint-Domingue in the quarter-century preceding the French Revolution. The flow of racial, geopolitical, and religious ideas from France into the colonies—from Montesquieu to Buffon and Grégoire, from the Enlightenment to revolutionary ideology—is analyzed here with a particular reference to the evolution, in terms of social standing and legal status, of all the social and ethnic components of colonial Saint-Domingue: Jews, free people of color, French whites. The first lines of the essay—which somewhat epitomize its main points—are worth quoting in full:

The case of Saint-Domingue's Sephardim illustrates that the story of the Jews in Europe's expansion westward is about more than the survival or mutation of deeply rooted family traditions. Old World questions about Jewish political identity did not disappear in the Americas. Rather, these persistent issues forced colonists and their children born in the New World to reconcile new European philosophies with American conditions. In the case of the largest slave colony in the Caribbean, Saint-Domingue's Jews helped translate emerging French nationalism into an attack on racial prejudice that eventually produced the Haitian Revolution. By raising complex issues of national identity and citizenship in French America after 1763, Sephardic merchants and planters provided a model for another group whose place in colonial society was equally ambiguous: Saint-Domingue's free people of color.

Garrigus's essay sets methodological guidelines that can be fruitfully applied to other situations, such as those of the Jews in Dutch and British America. Legal status, social aspirations, and economic positions interact in this analysis, and it appears clearly that a precise picture of the New Christian plight cannot be gained without simultaneously taking into account all of these factors. Saint-Domingue became the playground for ill-fated attempts at racial integration and for the formation of a "New White" elite with racial (and not necessarily religious) connotation. Finally, it was there that Jews and free men of color cooperated in the creation of Haiti, in 1804, "a new American nation with a racial identity all its own."

The Jews in Dutch America

Jonathan I. Israel, the author of a recent and comprehensive survey of Dutch history,[18] as well as several other groundbreaking works of socioeconomic and political history[19]—among them, the most challenging account of the social role of European Jewry in the early modern age[20]— opens the fifth section of this volume. His essay deals with the Jewish experience in Dutch America in its entirety, offering a panoramic view of the subject. Israel's essay shows how Jews could flourish in the Caribbean colonies under Dutch rule, constructing a powerful trade network and engaging in the production of sugar cane and other colonial goods. While the Caribbean Jews gained an overwhelming economic weight in the eighteenth century, the Jews in Dutch Brazil—for the relatively short span of time during which Brazil was under Dutch control, before returning to the Portuguese flag—thrived in the 1630s and 1640s. This period, studied by Israel mainly from a socioeconomic perspective, appears to be extremely interesting if also approached from a religious and social point of view. Under Portuguese rule, New Christians could not legally and openly practice their Jewish faith, whereas during the brief though intense period of Dutch control over Brazil, New Christians had the possibility of reverting to open Judaism. Did they do so? How many made this choice? The subject is of particular interest because this kind of sudden change of political rule is quite unique in Latin American history.

Israel's essay is mainly concerned, however, with economic matters. It depicts in great detail the differences between the two main Jewish communities in the Dutch Caribbean, namely Curaçao—the "Amsterdam of the Caribbean"—and Suriname, while offering also a brief sketch of Barbados and Jamaican Jewry. Its conclusions are of the greatest significance. In the first place, it appears clearly that in religious matters the Dutch were far less tolerant in the colonies than at home. The flourishing of Jewish trade was thus due more to a socioeconomic conjuncture than to a peculiarly liberal toleration policy. Furthermore, with pertinence to the Jews both in the brief Dutch-Brazilian period, and to the Caribbean Jews under Dutch rule, Israel highlights the ways in which Jews in "another environment" (to quote Robert Cohen) built a new kind of Jewish society, based on economic activities—such as tropical agriculture—quite different from any European model.

A closer analysis of the Jews in Dutch Suriname and Curaçao is provided by Wim Klooster, to whom we owe two outstanding recent publications on the colonial Dutch experience in the New World.[21] Klooster's essay—based on a vast amount of archival materials—portrays in detail the life of Jews in Suriname and Curaçao. The former constructed a remarkably solid agricultural colony, based on sugar cane; the latter instead developed, during the same period, a strong mercantile economy, originally based on smuggling. The experience in Suriname contradicts ipso facto the latent judeophobic assumption, commonly held in Europe at that time, that Jews could not practice agriculture and did not like it. It comes as no surprise that the Surinamese Jews sent a note of thanks to the Prussian writer Christian Wilhelm von Dohm, who, as late as 1781, published in Berlin a strong plea in favor of the betterment of the civil and legal conditions of the Jews in Europe. In that work Dohm maintained that the Jews could indeed be good farmers, as they were in biblical times. The case of Suriname and Curaçao Jewry well demonstrates the truth of all pro-Jewish literature from Simone Luzzatto in the early seventeenth century to Henri Grégoire in the late eighteenth: if granted a certain degree of toleration and liberty, Jews could substantially contribute to any kind of state economy. The staple market of Curaçao and the sugar plantations of Suriname were a convenient outlet for investments from Holland, when investment opportunities had decreased in the homeland. Well into the eighteenth century, these two Dutch-Jewish colonies flourished, starting to decline only in the last third of the eighteenth century in conjunction with a major decline in the world (and especially European) economy. Those colonial societies offered a splendid testing ground for daring businessmen and adventurers. Klooster's essay closes with a biographical sketch of one of these men (Felipe Henriquez, 1589–1656), who moved from marranism to international diplomacy, from smuggling to high society.

James Homer Williams's essay opens still another chapter in the history of the Jews in Dutch America. His perspective is comparative in its methodology and highly enlightening in its results. Williams takes into account side by side the development of the legal and social position of the Jews in Amsterdam and that of the Jews in New Amsterdam and Dutch Brazil. If compared to the situation in Amsterdam, the plight of the Jews in Brazil, and especially in New Amsterdam, appears to be far less happy. Especially in New Amsterdam the Jews faced a twofold hostility: on the one hand, they entered a market where Dutch merchants already held a prominent position; hence, there was no empty space for Jewish traders to conquer. At the same time, New Amsterdam's governor Peter Stuyvesant was a fierce enemy of the Jews—whom he constantly defined as a "deceitful race"—along with all faiths other than the Reformed. After 1664, when New Amsterdam fell into British hands, and was renamed, *faute de mieux*, New York, things started to change, and the Jews began to enjoy a much more tolerant regime. Williams carefully describes the parallel evolution of British policy toward the Jews at home and in the colonies; as a result, it seems clear that in New York Jews enjoyed a toleration even more advanced than was the case in London.

A different economic situation—namely, a broader array of opportunities—was to be found by the Jews in Dutch Brazil. Williams underlines the different personality of Brazil's governor, Johan Maurits, who was no less a Calvinist than Stuyvesant but far more oriented toward a pragmatic form of toleration. The West India Company encouraged Jewish migration to Brazil, where Jews could serve—as Williams describes it with a most acute definition—as "cultural brokers" with the Portuguese. The Calvinist zeal of Stuyvesant—at a time and in a city affected by a peculiar religious laxity that touched upon almost every faith and believer—prevented the Jews from blossoming in New Amsterdam. The moderate open-mindedness of Count Maurits, on the other hand, made Brazil a place where Jews were able to reach a remarkable degree of well-being. The "force of personality"—evoked here with the utmost opportunity by Williams, and a for a long time considered as a *quantité négligeable* by historiography—clearly played a major role in the two different destinies faced by the Jews in Brazil and New Amsterdam respectively.

The final essay of the "Dutch" section brings us a new and fresh perspective on Surinamese Jewry. Rachel Frankel offers here the fruits of her long-lasting, passionate involvement in the architectural history of "Jodensavanne," the flourishing Jewish colony on the Suriname River. The essay shows all the potential of architectural history as a form of, inter alia, historical anthropology of space. The focus is on the synagogue and the cemetery of the Jodensavanne. Though the model remained that of Dutch religious and civic architecture, the Jodensavanne Jews, freed from any external pressure and free to confer on public and private spaces new meanings and functions, erected their own synagogue in 1685, ten years after the construction of the main Sephardic temple in

Amsterdam. The synagogue, ideally located at the very center of a very linear village, served as a symbol of faith and social cohesion.

The differences characterizing this building, internally and externally, in comparison with the Amsterdam model are full of meaning; they point toward a new appraisal both of the social significance of faith in Suriname and of the social structure of the community. Here, Jews were not only free, but also at the top of the social hierarchy. Though a minority, they constituted the ruling class. The population counted an overwhelming majority of black slaves, few whites, and some Ashkenazi and even black Jews, the latter newly converted to the faith of the elite. Jews found themselves for the first time in a situation of privilege, certainly not shared by their co-religionists in even the tolerant United Provinces. For the first time in the Jodensavanne, according to Frankel's fascinating account, "Jews had the opportunity to design virgin landscape and construct it according to their needs, beliefs, and hopes."

Frankel's detailed description of Jodensavanne architecture provides a clear view of what this meant at a practical level. Of utmost interest also is the interaction—expressed even in architectural terms—between Jewish and African culture. There is evidence, such as in Paramaribo's (the capital city of Suriname) Jewish cemetery, that the two different cultures and religions found points of contact, especially anthropologically, for they took place in the exceptionally symbolic terrain of death and remembrance. Frankel's essay closes with an analysis of other important Surinamese synagogues, those of Paramaribo built in 1723 and 1735 respectively. Here, the space seems to lose, in its squared essentiality, all the messianic hopes and sense of freedom present in the Jodensavanne synagogue.

The Jewish Factor in the Atlantic Economy

The opening essay of this section, devoted to Jewish involvement in the Atlantic economy during the colonial era, is a definitive reassessment of the role played by Jews and New Christians in the Atlantic slave trade. This subject—which carries an enormous meaning not only at the historiographical, but also at the "ideological," public opinion level—has been addressed by a leading specialist in the history of the British involvement in the slave trade, and in the history of slavery in general. Seymour Drescher[22] provides a detailed analysis of the Jewish and New Christian participation in the Atlantic slave trade from the beginning until the late eighteenth century. His study takes into account not only purely economic factors, but also the ways in which those factors were interrelated with social background and legal distinctions using the classical division (in three phases) of the Atlantic slave trade: the first phase, from 1500 to 1640, during which a relatively minor number of black slaves were exported to the Americas; the second phase, from 1640 to 1700, which saw the number of slaves forcibly embarked to the New World triple in number; and the final phase, between 1700 and the British abolition of 1807, when the number of slaves exported from Africa reached a peak (6,686,000, according to the most accurate estimate, outnumbering by far the sums in the forced migrations of the two previous phases).

Drescher demonstrates that only in the second phase did Jews play a major role in the trade, especially in the Dutch Caribbean colonies. As for the first phase, he concludes that "the only accounts of prominent Jewish presence in this initial process of oceanic exploration and trade are related to the scientific and cartographic experts mobilized by Prince Henry the Navigator to track his African exploratory expeditions." The matter was different for the New Christians. They had a large share in the Iberian slave trade, which was never to be matched by that played by observant Jews, not even in the second phase of the Atlantic slave trade. According to Drescher, they could count on "trustworthy interlocking agents and trained apprentices," vital in this kind of trade. Furthermore, in broader terms, "if their quasi-pariah religious status kept them at least once removed from institutional power, that same status tended to make them most effective in a world where opportunities for long-term credit were dependent upon kinship and trust." Drescher also analyzes the function of the Jews in the French slave trade, identifying the Bordeaux Gradis family—an extremely interesting though rather unique case of extraordinary Jewish socioeconomic success—as one of the major slave traders in eighteenth-century France. In the last and massive phase of African slave traffic, however, the Jewish role was much constricted by the competition of other mercantile, often quasi-government, networks, and Jews clearly played a minor role in this trade.

On the other hand, Jews, and especially New Christians, played a very substantial part in a milder and less risky trade, that of sugar. James C. Boyajian, a leading authority on Portuguese economic history, particularly in its international dimension,[23] offers a carefully documented picture of Jewish and New Christian involvement in the sugar trade from 1550 to 1750. The essay shows how and why Jews and New Christians achieved a prominence in this particular trade. The New Christians had developed a production-trade cycle, financing sugar cane production through the slave trade, but also through the trade of sugar itself.

At a certain point between 1650 and 1750, when sugar consumption lost its luxury character and became, along with other colonial products, a staple consumed massively in Europe, its producers reached the peak of wealth. Boyajian highlights the international dimension of New Christian trade in the American colonies, the ways and routes that linked the West and the East Indies, and the value of the import of Oriental luxury commodities, such as silk, which became fashionable not only in Europe, but also among the New Christian elites in the New World. In general, the commercial activities of the New Christians followed the ebb and flow of Atlantic trade throughout the early modern era. At a certain point, with the possessions of Angola, Brazil, and Goa, the Portuguese could have—and indeed had—control over a large portion of international trade. It comes as no surprise that New Christians took advantage of this fortunate situation.

Ernst Pijning's[24] essay provides a close description of the New Christian sugar cultivators and traders in Brazil until ca. 1800. Here economic history is fruitfully intertwined with social and religious data. Pijning's study, which includes a detailed survey of the terminology that identified the social layers in Portuguese Brazil, is revealing of the social plight and mobility of the New Christian elite of traders and planters. New Christians generally wanted to be seen as Old, in order to ascend the social ladder and integrate into the majority. This was true especially for the elites: a phenomenon that broadly mirrored what was happening in Europe between 1750 and 1900, when socially prominent Jews, in order to increase their prestige and enter public careers, converted to Christianity. New Christians, already more or less forcibly converted for generations, had on the contrary to demonstrate to the external world that they could be considered in toto as Old Christians.

Pijning offers a fascinating view, almost from within, of Portuguese colonial society. He demonstrates that the Inquisition acted with the concealed aim of attacking an upwardly mobile socioeconomic cluster and that religious dogmatism served as an external justification. He also shows that, in spite of legal restraints, New Christians surprisingly succeeded in acquiring public office, which was a means of protecting themselves from the Inquisition and securing a firm place in the social hierarchy. Finally, it is of particular interest to learn that sugar cultivation, although less economically rewarding, enabled cultivators to gain much more prestige than they could have obtained by engaging in trade, a situation that once more reflects, in the New World, a common European mentality deeply rooted in the European upper class well into the nineteenth century.

Closing this section of the book, Pieter Emmer's study skillfully locates the "Jewish moment," from 1580 to 1650, in a broad, world-history context of the two expansion systems in the Atlantic. Emmer,[25] an authority on Dutch colonial and economic history, provides an international and comparative framework that enables us to understand the Jewish role in the Atlantic economy from a macro-historical perspective. His views, which could arouse vigorous debate among historians, help us to understand better the contents and general implications of what has been written by the other authors in the section. The essay displays in chrono-geographical detail the differences between the Iberian and the British-Dutch-French expansion systems, and the reasons that the Spanish economy never reached the prominence it could well have gained thanks to its immense possessions. It also shows why and how the Portuguese reached international prominence, which was later lost owing to the relative backwardness of their political and religious systems. Finally, the essay deals with the felicitous momentum of the Dutch economy between 1600 and 1650, and with the emergence of the British to international prominence in the late seventeenth and particularly in the eighteenth centuries. The role the Jews played in those macro-systems was dependent upon, and subordinate to, the trends of development and decline of those systems themselves. Rather than determining them, the Jews were, as individual economic agents, almost completely conditioned by them. The Jews, normally very flexible, could not adapt, however, to the new, global economic international system that emerged in the eighteenth century. In their capacity of economic actors, as were the Genoese, the British, the Germans, and so on, the Jews were affected by historical ebbs and flows. Their economic importance occasionally reached the highest peaks; occasionally, also, the global economic momentum was unfavorable to them: as in England before the expulsion of 1290, or during the Genoese prominence in world trade until 1600, or, to cite but another example, in Germany before and during the Weimar Republic. It is against this background of world history that the Jewish (and New Christian) socioeconomic factor must be located and understood.

The Jews in Colonial British America

The final section of this book contains a single essay. The research that has been done on the Jews in colonial British America is—relative to the actual number of Jews living in North America before 1800—immense. No more than two thousand were in North America before 1800, a figure comparable to the Jews living in the Italian Ghetto of Mantua alone at the same time. From Salo Wittmayer Baron to Jacob Rader Marcus, scholars of Jewish history have offered multiple accounts of this subject. They have dug out from archives and other repositories a huge number of documents, and published some of them. The flood of publications on the subject seems unlimited, and even major scholars normally more engaged with other subjects, such as Arthur Hertzberg, have devoted volumes to the Jewish experience in Anglo-America before and after the birth of the United States.

Still, as is always the case in historiography, a much plowed field has not, for that reason alone, to be deserted. The Jews in North America were far from isolated, and the vertical line of their trade to Central and South America, often involving New Christian partners, for instance, is fascinating, although not comparable, in scope, to the Atlantic "horizontal" routes.

It is a matter of pride to conclude this volume with an essay by Jonathan D. Sarna. His commitment to, and his knowledge of, American-Jewish history, from the colonial time to the present, is unsurpassed. Sarna's research encompasses a wide variety of aspects of this history, from the relationship with Israel to single case studies, such as Jewish communities (Cincinnati, Boston) and Jewish personalities. They are too numerous to quote in a single footnote.[26] His constant effort to overcome a parochial approach to Jewish history has become a model for scholarship. Attention to the interactions among cultures—and not only between a majority and a minority (concepts themselves particularly risky in the American "melting pot")—is heuristically and methodologically the most rewarding way not only to approach Jewish history but also to understand other histories, other stories.

Sarna's essay leads us back to the religious dimension of the Jewish experience in colonial America, that is to say, to the core of Judaism, for it can be argued that Judaism is first and foremost religion, faith—much more than the "ethnic" or "racial" or later "national" character, insofar as these factors can ever be separated from "religion." It is traditional religious observance that explains the unique bond of the people of Israel (at least from the Middle Ages, if not from 70 A.D.) that Sarna painstakingly traces, the peculiarities of North American colonial Judaism, and the multiple ways in which it "was becoming increasingly distinctive from its European counterpart." Jewish religion had to confront a new environment and a new society, and at the same time, the first Jews who migrated to the New World in the seventeenth century aimed at preserving Judaism, in its religious and messianic dimension, against the potential threat of this new, wild, and untamed environment. This was also true of the spiritual leaders of every religious minority that migrated to the New World. Thus, the leaders of the Jewish communities acted more in the religious than in the social and legal spheres. They did not maintain the overwhelming power of the European *kahal*, the communal organization that served as a guild, dominating every aspect of the life of families as well as individuals. Because of this difference in America, the violent confrontations between single individuals and Jewish communal authority, which we find in eighteenth-century Euro-Jewish history, did not take place in the Western Hemisphere.

Nothing comparable to a Jewish "state within the state" took root on American soil. Before and especially after the American Revolution, American Jewry tended to rely on the laws of the secular state for every aspect of their social life, whereas religion itself became an intimate way to preserve tradition and to adore God. Still, as Sarna brilliantly demonstrates, there were tensions between the "demands of Jewish law and the norms of the larger secular or Christian society in which Jews moved." "Religious laxity" was also very frequent. "Diversity" was a peculiar mark of distinction in American religious life in a more radical way than was the case in Europe, at least for the same period: "Within every community, even within many individual families, a full gamut of religious observances and attitudes could be found, a spectrum ranging all the way from deep piety to total indifference." At the same time, American colonial Jews—probably, but not necessarily, because of this phenomenon—"felt more comfortable interacting with Christians than Jews did in most parts of the world." Intermarriage between Jews and Christians—

a phenomenon not infrequent in Europe, but which required preliminary conversion to Christianity of the Jewish partner—was impressively recurrent, for 10 to 15 percent of all Jewish marriages in the colonial period were intermarriages, a figure not found anywhere else in the Jewish world.

A Milder Colonization

Jews and New Christians came to America along with all the other "nations," at the very beginning of the colonization. Contrary to the other nations—Spain, Portugal, France, Holland, Britain—they had no fleet or army, no West India Company or major public support, for they had no *state* of their own. In some of its peculiar traits their colonization of the New World followed the main character of every national colonization. Yet the fact that they did not have a nation-state at home fostered in them the desire to settle if not in their *own* state at least in a free country that could eventually become a secure haven to protect their faith and existence. This is precisely what happened in North America. In South America, after the revolutions of the nineteenth century, freedom of conscience was allowed, but anti-Semitism was and is still present to a degree unknown in North America. Jews came to America full of hope. Menasseh ben Israel's messianic and political work, *Hope of Israel*, which helped bring about the readmission of the Jews in Britain, also became (though without probably any direct or implicit reference to that work) the name of two important early synagogues in two major centers of American Judaism, Curaçao and Philadelphia. It is in the hope that this volume will help bring about better understanding and offer valuable insight into American Judaism—in its multiple interactions with Europe and the rest of the world—that I would like to close this introduction and invite the reader to approach the text.

Notes

1. This essay is dedicated to the memory of Antonello Gerbi and Giuliano Gliozzi. It was completed during my stay at The Institute for Advanced Study (Princeton) as a Member of the School of Historical Studies in the academic year 1998–1999.
2. James Romm, *The Edges of the Earth in Ancient Thought: Geography, Exploration and Fiction* (Princeton, 1992); *Herodotus* (New Haven, 1998).
3. Benjamin Schmidt, *Innocence Abroad: The Dutch Imagination and the Representation of the New World* (Cambridge, forthcoming).
4. David S. Katz, *The Jews in the History of England* (Oxford, 1994); idem, *Philo-Semitism and the Readmission of the Jews to England 1603–1655* (Oxford, 1982).
5. Patricia Seed, *Ceremonies of Possession in Europe's Conquest of The New World* (Cambridge, 1995).
6. Robert Rowland and Isabell Moll Blanes, eds., *La demographia y la historia de la familia* (Murcia, 1997); Robert Rowland and Renzo Derosas, eds., *Informatica e fonti storiche* (Bologna, 1991); Robert Rowland, *Antropologia, historia e diferenca: alguns aspectos* (Porto, 1987).
7. Lucette Valensi and Nathan Wachtel, *Memoires juives* (Paris, 1986) (English translation, Berkeley, 1991).
8. Nathan Wachtel, *Le Retour des ancêtres: les indiens Urus de Bolivie, XXe–XVIe siècle: essai d'histoire regressive* (Paris, 1990); *La Vision des vaincus: les indiens du Perou devant la conquête espagnole 1530–1570* (Paris, 1971) (English translation, New York, 1977).
9. Solange Alberro, *La actividad del Santo Ufficio de la Inquisición en Nueva España* (Mexico, 1981); *Inquisition et société au Mexique 1571–1700* (Mexico, 1988); *Les Espagnols dans le Mexique colonial. Histoire d'une acculturation* (Paris, 1992).
10. Eva Alexandra Uchmany, *La vida entre el Judaismo y el Cristianismo en la Nueva España 1580–1606* (Mexico City, 1994).
11. Günther Böhm, *Historia de los Judios en Chile* (Santiago, 1984); *Judios en el Peru durante el siglo XIX* (Santiago, 1984).
12. Anita Novinsky and Diane Kuperman, eds., *Iberia judaica: roteiro de memoria* (São Paulo, 1996); Anita Novinsky, *Inquisicão: rol dos culpados: fontes para a historia do Brasil (seculo XVIII)* (Rio de Janeiro, 1992); *Cristãos novos de Bahia* (São Paulo, 1972).
13. Geraldo Pieroni, *Les exclus du Royaume: l'Inquisition portugaise et le bannissement au Brésil, XVIIe siècle* (Paris, 1996). See also his *Purgatorio colonial: inquisicão portuguesa e degredo no Brasil* (Lisboa, 1994).
14. Gérard Nahon, *La Terre sainte au temps de kabbalistes 1492–1592* (Paris, 1997); *Métropoles et périphéries séfarades d'Occident: Kairouan, Amsterdam, Bayonne, Bordeaux, Jerusalem* (Paris, 1993); *Inscriptions hebraiques et juives de la France médiévale* (Paris, 1986). Nahon, together with Henri Méchoulan, has also provided the contemporary reference edition of a work most relevant to this text, *Hope of Israel* by Menasseh ben Israel (Paris, 1979). The introductory essay and the commentary by Nahon and Méchoulan have been translated into English, in the reprint of the 1652 English translation of the *Esperança de Israel* by Moses Hall (Oxford, 1987).
15. Silvia Marzagalli, *I negozianti delle città portuali in età napoleonica. Amburgo, Bordeaux e Livorno di fronte al blocco continentale 1806–1813* (Ph.D. diss., EUI) (Florence 1993).
16. Mordechai Arbell, *La Nacion. The Spanish and Portuguese Jews in the Caribbean* (Tel Aviv, 1981) (bilingual, English-Hebrew account of Arbell's archeological trips to the Caribbean islands); Mordechai Arbell, comp., *Spanish and Portuguese Jews in the Caribbean and the Guianas: A Bibliography* (Providence and New York, 2000).
17. John D. Garrigus, *A Struggle for Respect: The Free Coloreds of Pre-revolutionary Saint-Domingue 1760–1769* (Ph.D. diss., Johns Hopkins University) (Baltimore, 1998).
18. Jonathan I. Israel, *The Dutch Republic: Its Rise, Greatness and Fall 1477–1806* (Oxford, 1995).
19. Jonathan I. Israel, *Dutch Primacy in the World Trade 1585–1740* (Oxford, 1989); *Empires and Entrepots: The Dutch, the Spanish Monarchy and the Jews, 1585–1713* (London, 1990);

Conflicts of Empires: Spain, the Low Countries and the Struggle for World Supremacy 1585–1713 (London, 1997).

20. Jonathan I. Israel, *European Jewry in the Age of Mercantilism 1550–1750* (Portland, 1998).

21. Wim Klooster, *Illicit Riches: Dutch Trade in the Caribbean 1648–1795* (Leiden, 1998); *The Dutch in the Americas: A Narrative History with the Catalogue of an Exhibition of Rare Prints, Maps and Illustrated Books from The John Carter Brown Library* (Providence, 1997).

22. Seymour Drescher, *From Slavery to Freedom: Comparative Studies in the Rise and Fall of Atlantic Slavery* (New York, 1999); *Capitalism and Antislavery: British Mobilization in Comparative Perspective* (London, 1986); *Econocide: British Slavery in the Era of Abolition* (Pittsburgh, 1977).

23. James C. Boyajian, *Portuguese Trade in Asia under the Habsburgs 1580–1650* (Baltimore, 1993); *Portuguese Bankers at the Court of Spain 1620–1650* (New Brunswick, 1983).

24. Ernst Pijning, *Controlling Contraband: Mentality, Economy and Society in Eighteenth-Century Rio de Janeiro* (Ph.D. diss., Johns Hopkins University) (Baltimore, 1997).

25. Pieter C. Emmer and Femme Gaastra, eds., *The Organization of Interoceanic Trade in European Expansion 1450–1800* (Aldershot, 1996); Pieter C. Emmer et al., eds., *Wirtschaft und Handel der Kolonialreiche* (Munich, 1988); Pieter C. Emmer, *The Dutch in the Atlantic Economy 1580–1880: Trade, Slavery and Emancipation* (Aldershot, 1998).

26. But see, e.g., Jonathan D. Sarna, ed., *The American Jewish Experience* (New York, 1997); Jonathan D. Sarna and Nancy H. Klein, eds., *The Jews of Cincinnati* (Cincinnati, 1989); Jonathan D. Sarna, *Jacksonian Jew: The Two Worlds of Mordechai Noah* (New York, 1981); *Hebrew Sources in American History* (Cincinnati, 1981).

PART I

THE OLD NEW WORLD: IDEAS AND REPRESENTATIONS OF AMERICA IN EUROPEAN AND JEWISH CONSCIOUSNESS AND INTELLECTUAL HISTORY

– *Chapter 1* –

BIBLICAL HISTORY AND THE AMERICAS: THE LEGEND OF SOLOMON'S OPHIR, 1492–1591

James Romm

ONE CAN ONLY IMAGINE how delighted Columbus would have been to know that his discoveries would one day be studied in a city called Providence. To him, and to many of his contemporaries, the geography of the New World could best be understood within the framework of the Holy Bible, and within the historical scheme of a Divine Providence that had determined the fate of humankind from the moment of its creation. Moreover, the names of places were immensely important to Columbus and his age as signposts of how those places fit into biblical mythology— or into the body of myth and science inherited from Classical antiquity. Indeed, one wonders what he would have thought of the fact that this essay was first presented in a place called Salomon Hall. As I shall show in what follows, he would almost certainly have taken this name as proof that King Solomon had sent ships to the New World long before Spanish caravels went there, and would assert, as he did in fact believe, that his own travels were only a reprise or a reenactment of the voyages described in the Bible to the rich trading port of Ophir.

The name Ophir occurs at various points in the Hebrew Scriptures, though in two very different contexts. First, in an important chapter of Genesis (10:29) tracing the lines of descent begot by Noah, Ophir is named as one of the sons of Yoktan, a descendant of Noah's eldest son Shem. Later, in parallel passages of the books of Kings (1 Kings 9:26–28, 10:11, 10:22) and Chronicles (2 Chronicles 8:17, 9:10, 9:21) concerning the reign of King Solomon, the same name designates a place, the land from which Solomon's ships had brought back gold, silver, exotic animals, and a precious variety of wood called almug. Probably no connection should be drawn between the personal name and the toponym, as though the Ophir of Genesis were a settler of the land that bore his name[1]—though such links were commonly made by early interpreters in the cases of other Noachic descendants listed in the same passage of Genesis (indeed, the three sons of Noah were identified throughout the Middle Ages with the three parts of the Old World, a scheme we shall return to below). Significantly, the authors of the Septuagint and early commentators often write the name of the place as "Sophir" or "Souphir," whereas the name of the person never takes this form. However, Renaissance scholars who were unaware of this linguistic distinction made much of the apparent homonymy, as we shall see.

Incidental references elsewhere in the Bible (Is. 13:12, Job 28:16) speak of the "gold of Ophir" as a very fine gold, and an eighth-century B.C. Hebrew inscription found on a potsherd also contains this phrase in a similar context,[2] showing that the land of Ophir was well known in biblical times for its mineral wealth. Modern attempts to locate "King Solomon's mines" have been unsuccessful, though speculation has generally centered on southern Africa, Arabia, or the western coast of India. The trading port of Sofala in East Africa was recognized as a possible correlate as early as the sixteenth century (see below), while the Indian city called Souppara by Ptolemy (7.1.6) and Arrian has been championed by more recent interpreters.[3] The modern state of Israel, in an effort to link its own topography to the biblical past, assigned the name Ofira to the Red Sea port of Sharm el Sheik after capturing the Sinai Peninsula in 1948; but this was in fact the region where Solomon built and docked his treasure fleet, not the destination of its voyages.

Our purpose here, however, is not to join the modern debate over the location of Ophir but rather to survey its early history and examine how it figured into later thinking about the significance of the Americas. Already in the first few centuries A.D., Josephus and other commentators on the Bible placed Ophir in India, based on inherited notions about the riches of that fabled land. The Greeks had associated gold with India since the time of Herodotus, and Classical geographers sometimes imagined that an island called Chryse (Golden) lay opposite the mouth of the Ganges; Josephus seems to have equated this Chryse with Ophir.[4] Jerome, in his Latin translation of the Bible, once translates the phrase "gold of Ophir" to "gold of India." This tradition was not universally followed by later mapmakers, however, who seem to have been troubled at the thought of ancient vessels sailing so far. The author of the Hereford Map, for example, gives the name Ophyr to one of four imaginary islands in the Red Sea, a much closer destination for Solomon's vessels, docked as they were at the tip of the Sinai. However, Martin Behaim, whose 1492 globe is thought to have been known to Columbus, drew Ophir as an island in the mouth of the river Ganges, following the identification with Chryse first established by Josephus.[5]

Columbus himself took a strong interest in the question of Ophir's location, and, perhaps well before the Behaim globe was created, used the Book of Kings and the Book of Chronicles to support the hypothesis that he could reach Asia by sailing west. Columbus made many references to Ophir in his annotations to Pierre D'Ailly's *Imago Mundi* and Pius II's *Historia rerum ubique gestarum*, and on several occasions he quotes either the relevant passages of Scripture or the learned discussions he had looked up in Josephus and other commentaries.[6] None of these postils can be dated with any certainty, but some scholars believe they predate the first voyage to America; if this is the case, they show that passages from the Hebrew Bible helped convince Columbus that such a voyage was possible.[7] That is, according to how Columbus saw it, one could reach the east by sailing west—and the first place one would thereby arrive at would be the easternmost point of Asia, Solomon's Ophir. The Hebrew Bible thus should be counted among the ancient texts that informed the discovery of the Americas, as well as the more familiar Classical sources such as Aristotle, Ptolemy, and Seneca along with their medieval redactors.

Not only Ophir, moreover, but another then mysterious biblical locale, Tarshish, figured into Columbus's calculations concerning the feasibility of a voyage across the Atlantic. In one of his postils to D'Ailly's *Imago Mundi*, for instance, Columbus discusses the import of 2 Chronicles 9:21: "Solomon's ships went to Tarshish with the servants of Hiram; once every three years the ships of Tarshish used to come bringing gold, silver, ivory, peacocks, and apes." The Tarshish referred to here may be identified as the city of Tarsus in Asia Minor, or, alternatively, the Iberian port the Greeks called Tartessus.[8] But Columbus was more inclined to equate it with Ophir, especially since he had read elsewhere in the Bible (I Kings 22:48) that "ships of Tarshish" (meaning, perhaps, ships sturdy enough to reach Tartessus) were ordered to sail to Ophir for gold. Indeed, the two trade routes, already partly confused in the Hebrew Scriptures, came to be entirely conflated in Columbus's mind, as we can see from his notes to the *Imago Mundi*. Here Columbus cites two learned Bible commentators, Nicholas of Lyra and Jerome, who placed "Tarshish" neither in Asia Minor nor on the Atlantic coast of Spain but on the eastern fringe of Asia, based presumably on the fact that all the exotic trade goods mentioned in the *Chronicles* passage could be found there. Then, carrying the discussion further, Columbus cites Josephus, once again, for the idea that Ophir, too, belonged in India. The juxtaposition of the two hypotheses shows clearly the direction of Columbus's thinking: Both Tarshish and Ophir were in the Far East, and thus could be considered more or less the same place. Further speculation along these lines emerges from a presumably later work, the *Libro de las profecías*, in which Columbus (as we shall see below) argues strenuously that the Tarshish of the Bible is an island, just as Ophir was thought to be, and thus a different place than the city of Tarsus in Cilicia.

The crucial verse from Chronicles, therefore, with its mention of fleets returning from Tarshish "every three years," told Columbus something remarkable about the eastward extension of Asia. Interpreting this "three years" to mean the *duration* (not the frequency) of the round-trip voyages of the ships of Tarshish, Columbus concluded that the Asian land mass must be so vast as to require more than a year's travel between Jerusalem and its eastern edge (more precisely, a year and thirteen days, the figure he cites elsewhere in the *Imago Mundi* based on the biblical commentary of Jerome).[9] With so much of the globe taken up by Asia, he reasoned, the space left for the Atlantic Ocean must be narrow indeed. The same verse from Chronicles, moreover, is quoted by Columbus in a postil to the *Historia rerum*, along with a long excerpt copied out of Josephus's discussion of Solomon's fleet and its voyages to Ophir. Evidently, Columbus had done considerable research on the location of Ophir and Tarshish in an effort to prove to himself that the two places were one and that they lay so far to the east that a ship sailing westward could reach them.

After he had himself made that westward crossing, moreover, Columbus remained focused on King Solomon and Ophir in his thinking about where he had gone and what he had found. According to Peter Martyr, Columbus identified the island of Hispaniola with Ophir very early on in this thought process, perhaps at the first moment of discovery.[10] And other evidence attests that the idea stayed with him over the course of his life. In an undatable postil he wrote in his copy of Pliny's *Natural History*, he spoke of the first place he had found in the New World as "Feyti, or Ofir, or Cipangu, to which I have given the name Spagnola."[11] This note reveals Columbus's remarkable ability to entertain numerous diverse and conflicting geographic hypotheses at the same time; Ophir, traditionally located near India, could hardly be the same place as Cipangu, the name Marco Polo had given to the island of Japan. Moreover, the idea that either place would need to be renamed by Columbus—since both were well known and written of under their original names—also raises troubling questions. But what concerns us here is his readiness to identify as Ophir the island called Feyti by its inhabitants (the origin of the modern name Haiti). Moreover, in a letter to the Pope dated February 1502, Columbus repeats the identification of Hispaniola as both Ophir and Cipangu, and also adds two new identities, "Cethia" or Cethim and Uphaz—two more placeless biblical toponyms, the former an obscure island (Isa. 23:1–2, 23:12, Jer. 2:10–11), the latter, more significantly, a land from which gold is brought (Jer. 10:9).[12]

Columbus's ten-year insistence that Hispaniola was really Ophir, or Uphaz, or Cipangu—all places which were known to be rich in gold or other rarities—were on one level good public relations; after all, the sovereigns who were financing Columbus's journeys, Ferdinand and Isabella, had to be convinced that their efforts were worthwhile even though very little precious cargo had in fact returned to their shores. But it would be wrong to see Columbus as a mere self-promoter in his use of biblical names for his own discoveries. He was, after all, a man of deep piety and Christian faith who earnestly desired the universal triumph of the Catholic Church under the leadership of the Spanish monarchs—monarchs who had already struck a great blow on behalf of the Church by reconquering Granada from the Muslims, just before the first voyage to the New World.

Throughout his life Columbus exhorted Ferdinand and Isabella, and the Pope, to the further propagation of the faith and even the reconquest of Jerusalem from the infidels in a new crusade.[13] The gold he sought in the New World, or at times claimed he had found, was to serve as the endowment of this Christian mission. In this context, the legend of Ophir loomed large indeed in Columbus's mind, for it had not escaped the admiral's notice that, in the Books of Chronicles and Kings, Ophir's gold was used to finance the building of Solomon's temple in Jerusalem, and its precious almug wood actually served as the supports[14] for that holy structure.

The treasure from the new Ophir in the Americas, then, would serve to build a new temple in a newly sanctified Jerusalem. Such are the implications of the letter Columbus sent to Ferdinand and Isabella from his fourth voyage, the so-called *lettera rarissima*, dated 7 July 1503. In a famous passage of this letter, Columbus extols the power of gold to further the mission of the Christian faith. "O, most excellent gold!" Columbus writes. "Who has gold has a treasure with which he gets what he wants, imposes his will on the world, and even helps souls to Paradise." There follows a brief ethnographic note about the burial of gold among the Indians, and then, abruptly, Columbus turns his thoughts to King Solomon. Invoking yet again the well-worn passages from Chronicles and Kings, together with Josephus's commentary on them, Columbus reckons the golden treasure that Solomon collected from Ophir, the place Josephus had called Aurea, or "Land of Gold." "Josephus says that this gold was obtained in Aurea; if so, I declare that those mines of the Aurea are but a part of those in Veragua," Columbus writes, speaking of the South American coast he was then exploring. "Solomon *bought* all that gold, precious stones, and silver; but you may send orders to collect it if you see fit."[15] Then, citing a new biblical passage concerning the legacy of Solomon's father, King David, Columbus asserts that the gold used in building the Temple had come from the Indies, that is, from the lands known to Josephus simultaneously as Aurea and Ophir.[16] The endpoint of this convoluted train of thought suddenly becomes clear in the next sentence, startling in its clarity and conviction: "Jerusalem and the Mount of Zion are now to be rebuilt by Christian hands," as foretold in a psalm that, Columbus goes on to imply, foretold his own leading role in this enterprise.

Nor was this the largest of the spiritual implications Columbus saw in his supposed rediscovery of Ophir. For the rebuilding of the temple in Jerusalem, as Columbus knew from his readings of Scripture, was one of a series of events that would lead to the End of Days, the Apocalypse, and the universal reign of Christ on earth. Columbus's apocalyptic or messianic fantasies have been well documented in several recent studies, but the specific role within them of his thinking about Ophir has not as yet been fully explored. That role can be discerned not only from the *lettera rarissima* but also from the unfinished manuscript called the *Libro de las profecias*, compiled during the years 1501 to 1503 by Columbus, his son Ferdinand, and a Carthusian friar by the name of Gorricio.

In the final section of this work, Columbus and his collaborators trot out the familiar verses from Kings and Chronicles describing Hiram's treasure fleet and the voyages to Ophir, together with a new set of citations referring to Tarshish, the land from which Solomon brought silver.[17] Columbus, in his marginal annotations to these quotes, insists over and over on the insular character of this silver-bearing Tarshish, distinguishing it carefully from the city Tarsus in Asia Minor, so as to bolster the claim made in the postils to the *Imago Mundi* and repeated here in the *Libro* that Tarshish and Ophir are one and the same place. Columbus further identifies both places with yet another biblical island, Cethim, as he also does in his February 1502 letter to the Pope (written during the same period as the composition of the *Libro*). Though he does not here make any attempt to equate these places with Hispaniola, as he does in that letter, the implications of his thinking are clear within the messianic context of the *Libro* as a whole.

As noted in an important article by Pauline Moffitt Watts, many of the citations in this complex work speak of the recovery of Mt. Zion and the conversion of all humanity to one universal faith as signs of the coming Apocalypse.[18] In both cases, historical time is conceived of as returning to its beginnings as it comes to its end, uniting alpha and omega in one eternal circle. Columbus presumably thought of his voyages to Solomon's Ophir in similar terms: If a modern mariner were to recommence trading with ports forgotten since the ninth century B.C., the world would in some sense be restored to its biblical condition. Columbus becomes an avatar of the ancient past as well as a forerunner of the apocalyptic future—exactly the same combination of roles he took upon himself in his reinterpretation of a passage from Seneca's tragedy *Medea*, as I have discussed elsewhere.[19] Whereas, in his references to the *Medea*, Columbus identifies himself with Tiphys, the navigator who had once piloted Jason's epochal voyage and who (according to a spurious reading in the manuscripts of Seneca's play) would ply the seas once again at the end of that epoch, he seems in his treatment of biblical legend to have seen himself as a latter-day King Hiram, supplying naval wherewithal to a noble monarchy and collecting the riches required for a rebuilding of the ancient Temple.[20]

Columbus's idea of his discoveries as both a return to earliest biblical history and a step forward toward the Apocalypse assumed its most dramatic form during the third voyage, just before the compilation of the *Libro de las profecias*. In a justly famous passage of a letter to the Spanish sovereigns recounting this voyage, Columbus claims to have arrived at the very outset of biblical time, that is, at the earthly paradise of the Book of Genesis. He was in fact off the coast of the South American continent, at the mouth of what is now the Orinoco River—a river whose breadth and volume of fresh water, as Columbus realized, surpassed what was possible for any ordinary "island." His ideas about Ophir and Tarshish being thus inapplicable, Columbus began a new line of speculation about the geography of the earth. In his letter he explains to the Spanish monarchs that the globe is not quite spherical, as Ptolemy had believed, but rises to a summit in its Southern Hemisphere—a summit he compares, in a sublime pair of similes, to the stalk of a pear or the nipple of a woman's breast. Ptolemy had been oblivious of this elevation because he knew nothing of the Southern Hemisphere; Aristotle had speculated about it but had not known where to place it. Now Columbus claims to have found it, as proved by the immense flow of fresh water spilling down from its slopes. Then, in another awesome leap of mythic thinking, Columbus links this immense river with the four rivers said in Genesis to flow out of Paradise—another locale sought but not found by ancient authorities, though agreed by all to lie somewhere in the east.

Columbus then reasons that he is in fact sailing upward toward the summit of Paradise, which lies atop the stalk of the global pear or at the nipple of the breast, and that, though he can never approach the top, the river he has found must be flowing directly from that distant place. Whether or not the Admiral was aware that in medieval mythic geography the garden of Eden stands directly opposite Jerusalem on the other side of the earth, his "discovery" of Paradise on the third voyage seems closely connected with his growing apprehension of the coming End of Days. The return to the starting point of human history, in the biblical scheme that Columbus clearly adopts in the *Libro de las profecias*, signals and perhaps even initiates the approach of its close; the ends of the time line would be joined to form a circle, and the ancient kingdom of Jerusalem would be resurrected as the Christian New Jerusalem.[21]

Columbus, as many students of his writings can attest, had an astounding ability to find resonance between his own circumstances and the narratives of ancient myth, whether those of the Bible or of Greco-Roman antiquity. The legend of Solomon's treasure fleet was only one of the many tales that figured into his understanding of his life and discoveries, but an important one, given the support it lent to his presentiments of the Apocalypse and to his understanding of his own role in Christian eschatology. As a new Hiram, voyaging once again to Ophir and supplying the wealth needed to rebuild the ancient temple, Columbus saw himself taking part in a grand reenactment of a glorious moment in the biblical past; and such returns to early mythic patterns confirmed his belief that the ancient prophecies were being fulfilled and that history was at last reaching its end.

Ophir and Ethnography—the Later Sixteenth Century

Columbus indicates in the *Libro de las profecias* that the biblical prophets had foreseen not only his crossing of the Atlantic, but also his efforts to convert the inhabitants of the Americas to Christianity; but who were these inhabitants, in biblical terms? Columbus seems not to have been troubled by this question, since in his eyes the natives of the Americas were simply inhabitants of the Asian littoral or of the islands offshore— subjects, in other words, of the Great Khan (who had already become a target of Christian missionaries in the fifteenth century). Though preoccupied throughout his life with the *geography* of Scripture, Columbus had little interest in its relevance to *ethnography*; indeed, he seems not to have noticed, or not to have cared, that Ophir is not only a place but a person—one of the descendants of Shem, listed in the great roll call of Noah's offspring in chapter 10 of Genesis. Had he remarked on this homonymy, his lines of inference might have gone far indeed; as Samuel Eliot Morison has remarked, for Columbus, two plus two did not equal four, but rather twenty-two. It was left instead to those who followed Columbus, and who tried to assimilate his discoveries to their understanding of the world, to wrestle with the question of how the natives of the Americas fit into the biblical scheme of the peopling of the earth. Though few went as far as the Portuguese artist Vasco Fernandes, who in the early sixteenth century painted a Brazilian Indian as one of the three wise men adoring the Christ child, most had their own theories as to how the American natives were connected to the peoples of the Bible—theories that were hotly debated for more than a century after Columbus's death and that have continued to inform religious and racial mythology right up to the present day.[22]

Let us return for a moment to the interpretive dogma that underlies this debate. Since only Noah and his sons had survived the Flood, all the peoples of the earth had descended from them, according to the "family tree" of humankind in Genesis 10; only heretics like La Peyrère claimed that other, non-Noachic or Pre-Adamic peoples were included among the nations known to sixteenth-century Europeans. But the three sons of Noah had traditionally been linked to the three continents of the Old World, before the discovery of the New (Fig. 1.1).[23] How, scholars and clerics wondered, had one of Noah's descendants traveled into the New World so as to fill it with his offspring? And from which line had that ancient colonist come—from that of Japheth, Ham, or Shem? All the new tools of Renaissance humanism were brought into play in an effort to answer these questions. In the new age of printed books and of the revival of Classical learning, scholars and theologians had an immense array of material on which to draw in formulating their theories of Indian origins; and since all educated men were now being trained to read Greek, Latin, and Hebrew, a kind of pseudo-science of spurious linguistics and false etymologies came into play in support of these theories.

Guillaume de Postel, for example—a French scholar who had traveled to the East in order to learn and record Asian languages—showed in the treatise *Cosmographicae Disciplinae* (1561) how a little linguistic expertise could go a long, long way.[24] Postel constructed a bizarrely detailed scheme of the migrations of Noah's progeny across the face of the globe, and correlated these wanderings with the early human history recorded by Classical Roman mythologists like Cato the Elder. Noah, claims Postel citing Cato, was the same person known to the Romans as Janus, since Janus had traveled to Italy from Armenia, which is the landing place of Noah's Ark, and had been accompanied by a tribe called the Galli, whose

FIGURE 1.1 T-O map showing continents identified with the three sons of Noah, from 1472 Augsburg edition of Isidore of Seville, *Etymologiarum sive originum libri XX.* (Courtesy of The Newberry Library, Chicago)

name Postel derived from the Hebrew *gal* meaning "flood."[25] Having thus traced Noah, a.k.a. Janus, to Rome, Postel gives him a third name, Hattal, a Hebrew alias meaning "dew" or "mist," and derives the word "Italy" (or Hattal-y) from this name. The linguistic contortions get carried even further as Noah orders his son Japhet, who had accompanied him to Europe, to spread the three Hebrew letters of his name Hattal throughout the rest of the world. Thus Japhet, as he moved south into Africa and west beyond the shores of Spain, had named both the *Atl*as Mountains and the island known to Plato as *Atl*antis. It was but a short step from there to the New World, since the residents of Atlantis, according to Plato, had been great sailors and navigators who had explored the "true continent" lying to the west of their land. So the Atlanteans had colonized the *Atl*antic coast of the New World, spreading the seed of Japhet, along with the linguistic sign of his father, into the Caribbean and North America.

But Postel did not stop there, for he had yet to include the famous Ophir in his ethnographic scheme—and Ophir was, after all, a son of Shem, not Japhet. In yet a further extension of his etymological fancies, Postel traced Ophir to the Pacific shore of the New World, to Peru, or "Pheru," as Postel names it in an alternate spelling, presumably to bring the name into closer association with Ophir. Thus, whereas the line of Japhet had traveled west to reach the New World, the line of Shem had gone east, beyond the furthest shore of Asia. "Nam ex altera parte, nempe ab ortu, ex Semia Ophir in suam Pheru vel Peru possessionem venerat, qui rebus sacris praeesset" [For from the other direction, that is from the east, from Asia, Ophir came into his estate, Pheru or Peru, in order to be in charge of Divine matters], Postel wrote.[26] From this dual ethnography, Postel derives a remarkable Christian theology. The line of Shem, he explains, being descendants of Noah's blessed and first-born son, had been charged by their father with the Divine mission of spreading monotheistic faith throughout the world; their descendants, after all, had become the first Jews, many generations later. Thus, it was part of God's plan for the propagation of faith that the Shemites, too, had made it to the New World—"in order to be in charge of sacred matters," as Postel puts it.

Again turning to Roman mythology for confirmation, Postel notes that the great prophetess of ancient Rome, the Sibyl, had predicted the eventual triumph there of the Christian faith, another case in which an Asian and a descendant of Shem had spread monotheistic faith beyond the borders of his ancestral homeland. Noah, or Janus as he was known to the Romans, had evidently made his plan for the spread of monotheism clear to the Sibyl before his death. The arrival of Ophir in Peru had thus been an early forerunner of the journey of Christ's apostles to Europe and other pagan lands, and part of God's plan for the proselytization of His faith. "Nec enim fieri aliter potest, quin summus ille seculi aurei minister et institutor Ianus ita instituisset ut ubivis in toto orbe esset unus minister ex Semi auctoritate…. Sic in Atlantide est credendum ut ex Iectani filliis aliquis una cum Iapetitis fuerit missus, ita ut Peru posset esse Ophiri pars" [It cannot be otherwise but that that greatest overseer and founder of the Golden Age, Janus, thus established that everywhere in the whole world would be a single overseer from the high office of Shem…. Thus in the Atlantic region, it must be believed that someone from the sons of Jectan (i.e., the grandsons of Shem) was sent along with the Japhethites, in such a way that Peru became the inheritance of Ophir].[27]

The project of Postel's *Cosmographicae Disciplinae*—the tracing of all the wanderings and settlements of the sons of Noah in an effort to explain the location of the earth's races—was taken up ten years later by the learned Spanish humanist Benito Arias Montano in a treatise titled *Phaleg*. This treatise (named for one of the descendants of Noah—*phaleg* meaning "division" in Hebrew—because, according to Genesis 10, "in his days the earth was divided") was then included in Arias Montano's learned 1572 work, *Antiquitatum Iudaicarum*. Arias Montano had earlier learned Hebrew and had directed the immense Spanish Polyglot Bible of 1572 with its detailed commentary on many abstruse questions about biblical times.[28] In *Phaleg* he used his knowledge of Hebrew to assert not only that Ophir had founded Peru, which thereafter (as Postel implied) bore a metathesized version of his name, but that this South American land was known to the Old Testament under the name Parva'im. Parva'im, mentioned in the 2nd Book of Chronicles, is another unlocatable biblical toponym like Ophir or Uphaz, and, not surprisingly, another land from which gold was brought to Jerusalem in the days of Solomon. Arias Montano noted that the "-im" portion of this word could be understood as the Hebrew dual ending, and hence understood the name to mean "the two Parvas" or "the two Perus," and further interpreted this to mean "the two Americas." He writes, "Ophir... secundum abyssi magnae littora genus nomenque produxit suum, ad duas regiones angusto terrarum, sed longo Isthmo interiecto distinctas, quae ad Salomonis usque atque ulteriora etiam tempora integrum retinuere vocabulum Ophir; quod paulo post inversum utrique parti seorsum adscriptum est, atque alterutra pars Peru; utraque autem simul dualis numeri pronuntiatione Pervaim sive Parvaim dicta est" [Ophir ... carried forward his name and his race along the shores of the great abyss, and to the two regions of these lands separated by a long isthmus between; and these retained intact the name Ophir up to the times of Solomon and even afterward; but the name was shortly afterward reversed, and assigned to both portions of this region on their own; and so each part was called Pervaim or Parvaim, using the pronunciation of the dual number].[29]

In good scholarly fashion, Arias Montano illustrated the ethnographic scheme of *Phaleg* with a map (also published in his Polyglot Bible)[30] showing with numbers and letters the places to which each of Noah's sons, grandsons, and great-grandsons had migrated (Figs. 1.2 and 1.3). One can see from this map that he has postulated a land bridge across the Bering Strait (known to the Renaissance as the Straits of Anian), so as to make the intercontinental journey of Ophir possible. He has also been careful to give *two* locations for the number nineteen, designating Ophir's settlements in North and South America, to account for the dual form of the Hebrew word *parvaim*. This beautifully drawn map represents the first detailed attempt, so far as I know, to use cartography as a tool for investigating historical anthropology, and is also the first to posit a land bridge across the northern Pacific—the very route by which, as most scientists now believe, humankind crossed into the Americas.

But Arias Montano was not satisfied with merely tracing Ophir into the New World as Postel had done. He seems to have assumed that the descendants of Noah were listed by Genesis in geographic order, moving from west to east, and that therefore Ophir's eastward travels had been surpassed by those of his brother Iobab, represented as number twenty-one on the map, the last mentioned and therefore the easternmost Shemite. (An intervening brother, Havilah, represented by number

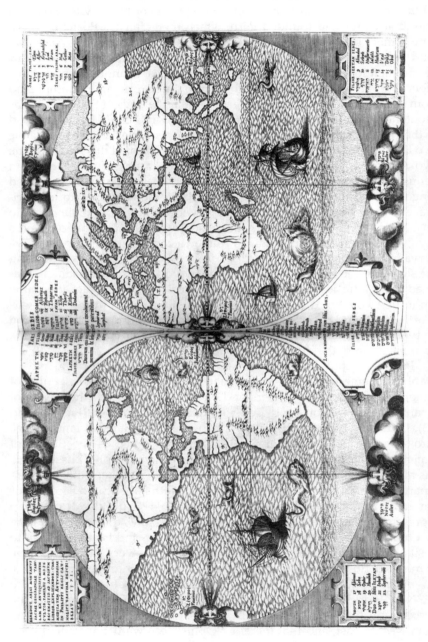

FIGURE 1.2   Ethnographic map of Benito Arias Montano, *Antiquitatum Iudaicarum Libri IX* (Lugduni Batavorum 1593).

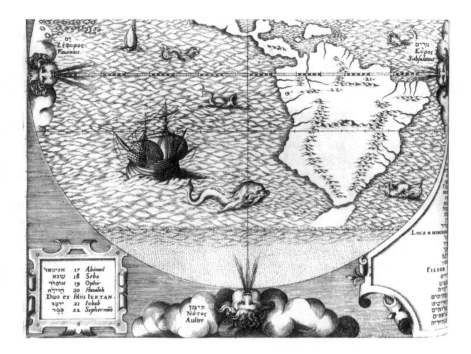

FIGURE 1.3   Detail of Montano map in Figure 1.2.

twenty, was situated by Arias Montano in the Asian land known to Genesis [2:11] as Havilah, and therefore this number alone does not fit the map's scheme of eastward progression.) Moreover, Iobab and his brothers, the sons of Ioktan, were said by Genesis to have settled in lands as far east as a mountain named Sepher, and even beyond that. If Iobab, then, had settled to the east of Ophir, the founder of Peru, then, reasoned Arias Montano, the Mountain of Sepher could only be the Andes range, represented by the number twenty-two here—the only physical feature included in the key to this otherwise purely ethnographic map. Here an etymological problem presented itself. Why, if Ophir had left such clear memorials of his name in "Peru" and "Parva'im," had the names of Iobab and the Sepher Mountain so entirely changed or perished? Arias Montano has a solution, which he proposes in the notes that accompany his ethnographic map. Under the rubric "Sepher Mountain" he admits that these peaks are "called Andes by our times," but adds: "In this part of the world there remains to this day a very ancient city Yuctan, which retains the name of the founder of this race." Iobab, in other words, had memorialized not himself but his father Ioktan in the New World, just as, according to Postel, Noah's son Japhet had spread his father's alternate name Hattal throughout the earth.[31]

Like Postel, Arias Montano made his ethnographic inquiries serve the purposes of a larger theology. In an extended discussion of the biblical Ophir—not just the person, but the place named for him, i.e., the destination of Solomon's treasure fleet—Arias Montano concludes that virtually all the gold known to antiquity had been brought out of this port and spread throughout the world. The other sources of ancient gold (rivers like the Pactolus and the Haemus), he reasons, simply could not have produced enough of the precious metal to account for the vast quantities spoken of in Greek, Roman, and biblical texts. A provident deity had created one source of gold for the entire earth, just as he had isolated its other resources in one land or another, in order to compel the races to share their goods and thus restore the original, Adamic unity of all humankind, Arias Montano argues. The three sons of Noah may have scattered in three different directions, but their descendants had been brought together again by their quest for natural resources like the gold of Ophir.[32] In this remarkable exegesis of the story of Solomon's ships, as noted in Gliozzi's study *Adamo e il nuovo mundo*, Arias Montano supplies a Divine mandate for the great commercial enterprise of his day, the systematic Spanish plunder of the gold of Mexico and Peru.

Such were the theological and eschatological themes that dominated the scholarly discussions of Ophir, the person and the place, in the third quarter of the sixteenth century, but in 1578 a new approach, more genuinely scientific and modern, was applied to the subject by the great Jesuit thinker and New World sojourner José de Acosta. In that year he published his Latin treatise *De Natura Novi Orbis*, later translated into Spanish and reprinted as the first two books of the famous *Historia natural y moral de las Indias*.[33] In two chapters devoted to the Ophir debate (1.13 and 14), Acosta attacked the etymological approach of bookish scholars such as Arias Montano and, in particular, dismissed the correlation of Yucatan with Ioktan as a mere linguistic coincidence. As for the derivation of "Peru" from "Ophir," Acosta put forth the devastating counterargument that the natives of South America, among whom he had done firsthand research, never used "Peru" themselves to refer to their own homeland, but regarded it as a Spanish term, derived accidentally from the name of a local river. Later commentators took up Acosta's argument and expanded it, producing a marvelous anecdote to explain the origin of the name "Peru": The first Spanish conquistadors to encounter a Peruvian native, as they sailed up one of the coastal streams, eagerly demanded to know where they were, and were told by the innocent native, "Beru, Beru," meaning "in the river." In another version of this story, designed to cast even greater ridicule on the Ophir-Peru etymology, the native whom the Spanish interrogated thought he was being asked for his own name, which happened to be Beru.[34]

It would require more space than this essay can accommodate to describe all the ingenious arguments Acosta brings to bear on the question of whether Solomon (or any ancient navigator) had sailed to the New

World, or whether the American Indians were descended from Ophir. Suffice it to say that he changed the framework of this debate forever, and that anyone who took part in it from that point onward had to wrestle with Acosta.[35] For example, the question of whether ancient navigators, who lacked the use of the compass to determine position at sea, were capable of making oceanic voyages was raised by Acosta for the first time, touching off a desperate search by Ophir-partisans through the Bible and Greco-Roman literature for references to the compass. Furthermore, Acosta pointed out the thereafter notorious problem that the New World contained animal and plant life unknown to the Old; surely, he argued, Solomon's ships had not brought llamas and jaguars with them on their voyages to the so-called land of Ophir. In the end, Acosta rules out the idea of ancient transoceanic voyages either in biblical or in Greco-Roman times, and supports the idea first raised by Arias Montano that early humans had crossed into the New World over a land bridge between Asia and North America. But he refutes the notion that any knowledge of the Americas had thereafter been passed back to Asia, so as to leave its traces in the Bible or in ancient Greek or Latin writings, in which, as a Jesuit scholar, he was thoroughly versed.

Though he arrives at these conclusions by keen scientific reasoning, Acosta was nevertheless a man of God, and in the final chapters of the *De Natura Novi Orbis* he, like Arias Montano and Postel before him, turns to theology as a way of understanding the meaning of Columbus's discoveries. God had revealed to Acosta's own Christian Age the great secret of the Western Hemisphere, a secret He had kept veiled from pagan and from Jewish antiquity. Indeed, the Divine Providence that had led Columbus to the New World was visible in the supernatural properties of the magnet, Acosta claimed, and of the compass fashioned from it. This strange, northward-pointing stone, without which oceanic travel was clearly impossible, embodied within itself the infinite wisdom and unfathomable mystery of the Divine mind, and demonstrated to Acosta that faith ultimately must take precedence over reason.[36] The discovery of the Americas proved to Acosta that his own era, the era of the magnetic compass, was the blessed Golden Age in which God had chosen to reveal the half of the globe kept hidden since its first creation.

The impact of Acosta's writings can be judged from the reaction it produced in one of his contemporaries, a figure who perhaps best preserves a sense of the intellectual and spiritual ferment surrounding the Ophir question in the Renaissance. Abraham Ortelius was neither a cleric like Arias Montano nor a philosopher like Acosta, but a humble map publisher and amateur humanist working in the town of Antwerp.[37] Ortelius is best known for his atlas of maps covering the entire earth, the *Theatrum Orbis Terrarum*, published in numerous editions and in various different languages from 1570 on; but he also produced a geographic reference work, the *Synonomia*, later renamed the *Thesaurus Geographicus*, a dictionary of ancient place names and their latter-day equivalents. In both

works, the *Theatrum* and the *Thesaurus*, Ortelius was forced to confront
the question of Solomon's Ophir and its relationship to Peru, but his comments reveal that he was confused about the issue and torn between conflicting arguments. Moreover, he changes his mind as the course of the
scholarly debate changes, as can be seen by comparing the various editions of his two principal works between 1570 and his death in 1598.[38]

In his first editions of the *Theatrum Orbis* and *Thesaurus Geographicus*,
published before Acosta's treatise had appeared, Ortelius cautiously
accepts the arguments of Postel and Arias Montano that ancient Ophir was
the modern Peru, although he also notes the opposition of Gaspar Barreiros, who had argued that King Solomon's gold mines should be located
in Indonesia instead.[39] Ortelius introduces yet a third possibility, based on
his own readings in the exploration literature of the day. In 1502, a Portuguese sailor named Thomas Lopez, who had accompanied Vasco da
Gama to Africa, recorded a peculiar encounter he had witnessed in the
trading port called Cefala or Sofala.[40] A group of Moors who resided there
approached da Gama and told him they had discovered native texts that
spoke of King Solomon's ships taking gold away from that spot once every
three years. Ortelius, noting that the region around Cephala is indeed rich
in gold, seems tempted to believe this curious account of Thomas Lopez,
which he had read in the great collection of explorers' logs published by
the Italian Ramusio. But his respect for the learning of Arias Montano wins
out, for the moment, and tilts the scales toward a Peruvian Ophir.

By 1596, however, Ortelius had read the writings of Acosta, and his
opinions about Ophir had shifted. Whereas formerly he had written, in
the Latin text of the *Thesaurus*, "Montani sententiam amplector," or "I
embrace the opinion of Arias Montano," he now changes the verb to a
subjunctive, "amplecterer"—"I *would* accept"—and adds, "if the vastness
of the intervening Ocean, which all antiquity judged to be unnavigable,
did not deter me." Ortelius goes on to cite Acosta's opinion regarding
ancient ignorance of the magnet as a decisive argument in the case. With
Arias Montano thus discredited, Ortelius turns back once more to his
own personal theory, based on Thomas Lopez's report of the writings
found in African Cephala. Ortelius now chooses to believe this report and
to identify Cephala with Ophir. Not only is this region rich in gold, as
Ortelius had mentioned already in 1578, but, as he now adds, it contains
ivory as well: "[T]he Scriptures report that Solomon got ivory from
Ophir, but ivory does not come from Peru, which never had any ele-
phants."[41] With such matter-of-fact reasoning and shrewd weighing of
the evidence, Ortelius reluctantly turns away from the idea of Solomonic
voyages to the Americas, an idea first proposed by Christopher Columbus more than a century earlier.

The humanistic and scientific approaches of men like Ortelius and
Acosta could not put an end to the line of speculation Columbus had
begun concerning the biblical identity of the Americas or the eschatological meaning of its "rediscovery." Indeed, as the Protestant Reformation

progressed and the response of the Church became harsher and more dogmatic, the debate surrounding Ophir took on religious and political significance far beyond what Columbus had ever imagined. Thus, toward the end of the sixteenth and the beginning of the seventeenth centuries, we find the idea of the New World as Solomon's Ophir promulgated by Church apologists and counter-reformists, in an effort either to demonstrate the infallibility of Scripture or to establish more firmly the continuities between the present and the ancient past.[42]

For example, at around the same time that Ortelius was abandoning the train of thought begun by Columbus, another writer, Thomas Bozio, was picking it up more or less exactly where Columbus had left off. In his religious treatise *De Signis Ecclesiae Dei* (1591), Bozio discusses passages from Hebrew Scripture that seem to refer to the Americas or to discuss its future role in world salvation, just as Columbus had done in the *Libro de las profecias*. And like Columbus, Bozio turns with intense interest to any passage concerning Tarshish or Ophir, in particular the verse predicting that "The kings of Tarshish and the islands shall bear gifts, and the kings of the Arabians and of Saba will offer presents" (Psalms 71:10)—a verse that Columbus had cited not once but three times in the *Libro*, more frequently than any other single verse.[43] Bozio explains that the verse clearly refers to his own times: "Regio namque Tharsis est illa, ad quam classis Salomonis, triennium totum in itinere ponens, appellabat.... Quocirca classis Lusitanica ... defert inde nobilissima atque ingentia munera ad nostras oras, quae Catholici nationi et sacris usibus maxime serviunt" [The land of Tarshish is that place at which the fleet of Solomon landed, spending a whole three years en route.... From these parts the Spanish fleet ... brings vast and very excellent "gifts" to our shores, and these serve the Catholic realm and its sacred purposes].[44] Not only had King David, the supposed author of this Psalm, correctly predicted the rediscovery of Ophir, but the eschatological meaning of his prophecy gave sanction, in Bozio's eyes, to the plunder of its gold by a Catholic country, Spain.[45]

In further support of the idea that Columbus's voyages had fulfilled a Divine mandate, Bozio proved that he could play scriptural word games as well as any of his humanist contemporaries. Citing a verse of Isaiah that refers to doves (*columbae* in Latin) and directly precedes another prophecy concerning the precious cargoes of the ships of Tarshish, Bozio claimed that the greatest of Hebrew prophets had here explicitly predicted that a man named Columbus would one day claim those riches.[46] Never mind that Isaiah's words had originally been written in Hebrew, not Latin!

We may be tempted to see the product of the fantastical and undisciplined Renaissance mind in this use of Scripture as a source of elaborately encoded prophecies with which to link contemporary events to remotest antiquity, but the same game is still being played today. As this essay was being prepared, a book called *The Bible Code* by Michael Drosnin, which rearranges the Hebrew letters of the Pentateuch into grids to produce prophecies concerning Hitler, Kennedy, and even Bill Clinton, stood in the fourth position on the *New York Times* bestseller list, with 350,000 copies in print in the U.S. and nine translations appearing in foreign countries. It seems that not only the late sixteenth century but also the late twentieth century sought a sacred text that contains within itself the pattern of all subsequent history and that gives eschatological meaning to an otherwise chaotic welter of world events. The oldest and most authoritative of "Western" writings, the Hebrew Bible continues to be our most popular refuge from this chaos, provides new "prophecies" of our experience as our methods of decoding it become more sophisticated. We continue to seek, as Columbus did five centuries ago and Bozio did a century later, a sense that our long voyage through history was foreknown to, and is guided by, a Divinity that shapes our ends.[47]

Notes

1. This point is stressed by Vassilios Christidès in "L'énigme d'Ophir," *Revue Biblique* 77 (1970):240–47. Christidès is to my knowledge the first scholar to take account of the interpretive consequences of the confusion of the two names; indeed, he points out himself (242 n. 14, e.g.) that other recent interpreters have persisted in this confusion.
2. Published by B. Maisler in *Journal of Near Eastern Studies* 10 (1951):266–69.
3. Especially Jacques Schreiden, "Les entreprises navales du roi Salomon," *Annuaires de l'Institut de philologie et d'histoire orientale et slave* 13 (1953):587–90.
4. See *Jewish Antiquities* 8.164, where it is unclear whether the Greek word *chrysen* should be treated as a proper noun. Other early commentators are cited by Christidès, "L'énigme d'Ophir," 241–44.
5. The note is quoted by E. G. Ravenstein, *Martin Behaim: His Life and Globe* (London, 1908), 94; see also G. E. Nunn, *Geographical Conceptions of Columbus: A Consideration of Four Problems* (American Geog. Soc. Research Series no. 14, New York, 1924), 75–76.
6. These and other annotations are discussed by Valerie Flint, *The Imaginative Landscape of Christopher Columbus* (Princeton, 1992), chap. 2, see esp. 54–55, 62, 70. The postils themselves can be found in Cesare de Lollis, *Scritti di Cristoforo Colombo* (vol. 1, part 2, of the larger *Raccolta di Documenti* [Rome, 1894]), and those Columbus made in his copy of D'Ailly are included in the edition of *Ymago Mundi* by Edmond Buron (Paris, 1930).
7. The position of Valerie Flint (*Imaginative Landscape*, 46–48) seems to me a reasonable one: Some of the postils to *Imago Mundi* and *Historia Rerum*, if not the other works annotated by Columbus, predate the first voyage, though others were certainly added later. The one postil that has been firmly dated is found in one of the *opuscula* in the D'Ailly volume, where Columbus refers explicitly to "this year 1491" (Pauline Moffitt Watts, "Prophecy and Discovery: On the Spiritual Origins of the Enterprise of the Indies," *American Hist. Rev.* 90, 1–2 [1985]:85–86).
8. Discussion of this point can be found in Rhys Carpenter, *Beyond the Pillars of Heracles: The Classical World Seen through the Eyes of Its Discoverers* (New York, 1966), 60f., 216–19.
9. Buron, *Ymago*, vol. 1, 306–7; translation quoted by Flint, *Imaginative Landscape*, 124.
10. Martyr cites this opinion in order to contest it in *Decades* I.3.1, an entry dated 13 November 1493; see the edition of J. Torres Asensio, vol. 1 (Madrid, 1892) 100.
11. De Lollis, *Scritti*, 472; see Flint, *Imaginative Landscape*, 70f. and 125.
12. De Lollis, *Scritti*, 164–66.

13. On this topic, see Pauline Moffitt Watts, "Prophecy and Discovery," 95–99, and chapter 3 of Delno C. West and August Kling, "The Piety and Faith of Christopher Columbus," an introductory chapter in their edition of *The* Libro de las Profecias *of Christopher Columbus* (Gainesville, Fla., 1991).
14. The Greek word in the Septuagint is *staseis* (2 Chronicles 9:10), presumably meaning pillars. However, it bears noting that the parallel passage in Kings (3 Kings 10:11 in the Septuagint) refers instead to *huposterigmata*, a rare word that can mean "supports" but is sometimes translated "stools."
15. Translations are those of Samuel Eliot Morison in *Journals and Other Documents on the Life and Voyages of Christopher Columbus* (New York, 1963), 383.
16. Both Morison (ibid., 385 n. 3) and Flint (*Imaginative Landscape*, 185 n. 7) mistakenly take the term "Aurea" in this passage as a reference to the Golden Chersonnese, thus obscuring the point behind Columbus's citations of Josephus. It was the link to King Solomon and the Temple at Jerusalem that made his discovery of the Veraguan (Ophirian) gold fields so important, as West and Kling recognized ("Piety and Faith," 62).
17. West and Kling, "Piety and Faith," 239–49.
18. Ibid., 92–94.
19. James Romm, "New World and *novos orbes*: Seneca in the Renaissance Debate over Ancient Discoveries of the Americas," in vol. 1 of *The Classical Tradition and the Americas*, eds. W. Haase and M. Reinhold (Berlin and New York, 1994), 81–84. See also Gabriella Moretti, "*Nec sit terris ultima Thule*: La profezia di Seneca sulla scoperta del Nuovo Mundo," *Columbeis* I (Publicazioni dell'Istituto di Filologia Classica e Medievale, Genoa, 1986), 95–106; and Diskin Clay, "Columbus's Senecan Prophecy," *American Journal of Philology* 113 (1992):617–20.
20. See West and Kling's discussion in "Piety and Faith," 61–63. The "fit" of the Solomon-Ophir myth with Columbus's voyage was not perfect, since Columbus himself, and others, had identified King Ferdinand of Spain with the biblical David rather than with Solomon, as West and Kling make clear. But Columbus also believed, as shown by the *lettera rarissima*, that Solomon had used the money bequeathed by his father David to construct the original Temple.
21. West and Kling, "Piety and Faith," 67–69. See also the discussion of Columbus's third voyage in Mary Campbell, *The Witness and the Other World: Exotic European Travel Writing, 400–1600* (Ithaca, N.Y., 1989), chap. 5, and in Margarita Zamora, *Reading Columbus* (Berkeley, 1993).
22. See the essay by David S. Katz in this volume, and Richard Popkin, "The Rise and Fall of the Jewish Indian Theory," in Y. Kaplan, H. Mchoulan, and R. Popkin, eds., *Menasseh Ben Israel and His World* (Leiden, 1989), 63–82.
23. Discussed by Don Allen Cameron, *The Legend of Noah* (Urbana, Ill., 1949), 85–89; more recently, see Benjamin Braude, "The Sons of Noah and the Construction of Ethnic and Geographic Identities in the Medieval and Early Modern Periods," *William and Mary Quarterly* 54 (3rd series, 1997):103–42.
24. On Postel's scheme of New World ethnography, see Giuliano Gliozzi, *Adamo e il nuovo mundo: La nascita dell'antropologia come ideologia coloniale, dalle genealogie bibliche alle teorie razziali (1500–1700)* (Florence, 1977), 29–30, 149–50.
25. Guillaume de Postel, *Cosmographicae disciplinae* (Basel, 1561), 27–30. The identification of Noah and Janus, which as far as I know originates with Postel, goes on to assume a prominent place in Renaissance scholarship, such that Sir Walter Raleigh felt compelled to refute it in his *Historie of the World* (1614).
26. Postel, *Cosmographicae disciplinae*, 32; see Gliozzi, *Adamo*, 29–30, 149–50. Though Postel's methods were far from scientific, his conclusions have recently been endorsed by a small group of anthropologists who believe that the Americas were settled by migrants from both Europe and Asia. A feature article by Douglas Preston in the 16 June 1997 issue of the *New Yorker* describes the controversy over the recent find of "Kennewick man"—a skeleton uncovered in Oregon and found to be more than 9,000 years old, yet clearly showing European-type facial features in its still intact skull. This

and other similar finds have convinced some anthropologists that the earliest settlers in the Americas were of European origin, and came to the New World either by crossing Asia and the Bering Strait or by walking over a then frozen North Atlantic. These first arrivals would subsequently have been overcome by other, later arriving groups of Asiatic stock.

27. Ibid. Of course, Postel's scheme ignores the obvious difficulty that the Aztecs of Peru were not monotheists at the time of the Spanish conquests. But Postel bypasses this point in silence, perhaps relying on reports of the advanced character of South American civilization, compared with that of the North, as proof of their kinship with the world's other "civilized" (i.e., monotheistic) races.

28. For Arias Montano's rather complicated blend of Erasmian humanism and Church orthodoxy in his approach to the Bible, see Marcel Bataillon, *Erasme et l'Espagne* (Paris, 1937), 765–67, 781–93.

29. Quoted from page 20 of *Phaleg*, published in Benito Arias Montano, *Antiquituatum Iudaicarum Libri IX* (Lugduni Batavorum, 1593).

30. Benito Arias Montano, *Biblia Sacra Hebraice, Chaldice, Graece et Latine*, tome VIII (Antwerp, 1572); Arias Montano, *Antiquitatum Iudaicarum*, 26f.

31. Discussed by Anthony Grafton, *New Worlds, Ancient Texts: The Power of Tradition and the Shock of Discovery* (with April Shelford and Nancy Siraisi) (Cambridge, Mass., and London, 1992), 149, and by Gliozzi, *Adamo*, 151–53.

32. Arias Montano, *Antiquitatum Iudaicarum*, 3–5.

33. José de Acosta, *Historia natural y moral de las Indias* (Salamanca, 1590); modern edition by E. O'Gorman (Mexico, 1962), and English translation by E. Grimson, *The Natural and Moral History of the Indies*, Hakluyt Society, ser. 1, no. 60 (London, 1880).

34. Gliozzi, *Adamo*, 158–59.

35. On the importance of Acosta, see Barbara Beddall, "Father José de Acosta and the Place of His *Historia natural y noral de las Indias* in the History of Science," pp. 12–98, in her edition of the work (Valencia, 1977).

36. Acosta, *Historia* 1, chaps. 16–17; see Romm, "New World and *novos orbes*," 112.

37. For an account of Ortelius's life, see C. Koeman, *The History of Abraham Ortelius and His Theatrum Orbis Terrarum* (Lausanne, 1964).

38. For a more extensive discussion of this comparison, see my "Abraham Ortelius as Classical Humanist: The Sixteenth-Century Debate over Ancient Discoveries of the Americas," *Allegorica* 15 (1994):49–69.

39. See, for example, the entry on Ophir in the first edition of Abraham Ortelius, *Synonomia geographica* (Antwerp, 1578). Barreiros's essay "De Ophyra regione" was published initially as part of that author's *Cosmographia* (Coimbra, 1561).

40. Lopez's account can be found in Giovanni Battista Ramusio's *Navigationi et viaggi* (Venice, 1550), vol. 1, no. 8, where the Sofala story appears on p. 134.

41. Abraham Ortelius, *Thesaurus geographicus* (Antwerp, 1596), s.v. "Ophir." Ortelius thought this entry definitive enough that he made cross-references to it in the later editions of two of his other geographic works, the *Theatrum orbis terrarum* (preface to the map of the New World) and the *Parergon* (preface to the map of *Geographia sacra*).

42. For a summary of this material, most of which falls outside the temporal limits of the present essay, see Gliozzi, *Adamo*, chap. 4, part 3, 162–74.

43. West and Kling, "Piety and Faith," 121, 243, 249. Other portions of Psalm 71 are cited in two other places in the *Libro de las Profecias*, making it, once again, the most frequently cited text in the compilation. The King James Bible has this psalm as Psalm 72.

44. Thomas Bozio, *De Signis Ecclesiae Dei* 20.6 (Rome, 1591), 333.

45. See Gliozzi, *Adamo*, 162–63.

46. Ibid.

47. See the commentary on the popularity of *The Bible Code* by critic Edward Rothstein, "Is Destiny Just a Divine Word Game?" *New York Times*, 12 August 1997, p. C11.

– Chapter 2 –

KNOWLEDGE OF NEWLY DISCOVERED LANDS AMONG JEWISH COMMUNITIES OF EUROPE (FROM 1492 TO THE THIRTY YEARS' WAR)

Noah J. Efron

Introduction

IN 1707, TOBIAS COHEN PUBLISHED *Ma'aseh Tuviyah*, a book that has justly been called "the most influential early modern Hebrew textbook of the sciences."[1] He described his own efforts without undue modesty: "I have composed a book containing the knowledge and scholarly disciplines that every literate man must know."[2] One of these "scholarly disciplines" was geography, and the "knowledge" needed by early eighteenth-century Jewish literati included rudimentary facts about the New World. Cohen devoted a small section of his book to what he called "the discovery of a new land on the continent of America, which was discovered by the foreigners." This is what he wrote, in its entirety:

> There is much I could tell about the new land, in their language Nuovo Mondo, but understand that it is not my intention [to do anything more] than spare you from the gentiles who deride our writers as knowing nothing about the ways of the world. Therefore I will tell you a small bit: how Christopher Colombus discovered it in the year 1492, by Christian reckoning, and after him, at the command of Frederick in the year 1600, Oliver from the land of Holland expanded it further and after him in our day a Spaniard whose name was Ferdinando de Cuéllar[3] expanded still further and up to our day, they spread throughout that land and the land is expansive before them, and they go and conquer and build store houses and fortresses. They also call them by the names of the Christian lands, and act according to their custom, and their dress is the dress of the foreigners of our day.[4]

Though it recounts little,[5] Cohen's account says much about what the New World meant to him, and about what he thought it meant to his Jewish contemporaries. Cohen included such elementary facts because he believed that his readers knew nothing at all about the Americas, even as late as the early eighteenth century. Cohen did not lament this, for he viewed the New World as a decidedly foreign affair.[6] He emphasized that the discoveries were achieved by "the foreigners," who quickly imposed their foreign names, customs, and dress. Being foreign, the discoveries and conquests were of little moment to Jews. The only reason why a Jew might need to know about America was to escape the ridicule of gentiles. Taken for its own sake, it was not an unhappy fact that Jews of his day neither knew nor cared much about the New World.

There is something surprising in this perspective, because by Cohen's time there were Jewish communities in hubs of New World trade, there were active Jewish communities *in* the New World, and the material and economic impact of the New World throughout Europe was certainly strongly felt in this period.[7] One might expect these conditions to stimulate greater interest than what Cohen observed and advocated.[8]

It may also be surprising to learn that even before these conditions existed, Jews in Europe were interested in the maritime explorations. At least eleven books with accounts of the voyages of discovery were produced by Jews in the period between 1492 and the start of the Thirty Years' War in 1618. At least six more books with such accounts remained in manuscript, several of which had wide circulation.[9]

More significant than statistics of this sort is the fact that virtually every Hebrew book that one might expect to include an account of the voyages of discovery did include one. With only two exceptions, the chronicles and historical accounts produced in the sixteenth century all included information about newly discovered lands.[10] So, too, did books with a significant natural philosophic or natural historic component.[11] It is hard to say how many Jews read these books, and harder still to say how many Jews learned about the New World from Latin or vernacular sources. A 1595 inventory of books owned by 430 Jewish families in Mantua included a total of sixty-three copies of four Hebrew books with significant accounts of the voyages of discovery. The inventory also included as many as fourteen copies of nine books in Latin or Italian that included such accounts.[12] The Mantuan community at this time was hardly representative and displayed more interest in contemporary liberal arts than most communities.[13] But it may give some measure of the order of magnitude in which accounts of the explorations found their ways into Jewish hands.

Despite this diffusion of accounts, Jewish interest in the voyages of discovery remained limited and idiosyncratic. Though the first Hebrew references to them appeared in manuscript not long after the voyages, the first printed accounts did not appear until the middle of the sixteenth century. Even these were neither widely nor closely read, so it was reasonable for a Jew writing near the start of the seventeenth century to note of the discovery of the New World that "this matter is a bit of a new thing for us [Jews]."[14] Accounts by Jews also tended to be sketchy, including little detail and often misinformation—discoveries in the New World and voyages to Africa and Asia were sometimes conflated or confused. Jewish accounts showed relatively little regard for the fortunes of the explorers or the outposts they established, and, more generally, showed little regard for the voyages and discoveries themselves. When Jews were concerned about adventures overseas, it was typically because of what these adventures implied for the Jews of Europe themselves.

This is hardly surprising. Scholars have long argued that the explorations and discoveries of the fifteenth and sixteenth centuries served to confirm European self-perceptions and beliefs about Europe, European history, and European faith.[15] There is nothing unusual, or particularly interesting, about people finding parochial meaning in far-flung events, or confirmation of old belief in new information. What is interesting, however, is the question of which parochial uses in the sixteenth and early seventeenth centuries Jews found for explorations and discoveries, and why. Overseas adventures were deemed significant by Jews most often for what they implied about the relationship between Europe's Jews and Europe's Christians.[16] For some, these adventures were a harbinger of forthcoming redemption; for others they were a sign of Jewish intellectual superiority; for still others they were a herald of increased collaboration between Europe's Jews and Christians. What all of these interpretations shared was a conviction that shifting world boundaries mattered to Jews, first and foremost, for what they might imply about the shifting social and intellectual boundaries between Jews and Christians in Europe.

Interpretations of the Discoveries of New Lands[17]

Interpretations in a Millennial Vein

In the earliest Jewish accounts, the voyages of discovery were sometimes seen as one among many signs that the End of Days was approaching. Though most accounts of this sort were produced by writers of Spanish descent, for whom the expulsion loomed large, the earliest was written by Abraham Farissol (1452–c.1528), who spent his childhood in Avignon (where his family had lived for a century or more) and most of his adult life in Mantua, Florence, and Ferrara.[18] Farissol's background is significant. In contrast to many of those who followed him, he made almost no reference to the expulsion from Spain (mentioning, in passing, only that the expelled Jews had settled in this or that location). As one might expect, the eschatological strains of this account were more muted and less fraught than those that would later be written by writers more directly affected by the expulsion.

Farissol's account of the voyages of discovery appear in a volume called *Iggeret Orhot 'Olam*, which he wrote in 1525, and which was first published in 1586 (see Figs. 2.1 and 2.2). As David B. Ruderman has shown, most of this account was drawn directly from a popular volume of the day compiled by Fracanzano da Montalboddo and entitled *Paesi novamente retrovati e nova mundo da Alberico Vesputio riorentino intitulato.*[19] It included descriptions of the Amerindians, emphasizing their odd sexual practices ("they use their women like animals," "a son will take his mother, a brother will take his sister," and so forth), their anarchic social organization ("they have no ministers or leaders or law or deity"), their lack of property ("they have no possessions that are theirs alone.... They eat and find sustenance together, and the men take [whichever] women come to hand"), their superior health ("they live longer than 150 years"), the richness of their wildlife ("there are great and excellent fish ... and species different than ours,... and forests filled with great and small predators), and their wealth in gems and metals ("there is endless excellent gold in the sand and ... precious stones ... and mother of pearl").[20]

All of this is familiar enough, and because it was translated and transcribed with little interpolation, it is hard to draw conclusions from this material about Farissol's own attitudes toward the discoveries, and those he was trying to inspire in his readers. More telling than his actual account, though, is the context in which Farissol chose to embed it.

Farissol positioned his accounts of the Amerindians between two chapters that represent his most novel and telling contributions to his book. The first of these concerned the Ten Lost Tribes and David Reuveni, a supposed emissary from these tribes who had appeared in Farissol's day. The last concerned the location of the Garden of Eden.

Farissol began his account of Reuveni as follows:

> For the benefit of this epistle that I, Abraham Farissol, have written to unveil for those who do not know geography, I chose to write this chapter about the travels of the Jew from the [Ten Lost] Tribes, or who may be from [the tribe of] Judah, who is called David b. Solomon Supreme Commander of Israel, who arrived and we saw in our regions, the region of Italy, how he came from the dessert [sic] of Habor, in his telling, and those who visited with him found peace for their souls, and rest from toils.[21]

Farissol's account was unembellished. He described how Reuveni arrived in Venice in 1523 and set out to enlist the weapons and soldiers of the Christian continent in a battle of his Jewish legions against the Muslims. Farissol recounted how Reuveni succeeded in gaining an audience with the Pope. Farissol himself neither endorsed nor rejected Reuveni's claims. For him, this was beside the point. "It is enough for us, in our exile in these regions," Farissol wrote, "that it was verified by many honest kings and the courts of Rome that the tribes of Israel still exist in great numbers and that they have many kings."[22]

FIGURE 2.1   Abraham ben Mordecai Farissol, [*Iggeret orhot 'olam*] (Venice, 1586). The title may be translated as *Epistle of the Ways of the World*.

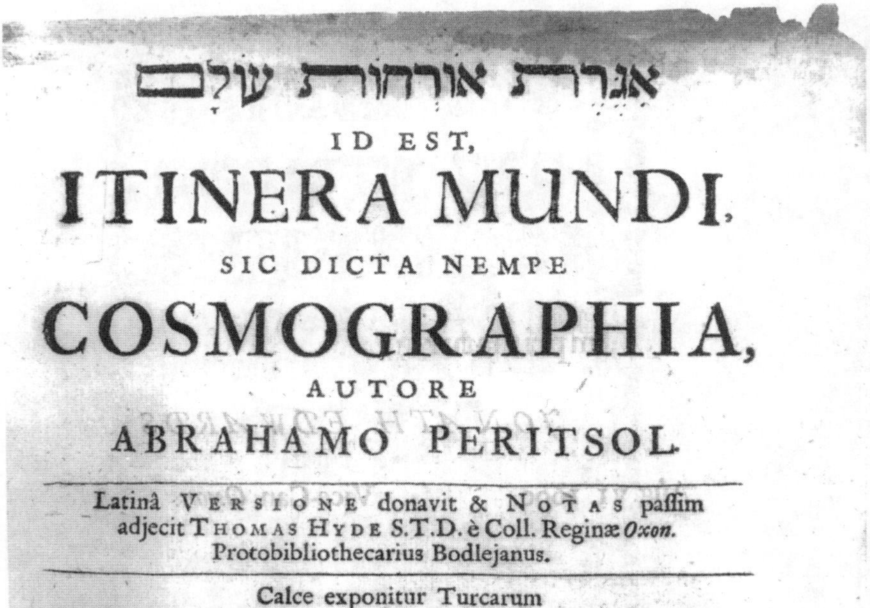

אִגֶּרֶת אוֹרְחוֹת עוֹלָם

ID EST,

ITINERA MUNDI,

SIC DICTA NEMPE

COSMOGRAPHIA,

AUTORE

ABRAHAMO PERITSOL.

Latinâ VERSIONE donavit & NOTAS paſſim
adjecit THOMAS HYDE S.T.D. è Coll. Reginæ *Oxon.*
Protobibliothecarius Bodlejanus.

Calce exponitur Turcarum
LITURGIA, PEREGRINATIO MECCANA,
ÆGROTORUM VISITATIO, CIRCUMCISIO, &c.

Accedit
CASTIGATIO
In *Angelum à Sto Joſeph,* al.diſtum *de la Broſſe,* Carmelitam diſcalceatum,
ſui Ordinis in Iſpahân Perſidis olim Præfeſtum.

Contentorum in Notis Elenchus Præfationem ſequitur.

OXONII,
E THEATRO SHELDONIANO, MDCXCI.
Impenſis *Henrici Bonwick* Bibliopolæ *Londinenſis,* apud quem proſtant ſub
Signo *Rubri Leonis* in Cœmiterio Paulino.

FIGURE 2.2 Abraham ben Mordecai Farissol, *Itinera Mundi* (Oxford, 1691). First published in Hebrew (Venice, 1586) under the title [*Iggeret orhot 'olam*]; translated into Latin by Thomas Hyde. This translation also included the original Hebrew text.

In his other original contribution to his book, Farissol brings to bear a rigorous combination of textual evidence with geographic and climatic evidence to determine the location of the Garden of Eden, a matter that "perplexed many scholars who did not know where it might possibly be."[23]

Both Farissol's presentation of the Garden of Eden and his presentation of Reuveni evinced confidence that elemental mysteries of the diaspora were being unraveled in his time, owing to the explorations and discoveries he described. It was in light of this confidence that Ruderman concluded that "Farissol was thrilled by the new discoveries because they offered unexplored possibilities for Jewish existence in other parts of the globe" and that he held the "hope that, with the location of the Ten Lost Tribes, Israel's redemption was near at hand."[24] One of the most enduring impressions produced by *Iggeret Orhot 'Olam* was that the world was being unveiled, and that a new order would soon emerge. Indeed, producing this impression seems to have been one of Farissol's principal goals. And his descriptions of the explorations and discoveries were among his principal means of creating this impression.

If, in Farissol's account, the voyages of discovery hinted or implied that the End of Days might be near, the eschatological significance of the explorations was more marked still in the works of three significant writers publishing in the 1550s: Solomon ibn Verga (fl. c. 1510), Samuel Usque (c. 1497–c. 1555), and Joseph b. Joshua ha-Kohen (1496–1578). Each of these men had direct links to the expulsions from Spain and Portugal. Ibn Verga had fled Spain for Portugal at the time of the expulsion, and was later forced briefly to live as a crypto-Jew in Portugal before finally settling in Flanders.[25] Samuel Usque was a Portuguese *converso*, whose family had also emigrated from Spain in 1492. Joseph ha-Kohen was born in Avignon to Spanish parents who had been expelled from Spain. He moved to Italy when he was five years old. Each of these men declared that the conversions and expulsions in Spain and Portugal provided his motive for writing historical accounts.[26]

The first two—ibn Verga and Usque—did not, in fact, recount the discovery of the New World in their essays (though they were often taken to have done so; as Joseph ha-Kohen believed, for instance, as I will describe below). But both were fully aware of the voyages of discovery, and each took these as yet another sign of the misery of Europe's Jews. Both wrote impassioned descriptions of the banishment of Jewish children from Lisbon by John II to the newly discovered island of São Tomé, off the coast of West Africa, as a site of exile. "The greatest of the enormous troubles [of the Lisbon persecutions] was the gathering of youths and casting them to the lost, uninhabited Islands," went ibn Verga's account. "[W]hoever has not seen the tears and wails of the women, has not seen or heard worry and grief and evil in his life."[27] Samuel Usque's description was no less dramatic:

> To my misfortune, the island of São Tomé had recently been discovered. It was inhabited by lizards, snakes and other venomous reptiles, and was

devoid of rational beings. Here the king exiled condemned criminals, and he decided to include among them the innocent children of the Jews.... Mothers scratched their faces in grief as their babies, less than three years old, were taken from their arms. Honored elders tore their beards when the fruit of their bodies were snatched.... One mother ... lifted her baby in her arms, and paying no heed to its cries, threw herself from the ship into the heaving sea, and drowned embracing her only child.... When those innocent children arrived at the wilderness of São Tomé, which was to be their grave ... almost all were swallowed up by the huge lizards ... and the remainder ... wasted away from hunger.[28]

While these descriptions did not concern the Americas, it is clear that the new discoveries played a role in defining the epoch that ibn Verga and Usque lamented. Usque begins his account of the "hardships we have been enduring" in the diaspora by invoking, at the start of his first dialogue, the new knowledge of far-flung places and the wealth that was accumulating in Europe from these places:

O Asia ... sown with precious gems and planted with rich and noble trees [and] infinite wealth and soft and marvelous fragrances.

O Africa ... pregnant with the finest gold ... buried wealth and the savory foods of Nature.

And Europe ... swelled by crafty stratagems ... into a terrestrial paradise....[29]

In light of the newfound marvels of the world, and the wealth Europe continues to wrest from its explorations, the state of the Jews is especially pitiable: "Now Europe, O Europe, my hell on earth, what shall I say of you, since you have won most of your triumphs at the expense of my limbs?"[30] For Usque, as for ibn Verga, the expansion of Europe was closely knit to the miseries that Jews had suffered since 1492. So, too, was it tied to their redemption. Now that some Jews had been cast to the newly discovered lands, and others have been discovered in far-flung places, Usque writes, the Jews have "run the entire gauntlet of misfortunes, and reached the end of [their] tribulations." Jews are returning "not only from all corners of Europe, but also from other parts of the world.... The ancients were unable to attain their proof, as were we, for we find ourselves living it in experience."[31] Again, the discoveries of Usque's day were associated both with the suffering of Jews, and with their incipient redemption.[32]

* * * *

THIS SAME ASSOCIATION was made by Joseph ha-Kohen, who wrote more in Hebrew letters than any of his contemporaries about the explorations and the New World. Joseph ha-Kohen included accounts (or at least mention) of the voyages of discovery in three compositions. In the last of these, his martyrology *Emek ha-Bakha* (finished in 1575, when he was 78 years old), he provided a spare paraphrase of Usque's description of São Tomé. (Joseph ha-Kohen's account was economical: for example, "And when they were in São Tomé, they became food for alligators, and the rest died of starvation."[33])

Joseph ha-Kohen's earlier two accounts included much more information and were less obviously martyrological. In these as well, however, his attitude toward the discoveries was ambivalent. The first of these accounts (and the most influential, for it was the only one to be printed and widely read in his century or the next) appeared in his chronicle, *Divrei ha-Yamim le-Malkhei Zarefat u-le-Malkhei Beit Ottoman ha-Togar*.[34]

Joseph ha-Kohen divided *Divrei ha-Yamim* into two unequal parts.[35] The first covers the period from the decline of the Roman Empire to the deaths of Maximilian I (in 1519) and Selim I (in 1520). The second volume, which was larger than the first, covers the thirty-three years between 1520 and the date of the book's completion. This lopsided division reflects Joseph ha-Kohen's conviction that the recent period was an important break from the past, that it signaled a new era. In it, he tells of the rise of Sulimann and of Charles V, the ascent of Luther, the burning of the Talmud, and other events of great, epochal significance.[36]

It is noteworthy that Joseph ha-Kohen chose to begin this volume with a relatively long account of the discovery of the New World, particularly because to do so he had to transgress the chronological ordering that was the organizing principle of the book, placing his account of the discovery of the New World between the death of Selim in 1520 and Magellan's voyage, which Joseph ha-Kohen also dates in 1520. That he chose to torture his chronology in order to begin the second volume, devoted to the new epoch, with accounts of the voyages of discovery and the discovery of the New World suggests that these were topics of some moment to him.[37]

The account in *Divrei ha-Yamim* emphasizes the rapaciousness of the Portuguese and Spanish crowns. It begins: "And it was in those days, the ships of the King of Portugal traveled to pillage plunder and to seize spoils in the land of Ethiopia...." He continues:

> and they came to Tarshish and Calcutta, which was ruled by the Turks, and they arrested their kings in shackles and their dignitaries in chains and the land was theirs and they made with the inhabitants a compact and they were servants to the king of Portugal to this day. And they brought from there spices and silver and gold and they filled their vaults....[38]

His description of the first voyages to the New World has a similar emphasis:

> And when the Spaniards were there, they conquered the inhabitants of the land and made them slaves and servants and they were subject to forced labor

to this day. The Spaniards also took their daughters to cook and to bake and they had no savior and the wailing of the inhabitants of this land wafted to the heavens.[39]

Likewise, his account of Magellan's voyage does not describe the circumnavigation, but focuses instead upon how the inhabitants of what would one day be known as the Philippines "prostrated themselves before [the Spaniards] and said, we are here to be servants to the Great Emperor, and he set them to hard labor."[40]

Joseph ha-Kohen's account, then, is ambivalent. It is in most ways a straightforward (though partial and highly selective) narrative of important voyages of discovery to Africa, India, and America. Its placement at the beginning of his chronicle of his own time suggests that Joseph ha-Kohen thought it of epochal importance. And its purposeful emphasis on the cruelty and rapaciousness of the Spanish and Portuguese echoes their cruelty and rapaciousness in expelling the Jews, an event that loomed larger than any other in Joseph ha-Kohen's historiography.

These impressions are further reinforced by Joseph ha-Kohen's massive unpublished compendium of edited translations about the voyages and the world they reveal, *Meziv Gevulot 'Amim*.[41] The compendium includes material taken from three works, Joannes Boemus's *Omnium gentium mores leges et ritus* (an "anthropological" work about the customs of Africans, Asians and Europeans[42]), and two books by Francisco López de Gómara: *La conquista de Mexico* (1552) and *La historia general de las Indias* (1554). Though Joseph ha-Kohen deleted much of the material he found in his sources, he added relatively few interpolations. When he did, his editorial choices again reflect some ambivalence about the events he was describing. He added the following to the end of his translation of Boemus (the body of which had *not* concerned the Americas):

> In our time, Columbus the Genoan discovered great islands and kingdoms in the west, the names of which were not known before this day. And many followed him from Spain. And they too found nations that Columbus did not see. And in all the lands of Peru in which there was gold ... they battled with the nations there. And they took them as servants, and they remain such to the kings of Spain to this day. And from there they bring gold every year.... And the worshipers of Ba'al that inhabited those cities prior to the arrival of the Spanish, they took out from darkness to the fog.... And they found nations of beastly people who eat human flesh to this day. The servants of the King of Portugal also discovered the island that is known today as San Thomé [sic]. And they found nothing there but the great fish that come out from the seas that are called *Lagartos*[43] and snakes and vermin and vipers. And the king sent there all those meant to be executed; he also sent Jews there. And they had no savior ... and the servants of the king of Portugal settled there. And they built houses to live in. And they worked their land. And the land gave fruit and they remained there safely.... They also planted sugar cane there. And they multiplied greatly. And they brought back the syrup which is called sugar to Portugal.[44]

Joseph ha-Kohen had interpolated the account that he found in Usque and would later include in *Emek ha-Bakha,* this time placing it in the New World.

The mere fact that Joseph ha-Kohen chose to produce these manuscripts at all attests to his interest in both the voyages of discovery and the exotica they uncovered. It also further attests to his belief that these were major events in history, connected to the changing order in Europe—an order that was at present unhappy for Jews, but one that, at the same time, might betoken dramatically different and perhaps better times to come.[45]

A decade after Joseph ha-Kohen died, Gedaliah ibn Yahyah, an Italian of Portuguese descent, published yet another compressed account of Jews exiled from Portugal to São Tomé.[46] In his continuation of the story of the expulsions, Gedaliah inserted the following notice about Columbus:

> In the days of Ferdinand and Isabella his wife, they sent Christofo Columbo, a commander and a great astrologer to the Islands across from the rivers of Ethiopia and many islands were found there which are called the "New World." And there are many Jews there, as can be seen in the books written about these voyages.[47]

Just what Gedaliah ibn Yahya meant by this last statement is unclear. Like Joseph ha-Kohen, ibn Yahya may have situated the São Tomé story in the New World. Whatever the case, it is not unreasonable to conclude that—like David Reuveni and Solomon Molkho—this event had eschatological resonance for him. In this, Gedaliah ibn Yahyah's accounts reprised the interpretation of the discoveries that one finds in Farissol, ibn Verga, Usque, and Joseph ha-Kohen, one that reflected some estrangement from the New World, but at the same time a belief that its discovery was one of many signs that a new, perhaps millennial epoch was approaching.[48]

* * * *

IT SHOULD BE NOTED that for none of these writers were the maritime explorations and discoveries a consuming concern, and none meditated much about their meaning. The discoveries did not function as explicit, singular symbols of Jewish degradation or of incipient salvation. At the same time, all of these writers included accounts of the discoveries because they did perceive these to have some meaning, which fit particularly well with what they were trying to achieve in their writing.

As has often been noted,[49] the chroniclers of the generations following the expulsion perceived themselves as living in a time that was uniquely pained and propitious.[50] The voyages of discovery highlighted both of these characteristics of the day. For all these writers, the fact that new worlds were being discovered was significant because it reinforced their feeling that they lived in a new, historically unique situation, and at the same time reinforced their conviction that matters were rolling toward a new and better millennial epoch.[51]

Nearer to the end of the sixteenth century, however, for Jewish writers with no immediate tie to the expulsions from Spain and Portugal, such a view held little attraction. Gone were most traces of millenarianism in their accounts of the New World. Gone, too, was the association of the discoveries with exotica like the location of the Garden of Eden or the location of the Ten Lost Tribes. The explorations were still interpreted as events with particularly *Jewish* significance, but this significance was now understood differently.

Interpretations in an Epistemic Vein

In his 1590 *Historia natural y moral de las Indias*, José de Acosta wrote:

> Having read what poets and philosophers write of the Torrid Zone, I persuaded myself that when I came to the Equator, I would not be able to endure the violent heat, but it turned out otherwise. For when I passed [the Equator] ... I felt so cold that I was forced to go into the sun to warm myself. What could I do then but laugh at Aristotle's *Meteorology* and his philosophy?[52]

Some Jews of the day had similar reactions, concluding that the discovery of the New World had given the lie to philosophic and natural philosophic texts that had long been held authoritative by many Christian and some Jewish scholars. Of course, these similar reactions had very different resonances for Jewish scholars than they might for Christian scholars. If for Acosta the discoveries might elevate the authority of observation and other new ways of gathering and producing knowledge, for Jewish scholars it served to denigrate the very notion that knowledge about the temporal world is of any value at all. If for some Christians the discoveries were taken to undercut the authority of ancient texts in favor of new ones, for these Jews it seemed to be a way to reinforce the authority of *Jewish* texts, particularly ancient ones. If for some Christian scholars the discoveries might invite a reordering of the hierarchies of scholarly authority, for Jews it might invite a conservative return to traditional texts treating traditional, unworldly subjects.

Tendencies like these can be discerned in the reaction of Judah Loew ben Bezalel (Maharal; c. 1526–1609) to the discovery of the New World, which he considered in the context of a long discussion of the arrival of the Messiah and the Ten Lost Tribes:

> And there are people who say that the scholars of the nations have recorded each and every place on the earth, and there are no more places that are not written in their books and everything is known to them, and there is no place in which the ten tribes are known [to reside]. But this is evidence of nothing,

they speak nonsense, because it is highly possible that there is a place in the world that is not known to them, as [for instance] if it is divided from inhabited areas by mountains or some such thing. And they have said that recently a place was discovered which they call in their language "New World" which was previously unknown, and it is likewise possible that another place will be found.[53]

Joseph ben Isaac ha-Levi expressed a similar view in his *Ketonet Pasim*. Astronomy, he wrote:

has not been perfected as have the other sciences.... For each one who comes in every succeeding generation disagrees with the other.... And so it is in the matters of inhabited lands: we have found inhabited lands in a region which astronomers had stated could not be settled, and these lands are called the "New World."[54]

For both men, the discovery of the New World (like the proposals of the Copernican and Tychonic systems) served notice that existing wisdom about the world, geography, and, more generally, natural philosophy and natural history was in principle unreliable and susceptible to change. If one New World had been discovered, so too could another one, and then another. The New World betokened the temporality of knowledge about the physical world, thereby diminishing its value. Rather than increasing the interest of such knowledge, the marvels that explorers discovered served only to circumscribe it.

The interpretations of Maharal and Joseph ha-Levi evince a certain alienation from the wisdom and undertaking of Christians, suggesting that the sorts of knowledge that Christians (and Jews who take interest in their philosophies) produce is different in kind, separate and inferior to that which Jews have traditionally produced and can produce. They suggest the existence of a gulf between the types of knowledge produced and imbibed by Christian scholars and the types that engage Jewish scholars.

Interpretations in an Irenic Vein

Other Jews of the day were persuaded that whatever gulf might exist between Christian and Jewish knowledge could be minimized and in certain realms entirely bridged. This persuasion informed very different attitudes toward the discoveries of the day.

Azariah de Rossi (1511–1578), as is well known, was castigated (most famously by Maharal) for incorporating information he found in gentile sources in his analyses of Jewish texts, including religious texts.[55] De Rossi, who spent the bulk of his life in Mantua and Ferrara, was himself highly versed in a variety of contemporary and ancient sources, as even a glance at his *Meor 'Einayim* makes clear, and he had significant contacts with Christian scholars. In light of his obvious predilections, it is not surprising that he planned to translate a portion of the Hermetic corpus into Hebrew.[56]

De Rossi was keenly interested in synthesizing scholarship of gentile and Jewish provenance. He was at pains to synchronize the intellectual tradition of the Jews with those of the Christians and of Classical culture, sometimes suggesting Jewish influences on Classical and Christian scholars[57] and sometimes gentile influence on Jewish luminaries.[58] In addition to highlighting mutual influences, de Rossi vigorously advocated harmonizing Jewish texts with the statements of the natural philosophers whenever this could be done without doing violence to statements rooted explicitly in Torah.[59] Indeed, de Rossi argued that it was valuable to use gentile sources, especially concerning natural philosophic questions, even to adjudicate questions, resolve confusions, and correct mistakes in Jewish sources.[60] Though he was persuaded that Judaism represented *prisca sapientia*, he at the same time believed that Greeks and Christians had inherited and much improved upon ancient Jewish wisdom.[61] De Rossi's penchant for apologetics has long been noted, and *Meor 'Einayim* does include passages insisting that Jews should know gentile languages and sources, strive to be good citizens, learn from gentiles, and at the same time demonstrate their wisdom to gentiles.[62] But de Rossi was driven by more than apologetic impulses. When he hoped that Christians would find value in his book, and when he explained that Jews were beholden by custom to pray equally for all nations, and when he insisted that Christian kings were guaranteed Jewish fealty, and so forth,[63] de Rossi was also expressing his sincere belief that Jewish and Christian scholars could and should maintain close relations marked by mutual respect.

The irenic impulses that I have been describing had much influence on de Rossi's interpretation of the voyages of discovery of his day. He begins his account by declaring that these voyages conclusively disproved Talmudic statements that implied the world is flat:

> If the scholars, may their memories be blessed, who believed that the earth is flat had been informed about what became well-known in our generations about the Spanish sailors who discovered the New World in the northern hemisphere the inhabitants of which find their perch opposite our feet ..., all of them, in a single voice, would answer and affirm for us the sphericality of the earth.[64]

He then describes at some length (though with an imperfect grasp of the details), Magellan's circumnavigation of the globe, completed by del Cano, concluding with a description of the crest, engraved with the statement *Primus circumdedisti me*, that the latter explorer received from Charles V. De Rossi then argues that, in fact, the New World was known to King Solomon:

> Believe with certainty that in the time of King Solomon this settlement was known and famous, and wayfarers regularly went to and fro to it for trade

and other purposes. And the land of Ophir and Paruvim from which the ships of Tarshish sailed once every three years as is written in the book of Kings and Chronicles would bring him gold and silver and spices and ivories and so forth, which are all things that in a period of time like that between leaving and returning is appropriate and these were brought too by [del Cano's] ship Victoria. There is no doubt that this is the country of Peru that is located in the aforementioned New World.[65]

This ancient Jewish knowledge had, in de Rossi's day, been perfected by Christian scholars: "Now from day to day they add to their expertise perfection and can go now in a single week a distance that in the days of the aforementioned caption and also perhaps in the days of Solomon they would need a month to traverse."[66] True to his predilections, de Rossi had given the New World an irenic spin, arguing that it was part of the body of ancient Jewish wisdom that in his day had been recovered and improved upon by the masterful Christian scholars in whose midst he lived.[67]

David Gans (1541–1613), a German Jew, educated in Poland, who lived most of his adult life in Prague, arrived at an interpretation similar to that of de Rossi, whose work he much admired. Like de Rossi, Gans wanted very much to promote joint Jewish-Christian scholarship; this was indeed the driving force behind his life's work. He believed that his relationship with Tycho Brahe and Johannes Kepler and other astronomers attending the court of Rudolf II might serve as a model for relations between other Jewish and Christian scholars.[68] Indeed, Gans described the entire history of astronomy as a history of joint activity and mutual influence between Jewish scholars, on the one hand, and Chaldean, Egyptian, Greek, Muslim, and Christian scholars on the other.[69]

Gans described the New World in both his extant works, a chronicle entitled *Zemah David* (1592) and an astronomic epitome named *Nehmad ve-Na'im* (prospectus, 1612; full text, 1743), and he may have written an independent volume about the voyages of discovery that has not survived. His accounts in the first book, which was published in Prague in 1592, were skeletal, and were excerpted from accounts he had found in German chronicles, as well as accounts by Joseph ha-Kohen and Azariah de Rossi. His accounts in the latter book, which he completed in 1612, were much richer and synthesized the findings of a number of contemporary cosmographies (see Figs. 2.3 and 2.4).[70]

In both sources, Gans approvingly cited de Rossi's conviction that the New World is the same as the biblical Ophir, suggesting that it was first discovered by Jews.[71] Though this original Jewish knowledge was now firmly in the hands of Europe's Christians, Gans still saw in the discovery of the New World many and varied opportunities for real collaboration between these Christians and Jews. When he realized, for instance, that the circumnavigation of the globe could create confusion about when to celebrate the Sabbath, Gans chose to consult Kepler about this *halakhic*

FIGURE 2.3 David ben Solomon Gans, [*Sefer Nehmad ve-Na im*] (Jessnitz, 1743). The title in English would be *A Pleasant and Agreeable Book*.

שער א

צורת ארבע יסודות ותשעה גלגלים הנזכרים

סימן יט״ ביאור קצת על הצורה הסמוכה :

בצורה הסמוכה למעלה תמצא המצער שלמם וחלקי המגלם שהם אורכם י״ל אקי״א ספרי״קן אשר איכותם יתבאר לפנים בפי׳ פ״א • ותרצאם בצירוף היפים כמו״כ שאותם הם בכירוסם מצורה חלי כדור הארץ • גם כלא וסרוף בצורת כדור ת׳ מהם כחו סבאחרנו כל זה למעלה בסי׳ כ׳ • למעלה מן היסודות הנרסקים וספ״ליריים סבצ נגלגלם לסבצ כוכבי לבת וחמרייסם נלגל הכוכבים תלגל סיתמי גם כ״מתף בצורה רסומים סנים עסר מזלות סני עעכ׳ים וסס על סתי כתינת כלסקת סמזלות הרסומים

כנגלגל סעלייו ואף שאין סם מלוי סוס כוכב כלל מכל מקוי רסומים סס סם בסכל כל תי״ב מזלות כאלו כיס קנועים סס וסס נקרחים המזלות הקבועים אשר לא ימירו ולא יחליפו ולא ירוו מצבם כל ימי עולם והבחינה הבנית סס המזלות הרסומים בנלבל הכוכבים אשר סם הקולו׳ בעצמם באמת אך הם כטיבות תנועת סכבידה ש׳ם נגלגל המזלות כנ״ל בסי׳ י״ל ולפנים כסער החמישי בסי׳ ק״י המזלות מתעמטוטים וימירו ויחליפו את מלכם ברחוק גדול רב כאוגן בקתום אשר בזמנינו במזלות הקבועים מעלוי סם ראס מזל סלה אשר כנגדו למטה בנלבל המזלות כיה ראוי כמו כן לכיות סם נ״כ מזל סלה אך מקמת התמוטטות ימלא אם כעת רחם מזל דנים אשר כזה יתבאר בסך סיטוב לפני׳ (כסי׳

problem rather than Maharal or Heller or Jaffe or any of the other rab-
binic luminaries with whom he had personal contacts.[72]

Even more than de Rossi, Gans emphasized the majesty of the
achievements of the Christian explorers. Gans begins his account in
Nehmad ve-Na'im by declaring that the discoveries reflect "great and
exalted wisdom, requiring the greatest contemplation."[73] Gans hails
Columbus as "a great scholar and philosopher," and Vespucci as "a wise
man of understanding and a warrior," and describes their patrons and
their voyages in heroic terms.[74]

Gans also emphasized that Jews of his day could understand and
even participate in the achievements of Christian explorers through globes
and maps. Gans included a detailed legend to a Hebrew *mappa mundi* he
had drawn, encouraging his readers to retrace the routes of the explorers.

> You the reader should know that these things [i.e., geographical facts] were
> unknown and mysterious to the early scholars; they labored and troubled
> over this all the days of their lives. Kings as well expended thousands and
> tens of thousands [to attain this knowledge]. And here [in maps] all of this is
> made known to us in our time wisely and easily, in such a way that every
> wise man can educate and explain to his small son and show him with his
> finger, in his own home and in his own room, most of the countries and
> inhabited places of the entire earth, with the borders of the seas. [He can do
> this] much better than if he traveled there with a wise, old man and saw it all
> with his own eyes.[75]

Thanks to the heroic efforts of Christian scholars, every child in *heder*
could now know the true geography of the world.

Gans was effusive about the discoveries since Columbus, but he
labored to ensure that this enthusiasm did not take on a millennial cast.
In contrast to Maharal, he insisted that the *entire* earth was in his day
charted.[76] He castigated Abraham Farissol and Abraham Zacut for suggesting that the Ten Lost Tribes might be found in the kingdom of Prester
John in Ethiopia.[77] For Gans, like some of the earlier writers I have discussed, the discovery of the New World was a sign of a changing world.
But for him, the change was anything but eschatological. For him, what
was developing—through continued collaboration of Jews and Christians—was a more miraculous and peaceable secular world for all.

Both de Rossi and Gans, then, tried to enlist Jews not only to marvel at
the new maritime discoveries, but also to *identify* with them and with the
explorers. They did this by insisting that Peru was the biblical Ophir, posit-
ing that Solomon had been the first to regularly voyage to the New World
(bringing back great treasures of gold). In so doing, they at the same time
implied a likeness between the recent kings of Spain, Portugal, France,
England, etc., and King Solomon. They did this also by encouraging Jews
to familiarize themselves with the discoveries, by referring to atlases, by
describing the voyages and the principal explorers, and especially by
insisting that these Christian discoveries and voyages were of great

moment to contemporary Jews, who reaped the intellectual and practical benefits of the maritime discoveries as did the Christians of their day.

De Rossi and Gans saw great value in Jews knowing (and teaching every schoolchild) about the new discoveries because they represented knowledge that ancient Jewish scholars had helped to produce and because they represented *human* knowledge of extraordinary *human* value that could be enjoyed equally by Jews and Christians. The discoveries were an excellent demonstration of the hope so fondly held by both men that in their day the mutual alienation that had for so long marked Jewish-Christian relations might finally disappear.[78]

Conclusion

The interpretations of the discoveries that I have presented were all parochial. Jewish interest in the New World was rarely interest in the New World per se, but rather in what it might mean back home in Europe. Jews who described the explorations and discoveries tended to impute to them special meaning for *Jews*. They used these events to cast light on questions that had long engaged Jews, and that had little or nothing to do with the events themselves.

None of this is surprising. Catholics and Protestants also often interpreted the explorations and discoveries in narrow and provincial terms.[79] What is most interesting about Jewish interpretations of these events is not that they are parochial or that they are incorporated into discourses that themselves have nothing to do with the discoveries but rather the specific parochial concerns they are taken to address.

In his study of Jewish accounts of the European expansion to America, Abraham Melamed found that Jews were "especially late in applying the discovery to the *Jewish question*."[80] This overlooked "Jewish question," for Melamed, concerned the "possible far-reaching implications ... the discovery of America [might] have for [Jewish] theological questions."[81] Melamed is right that the explorations and discoveries had no immediate impact on Jewish "theology." He argues further that when Jews *eventually* did "apply the discovery to the Jewish question," they did so in "two theological contexts: the *querelle* between 'moderns' and 'ancients,' and the question of the 'ten lost tribes.'"[82] Here Melamed is mistaken; the questions of whether or not the ancients knew of the New World and whether or not Jewish tribes had ever lived there are hardly theological questions at all. Sixteenth- and early seventeenth-century Jewish descriptions of the explorations and discoveries typically had little to do with theology.[83]

When Jews considered what these events might mean for the Jewish people, their conclusion was almost invariably that the explorations and discoveries illuminated not the relationship of Jews to their God but rather the relationship of Europe's Jews to Europe's Christians. Men like

Joseph ha-Kohen took these events as a further token of the mistreatment of Jews by Christians and, at the same time, as a harbinger of a new age in which such suffering would be ameliorated. Men like Maharal took them as a demonstration of the superiority of Jewish over Christian sapience. Men like Azariah de Rossi took them as a further demonstration of the complementarity of Jewish and gentile scholarship, and of the importance of Jews in any *translatio studii* account of the accumulation of human knowledge. In a world in which boundaries were radically changing, Jews found in the explorations and discoveries an opportunity to redefine the borders between Jews and Christians. Changes in world geography concerned Jews, but only insomuch as they affected the social geography of Europe.

Notes

1. David B. Ruderman, *Jewish Thought and Scientific Discovery in Early Modern Europe* (New Haven, 1995), 229.
2. Tobias Cohen, *Sefer Ma'aseh Tuviyah* (Bnai Brak, 1978; 1st printing: Venice, 1707), Author's Introduction, 26, col. 1.
3. "Oliver" probably refers to Olivier van Noort, who circumnavigated the globe between 1598 and 1601. (I am grateful to Dr. Norman Fiering for this identification.) Francisco Fernández de la Cueva Enriquez, Duqe de Albuquerque, Marques de Cuéllar was Capitan-General de la Nueva España at the start of the eighteenth century. See *Archivo Biográfico de España, Portugal e Iberoamérica (ABEPI)*, Fiche F 320, 293–327.
4. Cohen, *Ma'aseh Tuviyah*, 63a.
5. Later chapters supplemented this account with information about new herbs and medicines imported from America, which catalogued the virtues of sarsaparilla and sassafras (which purifies urine), tobacco (which, when smoked, purified within and without, especially the chest, head, and stomach, and when applied topically, reduced the pain of *podogra*, or podiatric gout), and more. See Cohen, *Ma'aseh Tuviyah*, 63a–64b.
6. There is some irony in this, in light of the passage in Jacob Aboab's introduction to *Ma'aseh Tuviyah*, in which he likens Cohen's greatness to the great heroism of Columbus. See Cohen, *Ma'aseh Tuviyah*, Introduction, 19, col. 1.
7. See the essays by Eva Alexandra Uchmany, Anita Novinsky, Silvia Marzagalli, Jonathan I. Israel, Pieter Emmer, James Boyajian, Ernst Pijning, and Seymour Drescher in this volume for more information about these developments.
8. Some of Cohen's contemporaries were certainly more interested in the New World; indeed, some made their fortunes in New World trade (see the essays cited in note 7, above). Cohen himself was interested in some of the goods procured there (see note 5, above). Still, there can be no doubt that Cohen, at least, took his readers to be ignorant of even the most rudimentary facts, and that he did not find this ignorance lamentable. The New World, Cohen believed, was of little inherent interest to Jews.
9. These books are described in some detail below. For other general surveys of accounts of the discoveries written by Jews, see Mendel Silber, "America in Hebrew Literature," *Publications of the American Jewish Historical Society* 22 (1914):101–37; Mendel Silber, "America in Jewish Literature," *Universal Jewish Encyclopedia*, vol. 1, 236–38; R. J. H. Gottheil, "Columbus in Jewish Literature," *Publications of the American Jewish Historical Society* 2 (1894):129–37; and especially Abraham Melamed, "Gilui America ba-Safrut

ha-Yehudit bi-meot ha-16–17," in *Be-'Ikvot Columbus: America 1492–1992*, ed. Miriam Eliav-Feldon (Jerusalem, 1996), 443–64.

10. About this genre, see Yosef Hayim Yerushalmi, *Zakhor: Jewish History and Jewish Memory* (Seattle and London, 1996; orig. pub., 1982), 54–75. The two exceptions are Abraham Zacut's *Sefer Yohasim* (1566) and Eliahu Capsali's *Seder Eliahu Zuta* (mss, pub. 1975). Capsali lived and wrote exclusively in the Ottoman Empire, where accounts of the explorations were fewer and harder to come upon. For the reception of the voyages of discovery in Ottoman culture, see Thomas D. Goodrich, *The Ottoman Turks and the New World: A Study of Tarih-i Hind-i garbi" and Sixteenth Century Ottoman Americana* (Wiesbaden, 1990); and Thomas D. Goodrich, *Ottoman Knowledge of Columbus and the New World in the Sixteenth Century* (Washington, D.C, 1991).

11. A noteworthy exception is Mattityahu Delacrut's *Zel ha-'Olam* (1733), which evinces no trace of the geographical discoveries of the fifteenth or sixteenth centuries. This is doubtless because the book is a fourteenth-century Hebrew rendition of an anonymous thirteenth-century French text. Why Delacrut chose not to interpolate contemporary material is impossible to say. About *Zel ha-'Olam*, see L. Zunz, "Essay on the Geographical Literature of the Jews from the Remotest Times to the Year 1840," in *The Itinerary of R. Benjamin of Tudela*, ed. A. Asher (New York, 1841), 264, 274–75.

12. The Hebrew books were *Iggeret Orhot 'Olam* (1586) by Abraham Farissol (of which twenty copies were distributed between seventeen families), *Meor 'Einayim* (1573–75) by Azariah de Rossi (of which twenty-nine copies were distributed between twenty-seven families), *Shalshelet ha-Kabbalah* (1587) by Gedaliah ibn Yahya (of which twelve copies were distributed among twelve families), and *Divrei ha-Yamim le-Malkhei Zarefat u-le-Malkhei Beit Ottoman ha-Togar* (1554) by Joseph ha-Kohen (of which two copies were held among two families). The list of Latin and Italian texts includes several that are difficult to identify. Among the texts, however, was Joannes Boemus's *Gli costumi, le leggi et l'usanze di tutte le genti* (1558), Pietro Martire d'Anghiera's *Historia de L'Indie occidentali* (1534), Giovanni Maria Bonardo's *La minera del mondo* (1585), Giacomo Gastaldi's *La universale descrittione del mondo* (1562), and a score of other historical, medical, and natural philosophical books that may well have contained mention or description of the New World. See the tables included in Shifra Baruchson, *Sefarim ve-Kor im: Tarbut ha-Keriah shel Yehudei Italiah be-Shilhei ha-Renesans* (Ramat Gan, 1993), 167, 172, 180–90.

13. Prof. Matt Goldish has recently begun a study of the meta-halakhic interests of Mantuan Jewry from this time.

14. David ben Solomon Gans, *Nehmad ve-Na'im* (Jessnitz, 1743), 27b. Though the first edition of *Nehmad ve-Na'im* was published in the middle of the eighteenth century, it was written in the years spanning from approximately 1590 to 1612.

15. See Anthony Grafton, April Shelford, and Nancy Siraisi, *New Worlds, Ancient Texts: The Power of Tradition and the Shock of Discovery* (Cambridge, Mass. and London, 1992), 1–10; as well as J. H. Elliott, *The Old World and the New: Cambridge Studies in Early Modern History* (Cambridge, 1970); G. Gliozzi, *Adamo e il nuovo mondo* (Florence, 1977); and M. T. Ryan, "Assimilating New Worlds in the Sixteenth and Seventeenth Centuries." *Comparative Studies in Society and History* 23 (1981):519–38, which are cited in Grafton et al., *New Worlds, Ancient Texts*.

16. Though this was not always the case. One also finds among Jews of the age some descriptions of the explorations and discoveries that differed in kind or emphasis from contemporary Christian accounts. Abraham Yagel's description of odd customs of Amerindians, for example, or Abraham Portaleone's description of the novel fauna of the New World are both the sorts of occasional descriptions of wonders and novelties that one might just as easily find in contemporary Latin or vernacular accounts. See Abraham Yagel ben Hananiah dei Goliccho, *Beit Ya'ar ha-Levanon*, Bodleian: Ms. Reggio 9 (Neubauer, 1304), chap. 106, 241a–242a.b.; and Abraham ben David Portaleone, *Shilte ha-Gibborim* (Mantua, 1612), 83a. On Abraham Yagel, see David B. Ruderman, *Kabbalah, Magic, and Science: The Cultural Universe of a Sixteenth-Century Jewish Physician*

(Cambridge, Mass., 1988). On Abraham Portaleone, and particularly the attitudes toward natural history, natural philosophy, and wonders of nature displayed in *Shilte ha-Gibborim*, see Matt Goldish, "The Sanctuary of Science: Rabbi Abraham Portaleone's Shilte ha-Gibborim," in *Volume Accompanying an International Conference on Jewish Responses to Early Modern Science (Jewish Treatments of Science from De Revolutionibus to the Principia and Beyond)* (Tel Aviv and Jerusalem, 1995).

17. I have found no discussion among Jews in this period in which the discovery of the New World was treated as distinct from other discoveries, particularly those in Africa and Asia. For Jews of this time, the expansion of Europe, the discoveries of new wonders, the growing knowledge of the earth, and the growing conviction that the earth was all known were all of particular moment and were often conflated. All the writers I will consider understandably viewed the explorations in Africa and Asia as a piece with those in lands previously unknown. The constant identification of the further exploration of known lands and the new exploration of new lands is perhaps best illustrated by Joseph ha-Kohen's decision to join into a single volume his translations of Boemus and Lopez de Gomara, the one being an account of the exotic habits of the three known continents, and the other being primarily an account of the conquest of the West Indies, or the new lands. This tendency was not unique to Jews. See, for example, Ilaria Luzzana Caraci, "Columbus' Outro mundo: The Genesis of a Geographical Concept," *Renaissance Studies* 6.3-4 (1992):336–51.

18. See David B. Ruderman, *The World of a Renaissance Jew: The Life and Thought of Abraham ben Mordecai Farissol* (Cincinnati, 1981).

19. Ruderman, *World of a Renaissance Jew*, 134, and especially 231n. 19. I have consulted an imperfect edition of this book printed in Milan in 1508 (and presently located in Harvard University's Houghton Library).

20. Abraham ben Mordecai Farissol, *Iggeret Orhot 'Olam* (Venice, 1586), chap. 29.

21. Farissol, *Iggeret*, chap. 14.

22. Ibid.

23. Ibid., chap. 30.

24. Ruderman, *World of a Renaissance Jew*, 137.

25. Solomon ibn Verga's biography has been a matter of some dispute. A good account can be found in M. Benayahu, "Makor 'al Megurashei Sefarad be-Fortugal ve-Zeitam aharei Gezeirat RaSaV le-Saloniki," *Sefunot* 11 (1978):233–65.

26. Solomon ibn Verga, *Shevet Yehudah* (Adrianople, 1554), Author's Introduction, 1; Samuel Usque, *Consolation for the Tribulations of Israel*, trans. Martin A. Cohen (Philadelphia, 1965; 1st ed., Ferrara, 1553), Prologue, 38–40; Joseph ben Joshua ha-Kohen, *Divrei ha-Yamim le-Malkhei Zarefat u-le-Malkhei Beit Ottoman ha-Togar: Milhamotehem Ve-Korotehem Ve-Hol Ha-Telaot Asher Matsu Et Am Yisrael Tahat Shevet Malkhutam* (Jerusalem, 1967; 1st ed., Sabbionetta or Venice, 1554), Frontispiece, Introduction, and 36b, and Joseph ben Joshua ha-Kohen, *Sefer Emeq ha-bakha* (Jerusalem, 1961; 1st ed., Vienna, 1852), 10.

27. Ibn Verga, *Shevet Yehudah*, chap. 57.

28. Usque, *Consolation*, Dialogue III, chap. 27, 201–2. See, too, the coda to this story, in which John II's son Alphonse was thrown off a horse and died at his own wedding in Divine retribution for this act of cruelty, Part III, 29. (Alphonse in fact died two years before the banishment from Lisbon.)

29. Ibid., Dialogue I, 43.

30. Ibid., 44.

31. Ibid., Dialogue III, 236.

32. Another sign of this incipient redemption, for Samuel Usque, was the Protestant Reformation. He opined that the new Lutherans had generations earlier been forcibly converted to Christianity. The Reformation was "an indication of the non-Catholic origin" of these people, and a sign that the strong-armed tactics of Christianity had begun to fail. See Usque, *Consolation*, Dialogue III, 185, 193.

33. Joseph ha-Kohen, *Sefer Emeq ha-Bakha*, 104–5.

34. Joseph ha-Kohen, *Divrei ha-Yamim*. About this book, its background, and its reception, see Reuven Michael, *Ha-Ketivah Ha-Historit Ha-Yehudit* (Jerusalem, 1993), 29–34.

35. This is true of the version that he brought to print. He later added a third part as well, which remained in manuscript until 1955. See Joseph ha-Kohen, *Divrei ha-Yamim*, and the Introduction there for the circumstances of its composition.

36. Joseph gives the numerological sign "yehash atidot le-mo" (from *Devarim* 32:35: "and he speeds what is forthcoming to them"), with its eschatological overtones, to date the book.

37. Or he could simply have been mistaken about the dates of the discovery. David Gans took him at his word when he was compiling *Zemah David*, and dated Amerigo Vespucci's voyages to 1520. But there is good reason to think that Joseph ha-Kohen was himself aware that the first voyages to the New World took place decades earlier than the placement of his account implies. First, he uncharacteristically omitted dates from all his accounts of voyages of discovery until he reached his account of Magellan. Second, Joseph ha-Kohen's entry was based on one or several books that were unlikely to report such skewed dating. It is likely that he already had a copy of Francisco Lopez de Gomara's detailed works when he composed *Divrei ha-Yamim*. It is difficult to believe, then, that he thought the New World had been discovered as late as 1520.

38. Joseph ha-Kohen, *Divrei ha-Yamim*, Part II, 1a.

39. Ibid., Part II, 1b.

40. Ibid., 2a.

41. *Meziv Gevulot 'Amim* was never published, and the precise date of its composition is impossible to determine. I consulted the manuscript in the Columbia University Rare Books Collection, sig. K82.

42. For an excellent short description of Boemus and this work, see Grafton et al., *New Worlds, Ancient Texts*, 99–100.

43. *Lagarto* is a generic term for a lizard. Joseph ha-Kohen was probably referring to alligators, known then as *lagarto de Indias*.

44. Joseph ha-Kohen, *Meiziv Gevulot 'Amim* (Columbia University: K82, 73a-b), reprinted in Rafael Weinberg, "Yosef ben Yehoshua ve-Sifro Meziv Gevulot 'Amim," *Sinai* 72, no. 7 (1973):363–64.

45. It is also significant that Francisco Lopez de Gomara's *Historia general de las Indias* itself had millenarian strains. Lopez de Gomara associated the Indies, for instance, with the mythical Atlantis. See Harold J. Cook, "Ancient Wisdom, the Golden Age, and Atlantis: The New World in Sixteenth-Century Cosmography," *Terrae Incognitae* 10 (1978):25–43.

46. Gedaliah ibn Yahya, *Sefer Shalshelet ha-Kabbalah* (Jerusalem, 1981; 1st ed., Venice, 1587), 273: "… and the [Portuguese] King investigated whether the exiles [from Spain] had paid the requisite head tax, and he found many of them who had not, and he was infuriated with them, and he took in bond, because they were poor, their sons from ages three to ten, and led them to an island called *Stomi* which was a thankless wasteland, owing to the alligators, which are poisonous snakes and serpents that kill. And he wanted to settle this island, but it was not worth his while, because most of them died from the snakes and some from hunger."

47. Ibid., 274.

48. Abraham Melamed has recently argued that the first Jew to view the discoveries of the fifteenth and sixteenth centuries in millenarian terms was Menasseh ben Israel, in the middle of the seventeenth century. Writing of Menasseh ben Israel, Melamed concluded that "thus, more than one hundred and fifty years after the great event [of the discovery of America], a direct link was finally forged between the discovery of America and the messianic question." (Melamed, "Gilui America," 464). Melamed is correct that Menasseh ben Israel's famous *Esperança de Israel* was the first to consider the idea that some among the Ten Lost Tribes had once lived in the New World (though Melamed overstates the Dutch rabbi's enthusiasm for the idea; see the excellent introduction to

Menasseh ben Israel, *The Hope of Israel*, trans. Moses Wall, ed. Henry Méchoulan and Gérard Nahon (Oxford, 1987; orig. English publ., London, 1652). Prior to 1650, Jewish millenarianism was in no way affected by the discoveries in the west, in Melamed's view, as evidenced by the fact that sixteenth-century inquiries into the location of the Ten Lost Tribes of Israel invariably concluded that they could be found in Asia or Africa. Melamed's distinction between the explorations to the east and those to the west is too sharp, however. As Gans's account exemplifies, Jews (like all other Europeans) tended to view the discoveries in the east and the west together. The voyages of discovery, put in the context in which they were perceived by their contemporaries, were interpreted in a millennial framework by the writers I have been describing.

49. For example, see Yerushalmi, *Zakhor*, chap. 3; Haim Hillel Ben-Sasson, "Dor Golei Sefarad 'al 'Azmo," *Zion* 26 (1961):23–34; and Reuven Michael, *Ha-Ketiva He-Historit Ha-Yehudit* (Jerusalem, 1993), chap. 1.

50. David Ruderman has rightly emphasized that these eschatological accounts were often, despite their martyrology, notably optimistic. Indeed, most of the accounts I have described see in the explorations and discoveries both exemplars of Jewish misery and, at the same time, significantly, hints of Jewish ascendancy.

51. The reactions that these writers had to the discoveries of their time were intriguingly similar to the reactions of many of the same writers to the Protestant Reformation. (About this, see Haim Hillel Ben-Sasson, "The Reformation in Contemporary Jewish Eyes," *Proceedings of the Israel Academy of Sciences and Humanities* IV [1971]:239–327.) None took the Reformation, in and of itself, as a clear sign of the End of Days (they had seen Hus and others, and indeed some contemporaries took Luther to be simply more of the same). For some, however, it did fuel a general feeling of millennial expectation. The same sort of attitude pertained to the explorations and discoveries. They did not occasion obvious shock or anxiety, but they did support the view (which owed more to the expulsions and the turbulence of the times for Jews than to anything else) that a new epoch had arrived, and that the old epoch, marked by countless persecutions and degradations in Europe, might be drawing to a close. Like the Reformation, the explorations mattered most to the writers I have been discussing for what they said about their times and for what they implied about how the lives and stocks of Jews might soon be changing.

   This view, of course, was not unique to Jews. See, for example, Leonard I. Sweet, "Christopher Columbus and the Millennial Vision of the New World," *The Catholic Historical Review* LXXII.3 (1986):369–82; and Cook, "Ancient Wisdom, the Golden Age, and Atlantis." It is certainly possible that Christian millennial interpretations of the explorations and discoveries served to reinforce similar interpretations among Jews.

52. Quoted in Grafton et al., *New Worlds, Ancient Texts*, 1, 99–100.

53. Judah Loew ben Bezalel, *Nezah Yisrael* (Bnai Brak, 1980; 1st ed., Prague, 1599), 156, col. 2. Maharal concluded that the Ten Tribes were not *geographically* isolated at all, but rather *metaphysically* isolated. No new discovery, then, could in principle shed any light on their whereabouts.

54. Joseph ben Isaac ha-Levi, *Ketonet Pasim* (Lublin, 1614), chap. 9, 13a-b. For a discussion of this passage, see Joseph Maurice Davis, "R. Yom Tov Lipman Heller, Joseph b. Isaac ha-Levi, and Rationalism in Ashkenazic Jewish Culture 1550–1650," Ph.D. diss., Harvard University, 1990, 320–21.

55. See Judah Loew b. Bezalel, *Be'er ha-Golah* (London, 1960; 1st ed., Prague, 1598), 126ff.

56. See Salo Wittmayer Baron, "Azariah de' Rossi: A Biographical Sketch," *History and Jewish Historians: Essays and Addresses*, ed. Salo W. Baron (Philadelphia, 1964), 167–73, and the references there.

57. For instance, Azariah de Rossi, *Meor 'Einayim* (Vilnius, 1865; 1st ed., Mantua, 1573–75), vol. 1, 85, in which he suggests Jewish influence on Hermes Trismegistus.

58. For example, ibid., vol. 2, 75, in which he suggest the influences of Ptolemy and Hipparchus on Talmudic scholars.

59. For example, ibid., chaps. 27 and 28, vol. 1, 254–64, and also vol. 1, 85.

60. See especially the second chapter of *Imrei Binah*, entitled, "The Necessity of Our Citing in Some Cases Evidence Which Is Not from Our Nation," in de Rossi, *Meor 'Einayim*, vol. 1, 68–76.

61. For example, ibid., 73–74.

62. See the discussions of de Rossi's apologetic tendencies in Robert Bonfil, "Some Reflections on the Place of Azariah de Rossi's *Meor 'Enayim* in the Cultural Milieu of Italian Renaissance Jewry," in *Jewish Thought in the Sixteenth Century*, ed. Bernard Dov Cooperman (Cambridge, Mass., 1983), 23–48; Salo Wittmayer Baron, "Azariah de' Rossi's Attitude to Life," in *History and Jewish Historians: Essays and Addresses*, ed. Salo W. Baron (Philadelphia, 1964), 174–204; and Salo Wittmayer Baron, "Azariah de' Rossi's Historical Method," in *History and Jewish Historians*, 205–39.

63. See Baron, "Attitude to Life," 187–88, and the notes there.

64. De Rossi, *Meor 'Einayim*, vol. 1, 145.

65. Ibid. The question of the locations of Ophir and Tarshish was also pondered by a variety of Christian scholars and explorers of the day. In 1526, Sebastian Cabot had sailed from Spain in search of Ophir and Tarshish in the Pacific. In 1568, Alvaro de Mendaña discovered islands that he was certain included the biblical sites, and for this reason named them the Solomon Islands. The hypothesis that the New World might contain Ophir was widely entertained through much of the sixteenth century. See the essay by James Romm in this volume.

66. De Rossi, *Meor 'Einayim*, vol. 1, 145.

67. Abraham Melamed has recently interpreted de Rossi's identification of Peru with the biblical Ophir very differently than I have. Melamed writes that de Rossi's statements must be seen as part of a debate about the relative status of ancient and modern scholars— what he calls "the *querelle* between 'moderns' and 'ancients.'" "Farissol, Joseph ha-Kohen and Tuvia ha-Cohen ('*harofeh*') adopted the radical position," Melamed writes, " which emphasized the superiority of the moderns. Azariah dei Rossi represented the more moderate position, namely that the moderns rediscovered what had been already known but forgotten" (Miriam Eliav-Feldon, ed., *Be-'Ikvot Columbus: America 1492–1992* [Jerusalem, 1996], xxi–xxii; and Abraham Melamed, "Gilui America," 451–59). The notion that de Rossi or Gans, who endorsed de Rossi's view, might champion the ancients over the moderns is inconsistent with the attitudes each man expressed throughout his writing. Both men believed strongly that recent achievements in natural philosophy and, more generally, in humane studies had outstripped those of the ancients. A more plausible explanation is that both de Rossi and Gans believed that the identity of Peru and Ophir enhanced the status of ancient *Jews* relative to modern *Christians*, but not that it demonstrated the superiority of the ancients to the moderns *in general*.

68. Noah Efron, "Irenism and Natural Philosophy in Rudolfine Prague," *Science in Context*, 10:4 (1997), 627–49.

69. David ben Solomon Gans, *Nehmad ve-Na'im* (Jessnitz, 1743), 8a–9b.

70. I have not been able to determine the exact identities of these sources.

71. David ben Solomon Gans, *Zemah David* (Jerusalem, 1983; 1st ed., Prague, 1592), Part II, 1533, 391; and Gans, *Nehmad ve-Na'im*, 28a.

72. Gans, *Nehmad ve-Na'im*, 29a.

73. Ibid., 27b.

74. Ibid.

75. Ibid., 29a.

76. Ibid.

77. Gans, *Zemah David*, Part I, [4]205, 48.

78. A similar view was later adopted by Judah Del Bene, among others. See Judah Del Bene, *Kissot le-Veit David* (Verona, 1646), 3:17, 42b. I am grateful to Prof. Ruderman, who drew my attention to this reference.

79. See the references cited in note 15.

80. Miriam Eliav-Feldon, ed., *Be-'Ikvot Columbus: America 1492–1992* (Jerusalem, 1996), xxi. The emphasis is mine.

81. Melamed, "Gilui America," 444.
82. Eliav-Feldon, *Be-'Ikvot Columbus*, xxi.
83. The single exception being when they were taken to supply further evidence for the coming of the Messiah. Yet even in this case, the events themselves were never taken to have explicit theological import. Rather, they were seen as one of many indications—the Christian Reformation was another, as were the large and small expulsions of the Jews in the fifteenth and sixteenth centuries, and there were many others as well—that the world was changing rapidly and dramatically. This broader phenomenon of widespread change was taken to provide evidence, though never theological justification, for the incipience of the Messiah's arrival.

– Chapter 3 –

JEWISH SCIENTISTS AND THE ORIGIN OF MODERN NAVIGATION

Patricia Seed

S TANDING ON THE WINDSWEPT SHORES of the Atlantic west of Lisbon in 1400, it would be hard to imagine the dizzyingly rapid set of changes that the next hundred years would bring. A simple fisherman watching the waters of the Tagus River slide smoothly into the Atlantic would have seen simple blue and white fishing boats setting out in search of sardines and tuna. His grandson, standing on those same shores a hundred years later, would observe a different scene. Alongside the customary low-slung blue and white fishing boats gliding out to sea would be tall-masted ships, called caravels and *naus*. These new, towering seagoing vessels would slip easily into the ocean, their long ropes slapping against the wooden masts as the sails were raised, sturdy sails snapping as they caught the wind, setting forth for worlds unimagined even a hundred years before. While the waters of the Tagus would glide into the North Atlantic on 1 January 1500 just as they had on 1 January 1400, the fisherman's grandchild standing at the mouth of the Tagus would know that a vast, previously unattainable world was now reachable beyond those shores.

In 1400, sailing anywhere in the world was still a matter of guesswork and approximation, but on the decks of the tall-masted ships in 1500 were men with devices capable of measuring location with numbers as accurate today as they were five hundred years ago. Also onboard these ships were charts and chart makers to accurately map uncharted lands; they could depict coasts as accurately as they appear on contemporary globes.[1] When some, not all, of the men on the departing tall ships eventually returned to the mouth of the Tagus, returning sailors brought back information that jolted the conventions by which medieval men and women had interpreted their world for centuries.

By the middle of the fifteenth century, the relatives of simple sailors who had put out to sea on those ships knew that widely held beliefs about the uninhabitable torrid zone were untrue, for they had seen densely inhabited regions of equatorial West Africa. Educated pilots also knew that Aristotle's assumptions about how to understand the earth (as qualities, not numbers) were wrong. If this were not enough, by 1501, one year after the start of the century, the Portuguese would become the first to know of the immense continents that lay across the ocean.

For Portuguese, not Spanish, navigators discovered the new land-masses of the Western Hemisphere. Christopher Columbus (a former longtime navigator for Portuguese leaders) by 1503 had merely discovered a handful of islands; on a single occasion he caught sight of a larger body, about which he could only speculate. Neither Columbus nor his Hispanic contemporaries had any idea of the size of the larger land-masses beyond.[2] Spaniards, for example, had no idea of the existence of Mexico until Cortés happened upon it in 1519, nearly thirty years after first landing in the Caribbean.

While Spanish navigators, like Columbus, cautiously crept around the nearby Caribbean guided by native pilots, Portuguese explorers boldly set forth on the unexplored and stormy seas of the North and South Atlantic. During the fateful voyages of Corte-Real and Gonçalo Coelho in 1501 and 1503,[3] only one and three years respectively after they first landed in the Americas, Portuguese scientists and officials learned there were not just islands but huge continents on the other side of the Atlantic. By 1503, Portuguese sailors, scientists, and mapmakers knew of the existence and were able to draw the contours of two major Atlantic coastlines, the very large landmasses of America north and south of the Spanish discoveries in the Caribbean—landmasses that a passenger on these voyages, Amerigo Vespucci, would subsequently publicize and christen "a New World."

While the Portuguese sailors had undeniable courage in setting forth onto open oceans that no one had ever sailed, they did not embark upon these expeditions foolishly. Rather, unlike many Western Europeans at the time, they were armed with a knowledge of oceanography and astronomy that would allow their caravels to set forth into the unknown stormy, and often dangerous, waters of the North and South Atlantic Oceans for weeks on end, while they mapped the coasts they encountered. Where did the mathematical precision in numbers and accurate charts come from? The answer is that the instruments and the calculations came from Jewish scientists on the Iberian Peninsula, heirs to (and innovators in) the great astronomical and mathematical traditions of the golden age of Arabic science. Using the achievements of this tradition, Jewish scientists expanded their horizons to create the mathematical equations and instruments for modern navigation, transforming sailing from guesswork into the precise proceeding that we recognize today.

The foundation of modern scientific navigation rests upon accurate understanding of both astronomy and mathematics. These sciences, however, were not well developed in fifteenth-century Christian Europe. During the Middle or Dark Ages, Christians produced little of enduring worth in physics, optics astronomy, mathematics, and medicine. By contrast, sustained innovation flourished in two influential centers in the Muslim-controlled world.

Between 800 and 1400 A.D., scientists in the Islamic world had invented algebra, taken the idea of the sine and developed trigonometry, transformed mathematical notation from the awkward Roman numerals to the forms we use today, and incorporated zero into counting systems. Al-Farabi calculated the circumference of the earth (close to its modern measurement), and other scientists created sophisticated instruments of astronomical observation from earlier primitive devices.

Science in the Muslim world showed another valuable characteristic as well. While Christian leaders kept their institutions of higher learning closed to Jews, Islamic leaders encouraged cooperation between Jews and Muslims in scientific inquiry. While Christians were welcomed into such dialogues as well, they rarely embraced the study of science with the same enthusiasm as did Muslims and Jews.

The scientific advances of Islamic and Jewish scientists did not continue forever. As the Muslim empire in Iberia (one of two major scientific centers) began to lose its territory and revenue, its scientific preeminence began to deteriorate as well.

New Christian overlords of what is now Spain proved less willing or less able to protect Jewish scientists from anti-Semitic elements in their midst. Pogroms in eastern Spain in 1391, in which a prominent Mallorcan astronomer was killed, began the exodus of Jewish scientists. As anti-Semitic agitation increased in Castile and Aragon, Portugal became the haven for Jewish scientists seeking refuge from increasingly anti-Semitic surroundings. Encouraged by the official toleration promoted by Catholic rulers in Portugal, Jewish scientists migrated to Portugal, where they could live in peace and tranquility.

Portuguese leaders—and Prince Henry, nicknamed the Navigator, in particular—had another reason for encouraging the immigration of Jewish scientists. Trying to develop a new route to the gold-producing regions of western Africa, he patronized seafaring expeditions off the African coast. But the challenges of navigating the mid-Atlantic proved seemingly intractable. More powerful tidal surges in the Atlantic than sailors had experienced in the Mediterranean made knowledge of the cycles of the moon imperative for the basic timing of entering and departing from ports. Welcoming Jewish mathematicians and astronomers with the knowledge of such cycles to Portugal created a critical mass of knowledge that would eventually contribute not only to the voyages to West Africa, but eventually to knowledge of how to sail around the world. Offering the prospect of both physical safety and a new scientific challenge, Portugal thus became an attractive place in which to settle for fifteenth-century Iberian Jews.

After Prince Henry's death, Jewish astronomers and mathematicians, drawing upon their own as well as their shared scientific traditions with Muslims, created lasting solutions to the problem of navigation in unknown waters. They created the modern science of navigation—the use of astronomical calculations to fix locations on the earth; they themselves, along with mathematical formulas, instruments, and charts, often piloted the giant tall-masted ships across the south Atlantic and eventually the world.[4]

The crowning achievement of Jewish scientists working for the crown of Portugal was the scientific determination of latitude—creating both the precise instruments and mathematical equations necessary to find the latitude (a numerical description) of unknown parts of the world.

While Babylonian and later Greek scientists had theoretically understood latitude and longitude coordinates for the heavens, they had never managed to apply them accurately even for the tiny part of the globe they knew, namely the Mediterranean; thus, latitude and longitude remained remote and abstract ideas known only to a few scientists. No means for accurately fixing latitude or longitude existed.

Jewish mathematicians on the Iberian Peninsula, however, recognized the theoretical potential of latitude and longitude for creating what we now know as celestial navigation, or the technical ability to determine precisely any location on the globe. But even more innovatively, the Jewish scientists in Portugal created a scientifically accurate means of navigation that did not require years of training and practice to use. Instead, they created both the necessarily precise instruments and the measurements that would allow any sailor with relatively brief training to determine a ship's position in an exact, scientific manner.

On the deck of a wooden caravel in the fog-shrouded morning calms in the equatorial Atlantic, or in the near gale force springtime winds off the Cape of Good Hope, sailors wanted more than prayers or even guesswork; they wanted the security that those guiding the boat knew both where they were and where they were going. And that certainty came from numerical calculations and measurements that could be repeated over and over again with the same results. Numbers, the Portuguese came to realize, could be used by anyone to navigate.

The proof of this novel insight had come dramatically in 1446. During an expedition to the west coast of Africa, arrows containing an unexpectedly deadly poison killed a landing team consisting of the captain, pilots, and leaders of the expedition. The sailors left guarding the ship observed with horror as, one after another, their leaders collapsed either dead or seriously injured from even slight contact with the venom. A sixteen-year-old boy with a rudimentary knowledge of astronomical navigation successfully piloted the expedition's ships back to Lisbon.[5] But while that knowledge was precise enough to be used to allow anyone to navigate, it could not be created by anyone.

To establish the measurements that would predict the sun's path in the sky and the correspondence to positions on the earth required intimate familiarity with mathematical specialties, such as trigonometry, and astronomical knowledge of the exact length of the solar year and of phenomena such as the precession of the ecliptic. Familiarity with such measures—widespread in the worlds of Jewish and Muslim scientists—was rare outside of occasional isolated individuals in the fifteenth-century Christian world. Indeed, the accurately calculated solar year—absolutely required for accurate measures of latitude—was not incorporated into Christian knowledge until 1583, over a century after a Jewish scientist in Iberia had created the first scientifically accurate means of finding latitude based upon a precise knowledge of the solar year.[6]

The knowledge, the data, and the manuals that provided the launching pad for modern nautical science were composed in Arabic and Hebrew. While Latin translations were made, the works translated were not always the ones needed to solve the problems presented by navigation. To provide a simple example, Al-Zarqel had proposed a method of using the first scientific instrument of navigation, the astrolabe, in the daytime. Alfonso the Wise had ordered this work translated into the *Libros de saber de astronomia*, but Al-Zarqel's solution for the daytime astrolabe was incorrect. The answer lay in a different approach, available only in Arabic and Hebrew, and understandable only to someone educated not in the Latinized universities of Western Europe but in the Hebrew-language schools of Iberian Jews.[7]

The role of Jews in introducing such changes in ways of thinking makes sense from yet another perspective. When we think of the stranglehold of religious orthodoxy that the Catholic Church exercised over scholarship during the Middle Ages, it makes sense that those who first openly contested the wisdom of church fathers in such matters would come from a tradition in which their authority was irrelevant. Who better than Jewish scientists to question widely repeated statements by prominent churchmen about the uninhabitable tropics? Who better than Jewish scientists to represent the earth with numbers when the Catholic establishment believed (following Aristotle) that the earth could only be understood qualitatively?[8]

During the early years of the fifteenth century, Portuguese monarchs began to draw upon Iberia's distinguished tradition of astronomical and mathematical learning to create scientific approaches to navigation, employing Jewish scientists on a regular basis. The kings consulted Jewish astronomers to establish more accurate timekeeping, to fix lunar cycles to determine high and low tides using the computations of the Mallorcan Jewish astronomer Abraham Cresques. Jewish scientists also began to instruct sailors prior to voyages in using the position of the guard stars around the Pole in nighttime navigation to pinpoint more specifically the direction of travel (e.g., southwest, northeast) or to describe the direction of a place relative to Lisbon using a primitive conception of celestial latitude, but all of these accomplishments were surpassed during the final three decades of the fifteenth century.

Beginning with the voyages of the shadowy Lopo Gonçalves in 1473/74,[9] the Portuguese approached a territory unknown by Classical Greek scholarship, unfamiliar even to the legendary Arab travelers and geographers of the Middle Ages.[10] They had reached territory that few in Europe had ever even imagined existed, and they had no models, charts, or even local nautical traditions to fall back on.

Previously, all of European sailing had been done in latitudes north of the equator—the Mediterranean, Red Sea, and even the northern reaches of the Indian Ocean all lie north of the equator—nor had Europeans often ventured by land south of the equator. Europe's overland traders with Arabia, Persia, and China primarily traversed terrain north of the equator.

By 1470, the Portuguese monarch's oceanic ambitions lay beyond the limits of existing seafaring knowledge and navigation organized around the Pole Star, which becomes invisible slightly south of the equator. Consequently, navigational computations by land and sea based on the fixed point of the north would no longer be useful.

While the challenges were great, so too were the potential rewards. Sailing south of the equator, Portuguese ships could reach the oft-traversed Indian Ocean where rare spices could be readily purchased. Lusitanian kings shared another ambition: finding the lost Christian kingdom of Prester John located somewhere in the Horn of Africa. Surprisingly, Jewish scientists shared this goal with the monarchs, for Portuguese Jewish folklore of the time held that a lost tribe of Israel—now identified as the Ethiopian Jews—was located in the same part of Africa as the Christian kingdom of Prester John.

In the years between 1473 and 1481, the Jewish scientific community on whom Portuguese monarchs relied for their scientific knowledge decided to use the position of the sun as the best measure of determining latitude south of the equator, for unlike the Pole Star, the sun was visible in both hemispheres.[11]

To transform this idea into a uniform set of numbers, however, Jewish scientists would have to overcome two major obstacles: one mathematical, and one practical. To find one's position on the surface of the earth from astronomical information, two separate measures had to be fixed. (Fixing two variables allows you to solve an equation for the third, which in this case was latitude.) Since sailors would be taking only a single measure—the position of the midday sun in the sky—they had to have an additional accurate measurement of where the noonday sun stood in relation to other objects in order to then determine the variable: latitude. Neither this equation nor the instruments to measure the angle of the midday sun existed in scientifically accurate forms.

Dealing with the mathematical obstacle required solving different problems. One of these difficulties was the absence of a concept of negative numbers, which would have made the equation far easier to solve. Negative numbers, however, did not come into existence until nearly two centuries later.[12] Furthermore, mathematical prediction of the sun's place in the sky on every day of the year demanded an absolutely precise solar calendar with accurate accounting of leap years. In 1473, the Jewish astronomer and mathematician Abraham Zacuto composed his *Rules for the Astrolabe*, the mathematically correct prediction of the sun's seasonal position in relationship to the earth.

With regard to the practical obstacle, in 1470 there was no instrument accurate enough to measure the position of the sun in the sky consistently and precisely. After experimenting with a number of different devices over the course of a decade (including Levi Ben Gerson's invention, the backstaff), the Jewish scientists working for the Portuguese king settled on remaking a traditional Iberian Islamic astronomical device, the astrolabe, as the most precise device for the purpose of fixing the exact angle of the midday sun above the horizon.

The astrolabe was a popular instrument for nighttime astronomical observation in Spain, but originally it could only be used to observe from specific latitudes. Changing one's latitude meant changing the plates, the largest and bulkiest part of the astrolabe, which typically extended between ninety-five and two hundred millimeters in diameter, and weighed between one and four kilos (roughly two to nine pounds).[13] The customary single latitude astrolabe would have been of no use to navigators or indeed to any traveler intent on exploring unknown regions and defining new latitudes. Furthermore, despite their beauty and complexity, many of the medieval land-use astrolabes were highly inaccurate.

In the eleventh century, two Muslim astronomers in Spain 'Ali ibn Khalaf and al-Zarqello, independently created the first universal astrolabes that could be used for nighttime observation.[14] Even with two models of a universal astrolabe that could potentially be used anywhere on the globe, the Jewish scientists collaborating with the Portuguese still faced an even more difficult task; they needed to transform the nocturnal astrolabe into an instrument of daytime observation.

The solution was found around 1480 by following a hypothetical suggestion originally proposed by Ibn Assafar, a twelfth-century Muslim astronomer from Cordoba. The Portuguese astronomers altered the design of the astrolabe so that when held by an outstretched arm at the waist, with the needle pointing to the sun, the sun passed through two small holes in small squares attached to the top and bottom of the needle. This produced a small circle of light (against the shadow of the squares), which fell upon numbers providing the height of the sun above the horizon.[15] The technique, popularly called "weighing the sun," avoided the difficulty of having to stare directly at the sun, as would have been necessary using the traditional nighttime astrolabe. In so doing, scientists were not only physically transforming an old-fashioned instrument; they were turning it into a device capable of accurately translating the height of the midday sun above the horizon into a number.

Thus, the two factors needed to determine latitude at sea in daytime were in place: a set of numbers indicating the position of the noonday sun for every day of a four-year cycle, as worked out by Abraham Zacuto, and an instrument that sailors could use to measure the sun's angle above the horizon. Using the sun's angle, and looking up the date of the solar calendar, ordinary sailors could then look up the latitude that would precisely describe where they or anyone else was standing anywhere on the globe with respect to the equator.

The earliest record of such use of an astrolabe and tables occurred in the 1480s. Diogo d'Azambuja captained the West African voyage of 1481 during which accurate latitudes were first fixed south of the equator. In 1485, José Vizinho in Guinea and in 1487 Bartholomeu Dias also calculated precise latitudes on land using the tables and new astrolabe.[16]

The new sun-measuring astrolabe had been designed only for use on land. It established the coordinates of a new place only once pilots were able to disembark. The final step in developing celestial navigation was finding a way to fix latitude while onboard ship. This process required maintaining the scientific precision of the new sun-oriented astrolabe while making the object both sturdy and stable enough to withstand the motion of a boat at sea.

In 1497, the Jewish astronomer Abraham Zacuto created the first mariner's astrolabe, handing it over personally to Vasco da Gama before the latter set sail on his first voyage to India and back.[17] This new nautical astrolabe was made of brass in the shape of a circle. It was thin and narrow at the top, where a ring was attached, and thick (and therefore heavy) on the bottom so it could remain stable on the high seas. On Cabral's voyage to Brazil and India, the *converso* scientist onboard, Master John, was surprised by the consistent results provided by the nautical astrolabe measurements on all five of the expedition's major vessels.

This modified and simplified, yet remarkably accurate, mariner's astrolabe soon became widely adopted in Western Europe together with Zacuto's accompanying mathematical tables. Shortly thereafter, Portuguese sailors began identifying their position anywhere on the earth by a set of numbers, not as a rare or unique event, but as common, everyday practice onboard ships. These latitude calculations (and accompanying charts) were so accurate that they would allow the able Portuguese pilot named Fernão Magalhães (better known in English as Magellan) to accurately fix the eastern boundary of the Portuguese and Spanish spheres set by the Treaty of Tordesillas, on the island of Melaku in what is presently Indonesia, during the voyage around the world of his little fleet.

The achievement of being able to find latitude at sea was soon reflected in more accurate maps. In 1504, Portuguese mapmakers—who also traced their scientific tradition from a Jewish founder or founders—constructed the first map of the world with accurate latitude lines. On that same map, they placed the first global prime meridian, the starting point for measuring longitude. This first global meridian ran through the Portuguese Madeira Islands, where it remained until 1884 when it was shifted to Greenwich, home of the nineteenth century's dominant naval power, England.

In determining longitude, the Portuguese Jewish scientists were never able to match the scientific precision of their multiple achievements with latitude. But João de Castro, Portugal's only prominent Christian astronomer, correctly declared in 1540 that clocks were the only way to solve the longitude problem. The clocks produced at the time, he noted, failed to meet the necessary standards of scientific accuracy.[18] In the meantime, they would continue to use astronomical calculations to estimate time, and thus successfully sail the world over.

Armed with accurate knowledge of the size of the earth and scientifically precise latitude, Portuguese officials knew that the only viable route to Asia lay around the southern tip of Africa. When approached by Christopher Columbus with his improbable suggestion that he could reach Asia by sailing west, the king and his largely Jewish scientific tribunal rightly derided Columbus's knowledge of the circumference of the earth as absurd. Given the size of the ocean lying between Portugal and Asia, no sailing vessel could carry sufficient supplies to last even the outbound portion of such a voyage.

Fifteenth-century Jewish scientists thus turned ancient notions into real usable knowledge of the earth. The idea of a coordinated geographical grid came from Ptolemy and the Alexandrian Greeks, but converting that idea into a working reality was the achievement of Iberia's Jewish scientists. They transformed latitude and longitude from little known and impractical oddities into realistic tools for navigation throughout the globe. While it was Galileo who most famously asserted that the book of nature is written in mathematics, we owe the origin of this understanding to Iberian Jewish mathematicians and astronomers who were the first to practically describe the world as a set of numbers. Their numbers were not abstract notions, but a concrete daily practice of finding latitude onboard the oceangoing ships of the fifteenth and sixteenth centuries.

The nautical voyages launched from Portugal after 1470 produced incontrovertible evidence not only that numbers could be used to describe the world, but also that in the real world of sailing, numerical indications and mathematically designed nautical charts were an immensely powerful means of survival and a successful means to reach the rest of the world.

Jewish scientists' expertise provided the basis for accurately locating the latitude of any place on the globe, and estimating longitude well enough for the world to be circumnavigated for the first time. For indeed, all the world soon adopted the methods created by Portuguese Jewish scientists, for the great advance of their methods was that they made scientifically accurate latitude accessible to everyone.

Given the extent of this achievement, it is easy to wonder why the Portuguese Jewish role has remained so little noticed, leading to the final, and perhaps most obvious, question: Why have the contributions of Jewish scientists at this time—mathematicians, astronomers, cartographers—been so little recognized before? There are many reasons, some perfectly innocuous, and others, unfortunately not.

In the first place, the fourteenth and the fifteenth centuries mark a significant decline for science in the Muslim world, a decline that corresponded to military defeats in Iberia and a simultaneous waning of Islamic influence. It should not be surprising that historians of Islamic science would concentrate instead upon the great achievements of the early and middle periods: the perfection of trigonometry and major achievements in refraction and optics. The fourteenth and fifteenth centuries offer nothing as stunningly original to the world of pure math or pure astronomy as do those earlier contributions.

Secondly, historians of European science, for similar reasons, have concentrated primarily upon the northern European tradition rather than looking southward in Europe. The modern academic study of the history of (European) science began in the nineteenth century, with many of its founding works coming from Germany. This field has concentrated upon innovations in mathematics and physics that took place primarily in northern Europe beginning in the seventeenth century.

As a result, Jewish scientific accomplishments in Portugal presently fall in between two distinct scholarly specializations, whose researchers concentrate on eras both well before and well after the Iberian innovations. Furthermore, since nearly all of the scholarly and technical work in this field has appeared in Portuguese, a language that few historians of science are familiar with, the terrain has often simply remained unknown in the English-speaking world. Daniel Boorstin, for example, was able to assert (quite inaccurately) in *The Discoverers*[19] that the process of discovering latitude was a simple, trivial matter, but such assertions are only possible if one has not delved into the scientific literature written in Portuguese, Arabic, and Hebrew. This literature reveals that the human and material costs of discovering latitude were high.

In addition to such linguistic and scholarly barriers, there are two additional factors, neither of which is entirely benign and both of which have prejudiced subsequent accounts of the role of the Jews in scientific and technical innovation. The first factor is a persistent Anglo-centrism, which Ian Hacking has characterized as the tendency to produce "sceptered-isle versions" of the history of science.[20] The tendency has become exaggerated when it comes to innovations at sea. When Great Britain became the dominant naval power at the start of the nineteenth century, British writers began to celebrate nautical achievements in which Englishmen played a critical role, even though as in the case of longitude they required a single mechanical invention rather than a major shift in forms and types of knowledge.[21] In a similar vein, the

Greenwich observatory's history of the prime meridian (the current starting point for measuring longitude) only in the 1990s began to include an
account of the international votes for and against Greenwich at the 1884
conference. Omitted entirely is the history of the prime meridian, and the
fact that moving to Greenwich entailed only an incremental shift—17
degrees east of where it was first placed by the Portuguese cartographer
Pedro Reinel in 1504 and had conventionally appeared on nautical charts
and world maps for nearly four hundred years.[22] The scientific advances
that made the maritime expansion of Europe technically possible originated in Portugal.

The final problem is that the scientific understanding of navigation
emerged on the border between two great competing political traditions—one Muslim, the other Christian. Since the innovators in the tradition of nautical science were Jewish, they have not been claimed
powerfully by either tradition. Even in Portugal, where one might expect
this scientific heritage to have been celebrated, remembrance has been
muted in regard to its Jewish origins. Portuguese historians of science
have downplayed, or even ignored, the Jewish faith of all of the mathematicians, pilots, and astronomers (save one) who invented nautical science in Portugal.

Indeed, nowhere in modern Portugal is there evidence or remembrance of this Jewish past. In the great monuments to the discoveries
along the banks of the Tagus, in the museums rightfully displaying the
technical and scientific achievements of the fifteenth century, there are no
Stars of David, no portraits of Jews or even of those forcibly converted
who remained behind for much of the sixteenth century to continue the
scientific tradition of their forefathers. Even in the National Maritime
Museum in Portugal, which contains exhibits of the scientific instruments
created by Jewish and *converso* scientists, the only portrait that hangs on
the walls is that of the lone Christian astronomer, João de Castro, who
wound up (by accident rather than design) in the astronomy and mathematics classes being taught the royal princes by a *converso* scientist.

Furthermore, in this present era of intense Muslim-Jewish hostility in
the Middle East, it has become immensely difficult to suggest that Jews
were the major conduit (and innovators of) a scientific tradition in astronomy and mathematics that was created and shared with the Muslim
world. Vehement Muslim-Jewish animosity has also rendered it politically
unpalatable to acknowledge that Jews transmitted the Islamic tradition of
astronomy and mathematics to Christian Europe, and transformed these
subjects into the modern science of navigation.

Therefore, it should not be surprising that the great achievements of
this era of Jewish scientific innovation and creativity are relatively
obscure at present. Emerging on the cusp of the decline of one great scientific tradition and the rise of another, the Iberian Jewish period was too
remote from the central and easily recognizable achievements of either
great tradition.

The evidence of the powerful and indispensable role of Jews in the invention of scientific calculations of latitude and in the invention of nautical science can be seen in the unnecessarily tragic decay of Portuguese science in less than a century after its powerful apogee. The rapid decline of Portuguese science paralleled the loss of its greatest figures to the expulsion or conversion decrees of 1497. As the heavy hand of the Inquisition fell increasingly upon the descendants and heirs of the fifteenth-century Jewish scientists, the sciences in which Portugal had once excelled, mathematics and astronomy, vanished. Pedro Nunes, the most justifiably famous of the sixteenth-century *converso* scientists, lamented that by the 1560s the training in mathematics elsewhere in Europe was surpassing that of Portugal,[23] but without the Jewish scholars who had introduced the subject, and with books on astronomy and mathematics increasingly subject to Inquisitorial confiscation, there was no likelihood of recovery.

Evidence of the achievements of those Jewish scientists remains in their invention of celestial navigation, the principles by which sailors still navigate in the event that their global positioning satellite receivers fail, for the modern science of navigation remains the single resounding success of a Judeo-Arab-Christian experiment in cooperation occurring in a tiny seafaring kingdom perched on the westernmost edge of Europe. Not only were there new routes, but also there were new continents. There was America. The shape of the known world had altered, and not long after 1500 even a simple fisherman standing on the banks of the Tagus knew it.

Notes

1. For the conformity of Portuguese nautical maps to elliptical (spherical) projections, see www.rice.edu/latitude.
2. Spanish maps, such as the Juan de la Cosa map, show only Caribbean shores, and even then the information is limited to the traditional sea routes of their native informants—north to Florida and south to what is now Venezuela.
3. Carlos Malheiro Dias, "A Expedição de 1501" and "A Expedição de 1503," *História da colonização portuguesa* (Porto, 1921–24), chaps. 8 and 10.
4. The pilot who gave the latitude of the discovery of Brazil was a *converso*, known only as Master John. Another of the great "converted" pilots was John of Lisbon (João de Lisboa).
5. Gomes Eannes de Azurara, *Crónica do descobrimento e conquista da Guiné* (Lisbon, 1985; orig. pub. 1453), cap. 86. The boy's age was not specified, but he was called a *moço,* a term used only for children aged sixteen and under.
6. The book is Abraham Zacuto's *Rules for the Astrolabe* (1476).
7. The more religiously fundamental members of the central synagogue in fifteenth-century Lisbon founded a separate school because science, not the Torah, was not the central educational focus of the main synagogue (the largest in Lisbon and in Portugal). It remains to be seen whether scientific instruction in the Jewish community was supplemented by tutoring—the means of educating members of the royal family in science.
8. Alfred W. Crosby, *The Measure of Reality: Quantification and Western Society, 1250–1600* (Cambridge, 1997), 13.

9. Junta das Missões geograficas e de investigaões coloniais, *Atlas de Portugal Ultramarino* (Lisbon, 1949), map 2.

10. J. Spencer Trimingham, "The Arab Geographers and the East African Coast," "Notes on Arabic Sources of Information on East Africa," in H. Neville Chittick and Robert I. Rotberg, eds., *East Africa and the Orient: Cultural Syntheses in Pre-colonial Times* (New York, 1975); Costa Brochado, *Historiógrafos dos descobrimentos* (Lisbon, 1960), 51.

11. João de Barros dates the decision to use the sun from the period after the discovery of Guinea: "verdade de caminho a altura [do sol] e muy certa mostrador." João de Barros, *Da Asia* (Lisbon, 1777–88), 24 vols., Dec. 1, liv. 3, cap. 2. See also Luís de Albuquerque, *Introducção a história dos descobrimentos portugueses*, 4a ed. (Lisbon, 1989), 201.

12. The process also required combining two separate mathematical series. The first series was the set of numbers derived from calculating the place of the sun relative to the equator; the second set required the accurate solar calendar to determine the date. These were originally put into two separate tables, and only subsequently combined (sometime between 1481 and 1485).

13. Joaquim Bensaude calculated the Arabic astrolabe of 95 to 125 mm in diameter, weighing 1 kilo; and that of 1632 being 184 mm in diameter and weighing 3.84 kilos. The Arabic ones are 360 degrees, the nautical ones go four times from 0 to 90 degrees. Joaquim Bensaude, *L'astronomie nautique au Portugal* (Berlin, 1915), 79.

14. Both astronomers dedicated their works to the penultimate Muslim ruler of Toledo before the Christian conquest. Emile Savage-Smith, "Celestial Mapping," in *History of Cartography*, ed. J. Brian Harley and David Woodward, vol. 2, pt. 1, Cartography in the Traditional Islamic and South Asian Societies (Chicago, 1992), 12–70, esp. 28–31.

15. An early sixteenth-century account describing how the Portuguese used this instrument is in the letter of Alessandro Zorzi, reproduced in Luís de Albuquerque, ed., *Portugal-Brazil: The Age of Atlantic Discoveries* (New York, 1990), 56–57. An early drawing illustrating how to use this astrolabe is in Pedro Nunes, *Tratado da sphera* (Lisbon, 1537).

16. Bensaude, *L'astronomie nautique*, 111. David Waters, "The Sea or Mariner's Astrolabe," *Revista da Faculdade de Ciencias*, vol. 39 (Coimbra, 1966):5–36.

17. Bensaude, *L'astronomie nautique*, 40, 79; Barros, *Asia*, Dec. 1, liv. 3, cap. 2, describes it as "3 palmos" in diameter but does not mention that Zacuto was its creator. Modern equivalents of these dimensions are from Roger C. Smith, *Vanguard of Empire: Ships of Exploration in the Age of Columbus* (New York, 1993), 56. Fourteenth-century astrolabes were usually more than double this size, 7 palmos. Millás, *Pedro el Ceremonioso*, 67–69. Luís de Camões's description of the "new astrolabe" (a "sage and wise invention") is thought to refer to Zacuto. Luís de Camões, *Os Luisadas* (Lisbon, 1584), canto V, stanza 25.

18. D. João de Castro, *Obras Completas de D. João de Castro*, ed. D. João de Cortesão and Luís de Albuquerque (Coimbra, 1968–76), vol. 1, 177–78, 286–89; Ramon Abadal y Vinyals, *Pedro el Ceremonioso y los comienzos de la decadencia politica de Cataluña* (Madrid, 1966).

19. Daniel J. Boorstin, *The Discoverers* (New York, 1983).

20. Classic examples of this tradition include Robert K. Merton, *Science, Technology and Society in Seventeenth-Century England* (New York, 1970), and Herbert Butterfield, *The Origins of Modern Science, 1300–1800* (New York, 1957). But even many more recent and sophisticated histories, such as Steven Shapin, *The Scientific Revolution* (Chicago, 1996), are oriented toward the English experience.

21. Dava Sobel, *Longitude: The True Story of a Lone Genius Who Solved the Greatest Scientific Problem of His Time* (New York, 1995); William Andrews, ed., *The Quest for Longitude: The Proceedings of the Longitude Symposium, Harvard University, Cambridge, Massachusetts, November 4–6, 1993* (Cambridge, Mass., 1993); David Waters, *The Art of Navigation in England in Elizabethan and Early Stuart Times* (London, 1958).

22. For close-up views of the prime meridian as it appeared in a 1517 Portuguese nautical chart, see www.ruf.rice.edu/~feegi/longitude.html.

23. Pedro Nunes, *Livro de Álgebra* (Anvers, 1567).

– Chapter 4 –

THE HOPE OF THE NETHERLANDS: MENASSEH BEN ISRAEL AND THE DUTCH IDEA OF AMERICA

Benjamin Schmidt

I

THE OLD TESTAMENT AND THE NEW WORLD combined in a number of curious ways in the culture of the seventeenth-century Dutch Republic. The mixture of the two, if sometimes improbable and somewhat infrequent, can be revealing nevertheless of the setting of religious history and the shape of geographic imagination in the early modern Netherlands. Consider, among the more exotic blends, the tropical *Sacrifice of Manoah* (1648) by Frans Post, a biblical landscape that stages the old in the new with remarkable effect (Fig. 4.1).[1] Against a broad and gently mountainous background, an episode of dramatic devotion takes place. A man and a woman—Manoah and his wife, as described in Judges 13—kneel before a stone altar on which a kid has just been sacrificed. Suspended within the pillar of gray smoke billowing up from their offering, an angel glances knowingly at the performance below while gesturing grandly toward the heavens above. The angel's baroque movement is mirrored by the theatrical reaction of Manoah, who gazes up in stylized awe. His wife, who wears an antique cloak of blue and a red blouse (costume and colors otherwise associated with the Virgin Mary) hides her head in her hands, less from shame than humility. For she, like her husband, has just learned that she will bear a child, as announced by the miraculously revealed messenger of God.[2]

The themes of the painting are spectacular—literally a spectacle of sacred theater—though Post's version goes beyond even the usual drama

FIGURE 4.1 Frans Post, *Sacrifice of Manoah*, 1648. (Courtesy of the Museum Boijmans Van Beuningen, Rotterdam)

of Baroque art. The story of the Sacrifice of Manoah—of the annunciation of a child to a barren woman of Israel and of her husband's elaborate thanksgiving—was not in fact a common theme in the visual arts; and, though a few precedents did exist, none even remotely resembles Post's composition. A late sixteenth-century engraved version by Hendrik Goltzius more typically neglects the actual sacrifice to underscore the scene of "annunciation" and the typological relevance the story had to the (New Testament) Annunciation.[3] In the middle of the seventeenth century, the theme received attention from Rembrandt and his circle, who tended to isolate the dramatis personae in a way that emphasized the quiet moment of prayer shared by the expectant parents rather than the sacrifice and its setting. Willem Drost's circa 1650 rendition presents a model of Protestant piety.[4] The painting that comes closest to the expansive grandeur of Post's arrangement was executed, about the same time, by Claes Cornelisz. Moeyaert (Fig. 4.2).[5] In this case, the central elements of the compositions do match—the ascending angel, the astonished Manoah, the sacrificial vessels—but the scenery places the action, literally, in a different world.[6] Moeyaert situates his biblical narrative in an Italianate landscape, amidst what are meant to pass for Classical ruins. The dramatic staging of the scene, like the historical context from which it derives, is meant to look old. Post, by contrast, locates the Old Testament story in what can clearly be recognized as the New World: the Israelites sacrifice along the coast of Brazil near Olinda, identified by the stout watch towers (whose stone form echoes that of the altar) typical of the region. Other Americana abound. The repoussoir framing the foreground swarms with South American flora, including a giant cactus on the left, ripe papaya and banana trees, and the thick tropical foliage that darkens the anterior. An iguana scavenges near a calabash in the center foreground, facing an armadillo peeking curiously out from the left. Indigenous birds hover over and perch upon the lush vegetation while others glide below, where a pair of natives appear busy with their work.[7]

Why would Manoah have journeyed to America? Partly because Frans Post did, between 1636 and 1644, as part of the entourage of Johan Maurits of Nassau, the governor of Dutch Brazil and a generous patron of the arts. Post (ca. 1612–1680) served as court artist for Johan Maurits, preparing for the prince both landscape paintings and topographical drawings of the region. Upon his return to the Netherlands, Post discovered a great interest in—and a strong market for—his tropical vistas and went into what might be called the Brazilian landscape business. His *Varzea Landscape with Plantation*, done eight years after his return, and his *River Landscape*, finished two years later, share with the Manoah composition a meticulous concern for native flora and fauna, which Post arranged in the *Varzea* landscape in a manner remarkably similar to that of his biblical painting (Fig. 4.3).[8] Both of these later paintings and the scores more like them that followed, however, came well after Post had established his workshop and reputation. The *Sacrifice of Manoah* represents one of the first canvases produced by the artist since his New World voyage and the only one, before or after, with an Old Testament subject. Later tastes and painterly habits explain only partially why Post (or his patrons) decided, precisely at that moment, to stage the Bible in America.[9]

Dutch colonial circumstances in 1648 and the political lessons insinuated by Manoah's sacrifice suggest more particularly why the painting may have taken the form it did. The child who was born to Manoah and blessed by the Lord, Samson, grew up to be the champion of the Israelites and scourge of the Philistines, who had tyrannized God's Chosen for forty years. A mere three years had elapsed since the Portuguese planters of

FIGURE 4.2   Claes Cornelisz. Moeyaert, *Sacrifice of Manoah*, ca. 1649

FIGURE 4.3 Frans Post, *Varzea Landscape with Plantation*, 1652. (Courtesy of the Rijksmuseum, Amsterdam)

Dutch Brazil had revolted against their governors, yet the latter-day Israelites—as the seventeenth-century Dutch liked to fashion themselves—desperately needed deliverance from the soaring costs, fiscal and political, of their overseas crisis.[10] Salvation, in other words, was projected onto Post's Brazilian landscape, in the hope that some new Samson might deliver the Netherlands from their latest antagonists. The Old Testament in this instance provided the allegorical as well as historical framework for Post's colonial narrative, while the New World provided—or so the Dutch, like Manoah, prayed—the site and the prospect of redemption.[11]

The themes of Divine history and heroic salvation shape the arguments of another Dutch work, produced around the same time and within many of the same contexts as Post's biblical landscape. Menasseh ben Israel's highly influential *Hope of Israel*—published originally in Amsterdam in 1650 and a dozen more times, in half a dozen languages, into the early eighteenth century—offered a timely reflection on Jews, America, and redemption by the leading Sephardi voice of the Netherlands.[12] In confident and learned prose, the author considers the tantalizing prospect of Old Testament Israelites residing in the New World: a remnant of the Ten Lost Tribes (this time Reubenites, Manoah having belonged to the tribe of Dan) holding out in the Cordillera mountains of New Granada, not far from present-day Medellin. Once again, the image of Jews in the tropics is presented as a propitious sign—the diaspora of the Jews to all corners of the world implied to Menasseh's readers the imminence of messianic redemption—and the work conveyed a heady message of religious salvation. More prosaically, it focused attention on the near disastrous state of Dutch Brazil and the plight of the Sephardi community living there, which faced the calamitous prospect of an ascendant Portuguese (meaning hostile) regime. Like Post's biblical landscape, Menasseh's literary evocation of Jews in America delivered a sermon of hope and deliverance against the backdrop of Dutch, and in this case Sephardi, aspirations in the New World.

This distinctive cultural geography shared by both the painter and the rabbi grew out of a larger context of Dutch politics and culture in the seventeenth century, and it is the purpose of this essay to explore further the Dutch background of Menasseh's American landscape. For a variety of reasons and purposes, the New World served as a site of salvation for the Dutch Republic, a place of promise, potential, and, most importantly, strategic support. This applied for Jews no less than gentiles, and Menasseh's case demonstrates nicely how Jews in the early modern Netherlands could partake equally, if also distinctively, of broader Dutch strategies of rhetoric and representation. Menasseh, who moved relatively easily between Jewish and Christian circles, constructed the New World in ways that reflected a traditional geographic discourse in the Republic that looked to America for redemption. Those Reubenites and Indians who suggested "the hope of Israel" resembled, in other ways, representations—or better, projections—of the New World and its natives as "the hope of the Netherlands." Menasseh's world, in this sense, featured a recognizably Dutch America.

It also featured a good deal more besides exotic Israelites, and this essay's focus on Menasseh's—and by extension Sephardi—geography represents something of a historiographic departure, both in terms of text and author. The *Hope of Israel* has traditionally been studied (and sensibly so) as a crucial chapter in the religious history of early modern Europe.[13] Menasseh's work ranks among the most influential documents of seventeenth-century Jewish history and certainly among the most widely read pieces of early Jewish Americana. In its day, it ignited a frenzy of messianic and millenarian speculation across the whole of Europe. This European, devotional context, however, has distracted attention from the *Hope*'s Amsterdam origins and the text's Dutch, no less than Dutch-Jewish, cultural context. Such a local reading of the text reveals, moreover, a somewhat more nuanced view of Menasseh himself and, by extension, of the Sephardi community in Amsterdam. Recent research has succeeded admirably in identifying, isolating, and analyzing the Sephardim of northwest Europe and particularly the "Portuguese Nation" of Amsterdam: the New Jewish immigrants of Iberian and *converso* origin who settled in Holland from the early seventeenth century.[14] To this lately improved understanding of *converso* identity, social history, and economic activity, this study seeks to add a further dimension to the Sephardi profile, a Dutch Republican dimension, by exploring the cultural and ideological contexts of Menasseh's geography. Tracking down Menasseh's Old Testament relations in the New World should lead back, in this way, to New Jewish culture in the Old.

II

The geography of the Netherlands broadened conspicuously beyond Europe during the late sixteenth century, a direct result of the Dutch Revolt against Spain (1568–1648) and the ferocious war of words waged by the rebel party. Already from the earliest years of the revolt, a distinctly Dutch idea of the New World developed when polemicists working for the Prince of Orange promoted the theme of "Spanish tyranny in America" as a means of blackening the reputation of their opponents. Spain's tenure in America had proven disastrous, it was argued, and much the same could now be expected from Philip II's regime in the Low Countries. "The Spanish seek nothing but to abuse our Fatherland as they have done in the New Indies," asserted a prominent group of nobles in 1568, in defiance of the government in Brussels.[15] "America," within this context, represented an ominous and foreboding future that awaited the Netherlands should the tyranny of Spain go unchallenged. The Habsburg "conquest" of the Low Countries, as the pamphleteers perceived it, threatened to bring the same miserable consequences to the Netherlands as the conquistadors had wrought in America. In his widely circulated *Apologie* (1581), Willem of Orange codified the image of parallel Spanish tyrannies when he detailed how the Habsburgs had "adjudged all [Netherlanders] to death, making no more account of you than of beasts … as they do in the Indies, where they have miserably put to death more than twenty millions of people, and have made desolate and waste thirty times as much land in quantity and greatness as the low country is with such horrible excesses and riots."[16]

From this assumption of mutual suffering evolved a more ambitious notion of a tactical alliance between those two "nations" that most intimately knew the misrule of Spain. Orange's assertion of shared anguish contained in it a considerable degree of sympathy for the Indians, who had experienced worse abuses, reportedly, than even the Dutch. It also implied a unique affinity between the rebels and the "Americans"—the Dutch typically lumped all the natives together—who were linked by their common hostility toward the Habsburgs. To the polemically agile mind, this suggested the further possibility of an "alliance": if the natives could be construed as cousins-in-suffering, might they not plausibly be represented as brothers-in-arms as well, or perhaps even partners in trade? This was the tack taken by Willem Usselincx (1567–1647) and a group of like-minded colonialists who insisted, by the early seventeenth century, that the Indians would welcome the Dutch as confederates and join with them in a campaign against the "universal monarchy" of Spain. Most of these authors, to be sure, advertised, too, the obvious religious and economic advantages of their program: God and gold. But they and Usselincx asserted also the moral duty of their readers to aid those American "allies," whose experience had bonded them to the Republic. "The pitiless slaughter of over twenty million innocent Indians who did [Spain] no harm," quoted Usselincx directly from the rebel's propaganda, "[demanded] God's righteous judgment." The creation of a Dutch West India Company was not just an opportunity, in this view, but an obligation born of the pledges of fidelity made by the rebels to their American brethren. "Our friends and allies will lose all faith in us," wrote Usselincx in the wake of truce negotiations (1606–09), "if they see that we, but for the sake of a specious title, abandon our own inhabitants and the allied Indians who have been so faithful and done us such good service."[17]

For a variety of reasons, Usselincx's vision turned out not to be the one adopted by the Dutch West Indian Company (WIC), founded upon the expiration of the Twelve Year Truce in 1621.[18] But his rhetoric and the image of America on which it was predicated did linger nonetheless in the minds of armchair travelers and colonial schemers, who persevered in their promotion of a singularly Dutch notion of the New World. Well into the 1630s and 1640s, America was featured as a site of peculiar attachment for the Republic. As late as the middle of the seventeenth century, the Indians continued to constitute the possibility of a special "alliance" with the Netherlands.

Two Dutch initiatives well illustrate the lasting power of this idea of America.[19] The first involved an official treaty designed to join the States General of the Republic with the "Serene Lords of Peru" (living, as was supposed, in Buenos Aires) in a bond of strategic assistance. Joan Aventroot, author of the document and a zealous warrior for the Reformed faith, proposed that the "Peruvians" held the key to Dutch salvation and that a cataclysmic uprising in America, triggered by the Dutch-Indian confederation, would displace the hegemony of the Habsburgs and the primacy of the Catholic Church. Aventroot's apocalyptic musings, remarkably, received the full backing of the States, which were not only committed to the treaty but even funded the printing of eight thousand copies, an unusually large run by early modern standards.[20] The second initiative came in 1643, when the Prince of Orange, in cooperation with the WIC, backed a plan to unite with the "Chileans" against Spain. Once again, official documents were drafted and this time delivered, reaching the western coast of South America with a fleet under the command of Hendrick Brouwer. In this instance, the Dutch in fact commenced negotiations and laid out to the bemused Araucanians the advantages of the proposed alliance. Yet, despite getting the natives to kiss the prince's letters of credentials, the Dutch could not ultimately get them to sign on, and the expedition ended with the desired alliance still elusive.[21]

Hope, nonetheless, remained high. Whatever the setbacks in America, the Dutch conceit of the New World remained notably viable back in the Old, rhetoric triumphing easily over reality. If by the middle of the seventeenth century the image of the New World had undergone certain adjustments—appeals to Chile and Peru had pushed the frontiers of the alliance to the farthest shores of the Western Hemisphere—it still retained considerable currency, especially among the many who wrote about, but never visited, America. This applied in particular to a circle of humanists and relatively broad-minded men of letters in or of Holland. Hugo Grotius (1583–1645), the noted jurist and diplomat who, though exiled from the Republic, participated actively in its world of letters, argued in a pair of Latin treatises published in the early 1640s that the native Americans had descended from "Norwegian" or Germanic tribes. This made them distant kinsmen to the Dutch, whom Grotius had elsewhere described as members of another Germanic tribe, the Batavians.[22] This patriotic argument resonated with Caspar Barlaeus (1584–1648), the humanist poet and author of a massive *Rerum per octennium in Brasilia* (1647) commemorating the colonial regime of Johan Maurits. In Barlaeus's rendition of events, the "progeny of Bato" (as he referred to the prince of Nassau) had successfully "civilized" and allied with the natives who, if not kinsmen per se, had shown themselves to be the stalwart supporters of the Batavians abroad. The prince's Brazilian triumph, in the context of Barlaeus's broader celebration of the Dutch Golden Age, represented yet another sign of the Republic's providential ascendance.[23]

III

By 1650, the year in which the *Hope of Israel* first appeared, the New World had become a familiar enough site on the horizons of the Netherlands. It had become, moreover, a site specific to the Dutch geographic imagination. "America" represented, firstly, a place of "Spanish tyranny," a topos that runs throughout Dutch Americana, from the rebels' polemics to the reports of Brouwer's expedition published in the middle of the seventeenth century. Consequently—and secondly—it also represented a place of anticipated succor. The notion that the Indians, as enemies of the Republic's enemy, would therefore be their friends is implicit in the colonialist pitch of Willem Usselincx and explicitly argued by the likes of Joan Aventroot. Aventroot's hope for a religious no less than military revolt in America suggests, thirdly, the theme of religious salvation in, or perhaps from, the New World. Notwithstanding the Portuguese crisis in Brazil, Barlaeus's paean to Johan Maurits fashioned Dutch triumphs in America as indicative of a redemption already in progress. In all events, Grotius, in construing the Americans as fellow *Germanii*, made their fate of direct concern to latter-day "Batavians."

Thus Dutch geography. What about Dutch-Jewish geography or at least "Menassean" geography? Menasseh ben Israel (ca. 1604–57) imagined the New World in a variety of forms. In a certain sense, America was a very real place for the Amsterdam rabbi, who, like many Dutch Sephardim, had material and even familial interests in colonization projects. Using as an intermediary his brother Ephraim, who left for the West Indies in 1639, Menasseh invested in America in the late 1630s, after a consolidation of the Amsterdam synagogues brought a substantial cut in his pay.[24] A few years later, he dedicated the second installment of his four-part *Conciliador* (1641) to "the most noble, most prudent and fortunate *señores* of the Council of the West Indies"—the directors of the WIC—and declared his intention to immigrate to Recife in Dutch Brazil.[25] Menasseh only just missed the honor of becoming the "first American rabbi," as Cecil Roth once put it, though not without a fair degree of relief. The privilege, as it turned out, went to his rival, Isaac Aboab da Fonseca, whose vacated position in the Amsterdam congregation *Talmud Torah* now fell to Menasseh. This meant a rise in salary, and it obviated the need to look westward for work. Yet Menasseh, it would seem, had never felt any great desire to go in the first place. "At present, in complete disregard of my personal dignity, I am engaged in trade," he wrote with resignation in 1639. "What else is there for me to do? I have neither the wealth of Croesus, nor the nature of a Thersites"—and apparently not the heart to forsake "this flourishing land of Batavia [Holland] for the distant parts of Brazil."[26]

From 1642, Menasseh's prospects of actually going to Brazil rapidly diminished. Yet, although America ceased to function for him as a "real" place to live, it continued to serve as a viable idea—as a geographic topos or construct—that was nonetheless compelling. This cultural sense of the

New World had, in part, been inherited from decades of Dutch Republican geography. Menasseh, whose family immigrated from Madeira to Holland when he was a boy, considered himself "Portuguese by birth but Batavian in spirit" and would have acquired by this time what might be called a Batavian world-view.[27] In part, too, this sense had further developed over the years from Menasseh's own involvement and interaction with the world of geography, which, apparently, interested him considerably. He took great pleasure, for example, in hearing of distant lands. Though personally not much of a traveler, he availed himself, as a rabbi and community leader, of the opportunity to interview others passing through Amsterdam and reportedly delighted in such vicarious voyaging.[28]

Menasseh also had notable contacts, both collegial and professional, with some of the leading intellectual figures of the Netherlands, including many who had written on matters American. Grotius, if not quite a friend, corresponded with Menasseh on questions of history and Scripture, as did the Amsterdam humanist Gerardus Vossius, whose children the rabbi tutored. When Menasseh contemplated moving to Brazil, these two humanists exchanged letters on the news, Grotius wishing for Menasseh good fortune in Brazil "from the bottom of my soul."[29] With Barlaeus, Menasseh enjoyed an exceptionally warm friendship, each scholar admiring the other's work. The esteemed Latinist composed a sonnet celebrating their extraordinary, interfaith relationship; and, after Barlaeus's untimely death in 1648 (just after completing his opus on Brazil), Menasseh wrote movingly on the bond he had felt with "the Virgil of our time."[30] As a printer, Menasseh came into contact professionally with those responsible for Amsterdam's voluminous production of maps, atlases, and travel narratives describing the New World. Johannes Janssonius, among the leading publishers of Dutch (and indeed European) Americana, printed an edition of Menasseh's *De Creatione Problemata* in 1636 and then engaged the rabbi, around 1650, to prepare a Spanish translation of the geographer's massive *Atlas Novus*. The work ultimately appeared in 1653, though Menasseh had completed his translation a few years earlier—more or less at the same time, that is, he was otherwise contemplating Jews in America.[31]

Most relevant perhaps were Menasseh's connections with literary Americana: with the actual descriptions of the New World, which he read, studied, and incorporated into his own writing. Evidence of his geographic expertise comes from the text of the *Hope* itself, which includes an impressive list of authors consulted whose work related to Europe's westward expansion. This list includes, naturally, a range of non-Dutch writers—many of whom, however, were popular in the Republic precisely for their unflattering accounts of the Spanish *Conquista*.[32] More to the point, it catalogues Menasseh's extensive familiarity with the leading Dutch authorities on America: the geographers Abraham Ortelius, Petrus Plancius, and Willem Blaeu (who was Janssonius's chief competitor in the business of cartographic publishing); Menasseh's colleague, Hugo Grotius, and the latter's opponent in the debate on Indian etiology, Joannes de Laet (who also wrote the standard seventeenth-century history of the New World); and, not least, Jan Huygen van Linschoten, whose turn of the century *Itinerario* provided the literary foundation for the Dutch overseas enterprise.[33] To be sure, dozens of other authorities—Dutch, Classical, and rabbinical—round off Menasseh's bibliography, and it makes little sense to read the *Hope* merely as a reflection of Dutch Americana. On the other hand, though, many more works read by Menasseh would hardly have merited mention—the polemical literature and anti-Spanish propaganda so ubiquitous in the Republic—so that the least that can be said is that Menasseh knew of and appreciated the Dutch vision of the New World.

IV

What difference would it have made that Menasseh's geography had a Dutch imprint? How would a Dutch idea of America have influenced Menasseh's hopes for his co-religionists? And why, most importantly, would America have featured in Menasseh's messianic musings in the first place?

The *Hope of Israel*, if not entirely about the New World, takes as its point of departure the arrival from America in the Netherlands of the worldly traveler, Antonio de Montezinos, his tale of New World encounter providing the basis for Menasseh's own meditation on messianic redemption. The work begins, in this sense, with a characteristically American story. The "Relation of Antonio Montezinos" narrates a marvelous adventure of high-altitude exploration, exotic intrigue, and apocalyptic implication. It describes how Montezinos—alias Aharon Levi, a New Christian merchant from the Portuguese town of Villaflor—experienced in the New World a series of encounters: with the Inquisition, with a native tribe of Quito, and with a Lost Tribe of Israel. Following these wondrous episodes, an excited Montezinos returned to Europe, where he reached Amsterdam in September of 1644 with news of his "extraordinary" journey. He delivered his testimony under oath to Menasseh (in his capacity as community rabbi); and, by all accounts, Montezinos sought neither profit nor material advantage for his sensational report. The story electrified all the same, exciting both the Amsterdam Jewish *kehilah* and the Protestant millenarian community. From Amsterdam the news spread rapidly across the rest of the Netherlands and Europe, so that by 1650, when Menasseh finally published it as part of his text, Montezinos's "Relation" had already achieved far-flung renown.[34]

It is by all measures an extraordinary narrative, which begins with a journey across the Cordilleras in Spanish New Granada, not far from the port of Honda and the present-day capital of Colombia, Bogotá. There, among his porters and guides, Montezinos meets a native cacique,

Francisco, who makes a seemingly offhand comment about the ill treatment of a "holy people ... most innocent," who would one day rise up and avenge the cruelty of their tormentors. Though this strange allusion stirs the marrano's imagination, he lets the comment pass. Upon his return to Cartagena on the Caribbean, however, a bout with the Inquisition and the solitude of his imprisonment jog Montezinos's memory and allow him to reflect on the Indian's curious remark. Released from the Inquisitor's jail, he tracks down Francisco in Honda, confesses to him his secret Jewish identity (and common antipathy toward the Spanish), and convinces the Indian to reveal the meaning of his earlier allusion.[35] This entails a week's trek into the mountains that brings the pair to a "broad river" (the Río Cauca) and face to face with two "brethren," who greet the weary travelers with a recitation, in Hebrew, of the Jewish profession of faith: "Hear O Israel, the Lord is our God, the Lord is One" (Deut. 6:4). These mysterious men, soon joined by others from the opposite bank of the river, deliver a fantastic oration in the ritualized form of nine propositions repeated by three hundred "brethren" over the course of three days. They proclaim themselves to be of the tribe of Reuben, and they request that Montezinos send twelve bearded emissaries, "skillful in writing," to join them for an event (undisclosed) of apocalyptic proportions. Later, Francisco explains that these men, among the earliest settlers of America, were descendants of the Children of Israel, miraculously delivered to that land by God. The twelve (Hebrew) scribes whom they sought were needed to help them and their Indian confederates rise up against the mutual Spanish enemy.[36]

Montezinos's testimony, remarkable in and of itself, seems all the more so for the way its themes fit so well—are *made* to fit so well—into the broader Dutch discourse of America. The geography of the itinerant marrano, as shaped by the Amsterdam rabbi, made perfect sense in the context of the Netherlands. Alliances forged in the New World, once again, presume to resolve problems emanating from the Old—or so it was hoped. Indians are enlisted by God's Chosen to overthrow the tyranny of Spain. In the case of Montezinos, an alliance between the Reubenites and the natives of Quito requires the added participation of twelve scribes (Amsterdam *hakhamim*?), which makes for a somewhat more triangular connection between the Old World, the New World, and the Old Testament wayfarers harbored in America. The effect, though, is much the same. The Indians will consent to join forces with the Jews/Dutch to wage war against that which by now rings familiarly as "the notorious cruelty [of] the Spaniards."[37] The purpose of this alliance also bears a striking resemblance to the central motif of Dutch Americana: salvation. In the case of the Israelites, the theme of redemption carries an emphatically messianic message. The Indians "shall be happy if [they] make league with [the Israelites]," since the Jews, freed from their bondage, "shall be lords of the world." The Dutch alliance with the Indians is similarly intended to free the Netherlands from its particular "bondage" (a word used repeatedly in Dutch literature), though for purposes perhaps more pragmatic—political and economic—than apocalyptic.[38]

In a number of ways, of course, the *Hope of Israel* had some plainly pragmatic purposes of its own that had nothing to do with the Netherlands. The treatise has traditionally been studied in the context of English religious politics and the author's subsequent efforts to win readmission of the Jews into the Commonwealth. In the dedication to the original Spanish edition, Menasseh refers to inquiries from Protestant divines, including "a man of letters and of quality in England" (the theologian John Dury) who had pressed him on the question of American Jews and thus induced the rabbi to publish. Menasseh dedicated the Latin and English editions of 1650 to the new English government, appealing to their "charitable affection," "that I may gain your favor and good will to our Nation, now scattered almost all over the earth."[39] The enthusiastic response of millenarians from the rest of Europe encouraged Menasseh to respond in print in such a way that cleverly harnessed (Christian) chiliastic energies to (Jewish) messianic ends. The *Hope of Israel* makes the strenuous argument that the presence of Reubenites in America boded best for Jews, not Christians; and the work certainly played a significant part in the expansion of Sephardi spiritualism in the middle of the seventeenth century.[40] Finally, and perhaps most practically, the presence of allies in America would have heartened the embattled Jewish community of Recife, mired for half a decade in a life and death struggle with the Portuguese. The *Hope of Israel* may not quite have announced the arrival of a Jewish-Indian cavalry, but it did offer solace and impart optimism to Jews, in Europe and America, by suggesting that an age of miracles might soon be upon them.[41]

It is the last of these purposes that may have been foremost on Menasseh's mind when he went to press in 1650—six full years after Montezinos's testimony—and that may suggest why he resorted, in all cases, to a distinctly Dutch idiom for his text. The directors of the Dutch West India Company had the capacity to offer Jewish colonists in Brazil something more concrete than solace and "hope"; and Menasseh, wisely recognizing this, resorted accordingly to a rhetorical style that made sense to a Dutch audience. The themes of the *Hope of Israel*, that is to say, are enunciated in the vocabulary of Dutch geography—in language, topoi, and motifs that derive, to a significant degree, from a Dutch polemical model—and in a manner that effectively linked the "hope of Israel" with a literary tradition of the Netherlands. Such a rhetorical strategy allied the Sephardi cause to that of the WIC. More generally, it affiliated the sacred history of the Jews and their hope for redemption with the patriotic historiography of the United Provinces and its well-established tropes of suffering, "alliances," and redemption. The hope of Israel, Menasseh asserted, resembled the hope of the Netherlands. And the New World, in this sense, promised salvation to Sephardi and Batavian alike.

In the end, what is so striking about the *Hope of Israel* is the many types of readers it could accommodate and the multiple layers of rhetoric and argument on which it rested. This is testimony to the skill of its author as a "conciliator": someone who moved easily between texts and sacred literatures (as Menasseh famously did) and someone who sought to reconcile ostensibly different goals and religious traditions (though with the Sephardi good always in mind). Menasseh's list of consulted "authors of other nations" demonstrates a catholicity of learning that stands out even in the relatively tolerant intellectual environment of the Dutch Republic.[42] It also demonstrates a remarkable rhetorical flexibility on the part of the author, as a Sephardi rabbi, to participate in and to exploit what might otherwise be considered alien idioms. Menasseh knew well how to use the language and topoi of others, and this allowed him to compose an outstandingly effective treatise—as the public success of the *Hope* well attests.

That Menasseh did move so easily within an otherwise distinctively Dutch discourse suggests, moreover, that the Sephardi "Nation" of Amsterdam need not be quite so isolated from its secular surroundings. Menasseh, it is true, was something of an exception within the Amsterdam Jewish community precisely for his connections to the Christian world of scholarship and even politics.[43] Yet he was not entirely alone in this regard. In the case of Uriel da Costa, whose heterodoxies sent convulsions through the community at about the time Menasseh came of age intellectually, influences came from further afield than simply the Netherlands.[44] The Holland-born Baruch Spinoza (who in all likelihood received his earliest schooling from Menasseh), though, participated from a very early age in the Dutch republic of letters. Like Menasseh, Spinoza showed himself able to move easily amongst the diverse philosophical and religious circles of Amsterdam. All of which is not to conflate the ecumenical use of learning (for orthodox ends) by Menasseh with the intellectual curiosity (for "impious" goals) of Spinoza. Rather, Menasseh's case and others show how the community of Amsterdam Sephardim, if forged by the unique *converso* experience, could be shaped all the same by the experiences, cultures, and (in Menasseh's case) geographies of those around them.[45]

In the final analysis, the geographic sensibilities expressed by the *Hope of Israel* say as much about the author and his world as they do about that distinctive New World he was describing. America, as imagined by Menasseh and his Dutch contemporaries, represented a hopeful and optimistic landscape that functioned perhaps better as an idea than a reality. The Amsterdam Sephardim, in the end, never sent twelve bearded scribes to the Cordilleras, just as the Dutch, despite their ongoing rhetoric, never finalized an alliance with their American Indian brethren. But over a period that extended from the late sixteenth through the mid-seventeenth centuries, the New World continued to offer the hope of redemption to Jew and Christian alike. Sephardi rabbi no less than colonial promoter appropriated the geography of America and the ever plastic image of its natives for their own ideological ends. The *Hope of Israel*, like so many other Dutch descriptions of the New World, provides evidence ultimately of both the rhetorical dexterity of its author and the singular malleability of his subject, America. By the remarkable combination of the two, the Old Testament had ended up in the New World.

Notes

For their helpful comments and suggestions on earlier drafts of this essay, I would like to thank Roger Diederen, David Katz, Hillel Kieval, Louise Townsend, and Ben Westervelt. Generous financial support came from the Keller Fund of the University of Washington.

1. Museum Boijmans Van Beuningen, Rotterdam (signed and dated, "F. Post 3.27.1648"). See Joaquim de Sousa-Leão, *Frans Post, 1612–1680* (Amsterdam, 1973), 26, 62–63; Erik Larsen, *Frans Post, interprète du Brésil* (Amsterdam, 1962), cat. no. 12; and Ernst van den Boogaart, ed., *Zo wijd de wereld strekt* (The Hague, 1979), 206.
2. Judges 13:20: "And when the flame went up toward heaven from the altar, the angel of the Lord ascended in the flame of the altar while Manoah and his wife looked on; and they fell on their faces to the ground." The drama of the story includes both the annunciation of the child to the couple and the climactic revelation of the angel to Manoah, who, while never quite doubting his wife, desired nonetheless confirmation of the Divinity of the message.
3. The image—signed "HGoltzius" and dated ca. 1586—was one in a series of six annunciations, half from the Old Testament and half from the New. See Walter Strauss, ed., *Hendrik Goltzius 1558–1617: The Complete Engravings and Woodcuts* (New York, 1977), esp. 373. There is an earlier engraving, also in the Mannerist style, by Maarten van Heemskerck (1498–1574), who worked in Haarlem just before Goltzius's arrival there ca. 1576–77.
4. F. Saxl, *Rembrandt's Sacrifice of Manoah*, Studies of the Warburg Institute, vol. 9 (London, 1939), reviews many of these paintings, engravings, and drawings, including images by Govaert Flinck, Barent Fabritius, and Willem Drost. The "Rembrandt" painting of Saxl's focus, though, is now attributed to Drost: *A Corpus of Rembrandt Paintings*, ed. J. Bruyn et al. (The Hague, 1982–), 3: 523–32. See also Christian Tümpel et al., *Im Lichte Rembrandts: Das Alte Testament im Goldenen Zeitalter der niederlandischen Kunst* (Munich, 1994), esp. 69–72. The Drost *Sacrifice of Manoah* is in the Staatliche Kunstsammlungen, Dresden.
5. *Sacrifice of Manoah*, ca. 1649 (whereabouts unknown; formerly coll. Baron Reedtz-Thott, Gaunö, Denmark), on which see Astrid Tümpel, "Claes Cornelisz. Moeyaert," *Oud Holland* 88 (1974):1–163, esp. 119–22 and Fig. 166.
6. Moeyaert, who had a successful career as an Amsterdam portraitist, has in fact been credited with the figures in the Boijmans painting. Other candidates include Flinck and Ferdinand Bol, though their high reputations at this time (especially Flinck's) may have precluded their contributing to a relatively minor composition. See Albert Blankert et al., *Gods, Saints, and Heroes: Dutch Painting in the Age of Rembrandt* (Washington, 1980), 266.
7. The region, more generally, was described as "the Paradise of Brazil" by the leading chronicler of Dutch America, Johannes de Laet, who happened also to be a *bewindhebber* (director) of the Dutch West India Company. See Johannes de Laet, *Historie ofte Iaerlijck verhael van de verrichtinghen der Geoctroyeerde West-Indische Compagnie* (Leiden, 1644), and cf. 192 on the captaincy of Pernambuco, in which Olinda was centrally situated.

8. Frans Post, *Varzea Landscape with Plantation* (Rijksmuseum, Amsterdam) and *River Landscape* (Scheepvaart Museum, Amsterdam). Both paintings are signed and dated, 1652 and 1654 respectively. The 1652 landscape was very likely commissioned by Peter Hagen, a former councilor in Brazil (De Sousa-Leão, *Post*, 69).

9. This issue has been left largely unexplored in the literature—both on Post and on the Dutch in Brazil. See, for example, C. R. Boxer, *The Dutch in Brazil, 1624–54* (Oxford, 1957); C. M. Schulten, *Nederlandse expansie in Latijns Amerika: Brazilië 1624–1654* (Bussum, 1968); and the art historical literature cited above (note 1). Post's biblical exoticism, as such, has gone unremarked as well, notably in two recent studies of Dutch biblical painting in the mid-seventeenth century: Christian Tümpel et al., *Het Oude Testament in de schilderkunst van de Gouden Eeuw* (Amsterdam, 1991), and Tümpel, *Im Lichte Rembrandts*.

10. This political reading of the painting was first suggested in A. B. de Vries, ed., *Maurits de Braziliaan* (The Hague, 1953), 41, no. 17.

11. De Laet seemed also to have recognized some of the spiritual qualities of Post's Brazilian site by prominently noting, in his description of Olinda, "the beautiful and well-built Jesuit monastery," the Capuchin and Dominican monasteries, the Carmelite nunnery, and diverse other churches—all of which graced the contested settlement (De Laet, *Iaerlijck verhael*, 191).

12. The work was published simultaneously in Spanish and Latin as *Miqweh Israel. Esto es Esperança de Israel* and *Miqweh Israel. Hoc est Spes Israelis* (both Amsterdam, 1650), thus assuring a wide audience both within and without the Sephardi community of Amsterdam. All told, at least thirteen editions appeared through 1723 in Latin, Spanish, English, Dutch, Yiddish, and Hebrew. For a complete bibliography, see J. H. Coppenhagen, *Menasseh ben Israel: Manuel Dias Soero, 1604–1657: A Bibliography* (Jerusalem, 1990).

13. See, for example, the essays in Yosef Kaplan, Henry Méchoulan, and Richard Popkin, eds., *Menasseh ben Israel and His World* (Leiden, 1989); and the superb Introduction by Henry Méchoulan and Gérard Nahon in Menasseh ben Israel, *The Hope of Israel*, ed. Méchoulan and Nahon (Oxford, 1987), 1–95. Menasseh's campaign to win admittance into England for the Jews (and the millenarian context of these efforts) are examined in David Katz, *Philo-Semitism and the Readmission of the Jews to England 1603–1655* (Oxford, 1982); idem, *The Jews in the History of England* (Oxford, 1994), esp. 106–44, with an updated bibliography; and Lucien Wolf, *Menasseh ben Israel's Mission to Oliver Cromwell* (London, 1901). For an excellent study that relates Menasseh's messianism specifically to events in Brazil, see Jonathan Israel, "Dutch Sephardi Jewry, Millenarian Politics, and the Struggle for Brazil," in *Skeptics, Millenarians and Jews*, ed. Jonathan Israel and David Katz (Leiden, 1990), 76–97. Dutch millenarianism is considered in this context by Ernestine G. E. van der Wall, "The Amsterdam Millenarian Petrus Serrarius (1600–1669) and the Anglo-Dutch Circle of Philo-Judaists," in *Jewish Christian Relations in the Seventeenth Century*, ed. J. van den Berg and van der Wall (Dordrecht, 1988), 73–94; and idem, "Three Letters by Menasseh Ben Israel to John Drurie," *Nederlands Archief voor Kerkgeschiedenis* 65 (1985):46–63.

14. The literature is voluminous. For the *converso mentalité*, see Miriam Bodian, "'Men of the Nation': The Shaping of *Converso* Identity in Early Modern Europe," *Past and Present* 143 (May 1994):48–76; and idem, *Hebrews of the Portuguese Nation: Conversos and Community in Early Modern Amsterdam* (Bloomington, 1997). Social and religious issues are addressed in two useful overviews by Yosef Kaplan, "The Portuguese Community in Amsterdam in the Seventeenth Century: Tradition and Change," in *Society and Community*, Proceedings of the Second International Congress for Research into the Sephardi and Oriental Heritage, ed. A Haim (Jerusalem, 1991), 141–71; and "The Intellectual Ferment in the Spanish-Portuguese Community of Seventeenth-Century Amsterdam" [Hebrew], in *Moreshet Sepharad: The Sephardi Legacy*, ed. Haim Beinart (Jerusalem, 1992), 600–621. For the economic activities of the Sephardim, see the essays collected in Jonathan Israel, *European Jewry in the Age of Mercantilism, 1550–1750* (Oxford, 1985); idem, "The Economic Contribution of Dutch

Sephardi Jews to Holland's Golden Age, 1595–1713," *Tijdschrift voor Geschiedenis* 96 (1983):505–36 (reprinted in the very useful *Empires and Entrepots* [London, 1990]); and D. M. Swetschinski, *Reluctant Cosmopolitans: The Portuguese Jews of Seventeenth-Century Amsterdam* (London, 2000). A fine survey of the state of research (with extensive bibliographies) can be found in J. C. H. Blom, R. G. Fuks-Mansfeld, and I. Schöffer, eds., *Geschiedenis van de Joden in Nederland* (Amsterdam, 1995), esp. in the essays of D. M. Swetschinski ("Tussen middeleeuwen en Gouden Eeuw, 1516–1621," 53–94), J. I. Israel ("De Republiek der Verenigde Nederlanden tot omstreeks 1750: Demografie en economische activiteit," 97–126), and Y. Kaplan ("De joden in de Republiek tot omstreeks 1750: Religieus, cultureel en sociaal leven," 129–73). See also the synthetic overview of R. G. Fuks-Mansfeld, *De Sephardim in Amsterdam tot 1795* (Hilversum, 1989).

15. "Verbintenis van eenige Eedelen," in J. W. Te Water, *Historie van het verbond en de smeekschriften der Nederlandsche edelen ter verkrijging van vrijheid in den godsdienst en burgerstaat in de jaren 1565–1567,* 4 vols. (Middelburg, 1779–96), 4:61. Further examples are discussed in Benjamin Schmidt, "Tyranny Abroad: The Dutch Revolt and the Invention of America," *De Zeventiende Eeuw* 11 (1995):161–74.

16. *Apologie of Prince William of Orange against the Proclamation of the King of Spaine,* ed. H. Wansink (Leiden, 1969), 53–59 (with slight changes in the punctuation). Like many of the rebel propagandists, Willem targeted a broadly international audience and had the *Apologie,* originally published in French, translated immediately into Dutch, German, Latin, and English. Willem's point was reiterated a few months later by the States General in their official abjuration of Philip II, which similarly accused the Spanish monarch of seeking "to abolish all the privileges of the country and have it tyrannically governed by Spaniards *like the Indies*" (emphasis added). See the *Plakkaat van Verlatinge 1581,* ed. M. E. H. N. Mout (The Hague, 1979), esp. 97, 99, 105, 117.

17. *Levendich discours vant ghemeyne Lants welvaert, voor desen de Oost, end nu de West-Indische generale compaignie aenghevanghen* (1622), sig. [C4] v; *Memorie vande ghewichtighe redenen die de heeren Staten Generael behooren te beweghen, om gheesins te wijcken vande handelinghe ende vaert van Indien* (1608), sig. iij-r; and cf. the *Onpartydich discours opte handelinghe vande Indien* ([1608?]), sig. Aij-r, which speaks of an "alliante" with the Indians.

18. Briefly, a sluggish subscription rate induced the directors to focus more squarely on economic issues—though political rhetoric did remain part of their pitch. Debates over the Company's origins can be found in W. J. van Hoboken, "The Dutch West India Company: The Political Background of Its Rise and Fall," in *Britain and the Netherlands,* ed. J. S. Bromley and E. H. Kossmann (London, 1960); and J. G. van Dillen, "De West-Indische Compagnie, het calvinisme, en de politiek," *Tijdschrift voor geschiedenis* 74 (1961):145–71. Also useful for the early development of the WIC are Simon Hart, *The Prehistory of the New Netherland Company* (Amsterdam, 1959); P. J. van Winter, *De Westindische Compagnie ter kamer Stad en Lande* (The Hague, 1978); Ernst van den Boogaart, "De Nederlandse expansie in het Atlantisch gebied, 1590–1674," *Algemene Geschiedenis der Nederlanden,* 15 vols. (Haarlem, 1977–83), 7:220–54; and Henk den Heijer, *De geschiedenis van de WIC* (Zutphen, 1994). The classic biographies of Usselincx are J. Franklin Jameson, *Willem Usselinx: Founder of the Dutch and Swedish West India Companies,* Papers of the American Historical Association, vol. 2, no. 3 (New York, 1887); and C. Ligtenberg, *Willem Usselinx* (Utrecht, 1914).

19. Both are discussed at greater length in Benjamin Schmidt, "Exotic Allies: The Dutch-Chilean Encounter and the (Failed) Conquest of America," *Renaissance Quarterly* 52 (1999):440–73.

20. Joan Aventroot, *Sendt-brief aen die van Peru, met een Aliance van de … Heeren Staten, der Vereenigder Provintien des Nederlands* (Amsterdam, 1630). Aventroot had attempted to forge an American alliance a few years earlier, when he provided the Nassau Fleet (mid-1620s) with special directives for negotiating a confederation with the natives. See the "Instructie voor u, Jacques l'Hermite, vanwegen de Ho. Mo. Heeren, de Staten-Generaal" and the "Instructie voor den Generael" in *De reis om de wereld van de Nassausche*

Vloot 1623–1626, ed. W. Voorbeijtel Cannenburg, Werken Uitgegeven door de Linschoten-Vereeniging, vol. 65 (The Hague, 1964).

21. See the published journal of the voyage, *Journael ende historis verhael van de reyse gedaen by oosten de Straet le Maire, naer de custen van Chili, onder het beleyt van den Heer Generael Hendrick Brouwer, inden jare 1643 voor gevallen* (Amsterdam, 1646), as well as the overly confident *Tydingh uyt Brasijl aende Heeren Bewinthebberen van de West-Indische Compagnie, van wegen den tocht by den Generael Brouwer nae de Zuyd-Zee gedaen* (Amsterdam, 1644), which prematurely announced a Dutch success in the region.

22. Hugo de Groot, *De origine gentium Americanarum dissertatio* (Paris, 1642) and *De origine gentium Americanarum dissertatio altera, adversus obtjectatorem* (Paris, 1643), which responds to Joannes de Laet, *Notae ad dissertationem Hugonis Grotii* (Amsterdam, 1643). De Groot laid out his view on the origins of the Dutch Republic in the *Liber de antiquitate reipublicae Batavica* (Leiden, 1610), which was published around the same time that Abraham van der Myl (Mylius) was drawing a linguistic link between the "Teutonic" races (especially the Cimbri, progenitors of the Dutch) and the Indians: *Lingua Belgica* (Leiden, 1612). G. Gliozzi argues that Grotius, at the time an ambassador for the queen of Sweden, meant to bolster his patron's claims to lands in North America: G. Gliozzi, *Adamo e il nuovo mondo: La nascita dell'antropologia come ideologia coloniale* (Florence 1977). J.-P. Rubiés sees Grotius's and de Laet's debate in the context of a Dutch religious dispute over Calvinist orthodoxy: "Hugo Grotius's Dissertation on the Origin of American Peoples and the Use of Comparative Methods," *Journal of the History of Ideas* 52 (1991):221–44. In emphasizing economic and religious concerns, Gliozzi and Rubiés both underestimate, and therefore overlook, the intense and intensely nostalgic patriotism nurtured by de Groot for that which he considered, to the very end, his *patria*, namely Holland.

23. Caspar Barlaeus, *Rerum per octennium in Brasilia et alibi nuper gestarum, sub praefectura … J. Mauriti* (Amsterdam, 1647). The work contained dozens of engravings based on drawings made in situ by Frans Post.

24. For biographical details, see Cecil Roth, *A Life of Menasseh ben Israel, Rabbi, Printer, and Diplomat* (Philadelphia, 1934), esp. 51–53; and Méchoulan and Nahon, "Introduction," 39–40. Menasseh's concern for the Dutch colonial enterprise is treated by Jonathan Israel, "Menasseh ben Israel and the Dutch Sephardic Colonization Movement of the Mid-Seventeenth Century (1645–1657)," in Kaplan et al., *Menasseh*, 139–63. More generally, see Arnold Wiznitzer, *Jews in Colonial Brazil* (New York, 1960).

25. Menasseh ben Israel, *Conciliador o de la convenecia de los Lugares de la S. Escriptura que repugnantes entre si parecen*, Part 2 (Amsterdam, 1641). The dedicatory epistle also contained a glowing account of the Republic's recent naval triumphs in Spanish American waters.

26. Menasseh ben Israel, *De termino vitae: libri tres* (Amsterdam, 1639), 236 (cited in Roth, *Menasseh*, 53; and cf. ibid., 59–61, for Menasseh's warm feelings for "Batavia" and for Aboab's rabbinical first).

27. Menasseh, *Conciliador*, Part 2, "Epistola dedicatoria." There is still some dispute regarding Menasseh's birthplace. Roth, who favors Madeira, reviews the source material in an extensive note: Roth, *Menasseh*, 28–30. Méchoulan and Nahon (Introduction, 23) hedge their bets, emphasizing, in all events, the *converso* background of the Soeiro family and the youth of Menasseh upon his arrival in the Netherlands. See also H. P. Salomon, "The Portuguese Background of Menasseh ben Israel's Parents as Revealed through the Inquisitorial Archives at Lisbon," *Studia Rosenthaliana* 17, no. 2 (1983): 105–46.

28. As noted in his *Sefer Nishmat Hayyim* [Hebrew] (Amsterdam, 1651) and cited in Roth, *Menasseh*, 45.

29. These relationships are well reviewed in Roth, *Menasseh*, 143–48. See ibid., 59, for the letters exchanged between Grotius and Vossius (January and February 1640); and cf. Edwin Rabbie, "Hugo Grotius and Judaism," in *Hugo Grotius Theologian: Essays in Honor of G. H. M. Posthumus Meyjes*, ed. Henk J. M. Nellen and Edwin Rabbie (Leiden, 1994), 99–120, for a more skeptical view of Grotius's relationship with his Jewish colleague.

30. Barlaeus's sonnet appears in the prefatory materials to Menasseh's *De Creatione Prob-lemata XXX* (Amsterdam, 1635). More generally, see F. F. Blok, "Caspar Barlaeus en de Joden: De geschiedenis van een epigram," *Nederlands Archief voor Kerkgeschiedenis* 63 (1976–77):85–108 and 179–209; and Roth, *Menasseh*, 152–54.

31. The Spanish Janssonius—*Nuevo Atlas o Theatro de Todo el Mundo de Juan Janssonio* (Amsterdam, 1653)—is discussed by J. Werner, "Universiteitsbibliotheek van Amsterdam ontvangt een Spaanse Janssonius," *Caert-Thresoor* 4 (1985):10–11; and A. K. Offenberg, "Some Remarks Regarding Six Autograph Letters by Menasseh ben Israel in the Amsterdam University Library," in Kaplan et al., *Menasseh*, 191–98. Joan Blaeu, the Netherlands' other leading geographer/publisher, also had dealings with Menasseh, in his case regarding an edition of the *Conciliador* (Roth, *Menasseh*, 171).

It is perhaps worth noting one further cultural contact, who collaborated with Menasseh on matters related both to scholarship and printing (he produced images for the *Piedra gloriosa* [Amsterdam, 1655]), namely, Rembrandt van Rijn. For a recent study of their personal and professional relationship, see Michael Zell, "Protestant Imagery and Jewish Apologetics: Rembrandt's Encounter with Rabbi Menasseh ben Israel" (Ph.D. diss., Harvard University, 1994).

32. Notably "Alonsus de Erzilla [Ercilla y Zúñiga]," whose epic *La Araucana* describes the heroic resistance of the native Chileans against the Habsburgs (Spanish ed. pub. Antwerp, 1586 and 1597; Dutch trans. pub. Rotterdam, 1619) and "Garcilassus [Garcilaso] de la Vega [Inca]," whose highly ambivalent account of the *Conquista* (the author was half-native) was widely cited in the United Provinces.

33. Menasseh, *Hope*, 103–4.

34. Ibid., 105–11. See also Méchoulan and Nahon, Introduction, 68–76 (citing the Gemeentearchief of Amsterdam on Montezinos's notable absence from the register of alms recipients); and, for biographical details, the fascinating account of Elizabeth Levi de Montezinos, "The Narrative of Aharon Levi, alias Antonio de Montezinos," *American Sephardi*, 7-8 (1975):63–83. Antonio, who claimed to be forty years old at the time of his Amsterdam visit (1644), actually returned the following year to Dutch Brazil, where he lived for two more years, dying before the Jewish community there began its own register.

35. In order fully to gain Francisco's confidence, however, Montezinos must first "go native": abandon his Spanish cloak and sword, wear instead the native "alpergatos" (linen shoes), and swear to eat only roasted maize. See the version of the story (based on a French ms. copy sent by Menasseh) in Thomas Thorowgood, *Iewes in America, or, Probabilities That the Americans Are of that Race* (London, 1650), 129–[138].

36. Records of the Holy Office of Cartagena de las Indias confirm at least part of Montezinos's tale. See Montezinos, "Narrative," which traces Inquisition documents concerning "Antonio Montessinos, born at Villaflor" and discusses family traditions related to the affair.

37. Menasseh, *Hope*, 105 and passim. Menasseh's dark vision of "Spanish tyranny" reappears in numerous of his other writings. See, for example, the "Epistola dedicatoria" of the *Conciliador* (pt. 2), in which he acknowledges the Dutch role in protecting the Jews from the Inquisition: "We were protected from Spanish tyranny, and for that neither I nor my co-religionists will ever be able to thank you [the United Provinces] enough."

38. Menasseh, *Hope*, 110. On the metaphor of bondage (or slavery) as used in contemporary narratives of the Dutch Revolt, see Simon Schama, *The Embarrassment of Riches: An Interpretation of Dutch Culture in the Golden Age* (New York, 1987), 81–93.

39. See the "Epistola dedicatoria," in Menasseh, *Esperança de Israel*; and the "Epistle Dedicatory," in Menasseh, *Hope*, 99–100. Important studies that place the work in this English context include Roth, *Menasseh* (cf. 181–202); idem, "The Resettlement of the Jews in England in 1656," in *Three Centuries of Anglo-Jewish History*, ed. V. D. Lipman (London, 1961), 3–25; Wolf, *Menasseh ben Israel's Mission*; and Katz, *Philo-Semitism*. Menasseh later attempted to play the Swedish card as well; see David Katz, "Menasseh ben Israel's Mission to Queen Christina of Sweden, 1651–1655," *Jewish Social Studies* 45 (1983):57–72.

40. This is the central theme of Méchoulan and Nahon (Introduction), who correctly point out that Menasseh made the case *not* (as has traditionally been argued) that Indians were Jews, but rather that Jews lived *among* the Indians. The Israelite's miraculous dispersal to the farthest corners of the world, New and Old, was a sign of the imminent messianic redemption.

41. Israel, "Dutch Sephardic Colonization," and idem, "Dutch Sephardi Jewry," which include discussions of the messianic moment of 1645–50.

42. Compare, in this regard, the case of Barlaeus, whose open-minded sonnet dedicated to Menasseh (which suggested that Jews and Christians might coexist as "friends before God") brought in fact a hail of accusations upon the embattled Latin—and, nota bene, Remonstrant—scholar.

43. It was Menasseh who received the stadholder Frederick Henry (accompanied by Queen Henrietta Maria, wife of Charles I) in the Amsterdam synagogue in 1642. He communicated also with Christina of Sweden (see note 39 above) and, of course, with Oliver Cromwell.

44. See the recent edition of Uriel da Costa, *Examination of Pharisaic Traditions*, trans. H. P. Salomon and I. S. D. Sasson (Leiden, 1993); as well as Carl Gebhardt, *Die Schriften des Uriel da Costa* (Amsterdam, 1922).

45. Bodian (*Hebrews of the Portuguese Nation*), while making a convincing case for the distinctiveness of the Amsterdam "Men of the Nation," also acknowledges a number of significant points of cultural contact between the "Portuguese" Sephardim and the Dutch. Among these was a shared idiom of antipathy directed at Iberian Catholicism and even a certain overlap in the construction of "foundation" histories (see especially her third chapter, "The Dutch Context," in ibid., 53–75). Bodian also indicates the possible channel for this interaction—literature—and notes that Menasseh's rival, the rabbi Isaac Aboab da Fonseca, likewise read widely in Renaissance literature, both secular and sacred.

Chapter 5

ISRAEL IN AMERICA: THE WANDERINGS OF THE LOST TEN TRIBES FROM MIKVEIGH YISRAEL TO TIMOTHY MCVEIGH

David S. Katz

R OYAL FAMILY TREES in the early modern period often began with Adam and Eve, and carried on without shame to the most contemporary representatives of that illustrious lineage. In principle, this was easily accomplished. Everyone knew that Noah had divided the world among his three sons, each of whom was given divine title either to Europe (Japheth), Asia (Shem) or Africa (Ham).[1] The discovery of the American Indians, however, demanded a bit of creativity, since there was no apparent mention of the New World in Genesis, so distant as it was from the scene of biblical events. Columbus himself had no difficulty with their discovery. He died in the belief that he had landed on the east coast of Asia: the Indians were Asiatics, and their presence was interesting but unremarkable. Columbus reported in his journal that when he sent a reconnaissance party into the interior, he included one Luis de Torres, a *converso* who "understood Hebrew and Chaldean and even some Arabic." Torres was meant to be the interpreter should the expedition encounter any Hebrew-speaking Indians.[2] It was entirely possible, Columbus reasoned, that these strange people might be the barbarized descendants of the Ten Tribes of Israel whose fate was described in the biblical canon itself.

Although some proto-anthropologists, such as Isaac la Peyrère in seventeenth-century France, suggested that the American Indians might be entirely outside the Scripture story, virtually all those who wrote about the origin of the American Indians agreed that they must in some way be

descended from Adam and Eve, if not from Noah as well. The chief difficulties were to describe the route of migration and to fit the chronology
within the accepted timetable of Genesis.[3] The identification of Indians
with the Lost Ten Tribes was one convenient and popular solution that
found advocates not only in the Spanish-speaking world, but also in England and continental Europe.[4] But there have been other candidates for the
descendants of the biblical Israelites, most notably the British people and
the white Anglo-Saxon citizens of the United States of America. What
gives this curious and somewhat comical academic dispute historical bal-
last, however, is that the early modern myth of Israel in America would
not only survive the Enlightenment, but would also become the ideological underpinning both of a major American religion and of twentieth-century racist groups such as the Aryan Nations and the Christian Identity
movement, from whose ranks emerged Timothy McVeigh, who was convicted for the 1995 bombing of the federal building in Oklahoma City.[5]

I

Speculations concerning the possible identification of the Lost Ten Tribes
of Israel with the American Indians may have been in the air since
Columbus, but they took on a renewed urgency in 1644, when a marrano
named Antonio de Montezinos, recently returned from Quito Province in
Ecuador, testified under oath before the Amsterdam Rabbi Menasseh ben
Israel (1604–1657) that he had met Israelites of the tribe of Reuben there,
living secretly, deep in the interior of the territory. Montezinos had made
a good choice in selecting Menasseh as his witness, for in many respects,
the Dutch rabbi had become the Jewish ambassador to the gentile intellectual world.

Montezinos's testimony before Menasseh ben Israel was both fantastic and exciting. Montezinos recounted his arrival at the secret kingdom
where the inhabitants repeated the Jewish credo, the *Shema,* along with
nine vague remarks and prophecies, but refused to allow him to cross the
River Sambatyon bordering their country. Montezinos estimated that he
spoke with nearly three hundred Israelite American Indians during his
three days there, but they would see him only in small groups and
declined to elaborate on their nine cryptic statements.[6] Menasseh himself
published the full account in his book *The Hope of Israel,* which appeared
in Amsterdam in Latin and Spanish in 1650, and in London the same year
in an English edition, translated by Milton's friend Moses Wall; a second
English edition is dated 1652 (see Fig. 5.1).[7]

Menasseh's little book reinvigorated the issue of the Lost Ten Tribes
and gave the debate a text over which it could center. Menasseh, in turn,
was instantly famous, especially in the circle of English philosemitic intel-
lectuals who believed that the conversion of the Lost Ten Tribes was a
harbinger of the conversion of the European Jews, which in turn was a

FIGURE 5.1 Menasseh ben Joseph ben Israel, [*Sefer Mikweh Yisrael*] (Amsterdam, 1697). *The Hope of Israel* was first published in Spanish as *Esperança de Israel* (Amsterdam, 5410 [i.e., 1650]).

prelude to the Second Coming and the millennium, when Christ would rule on earth for a thousand years with his saints. Menasseh, on the other hand, had no intention of converting to Christianity, but relied on the book of Isaiah, which prophesied that the Lord would "assemble the outcasts of Israel, and gather together the dispersed of Judah from the four corners of the earth" before the coming of the Messiah. Russia and Palestine might be two corners; South America might be a newly discovered third. England was probably the fourth, in part because its designation in medieval Hebrew literature was often "the end of the earth," a Franbreu translation of "Angleterre."[8]

It was the issue of the Lost Ten Tribes, then, that caused the rise of Menasseh ben Israel, following neatly upon his fall. The discovery of the Lost Tribes enabled an unemployed and underpaid Dutch rabbi to connect with circles in London who hoped that by readmitting the Jews to England and converting them to true and pure English Protestant Christianity, the Second Coming of Christ would be brought closer. There was an identity of purpose between Christian and Jew in seventeenth-century England, which was already sensitized to philosemitism on the basis of the values of the Renaissance and the Reformation common to Northern European culture.[9]

II

The chimera of the Lost Ten Tribes stayed fresh and survived as a powerful force, especially among those groups that stressed the inerrancy of the Bible and refused to accept the new biblical criticism, and even more so among those denominations that gave the Jews, with or without the Lost Ten Tribes (and sometimes the Israelite American Indians), a critical role to play at the End of Days. The first of these religious groups was the Mormons, whose truths were revealed to Joseph Smith on 21 September 1823 by the angel Moroni, son of Mormon. Written on gold plates in the Reformed Egyptian language, these truths could be deciphered with the aid of an accompanying pair of eyeglasses made from two transparent stones, the Urim and Thummim described in the Old Testament. Only four years later was Smith allowed to take possession of the plates and to begin the process of translation.

The result was the Book of Mormon, a 275,000-word chronicle about the inhabitants of pre-Columbian America. The story begins in 600 B.C. in Palestine, when a group of Israelites is inspired to leave Jerusalem immediately before the Babylonian invasion. They flee by caravan to the Indian Ocean and then by boat to the Promised Land on the west coast of North America. There they split into two contentious groups, the Nephites and the Lamanites, who spend centuries building a civilization and fighting with one another. Following His crucifixion and resurrection, Christ appears to them in America, announcing that He will also visit other remnants of the Lost Ten Tribes of Israel. "I go unto the Father," He told them as He prepared to leave, "and also to show myself unto the lost tribes of Israel, for they are not lost unto the Father, for He knoweth whither He hath taken them." The Nephites and the Lamanites live in harmony after the divine visitation for about two centuries, then begin warring again; finally, in about 421 A.D., the Nephites are totally vanquished and destroyed. The victorious Lamanites, however, gradually sink into barbarism, lose their fair skins, and become the ancestors of the American Indians. Moroni, the last prophet of the exterminated Nephites, buries the history of the American Israelites in the Hill Cumorah, where it remains until revealed to Joseph Smith in 1823. As is fitting for the first genuine indigenous American variety of Christianity, America is given a starring role: it had been the scene of Christ's work on earth as much as in Palestine, and would be once again as the true American church arises against the apostate churches of ungodly Europe.[10]

The Articles of Faith of the Church of Jesus Christ of Latter-day Saints made quite clear the role that the Jews and the Lost Ten Tribes were expected to play. The tenth of thirteen articles affirms: "We believe in the literal gathering of Israel and in the restoration of the Ten Tribes; that Zion will be built upon this [the American] continent; that Christ will reign personally upon the earth; and, that the earth will be renewed and receive its paradisiacal glory."[11] This Zion was revealed to be Jackson County, Missouri, confirmed by revelations received by Joseph Smith.[12]

The Mormon attitude to the Bible was somewhat less straightforward. As Joseph Smith explained it in 1842, "We believe the Bible to be the word of God as far as it is translated correctly."[13] Believing the Bible to have been incorrectly translated, Smith began the work afresh as early as 1830, producing a text that is not a genuine translation, but the Authorized Version amended, with certain passages corrected and others expanded. Since Smith had no knowledge whatsoever of either Hebrew or Greek, he was forced to rely on inspiration. This claim was problematic, to which one might only reply, "Judge not, that ye be not judged," or as Smith elegantly put it, "Judge not unrighteously, that ye be not judged; but judge righteous judgment."[14]

For the Mormons, then, the Jews form an essential part of their theology, and the fate of the Lost Ten Tribes is one of the pillars of their version of history. The Mormons remain steadfastly philosemitic and supportive of Jewish temporal interests, especially the welfare of the modern state of Israel, which most Protestant groups have come to see as part of the divine plan rather than as a human attempt to jump the gun. A vast and beautiful Mormon college sits on Mount Scopus in Jerusalem, built only recently and with full support from one of Israel's previous right-wing nationalist governments. As we shall see, however, the Mormons did not have a monopoly on the Lost Ten Tribes. By the beginning of the twentieth century, the missing Israelites would be enlisted into the ranks of the Christian Identity movement, whose fruits would include both rabid anti-Semitism and the ideological politics behind many of the so-called "militias" in the United States.

III

Perhaps the most eccentric messianic theory that emerged during the nineteenth century was the one usually known as British Israelism. The concept, in brief, is that the British, or perhaps the Anglo-Saxon races in general, are the literal descendants of the Lost Ten Tribes of Israel, and therefore all of God's biblical promises apply to them and not to the modern Jews. It is the Anglo-Saxons who are the Chosen People, as demonstrated not only by evidence in Scripture, but also by anthropological investigations of the historical migrations of the Lost Ten Tribes since their Babylonian captivity in the sixth century B.C. The modern Jews, the offspring of those who rejected Christ, are therefore excluded from God's Grace, while the British, the descendants of those Jews who did not have the opportunity of hearing the message of Jesus, have the best of both Jewish and gentile worlds: they are the heirs of promise and saved by Christ's blood as well.

The true ideological founding father of British Israelism was John Wilson (d. 1871), the son of an Irish weaver. Wilson conceived the idea that the English were the true and literal descendants of the Lost Ten Tribes of Israel, and promulgated this view in lectures in Dublin and elsewhere in Ireland between about 1840 and his death thirty years later. He seems to have met with great success, peppering his lectures with other fashionable subjects, especially phrenology.[15] Wilson's ideas were clearly expressed and his thesis easily explained.

> He agrees with those who apply to these Christian nations many of the prophecies respecting Israel, believing, as he does, that these nations have not merely come into the place of ancient Israel, but are truly the seed of Abraham according to the flesh—are of the so-called "lost house of Israel," the leading tribe of which was Ephraim. These nations have been brought forth at the time and in the place predicted; they are the modern nations of Europe, and especially those of Saxon race.

In the early editions of his lectures, Wilson saw the British as only one of the Israelitish heirs, along with the Germans and the Scandinavians. By the fifth edition of 1876, however, England had moved up to a special and unique position, demonstrated not only by her extraordinary maritime skills, but also by the rise of America as her brother Menasseh.[16]

Wilson proved his thesis that the English were the lineal descendents of the lost tribe of Ephraim in various ways. Like the Spanish theologians who saw in the American Indians traces of the biblical Jews, Wilson gave pride of place to cultural comparison and linguistic analysis. The name "Britain" itself derived from the Hebrew word for covenant, *brit*. Other traces of the Lost Israelites could be found elsewhere in Europe, such as the remnants of the tribe of Dan, whose legacy survived in places like the River Don, the city of London, and of course, the River Danube. The word "cossack" was a corruption of *goi-izak*. Even the title of the song "Yankee Doodle" is not originally American: "The name seems to be a Hebraic nursery epithet of endearment, and it would be interesting to trace the history of the tune, still more remotely."[17] As if part of a dark prophecy, Wilson also demonstrated the veracity of British Israelism with a large dose of racial reasoning, which gave pride of place to "the European branch of the SEMITIC race" in England and America. As we shall see, this racist element of British Israelism would become dominant in the transfiguration of the theory into the Christian Identity movement in the United States.[18]

Not content with merely identifying the whereabouts of some of the Lost Ten Tribes, Wilson also sought to transform his discovery into a practical program for retaking the land of his fathers, promoting a sort of British Israelite Zionism. "The land of Israel is a rich epitome of all lands," he wrote with the confidence of one who had never been to the Middle East, "and of all countries it is the most centrally placed in respect to both land and water. Especially is this the case with regard to the different offshoots of the British Empire; so that in going there, we are, as already noticed, only removing into the midst of our family, to invite its several members to draw more closely around us." He further noted: "What was regarded a few years ago as a wild dream is now merely a rational expectation." All that was required was for the British to conquer Palestine from the Turks. "There is no time to be lost," Wilson warned.[19]

Although Wilson was content to spread his ideas as special (paid) lecturer, he made no attempt at first to establish a religious sect or even a group of fellow believers. It was only in 1871 and 1872 that such a plan evolved, and the Anglo-Ephraim Association was founded at meetings presided over by Bishop Gobat of Jerusalem. Wilson, after all, earned his living by promoting a historical theory, which by itself did little to threaten the mainly middle-class Victorians who came to see the show. Even those who were convinced by his exegesis were not really required to do anything but merely to appreciate the demonstrated fact that they were the descendants of the Lost Ten Tribes and that God had promised to them His love and protection. Joining a club would not bring forward the Second Coming by a single day. Nevertheless, from the early 1870s a number of small associations of like-minded believers did emerge, and British Israelism was launched as a movement.

John Wilson's reluctance to form an organized movement makes Edward Hine (1825–1891) the first proper Anglo-Israelite. He had left school at age twelve and worked his way up in the late 1860s to deputy manager of the "Penny Bank." But the key event in his life occurred in 1839 when at the age of fourteen he heard Wilson lecture in Aldersgate Street and became convinced about the truth of British Israelism.[20] He gave his first lecture on the subject in 1869 and published it at the same time, only two years before Wilson's death, making him in a sense the man to whom the torch was passed.[21] Hine was eventually supplanted by Edward Wheler Bird, born in India in 1823, the son of a well-known provincial judge. Bird passed his exams in England at the age of nineteen, and entered the Indian Civil Service, retiring to Bristol in 1868 from a senior position. In England he quickly became involved in various evangelical activities, including the Society for Promoting Christianity Amongst the Jews, the Bible Society, and others. In 1874, he chanced upon one of John Wilson's books and became an enthusiastic supporter of British Israelism, becoming chairman of the Bristol and Clifton Anglo-Israel Association in April 1875. Edward Hine himself moved to the United States and, as we shall see, had more success in that particular Anglo-Saxon territory.

IV

While British Israelism would degenerate in England to being yet another eccentric fringe movement, its transplantation to the United States in the 1880s not only ensured its survival but also enabled it to merge with other biblical interpretations such as Millerism, dispensationalism, and Christian Aryanism to produce a potent variety of revolutionary messianism and virulent racism. If Britain was Ephraim, then the United States was Menasseh, another Lost Tribe and heir to the promises of Abraham. The same themes that had been discussed by John Wilson on an exegetical or intellectual level took on a greater meaning in the New World. After all, was not the very name of "America" merely a corruption of the Hebrew words *am-erik*, "the country of [Leif] Erik[son]"? Looking at all of this evidence together, who could not but conclude that the British and the Americans were the true Chosen People of God, and that the biblical promises applied to them alone?

But most fascinating was the introduction of pyramidology to the British Israelite scheme. Although this was certainly not a uniquely American phenomenon, it was introduced into the movement at the time of its transplantation to the United States, and thus became a key issue from its inception there. Nearly all pyramid enthusiasts are Anglo-Israelites, so the concepts have remained intertwined. Pyramidology is an old concept, proclaimed by no less than Isaac Newton and many others. The basic idea is that the Great Pyramid is God's original record of biblical revelation, presented in symbols and terms of modern science and preserved in the stones of the pyramid itself. Just as God recorded His revelation in the form of words in the Bible, so too did He give us the same information in stone, which can be deciphered through mathematics and an understanding of the measurements of the Great Pyramid. Since biblical interpretation is never perfectly clear, we are almost compelled to seek further information in the dimensions of the Great Pyramid.[22]

In practice, what this means is understanding that there is such a thing as a "pyramid inch," 1.00106 British inches, an exact twenty-fifth part of the Sacred Cubit (25.0265 British inches), which conveniently is precisely one ten-millionth of the earth's mean polar radius. The builders of the Great Pyramid constructed that massive edifice so that each pyramid inch (especially in the ascending and descending interior chambers) would signify a single year in the history of humankind. In this way, we can trace the entire history of the world from the beginning of the "Adamic race" in about 4000 B.C. to its conclusion in about 2000 A.D., when humankind will become extinct in the millennial Sabbath. The Great Pyramid documents the dates of the Flood (2352 B.C.), the Exodus (1513 B.C.), the life of Christ in great detail, the war between the United States and Mexico (1846), the repeal of the British Corn Laws (also 1846), World War I, and the abdication of Edward VIII (1936). The Great Pyramid can also be used efficiently for the prediction of future events. Adam Rutherford, the great pyramidologist of the 1930s, predicted the creation of the State of Israel "after 1941," and the establishment of Christ's millennial reign on earth at 21 September 1994 on the autumnal equinox.[23] Peter Lemesurier, Rutherford's successor, has since corrected that happy date to 2 July 2989.[24]

Who built the Great Pyramid? It is named for the Pharaoh Cheops, but perhaps the builder was Enoch, who led the Shepherd Kings to Egypt and lived for 365 years, symbolically the same number of days in a single year. Perhaps the builder was Melchizedek, who was really Job. But two things are clear, as Adam Rutherford put it: "… that the Great Pyramid in Egypt is a Divinely designed monument and that it is truth in structural form." In other words, he says, "the teaching of the Bible and that of the Pyramid are identical in every particular, the one in words, the other in stone."[25] No wonder the British Israelites listened so carefully.

V

One of the first Americans to promulgate the British Israelite view was Lt. Charles A. L. Totten (d. 1909), an artillery officer who was in charge of military instruction at Yale between 1889 and 1892 and who wrote a number of texts on this important subject. When the British Israelite leader Edward Hine came to the United States in 1884, he linked up with Charles Totten and stayed with him in New Haven. Hine enjoyed the opportunity to re-create himself in this virgin land and made a new career, lecturing over the next four years up and down the eastern seaboard and into Canada and the upper Midwest about the true destiny of the British people and their American brethren, before returning to England in February 1888. Eventually, groups devoted to this ideology were also formed in the western United States and Canada, centering around Vancouver, Portland (Oregon), and Los Angeles, which has remained its core.[26]

While many of the British Israelites regarded the tribe of Judah, the modern Jews, as having no part in God's inheritance, there was no intrinsic reason why this particular ideological bent should have become essentially anti-Semitic. The transformation of warmly philosemitic British Israelism into dangerously anti-Semitic Christian Identity is in itself almost an accident of history, the result of its adoption by religious and political activists whose thinking was already moving along racist lines. Among those earliest writers responsible for this development was Reuben H. Sawyer (b. 1866), a minister in Portland, Oregon, where he led an active Anglo-Israel Research Society. Sawyer lectured throughout the Northwest and helped establish the British Israel World Federation in London in 1920. At the same time, Sawyer found the leisure to serve as leader of the Ku Klux Klan in Oregon from 1921 to 1924.[27]

Many others apart from Sawyer saw the Jews as virulent opponents who were trying to usurp the role of Chosen People from the rightful representatives, the British and Anglo-American white Christians. This was due in part to the efforts of Gerald L. K. Smith (d. 1976), a former associate of Huey Long, the populist politician from Louisiana who was assassinated there in 1935. By World War II, Smith was the most notorious anti-Semite in America, and in the early 1950s, he moved his operation to Los Angeles, where he pushed Anglo-Israelism into a more overtly anti-Semitic stance by encouraging its association with the growing Christian Identity movement.[28]

In any case, Los Angeles became a center of the British Israel movement in the 1930s and 1940s, with conferences held there annually between 1945 and 1947. Gradually the California-based movement lost its links with the organizations in England, and even with followers on the East Coast of the United States. It fused instead with the very anti-Semitic Christian Identity movement then underway, a process which Gerald L. K. Smith actively encouraged.[29]

In the 1950s, some people with connections to Gerald L. K. Smith and the racist interpretation of British Israelite views appeared on the scene in the Los Angeles area, such as William Potter Gale (1917–1988) and Wesley Swift (1913–1970). Swift, the son of a Methodist minister in New Jersey, had begun his career in the (Pentecostalist) International Church of the Foursquare Gospel of Aimee Semple McPherson. Swift withdrew and set up his own church on the outskirts of the Los Angeles area, first calling it the Anglo-Saxon Christian Congregation, and later changing its name to the Church of Jesus Christ Christian—in this way emphasizing the Identity position that Jesus was not a Jew.[30] William Potter Gale also had a lasting influence. His own background was in the military, having been a colonel on General MacArthur's staff in World War II and later serving in the Philippines. Gale came across Christian Identity writings in the early 1950s and helped found the Christian Defense League (CDL) in the early 1960s. The first president of the CDL was Richard Grint Butler, who, after Wesley Swift's death in 1970, set up a church in Idaho with the identical name—the Church of Jesus Christ Christian—and united it with the movement known as Aryan Nations, one of the most dangerous, openly racist organizations operating in America today.

Gale was also one of the founders of the Posse Comitatus, which was established in about 1969 in Portland, Oregon.[31] The group remained obscure until 1975, when the FBI was informed that they intended to assassinate Nelson Rockefeller. An investigation revealed that the group was active in twenty-three states. One of their leaders, James Wickstrom, had a Christian Identity ministry in Wisconsin, and by 1984, prominent Aryan Nation figures were active in the group.[32] According to the ideology of the Posse Comitatus, the Jews are the children of Satan, and the blacks are "mud people." They also insist that since the United States was founded as a Christian commonwealth, it should be run as a Christian country for Christians alone. Furthermore, they argue, since the largest legitimate governmental unit is the county and the highest American official is the sheriff, no law enforcement authority above the level of the county sheriff's posse has any standing in the United States Constitution.[33]

Various strands of millenarian theorizing were therefore brought together in postwar America, fusing with new versions of anti-Semitism, pre-Adamite racism, British Israelism, neo-Nazi Aryanism, and other ideologies to form the central tenets of the militant revolutionary messianists. Those attracted to such ideologies saw the United States change from a society dominated by white male Christians to one incorporating blacks, Hispanics, Jews, and women in positions of power and authority. On the outside, the Communist menace seemed to be looking for any opportunity to destroy an American society already decimated from within. These groups created a unique amalgam of various theories and ideologies, combining existing ideas with conspiracy theories about the subversive activities of Jews, Freemasons, and Communists. The civil rights movement and its successes made many people feel even more dispossessed, since they believed that they would have to fight for the very survival of the Christian white American world against the government of the United States, which was no longer legitimate, having abandoned its responsibility to those who should not have been given any power at all.

It was this sort of world-view that led to the proliferation of military survivalist groups, the militias, the Posse Comitatus, the Freemen, and others who began to prepare for the Battle of Armageddon, or something like it, on American soil.[34] Many of the militia groups are primarily survivalist in nature and are more interested in opposing gun control than in promulgating a more complicated ideology.[35] Their ideology, or theology, is based in large part on a combination of British Israelism, dispensationalism, and other concepts. They find their authoritative literature in the writings of people like Nesta Webster (1876–1960), the English conspiracy hunter,[36] and Eustace Mullins (b. 1923), the scourge of the Jews and the Federal Reserve Bank;[37] in the apocalyptic, racist novel *The Turner Diaries*;[38]

or in the works of groups, like the Christian Reconstructionists, that advocate promulgating God's law as the law of the land.[39]

In the writings of these militant groups we hear the echo of the more benign theories of the sixteenth and seventeenth centuries. Consider, for example, the statement by Richard Grint Butler, the leader of the Aryan Nations, based in Hayden Lake, Idaho. "We believe that the true, literal children of the Bible are the 12 tribes of Israel," he wrote, "which are now scattered throughout the world and are known as the Anglo-Saxon, Celtic, Scandinavian and Teutonic people of the earth." Furthermore, he tells us, "All races did not descend from Adam. Adam is the father of the White Race only," and "the Jew is the adversary of our race and God." The children of Satan are alive and are causing a variety of dangerous troubles. In the end, there will be an accounting by Yahweh in which those who have followed His Law will be redeemed, and the rest sent to eternal damnation.[40] So too do we find similar sentiments expressed in the statement of belief of the Church of Israel at Schell City, Missouri, which includes the pledge: "We believe that Adam is the father and beginning of the Caucasian race and of no other race. We believe that all of the non-white races were on earth before Adam." The Chosen People are the Israelites who are "today identified among the Anglo-Saxon-Germanic-Scandinavian-Slavonic kindred peoples." The Jews are not Israelites, not Adamites, not of the Tribe of Judah, but the "Jews of today are the Canaanite, Edemite, Amalekites and other related peoples identified in the world today as Zionists, Khazars and other related terms."[41]

This view, a school of thought that could be designated "Christian Aryanism," is more than the product of contemporary extremism; it is a fascinating amalgam of much earlier messianic ideologies and theologies. British Israelism is obviously the key ingredient despite the fact that many of the Christian Aryans are unaware of their connection with that rather esoteric English system of belief and most would be appalled to learn how Rabbi Menasseh ben Israel had contributed to their very existence.

VI

Thomas Fuller, in his massive seventeenth-century illustrated geography of the Holy Land, could not but reflect on the deep significance of the Lost Ten Tribes. "Strange!" he exclaimed,

> that the posterity of the two tribes (*Judah* and *Benjamin*) should be found (almost) *every where*, whilest the offspring of the *ten Tribes* are found *no where*!... Not, that he hath utterly extinguished the *being* (an opinion as unreasonable, as uncharitable) but hath hitherto concealed the *known being* of so numerous a nation, whom we may call the *lost-lost sheep of Israel* both in respect of their spirituall condition, and corporall habitation.[42]

The wanderings of the Lost Ten Tribes in America, as we have seen, began with the enchanted gaze of the very first European explorer to behold the New World. The Israelite sojourn took on messianic significance with the congruence of Jewish and Christian interpretation in the England of Menasseh ben Israel and Oliver Cromwell.

When the Israelites adopted British and then American nationality in the nineteenth century, they unwittingly set the stage for anti-Jewish sentiment and for a racist ideology that would ultimately lead to violence. The transformation of the British Israelites into the Aryan Nations is only one of the bizarre developments in the history of messianic revolution and perhaps the aspect of our story with greatest contemporary relevance. The very notion of an Aryan race grew out of a misunderstanding of the eighteenth-century discovery by another Englishman named Sir William Jones (1746–94) that many European languages share a common origin in Sanskrit. It was a short but crucial step for others to posit the existence of a superior Aryan race of Indo-Europeans who spoke the mother tongue of Europe, an idea with dangerous consequences once it became part of the Nazi theory of race.

Yet it is less recognized that the even older English theory of British Israelism also underwent a deadly revision, whereby its later adherents in the United States began to argue that the biblical promises God made to the Israelites applied literally to their progeny alone, the white Anglo-Saxon Protestants of America, and that on this basis they might take any action to protect their "race." The so-called militia movement in the United States draws its ideology from British Israelism, and without understanding this obscure English theory, we can never comprehend the crimes that were committed at Oklahoma City in 1995. One need not argue that Columbus was the ideological precursor of Timothy McVeigh to concede that the transformation of the Israelites from American Indians to British Imperialists and back again to British Americans makes the parting of the Red Sea look like a pleasant walk on the beach.

Notes

1. Gen. 9: 18–19.
2. *The Journal of Christopher Columbus*, ed. C. Jane and L. A. Vigneras (London, 1960), 51, 206. Cf. A. B. Gould y Quincy, "Nueva Lista Documentada de los Tripulantes de Colon en 1492," *Bol. de la Real Acad. de la Hist.* 75 (1924):34–49.
3. See Richard H. Popkin, *Isaac La Peyrère (1596–1676): His Life, Work and Influence* (Leiden, 1987).
4. See generally, David S. Katz, "The Debate over the Lost Ten Tribes of Israel," in *Philo-Semitism and the Readmission of the Jews to England, 1603–1655* (Oxford, 1982), chap. 4.
5. For more of these connections, see David S. Katz and Richard H. Popkin, *Messianic Revolution: Radical Religious Politics to the End of the Second Millennium* (New York, 1999).

6. "The Relation of Master Antonie Monterinos," *Ievves in America*, ed. T. Thorowgood (London, 1650). Cf. Menasseh ben Israel, *The Hope of Israel*, ed. Henry Méchoulan and Gérard Nahon (Oxford, 1987), 105–11.
7. For the publishing history of *The Hope of Israel*, see the edition of Méchoulan and Nahon, ix–xi.
8. Isa. 11:12; Deut. 28:64; Cecil Roth, "New Light on the Resettlement," *Trans. Jew. Hist. Soc. Eng.* 11 (1928):113–14.
9. See generally David S. Katz, *The Jews in the History of England, 1485–1850* (Oxford, 1994).
10. Most of this narrative comes from the first book of Nephi, in *The Book of Mormon* (Palmyra, 1830), and the introductory material therein, which is part of the canon. See also Whitney R. Cross, *The Burned-Over District* (Ithaca, N.Y., 1950); Fawn M. Brodie, *No Man Knows My History: The Life of Joseph Smith, the Mormon Prophet* (New York, 1946); Leonard J. Arrington and Davis Bitton, *The Mormon Experience: A History of the Latter-day Saints* (London, 1979); and J. L. Brooke, *The Refiner's Fire: The Making of Mormon Cosmology, 1644–1844* (Cambridge, 1994).
11. The articles of faith are signed by Joseph Smith, and are often printed in the *Book of Mormon*.
12. *The Book of Mormon*, III Nephi 20:29–33; 21:23–26.
13. Quoted in Arrington and Bitton, *Mormon Experience*, 30.
14. Joseph Smith's new translation is published by the Reorganized Church of Jesus Christ of Latter-day Saints (Independence, Missouri). See R. J. Matthews, *"A Plainer Translation": Joseph Smith's Translation of the Bible* (Provo, Utah, 1975).
15. John Wilson, *Lectures on Ancient Israel, and the Israelitish Origin of the Modern Nations of Europe* (Cheltenham, 1840); idem, *Lectures on Our Israelitish Origin* (5th ed., London, 1876); the preface from the first edition is dated Liverpool, August 1840. The fifth edition included a biographical sketch of Wilson, "The Re-Discovery of Our Israelitish Origin," 411–42, in which it is claimed that "Mr Wedgwood's 'Book of Remembrance,' also, did not come into his hands till long after the publication of the second edition of 'Our Israelitish Origin.'" Cf. John Wilson, *Sixty Anglo-Israel Difficulties Answered. Chiefly from the correspondence of the Late John Wilson, compiled by his daughter* (London, [1878?]); idem, *The Book of Inheritance; and Witness of the Prophets, respecting Ephraim, and the Raising up of Israel* (London, 1846). Wilson also attempted to start a couple of monthly magazines—*The Time of the End and Prophetic Witness* (1844) and *The Watchmen of Ephraim* (1866–68)—but these failed within a relatively short time.
16. Other contemporaries who emphasized Britain as the sole heir include R. Govett, *English Derived from Hebrew: With glances at Greek and Latin* (London, 1869); F. R. A. Glover, *England, the Remnant of Judah and the Israel of Ephraim* (London, 1861); the author describes himself as sometime chaplain to the British consulate at Cologne, and he would later be active in the British-Israel movement as well.
17. Wilson, *Lectures*, 192–93, 197, 229–31, 293, 302–99.
18. Ibid., chap. 2: "Relation of Abraham's Posterity to the Three Grand Races of Mankind." For more on Christian Identity, see below.
19. Ibid., 391, 397–98. Cf. John Wilson's *The Millennium, or, World to Come; and its relations to preceding dispensations* (Cheltenham, 1842), with a chart of the Dispensations (76); idem, *The Mission of Elijah to Restore All, previous to our Lord's Second Advent* (London, [1861]); idem, *England's Duty in Relation to the Christians of Turkey* (London, [1876?]); idem, *A Vindication of Christ's character as the Prophet* (London, 1878).
20. See Edward Hine, *Memoirs, and a Selection of Letters* (London, 1909).
21. Edward Hine, *The English Nation Identified with the Lost Ten Tribes of Israel, a Lecture* (Warrington, 1872). Cf. idem, *Seventeen Positive Identifications of the English Nation with the Lost House of Israel* (London, 1870); idem, *Twenty-Seven Identifications of the English Nation with the Lost House of Israel* (7th ed., London, 1870); idem, *Forty-Seven Identifications of the British Nation with the Lost Ten Tribes of Israel* (London, 1874).
22. Generally, see P. Lemesurier, *The Great Pyramid Decoded* (London, 1977).

23. See the voluminous writings of Adam Rutherford of the Institute of Pyramidology at Stanmore, London, in the 1930s, especially his monumental *Anglo-Saxon Israel or Israel-Britain* (4th ed., Stanmore, 1939; 1st ed., 1934), subtitled "A Call to all the Anglo-Saxon, Celtic, Dutch and Scandinavian nations with A Special Call to Iceland." Iceland, indeed, was one of his favorite subjects, about which he published many books on everything from that country as the key to biblical prophecy to its transportation system. The predictions cited above are on pages 556, 569, 579–89, 613, 615, 620, 630, 655, 656, 676.

24. See generally the ultimate pyramid book, P. Lemesurier, *The Great Pyramid Decoded* (London, 1977), esp. 181.

25. Rutherford, *Anglo-Saxon Israel*, 329.

26. Generally, see Michael Barkun, *Religion and the Racist Right* (Chapel Hill, N.C., 1994), 20–21.

27. Barkun, *Racist Right*, 22–23.

28. Generally, see G. Jeansonne, *Gerald L. K. Smith: Minister of Hate* (New Haven, 1988).

29. Barkun, *Racist Right*, 54–67, and generally chap. 4, "Creating Christian Identity, 1937–1975."

30. Cf. Wesley A. Swift, "Was Jesus Christ a Jew?"; Aryan Nations Internet site.

31. For more on Pelley, see E. V. Toy, "Silver Shirts in the Northwest: Politics, Prophecies, and Personalities in the 1930s," *Pacific Northwest Quarterly* 80 (1989):139–46; and Barkun, *Racist Right*, 91–96.

32. Barkun, *Racist Right*, 217ff. Many of these Posse Comitatus groups have web sites, such as "The Watchman: The Voice of the Christian Posse Comitatus" in Pennsylvania. Mark Thomas, its editor, proclaims that "I am a Two-Seedline Identity minister and was ordained by Pastor Butler at Aryan Nations in 1990."

33. A full statement of their political, economic, and legal views, taken from a pamphlet issued in Oregon in the 1980s, appears in *Extremism in America: A Reader*, ed. L. T. Sargent (New York, 1995), 343–50. Cf. T. Heath, "A Law of Their Own," *Newsweek* (25 September 1995):27. See also the web site of "The Fully Informed Jury Association" (FIJA), which proclaims as its object "to re-establish the trial jury not only as the decider of justice in the case before it, but as a commentator on the law itself, so that lawmakers enjoy ongoing access to the will of the people, expressed through the verdicts of citizen juries." The concept of "leaderless resistance" is one developed recently by Louis R. Beam, a former Texas Ku Klux Klan member who also lives in Idaho; K. Schneider, "Bomb Echoes Extremists' Tactics," *New York Times* (26 April 1995), A22; T. Reiss, "Home on the Range," *New York Times* (26 May 1995); G. Niebuhr, "Sandpoint Journal: Spreading a Message of Love Where Hate Has Found a Home," *New York Times*, 29 October 1995, 1.24; and generally on Beam, M. Dees, *Gathering Storm: America's Militia Threat* (New York, 1996).

34. Generally, see the Anti-Defamation League [B'nai Brith] Fact Finding Report, *Armed and Dangerous: Militias Take Aim at the Federal Government* (New York, 1994); J. Coates, *Armed and Dangerous: The Rise of the Survivalist Right* (New York, 1987); and Dees, *Gathering Storm*. See also J. Smolowe, "Enemies of the State," *Time* (8 May 1995):58–69; J. Thomas, "Kansas City Journal; Militias Hold a Congress, and Not a Gun is Seen," *New York Times*, 1 November 1996, A20; A. W. Bock, "Weekend Warriors," *National Review* 47 (29 May 1995):39–42; C. J. Farley, "Patriot Games," *Time* (19 December 1994):48–49; G. Wills, "The New Revolutionaries," *NY Rev. Books* 42 (10 August 1995):50–52; P. Doskoch, "The Mind of the Militias," *Psychology Today* 28 (July/August 1995):12–14; M. Barkun, "Militias, Christian Identity and the Radical Right," *Christian Century* 112 (2–9 August 1995):738–40; idem, "Millenarian Aspects of 'White Supremacist' Movements," *Terrorism and Political Violence* 1 (1989):409–34; J. Kaplan, "A Guide to the Radical Right," *Christian Century* 112 (2–9 August 1995):741–44; M. Janofsky, "Groups Gain New Members Since Attack," *New York Times*, 18 June 1995, 1.19; P. Applebome, "Radical Right's Fury Boiling Over," *New York Times*, 23 April 1995, 1.33.

35. See, for example, the Militia of Montana (MOM)—"we are everywhere"—especially their Internet site. Generally, see M. Cooper, "Montana's Mother of all Militias," *Nation* 260 (22 May 1995):714ff.; M. Kelly, "The Road to Paranoia," *New Yorker* 71 (19 June 1995):60–64;

D. Voll, "At Home with M.O.M.," *Esquire* 124 (July 1995):46–49; cf. an account of the visit of their leader John Trochmann to Yale University in October 1995: Y. Cheong, "Militia Chief Assails Federal Stewardship," *Yale Daily News*, 27 October 1995. Trochmann was a featured speaker at the Aryan Nations congress in 1990, and has been to the compound at Hayden Lake four or five times by his own admission: D. Junas, "The Rise of the Militias," *Covert Action Quarterly* [n.d.: Internet repr.]. For information on the Michigan Militia Corps, see T. S. Purdum, "Clinton Assails the Preachings of the 'Militias,'" *New York Times*, 6 May 1995, 1.1; M. Janofsky, "'Militia' Man Tells of Plot to Attack Military Base," *New York Times*, 25 June 1995, 1.14. For "E Pluribus Unum," another patriot group, see M. Janofsky, "Demons and Conspiracies Haunt a 'Patriot' World," *New York Times*, 31 May 1995, A18. Generally, see M. Navarro, "At Fair for Survivalists, Fallout from Oklahoma," *New York Times*, 12 June 1995, A10.

36. Nesta H[elen]. Webster, *Secret Societies and Subversive Movements* (London, 1924), repr. in at least seven editions. Cf. her book, *World Revolution: The Plot Against Civilization* (London, 1921), also in editions at least until 1971; and especially her *Surrender of an Empire* (3rd edn, London, 1931), chap. 19: "The Surrender to Zionism." See also T. P. Weber, "Finding Someone to Blame: Fundamentalism and Anti-Semitic Conspiracy Theories in the 1930s," *Fides et Historia* 24 (1992):40–55.

37. Eustace Clarence Mullins, *A Study of the Federal Reserve* (New York, 1952), with further editions at least in 1954, 1971, and 1983; idem, *The New History of the Jews* (Staunton, Va., 1968), published by the International Institute of Jewish Studies. Other works by him in this vein include: *Murder by Injection: The Story of the Medical Conspiracy Against America* (Staunton, Va., 1988); *The Rape of Justice: America's Tribunals Exposed* (Staunton, Va., 1989), and *A Writ for Martyrs* (Staunton, Va., 1985).

38. *The Turner Diaries* was written by William L. Pierce, a former physics professor from Oregon State University, and an aide to George Lincoln Rockwell of the American Nazi Party. Pierce founded a group called the National Alliance in Hillsboro, West Virginia, and published this work in serial form in its magazine *Attack!* between 1975 and 1978, and as a paperback book in 1978. It was republished by Barricade Books in New York in 1996, ironically by a Jewish publisher named Lyle Stuart who in an introduction to the paperback edition explains why he thought it important to make the book available to the general public.

39. On Christian Reconstructionism generally, see Bruce Barron, *Heaven on Earth: The Social and Political Agendas of Dominion Theology* (Grand Rapids, Mich., 1992); D. A. Rausch and D. E. Chismar, "The New Puritans and Their Theonomic Paradise," *Christian Century* 100 (3–10 August 1983):712–15; A. Shupe, "The Reconstructionist Movement on the New Christian Right," *Christian Century* 106 (4 October 1989):880–2; R. J. Neuhaus, "Why Wait for the Kingdom? The Theonomist Temptation," *First Things* 3 (1990):13–21; D. A. Oss, "The Influence of Hermeneutical Frameworks in the Theonomy Debate," *Westminster Theological Journal* 51 (1989):227–58.

40. The full text is given in *Extremism in America: A Reader*, ed. L. T. Sargent (New York, 1995).

41. Ibid., 334

42. Thomas Fuller, *A Pisgah-Sight of Palestine* (London, 1650), 193.

PART II

IDENTITY AT STAKE: CONCEALING, PRESERVING, AND RESHAPING JUDAISM AMONG THE *CONVERSOS* AND MARRANOS OF SPANISH AMERICA

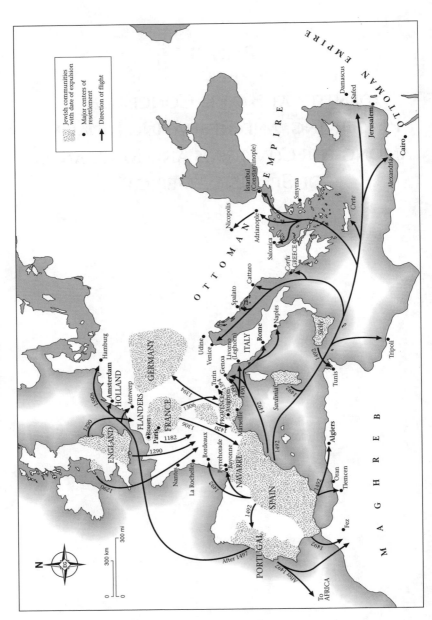

MAP 7 Expulsion of the Jews in Europe. Adapted from a map in Martin Gilbert, *The Atlas of Jewish History* (1992).

– Chapter 6 –

NEW CHRISTIAN, MARRANO, JEW

Robert Rowland

I

A DEQUATE DISCUSSION of the role played by Jews in the making of the New World depends on prior clarification of a difficult question—that of defining precise and unambiguous criteria for establishing whether and in what sense a given individual is to be regarded as a Jew. This question does not arise in relation to Jews from Central and Eastern Europe; it can be answered in relatively straightforward terms in the case of Jews of Iberian origin who, before leaving Europe or after arrival in America, were members of formally recognized or tacitly tolerated Jewish communities. But in the case of Spanish or Portuguese "New Christians,"[1] before the end of the eighteenth century, the question is a decisive one. In Spain and Portugal, and in their respective empires, there had officially been no Jews since the end of the fifteenth century, after which only those Jews who had—voluntarily or otherwise—been converted to Catholicism (and their Catholic descendants) were allowed to remain. Since all were nominally Catholics, they were under the jurisdiction of the Inquisition and liable to prosecution if accused of any act or utterance that could be interpreted as evidence that their Catholicism was insincere.

Thus, the only observant Jews who remained in the Iberian world were, of necessity, clandestine Jews, vitally concerned with dissimulating their religious sentiments and practices. In consequence, little evidence has survived concerning them that was not produced by the Inquisition in its attempt to root out and suppress the remnants of Iberian Judaism. Genealogical inquiries conducted in relation to candidates for admission to military orders or appointment to certain posts shared the same frame of reference. Independent evidence on the survival of Judaism in the Iberian Peninsula is for the most part simply not available.

In both Spain and Portugal, it is clear that not all the descendants of those converted during the fifteenth century remained faithful to Judaism, and the fact that an individual was entirely or partly of Jewish descent does not by itself mean that he considered himself, or was considered by others, to be a Jew.[2] The descendants of converted Jews were, it is true, subject to various forms of discrimination on account of their "impurity of blood," and were regarded as inherently suspect in matters of faith; but this does not justify the presumption on the part of historians that such prejudices and suspicions had any kind of basis in fact.

Many New Christians whose families had long before lost contact with the Judaic tradition found themselves falsely accused by enemies or rivals of secretly practicing Judaic rites and ceremonies. As numerous contemporaries pointed out, the procedures of the Inquisition were such that a person falsely accused of reverting to Judaism could only with great difficulty demonstrate his or her innocence, and so great were the risks of attempting to do so that many preferred to offer the Inquisitors a false confession, including an imaginary list of accomplices. In that way, they could hope to escape with only the loss of their goods and other relatively minor penalties, instead of risking condemnation to death as a *negativo*. In such circumstances, neither the accused's confession to Judaic beliefs or practices nor the information provided about other individuals can be regarded as reliable evidence.

The persistence of Judaism among Iberian New Christians, as recounted in Inquisitorial records, cannot thus be taken at face value. There can be no doubt that many succeeded in maintaining a form of clandestine religious practice, but we can be equally sure that not all New Christians did in fact remain secretly faithful to Judaism, and that the generalized suspicion directed against them on grounds of their Jewish descent was often quite unfounded. We can also be sure that not every confession to having practiced Judaism in secret and not every accusation made during interrogation had a factual basis. As we shall see later, in some cases there can be little doubt that Judaic religious observance and practices did survive in Spain and Portugal well into the eighteenth century, but we do not possess unambiguous criteria for deciding which accusations and confessions were true, and which were, on the contrary, a by-product of Inquisitorial procedure or generalized anti-Judaic prejudice.[3] The nature of our sources is such that unless considerable care is exercised they will only confirm our presuppositions and appear to demonstrate, as the case may be, either that most of the New Christians denounced to the Inquisition were crypto-Jews attempting to remain faithful to ancestral traditions, or that they were the innocent victims of anti-Judaic prejudice, false accusations, and the perversity of Inquisitorial procedure.

In some ways the situation is analogous to that faced by the historian who reads some of the strangely repetitive confessions of those accused of witchcraft in sixteenth- and seventeenth-century Europe. Some authors have accepted the reality of the accusations and confessions, and for them, as for early modern demonologists, the standardized nature of the confessions is merely evidence of the strength and influence of the "innumerable army of Satan." Most historians, however, have been convinced of the unreality of witchcraft and the impossibility of many of the actions described in the confessions. Their skepticism, or downright disbelief, leads them to seek an external explanation for the stereotyped character of the confessions in the very nature of the repression directed against suspected witches. According to this interpretation, those accused of witchcraft were responding under torture to the same leading questions posed by judges who had all read the same treatises on witchcraft. The standardized representation of witchcraft—and the role in that representation of the witches' Sabbath—could thus be attributed to the ways in which the repression of witchcraft was organized by lay and ecclesiastical courts. In both cases, the interpretation of the evidence and the overall conception of what has to be explained are determined by preconceptions regarding the reality of witchcraft.[4]

Likewise, in the case of the New Christians the same judicial records can be read in entirely different ways depending on the preconceptions of the historian. For some, the schematic list of stereotyped "Jewish practices" to be found in the majority of confessions is evidence of an attempt to maintain ancestral traditions under adverse conditions, with few possibilities of exchanging information with other clandestine Jews, let alone of contacting Jewish communities abroad. For others, those very same characteristics are evidence of a process of labeling—in which stereotyped attributes projected onto a minority from without are apparently confirmed in "confessions" extracted by interrogation and torture—and thus cannot be accepted uncritically as evidence of the persistence of Judaism in early modern Spain and Portugal.

As in the case of the beliefs and practices attributed to witches in early modern Europe, it is not possible to verify the factual basis underlying the accusations of "Judaism" directed against New Christians. Clarification of the issue (which must in any case be indirect) can only be provided by closer attention to context: to the changing situation of New Christians in Iberian society, to the role played by the Inquisition at a given time and place, and to the circumstances surrounding individual acts of accusation.

II

The first aspect to be considered in this respect, even though it might almost appear too obvious to be worth mentioning, is that of the legal status of Jews in relation to the Inquisition. The expulsion and forced conversion of Spanish and Portuguese Jews and the persecution of "Judaism" by the Iberian Inquisitions have tended to overshadow the fact that Jews were not, in principle, under Inquisitorial jurisdiction at all. According to the Bull *Antiqua Iudaeorum improbitas* of Pope Gregory XIII, Jews, Muslims, and other non-Christians were not ordinarily subject to the Inquisition. In themselves, the religious beliefs or practices of non-Christians who had been allowed to reside in a given territory were of no concern to the Inquisition as long as they remained circumscribed to the domestic sphere or to their areas of segregated residence.[5] In certain cases, however, particularly when the nature of their relations with the Christian population was thought to endanger the latter's faith, the Inquisition was entitled to intervene. This could occur if, for example, Jews attempted (or were accused of attempting) to induce converts to return to the old faith, and in fact it was ostensibly because of the influence they were thought to be exerting over the large number of Jews who had converted to Catholicism during the fifteenth century that the remaining Spanish Jews were expelled in 1492.

The situation of converted Jews and their descendants was quite different. All those who had been baptized as Catholics were under the jurisdiction of the Inquisition. Many New Christians in fifteenth-century Spain (and to a much lesser extent in Portugal as well) were accused of having feigned an opportunistic conversion while continuing to practice Judaism in secret in order to gain access to posts from which Jews were barred. The same accusations were formulated against the descendants of such converts, who although baptized as Catholics were suspected of having been brought up secretly as Jews and were accused of maintaining allegiance to the "law of Moses" and performing Judaic rites and ceremonies. Formally, such behavior on the part of a baptized Catholic would constitute apostasy from the faith, and could be punished as heresy by the Inquisition. The need to root out such heresy among New Christians was invoked to justify the introduction of the Inquisition in Castile at the end of the fifteenth century, and the creation of the Portuguese Inquisition in 1536 was based on similar considerations (Fig 6.1).

What this implies is that all relations between the Inquisition and Jews—whether those living openly as such (where this was permitted, as in many parts of Italy), or those maintaining, as in the Iberian Peninsula, a clandestine Jewish identity and religious practice—reflected and arose out of the relations that existed between Jews and Catholics: in the first case, between the Jewish and Christian (or New Christian) communities; in the second, between each individual's public identity as a Catholic New Christian and his or her secret (or familial) identity as a clandestine Jew. The evidence provided by Inquisitorial sources, consequently, refers in the former case to the relations between Jews and Christians, in the latter, to the relationship between individuals' Jewish and Catholic identities. Such sources do not provide evidence about the identities and beliefs of Jews as such.

Furthermore, that New Christians' relations with the Inquisition derived essentially from their (actual or suspected) dual identity as Catholics and Jews is a fact reflected not only in the nature of Inquisitorial

FIGURE 6.1   The inquiry. J. Baker, *A Complete History of the Inquisition in Portugal, Spain, Italy, the East and West Indies* (London, 1736).

sources. The presence and activity of the Inquisition reinforced that duality. Sincere converts to Catholicism and their descendants knew that at any time they could be suspected and accused of clandestinely maintaining a Jewish identity and allegiance, while those New Christians who did in fact succeed in maintaining some kind of Jewish identity were forced to engage in constant dissimulation. Thus, in one way or another, all Iberian New Christians were Judeo-Catholics.

III

But the Inquisitions of early modern Spain, Portugal, and Italy were not, of course, only concerned with the religious beliefs and practices of converted Jews and their descendants. They were concerned—in relation to the Catholic population under their jurisdiction—with all kinds of beliefs and practices that could in one way or another be construed as heretical. A second aspect that has to be considered in discussing the relation between New Christians of Jewish origin and the Inquisition is the specific importance of accusations of Judaism among the latter's repressive activities.

The Inquisition has traditionally been analyzed in terms of its role in attempting to prevent and repress religious dissent. Such a characterization, which reproduced the Inquisition's own definition of its role in society, located the study of the Inquisition firmly within the history of ideas and concentrated attention on its victims, on a relatively small number of celebrated trials, and on the struggle for freedom of expression and of religious belief.

Over the past twenty years a different approach has emerged based on statistical analyses of the activity of individual tribunals. In 1978 Gustav Henningsen and Jaime Contreras pointed out, in a seminal paper presented at a conference on the Spanish Inquisition held in Copenhagen,[6] that less than half of those tried by the tribunals of the Spanish Inquisition between 1560 and 1700 had been accused of formal heresy (including Judaism and Mohammedanism). The majority of trials were for minor offenses such as bigamy, blasphemy, and various forms of superstition. Furthermore, there were considerable differences between one tribunal and another. These results cast some doubt on the assumptions underlying the more traditional approaches and encouraged other scholars to undertake similar analyses of the Roman and Portuguese Inquisitions.

The results show very clearly that the activity of the Inquisition cannot be reduced to a single model.[7] In Northern Italy, for example, repression was at first directed primarily against the influence of the Reformation: those accused of Protestantism represented 68 percent of those tried in Venice between 1547 and 1585, and 53 percent of those tried in Friuli between 1557 and 1597. In Naples, on the other hand, the principal offenses between 1564 and 1590 were witchcraft and illicit magic (24 percent), whereas those accused of "Lutheranism" were no more than 3 percent. By the seventeenth century the magical arts had become a central preoccupation of the Inquisition in Northern Italy as well.

In Spain, the pattern was quite different, with significant variations between individual tribunals. Even though our information regarding the first wave of terror is far from complete, it is clear that the Inquisition's victims were, between 1480 and 1530, nearly all New Christians accused of having remained secretly faithful to Judaism. According to one estimate, there were 3,196 trials and 283 executions in Toledo during this period, with 87 percent originating in accusations of Judaism.

In the following period, when our information is more complete, a different picture emerges. Between 1540 and 1700, in nineteen tribunals of the Spanish Inquisition, 24 percent of the trials were for Mohammedanism, 10 percent for Judaism, and 8 percent for Protestantism. The remaining trials, as has been mentioned, were for minor offenses. Mohammedanism accounted for 29 percent of trials in Aragon and 18 percent in Castile.

Conversely, accusations of Judaism were responsible for 18 percent of the trials in Castile, but only 4 percent of those in Aragon.[8]

As in Italy, the pattern of repression changed over time. During the initial decades, Judaism was the central preoccupation almost everywhere. The second half of the sixteenth century saw continued repression against the *moriscos* (descendants of converted Muslims) of Aragon and Granada, but the other tribunals began to concern themselves with the relatively minor offenses of the Catholic ("Old Christian") population and with what has been termed the "administration of the Faith."[9] Cases of suspected Lutheran heresy remained relatively rare. During the seventeenth century and until the decline of the Inquisition in the eighteenth century, accusations of Judaism became once again frequent. This time the victims were mostly New Christians of Portuguese origin who had come to Spain or to the Spanish Empire for economic reasons or to escape the greater severity of the Inquisition in Portugal.

The Portuguese Inquisition was, in fact, something of an exception in the context of the three early modern Inquisitions. After its comparatively belated creation in 1536, there was no initial wave of terror, as in Spain, and the intensity of repression remained relatively stable from the middle of the sixteenth to the end of the seventeenth centuries, declining gradually as the eighteenth century wore on. Even during the years between 1675 and 1767, before the reforms introduced by the Marquis of Pombal, the three Portuguese tribunals completed an average of fifty-nine trials a year. From 1536 to the time of those reforms, which among other things abolished the legal distinction between Old Christians and New Christians, the Portuguese Inquisition was overwhelmingly preoccupied with the eradication of Judaic beliefs and practices among members of the New Christian population. In the Lisbon tribunal, whose jurisdiction extended to Brazil and West Africa, accusations of Judaism constituted 68 percent of all trials between 1540 and 1629. In the Coimbra tribunal they represented 83 percent of all trials between 1566 and 1762. In Évora, between 1553 and 1668, the proportion was 84 percent.

The contrast with Italian and Aragonese tribunals, and even with those of neighboring Castile, is evident. Given the unified doctrinal and institutional framework that regulated the activity of *all* the early modern Inquisitions, it is clear that such differences need to be explained contextually, in terms of both time and place, and that the extreme specialization of the Portuguese tribunals in the offense of Judaism can only be understood in the light of the specific situation of the New Christians in Portuguese society between the end of the fifteenth and the middle of the eighteenth century.

IV

At the root of that specificity lay the contrasting experiences of Spanish and Portuguese Jews in the preceding century. In Spain, the massacres of

1391 and the climate of continuing hostility toward Jews that ensued had provoked a wave of conversions to Christianity. Many *conversos* subsequently came to occupy positions that had been barred to them before conversion, and they were, as has been mentioned, repeatedly accused of having feigned conversion precisely in order to gain access to such positions. Such accusations aggravated tensions that had their origins in the role played by many *conversos* in the urban economy and on many occasions degenerated into episodes of violence. At a different level, as in the case of the anti-*converso* statutes of Toledo in 1449, there were attempts at instituting new forms of exclusion against the descendants of converted Jews. The situation in many regions of Castile at the accession of Ferdinand and Isabella in 1475, just before the establishment of the Inquisition, has been aptly described as one of latent, or even open, civil war.[10]

In Portugal the situation was quite different. Portugal, like Spain, had a proportionately significant Jewish population. Toward the end of the fifteenth century they may have numbered thirty or forty thousand, between 3 percent and 4 percent of the population. Most of them were artisans and tradesmen, and they thus represented a higher proportion of the population in urban settlements—in many places, probably well over 10 percent.[11] They were under the king's protection, and in 1392, just at the time that many Spanish Jews were being murdered or forced into conversion, the Portuguese legislation designed to protect Jews was confirmed.[12] Only during the second half of the fifteenth century, with the arrival of increasing numbers of both Jewish and *converso* refugees from Spain, were there signs of growing intolerance, but as a rule, the immigrants were readily integrated into the Jewish or Catholic population. Unlike Spain, fifteenth-century Portugal did not have a "*converso* problem."

As tension in Spain became more acute, and particularly after the introduction of the Inquisition, the influx of Spanish Jews and *conversos* into Portugal increased dramatically, provoking reactions in Oporto and Lisbon. In 1488, the king forbade the entry into Portugal of any more Castilian *conversos* and simultaneously encouraged the emigration, mainly to Northern Europe, of those who had sought refuge in Portugal.[13] Nevertheless, after their expulsion from Spain, King John II agreed to allow Spanish Jews to settle in Portugal. The sources and historians disagree as to the exact number of those who sought refuge in Portugal, but their arrival probably doubled the overtly Jewish population.[14]

There is no need to repeat here the well-known story, told in different but equally dramatic ways by Damião de Góis and Samuel Usque,[15] of how the marriage of the new Portuguese king, Manuel, to Ferdinand and Isabella's daughter was made on condition that the Jews be expelled from Portugal as well, or of how the king, having decreed the expulsion in 1497 of all Portuguese and Spanish Jews who did not accept conversion to Christianity, did all he could to prevent their departure and subjected them to forced baptism.

Whatever the motives–and it is likely that they were at least in part economic—there can be no doubt regarding the policy adopted by the Portuguese crown in relation to the newly "converted" Jews: they were encouraged to become fully integrated into Portuguese society. Even before the date fixed for expulsion, and in an attempt to dispel fears that they might, like the Spanish *conversos*, become subject to the Inquisition, the king determined that those who accepted conversion would not be subject, for twenty years, to any kind of inquiry regarding their religious beliefs and practices. Furthermore, all forms of socioeconomic discrimination against New Christians (except, at first, for the prohibition against leaving the realm) were abolished. It was assumed—or hoped— that if they were not treated differently, they would, within time, become good Catholics. The same assumption seems to have underlain the extraordinary (but now lost) law of 1498 prohibiting marriages between New Christians: it appears to have been assumed that in a mixed marriage there would be a greater chance of the children being brought up as Catholics.[16]

The year 1507 saw the lifting of the prohibition against leaving Portugal and a renewal of the undertaking that New Christians would not be subject to investigation in matters of faith. Five years later, the undertaking was renewed for a further sixteen years. Some Jewish authors referred to King Manuel as "the pious King"; according to others, he was referred to in some New Christian families as *"El-rei judeu"* ("the Jewish King").[17]

In general terms, the policy appears to have been relatively successful, and, with the obvious exception of the Lisbon massacre of 1506, which was severely punished by the king,[18] there was little evidence in early sixteenth-century Portugal of the kind of open tensions and violence that had scarred Spanish society during the fifteenth century and prepared the way for the introduction of the Inquisition.

There can be no doubt, however, that only partial integration was achieved. Latent tensions, due in part to economic rivalry, persisted between sectors of the Old Christian population and the converted Jews. Indicative of this is the way Jews and New Christians are depicted in the plays of Gil Vicente. In those with a religious theme, we find the usual— and insulting—medieval stereotypes, but in his profane plays the Jews are authentic popular characters, very much a part of community life. Even when depicted in caricature, Gil Vicente's Jews are real people.[19]

The persistent tensions and the example offered by neighboring Spain lent support in some quarters to the idea of introducing the Inquisition, but opinions were divided and policy was contradictory. As early as 1515, on the grounds that large numbers of *conversos* were entering Portugal clandestinely from Spain, King Manuel had approached the Pope with a view to establishing an Inquisition in Portugal. The proposal met with considerable opposition in court and was abandoned.

After Manuel's death, King John III twice renewed the guarantees given to the New Christians by his predecessor—first in 1522, then again in

1524. At the same time, yielding to increasing pressure and using as a pre-text the agitation provoked among New Christians by the messianic preaching of David Reubeni,[20] he began to negotiate with Rome. In 1531 he succeeded in obtaining from the Pope a Bull appointing an Inquisitor in Portugal and removing questions of faith from episcopal jurisdiction, but the Bull was revoked a year later without ever having been published in Portugal. It was only after another five years of negotiations that, in spite of the diplomatic and financial efforts of the New Christians' representa-tives in Rome, he succeeded in obtaining from Pope Paul III a Bull estab-lishing an Inquisition in Portugal, with three Inquisitors appointed by the Pope and one by the king. The Bull was published in Évora in 1536, the first auto-da-fé was held in Lisbon in 1540, and by 1541 tribunals had been established in Lisbon, Évora, Coimbra, Oporto, Tomar, and Lamego.[21]

The apparent similarity between developments in Portugal and in Spain—and in particular the introduction in Portugal of an Inquisition according to the Spanish model, concerned primarily with the "Judaism" of New Christians—should not be allowed to obscure the differences between the two situations. As we have noted, Portugal, unlike Spain, did not have a *"converso* problem" during the fifteenth century. Whereas in Spain mechanisms of exclusion had been instituted in some places as early as the mid-fifteenth century, the Portuguese crown chose to encourage and even to impose integration of the New Christians into Catholic Portuguese society. The Inquisition in Spain was established at a time when Judaism was still officially admitted. In Portugal, it was introduced forty years after the forced conversion of the Jews; during that time New Christians were officially allowed to maintain Judaic religious practices in the secrecy of their homes. An entire generation was brought up in a context of religious and cultural dualism: in public they were required to behave as Catholics; in private they were allowed to maintain a separate Jewish identity.

By 1530, the differences had become even more marked. In Spain, those *conversos* who remained had for the most part become sincere practicing Catholics; the remainder had either left the country or had fallen victim to the Inquisition.[22] In Portugal, the Inquisition had not yet been introduced, and an unknown, but clearly very significant, propor-tion of the New Christians maintained a separate Jewish cultural and religious identity.

We have no direct evidence regarding the exact proportion of New Christians in the Portuguese population between the sixteenth and eigh-teenth centuries, nor do we have any direct indication regarding the pro-portion of New Christians who maintained allegiance to Judaism. We do have some indirect evidence regarding the extent of intermarriage between New Christians and Old Christians during the sixteenth and early seventeenth centuries, and this evidence, combined with what we know about the number of New Christians at the end of the fifteenth century, can provide a relatively secure basis for estimates of the propor-tion of New Christians in the population at later periods.

In 1630, a group of fifty-three New Christians presented themselves before the Lisbon Inquisitors and confessed to remaining faithful to Judaism.[23] On this occasion, perhaps because these confessions were to constitute the starting point for an investigation, the Inquisitors were careful to note the precise genealogical status of each individual. Seven (13.2 percent) were described as being full New Christians; eight (15 percent) were recorded as one-eighth New Christian; and the remaining thirty-eight (71.7 percent) were variously described as three-fourths, one-half, three-eighths, one-fourth, or simply "part" New Christian.

A few years later, a total of ninety-six New Christians, convicted of Judaism, were sentenced at the auto-da-fé celebrated in Lisbon on 3 August 1636. Of these, no more than twenty (20.8 percent) were full New Christians; one was described as one-eighth New Christian; and the remaining seventy-five (78.1 percent) were either one-half, one-fourth, or "part" New Christian.[24]

If we accept that these two groups were a representative sample of the entire New Christian population at that time, these figures imply that, on average, for the first four generations after the forced conversion at least 20 percent of all marriages involving New Christians (defined as all descendants of the converted Jews, including those issuing from mixed marriages) were with Old Christians.[25] After four generations, in fact, that degree of exogamy in each generation would imply that those of pure Jewish descent represented 19.8 percent of the—now much larger— New Christian population; 11.2 percent would be, to use the Inquisitors' categories, one-eighth or one-sixteenth New Christian; and the remaining 69.1 percent would be between one-half and one-fourth New Christian. These figures are sufficiently close to those observed in the 1630s for us to be able to accept the figure of at least 20 percent as a realistic estimate of the degree of exogamy practiced by the New Christians during the sixteenth and early seventeenth centuries.[26]

Without mixed marriages, the proportion of New Christians in the population would, other things being equal,[27] remain constant. With intermarriage, however, the proportion of those of *pure* Jewish descent would decline from generation to generation, at the same time as the proportion of those who were *partly* of Jewish descent increased. Since anybody who was even in part descended from the converted Jews was formally classified as a New Christian, intermarriage implied an increase, in each generation, of the proportion of the population who were formally considered to be of "impure blood" and inherently suspect in their adherence to Catholicism.

At the end of the fifteenth century, as we have seen, the New Christians represented about 8 percent of the Portuguese population. In urban settlements, where they were concentrated, the proportion was certainly higher. If on average and in each generation 20 percent of all marriages involving New Christians were with Old Christians, then after four generations, or about 120 years, the proportion of the entire population classifiable as "New Christian" would have doubled. By 1620, they would have constituted 16.6 percent of the population, although, as we have seen, no more than one-fifth of them would by then have been of pure Jewish descent.

By 1740, if the same proportion of mixed marriages had been maintained over the following four generations, those of pure Jewish descent would have represented no more than 3.9 percent of the New Christians; but the latter—still defined as all those descended in some degree, however remote, from the original Jewish converts—would by then have represented no less than 34.4 percent of the Portuguese population and well over half of the urban population. This situation was in no way comparable to that found in either Spain or Italy, and goes some way toward explaining the peculiarities of the Portuguese Inquisition.

V

An overwhelming proportion of those sentenced by the Portuguese Inquisition between 1540 and the middle of the eighteenth century were, as we have seen, accused of "Judaism." With few exceptions, the practices of which they were accused (and to which they almost invariably confessed) had been described in a document published in 1536 when the Portuguese Inquisition was initially established. This *Monitório do inquisidor geral*, as it was known, purported to describe the external signs through which a crypto-Jew could be identified. But instead of being a description of the religious practices of Portuguese New Christians a generation after their conversion, it is, in fact, a compilation of earlier Spanish Inquisitorial documents dating back to the late fifteenth century.[28] As represented in the *Monitório*, the "Judaism" of Portuguese New Christians consisted of the following rites and observances: observing the Sabbath by doing no work and putting on clean clothes or jewels on Saturdays; cleaning the house on Fridays; preparing food on Fridays for the day after; slaughtering animals in the Jewish manner; not eating bacon or other forbidden food; practicing the Great Fast of September, that of Queen Esther and certain other fasts; celebrating the Easter of the Jews; practicing certain funerary rites; practicing circumcision; blessing their children without making the sign of the cross. More generally, in a clear transposition of Catholic religious conceptions, they were accused of "seeking the salvation of their souls in the Law of Moses." Although there are a few cases in which the accused confessed to practices and observances not described in the *Monitório* and similar documents, the vast majority of cases consist of accusations as stereotyped as these: the prisoner, a New Christian, would typically be accused by neighbors of being ill-disposed toward the Catholic faith, of not eating pork, and of putting on a clean shirt on Saturdays; he would end up by admitting this, together with some other practices repeatedly mentioned in Inquisitorial edicts; and finally he would provide a list of people with whom he had made mutual declarations of faith in the law of Moses.

In the vast majority of cases, the records of the Inquisition thus provide very little objective information regarding the Judaism practiced by Portuguese New Christians. As in the formally similar cases of early modern witch trials or those of sixteenth-century Italian "Lutherans,"[29] the accusations reflect the preconceptions of the Inquisitors as much as the actual behavior or beliefs of the accused.

It should be remembered that the Inquisition was finally established in Portugal almost a half-century after the forced conversion of 1497, and that all but a very few of its victims, even in the initial years, had been formally brought up as Catholics. Relegated to the domestic sphere, their Judaism—which after 1536 was, in addition, a source of potential danger—became progressively more simplified, and some practices, like circumcision, had to be abandoned altogether. As those who remembered the original traditions and rites became older and died, there inevitably arose a problem of cultural transmission. In the records of the Coimbra Inquisition in the second half of the sixteenth century, for example, there are references to young men who used to attend autos-da-fé so as to learn the prayers mentioned in the sentences of the condemned, because in their hometowns there was nobody still alive who knew them.[30]

This example underlines the fact that the Judaism of Portuguese New Christians was not simply a tradition transmitted from generation to generation within the protective walls of their homes. It was also a cultural representation held up to them, as in a deforming mirror, by the Inquisition and by the rest of society. Given the difficulties of clandestine cultural transmission, it was inevitable that many New Christians should come to recognize themselves in the representation of Judaism that was repeatedly held up to them from outside, whether in the stereotyped formulae of the accusations or in the spectacular rites of the Inquisition.

VI

According to the rules of Inquisitorial procedure, somebody who persisted in denying an accusation of heresy that the Inquisitors considered to have been proven could be considered a *negativo* and, even if this were the first offense, sentenced to be burned. This was because a refusal to confess indicated lack of repentance, and an unrepentant heretic could not be reconciled with the Church and readmitted into the Christian communion. Likewise, someone who made an incomplete confession, omitting the names of accomplices, for example, could be considered *diminuto* and suffer the same penalty. Under these circumstances, it was in the accused's interest to confess and denounce all those whom the Inquisitors regarded as his or her accomplices, since after a full and satisfactory confession, with appropriate signs of repentance, the accused would normally be admitted to reconciliation. After publicly abjuring his or her errors and being subjected to different forms of penance, the accused would then be released. Although the goods of those reconciled after confessing to heresy would be confiscated, this was obviously preferable to the sentence that awaited a *negativo* or *diminuto* (Figs. 6.2, 6.3, and 6.4).

In the case of a New Christian who had effectively maintained a dual religious allegiance—Catholicism in public, Judaism in private—the situation was clear. If accused and arrested, he could either make a full confession, naming all those who had participated in Judaic rites with him, or he could deny the accusation and run the risk—should the evidence against him be considered sufficient—of being considered *diminuto* or *negativo*. But a New Christian who had been *unjustly* accused of Judaism faced the same dilemma in a different form: he could either attempt to refute the accusation and risk being considered *negativo*, or he could attempt to make up a false confession and list of accomplices. Since the prisoner was kept in the dark both in regard to the offenses of which he was accused and the identity of his alleged accomplices, this was a risky strategy to adopt; if the prisoner had been accused as an accomplice by another New Christian but did not include the latter in his own list of accomplices, or if he failed to include a rite or ceremony in which he had been accused of participating, he might still be considered *diminuto*.

The perversity of this procedure gave rise among New Christians to concerted strategies of mutual self-defense. Those fearing the likelihood of arrest, usually a group of close kin, would agree among themselves as to what offenses should be admitted and as to who should be accused as an accomplice. The latter, knowing in advance that they would be accused, would attempt to forestall arrest and secure more favorable treatment by presenting themselves "spontaneously" to the Inquisitors as soon as a kinsman was arrested and making the prearranged confession and accusations. As the various confessions corroborated each other, there was hope that they would be accepted by the Inquisition as sincere and complete. Once those involved had been released, however, they would be branded as confessed heretics and marginalized. They might attempt to salvage what they could of their possessions and seek refuge abroad; alternatively, they could remain in Portugal and rely on the protection and solidarity of their kin network and the New Christian community. But in either case, they would have been definitively excluded from normal social relations with Old Christians and forced into close dependence on the New Christian community, even if originally innocent. Under such circumstances, even New Christians who had virtually lost contact with the original Jewish tradition might rediscover a Judaic identity, accepting with pride the stereotyped label thrust upon them by the Inquisition and by Old Christian society, and even, in some cases, undergoing conversion to Judaism in Amsterdam or London.[31] It is in this sense that the New Christians used to argue that the Inquisition was a *fábrica de judeus*.

P. 313.

A Man condemned to be burnt but hath escaped by his Confession.

FIGURE 6.2 "A man condemned to be burnt but hath escaped by his confession." J. Baker, *A Complete History of the Inquisition in Portugal, Spain, Italy, the East and West Indies* (London, 1736).

P.377.

Por hereje negatiuo morre o queimado

The Samara worn by a Relapse or Impenitent &c. going to be burn'd.

FIGURE 6.3 The "samarra" worn by those sentenced to the stake. J. Baker, *A Complete History of the Inquisition in Portugal, Spain, Italy, the East and West Indies* (London, 1736).

The Processioning of ye Act of Faith.

FIGURE 6.4 An auto-da-fé. J. Baker, *A Complete History of the Inquisition in Portugal, Spain, Italy, the East and West Indies* (London, 1736).

VII

As I. S. Révah clearly perceived, there is little point in judging the religion of the New Christians by reference to Orthodox Judaism. Despised by the Old Christians, they rejected the Catholicism that excluded them; cut off from the Judaic tradition and from Jewish communities abroad, they tried to reconstruct a Jewish identity from the fragmented elements they had at hand, many of which reached them filtered and distorted by the Inquisition. Theirs was, he argued, a *potential* Judaism, defined less in terms of faith or knowledge than in terms of will. It was this will to be Jewish that explains, in his view, the return to Judaism of many New Christians who in the seventeenth and eighteenth centuries left Portugal and sought refuge in one of the Jewish communities abroad.[32] Révah's definition of "marrano religion" as a Judaism of the will is undoubtedly correct, as is his recognition that the marrano will to be Jewish was in many cases a direct response to the arbitrary injustice of Inquisitorial persecution and to what he terms the "racism" of Spanish and Portuguese society. Despite his perception of the role of the Inquisition in shaping the representation of Judaism that was common to Old and New Christians alike, he tended to take that role as given and to define the problem primarily as one of the transmission of a religious and cultural identity under conditions of persecution.

This "essentialist" perspective does not give due weight to the implications of the demographic factors mentioned earlier, and in particular to the consequences of intermarriage between Old and New Christians. As we have seen, the proportion of "pure" New Christians among those accused and condemned for Judaism in Lisbon in the first half of the seventeenth century implies that, on average, at least 20 percent of all marriages involving New Christians during the first four generations will have been mixed marriages. This degree of intermarriage implies, as we have seen, that the proportion of the Portuguese population who were formally of "impure blood," and hence subject to discrimination, will have increased from 8 percent in 1500 to about 17 percent in 1620 and—assuming the same degree of intermarriage over the following generations—to over 34 percent in 1740. It was inevitable, under these circumstances, that the Jewish cultural and religious identity preserved by a very significant proportion of the first New Christian generation—as Samuel Usque put it, they did not "change the secret of their souls"[33]—should have become progressively more diluted as parents neglected, by choice or by fear, to pass on the Jewish cultural and religious traditions to their children.

This dilution was not uniform. In some cases, we can be sure that Jewish religious observance—including the details of the religious calendar—was preserved well into the eighteenth century. The case of António José da Silva, the playwright known as "o Judeu," is emblematic. His family was caught celebrating Yom Kippur on 5 October 1737, but the Inquisition, which always referred to Yom Kippur as "the Great Fast of September," did not realize what was happening; when "o Judeu" was in fact condemned to death, the charges against him consisted only of the Jewish fasts he was—perhaps falsely—accused of having observed later while in prison.[34]

In other cases we can almost observe the process of dilution and contamination of the original tradition. In several sixteenth-century trials, for instance, we find references to the Torah. In a trial of 1562, it is described as a roll of parchment that was shown to those who used to gather in the accused's home and was then put away.[35] In 1557, we are told of a room "where they worship the *Toura*."[36] The use of the vernacular form Toura, which could also mean "cow," paved the way for a semantic contamination. In 1634, in Évora, a twelve-year-old girl confessed that her mother had taught her a prayer that was to be recited "to the golden calf."[37] In 1609, in Covilhã, we find a silver statuette of a female calf (*bezerrinha de prata*) carefully preserved and transmitted from generation to generation by a New Christian family.[38] In northeastern Brazil at the end of the sixteenth century, a clay statuette in the form of a cow is described to the incredulous Inquisitorial Visitor in an accusation as being "the Toura of the Jews."[39] Some time later, still in Brazil, we find references to a "Confraternity of the Toura," organized and financed by New Christians.[40]

It is clear that transmission of the Jewish cultural and religious tradition was selective. In some family lines it would be kept alive, in others it would die out. It is likely that, as among the Xuetes of Majorca, marriage alliances were consciously and selectively used to preserve a hard crypto-Judaic core: some children would be married within the group, and would be given religious instruction; others would be allowed to marry outside the group to non-Judaizing New Christian families or to Old Christians, and from these such dangerous instruction would be withheld.[41]

Given such forms of selective transmission, the tradition could at any time be reactivated even in a family where it had died out. An individual unjustly accused of Judaism, for example, and forced to make a false confession would be publicly branded as a New Christian and heretic and be forced to seek support from other New Christians. In due course, he might reclaim his Judaic identity, seeking out elements of the tradition from a branch of the family or from other families in which it had been preserved, or simply adopting the representation of Judaic rites and ceremonies that had been held up to him by the Inquisition. In such a situation, as Révah perceived, the tradition could be reactivated by Inquisitorial persecution. Such mechanisms will have been all the more important and significant as the Jewish tradition became progressively more diluted with each generation in a constantly increasing New Christian population, while the Inquisition and Old Christian society continued to discriminate on grounds of "purity of blood" against all known descendants of converted Jews, however remote the genealogical link, and however diluted their Jewish identity. The relative importance of the inherited tradition and of the externally imposed label will have changed dramatically over time.

Because of this, more attention needs to be given to the factors underlying the two elements that Révah and other authors have taken as given: the social context out of which accusations of Judaism against New Christians continued to arise and the mechanisms underlying the survival of the Inquisition itself.

VIII

If the persistence of a Judaic identity among New Christians can be explained, at least in part, by the fact that it was constantly being held up to them and imposed by the Inquisition, by Old Christians, and by the discrimination to which they were subjected, what explains the persistence of the Inquisition itself? Was it simply the case of an institution that, to guarantee its own survival, needed to maintain its rhythm of activity and hence to "manufacture" crypto-Jews? Or are there other reasons that can explain the institution's longevity?

Between 1570 and 1770, the number of "Familiars" (lay collaborators) of the Portuguese Inquisition increased uninterruptedly. Between 1621 and 1670, an average of forty-six "Familiars" were appointed every year; between 1671 and 1720, 110; and between 1721 and 1770, 174 every year. During the same period, there was an analogous expansion of the Inquisitorial bureaucracy: from 1621 to 1670 and 1721 to 1770 the number of *comissários* (local delegates) increased from 297 to 1,011 and the number of *qualificadores* (theological consultants) increased from 110 to 419. But this expansion of the bureaucratic apparatus did not meet any functional need. During the same period, the number of Deputies and Inquisitors remained stable, increasing from 117 to 119, while the number of those sentenced actually fell from 11,154 to 3,895.[42]

It is clear that the Inquisition was being used, on a massive scale, as a means of social affirmation and mobility. Appointment to any Inquisitorial post required a detailed investigation of the genealogies of the candidate and his wife to determine whether there was any trace of "infected blood." With the passing of time, not having in the family any "Familiar" or other official of the Inquisition could give rise to suspicion, and as a result, the social status of individuals and their families depended crucially on the result of these inquiries. The advantages of posts in the Inquisition, like membership in military orders, did not derive only from the significant privileges that they conferred, but above all from the fact that not everybody could have access to them.[43]

"Familiars" were recruited at almost all levels of society. Although the proportion of artisans decreased after the end of the sixteenth century and the proportion of merchants increased significantly during the eighteenth, the social origins of the Inquisition's "Familiars" were always varied. And although the numerical importance of each group—and in particular of the *lavradores* (farmers)—was very different from one case to another, in general the Inquisition recruited its "Familiars" in the same social groups in which it sought out its victims.[44] In each one of these groups the title of "Familiar" will have accentuated the division between New Christians and Old Christians, preventing it from disappearing with time.

The persistence of this distinction in a society in which, by 1740, those who could in principle be branded as New Christians represented one-third of the population—and over half of the urban population—was structurally related to the persistence of the Inquisition itself and to the functions it performed in delineating social groups, the criteria for social status, and strategies of social advancement. As time went on, the "Jewish question" in Portugal became less and less a religious question and more and more a question of relations between social groups at all levels of society.

IX

These issues are obviously crucial for our understanding of early modern Portuguese society and the role played by the Inquisition. They are also crucial for our understanding of the meaning to be attached to accusations of crypto-Judaism directed against New Christians at all levels of society. Less obvious, perhaps, is their immediate relevance to our understanding of the role played by Iberian Jews in the making of the New World. It should be remembered, however, that Portuguese New Christians were not only important in colonial Brazil. They also constituted a large proportion of the *converso* merchants active in the Spanish possessions in Central and South America. The Jews who moved from Amsterdam to Pernambuco then to the West Indies and North America were also to a large extent of Portuguese origin.

As was pointed out earlier, the Spanish Inquisition's persecution of native *conversos* had more or less come to an end by the middle of the sixteenth century. There followed a period when it was more concerned with the minor offenses of Old Christians and, in Aragon, with *moriscos*. The Spanish tribunals (and in particular those of Castile and Spanish America) only resumed their persecution of Judaism when, after 1580, significant numbers of Portuguese New Christians moved into Spain and the Spanish dependencies. A very large proportion of those tried for Judaism by Spanish tribunals throughout the Americas in the seventeenth and eighteenth centuries were, in fact, Portuguese or of Portuguese origin.

This implies that the experience of Portuguese New Christians—and in particular the mechanisms underlying the transmission and social construction of their Jewish religious and cultural identity—is directly relevant to our understanding of the role played by New Christians or marranos throughout the Americas. Unlike the victims of the first phase of the Spanish Inquisition (1480–1530), whose Jewish identities were seldom in any doubt, the Portuguese New Christians and marranos of the seventeenth and eighteenth centuries, regardless of whether or not they attempted to maintain Judaic observance, were the product of a complex process in which both their Catholic and their Jewish identities were deeply intertwined. As numerous authors have pointed out,[45] the inner experience of these New Christians and marranos was profoundly marked by the duality and ambiguity of their Judeo-Catholic cultural and religious identity. To examine their role in the making of the New World exclusively in terms of that identity's Jewish component is to tell only part of the story.

Notes

1. Converted Jews and their descendants were usually referred to as *conversos* in Spain and *Cristãos novos* in Portugal. Both terms could also be used to refer to converted Muslims, and in Spain the more specific term *Cristiano nuevo de judío* was sometimes used. I shall here use the generic term "New Christian" to refer to converted Jews and their descendants in both countries. Following Israel S. Révah, "Les Marranes," *Revue des Etudes Juives* 118, no. 1 (1959–60):29–77, I shall reserve the term "marrano" for those New Christians who consciously attempted to maintain, however imperfectly, some form of Judaic religious observance and identity.
2. Whether he would be so considered by Jewish communities and religious authorities outside Spain or Portugal is a separate question which cannot be dealt with here. The best general account in English of the "marrano question" is still Yosef H. Yerushalmi, *From Spanish Court to Italian Ghetto. Isaac Cardoso: A Study in Seventeenth-Century Marranism and Jewish Apologetics* (New York and London, 1971), chap. 1.
3. Despite the contemporary overtones of terms like "purity of blood," the notions of anti-Semitism and racism are out of place in the context of early modern Spain and Portugal.
4. Cf. Robert Rowland, "Fantasticall and Devilishe Persons: European Witch-Beliefs in Comparative Perspective," *Early Modern European Witchcraft. Centres and Peripheries*, ed. B. Ankarloo and G. Henningsen (Oxford, 1990), 161–90.
5. See Nicolaus Eymericus, *Directorium Inquisitorum* (Rome, 1578), 244ff.; Cesare Carena, *Tractatus de Officio Sanctissimae Inquisitionis et modo procedendi in causis fidei* (Cremona, 1655), 251–55; [Eliseo Masini], *Sacro Arsenale, ovvero Prattica dell'Officio della S. Inquisitione* (Genoa, 1625), 19–20; and, for an overview of the situation in the late medieval period, Kenneth R. Stow, "Ebrei e inquisitori. 1250–1350," *L'Inquisizione e gli ebrei in Italia*, ed. M. Luzzati (Rome-Bari, 1994), 3–18.
6. Jaime Contreras and Gustav Henningsen, "Forty-four Thousand Cases of the Spanish Inquisition (1540–1700): Analysis of a Historical Data Bank," in *The Inquisition in Early Modern Europe: Studies on Sources and Methods*, ed. G. Henningsen and J. Tedeschi (Dekalb, Ill., 1986), 100–130.
7. These results—derived from research by E. W. Monter, J. Tedeschi, J. P. Dedieu, J. Demonet, G. Henningsen, J. Contreras, J. Veiga Torres, and A. Borges Coelho—are conveniently summarized in Francisco Bethencourt's major comparative study, *História das Inquisições. Portugal, Espanha e Itália* (Lisbon, 1994), 268–84 (French trans., *L'Inquisition à l'époque moderne. Espagne, Portugal, Italie, XVe–XIXe siècle* [Paris, 1995]).
8. The Aragon Secretariat included the tribunals of Barcelona, Logroño, Majorca, Sardinia, Sicily, Valencia, Saragossa, Cartagena de Indias, Lima, and Mexico; that of Castile the tribunals of the Canary Islands, Córdoba, Galicia, Granada, Llerena, Murcia, Seville, Toledo, and Valladolid.
9. Jean-Pierre Dedieu, *L'Administration de la foi. L'Inquisition de Tolède, XVIe–XVIIIe siècle* (Madrid, 1989).
10. Antonio Domínguez Ortiz, *Los Judeoconversos en España y América* (Madrid, 1988), 26.
11. Cf. Maria José Pimenta Ferro Tavares, *Os Judeus em Portugal no Século XV*, vol. 1 (Lisbon, 1982), 74. According to the earlier estimates of João Lúcio de Azevedo, *História dos Cristãos Novos Portugueses* (Lisbon, 1921), 43, they numbered 75,000, but such an overall figure would have implied inordinately high proportions of Jews in urban settlements, and must surely be regarded as excessive.
12. These legal provisions were based on Pope Boniface IX's Bull of 2 July 1389. According to the *Ordenações Afonsinas* (II, 120), no Christian was allowed to kill or wound a Jew, steal his goods, or offend his customs; nor could he violate Jewish cemeteries (on the pretext of hunting for buried treasure), disturb the feasts of the Jews, or force any Jew to perform any kind of service or forced labor. See M. Kayserling, *História dos Judeus em Portugal* (São Paulo, 1971; orig. ed. Leipzig, 1867), 39.
13. Tavares, *Judaísmo e Inquisição* (Lisbon, 1987), chap. 1.

14. According to the most recent estimate by Tavares, they numbered no more than twenty or thirty thousand. Among contemporaries, Abraão Zacuto speaks of 120,000 individuals, Damião de Góis of 20,000 families. The Spanish chronicler Bernáldez claimed that 93,000 crossed the frontier. These high figures have sometimes been uncritically accepted by modern historians, but they would imply that the number of Jews in Portugal had risen, in the space of a few years, from 3 or 4 percent to about 15 percent of the total population, and from perhaps 8 percent to about 30 percent of the population in many urban settlements. This was clearly not the case, and such high figures must be regarded as an exaggeration. Cf. Tavares, *Os Judeus*, 252–57, and Azevedo, *Cristãos Novos*, 20–22.

15. Damião de Góis, *Crónica do Felicíssimo D. Manuel* (Coimbra, 1949); Samuel Usque, *Consolaçam às Tribulaçoens de Israel*, 3 vols. (Coimbra, 1908).

16. Tavares, *Judaísmo e Inquisição*, 41–51; cf. Cod. RES 863, fol. 1, Biblioteca Nacional de Lisboa (BNL). The law was still officially in force in the early years of the sixteenth century—there are cases on record of New Christians asking for permission to marry among themselves—but does not appear to have been seriously enforced.

17. Kayserling, *História dos Judeus*, 154.

18. Contemporary estimates of the number of New Christians who lost their lives range from 1,900 (Damião de Góis) to 4,000 (Samuel Usque). Fifty of those held responsible for the massacre were condemned to death. The population of Lisbon lost some of its privileges, and the city was subjected to a heavy fine.

19. Paul Teyssier, *La langue de Gil Vicente* (Paris, 1959), chap. 4.

20. See Lea Sestieri, *David Rubeni. Un ebreo d'Arabia in missione segreta nell'Europa del '500* (Genoa, 1991).

21. The latter three tribunals were in existence for only a short time. In 1558 a fourth tribunal was established in Goa, with jurisdiction over East Africa and the entire Orient. On the establishment of the Portuguese Inquisition, see Alexandre Herculano's classic *História da Origem e Estabelecimento da Inquisição em Portugal* (Lisbon, 1854–59).

22. A few isolated communities remained, which the Inquisition would discover and dismantle in the following decades. For an overview, see J. Contreras, "Estructura de la actividad procesal del Santo Oficio," in *Historia de la Inquisición en España y América*, ed. J. Pérez Villanueva and B. Escandell Bonet, vol. 2 (Madrid, 1993), 621–27.

23. The list is reproduced in Cod. RES 863, fols. 97–98, BNL. As the individual trials have not been analyzed, we cannot be sure that this group constituted a representative sample of the New Christian population in Lisbon, but the fact that they confessed "spontaneously," possibly fearing that they might be accused by others (cf. section VI) suggests that they were at least representative of the kind of New Christian who could plausibly be accused of Judaism.

24. Cod. RES 863, fols. 119–23, BNL.

25. If those of pure Jewish descent represented no more than one-fifth of those accused and sentenced for Judaism, it is very unlikely that they could at the same time have represented a higher proportion of the entire New Christian population. The figure of 20 percent should thus be regarded as a minimum estimate of the proportion of mixed marriages.

26. It comes as something of a surprise, after these figures, to discover that by the eighteenth century the vast majority of those accused of Judaism and sentenced by the Inquisition were described simply as "New Christian": 93.7 percent of those sentenced at the auto-da-fé held in Lisbon on 19 October 1704, or 84.9 percent in that held on 25 July 1728 (Cod. RES 863, fols. 353–56, 437–39, BNL). It is possible that, as in Majorca, selective marriage strategies on the part of some New Christian families could have led to the constitution of an endogamous Judaizing sub-group within the New Christian population (cf. Enric Porqueres, *Lourde alliance: mariage et identité chez les descendants de juifs convertis à Majorque [1435–1750]* [Paris, 1995]), but it is also possible that by then genealogical subtlety had been abandoned and that the term "New Christian," without qualification, was being applied indiscriminately to practically all those of

known Jewish descent. In either case, the Judaic identity of condemned New Christians cannot simply be taken as given. Cf., however, Révah, "Les Marranes," 50, who interprets these figures as signifying that even as late as the eighteenth century "Portuguese crypto-Judaism had preserved a fairly remarkable degree of racial homogeneity."

27. On the assumption, in particular, that demographic rates were broadly comparable among the two sub-populations.

28. The contents of this document have been analyzed in detail by H. P. Salomon, "The 'Monitório do Inquisidor Geral' of 1536: Background and Sources of Some 'Judaic' Customs Listed Therein," *Arquivos do Centro Cultural Português* 17 (1982):41–64, which also reproduces the original text.

29. Cf. Rowland, "Fantasticall and Devilishe Persons," and Silvana Seidel Menchi, *Erasmo in Italia* (Turin, 1987).

30. Elvira Cunha de Azevedo Mea, "Orações judaicas na Inquisição portuguesa—século XVI," in *Jews and Conversos: Studies in Society and the Inquisition*, ed. Y. Kaplan (Jerusalem, 1981), 158.

31. The strategy is described in full in a manuscript written about 1735 by the celebrated New Christian physician Ribeiro Sanches, who was brought up as a Catholic and unjustly denounced to the Inquisition by a cousin. He fled to London, where he was converted to Judaism, but he later returned to Catholicism and became physician to Catherine of Russia. See A. N. Ribeiro Sanches, *Christãos Novos e Christãos Velhos em Portugal*, ed. Raul Rego (Oporto, 1973).

On the extent to which Jewish identities and traditions had in some cases to be reinvented, see now Miriam Bodian, *Hebrews of the Portuguese Nation: Conversos and Community in Early Modern Amsterdam* (Bloomington, 1997).

32. I. S. Révah, "Les Marranes."

33. Usque, *Consolaçam*, 3:32.

34. Révah, discussion in A. J. Saraiva, *Inquisição e Cristãos Novos*, 2nd ed. (Lisbon, 1985), 284–86; J. Lúcio de Azevedo, *Novas Epanáforas* (Lisbon, 1932), 143–218.

35. Processo N° 1266, Inquisição de Lisboa, Arquivo Nacional da Torre do Tombo (ANTT).

36. Processo N° 236, Inquisição de Lisboa, ANTT.

37. António Borges Coelho, *A Inquisição de Évora*, vol. 1 (Lisbon, 1987):363.

38. *Denúncias em Nome da Fé. Perseguição aos Judeus no Distrito da Guarda de 1607 a 1625*, ed. Maria Antonieta Garcia (Lisbon, 1996), 70–71.

39. *Primeira Visitação do Santo Ofício às Partes do Brasil pelo Licenciado Heitor Furtado de Mendonça. Denunciações de Pernambuco, 1593–1595*, ed. R. Garcia (São Paulo, 1929), 38.

40. Anita Novinsky, *Cristãos-Novos da Bahia* (São Paulo, 1972), 159.

41. Porqueres, *Lourde alliance*.

42. José Veiga Torres, "Da Repressão Religiosa para a Promoção Social. A Inquisição como instância legitimadora da promoção social da burguesia mercantil," *Revista Crítica de Ciências Sociais* 40 (1994):109–35.

43. See the excellent study by Fernanda Olival "O acesso de uma família de cristãos novos portugueses à Ordem de Cristo," *Ler História* 33 (1997):67–82.

44. We do not, at present, have sufficient information for a rigorous statistical comparison. Cf., however, the figures given by Borges Coelho (*Inquisição de Évora*, 1:383) and by Veiga Torres ("Repressão Religiosa," 133). Of 5,382 individuals tried by the Évora Inquisition between 1537 and 1668, 22 percent were merchants or tradesmen, 42 percent artisans, 9 percent farmers, and 4 percent laborers. During the same period farmers made up almost half the number of "Familiars," whereas artisans, merchants and *fidalgos* made up, respectively, 15 percent, 13 percent, and 6 percent. Between 1721 and 1770 the proportion of farmers had fallen to 28 percent, while the remaining three groups now made up, respectively, 6 percent, 37 percent, and 5 percent.

45. See, for example, Novinsky, *Cristãos Novos*, and Nathan Wachtel's contribution to this volume.

– Chapter 7 –

MARRANO RELIGIOSITY
IN HISPANIC AMERICA IN THE
SEVENTEENTH CENTURY

Nathan Wachtel

WHAT IS MARRANO RELIGIOSITY? We can legitimately discern among New Christians throughout the Iberian world beliefs and practices that indicate the persistence of a possible crypto-Judaism. But does it suffice merely to make an unquestioning inventory of such elements? For indeed, the range of beliefs held by New Christians was not limited to the clandestine pursuit of more or less impoverished Judaizing practices. Hence, we must avoid using the reductive schemas of an apologetic history and instead restore to marrano religiosity its full measure of complexity and diversity. We must cover a broad spectrum between two poles—that of actual fervent Judaists and that of sincere Christians—with a whole series of intermediate cases and syncretic combinations.

Conversos can be distinguished from Old Christians both negatively and positively: legally, the "pure blood" statutes left them (in principle) relatively marginalized; but we know that in social terms the New Christians were united in vast networks reinforced by kinship and marriage, and that this solidarity was reinforced to varying degrees by the shared feelings of a community of memory. But what about their religious beliefs? In seeking to answer this question, we are confronted with a paradox, arising from the complex and manifold forms of religious life. On the one hand, there is a (potentially) common body of Judaizing practices, and on the other, extreme diversity among various individuals, groups, places, and periods under consideration. It is as if the very object of our study dissipates before our eyes. The essential point is in the paradox itself: what is specific about the religious domain of New Christians is precisely the tension they experienced between two religions—Judaism and Christianity—with all the resultant doubts, hesitations, vacillations, and at times skeptical detachment, as well as the "interferences," cross-fertilization, and dual sincerity.

Here a brief consideration of terminology is in order. It is no accident that the terms "marrano" and "marranism," despite their once pejorative connotations, have come to be accepted for the sake of convenience: they correspond to an objective reality, that of a certain religiosity. By religiosity, I mean not a religion as clearly defined by theological doctrine, but rather a set of concerns, practices, and beliefs grouped together in a configuration made up of various, even contradictory, elements whose diversity does not preclude a kind of unity—a generic style that makes it possible for us to identify and label it with a specific term, in this case "marrano."[1]

Marrano religiosity as it pertains to the New Christians in Hispanic America, and more particularly in New Spain, during the first half of the seventeenth century is the focus of this essay.[2] The overwhelming majority of the New Christians—Judaizing or otherwise—who came to the American continent in large numbers, particularly starting in 1580 with the Union of the Two Kingdoms, were of Portuguese origin. Many of them were the descendants of Spanish Jews who had originally fled to Portugal in 1492, sometimes making a detour through Spain again for one or two generations before ultimately pursuing their migration as far as the New World. In the American context, these *conversos* exhibited very particular characteristics: like the Amerindian societies, but in a very different milieu, they constitute a virtual laboratory for the study of problems related to acculturation processes, syncretic phenomena, and cultural *métissage*.

In the Americas—which were open to new arrivals but which retained a population that, despite the demographic catastrophe, remained predominantly indigenous—heterodox beliefs and practices could indeed escape detection and denunciation more easily than in the metropolis (all the more so because the jurisdiction of the Inquisition tribunals extended here over vast areas). Conversely, in those faraway lands to which Hebrew literature made its way only surreptitiously, and exceptionally at that, it was difficult to sustain a Jewish Orthodox tradition. Thus the New Christians who immigrated to Hispanic America had recourse to a whole range of multiple syncretic combinations, which we shall examine more closely in order to discover the specific characteristics of marrano religiosity.

The Range of Beliefs: Christian Influences

By definition, the *conversos* had received some Christian education that had inevitably left traces, even to the point of stamping their personalities with indelible mental reflexes. There are many accounts describing the shock experienced by an adolescent to whom a parent had suddenly revealed that everything the child had previously learned, and in which he ardently believed—Jesus Christ, the Virgin Mary, the Holy Trinity, the saints, and so forth—was false and that salvation was to be found not in the "law of Jesus" but in the "law of Moses." Such expressions were not confined only to the vocabulary of the Inquisitors; they were totally assimilated by the New Christians as well, whatever the nature of their faith. What was at stake was still the salvation of the soul: this peculiarly Christian concern formed the basis for a range of beliefs within which the alternatives were arrayed, along with the doubts and hesitations of those who, from the moment of revelation on, found themselves faced with a dramatic choice.[3] Often a single family would be split into sincere Catholics and fervent Judaists, the relations between them oscillating between mutual distrust and compromising solidarity. Sometimes parents would argue over their children's education, as in the example of Antonio Diaz de Caceres and his wife Catalina de León de la Cueva (the sister of the famous Luis de Carvajal El Mozo). Their fourteen-year-old daughter, Leonor de Caceres, reported a remarkable episode:

> One day, in the presence of the said Doña Mariana (who was quite crazy) and the said Doña Anna, Antonio Diaz fought at length with Doña Catalina because she made her [Leonor] fast during the holy days of the Lord and he ordered her [Leonor] to get dressed, saying, "Stand up, you bad woman of poor breeding, and do not ever return to this house" and so Ysabelica *china*, who is now dead, dressed her and she went with her father down to the street corner where she said to the said Antonio Diaz, "My Lord and father, where are you taking me so that I might cry in someone else's home?" and the said Antonio Diaz responded, "Be quiet, you sly vixen of poor breeding. I am taking you to Machado's house." And as she knew not who he [Machado] was, she cried, and the said Antonio Diaz shed tears when he heard her ask where he was taking her so that she might cry in someone else's home, and he took her back to her mother's house, saying, "Go on, you poorly bred woman and thank God for what you said to me, for it is because of this that I am taking you to this bad woman," and her father, the said Antonio Diaz, left her at the door and went about his business.[4]

Let us take another example that illustrates the persistence of Christian practices in the midst of Judaizing observances, or rather, in this case, a Judaizing reinterpretation of Christian practices and beliefs. This is the case of Antonio Fernandez Cardado, born in Moral in La Mancha (of parents native to Portugal). After a complicated itinerary that took him through Bordeaux and Saint Jean de Luz, he arrived in Spain in 1613. He amassed some capital by working as a peddler between Vera Cruz and Puebla, and then opened a wholesale supply company in Mexico, extending his business to Tlaxcala and the mining town of Pachuca. When he ended up in front of the Inquisition tribunal in 1634, this is how Cardado described his conversion to Judaism:

> The said Talaveras, his cousins, told this confessant that the law of Jesus Christ was not the good one and that there was only one God who was to be adored, and that the Messiah had not come, nor was Jesus Christ the Messiah, although they said that there was a Holy Ghost who had spoken through the prophets and patriarchs of the old law.[5]

Thus, at the very moment when the reconversion took place, as Jesus Christ was rejected, there remained a trace of Christian doctrine in the presence of the Holy Ghost transposed onto the Old Testament. Antonio Fernandez Cardado went on to say that, as a child, in the school where he was taught by priests to read and write, he had learned a prayer that the children had recited every afternoon, and he repeated it to the Inquisitors: "We pray to you that you have mercy on us and the souls of our deceased relatives and friends, and please Lord, save them from the pain they suffer and take them to your Holy Kingdom. Amen Jesus."[6] Antonio Fernandez Cardado added that he remained quite attached to this prayer and that he continued to recite it even after his conversion to the "law of Moses," although he took care to stop before he got to the "Amen Jesus" with which it ended. However, sometimes he would slip and unintentionally utter the final "Amen Jesus" without meaning to; the mechanism of a prayer learned by heart, inculcated at an early age, reproduced itself like a reflex.

Let us note further how Antonio Fernandez Cardado excused himself for making these slips: his real intention, he insisted, was truly to pray as one who observes the "law of Moses" and to address the God of Israel exclusively.[7] So even in private prayer he maintained a mental reservation and drew a distinction between the words he actually uttered and the faith within his heart of hearts; in other words, there was a discrepancy or gap between the prayer as literally expressed and his inner feelings, the authentic faith that alone guaranteed salvation. Antonio Fernandez Cardado's observation is similar to certain admissions concerning the Christian confession: those *conversos* on trial often related how, when they went to church for the purpose of confessing, it was because they were obliged to keep up appearances. Although they confessed to the priest, they too had mental reservations, taking care to think of the God of Israel to whom their prayers were really addressed (and to whom they had prayed beforehand in order to ask for forgiveness).

Another type of ambiguity is illustrated by a scene that was played out in the house of Simon Vaez Sevilla, one of the richest business men in New Spain during the 1630s. The occasion was a Passover celebration, in a ceremony at which Blanca Enriquez was officiating. Considered a "dogmatist" and rabbinist, she was the mother-in-law of Simon Vaez Sevilla and had been imprisoned and tortured in the dungeons of the Inquisition in Sevilla. The faithful gathered together in the back room of the house where Blanca Enriquez proceeded to distribute the unleavened bread that had been secretly prepared. They lined up before her, one behind the other; for each of them, she broke off a small piece of unleavened bread and placed it in the worshipper's mouth, according to, and as if in atonement for, the Christian model.[8]

* * * *

IN ORDER TO BROADEN the scope of our study, let us consider the extremely complex case of Manuel Bautista Perez, a powerful merchant in Lima (and the Peruvian counterpart, in the 1620s and 1630s, of Simon Vaez Sevilla).[9] An examination of his commercial practices is not the focus here, but it is known that he made his fortune through the African slave trade and through smuggling.[10] Now this slave trader was also a well-read man: along with his collection of 125 paintings, Manuel Bautista Perez possessed a library of 155 volumes;[11] the inventory of these works shows that 19 percent consisted of *belles lettres*, 62 percent were secular works (including history, law, philosophy, and so forth), and only 18 percent belonged to the religious domain. Compared to other personal libraries of the same period, religious works represented a relatively minor part of Perez's collection.

Among the secular works, which made up the majority of the books, one genre predominated—history, with forty-seven titles, or about one-third of the total collection. This interest in the things of the past indicated on Manuel Bautista's part certain preoccupations that are probably connected somehow to his status as both *converso* and Portuguese. Indeed, a significant proportion of these history books deal with the expeditions of discovery and conquest undertaken by the Portuguese in the fifteenth and sixteenth centuries, for example, Diogo de Couto's *Decades*, published in Lisbon between 1602 and 1614; the *History of the Moluccas*, by Bartolome Leonardo Argensola (Madrid, 1609); or again the famous *Travels in China* by Fernâo Mendes Pinto (Lisbon, 1628). Manuel Bautista Perez directed his curiosity toward the knowledge of distant lands, the latest discoveries, and the learned publications of his time.

While the religious part of his library was not abundant, its contents were no less telling. Apart from works of hagiography, there were treatises on Christology and Marian cults, a set of themes and beliefs specifically rejected by Judaists. Thus we note two books on the life of Christ, one by Cristobal de Fonseca (the first part published in Toledo in 1596 and the second in Lisbon in 1602), the other by Juan Arze de Solorzano (Madrid, 1605). Other works take up the debate over the conception of the Virgin, for example, the *Concepción de Maria Purisima*, by Hipolito de Olivares y Butron (Lima, 1631), and *Nombres y atributos de la Virgen*, by Alonso de Bonilla (Baeza, 1624). We also note the presence of a *Treatise on the Communion* by Fernando Quirino de Salazar (Madrid, 1622).[12] In other words, Manuel Bautista Perez's interests as far as theology is concerned seem to be concentrated around issues that differentiate the "law of Jesus" from the "law of Moses." Several accounts also relate his conversations with the Dominican Fray Blas de Acosta, who responded to his questions (*dudas*) relating to the Trinity, the Virgin, and the incarnation of Christ.[13] This set of preoccupations suggests a religious anxiety that appears quite different from the attitudes of the most radical Judaists (for example, that of Francisco Maldonado de Silva, condemned to the same auto-da-fé in 1639), who categorically denied the founding mysteries of Christianity.

We may well wonder whether these theological interests and the manifestations of Christian faith evinced rather ostentatiously by Manuel Bautista Perez were not intended to mask his crypto-Judaism. We do know, however, that—again, unlike Francisco Maldonado de Silva—Perez always, even under torture, denied having observed the "law of Moses": in fact, he was condemned as a *negativo*. It is true that many other accounts adduced at his trial report scenes and conversations that rendered him highly suspect.[14] But suspect of what, precisely? Some of his own notations attest to his being clearly aware that the Judaizing practices of his friends in Lima were extremely impoverished, being reduced to banal stereotypical formulas: "All that they know of the Law of Moses is very limited because Jewish practices here are not known because they have never seen anyone who knows more than to fast on Tuesdays and Fridays."[15] The numerous meetings held in his house were devoted essentially to recollections of these ceremonies, as if the rite were, under the circumstances, reduced to speech and to memory. In this sense, the crypto-Judaism of Manuel Bautista Perez, if crypto-Judaism it was, would seem to have been based more on the cult of memory than on an authentically religious faith, thus prefiguring, in its way, a quasi-secular Jewish consciousness.

The complex personality of Manuel Bautista Perez leads us to ask, with respect to him and to many others condemned by the Inquisition, whether he was a Jewish martyr or a Christian martyr. The answer, in his case, is not obvious, but it is not implausible to suppose that he was the victim of a dual sincerity—straddling two different standards while experiencing doubts and uncertainty about both of them.

Diverging Representations of the Afterlife

Let us return to Mexico and to the statements made by Antonio Fernandez Cardado. The anecdote concerning his slip in uttering "Amen Jesus" at the end of a prayer reaches much deeper than its superficially amusing aspect. If Cardado remains attached to the prayer he learned in childhood, this is clearly because of its content, the object of the prayer, which is a plea for mercy for the souls in Purgatory. The notion of Purgatory, of course, is a relatively late development and a distinctively Christian one.[16] If a kind of equivalent is sometimes found in Jewish conceptions at that time (particularly in the cabalistic tradition), these concepts nevertheless take quite different forms. As for the representations of the afterlife as understood by the New Christians of New Spain during the same period, they appear to be extremely varied, running the gamut from belief in the immortality of the soul to the more or less radical negation of such immortality.

We will consider only a few examples here. While Antonio Fernandez Cardado continues to believe in Purgatory, the same is not true of his nephew Francisco Botello, who explicitly denies its existence. In fact, properly speaking, Botello's beliefs concerning the destiny of souls appear to be more consistent with the Jewish idea of the necessity of the Messiah's coming before the "gates of heaven are opened," although there are also references to the "Elysian Fields" with connotations evoking the ancient world. As for hell, it most certainly exists, but it is reserved for Christians who are condemned to it for their idolatry:

> And the said Francisco Botello affirmed that there was no purgatory because those who died went to a place, which he understood was called the Elysian Fields, and they would remain there until the Messiah came to take them to heaven, and when he heard of one who had died and it was believed that God has received him in heaven, Francisco Botello laughed because he said the time had not come to open the gates of heaven. Even though they were not Christians they could not go to heaven because all Christians were going to hell for being idolatrous and worshipping wooden images of Jesus Christ and the saints.[17]

The equivalent of Purgatory that is found in the case of Margarita de Rivera bears more resemblance to the Cheol of some Jewish traditions: after death, the soul remains there for a period limited to one year; this is also a period of mourning with its attendant fasts, intended to ensure the salvation of the soul of the deceased.

> It is a constant among observants that the souls of the deceased, who are also observants, remain a year and a day suffering the punishments which God our Lord sees fit to give them ... and in this way the fasts that are assigned are performed specially for the benefit of the souls before the year and a day, so they might escape those punishments, since after the year and a day are up, the fasts are useless.[18]

Yet another version is put forth by Antonio Vaez Casteloblanco. The elder brother of Simon Vaez Sevilla, he was considered by the Inquisitors to be one of the principal "dogmatists" of the marrano community in Mexico. In his representation of the hereafter, not only is Purgatory absent, but hell also is nonexistent: "And he said to this confessant concerning the Law of Moses ... that no one who observes it will be condemned [to hell] nor either are Christians because there is no hell, and the Christians [who believe in it] are like beasts lacking understanding."[19] Unfortunately, Antonio Vaez Casteloblanco does not expand upon this conception, but his derogatory remark about Christians leads one to suppose that, at least so far as they were concerned, he believed their souls to be mortal and their situation to be accurately described by the famous saying, *no hay mas que nacer y morir* ("there is no more than living and dying")—a watchword, in the eyes of the Inquisitors, for Judaizing heresy. In other words, the problem here of the immortality of the soul gives rise to a sort of compromise through juxtaposition, since two different destinies were possible after death: the first, reserved for one part of humanity—namely Christians—was the void; the second, for another part—those who observe the "law of Moses"—was guaranteed salvation.

An example that takes us to the end of the seventeenth century completes this picture of the diversity of representations of the afterlife: this is the case of Fernando de Medina, a recent arrival in Mexico who had lived there for only four years before being imprisoned by the Holy Office in 1691. He had actually been born in the marrano community of Peyrehorade in southwestern France (where he had been both baptized and circumcised); at the age of twelve, he left for Spain, where he resided for about twenty years before emigrating to Mexico to escape his debt collectors. The numerous contradictory statements made by Fernando de Medina in the course of his trial are difficult to interpret. While the Inquisitors did not hesitate to attribute his frequent sarcasm and blasphemy to intentionally feigned madness, it nevertheless seems likely that he was indeed suffering, at least temporarily, from some mental disturbance. Still, on the question of the destiny of the soul, he clearly and coherently put forth a world-view that excluded any belief in an afterlife:

He did not know whether there was a God or not.[20]

What salvation of the soul, because the soul was the spirit and when the body died, the spirit also died, [and the spirit] was what he understood to be the soul.[21]

And he believed that there was nothing more than the present and no sin greater than doing harm to another, and such a sin called for punishment in this life as there was no other and that the judges and superiors there are in the world who govern the republic must reward the good in this life.[22]

Fernando de Medina's denial of the immortality of the soul is far more radical than the partial denial made by Antonio Vaez Casteloblanco, since the former encompasses all of humanity, including those who observe the "law of Moses" as well as those who follow the "law of Jesus"; but Medina's denial also fit within a context of unbelief in the vulgar sense (*no hay mas que nacer y morir*) rather than within the framework of a more learned tradition of skepticism, to which Fernando de Medina's scanty education would scarcely have allowed him access. Other statements of his suggest a certain relativism in the matter of religious loyalty,[23] which is in keeping with his thinking based on atheistic materialism.

The Rejection of Image Worship

Let us return to the first half of the seventeenth century in Mexico. We have seen that Francisco Botello condemned Christians to hell for their idolatry. This leads us to another major theme, one of the most fundamental elements of marrano religiosity: the rejection of image worship. This refusal found expression in scorn and mockery, such as we know Blanca de Rivera and her daughter indulged in while watching Holy Week processions with statues of the saints, the Virgin, and Christ pass by their windows.[24] Did their aversion go as far as sacrilege, provoking insulting or violent gestures such as spitting upon images or subjecting them to flagellation? Such accusations frequently appear in the documents of the Inquisition, and we must consider whether they are slanderous or not. While the sincerity of certain witnesses (often household servants) is dubious in some cases where such practices are described, many indications seem to confirm that they did indeed occur (even if they were perhaps not as widespread as claimed by the denunciations).

Let us look at a few more examples. This type of insulting gesture is mentioned at the end of the preceding century, even in the entourage of Luis de Carvajal El Mozo, whose piety bordered on mystical illuminism, but who turned his back on images of the Virgin and the saints when praying in his own home:

> And so they had images of Our Lady of the Conception and of Pity and other saints in Santiago's chapel in order to keep up appearances because they revered them as idols and when they prayed, they turned their backs to them, and she saw the said Luis de Carvajal, Doña Catalina her mother, Doña Francisca her grandmother, and Doña Ysabel her aunt, spit on the images, saying, "I do not know for what reason we have these idols."[25]

In the 1630s and 1640s, Blanca de Rivera and her daughters, once again, were accused of striking a crucifix with a whip.[26] Likewise, Duarte de Leon Jaramillo and his wife Isabel Nuñez "flagellated an image of Christ and dragged it across the room."[27] Regarding this last case, one account deserves to be quoted at length: firstly, because it is an extraordinarily vivid recreation of a scene from daily life portraying children in a Mexican street; and secondly, because the plethora of lifelike details suggests that the narrative could not have been purely and simply invented by Inquisitors running short of accusations. Here, then, is the record of the account by Maria de Luna y Vilchas, who was eighteen years old in 1648. She was about eight years old when the incident, ostensibly about sweets, took place:

> She said that she knows very well that a little more than ten years ago, the said Duarte de León and his wife, Ysabel Nuñez, and their daughters, Clara Antonia and Ana, and their sons, Francisco, Simon and Jorge, the smallest, had all been condemned by the Inquisition with *San benitos* ... because they lived as

neighbours for years on Azequia Real Street, and it was common for this witness and her sisters, Francisca and Petronila, to be friendly with all of the sons and daughters of the said Duarte de León because as children they had all been raised together and she remembers that about ten or more years ago, Jorge came across this witness in the doorway of the store where her father, Juan de Vilches, held the right to sell ice, and he said to the witness, "Give me a piece of ice and I will tell you something," and the witness, standing in the doorway, said to him, "I won't give you any ice unless you tell me." So the said Jorge said that his father, Duarte de León, flagellated a Holy Christ with a barbed wire whip at night in the chamber where he slept ... and without asking any more questions, nor saying another thing to him, the witness gave Jorge the piece of ice that he had asked for.[28]

If we admit that such sacrilegious practices did take place, how are we to understand them? Why insult images, if one considers them to be no more than lifeless paintings on pieces of wood? The aggressive gesture, in the circumstances described, takes on a ritualistic quality that implies, paradoxically, that the images are thought to possess a certain power or at least that this black magic is expected to have some effect. In other words, the aggression is also a transgression, insofar as it betrays a form of adherence to the dominant beliefs, that is, Christian beliefs; but the adherence is inverted.[29] Confirming this is an observation that Juan Pacheco de León (a native of Livorno, where he was educated in the Jewish community) made when he was accused of participating in such sacrilegious rites at the home of Simon Vaez Sevilla. Although in his refutation he admits that he does not believe in Jesus Christ, he denies ever having committed blasphemy; his argument is based on a telling comparison between the Jews of his native land, Italy, and those of the Iberian territories where they were obliged to convert to Catholicism:

> And although it is true that he did not believe in Our Lord Jesus Christ and believed the images to be merely sticks and paintings, he has never blasphemed Jesus Christ Our Lord, nor the Holy Virgin, nor any of the saints in heaven, because there in his native land they only cared about teaching the old law and observing its commandments, performing the rites and ceremonies while awaiting the Messiah, but they have nothing to do with Jesus Christ Our Lord, seeing as the Jews who whip Christs and perform other crimes of that sort are those who live here as Catholics, because they are the worst, and those who go to live in those lands are the most unlawful, they are held in low esteem by other Jews.[30]

Juan Pacheco de León's remarks are of a general nature (he avoids commenting on the specific point of subjecting the image of Christ to flagellation in the home of Simon Vaez Sevilla), but his distinction between Jews who could freely profess their faith in certain European countries (*allá*, there) and those in Mexico or Spain (*acá*, here) who were obliged to conceal it, in fact corroborates the accusation: the latter Jews were the ones guilty of sacrilegious offences, and if they behaved thus, he says explicitly, it was because "they live like Catholics." Marked by their Christian education, imbued with the beliefs that surrounded them, and suffering from persecution at the hands of the Inquisition, they expressed their hatred and resentment through such gestures. Secrecy and repression led them to assert their true faith in this perverted manner, and when they were back in Jewish communities in Europe (or Muslim lands), they were treated with scorn.

Transgressive behavior directed at images can therefore be considered as one form—here superstitious or magical—among many syncretic combinations that are found in such wide variety among the New Christians. Marrano religiosity, however, is so diverse, complex, and contradictory that other forms of syncretism concerning their attitudes toward images call for some nuances and corrections. Let us once again return to Francisco Botello, who condemned all Christians to hell for their idolatry. What do we find in his home, or more precisely, in the bedroom of a member of his household, his nephew Baltazar de Burgos? Two tapestries whose images, while they do not represent Christian saints, portray none other than King David and Saint Moses. By custom, the members of Francisco Botello's family would light a candle in honor of these figures.[31] Another image of Moses, described in a passage that includes a striking detail, was recorded as being in the house of Isabel de Medina: "She had a tapestry painted with Saint Moses ... with Jewish garments and some rays on his head in the form of horns, with the tablets of the law in his hands."[32] Is it surprising that among these Judaists in Mexico the representation of Saint Moses, with horns on his forehead, is none other than a traditional image of Christian iconography?

This image of Saint Moses preserved by Isabel de Medina was supposed to assist childbirth, and it was to this image that Juana Enriquez, the wife of Simon Vaez Sevilla, addressed her prayers before the birth of her son. Let us trace her comings and goings and examine more closely the details of the rituals she engaged in at that time. Juana Enriquez did not limit herself to praying to Saint Moses in her prayers; nor is it surprising that she associated a Christian saint with a Jewish "saint." One account tells us explicitly that she also went to church—the church of San Francisco; that there she prayed to San Antonio (Saint Anthony); and that afterward, as was the custom among pregnant women in the marrano community, she performed a novena to Saint Moses.[33] This association of two "saints," one from the Old Testament and another from the New Testament—the first worshipped in secret and the second in public—represents another remarkable case of syncretic combination.

The Special Characteristics of Marrano Fasting

The theme of marrano fasting, which is among the most frequently recurring charges in the Inquisition trials, is no less complex. It is well known that fasting was one of the principal rites practiced by Judaists, who undertook it not only on the occasions of the yearly holidays of obligation, such as Yom Kippur or the commemoration of Queen Esther (to whom the marranos evinced a particularly fervent devotion), but also quite frequently in the course of ordinary weeks, up to two or three times a week, preferably on Mondays and Thursdays. (In keeping with the "Jewish custom," this involved a full twenty-four-hour fast lasting from dusk to the following dusk.) The worshipper who manifested his piety in this way might be motivated by a variety of goals: to implore forgiveness for his transgressions, to pray for the salvation of souls or the coming of the Messiah, or simply to manifest his faith in the "law of Moses." More prosaically, a fast might serve to request that a disease be cured, or that a journey or business deal meet with success. The frequency of this fasting can be explained first of all in practical terms: it was a rite that could be observed quite discreetly and was thus in keeping with the marrano style. It was easily kept secret because it could not be detected externally. Of course, those who fasted ran the risk of arousing the suspicions of the domestic servants, which is why Simon Vaez Sevilla, for example, made a show of quarrelling with his wife before fasting so it would appear to the servants that he was too angry to eat; alternatively, he would pretend to be ill.[34]

Fasting as practiced by these Judaizers was distinguished by special traits that suggest a specifically marrano religiosity. The first such trait was the state of spiritual exaltation it brought about, enabling the worshipper to leave behind the limits of the human condition and ascend to a state of quasi-mystical communication with the Divine. Thus, accounts concerning Leonor Nunez, one of the "rabbinists and dogmatists" in Mexico, the mother-in-law of Tomas Treviño de Sobremonte (himself the leader of another marrano group), described her as a "saint" whose fasts transformed her into a virtual "angel" on earth, allowing her to attain a state of "grace":

> On that day and on many other occasions when we performed the *Cro*, Tremiño said to my mother that she seemed to him like a beautiful and transparent image and his mother-in-law replied, "Son, if I were to die now, I would go straight to heaven because when I do this, it seems that I am in a state of grace."[35]

Fasting among marranos in New Spain is distinguished by yet another trait that is more paradoxical: it was devoid of any of the forms of asceticism, mortification, or vilification of the body that accompanied certain Christian practices. Quite the contrary, among marranos the experience of fasting could include a certain sensual, even erotic, exaltation. Indeed, fasting together was considered as a mark of trust or affection: the secret was shared with the family, friends, or even more significantly, with lovers. For a suitor, inviting a young woman to fast with him was a way of declaring his feelings. This was true to such an extent that, in communications among prisoners held by the Inquisition, code words for fasting (such as *cro,* or *suchil*) were used ambiguously to signify not only "fasting" but also "making love."[36] Was this fleshly dimension of the rite inspired by certain illuminist tendencies? The practice of fasting presents another of the many forms of syncretism developed by the Judaists of Mexico.

Messianisms

Frequent fasting was also viewed as a means of promoting the coming of the Messiah. This aspiration was by definition an essential component of marrano religiosity since it formed the basis for rejecting Jesus Christ and for believing that salvation was ensured only by following the "law of Moses." Yet, as paradoxical as it may seem, the messianism found among the Judaists of Mexico also embraced certain hybrid forms, to the point of being permeated at times with Christian representations or conceptions. This phenomenon is aptly illustrated by the case of Juana Enriquez, whom we have already seen praying to Saint Moses and Saint Anthony for the successful outcome of her pregnancy. It should be recalled that Doña Juana was not just any pregnant woman. She belonged to a well-known and respected family (several members of whom were condemned by the tribunals of the Inquisition in Lisbon, Seville, Cartagena, and Lima), and in the marrano communities of Mexico, there was talk of the long-awaited Messiah being born in the Americas to the Enriquez family.[37] Impelled by this fervent hope, Doña Juana directed her prayers toward the "saint" of the Old Testament and the "saint" of the church. A further detail is to be noted in the exceptional case of Doña Juana: the account specifies that special respect was due to her as the Mother of the Messiah (*Matriz*). The syncretic process is therefore not limited here to the sanctification of Moses, nor to the association of Saint Moses and Saint Anthony; it leads to a sort of analogy between Doña Juana and the Virgin Mary:

> The aforementioned Doña Juana had gone to San Francisco to pray to San Antonio, and had returned, to come and pray to Moses so that he would grant her a good childbirth and, before giving birth, she had to go nine days and pray to him, as the pregnant women usually went to visit that Moses, and she was given to sewing small shirts for the heir which was to be born and which was to be the Messiah, and they were to raise him according to their customs, and they were to respect her as the Mother of the Messiah.[38]

A similar phenomenon can be observed in a striking scene described by several witnesses. The protagonist in this scene is none other than Blanca Juarez (Blanquita), the niece of Juana Enriquez. The latter did indeed give birth to a son, Gaspar, who ultimately failed to live up to the rather unreasonable hopes that had been placed on him. According to a revelation made by an angel to the "dogmatist" grandmother Blanca Enriquez, the Messianic aspiration was transferred to one of her grandchildren, the pious Blanquita, herself the daughter of Dona Juana's sister Rafaela Enriquez. A ritual consisting of prayers and fasting was practiced, once again, in order to bring about the desired event. In Doña Rafaela's house, this time, but still under the guidance of the grandmother Doña Blanca (as with the distribution of the unleavened bread), a dozen women gathered one afternoon after having performed the ritual ablutions. They stripped the young Blanquita, purified her, clothed her in a white tunic, adorned her, and finally, by candlelight, formed a circle around her, praying and fasting until the evening that she would give birth to the Messiah. The entire ritual had an aspect of "adoration" of the young woman who was to be the Messiah's Mother:

> That when Doña Rafaela Enriquez lived opposite San Lorenzo, one afternoon she had a light lunch and party at which all of her female relatives were present but no men, and in order to celebrate, first they all bathed and cleaned themselves very well, and then they fasted at their own leisure without anyone outside knowing, and they undressed Blanca Xuarez, and cleaned and washed her well, dressing her in a very pretty white garment, and they sat her in the middle of the drawing room, all adorned, and they all prayed to ensure that the Messiah be born to this Jewess, and her grandmother, the dogmatist, said that an angel had revealed this to her.[39]

> She completely undressed her daughter Blanca and having put a white tunic on her, they placed her on an altar and worshipped her.[40]

Dona Juana Enriquez's prayers, along with the ceremony in honor of Blanquita Juarez, indicate that the coming of the Messiah was conceived as imminent. Other accounts confirm this belief: there were rumors that an astrologer had forbidden his son to become a priest, for "the law of Jesus was to last only a little while longer," and that, according to another astrologer, "a change in the law [*mudança de leyes*] was to take place before long."[41]

Likewise, among the entourage of Simon Vaez Sevilla in particular, it was announced that the observance of the "law of Jesus" was coming to an end, and that all men would henceforth obey one law only—"the ancient written law." The date of the event was even specified: it was to take place "in 1642 or 1643."[42] Why this date rather than 1648, the year that certain Jewish cabalistic traditions in Europe considered to be auspicious for the Judgment and resurrection of the dead?[43] Was the Mexican prediction linked locally to the beginning of the first wave of arrests of Judaists in New Spain? This was perhaps suggested by the idea, voiced by Antonio Vaez Casteloblanco (the brother of Simon Vaez Sevilla), that the Messianic era would be preceded by great misfortunes and that these tribulations were none other than the Holy Office's "filling the prisons" with the Judaists of Mexico: "The aforementioned Antonio Vaez Castelo-blanco said to them that the people of this land had to become like us and of one single law … and also that before this happened, the prisons of the Holy Office would be filled with people imprisoned for being observants of Moses' law."[44]

As a corollary, we note the diffusion of apocalyptic themes, in expectation of the return of Elias and Enoch, and even the knowledge of a cabalistic symbol (which recurs twenty years later in the movement of Sabbataï Tsevi):[45] when the new era begins, the witness specifies, those following the "law of Moses" will have to dress in red, the color of Judgment. These indications are supplied by Margarita de Rivera, a believer who was herself uneducated; it is noteworthy that she in turn drew her information from what she had heard in the house of the same Simon Vaez Sevilla, whose circle was by all evidence particularly active with respect to Messianic speculation:

> That this confessant had said that the law had to be one and that Elias and Enoch would come and other things of the sort, the truth of the matter is that six months before this prisoner was arrested, while she was in the drawing room of Simon Vaez Sevilla's house one night with Doña Juana Enriquez and Simon Vaez Sevilla, her husband, and Gaspar Vaez, their son, Juan Mendes Villaviciossa entered … and Juan Mendes responded that he was glad … that there should be rejoicing, the law which was observed had to become one single law and be the law of Moses, which was the good one, and that those who observed it then had to dress in red, which pleased all of them very much.[46]

The problems of Messianic chronology lead us to wonder, in parallel, about a possible connection with the great political event of 1640: the restoration of Portuguese independence. Such a line was present in the minds of the Inquisitors, since their aim was to repress the "Great Conspiracy." It seems unlikely that the New Christians of Mexico would have been involved in any conspiracy against the Spanish crown, but it is true that they were connected with a vast international network and that they maintained business relations with the enemies of Spain. Further still, numerous accounts attest to their loyalty toward the Lusitanian crown, and it is therefore not surprising that they also participated in another major Messianic movement, a specifically Portuguese one known as Sebastianism. This involvement is confirmed by certain commentaries on the political events of their home country in which one encounters not only the old medieval idea of the decline and fall of Spain, but also the notion (proper to Sebastianism) of the glorious destiny of the king of Portugal who was to be called upon to reign over the whole world until the end of time. It is advisable to distinguish between Portuguese and Jewish messianism, but a certain interconnection or "interference" between the two perspectives can be clearly discerned among the Judaists in Mexico. Such interferences can be found, for example, in the conversations between Maria de Campos and Francisco de

Léon, which clearly associate the restoration of the Lusitanian kingdom with the redemption of the Jewish people, or at least the beginning of their redemption, since the king of Portugal would then, they hoped, protect them from persecution by the Inquisition, deliver them from their present captivity, and even avenge them.

> And that Spain was coming to an end, and was very wretched and that it would never hold up its head again, and Maria said to him, "This news makes me very happy, and tell me, how are Portugal and our kind faring?" And the man replied, "Very vigorous and much fortified, with many people and he will be the one who will rule until the end of time," and Maria said to him, "God save our King and Lord and keep him many years in his kingdom, and not that King of Spain who is without a rightful title, possessing that which was not his, each should enjoy that which corresponds to him, and be it that Ours is forever and becomes the ruler of all, and wins this and destroys this house, and that we all see ourselves freed from the power of these wicked people, and that our injuries be avenged, and that we be taken out of this captivity.[47]

Other commentaries, in analogous fashion, explicitly connect the "change of law," the Lusitanian restoration, and the suppression of the Inquisition, which had supposedly come to an end in Portugal (as in Granada as well).[48] It is probably not a question of syncretism strictly speaking, but if Jewish messianism and Portuguese messianism did not fully merge, they did give rise to hybrid forms by mixing at least partially, overlapping and intertwining in such a way as to give marrano religiosity some of its specific traits.

* * * *

I HAVE PLACED PARTICULAR EMPHASIS on the syncretic aspects of marranism in order to show one of its essential characteristics, which distinguishes it from crypto-Judaism per se. Of course, marrano religiosity, in its diversity and complexity, cannot simply be reduced to these intersections or interpretations: it encompasses all the possible cases, including that of authentic Judaism, but also attitudes of doubt and hesitation, and finally the processes of separation from both the "law of Moses" and the "law of Jesus." This last aspect, which is also specific to marranism, is what I would like to emphasize in my conclusion, for it too results from the tension between two religions: the vacillations and variations, the dual sincerities, are a way of reckoning with polemical arguments that stand in opposition to each other, such that their reciprocal neutralization may lead, if not necessarily to disbelief and to skepticism, at least to a certain religious relativism. Along these lines, it can be argued that the New Christians contributed considerably to the emergence of modernity in the Western Hemisphere, not only in the economic arena, but also in that of religious and intellectual history.

Let us consider once again the case of Francisco Botello, who died at the stake in 1659 and whom the chronicler of the auto-da-fé described as "the most hardened Jew of all those who were punished by the Holy Office over the centuries."[49] When he wished to affirm his adherence to the "law of Moses," he did so using aphorisms that do not refer exclusively to belief in the God of Israel: "let each man be what he is; whomever I follow, I follow; whomever I belong to, I belong to";[50] or again: "let each man keep what comes to him";[51] "whatever one is, one must die as one is."[52] The identity thus claimed is received by birth, and it includes a collective dimension: the individual is defined in relation to the group into which he is born, to which he is bound in solidarity, and from which he receives a heritage that must be "preserved and honored."[53] Now this conception of identity applies to all human groups: taken generally, it legitimates all faiths (Jewish faith for Jews, Christianity for Christians) so that ultimately all religions are equal. In fact, at the very moment when Francisco Botello was expressing regret that his Old Christian wife, Maria de Zarate, observed another law, he praised her with this surprising statement: "and if everything that she did in her law, she did in our own, she would be a saint and would be canonized."[54] This husband and wife most likely had occasion to discuss their respective beliefs, and they seem to have agreed upon a sort of parallelism: let each one follow the law of the community to which he or she belonged. Indeed, Maria de Zarate (not only an Old Christian, but born to a family that took pride in being related to Juan Martinez Siliceo, the famous Archbishop of Toledo) gave voice to a sentiment in tune with the one her husband had expressed: "Let each one follow the law he chooses … God the Father is not angry with those who serve God the Son, nor is God the Son angry with those who serve God the Father."[55] In the case of Maria de Zarate, the idea of reciprocal tolerance goes so far as to include a defense of "free choice" in religious matters.[56]

This relativism took a more radical form forty years later when Fernando de Medina voiced his belief that "men can find their salvation in all laws and all sects,"[57] even as he drifted into a materialism that was at least agnostic. The term "salvation" is not to be understood here in its religious meaning, since, as we have seen, the author of these universalist views does not believe in the immortality of the soul: it is the futility of being concerned with one's destiny in an afterlife that makes all religions equal in his view, and that means justice can only be immanent, thanks to instituted laws. But while ritual practices and the properly religious content of Judaism were blurred, Fernando de Medina's sense of identity was accompanied by an even more vital idea of "nation," which was thereby secularized, rooted in collective memory, implying only moral obligations: loyalty to ancestors, solidarity with members of the marrano diaspora, and reverence for the "natural name that was given us at birth,"[58] that is, the Jewish name conferred by a history conceived as nature. When belief in God disappears, religious faith becomes faith in memory.

Notes

Translated from the French by Jennifer Curtiss Gage. Spanish quotations translated by Carrie Chorba.

1. The term "marrano" has therefore a much wider connotation than crypto-Judaism in the strict sense of the word.
2. I focus my attention on the New Christians of New Spain in the first half of the seventeenth century mainly because the series of Inquisition trials in the Mexican archives (especially those produced by the repression of the "Great Conspiracy") are extraordinarily rich in evidence. From time to time, however, to supplement the picture, I shall stray outside this main period and geographic area (cf. below, the example of Manuel Bautista Perez in Peru).
3. It is true that when the accused alluded to their hesitation regarding the two "laws," this was on many occasions part of their defense strategy. Nevertheless, the terms they use and the context entitle us to give credence to their statements. For example, in the Archivo General de la Nación de México (hereafter AGN), *Inquisición*, Trial of Antonio de Caravallo, vol. 406, fol. 272r: "aunque conocía que la ley de Moysen era contraria a la de nuestro Señor Jesu Christo nunca la ha dejado sino que sin distincion las guardaba entrambos." Similarly, further on, fol. 276r: "a seguido la ley de Moysen y la de nro Señor Jesu Christo teniendolas emtrambas por buenas para la saluación de su alma." And again, the statement of Isabel Tinoco (aged 16), vol. 395, fol. 237r: "pero que ni en ella [la ley de Moysen] ni en la de nro Señor Jesu Christo hauía estado firmamente asentada, porque le faltaba la razon y el discurso, viviendo entre dos aguas."
4. AGN, *Inquisición*, Trial of Ruy Diaz Nieto, vol. 157, exp. 1 (unpaginated): "y un dia en presencia de las dhas doña Mariana y doña Anna estando la dha doña Mariana loca riño mucho el dho Antonio Diaz a la dha doña Catalina porque hacia ayunar a esta los dias grandes del Señor y mando a esta que se vistiesse diziendole levantate mala hembra de mala casta que no volveras más a esta cassa y a esta la vistió Ysabelica china ya difunta y se fue con el dho su padre ya a la esquina de la calle dixo esta al dho Antonio Diaz Señor padre a donde me lleva V. Md para que yo ande llorando en cassas ajenas y el dho Antonio Diaz le respondió calla buena pieça de mala casta que a cassa de Machado te llevo sin sauer esta quien fuesse el dho y esta lloró y al dho Antonio Diaz se le saltaron las lagrimas quando oyó a esta que dixo que para que la llevaba para que anduuiesse, llorando en cassas ajenas y la volvió a cassa de la dha su madre diciendole anda mala casta agradesçe a Dios lo que me aveis dho que por eso os lleuo con aquella mala hembra y dexando a esta en la puerta se fue a sus negoçios el dho Antonio Diaz su padre de esta."
5. AGN, *Inquisición*, Trial of Antonio Fernandez Cardado, vol. 378, exp. 1, fol. 176r: "Los dhos Talaveras sus primos comunicaron a este confesante de que la ley de Jesu Christo no era la buena y que no avía más que un dios a quien se avía de adorar, y que el mesias no avía venido, ni Jesus Cristo lo era, aunque dixeron que auía espiritu santo, el qual hablabla por boca de los profetas y patriarchas de la ley antigua."
6. Ibid., fol. 305v: "Rogamos a ti mismo que ayas misericordia de nos y de las animas de nuestros difuntos parientes y amigos, y plegate Señor de las sacar de las penas en que estan y llevarlas a tu Santo Reyno Amen Jesus."
7. Ibid., fol. 180v: "y que esta oración como la a referido la decía los más dias asta que tuuo noticia y le enseñaron la ley de Moysen y la creyó que despues aunque la dezía quitaba la palabra (Amen Jesus) porque le parescía que en toto lo demas hablaba con el Señor y su yntención era de hablar con el como observante de la ley de Moysen y aunque algunas vezes pronunciaua el Amen Jesus como la auía aprendido su yntención no era sino dezirlo como los observantes de la dicha ley de Moysen." Similarly, fols. 305r–305v.
8. AGN, *Inquisición*, Trial of Micaela Enriquez, vol. 397, fol. 266v: "y hiço el pan cenceno que era unas torticas de arina … Dandole un pedaçito de una de ellas no consintiendo

que la dha Micaela Enriquez la tomase en la mano sino que la misma dha su madre se la daba en la boca como cuando comulgan los cristianos diciendole çiertas palabras en remedio de la comunión de la santa iglesia catolica, que dan los sacerdotes de ella." Cf. also the trial of Rafaela Enriquez, vol. 402, fol. 128v (testimony of Pedro Tinoco): "un bocado de aquel pan ... y la dha su abuela se lo dió a este confesante con su propia mano poniendoselo en la boca como quando se da la comunion a los cristianos."

9. The bulk of the Inquisitorial archives of the Lima tribunal have unfortunately disappeared, but by good luck the proceedings of the trial of Manuel Bautista Perez were sent to the Supreme Council in Madrid. They are catalogued in the Archivo Histórico Nacional (hereafter AHN) in bundle 1647, n°13. The document, 457 folios in length, is almost complete.

10. Cf. Frederick Bowser, *The African Slave in Colonial Peru, 1524–1650* (Stanford, 1974), 61ff, and tables and graphs in Appendix B, 342–45.

11. Cf. Gonçalo de Reparaz, *Os Portugueses no Vice-Reinado do Peru (Seculos XVI y XVII)* (Lisbon, 1976), 105–9. Pedro Guibovich Perez has analyzed the library of Manuel Bautista Perez in "La cultura libresca de un converso procesado por la Inquisición de Lima," *Historia y Cultura. Revista del Museo Nacional de Historia* (Lima, 1990), 133–60.

12. Ibid.

13. AHN, *Inquisición*, leg. 1647, n°13, fol. 104.

14. Ibid., n°16, for instance, fol. 60v: "que nunca comían el quarto trasero de ningun genero de carne ... la carne que comian la echavan a desangrar el día antes."

15. Ibid., n°13, fols. 197r–197v, testimony of Amaro Dionis: "todo quanto savían de la ley de Moysen era por mayor porque las ceremonias de los judíos aca no se sauían porque nuna avía visto persona que supiere más que ayunar martes y viernes."

16. Cf. Jacques Le Goff, *La Naissance du purgatoire* (Paris, 1981).

17. AGN, *Inquisión*, Trial of Francisco Botello, vol. 457, fols. 525r–526v: "y afirmaba el dho francisco botello que no avía purgatorio porque los que morían iban a un campo que entiende se llama campo eliseo y que alli estaban hasta que viniese el mesias para ir al cielo; y quando oía decir de alguno que avía muerto y que confiaba en dios que estava en el çielo se reía el dho francisco botello porque decía que no avía llegado el tiempo de abrirse las puertas del çielo; y que asi no podían yr al çielo aunque no fuesen christianos porque todos los christianos se yban al infierno por ser ydolattras en adorar las imagenes de Jesu Christo y de los sanctos echas de palo."

18. AGN, *Inquisición*, Trial of Margarita de Rivera, vol. 408, exp. 1, fol. 342v: "es cosa constante entre los observantes que las almas de los difuntos que lo son estan año y día padeciendo penas que Dios nuestro Señor se sirbe de darlas ... y que assi los ayunos que dejan mandados se hagan por sus almas precisamente se an de hacer antes del año y día porque aprovechen a salir de aquellas penas, y que despues del año y día no sirben."

19. AGN, *Inquisición*, Trial of Antonio Vaez Casteloblanco, vol. 413, fols. 131v–132r: "y que dixo a este confesante tratando de las cosas de la ley de Moysen ... que ninguno de los que guardavan se condenaba ni tampoco los christianos porque no havía ynfierno y que los christianos eran como las bestias sin entendimiento."

20. AGN, *Inquisición*, Trial of Fernando de Medina, vol. 681, fol. 106r: "no savía si havía Dios o no."

21. Ibid., fol. 106v: "que saluación de anima, porque la alma era espiritu y muriendo el cuerpo se acauaua y moría el espiritu que era lo que el entendía por alma."

22. Ibid., fol. 106bis r: "y que entendía que no hauía más que el presente ni mas pecado que hazer daño al proximo el cual pecado se hauía de castigar en esta vida pues no auía otra y premiar en ella al bueno los jueces y superiores que ay en el mundo y gobiernan la republica."

23. AGN, *Inquisición*, Trial of Fernando de Medina, vol. 704, fol. 336r, fol. 367v.

24. AGN, *Inquisición*, Trial of Margarita de Rivera, vol. 394, exp. 2, fols. 370r–370v.

25. AGN, *Inquisición*, Trial of Ruy Diaz Nieto, vol. 157, exp. 1 (unpaginated): "y si tenían ymagenes de Nuestra Señora de la Concepción y de la Piedad y de otros santos en la sala de Santiago por cumplimiento porque los tenían por idolos y quando rezaban los

bolvían las espaldas y vío esta a los dhos Luis de Carvajal doña Catalina su madre de esta doña francisca su abuela doña ysabel su tía escupir a la dhas ymagenes diziendo no se para que tenemos estos idolos."

26. AGN, *Inquisición*, Trial of Margarita de Rivera, vol. 394, exp. 2, fols. 285r–286v, 451r–452v.
27. AGN, *Inquisición*, Trial of Isabel Nuñez, vol. 401, exp. 1, fol. 17v.
28. AGN, *Inquisición*, Trial of Jorge Duarte, vol. 431, exp. 4, fols. 106r–106v: "dixo que conoce muy bien abra mas de diez años a los dhos Duarte de León e Ysabel Nuñez su mujer y a sus hijas Clara Antonia y Ana y a sus hijos Francisco y Simon que todos han salido penitenciados con san benito y a Jorge que es el más pequeño ... porque vivían pared años en la calle de la Azequia Real y de ordinario esta declarante y sus hermanas Francisca y Patronila tenían amistad con todos los dhos hijos y hijas del dho Duarte de León como muchachos que e criaban juntos y se acuerda que abra diez años dhos poco más o menos que el dho Jorge alló a esta declarante en la puerta de la calle de la tienda donde su padre Juan de Vilches vende la nieve por tener el estanco della y la dixo estando parada a la puerta y solos dame un pedacito de nieve y te diré una cossa y esta declarante le dixo no te e de dar la nieve hasta que me lo digas y entonces le dixo el dho Jorge que el dho su padre Duarte de León açotaba a un Santo Christo de noche en el aposento donde dormía con una disciplina de alambres ... y sin preguntarle más esta declarante ni decirle otra cossa el dho Jorge le dio el pedaçito de nieve que le havía pedido."
29. Cf. Solange Alberro, *Inquisition et société au Mexique (1571–1700)* (Mexico, 1988), 213.
30. AGN, *Inquisición*, Trial of Juan Pacheco de León, vol. 400, exp. 2, fols. 705r–705v: "y aunque es verdad que no creía en nuestro Señor Jesu Christo y tenía a las imagenes por palos y pinturas, nunca ha blasfemado de Jesu Christo nuestro Señor, ni de la Virgen Santíssima, ni de los santos del cielo, porque alla en su tierra solo cuidan de enseñar la ley vieja y en guardar sus preceptos haciendo sus ritos y ceremonias esperando el Mesias, pero no se meten con Jesu Christo nuestro Señor, que los judíos que azotan Cristos y hazen otros delitos de esta calidad serían aca y viven como catolicos, porque son los peores, y en yendo a vivir en esas tierras son los mas desaforados y los tienen los otros judíos por gente de poca importancia." This trial has been published by Boleslao Lewin in *Singular Proceso de Salomon Machorro (Juan de León), Israelita Liornes condenado por la Inquisición (México, 1650)* (Buenos Aires, 1977). For the passage quoted, cf. also, Solange Alberro, *Inquisition*, 213.
31. AGN, *Inquisición*, Trial of Francisco Botello, vol. 403, exp. 1, fols. 262r–263r.
32. AGN, *Inquisición*, Trial of Pedro de Espinoza, vol. 403, exp. 1, fols. 159v–160r: "tenía en un guardamesi pintado al Sancto Moysen ... con vestiduras judaïcas y unos rayos a manera de cuernos en la cabeça con las tablas de la ley en las manos."
33. AGN, *Inquisición*, Trial of Juana Enriquez, vol. 400, exp. 1, fols. 88r–88v.
34. AGN, *Inquisición*, vol. 398, exp; 1, Trial of Simon Vaez Sevilla: "y que el dho Simon Vaez era judío tan cauteloso y recatado que cuando en compania de su mujer Juana Enriquez había de hacer los ayunos de la ley de Moysen ... fingían alguna riña, o enojo, con que se retiraba a su escritorio el dho Simon Vaez para que los criados atribuyesen el no comer a los enojos fingidos siendo verdaderos ayunos."
35. AGN, *Inquisición*, "Diez cuardernos de comunicaciones de carceles," vol. 423, exp. 3, fol. 130r: "aquel día y en otras muchas ocaciones quando hacíamos el *Cro* le decía Tremiño a mi madre que le parecía una imagen linda y trasparente y lo que su suegra le respondió fue hijo si agora me muriera me iba derecho al Cielo porque quando hago esto me parece que estoy en la gloria."
36. The ambiguity of the term *Cro* is suggested in numerous instances. Here are a few examples taken from the accounts of Leonor Vaez in AGN, *Inquisición*, "Diez cuadernos de comunicaciones de carceles," vol. 423, exp. 3. Regarding the love affair between her sister Maria Gomez and Melchor Rodriquez Lopez: "tambien en mi cassa se vieron muchas veçes y se goçaron Melchor Rodriguez y mi hermana Maria y alli hiçimos el *Cro* dos o tres veçes y todos los días me vía y me socorría con lo que podía y yo le decía oy es buen día," fol. 187r. And again, on the same subject: "que Melchor Rodriguez una

vez que el supo que tremiño auía ydo a la tierra adentro fue a mi cassa y me dixo por vida tuia que me has de hacer un favor ... y que el dho Melchor Rodriguez le dixo que le ruegues a tu hermana Maria supuesto que no esta aqui su marido que se vaya a mi cassa y tu con ella por ocho o quince dias ... y que fueron en casa de Melchor Rodriguez y que estuvieron alla muchos días y que las regaló mucho y que hicieron el *Cro* más de doçe veces y que todas la veces que hacían el *Cro* se bañauan y limpiauan y ponían ropa limpia de Melchor Rodriguez porque no inbiaramos por ropa y lo hiçimos como se debe haçer y mi madre y yo y Maria y Melchor Rodriguez y un amigo suyo de España llamado Sebastian Riveros muy a puerta cerrada y nos regaló mucho y nos holgamos de todas maneras porque de día hacíamos el *Cro* y de noche dormía Maria con Melchor Rodriguez y yo con el Sebastian Riveros que era muy lindo moço y no emos tenido mejores dias," fols. 244r–244v. The term *Cro* can be said to have a narrow sense (fasting exclusively) and a broader sense, as another episode involving Isabel de Caravallo and Pedro de Guevara shows: "y que guebara enamoró a la coxa mujer de caravallo y que ella le dixo a guevara que se dexase deso que estaba muy bien ocupada con amigo suyo ero si quería amistad con ella y con su marido o padre y madre para declararse con ellos par hacer el *Cro* que eso si, que tendría entrada en su cassa el y su compañero Amesquita y todo regalo para el *Cro* y no para otra cosa," fol. 192r. Pedro de Guevara appears to be just as unsuccessful with the narrator Leonor: "y luego gueuara enamoró a mi y le dixe que no se cansase que yo era muger honrrada que en cuanto el *Cro* cuanto el quisiera y lo hiçe muchas veçes con el," fol. 192r.

37. This belief peculiar to Judaizers in New Spain was not confined to the Enriquez family alone (i.e., the entourage of Simon Vaez Sevilla); it was also widespread in many other circles. It has, for instance, been detected in the "dogmatist" Leonor Nuñez (mother-in-law to the famous Tomas Treviño de Sobremonte); cf. AGN, *Inquisición*, Trial of Leonor Nuñez, vol. 379, fol. 233r: "que Duarte de León, Isabel la de Luis Perez y Leonor su madre se enserraban en el almaçen del dho Duarte de León. Y que la dha Leonor Nuñez dixo a uno de los hijos, que nombró, del dho Duarte de León, que estaban esperando su Messias que hauía de nacer de uno de ellos."

38. AGN, *Inquisición*, Trial of Juana Enriquez, vol. 400, exp. 1, fols. 88r–88v: "la dicha dona Juana, que avía ido a San Francisco a reçar a San Antonio, y que de vuelta avía de venir a reçar a Moysen para que la diese buen parto, y que antes de parir avía de yr nueve dias, que suelen andar las preñadas a visitar al dicho Moysen, y reçarle, y que le avía dado a coser unas camisitas para el heredero que avía de nacer que era el Mesias, y lo avían de criar a su usança, y que a la dha persona le avían de respetar como a Matriz."

39. AGN, *Inquisición*, Trial of Blanca Juarez, vol. 487, fol. 437r: "que quando doña Rafaela Enriquez vivía frontero de San Lorenzo hauía hecho una tarde una merienda y fiesta en que se hauían hallado todas la mugeres de su parentela sin níngun hombre y que para celebrar la dha fiesta se hauían bañado primero todas y se hauían limpiado muy bien, y luego ayunaron muy a su gusto sin que lo supiera nadie de fuera, y que a la dha Blanca Xuarez la desnudaron, y pusieron muy limpia y muy aseada y la vistieron una bestimenta blanca muy linda, y la sentaron en medio del estrado muy adereçada y se pusieron todas en oración asegurando que desta judía havia de nacer el Mesias, y en especial la dogmatisadora de su abuela que decía que se lo avía revelado el angel."

40. AGN, *Inquisición*, Trial of Rafaela Enriquez, vol. 402, fol. 270r: "que ella desnudada en carnes a su hija Blanca y poniendola una tunica blanca puesta en un altar la adoraban."

41. AGN, *Inquisición*, Trial of Pedro de Espinoza, vol. 403, fol. 73r (statement of Violante Juarez dated 27 November 1642: "Y que un mes antes que la prendieron oío decir a Manuel de Mella su marido que hablando con Pedro de Espinoza que hauía llegado a aquella ciudad ... que un astrologo desta çiudad no hauía querido que un hijo suyo se ordenase porque hauía de durar poco la ley de Jesu Christo y que un veçino desta çiudad llamado fulano de la Calua ... le hauía dicho al dho Manuel de Mella que otro astrologo tenía un repertorio ... en el qual preuiene que muy en breue a de tener mudança de leyes."

42. AGN, *Inquisición*, Trial of Margarita de Rivera, vol. 394, fol. 373r: "y que se esperaua el Messias prometido en la ley, y que su venida auía de ser por el año passado de mil seiscientos y quarenta y dos, o quarenta y tres, con que se acabaría la ley de nro Señor Jesu Christo y sería una sola ley antigua escrita."

43. Cf. Gershom Sholem, *Sabbataï Tsevi. Le Messie mystique, 1626–1676* (Paris, 1983), 99ff.

44. AGN, *Inquisición*, Trial of Antonio Vaez Casteloblanco, vol. 489, fol. 314r: "el dicho Antonio Vaez Casteloblanco les dezía que toda la gente de esta tierra había de venir a ser como nosotros y de una ley … y que asimismo dixo que primero que esto se cumpliese se hauían de llenar las carceles deste Santo Oficio de gente pressa por observantes de la dha ley de Moysen." Cf. also the Trial of Margarita de Rivera, vol. 394, fol. 415r.

45. Cf. Sholem, *Sabbataï Tsevi*, 599–600.

46. AGN, *Inquisición*, Trial of Margarita de Rivera, vol. 408, fols. 316r–316v: "que esta confesante auía dicho que la ley auía de ser una y que auía de venir elias y enoch y otras cossas de esta traza, y la verdad de esto es que seis messes antes que esta rea fuese pressa, estando en casa de Simon Vaez Sevilla una noche en la sala del estrado juntamente con doña Juana Enriquez y el dho Simon Vaez Sevilla su marido y Gaspar Vaez si hijo, aserttó a entrar Juan Mendes Villaviciossa … y el dho Juan Mendes respondió que se holgaba … para el rregusijo que havían de tener pues la ley que se guardaba havía de ser presto toda una y la de moysen que era la buena y se havían de vestir entonces todos de colorado los que la guardauan de lo qual se alegraron todos mucho."

47. AGN, *Inquisición* (Riva Palacio), Trial of Maria de Campos, vol. 23, exp. 2, fols. 2r–2v: "que España se iba acabando y estaba muy desdichada y que no alzaría cabesa en su vida, y Maria le dijo mucho me huelgo con esa buena nueba y dime Portugal y nuestro Rey en que alturas se hallan? Y el hombre le respondió, muy pujante, y muy fortaleçido y con mucha gente y sera Rey de acqui a que se acabe el mundo y Maria le dixo Dios aiude a nro Rey y Señor, y lo conserve muchos años en su Reino, y no que estaba el de España con mal titulo poseiendo lo que no era suyo, cada uno goze lo que le toque, y el Nuestro sera para siempre y venga a ser Rey de todo, y gane esto y asuele esta cassa, y nos veamos todos libres y fuera del poder de esta mal gente, y vengue nuestros agravios y nos saque de este captiverio."

48. AGN, *Inquisición*, Trial of Pedro de Espinoza, vol. 403, fol. 73r (testimony of Violante Juarez): "y de lo demas que les oió en aquella ocasion çerca de que ya no hauía Inquisición en Portugal y Granada."

49. Cf. Jose Toribio Medina, *Historia del Tribunal del Santo Oficio de la Inquisición en México* [1905] (Mexico, 1987), 309: "Francisco Botello el más endurecido judío de cuantos en muchos siglos se habran visto castigados por el Santo Oficio, sin ser posible con el que nombrase a Jesus ni a la Virgen Santíssima su madre, se dejo abrasar vivo."

50. AGN, *Inquisición*, Trial of Francisco Botello, vol. 457. These statements are taken from the "confidences" exchanged between Francisco Botello and Juan Pacheco de Léon while in prison. These "confidences" have been published by Boleslao Lewin, *Confidencias de dos cripto-judios en las carceles del Santo Oficio (México, 1645–1646)* (Buenos Aires, 1975). Cf. here, page 65: "eso si, estar cada uno lo que es y con quien vengo, vengo; y cuyo soy, soy"; similarly, page 121: "eso si es lo que importa, y con quien vengo, vengo, y cuyo soy, soy."

51. Ibid., 139: "hacía muy bien como bueno y como quien es, guarde cada uno aquello que le toca me parece muy bien."

52. Ibid., 150: "ya que lo son mueren como son."

53. Ibid.: "cada uno se precie de quien es y de lo que guarda."

54. Ibid., 174: "que estaba con una mujer muy caritaiva y limosnera, que hacía todo el bien que podía, y muy observante de su ley de ella (que es la de los cristianos) … y si lo que ella hace de su ley lo hiciera de la nuestra fuera una santa y estuviera canonizada."

55. AGN, *Inquisición*, Trial of Maria de Zarate, vol. 1500. The trial has been published by Boleslao Lewin as *La Inquisición en México. Racismo inquisitorial (El singular caso de Maria de Zarate)* (Puebla, 1971). Cf. page 61: "y que no se enojaba Dios padre que sirviesen los hombres a Dios hijo, ni tampoco se enojaba Dios hijo de que sirviesen al Padre."

56. Ibid., 61: "que Dios no quería que se forzase el libre albedrio del hombre sino que siguiese la ley que quisiese." To Francisco Botello's aphorism cited earlier, we can add the following remark: "[los cristianos] adoran sus cosas como nosotros las nuestras" (Lewin, *Confidencias de dos criptojudios*, 95).

57. AGN, *Inquisición*, Trial of Fernando de Medina, vol. 704, fol. 367v: "dijo que en todas leyes y sectas se podían salvar los hombres."

58. AGN, *Inquisición*, Trial of Fernando de Medina, vol. 681, fol. 108v: "que es ley que entre nos esta que la llamamos de unome [sic], el señalado de nuestras antiguedades y del tiempo presente por mantenedor de la casa con nombre natural de nacimiento, el qual se hace mención diaramente y se venera sobre todos los demas."

– *Chapter 8* –

CRYPTO-JEWS AND THE MEXICAN HOLY OFFICE IN THE SEVENTEENTH CENTURY

⊘Ӿ⊚

Solange Alberro

Antecedents and the Original Alternative

A LTHOUGH *CONVERSOS* secretly practicing Judaism began arriving at the very beginning of the conquest and colonization of what would soon be called New Spain, their presence—if not massive, at least established—was not registered until the 1580s. The union of the Castilian and Portuguese crowns between 1580 and 1640 made the passage to America possible for families that, after the expulsion from Spain decreed by the Catholic monarchs in January 1492, had taken refuge in Portugal, a kingdom initially more tolerant toward Jews. From 1496 onward, however, a repression even more severe than that which had preceded and accompanied their expulsion from Spain was unleashed upon the *conversos* of Portugal. Families that were able to fled once again. They sought refuge in some of the cities of southwestern France, in England, in the Low Countries, in some German ports, and, not long after, in the cities of northern Italy, not to mention in countries of the Middle East and of the Maghreb. Nonetheless, many stayed in Portugal, learning to live through and survive clandestine situations made extremely difficult by the Portuguese Holy Office, which acted against them with relentless harshness. These were the families and individuals who took advantage of the politically favorable conditions afforded by the union of the two crowns in 1580 to return to Castile, from where their ancestors had fled a century before.

Many headed for Seville, where they frequently re-encountered close and distant relatives and acquaintances, and where some had also lived for varying amounts of time. Although some chose to settle in the great

Andalusian port (which, because of its intense and monopolistic trans-oceanic relations, afforded many commercial and artisanal opportunities to the newly arrived), others awaited the possibility of emigrating to America. Despite their generally Castilian origins, in Seville they were considered "Portuguese" for having lived for a century in the Lusitanian kingdom, whose language they had adopted. For these *conversos*, New Spain, with its economic boom, was one of the most attractive destinations.

It is well known that in the fateful winter of 1492, a pressing dilemma was imposed upon the Jews of Castile: receive baptism or go into perma-nent exile from the land where, for centuries, they had lived and often prospered. Tens of thousands, placing loyalty to their religion above all other considerations, accepted the second alternative. But why did oth-ers, perhaps in as great a number as the first, decide to stay in Spain? Of those who stayed, an undetermined number—perhaps in despair from the persecutions suffered because of their Jewish faith in the previous century—accepted baptism and became New Christians, hoping to escape persecution and discrimination forever by assimilating defini-tively into the Christian majority. This assimilation would never be com-plete, since for generations thereafter the stigma, the suspicions, and the restrictions on holding office or receiving distinctions would weigh on *converso* descendants. Alternatively, others, in numbers also impossible to estimate, received baptism simply as a strategy for continuing to practice Judaism clandestinely. These individuals—since we cannot speak here of whole families—are the ones that make us ask: How could they believe that they could escape popular and inquisitorial vigilance—which we will soon see was one and the same—so as to continue practicing with impunity the necessary Jewish rites? How could they hope to preserve their ancestral religion without the help of rabbinical authorities and the traditional formative experiences?

Such crypto-Judaism and the questions it raises appeared in Portugal a few years later when relentless repression was waged on overt Judaism, and again in the last decades of the sixteenth century when whole families and isolated individuals opted to cross the ocean and try their luck in Peru or New Spain. In effect, the Jews who remained practicing Jews despite their baptism—first in Castile, then in Portugal, and finally in New Spain and all of the Spanish Empire—knew well that they would always be sub-ject to Inquisitorial persecution. This persecution was especially fearsome because they would then be dealt with as *relapsos*. Why not choose, in 1492, in 1496, or at the end of the seventeenth century, to relocate to a country or city where the possibility existed of openly being Jewish?

America: Reasons for the Choice

To answer this question, it is necessary first to look at a cultural consid-eration never explicitly mentioned by the people concerned—since they would not have been conscious of it—but that permeated their way of living and being. Our *conversos* were Mediterranean; more specifically, they were Iberian, since the adjective "Spanish" still lacked meaning at that time. They were accustomed to a way of life and of conviviality that included habits of all kinds: social, familial, and personal, including such matters as love relations, taste in clothing and jewelry, celebrations, types of cooking, values such as "honor," and more generally, we may surmise, extroverted behavior characterized by informality and warmth. Although they never specifically mentioned this, it is probable that these crypto-Jews preferred to preserve what we today call their culture—their Spanish and/or Portuguese culture, the drinking of wine and the singing of verses of Lope de Vega accompanied by a guitar—to greater security in a different environment. It was always the case that one of the twenty-some tribunals of the Holy Office was stalking the crypto-Jews of the kingdoms that depended upon the Castilian and Portuguese crowns.[1] These Jews were, nonetheless, in their natural and traditional medium where they were more likely to recognize the threats, delude the authorities, and even beat the dangers that they had learned to evade since at least the fourteenth century.

At the end of the sixteenth century, there were compelling incentives for those who embarked in greater numbers in Seville for the remote American possessions. A major inducement for any Iberian was the possibility of becoming rich. The entire American continent has always inspired—up to the present—great dreams among immigrants of all classes and origins, who hope to try their luck and remake their lives. New Spain at the end of the sixteenth century, with its Asian dependency of the Philippine Islands, and Peru in the mid-seventeenth century, with its silver mines, captured the expectations and imaginations of thousands of Iberian migrants—among whom were more than a few secret Jews— who, one way or another, set out toward the sea.

New Spain, with its booming mining industry and noteworthy expansion toward the north and to the Philippines, was especially attractive. First, it offered many readily available commercial opportunities. The capital of the viceroyalty, the big cities like Puebla, and the mining camps (especially the ones in the north) held a population that was thirsty for luxury goods and possessed the means to acquire them. Also, it was tempting, though risky, to look for pearls in the Rio de la Hacha— on the north coast of present-day Colombia—and for the emeralds of New Granada, or to acquire the most precious stones, cloths, and commodities from Europe and Asia to sell for great profit in New Spain.

The inventories of the great *converso* merchants who lived in New Spain in the mid-seventeenth century reveal the extensive commercial activities they were engaged in. To this mercantile business must be added the flourishing but horrible trade in Africans—a commerce to which some of the most prominent members of the Portuguese-Castilian *converso* population established in the viceroyalty were dedicated. Those who looked for a fortune on American soil that was as quickly made as it was great pretended, or perhaps actually believed, that after achieving it, they would live in countries where they could openly practice the religion of their ancestors. This dream was seldom realized, for as these *conversos* became wealthy, either they continued increasing their estates, following human nature, or they felt so rooted in New Spain that they no longer desired to leave. When the persecutions associated with the so-called "Great Complicity" or "Great Plot" were unleashed in the years from 1642 to 1649, there were at least a dozen prosperous Jewish merchants and traders who could easily have left the viceroyalty and their Iberian possessions to live comfortably in countries where they would not have been disturbed for being Jews.[2]

On the other hand, American kingdoms like Peru, New Granada, and New Spain, although subject to tribunals of the Holy Office, offered singularly more favorable environments than the metropolis for the clandestine practice of Judaism. In America, Inquisitorial districts were thinly administered because of their size, their geographic diversity, and the weakness of institutional networks in general. The Mexican Holy Office's district stretched from New Mexico to Nicaragua, and included even the remote Philippine Islands. The tribunal itself was composed of three Inquisitors who never left the capital, unlike their metropolitan counterparts who were obligated to periodically visit their districts. Thus, Jews established in a mining camp or *hacienda*, or better, those who traveled from place to place as their commerce dictated, could easily escape any vigilance. It can even be asserted that only bad luck could reveal their practices in regard to foods, fasts, prayers, and other observances of their faith. This was particularly the case in New Spain where the population, in comparison with that of Spain, generally lacked the religious sophistication to detect such clandestine activities.

In effect, Spaniards who theoretically had the religious training necessary to notice heterodox religious behavior or statements were always a minority in New Spain. What is more, these Spaniards were often isolated, especially in the mining camps and outlying regions. They did not necessarily always collaborate wholeheartedly with civil and religious authorities, who were not always present. Hence, it was ordinarily only in the cities that conditions existed to sustain and carry out the vigilance and denunciations of the Inquisition.

Aside from these few peninsular Spaniards, much of the population consisted of the *castas*[3] and the indigenous masses whose Christianization and consequent Westernization were as recent as they were superficial. These majority sectors of the population were largely incapable of discerning heterodox behavior. When they denounced what looked to them like heresy, it was done with an ulterior motive—as was the case with slaves, who turned in their masters for reasons as varied as they were obvious—or the denunciation was without foundation. In effect, the general population of New Spain could not collaborate effectively with the Inquisitorial apparatus, in contrast to the Old Christians of the Iberian Peninsula—a circumstance obviously very favorable to crypto-Jews.

The immensity of the territory, the weakness of institutional networks, especially of the Inquisition, and the consequent lack of effective control have been noted. Moreover, it was always feasible, when imminent danger was suspected, to make oneself "absent" (*ausentarse* was the term preferred at the time), that is, to hide in a remote region, or even another American or Asian country, and take refuge in a new identity. The many proceedings "in absentia" conducted by the Mexican Holy Office against Jews testify plainly to this device. Although some of these proceedings refer to individuals who had died before the time of the trial, others concerned people who were quite healthy but had left the viceroyalty, either for business reasons or because they fled when they sensed danger.

The Coexistence of Jews and the Inquisition in New Spain

Surviving under the Inquisitorial gaze meant above all else escaping the curiosity and vigilance of the others: the Old Christians, the mass of *castas*, and the indigenous population. Like its Iberian counterparts, the sleepy and simple colonial tribunal could not function without denunciations by good Christians; denunciations were the raw material indispensable to any further proceedings capable of resulting in a trial. Meanwhile, backed by their lengthy experience in Spain and Portugal, the crypto-Jews who had settled in the viceroyalty practiced all manner of precautions and deployed a vast quantity of subterfuges to parallel the behavior of others—to appear to be obedient and even conformist Christians. In an ancien régime society, and moreover one with a Mediterranean culture, appearances were fundamental, prevailing over any other distinctions.

It is difficult to create even a preliminary list of the various wiles by which the *conversos* of New Spain managed to deflect the outsider's scrutiny. The very diversity of the situations and of the psychological mechanisms employed contributes to this difficulty. Nonetheless, we can establish a clear distinction first between men and women, and second between rich and poor. Men, for example, especially if they were wealthy, participated in the full socioeconomic life of the viceroyalty. Often engaged in business away from home, they had constantly to deal with Christians and found themselves frequently obligated to share their habits—foods, religious practices, social customs—and perhaps develop personal friendships with them that would be impossible to avoid in Hispanic culture. Thus, a renowned merchant might drink chocolate with a religious dignitary even while he should be fasting according to the Jewish calendar. He could be a member of an exclusive Catholic brotherhood with the aim of maintaining necessary social relations, and would not avoid inviting Christians to a wedding celebrated within the family.[4]

Conversely, women, especially poor women, enjoyed wide freedom of action by remaining at home. Even though the stereotype of the Spanish woman rigorously cloistered in her home was far from the reality in the American viceroyalties, it is a fact that Jewish women essentially functioned in the family and domestic sphere, unlike their husbands, brothers, and sons. This was the case even among those who saw themselves obligated to undertake some kind of remunerative activity because they had been abandoned or left destitute. The Rivera family, for example, composed of a mother and four daughters, supported themselves at home through small-scale artisanal work. Women in general—and the poor in particular—tended to be less restrained and cautious in Jewish religious practices than men because their actions were not as exposed to the outsider's gaze.[5]

To appear to be good Christians, it was essential to comply with the strictest and most public Catholic obligations: baptism, mass, confession, taking communion on Easter, and extreme unction. Moreover, it was helpful for one's image to participate in Holy Week processions, to carry a rosary, to have one or another religious paintings and a crucifix in the home, and to remember to utter the appropriate sacred formulas at the ends of certain sentences, for example when someone sneezed. The vast majority of Portuguese Jews sought to fulfill these norms meticulously, all the while inventing thousands of ways to evade, counteract, or invalidate their form and meaning. While listing and describing these numerous strategies is outside the scope of this essay, we can simply say that the inventiveness crypto-Jews mustered in order to seem Christian can only be compared with the capacity they showed to conceal their Judaism.

There were some religious commandments that were difficult to adhere to while being concealed. These had to do with codes guiding food and ritual cleanliness. The thorniest had to do with the Jewish prohibition against consumption of pork in all its forms, a practice that reasonably aware Christians noticed first because it was the most plainly identifiable. Jews tried to eat only in their own home or in the home of another Jew. The presence of slaves constituted a constant danger, since they could turn in their masters. In this case, one took refuge in the excuse of endemic stomach problems, one discreetly fed the forbidden meat to domestic animals, or one simply pretended not to like the food. With regard to the ritual sacrifice of fowl, bleeding of meat, eating only fish with scales, or cleaning a leg of lamb, Jewish women shielded themselves behind practical explanations to allay suspicions: as they explained it, meat prepared this way or that way tasted or cooked better.

Being unable to carry out properly the various Jewish celebrations in a society with a Christian majority, Jews compensated for the absence of these observances by undertaking a great number of fasts. Fasts had the significant advantage of being very difficult to identify as heterodox behavior, and, as a form of penance, they may have helped Jews to cope with the guilt of the necessary deviations from Jewish law and practice.

It was easy for a merchant invited by a Christian colleague to sit at his table to avoid eating by saying that he had already eaten at home or was indisposed. If it was impossible to observe the fast that corresponded with a certain Jewish holiday, the merchant could pay some poor woman from the community to fast on his behalf.[6] Through this transaction, he met his religious obligation, the woman received some charity, and appearances, always vital, were maintained: no one would suspect that the merchant in question had contrived to reconcile the unreconcilable.

Although it was feasible to comply with attendance at masses and with the celebrations of the majority of Catholic practices in such a way that others would suspect nothing, and though there were mechanisms for satisfactorily negotiating the proscriptions of Jewish law, celebrating the Shabbat (the Sabbath) entailed serious dangers. Some of the major holidays, like Yom Kippur, Rosh Hashannah, Hanukkah, and Passover, coincided in large part with Christian holidays, and, as a result, their discreet observance easily passed unnoticed. But this was not the case with the Shabbat: the Jewish Saturday of rest could not but contrast with the Christian Sunday. There was little that could be done to hide the Friday ablutions, the changing of underwear and bedsheets, and the candlelight dinner at dusk with the whole family in attendance and perhaps some relatives and friends. All that could be done was to remove the slaves, some matron dismissing them from the house so the family could be free of their gaze.[7] The weekly celebration of the Shabbat was the most dangerous of observances because there was no way to disguise it as a Catholic practice; the only recourse was to carry it out with extreme caution and to reduce it to a few discreet practices.

In very broad terms, these were the main contrivances that the *conversos* resorted to so that they would appear to be like the rest of the European inhabitants of New Spain. With these precautions, they handily achieved their ends, and, though they were generally recognized as "Portuguese" because they frequently spoke the language and preserved certain Portuguese customs, rarely were they discovered to be practicing Jews.

Aside from subterfuges designed to deceive the bulk of the Christian population, there were other contrivances, less frequent and more exclusive, that were used to establish privileged relationships with the Church in general and with the members of the Holy Office's tribunal. These privileged relationships were intended to protect against any sort of suspicion in matters of faith. At least some *converso* families went beyond participation in the Catholic ceremonies and customs we have just mentioned or membership in some particularly exclusive religious brotherhood. From the Carvajal family of the sixteenth century and the Campos of the seventeenth century, one member actually became a priest or friar in a religious order. Such a step doubtlessly resulted from complex motives, among which we must stress the following. First, it is clear that after 1492 and the consequent acceptance of baptism by those who chose to stay in the Spanish Empire, some individuals genuinely embraced Catholicism, as attested by the high proportion of clergymen, including mystics, whose families were of known Jewish origin. We must recognize that an unspecified number of New Christians not only developed into true Christians but also into figures distinguished among their counterparts for the intensity and quality of their religious fervor. Without a doubt, however, there also existed an actual strategy that consisted of "sacrificing" a member of the family by handing them over to the Church, so that the whole group would be symbolically exempted from suspicion on questions of faith. The cases of Iberian clergymen who were punished for continuing to practice Judaism despite their robes allows us to believe that this was one of the mechanisms that some families resorted to in order to secure their survival and social status.

What is more, in American viceroyalties such as New Spain, the colonial reality provided other opportunities to establish acceptable, if not cordial, relations within ecclesiastical and Inquisitorial spheres. In the midst of the indigenous peoples and the ever growing number of *castas*, the Spaniards, Portuguese, and the handful of other Europeans who settled there—when they belonged to social sectors of a certain status—tended to merge into a single category: that of rulers, automatically identified as Old Christians and frequently adorned with a fictitious heraldry. In America, as we know well, traditional social barriers were largely erased by the amassing of money. The low-born wealthy merchant or slave dealer could, with impunity, adopt the lifestyle of the Iberian nobility with whom he had struck up social relations, and he might even marry into this group. There is nothing strange, therefore, in the fact that people like Simón Váez Sevilla or Sebastián Váez de Acevedo would deal with Inquisitors, give them expensive gifts, or even ask them for favors. Acevedo, for instance, did not hesitate to ask the Mexican Holy Office tribunal to warehouse goods he had brought from the Philippines in order to hide them from the royal tax auditor.[8]

Such relationships could eventually carry over into participation in family life, as evidenced by the presence of several Inquisition officials at the funeral rites of the famous dogmatist Blanca Enríquez. The Enríquez family must have realized the danger posed by the presence of these officials at an event in which several rituals that were carried out stood to raise reasonable suspicions. Indeed, the good relations with Inquisition officials seems outright bizarre when we look at the relationships of the daughters of Blanca Enríquez. Micaela and the charming Rafaela, though devout Jews, became close friends of the Inquisitorial notary Don Eugenio de Saravia and of the Inquisitor Don Francisco de Estrada.[9] Again, supposing that the officials did not harbor the slightest doubt about the orthodoxy of the sisters—which seems unlikely, as we shall see—how can we explain this dangerous familiarity on the part of practicing Jews with men known to be potential persecutors? Aside from the reasons already discussed, such as families placing some of their members among the ranks of the church, and aside from quite individual motives, such as the flirtatiousness of confident women accustomed to breaking hearts, we glimpse here a class complicity among the ruling elite of colonial society and, in the end, a process of assimilation of some crypto-Jews into a majority-Christian society.

The Holy Office and the Jews: "All was quiet"

For their part, it seems that the Inquisitors had established a modus vivendi with those who should normally have inspired the Inquisition's concern, if not outright suspicion. The Holy Office had not ignored the fact that Jews were present in the viceroyalty from the beginning, and the persecutions at the end of the sixteenth century—in particular, the spectacular case of the Carvajal family in 1596—demonstrated that groups of crypto-Jews had settled in different parts of the country. But aside from a small upswell of Inquisitorial activity in the beginning of the seventeenth century, which was really the tail end of earlier persecutions, in the succeeding decades there were no alarming measures taken against the "Portuguese," who continued arriving in ever greater numbers to the American kingdoms.

There were denunciations that revealed situations that should have inspired at least the curiosity of the Inquisition. In 1622, for example, an anonymous tip sent to the tribunal revealed the existence of a synagogue on Calle de Santo Domingo, just two doors down from the Inquisition's offices. Any passerby could hear the prayers of the devout congregated there for the Shabbat, and by then there were maybe between fifty and one hundred "Portuguese" living in the capital. This information was filed away, without so much as an investigation.[10]

Three years later, an informer appeared before the tribunal who was a person of responsibility, this time providing his name: he was the head administrator of the Mexico City Treasury. He had worked for some months as a cashier in the household of the wealthy merchant Simón Váez Sevilla, which allowed him to observe actions and situations that left no room for doubt. The family never ate pork in any form, they used oil instead of lard for cooking, Simón Váez ate meat on Fridays, his wife did not regularly attend church nor pray with the rosary, the couple lived in isolation and associated with people already punished for being Jewish. This accusation was not successful either.[11]

Ten years later in 1635, in the same month of August when the crackdown against the "Great Complicity" was taking place in Peru, the Mexican Inquisition received new accusations against Simón Váez Sevilla, his wife, and his sister, Elena Váez. The sister was accused of not eating bacon, bleeding meat before cooking it, using beef marrow or oil instead of lard, not attending mass, and ridiculing an image of Christ. Váez's wife, Juana Enríquez, was accused of performing Jewish funeral rites—washing the body and dressing it in a shroud of new cloth—upon a deceased nephew, the son of her sister-in-law. One of the witnesses called by the tribunal in reaction to these weighty allegations informed the Inquisitors that on Good Friday and the Thursday before it was customary at the Váez household to whip the slaves and that Simón Váez did not stop washing himself, in contrast to what Christians did during those days of mourning. Despite what was going on in Peru at the same time, these accusations were filed away without further repercussion.[12] What is more, they were filed away even though twelve other Jews had been reconciled and another five relaxed in effigy in the auto-da-fé on 2 April 1635. It is clear that the persecution waged in New Spain was insufficient to destroy the flourishing crypto-Judaic community and that the Inquisitors were not disposed to act vigorously against it. Nonetheless, the accusations that kept arriving were filed away with the rest, awaiting the fateful day when they would be dug up.

Without saying that relations between the Portuguese Jewish community and the Inquisitors were actually "tight" or even cordial, it can be asserted that during the decades between 1620 and 1640 some Inquisitors and Jews knew each other well and tried to get along through a modus vivendi that excluded neither judicial hearings like those in 1635 nor private understandings that ranged from criminal conspiracies to personal relationships. This was the case because, despite the existence of clandestine religious heterodoxy no doubt less important in the New World than in the Old, Inquisitors and crypto-Jews belonged to the same ruling elite.

We will not reiterate here the many complex reasons why this precarious equilibrium broke down after having endured throughout almost the entire first half of the seventeenth century. It suffices to remember that the change occurred because of political events in the mother country and the role played by certain key individuals such as Count-Duke Olivares, Bishop Juan de Palafox, Viceroy Marquis de Villena, and the Inquisitors Arce Reinoso at the *Suprema* (the Supreme Tribunal of the Inquisition in Spain), and Juan Sáez de Mañozca in New Spain. It was also caused, in a fundamental sense, by the deep schism within New Spain's crypto-Jewish community along the lines of rich and poor and, within these groups, by the dilemma of remaining true to their faith while continuing to be the Iberians that they also were. In the unique political circumstances of 1640, these factors combined to destroy forever the already strained dynamics of the *converso* community in New Spain.[13]

Although the community as such was irreversibly destroyed, the individuals that it comprised for the most part survived. In the mid-seventeenth century the Jewish population of New Spain probably numbered between 150 and 250 people—a loose approximation given the semi-clandestinity they maintained. Of these, only a portion was arrested, and outside of those who were burned at the stake—some twenty or twenty-five at the most—the great majority were reconciled and theoretically condemned to exile from the viceroyalty in Seville and in Madrid.[14]

Nonetheless, few ever embarked for Spain to fulfill their sentences. Most opted to stay in New Spain. While we cannot speak of a Jewish community after 1650, the individuals remained under different identities and far from the capital, and continued to observe their religion to the extent that they could or that they chose to.

Final Considerations

Like their equals in Iberia, the crypto-Jews who settled in New Spain tried to immerse themselves in the society of the Christian majority, and, by and large, they succeeded. Their long experience at evading the curiosity and vigilance of the Christian population in general, the relative inability of the bulk of the population to recognize their heterodox practices, the weakness of institutional networks—especially the Inquisition's—and finally, the elite status that they shared with other Europeans gave them a good chance of surviving, as had been their hope when they embarked for America. Had it not been for the great persecution that was unleashed in the mid-seventeenth century, which ended their existence as a group, it is likely that they would have continued living in the tolerable environment that had existed until then.

Today, the only officially recognized Jewish communities in Mexico are those of the Sephardic descendants of immigrants from the old Ottoman Empire and the more recent Ashkenazim, who settled after the advent of Nazism in Europe. It might be asked: What would have become of the "Portuguese" from the years between 1580 and 1640 had they not been persecuted and dispersed in the mid-seventeenth century? Two answers seem possible. First, according to the historical record, isolated individuals secretly continued the practices they considered fundamental to Judaism and tried to pass on some rites. These now survive merely as cultural fragments within families that have otherwise lost their historic memory of their remote identity.

On the other hand, it is doubtful that the *converso* community as it stood at mid-century could have sustained itself indefinitely. The differences and latent antagonisms between rich and poor coincided in large part with the differences between men and women, and in the end made for a religious practice that was locked into the home and managed by women. The lack of sacred texts, rabbis, and formal teaching condemned Jewish religion to the status of being little more than a series of domestic rituals; for some, it became a faith whose characteristics and requirements were strictly personal. A merchant like Tomás Nuñez de Peralta exemplified this outcome. Scolding his wife for frequent and dangerous indiscretions, he told her one night: "For fifteen years, I have done nothing more than commend myself to God while I go about my business, and having Him in my heart is enough."[15] Obviously, this type of religiosity held more in common with the beliefs of enlightened elites of the eighteenth century than it did with commonly accepted practice among both Christians and Jews in the seventeenth century. In sum, there were factors at the heart of the crypto-Jewish community of New Spain that augured its probable disintegration over time, under the inevitable impact of deliberate, although unintended, assimilation.

Finally, and paradoxically, the only way for the community to survive was specifically under the pressure and vigilance of the Inquisition. After the original alternative—baptism or exile—Iberian crypto-Jews had implicitly accepted living in isolation, out of touch with broader Jewish religious currents and deprived of their theological and cultural infrastructure. They accepted the task of seeming to be what they were not and hiding what they really were, in effect being both Christian and Jew at the same time. In this sense, they were true cultural *mestizos*, rejected by both religions, each equally driven by purity and orthodoxy. These *conversos* established a modus vivendi that we could well call a marrano (or *converso*) culture, the focal point and defining element of which seems to have been ... the Holy Office.

In the *converso* world of both vital and deadly appearances, of contradictions and of existential schisms, only the tribunal was an absolute and constant point of reference. What it represented became the only factor drawing together sectors, families, and individuals unavoidably torn by contradictory and opposing forces. As Jean Paul Sartre showed in his classic *Anti-Semite and Jew*, it is the anti-Semitic assault that, in situations that favor the assimilation of Jews, reminds them of who they are. In this sense, the Holy Office of the Inquisition was the main force that reminded the *conversos* that they were Jews and obligated those who were on the verge of forgetting to remember.

This marrano culture—or *marranismo*, if you will—was characterized by secrecy, clandestine activities, and constant fear in the face of danger. To live and to endure demanded rejecting and even mocking the Christianity imposed upon them. Only in this way could the crypto-Jews preserve their specificity, and it is interesting to note that the Holy Office's tribunal and its inherent anti-Semitism played exactly the same role for the nascent Creole identity.[16]

As the great persecution of the Portuguese in the capital of New Spain wound down, the first herald of militant creolism, Miguel Sánchez, brought to light his *Imagen de la Virgen María ...*, in which he proclaimed the Virgin of Guadalupe's meaning and mission for the Mexican nation. The clergyman could not help drawing a relationship between the Guadalupean miracle and the autos-da-fé conducted at the time. Under his pen, the penitent crypto-Jews that were the "enemies of our holy faith" were also "strangers and foreigners ... without original roots in this land."[17] In this way, the Catholic faith became a characteristic of "this land" and therefore of its sons, who opposed themselves to the "enemies of our holy faith." If the crypto-Jews on their part needed the Christians, headed by the fearsome Inquisition, to preserve themselves as such, the

New Spain Creoles also needed the crypto-Jews in order to vivify their nascent identity.

These considerations lead us to believe that as long as the Holy Office maintained some sort of pressure over them, real or imagined, the Portuguese of New Spain would retain their cohesion; inevitably, they drifted toward a syncretism and assimilation, but their Jewishness should not be questioned. The persecutions of the 1640s probably accelerated the process of assimilation, annihilating the community and dispersing its individuals. But in so doing, the Holy Office, whose purpose was the eradication of that community, signed its own death sentence. The Jew and the Inquisitor did not exist except in relation to each other; after the disappearance of the first, the second became superfluous.

The reciprocity of this relationship between Jew and Inquisitor was perceived by those Jews who were living in communities in which they could openly practice their faith. According to Juan Pacheco de León, the Jews of Livorna, Italy, for example, looked down upon the marranos that had remained in the Spanish Empire to such a degree that when they encountered one, they hurriedly denounced him before the bishop, accusing him of being a bad Catholic.[18] The sharpest Inquisitors also perceived this, and Juan Sáenz de Mañozca, the main figure behind the persecution of New Spain's marranos in the mid-seventeenth century, wrote the following to the *Suprema*, at the end of the intense years from 1642 to 1649: "With the complicities of 1649 concluded, this Inquisition returned little by little to that earlier slackness."[19]

Notes

1. Theoretically, the Spanish Empire was formed by several kingdoms that were ruled by their own laws, usages, and authorities. The term "colony" from the English language appears only with the Bourbon dynasty in the late eighteenth century, when the Spanish crown aimed to administer its possessions in a systematic and rational way.
2. For the socioeconomic situation of the marrano community of seventeenth-century Mexico. Stanley Hordes, "The Crypto-Jewish Community of New Spain, 1620–1649: A Collective Biography" (Ph.D. diss., Tulane University, 1980); Seymour Liebmann, *The Jews in New Spain: Faith, Flame and the Inquisition* (Coral Gables, 1967), passim; and for most of these items, Solange Alberro, *Inquisición y sociedad en México 1571–1700* (Mexico, 1988). There is a French version, *Inquisition et Société au Mexique, 1571–1700* (Mexico, 1988). In this paper, the citations are from the Spanish version.
3. The *castas* are the different groups of *mestizos* who were the issue of relations between Indians, Europeans, and Africans in Spanish America. It is not a formal system but a common way to name the different offspring, from their somatic characteristics.
4. Cases of Thomas Núñez de Peralta, Mathias Rodríguez de Olivera, and the Enríquez family of Mexico. See Alberro, *Inquisición*, 425.
5. Ibid., 444–45.
6. Ibid., 443.
7. Cf. the case of Blanca Enríquez. Alberro, *Inquisición*, 420.
8. Ibid., 46–47.
9. Ibid., 47–48, 426. Rafaela Enríquez had an affair with the Inquisitorial notary, Eugenio de Saravia.
10. Alberro, *Inquisición*, 536.
11. Ibid., 536–37.
12. Ibid., 539–40.
13. Ibid., 533–94.
14. In such cases, they were forbidden to stay in the viceroyalty itself, the whole Indies, the court of Madrid and the city of Seville, the main departure port for America, but they were allowed to live in any other place in Spain.
15. Alberro, *Inquisición*, 425.
16. The term "Creole" ("criollos") refers to descendants of Spanish or French parents, born in Spanish or French American territories and the Philippines Islands. The "criollos" were also called "American Spanish," in opposition to the "peninsular Spanish."
17. Miguel Sánchez, *Imagen de la Virgen María Madre de Dios de Guadalupe ... México, Imprenta de la viuda de Bernardo Calderón, 1648*, in Ernesto de la Torre Villar and Ramíro Navarro de Anda, *Testimonios históricos guadalupanos* (Mexico, 1982), 173. "Enemigos de nuestra santa fé, sin raíces originarias desta tierra ... extraños peregrinos y advenedisos."
18. Alberro, *Inquisición*, 438.
19. Ibid., 584. "Conclusa la complicidad por abril 649 se fue volviendo poco a poco esta Inquisición a aquella flogedad antigua."

Chapter 9

THE PARTICIPATION OF NEW CHRISTIANS AND CRYPTO-JEWS IN THE CONQUEST, COLONIZATION, AND TRADE OF SPANISH AMERICA, 1521–1660

Eva Alexandra Uchmany

Introduction

MODERNITY EXCLUDED THE JEWS from one of its biggest enterprises: the discovery, conquest, and colonization of America. Notwithstanding, the Jews found ways to participate in this adventure, although in Christian garb. The persecutions and social pressures lived through by the Jews from Castile, and in minor form by Aragonese Jewry, during their last hundred years in the Iberian Peninsula forged a tendency in the baptized and their successors, the New Christians, to assimilate into the religion of the majority. It was a span of time in which almost two-thirds of the Hebrew nation converted to Christianity, by coercion or voluntarily.

The case of Portuguese Jewry, as is well known, was very different. The whole Hebrew nation of Portugal was forced, in a very short span of time—almost in one day—to accept a religion in whose authenticity they did not believe and to the popular culture and liturgical forms of which they had had no time to assimilate. Because of this violation of their consciences, the immense majority of the Portuguese Jews never abandoned their ancestral religion, but rather only changed their external identity. Although they tried to appear to be good and devout Christians in the eyes of their neighbors and of spies, in the intimacy of their homes they remained Jews and continued to educate their children in Jewish customs and religion. Due to the different circumstances in which the conversion of the two groups took place, and also because the Portuguese New Christians, who were in the majority crypto-Jews, arrived in New Spain and Spanish America mostly in the second half of the sixteenth century, this essay will be divided into two corresponding sections.

The New Christians of Spanish Origin

Imitating the Portuguese venture into the Atlantic Ocean, the Spanish discover and colonization of the New World was undertaken as a capitalist enterprise. So it is not strange that the New Christian Luis de Santángel,[1] a major entrepreneur and financier of the Spanish crown, invested in the first voyage of Columbus, who intended to arrive in the East by sailing west. Certainly, Santángel and his associates had also endeavored to share in the rich Portuguese Atlantic trade.

In the four voyages of Columbus, several New Christians were present and also one *converso*. The latter was Luis de Torres from Murcia, who knew Hebrew and Aramaic, languages that might have been understood in the Indian Ocean and were the first spoken in the New World by a European: Columbus, who thought he was near the territories of the Grand Khan, had sent de Torres to explore the first major island of the West Indies that they discovered and named Hispaniola.[2] Before returning to Spain, Columbus left behind thirty-nine men, among them Luis de Torres, to colonize the island. All were killed by the indigenous people.[3] In the first and last voyage a crypto-Jew was also present—the apothecary Maese Bernal, who was later tried by the Inquisition for Judaizing.[4]

The Favorites and the Prohibited

In 1501 the Catholic king excluded from the West Indies adventure all the converted Jews and New Christians who had been punished for Judaizing during the preceding ten years. In the Archive of the Indies there is a list (*Padrón de Conversos*) with more than five hundred names from the province of Seville alone.[5] In this *Padrón* are listed many families whose members later played a major role in the conquest, colonization, and Christianization of the New World. Such was the case of the family of Fray Bartolomé de las Casas, the great protector of the American Indians, who arrived in America in the company of his father Pedro de las Casas in the second voyage of Columbus.

The king rigorously punished transgressors against the faith. He confiscated their property, excluded them from any honorable office, and prohibited them from trading with the Indies. But the decree did not include the favorites: the relatives and friends of the New Christian Lope de Conchillos, secretary of the council of Castile, and those of the queen's secretary Miguel Pérez de Almazán. The family of Alonso de Ávila, who had been one of the *converso* secretaries of Queen Isabel, was also not discriminated against, although his cousin and namesake had been penalized by the Inquisition and appears in the *Padrón de Conversos* as number 70. Indeed, this former secretary of the Queen was able to get a good post for his cousin Gil González de Ávila, who in 1509 was appointed royal accountant in Hispaniola.[6] In 1511 Gil González transferred this post to his nephew Alonso de Ávila and left for Cuba. In 1514 King Ferdinand dubbed him Knight of Santiago and sent him to outfit an expedition to locate a strait between the two oceans. While searching for the strait, Gil González conquered Costa Rica, Nicaragua, and part of Honduras, where he clashed with the captains of Cortés, who claimed the territory for themselves.

A few years later, the royal accountant Alonso de Ávila enlisted in the army of Hernán Cortés as captain. The conquistador appointed him the first bookkeeper of the recently founded city of Veracruz and of the whole army during the conquest of Mexico, and later sent him, with the treasury of Motecuhzoma, as his procurator to Spain. In 1528 Alonso de Ávila enrolled with Francisco de Montejo for the conquest of Yucatán. His brother, Gil González de Benavides de Ávila, also played an important role in the conquest of Mexico. Both of them were harassed by the primitive Inquisition in New Spain, headed by Fray Juan de Zumárraga, the first bishop of New Spain: Gil González de Benavides in 1527 and his brother Alonso ten years later.

Like many New Christians, they had an eclectic approach toward matters of faith. In 1537 Alonso de Ávila was accused by Bishop Zumárraga of keeping a crucifix under his writing desk and stepping on it.[7] Indeed, this was a classical accusation against many Jews and New Christians, and served the Inquisitor as a defamatory libel against the former royal accountant and conqueror of Mexico and Yucatán.[8] Zumárraga hated Ávila because he dared to warn his good friend, the New Christian Gonzalo Gómez (founder of the town Guayanguareo, now the city of Morelia, the capital of the state of Michoacán), that the apostolic Inquisitor was going to arrest him.[9] Definitely, no true Old Christian would do such a favor for a New one.

Some time later, after degrading and shaming the New Christians, the Catholic king secularized the sanctions of the 1501 decree and offered to rehabilitate lost civil rights for a large sum of money. Indeed, the king sold to the enabled (*inhábiles*) papers that restored to them their lost honors. In 1508, those reconciled by the Inquisition from the province of Seville alone paid 20,000 golden ducats to Ferdinand for the return of their confiscated property. A year later, in 1509, the Catholic king collected 80,000 ducats selling them the rights to hold public office and to trade with the Indies. The New Christians seized these opportunities with both hands.

Many names that appear in the *Padrón de Conversos* are found in the "Catalogue of Passengers to the West Indies,"[10] and similar lists. A large number of them arrived in 1514 with the expedition of the New Christian Pedro Arias de Ávila, or Pedrarias Dávila, appointed by the king as governor of Castilla de Oro. He was the grandson of Diego Arias, who had embraced Christianity in the first decades of the fifteenth century and became the Chancellor of the Exchequer of Castile; all of his family became ennobled and related to the crown.[11] A significant number of New Christians who came with Pedrarias took part in different expeditions and were involved also in the conquest of Mexico and Peru, as was the case of the brothers Juan de Orgoñoz and Diego Méndez, who were present at the conquest of Cuzco. Others were appointed as royal accountants and public and royal notaries.

Some were engaged in finance or trade with the West Indies. From this group I will mention only Juan de Córdoba, registered in the *Padrón de Conversos* as number 286, one of the most prominent New Christians in Seville, who later managed to be one of the twenty-four city magistrates, or councils of the city. In 1519, Juan de Córdoba lent to Hernán Cortés a large sum of money to carry out the conquest of Mexico.[12] The loan was given to Cortés thanks to his relative, licentiate Francisco Núñez de Valera, a prominent New Christian from Salamanca, who was married to Cortés's father's sister Inés Gómez de Paz.[13] Núñez, in whose house Cortés lived during his student years at the University of Salamanca, was the conquistador's private procurator in Seville and in the royal court.[14] In 1522, licentiate Núñez sent Rodrigo de Paz, his oldest son, to Mexico, carrying the royal appointment for Cortés as captain general and governor of New Spain. At the same time, the New Christian Rodrigo de Paz was also the courier of the royal decree that ordered Cortés to expel from his recently acquired overseas domains all settlers with Jewish and Moorish origins.[15] Such contradictions amplified the already bizarre reality lived by many in Spain, which after 1522 was exported to New Spain.

Cortés favored Rodrigo as well as his brothers Alonso de Paz and Adrián and Juan Núñez, his sister Ana Núñez, and her husband Christóbal de Salamanca, who traveled together to Mexico. To all of them he conceded various Indian villages. Indeed, Rodrigo de Paz owned, three years later, several houses and sixteen shops in Tenochtitlán (as Mexico City was still called in the documents of those years),[16] and slaves that he exploited in his mines.

When he began the conquest of the Hibueras,[17] Cortés made Paz the administrator and keeper of his estates and fortune. After the conqueror left the city with his expedition, the political situation changed in Mexico. The royal officials, mortal enemies of the conquistadors, took the government into their own hands, confiscated the property of Cortés, and tortured his loyal cousin Rodrigo de Paz, burning his feet and legs. On 16 October 1525, Rodrigo was executed on the gallows,[18] accused of hiding the conquistador's treasury.

The Prohibited

The royal decree that Rodrigo handed to Cortés in late 1522 was issued on 25 September of the same year by Charles I, who had recently become the king of Spain. Charles of Flanders, educated to distrust the converted Jews, changed the crown's policy toward the New Christians. In 1518 he prohibited any person, once punished by the Inquisition, from embarking for the West Indies. The New Christians protested, alleging that free traffic to the Caribbean Islands was a privilege they had paid for. The king ordered an investigation into the matter, wishing to know more than anything else if all of them had paid their debt to the crown. While the inquiry lasted, the way to the Indies remained open. But after 25 September 1522, all people of Hebrew origin were forbidden to cross the Atlantic Ocean. Subsequent laws ratified this sanction and extended the prohibition to grandchildren and great-great-grandchildren of any Jew.

Most of the conquistadors and royal officials disobeyed these prohibitions and did not publish the royal bans. They feared provocation, quarrels, and discord in their armies; moreover, some of them had Jewish ancestors. Many New Christians who had gained access to the West Indies before 1518 managed to conceal their origins by changing their identity and profession. They made every effort to appear to their neighbors as Old Christians. A good number of them succeeded, but some did not. These unfortunates were harassed and paid for their ascendancy with their lives.

Such was the case of the Alonsos, Hernando and Martín, natives of the province of Huelvas, from the villages Niebla and Palos. Both embarked in 1518 for Cuba. Hernando, a blacksmith by trade, worked under the orders of Martín López in building the brigantines that played such an important role in the conquest of Mexico-Tenochtitlán, and took part also in the pacification of Pánuco. For all these services he was granted the signory of Actopan as an *encomienda*.[19] From 1524 to 1528 he devoted himself to mining and cattle-raising, which enabled him to obtain a monopoly on the meat supply for Mexico City. In the early autumn of 1528 he was accused of Judaizing in Cuba. Supposedly, he assisted in a Passover ceremony, sang "Bzet Israel," and did not permit his wife to go to church during her period. In this case he confused the synagogue with the church, to which he might have attributed a biblical ordinance. Some witnesses said, however, that he was simply very jealous of Isabel de Aguilar, his young and beautiful wife.[20] In any case, in 1528 the Dominican Santa María burned him, almost without a trial,[21] in the first public auto-da-fé celebrated in New Spain, together with Gonzalo Morales, a shopkeeper. Gonzalo's brother, Diego, condemned for blasphemy and for suspicion of being a Judaizer, was present with tied hands fastened to pincers clipped to his tongue and connected with a rope to a tree. This situation barely permitted him to put his feet on the ground and left him hanging in the air during the four long hours that the ceremony took place. He survived six other autos-da-fé in the following twenty years in which he was accused time and again for the same sins.[22]

One of the notable figures in the auto-da-fé was Diego de Ocaña, public notary, who served as secretary to the governor of New Spain, Alonso de Estrada, and who belonged to the group of royal officials opposed to Cortés. Alonso de Estrada, born in Ciudad Real, a natural son of King Ferdinand and a Jewish lady,[23] was married to Marina de la Caballería, daughter of a famous New Christian family that embraced Christianity sometime at the beginning of the fifteenth century. The governor sent his cousin, Diego de Mazariegos, to subdue and settle the province of Chiapas. The names of the conquerors and colonizers of Chiapas coincide, in their totality, with the names of those sentenced by the Inquisition in Ciudad Real, including the name of Diego de Mazariegos.[24] The children of those condemned and defamed by the Inquisition were determined to make a new life, far from the metropolis, in the most remote corners of the Spanish Empire.

From the accusations against Diego de Ocaña, it can be understood that he was still bound to Jewish dietary laws, avoiding non-*kasher*[25] fish and sacrificing chickens according to the "law of Moses." He used to shout in the jail: "I am telling you, wall, not to confess because the witnesses are dead."[26] Nevertheless, thanks to his friendship with the governor and other important people of that time, he was reconciled and condemned only to spiritual penitence and to wearing a *sambenito* all of his life. But the public humiliation to which this intelligent man was exposed, and the shameful garment that he was obliged to wear, which exhibited him to all the people as an infamous heretic, destroyed him morally.[27]

In those same years, Martín Alonso Alemán (the relative of the above mentioned Hernando Alonso), who appears in the *Padrón de Conversos* as number 172, was engaged in pearl fishing and trade in the Caribbean. In 1527, he was elected mayor of Cubagua, an honor that provoked the envy of some Old Christians. In December 1528 he was assassinated by Pedro de Barrionuevo, a native of Soria, who was convinced that stabbing to death a descendant of a Jew was not a sin.[28]

The royal prohibitions and the changing mood in the colonies have been closely linked to the battles between Old Christians and New Christians over positions of honor and wealth in the Church and the realm. By means of the "Statutes of Purity of Blood," the middle-class Old Christians tried to oust the New Christians from all the opportunities that their time offered to entrepreneurs. The "Statutes" were adopted by the mendicant orders, who themselves were sons of the middle-class bourgeoisie, by the city councils almost everywhere, by the Council or Cabildo of the Toledo Cathedral, and so forth. Through the "Statutes," the descendants of Jews were absolutely excluded from the Colegios Mayores, whose graduates were accepted automatically to all the important bureaucratic posts in Spain and in the colonies, including the tribunal of the Inquisition. On the basis of the "Statutes," even those New Christians who had only a few drops of Jewish blood in their veins could not be trusted and were condemned to live on the margins of society, despite their sincerity as Christians.

For example, Dr. Antonio Robles, who was born in 1544 in San Lúcar de Barrameda and had been brought by an uncle to New Spain as an infant, graduated in canon law and theology at the University of Mexico and was honored with the chair of theology at the same institution. In 1592 he was appointed attorney of the tribunal of the Holy Office. An extensive inquiry into his origins started instantly. A year later, testimonies showing he was "unclean" reached the Inquisition of New Spain. Indeed, it was public and notorious knowledge to everyone in San Lúcar de Barrameda that Robles's grandparents from his father's side, Hernando Ortiz and his wife Violante Hernández, were descendants of converted Jews. Hernando Ortiz was even nicknamed in the town as "the king of the Jews." On 1 December 1592, the day that this information arrived, Dr. Antonio Robles was suspended from all his positions, and his sisters and cousins, married to the best of New Spain's families, became defamed.[29]

In the hostile environment that reigned in the Spanish Empire during and after the Council of Trent (1545–63), the New Christians of Spanish origin had only one desire: to acquire by any means the documents that would demonstrate their "purity of blood." Sometimes they were lucky and succeeded in acquiring the desired paper, but even this was not a guarantee for a peaceful life. Dr. Christóbal de Miranda, posted as the dean of the cathedral of Yucatán, arrived in the company of his father in Veracruz in the early 1570s. Some time later he was also appointed commissary of the Inquisition in Yucatán. Due to his new position, according to the practices of the Holy Office, a second exhaustive inquiry was made about his ancestry. As a result, it came out that both the paternal and maternal grandparents of this theologian had been punished and burned at the stake in the port of Santa María, near Seville, as "dogmatic Judaizers."[30]

The Portuguese Presence: The Doubly Prohibited

From the year 1560 small Portuguese communities spread all over Spanish America. Most of these colonizers were New Christians who hoped to evade the tribunals of the Inquisition in Portugal and, at the same time, were attracted by the discovery of the rich silver deposits in New Spain and the region of Potosí. Furthermore, the conquest of the Philippines opened a new route to the east and that meant a wide sphere of action for many entrepreneurs. Also, some New Christians had relatives and friends who were in the service of the Portuguese crown or went as merchants to the Lusitanian outposts in Southeast Asia. The immense majority of them rejected assimilation and tried to survive, given the circumstances, as Jews in Christian garb. Due to the necessarily secret aspects of their lives, they are properly called crypto-Jews.

At the same time they were the "doubly prohibited," since the prohibition against settling in Spanish America not only included the descendants of Jews but also was extended to foreigners. Their presence was ultimately detected by the tribunal of the Inquisition established in Lima, Peru, in 1570. A group of persons was denounced "for taking out the sinew from the lamb's thigh,"[31] a Jewish custom well known to the Spanish Inquisitors. The rite was practiced in remembrance of Jacob's fight with the Angel. Unable to defeat Jacob, though he hit his thigh, the Angel, after blessing him, changed Jacob's name to Israel, meaning literally the undefeated, the victorious one. This story, relating to the origins of the Hebrew nation and to the promise given by God to Abraham, evolved during the following centuries into the belief in messianic redemption in history.[32] Taking out the sinew from the lamb's thigh was the first and last Jewish rite detected by the Inquisition in Spanish America. Due to its antiquity and meaning, even New Christians who were assimilated to the religion of the majority, as was the physician Alfonso de Rojas, the grandson of Fernando de Rojas, the famous *converso* author of the fifteenth-century novel *La Celestina* (1499), still felt bound to this Hebrew rite in the last decade of the sixteenth century.[33]

In 1580 Philip II of Spain seized the Portuguese crown and became Philip I of Portugal. It was sixty years before the Lusitanians regained their autonomy. During this period of the United Crown, that is, between 1580 and 1640, Portuguese settlers abounded in Spain and its overseas colonies. Many of them migrated to Spain from Portugal and from there ventured to Spanish America. Others, who had fled Portugal in previous years and settled temporarily in Jewish quarters and ghettos in Italy and other places, also found their way to the Spanish overseas domains. The anti-Jewish rules imposed by several popes of the Counter-Reformation made their lives so miserable in the overcrowded ghettos that many left the intolerant European Christian kingdoms and settled in the territories of the Ottoman Empire; others returned to the Iberian Peninsula and embarked to the East or West Indies, as was the case of Ruy and Diego Díaz Nieto.[34]

Juan Rodríguez de Silva had lived in France, Italy, and in the Ottoman Empire. He married in Salonica, where he left his wife and traveled once again to Italy, and from there to Spain, from which he embarked for the West Indies. He set up shop as a soap manufacturer in New Spain, fleeing when the officers of the Inquisition began looking for him. He was burned in effigy, as all absent persons were, in the auto-da-fé celebrated in Mexico City in 1596 and thus became in life a dead man in the Iberian empires.

His friend Jorge de Almeyda lived in Ferrara until 1570. When life became difficult for the Jews in the duchy of D'Este, due to one of the economic crises caused by the wars with the Turks, he left with his family for New Spain, where he dedicated himself to mining. His cousin, Blanca Rodríguez, settled in Seville where she opened an inn at which many crypto-Jews stopped on their way to and from America. For them *kasher* food was served. Almeyda fled from Mexico in 1590 after the Holy Office apprehended his wife Doña Leonor, one of the daughters of the Carvajal family, whose members were burned at the stake in the terrible autos-da-fé celebrated in Mexico City in 1596, 1601, and 1649. Doña Leonor was sacrificed together with her mother, Doña Francisca, and her sisters, Doña Catalina and Doña Isabel, and brother Luis.[35] In 1594 Almeyda was still in Madrid, and thanks to his good connections with some people in the royal court, he got a contract to carry merchandise from Angola to Cartagena. After the sacrifice of the Carvajal family he went back to Italy and years later embarked for the East Indies.

New Christians often developed the ability to slip in and out between Christian and Jewish societies. They knew how to behave properly in both the synagogue and the church, and they also had mastered several languages. This ability—born in them as a consequence of religious coercion—permitted some of them to leave behind for a while the miserable social and economic situation of the ghettos and to search for better opportunities in the Iberian empires. For example, Diego Pérez de Albuquerque, born in Bordeaux and raised in Rouen, France, arrived in New Spain in 1618. He lived in Puebla and Mexico City, and finally settled in the mining center of Zacatecas, where he opened a shop. Soon after, however, he found himself in 1624 in the secret jails of the Holy Office. Alvaro Méndez, arrested in Lima, Peru, in 1631, had formerly lived in France and had sent money to relatives in Amsterdam. Julián Alvarez came to Mexico from Holland. Luis Franco Rodríguez, a resident in Cartagena de Indias who had brothers in Holland, yearned throughout his whole life for a comfortable economic situation that would permit him and his family to live freely as Jews.[36]

Many crypto-Jews had seemingly lost the ability to put down roots anywhere and wandered from one place to another. This was the case of Balthazar de Araujo, descendant of Abraham Senior, chief rabbi of Castile, supplier of the armies that conquered Granada, and one of Queen Isabel's loyal advisors. To keep this ancient servant with her, the Catholic queen did the impossible and compelled him, together with his son-in-law Meir Melamed, to a baptismal font. They took the name of Núñez Coronel and Pérez Coronel, respectively. A branch of this family, trying to live in accord with the "law of Moses," moved to Portugal, from there to Bayonne, and later to Galicia. In this kingdom, the tribunal of the Inquisition was formally introduced in 1562 and began its functions only in 1574.[37] When life for the crypto-Jews became dangerous there, the mother of Pérez Coronel, alias Araujo, moved to Flanders and from there to Venice, where she had her sons circumcised and gave them Jewish names. Balthazar was called Abraham Senior after his illustrious ancestor. In Venice and later in Salonica, and then in Constantinople, he studied in a yeshiva,[38] together with his brethren. After that he moved to Cairo; later he settled in Alexandria, and from there he returned to Bayonne, but out of fear of the Holy Office he went back to Constantinople. Nevertheless, he "felt a desire to see the world" and once again crossed the Balkans, traveling through Italy and Spain, and finally embarked for the West Indies. In 1634 he was apprehended by the Holy Office in Cartagena de Indias.[39]

Travelers like Coronel Senior and others, such as those mentioned above, infused new life into the small crypto-Jewish communities spread over the Spanish overseas domains in the main cities and mining centers, and kept them in constant communication with the intellectual centers of Judaism. Occasionally, these men, such as Juan Pacheco de León, who came to Mexico in 1639 from Livorno, Italy, became the spiritual guides for some groups of their co-religionists.

Moreover, all these Jews carried books printed in Ferrara, Venice, or some other cultural metropolis, which found their way to the most remote corners of the Spanish Empire. Manuel de Paz, imprisoned in Lima in 1634, had one of these Hebrew-Spanish bibles.[40] The physician Blas de Paz Pinto, who converted his house in Cartagena de Indias into a synagogue, owned not only a Hebrew bible but a prayer book from which a member of the community was reading the appropriate portion every afternoon to an audience of ten or more men gathered for *Maariv*.[41] They were observed, from a small window on the roof of the house, by two black slaves: Rufina and her lover, the sorcerer Diego López. That the slaves were unable to understand the language of the prayers[42] suggests that they were read in Hebrew. In 1637, Simon Váez Sevilla was denounced by his "godfather" Pedro de Navia for displaying a Hebrew-Spanish bible on his desk.[43] These types of books circulated also in the Philippines, Macao, Malacca, Cochin, and Goa.

One of the main characteristics of the period of the United Crown was that the majority of the crypto-Jews actually tried to fulfill the commandments of the Torah, or the "law of Moses." All of them observed Shabbat (the Sabbath), though the men made a pretense of going to their business places so that they would not be noticed. For the women it was easier to pretend that they were sewing or embroidering without doing anything. A substantial number of them abstained from eating prohibited food, although they served bacon when they had visitors, calling pork, ironically, *ejecutoria*, a nobility coat. In his great novel, Miguel Cervantes de Saavedra, who was a New Christian and because of it banned from migrating to New Spain, makes Sancho Panza, the armor-bearer of the errant knight Don Quixote, who was aspiring to the governorship of an island, say that he deserves the honor because he is full of ham and bacon from the four sides of his ancestors. "I am an Old Christian and to be a Count it is enough," Sancho asserts. Cervantes-Quixote answers him: "Look, Sancho, it is not the blood you inherit, but the virtue you acquire that matters. Virtue has inherent worth; blood does not."[44] Notwithstanding, it was Sancho's statement that became the opinion of the majority in sixteenth-century Spain and its dominions.

To the extent that circumstances permitted, crypto-Jews of Portuguese origin celebrated the three major annual holidays, namely *Pesah*, *Shavuot*, and *Sukkot*. They strictly fasted on the "Great Day of the Lord," as they called *Yom Hakkipurim*, and at the "Fast of Esther." Due to the religious oppression in which crypto-Jews lived, Queen Esther was considered by them one of the greatest Hebrew heroines because she had saved her nation from destruction. Many of them fasted Mondays and Thursdays, the days when the reading of the Torah is performed in the synagogues. By means of fasting they asked God to forgive them their transgressions, that is, their living in Christian garb. On the eves and ends of the fasts, they dined only on Lenten dishes, such as vegetables, fruit, fish, eggs, and cheese, as many Sephardi families still do to this day. On the occasion of these banquets, the family and a small group of friends would gather to discuss the "law of Moses," reiterating that "this law is the right one and the only one by which man could be saved."

The subject of the Messiah came up in all meetings, since everyone yearned for a quick redemption of Israel. Some even predicted the date of his arrival. Manuel Díaz, sacrificed at the auto-da-fé celebrated in 1596, calculated that the Messiah would appear by the year 1600. During his imprisonment, Manuel dreamed that the Anointed One of the House of David had opened the doors of the Inquisition's secret jails. Seeing himself outside and free, he said to some acquaintances: "Look, God took up his cause."[45] With this belief in his heart, Luis de Carvajal, during his second imprisonment, confronted the Inquisitors and tried to convert them to Judaism.

Others believed that the Savior would be born into a crypto-Jewish family. In 1620, when Juana Enríquez was pregnant with her son Gaspar, it was believed that she would give birth to the Redeemer because she strictly observed the *Mitzvoth* and because her husband, Simon Váez, was descended from the tribe of Levi. When Gaspar did not turn out to be the Messiah, other virtuous women were considered as possible mothers of the Savior. Certainly, every irregular and strange happening was seen as a sign of His impending arrival. Simple as well as educated men believed with all their hearts that God had not forgotten His people. Thanks to this deep and genuine faith, which was at the same time the kind of futuristic ideology that helps people to cope with tragedies, the survivors of the autos-da-fé—in which their family and friends had been devoured by flames—had the strength and energy to educate their children in their ancestral creed. For fear of being discovered, the crypto-Jews educated their small children as Christians. They revealed their children's true identity and initiated them into Judaism when they reached the ages of twelve and thirteen. The teaching generally began a few weeks before the fast of *Yom Hakkipurim*. In this way the bath mitzvahs or the bar mitzvahs, after fasting for the first time, became members of their small communities.

Though I have treated the period of the United Crown as one epoch, this span of time should be divided in two stages. The first one extends from 1580 until 1606, when the survivors of the three big autos-da-fé celebrated in New Spain (in 1590, 1596, and 1601) and those punished in that decade in Peru and Goa benefited from the general pardon extended to them by Pope Clement VIII. Thanks to the 1,800,000 golden ducats that they paid to Philip III, of which the Holy See got a part, the New Christians had been absolved from their sins and were reintegrated into civil society.[46]

The second stage extends from about 1610 until 1635 in Peru and Cartagena de Indias,[47] and from the same time more or less in New Spain until 1642, with small autos-da-fé in between. In this span of time, many New Christians and crypto-Jews settled once again in the Spanish overseas dominions. Some of them amassed great fortunes, especially those who were engaged in the Atlantic trade. Some very few also ventured into the Pacific trade. Their Lusitanian origin as well as their fortunes provoked envy and jealousy among royal officials. The governor of Panama, Francisco Valverde Mercado, expressed the feelings of many when he wrote to Philip III in the first half of the seventeenth century that "today the traders of the Indies are the Portuguese because they have the *asientos* [contracts] for supplying slaves and the dispatch of the fleets and squadrons on the good journey, of which all trade depends, and of this nation there have been many Jewish merchants around here who live within their Law and they, upon getting rich, go to other kingdoms before they fall into the hands of the Inquisition."[48] Nevertheless, the sad truth is that most of them, together with their fortunes, did fall into the hands of the Inquisition.

The most important distinction between the crypto-Jews of the sixteenth and the seventeenth centuries was the difference in their intellectual level. The first wave of crypto-Jews had access to the Jesuit colleges because the *Societatis Jesus* did not introduce to their order the "Statutes of Purity of Blood" until 1570. Therefore, a good number of New Christians studied in their colleges and also in the Spanish universities, which never introduced the "Statutes" and remained universal—especially the University of Salamanca, at which several crypto-Jews got their degrees in medicine and law. Due to this policy, a notable number of them mastered Latin.

The second wave of New Christians and crypto-Jews had less opportunity to be educated in similar institutions, though a small number of them studied law in Salamanca, as was the case of Tomás Treviño Martínez de Sobremonte, who must have been a good Latinist, since he studied *Utroque Jure* (Roman and canon law) in the above mentioned university. It must be also said that Treviño was one of the most learned and devoted Jews of his time in New Spain. During his last seven years, spent in the secret jails of the Holy Office (1642–49), he refused to eat food prohibited for a Jew; and when he was asked, in the last minutes of his life, to take a cross in his hands as a sign that he was repentant for his sinful and wicked Jewish life, he refused to do so. Due to this refusal, he was burned alive.[49] The Inquisition extended its merciful hand only to those who in their last seconds appeared to be repenting for their sins and asked for clemency. As an act of Christian-Inquisitorial charity, the penitents were strangled before the wood on which they were standing was set ablaze.

The Collapse of the Crypto-Jewish Communities in Spanish America

In 1634 a young man who had recently arrived in Peru from Portugal was arrested in Lima. He was brutally tortured and, when lying on the rack, confessed his Jewishness, concurrently becoming a witness against other co-religionists. In this way he initiated a series of persecutions that culminated in the auto-da-fé celebrated in Lima in 1639 in which most of Peruvian Jewry was exterminated. During that same span of time, the community of Jewish merchants at Cartagena de Indias almost vanished.

The destruction of the crypto-Jewish community in New Spain began in 1641 when Gaspar de Robles, a member of the large López-Méndez-Enríquez family, who had been introduced by his uncles to Judaism in Angola, as other young people were, changed his creed and, as a sincere Catholic, denounced them as Judaizers.[50] During the course of the year 1642, the secret jails of New Spain's Inquisition swelled with crypto-Jews. During the four autos-da-fé celebrated between 1646 and 1649, more than 188 Judaizers were displayed and punished in these processions. This includes the living and the dead, since those who expired in jail or elsewhere were ignited in effigy along with the boxes that contained their exhumed bones from the different churches and graveyards of the city.

It should be underscored that 90 percent of the men condemned in the several autos-da-fé that were celebrated in Peru, Cartagena de Indias, and New Spain had been circumcised. A notable number of them went through this rite in Amsterdam, and others had their circumcisions performed in New Spain and Peru.[51]

The autos-da-fé had disastrous economic consequences in Spain as well as in the viceroyalties. The seizure and confiscation of property carried out in Peru between 1637 and 1639 caused the bankruptcy of the only bank that existed in those times in Lima.[52] The confiscated property in Cartagena de Indias and New Spain, which included a great amount of merchandise belonging to important brokers in Seville, was never paid back to them, and therefore caused their ruin. The seized property was partially sold at public auctions, and the money was used for current necessities of the Holy Office, such as ornaments for chapels and churches. The rest was invested in state bonds on the public debt, called juros, which paid their holders an annual revenue of 7 percent. In sum, the confiscations not only ruined big commercial houses in Seville and some great merchants in the colonies, but it changed active capital into passive in Spain and her overseas domains. Finally, the confiscations caused mistrust among the big financiers and entrepreneurs, mostly New Christians, some of whom were fortunate and fled with their capital to the Low Countries and England, kingdoms that were enemies of Spain.

The survivors of the last autos-da-fé celebrated in the Spanish American tribunals, who were considered potential heretics, were expelled from that part of the world. For both those who were honorable and prosperous subjects of the crown and others who were poor and degraded pariahs, it was not easy to abandon the land in which they had lived for decades. Most of them, though they wanted to leave the place of their sufferings, lacked the means to do so. They left the secret jails of the Inquisition with only the ragged clothes on their backs, which occasionally were covered with the *sambenito*. Many of them, including Juana Enríquez, the wife of Simon Váez Sevilla, had started their new life with only a *sambenito*, since their rags were destroyed the day following the auto-da-fé. Indeed, Juana, like most of those reconciled into the bosom of the Catholic Church, was condemned to get two hundred lashes for having communicated with her fellow prisoners during her years of confinement in jail. This punishment was applied by mounting the victim on a donkey in the public streets of the city. The executioner was rewarded by the spectators of this show with generous tips for every good flog.

All of the survivors had to beg in the street or seek loans to pay their passage to Spain. At the same time, the captains and sailors rejected them and refused to allow them on their ships, believing that having heretics on board could cause some misfortune to befall them on the high seas. But the Holy Office was implacable. It forced the owners of the vessels to obey their orders under penalty of a fine of two hundred ducats and the threat of excommunication.[53]

Nevertheless, small groups of crypto-Jews found ways of remaining in America. Terrible was their fate if, through misfortune, they were to fall once again into the grasp of the Holy Office. This happened to some of them, and their destiny was the flames. In 1659, in the auto-da-fé celebrated in Mexico City, two old men, Diego Díaz and Francisco Botello, who had nowhere to go, were reduced to ashes together with other heretics. Diego Muñoz de Alvarado, who was once mayor of the city of Puebla, was condemned as a Judaizer in June 1684 more because of his multiple holdings and possession of 100,000 pesos in cash than because of heresy. One of the last Jews sent to a pyre in Spanish America was Fernando de Medina, alias Moisés Gómez, a native of Bordeaux, France. He was linked to the tobacco monopoly, the administration of which was still in the hands of Portuguese financiers who, as has been noted, were in the majority New Christians. He was burned alive in a private auto-da-fé celebrated on 14 June 1699 in Mexico City.

By the eighteenth century, Spanish America was almost clean of Jews. The New Christians that had not abandoned this part of the world were, in general, already assimilated into the society of the Old Christians. Even the term "New Christian" fell into disuse in the Spanish colonies. The inhabitants, who had never seen a living example of a Jew, but who attended the religious theater and walked in the solemn processions during Holy Week, considered the Jew to be a mythical being who personified the concept of evil in history. Indeed, the Jew was identified with the devil and was believed to have a tail and horns. Concepts like these also prevailed in the first decades after the independence of Mexico—and of

Spanish America as a whole—until liberal ideas gained ground and different states issued laws establishing religious tolerance. The Inquisition, from its establishment in New Spain and the viceroyalty in Peru, formed and manipulated public opinion through the periodic publication of the Edicts of Faith, which were read in all the churches, including the smallest ones in the vast Spanish domains, and by this means transformed not only the Jews but also the English, Dutch, and other non-Catholics into demons and villains. When some French and even English came to New Spain with the Bourbon regiments in the second half of the eighteenth century, the Mexican Inquisitors wrote to the king in 1770, asking him to prohibit foreigners from passing to the Indies. The Holy tribunal feared that the foreigners' presence would "undetectably dispel among the majority of the inhabitants of this Kingdom the horror and abomination that they have against this nation [the English] only because of the idea that they are heretics and enemies of the religion and the Church."[54]

Notes

1. "Lineage of Santángel" in *Libro Verde de Aragón*, reproduced partially by Manuel Serrano y Sanz, *Orígenes de la Dominación española en América* (Madrid, 1918), 494–501; "Summary and Memory of the Converted Jews, Neighbors of the City of Zaragoza, Which Were Burnt in Person or in Statue, or Punished by the Inquisition between 1483–1504," in José Amador de los Ríos, *Historia Social, Política y Religiosa de los Judíos en España y Portugal* (Madrid, 1960), 756, 1010–22.
2. Fray Bartolomé de las Casas, *Historia de las Indias* (Mexico, 1996), vol. 1, 226–27.
3. Alice B. Gould, *Nueva Lista documentada de los tripulantes de Colón en 1492* (Madrid, 1984), 53–54. De Torres converted sometime in 1492, before the expulsion of the Jews from Spain, and enlisted himself with the Adelantado of Murcia, Don Juan Chacón. He was asked to cross the Atlantic Ocean with Columbus because of his knowledge of Hebrew and Aramaic. He traveled on the boat *Santa María* and was left in the first colony founded by Columbus in the New World, named Navidad, where he was killed by the Indians together with his companions. Bartomomé de las Casas, *Historia*, vol. 1, 239.
4. Antonio Domíguez Ortiz, *Los judeoconversos en España y en América* (Madrid, 1971), 49–50.
5. Claudio Guillén, "Un padrón de conversos sevillanos," in *Bulletin Hispanique* (Bordeaux, 1963), T. 65, 40–85.
6. The names Alonso de Ávila and Gil González de Benavides de Ávila were used very frequently in the same family, the name passing mostly from an uncle to his cousin. The same was the case in the family of the Santángels, mentioned above.
7. "Inquiry of the Holy Office against Alonso de Ávila ... Mexico, 1537," Archivo General de la Nación de México, further AGNM, Inquisition, further Inq., Index of the first volume of the Inquisition files.
8. Returning from Spain, Alonso de Ávila enlisted under Francisco Montejo and in 1528 took part in the conquest of Yucatán.
9. Eva A. Uchmany, "De algunos cristianos nuevos en la conquista y colonización de la Nueva España," *Estudios de Historia Novohispana* (1985):265–318; and "Proceso de Gonzalo Gómez por palabras malsonantes, México 1536," AGNM, Inq., vol. 2, exp. 2.

10. Cristóbal Bermúdez Plata, *Catálogo de pasajeros a Indias durante los siglos XVI, XVII y XVIII* (Seville, 1964), 2 vols.
11. Amador de los Ríos, "Historia," 623–27.
12. Ruth Pike, *Aristócratas y comerciantes, la sociedad sevillana en el siglo XVI* (Barcelona, 1978), 105.
13. Francisco López de Gómara, *Historia General de las Indias* (Barcelona, 1954), vol. 2, 4, 299.
14. "Testamento de Hernando Cortés," in *Cartas y Documentos de Cortés* (Mexico, 1963), 499, 508, 514, 570, 589.
15. Bernal Díaz del Castillo, *Historia Verdadera de la Conquista de México* (Mexico, 1960), vol. 2, 161–63.
16. "The Will of Rodrigo de Paz, Native of Salamanca, September 23, 1525" and "Nuevo Codicilo de R. de Paz, September 30, 1525," in A. Millares Carlo and J. I. Mantecón, *Indice y extractos de los Protocolos del Archivo de Notarías de México, 1524–1528* (Mexico, 1945), vol. 1, 42–44, doc. numb. 74. and doc. numb.96.
17. Hibueras is today's Honduras and part of Nicaragua. In this unfortunate expedition Cortés lost his governorship in New Spain.
18. Millares Carlo and Mantecón, *Indice y extractos*, note at 57.
19. An *encomienda* included land, water, and Indians, whose labor was the main capital of the conquistador (*encomendero*). The granting of an *encomienda* was limited in time: a span of years or one or more lifetimes.
20. "'Statements of Bartolomé González and Pedro Vázquez de Vergara,' Companions of Hernando Alonso in the Conquest of Mexico," in "Diligencias sobre los Sambenitos antiguos y renovación de ellos y postura de los que se han relaxado y requeridos por este Santo Oficio, Mexico, 1574," AGNM, Inq., vol. 77, exp. 35. (This was an Inquisitorial list of all those punished by the Inquisition in Mexico, including those condemned to death. They were given over to secular justice to execute the terrible order to burn them at the stake. This was done in the late afternoon, after the reading of their sentences came to an end. The formal tribunal was establish in Mexico in 1571. After an exhaustive investigation into all those convicted, the penitential garment (*sambenito*) of the convicted was displayed in the cathedral of the city, so that they and their families would live in shame for generations. The *sambenito* in itself was an overgarment marked with a cross of Saint Andrew, on which the sentence of the convicted was painted.)
21. According to Don Sebastián Ramírez de Fuenleal, archbishop and Inquisitor of Santo Domingo, who became in 1530 the president of the Royal Audience of New Spain, in "Statements" of the above mentioned witnesses.
22. Uchmany, "De algunos," 301–2.
23. Francisco Fernández del Castillo, "Alonso de Estrada, su familia," in *Memorias de la Academia Mexicana de la Historia* (Mexico, 1942), T. I., 398–431; Norberto Castro y Tosi, "Verdadera paternidad de Alonso de Estrada," in *Revista de Indias* (Madrid, 1948), vol. 9, 1011–26.
24. Gudrun Lohmeyer, personal communication, and Master's Degree thesis on the conquest of Chiapas. Haim Beinart, *Records of the Trials of the Spanish Inquisition in Ciudad Real, 1483–1525* (Jerusalem, 1974–85), 4 vols.
25. *Kasher* is the Hebrew word meaning "pure, not contaminated" according to Jewish dietary ordinances. Deformation of the word "Kosher," as used in Yiddish.
26. Uchmany, "De algunos," 301–2.
27. "Testamento de Diego de Ocaña, México 1533," in *Vida Colonial*, publication of the AGNM, 1933, numb. VIII, 3–15.
28. Enrique Otte, *Las perlas del Caribe: Nueva Cádiz de Cubagua* (Caracas, 1977), 198–99.
29. Javier E. Sánchiz Ruiz, "La limpieza de sangre en la Nueva España, El funcionariado del Santo Oficio de la Inquisición, siglo XVI," Master's Degree thesis, 1990, UNAM, unpublished, 109–12.
30. "Letters, Testimonies and Information" on Doctor Christóbal de Miranda, from the year 1577, in AGNM, Inq., vol. 79, exp. 10; vol. 80, exps. 8,9,10, 11 and 21; vol. 82, exp. 34; and from the year 1579, vol. 82, exp. 14.

31. José Toribio Medina, *Historia del tribunal de la Inquisición de Lima, 1596–1820*, ed. Marcel Bataillon (Santiago de Chile, 1956), 175–76.
32. This concept is discussed in Eva A. Uchmany, *La vida entre el Judaísmo y el Cristianismo en la Nueva España, 1580–1606* (Mexico, 1992, 1994), 158–59.
33. Uchmany, *La vida*, 158–59.
34. Uchmany, *La vida*.
35. Ibid.
36. Eva A. Uchmany, "The Periodization of the History of the New Christians and Crypto-Jews in New Spain" in *New Horizons in Sephardic Studies*, ed. Yedida K. Stillman and Georges K. Zucker (Albany, 1993), 113.
37. Jaime Contreras, *El Santo Oficio de la Inquisicien de Galicia*, Madrid, 1982, 39–65.
38. "Yeshiva" is a rabbinical school.
39. "Testification of Balthazar de Araujo against Luis Franco Rodríguez, 1634," in Manuel Tejado Fernández, *Aspectos de la vida social en Cartagena de Indias durante el seiscientos* (Sevilla, 1954), 322–24.
40. Medina, *Historia*, vol. 2, 93.
41. *Maariv* is an evening prayer.
42. "According to the testimony of the sorcerer Diego López, the man who was reading from the book was young, about 23 years old, of dark complexion and a newcomer in Cartagena," in Manuel Tejado Fernández, *Aspectos*, 200.
43. Eva A. Uchmany, "Simón Váez Sevilla," in *Estudios de Historia Novohispana* (Mexico, 1987), vol. 4, 307–22.
44. Miguel de Cervantes Saavedra, *El ingenioso caballero Don Quijote de la Mancha*, chap. 42.
45. Uchmany, *La vida*, 87–88.
46. Ibid., last chapter and enclosed documents.
47. In 1610 a third tribunal of the Holy Office was establish in Spanish America.
48. "Letters of don Francisco de Valverde Mercado, Puertobelo, 1 and 30 of July, 1606," Archivo General de Indias, Seville, Audiencia de Panamá, exps. 718 and 725.
49. "Causa Criminal contra Tomás Treviño de Sobremonte, por judaizante, Oaxaca, 1625"; and "Segundo Proceso Criminal …, México 1642," in *Boletín del Archivo General de la Nación* (Mexico, 1935), T. VI, no, 1, 2, 3 and 1936, T. VII, 1, 2, 3.
50. "Testification of Gaspar de Robles, México 1641," AGNM, Inq., vol. 390, exp. 11, and "Proceso criminal contra Francisco Home alias Vicente Enríquez por judaizante," vol. 391.
51. Description or *Relación Sumaria* of the autos-da-fé celebrated in Mexico City in the years 1646, 1647, 1648, and 1649. These books, best-sellers in their time, were written by Don Pedro de Estrada y Escobedo, member of the administration of the cathedral of Mexico City, and brother of Francisco de Estrada y Escobedo, one of New Spain's Inquisitors at the time. The auto-da-fé celebrated in Lima, Peru, was described by the Presbyter Fernando de Montesinos, a "Familiar" (lay collaborator), of the tribunal of Lima. The books were published in the printing houses of the Holy Office, and most of them include the sermon that was preached during the autos-da-fé. Some of these *Relaciones* survived, and a copy can be found in The John Carter Brown Library.
52. "Letter from the Inquisitors of Peru to the Supreme Council of the tribunal … giving statement of the bankruptcy of the Bank of Juan de la Cueva," in *Archivo Histórico Nacional*, Madrid, Inq., libro 1040, fs. 423–25.
53. "Letters and orders, Mexico 1649," annexed to the "Proceso criminal contra Simín Váez Sevilla por judaizante, Mexico 1642," AGNM, Inq., vol. 398, exp. 1.
54. José Toribio Medina, *Historia del tribunal del Santo Oficio en México* (Mexico, 1952), 293.

– Chapter 10 –

CRYPTO-JEWS AND NEW CHRISTIANS IN COLONIAL PERU AND CHILE

Günter Böhm

IN 1947 WHEN I SUBMITTED to the Chilean Historical Society the manuscript for my book *Los Judíos en Chile durante la Colonia*,[1] I thought that
I had exhausted all available documentation on the subject in Chile—
going beyond even José Toribio Medina's legacy of work on the Inquisition, which forms part of the treasures in the National Library in
Santiago. The response I received from Chilean historians such as Carlos
Larraín de Castro seemed to confirm my belief.[2]

Now, fifty years after beginning my research on the presence of Jews
in colonial Peru and Chile, I must admit that many related questions have
yet to be resolved. Because we have no knowledge of any testimony from
the accused or their contemporaries, the history of the Jews must be
found almost exclusively in the acts and proceedings of the Holy Office
of the Inquisition's tribunal. The information in the acts of the tribunal in
Lima leads us to believe that no more than 250 people were accused of
having Jewish origins between 1569—the year that this tribunal was
established in Lima (Fig. 10.1)—and 1690. Of this sum, scarcely a dozen
cases occurred in the territory of present-day Chile. We may never know
with certainty the exact number—or even an approximation thereof—of
Judaists who settled temporarily or permanently in these territories.
Here, I will put forth a few of the reasons for which we do not have more
records concerning the real number of Jewish converts (*conversos*) or clandestine Jews in colonial Chile and Peru at our disposal.

To begin, I must mention that several decades passed after the conquest of these two countries and after the constitution of the tribunal of
the Holy Office of the Inquisition in Lima before any denouncements

FIGURE 10.1   Royal letters patent establishing the Holy Office of the Inquisition in Chile. Madrid, 25 January 1569.

against Judaizers were received. The tribunal's early activities were primarily concerned with combating heresy and sins against the holy Catholic faith, as well as staving off Protestantism's possible infiltration into the region—which, it was thought, might be brought in by crew members of foreign vessels.

During the sixteenth century, numerous *conversos* were able to proceed into the territory of Chile, owing to the lack of European inhabitants and the absence of a local tribunal, for here there were only commissioners who had been named by the headquarters. Years later, often after their deaths, the true origins of many of these crypto-Jews were revealed only because their names appeared in generally anonymous, libelous pamphlets.

An example of this is provided by the case of Rodrigo de Orgoños,[3] a member of the small army that accompanied Diego de Almagro on his 1535 exploratory expedition to Chile. Born in Oropresa in the diocese of Toledo, Spain, he was the legitimate son of Alfonso Jiménez, a Jewish cobbler, and Beatríz Dueñas. While serving in Italy, this Spanish soldier adopted the surname of a modest hidalgo from Oropresa, claiming to be his illegitimate son and demanding legal recognition as such in return for a large sum of money and a yearly allowance. Whatever the truth, Juan de Orgoños denied any relation to Rodrigo and publicly declared, "What an annoying Jew; he is not my son, and I thank God for that fact."[4] Naturally, the records that contain this information were unknown in Chile and Peru during Orgoños's stays in both countries.

Years later, another Spanish soldier, Diego García de Cáceres, served with the conqueror of Chile, Pedro de Valdivia, and soon after, in 1583, became acting governor. Two of Chile's founding fathers, José Miguel Carrera and Diego Portales, number among García de Cáceres's descendants.[5] A full four centuries after García de Cáceres arrived in Chile, his Jewish origins were revealed with the discovery and publication of a text in Lima. The work had been written in 1621—many years after the death of García de Cáceres—by Pedro Mejía de Ovando, and was therefore known as "La Ovandina." In this work, Ovando claimed to know of a list of families who had assumed noble titles through payment of huge sums of money. Among them was the García de Cáceres family, as this passage from the proceedings shows: "Ramiro Yañez de Saravía, married in the kingdom of Chile to Doña Isabel de Cáceres y Osorio, daughter of Diego García de Cáceres of Plascencia where he and his descendants are publicly deemed new Christians, descendants of Jews."[6] Thanks to documents that still exist in Spain, it has been proven that Diego García was neither a hidalgo nor from Cáceres, as Ovando had claimed.

A 1570 letter to the General Inquisitor referring to both Chile and Peru confirms the ease with which Spanish *conversos* arrived and resided in colonial Chile, saying, "with respect to the few Spaniards in these parts, there are two times as many converts as in Spain."

Of equal importance is the case of the soldier Luis Duarte, son of a Portuguese Jewish *converso*, who changed his surname to Noble and was baptized by a clergyman who had been "degraded for being a Judaizer." Despite the fact that he had been denounced as a Jew in the port of Buenos Aires, Luis Noble was able to travel to Peru where, in 1608, he had no problem enlisting in a troop that was then sent from the port of Callao to Chile. In the middle of 1614 he returned to Peru. His Jewish origins would never have been known had it not been for the fact that, in dire need of sustenance, he robbed a church. As a result, he was captured and tried in the tribunal of the Holy Office in Lima, wherein he was forced to acknowledge his true origins.[7]

As a result of the temporary unification of the two Iberian crowns between 1580 and 1640, a significant number of Portuguese New Christians began to flock to Spain's New World dominions. They were assured residency within Hispanic territories through legally obtained authorizations despite the fact that they were considered foreigners. These Portuguese first headed to Brazil and, by way of the port of Buenos Aires, moved on to Córdoba, Tucumán, and the silver mines in Potosí. Often they continued on to Peru and Chile. Documents received by the Inquisition's tribunal in Lima constantly complain of their presence. For example, one written document affirms "that through the port of Buenos Aires in the province of Río de la Plata enter many Portuguese from the Hebrew nation" and earnestly demands that they be stopped from entering the region.

The surgeon Diego Núñez de Silva (father of the martyr, Bachelor Francisco Maldonado de Silva, whom I discuss below) must have traveled this very same route. Around 1580 in San Miguel de Tucumán, he married an Old Christian, the daughter of one of the conquerors.[8] Many other Portuguese followed the same path as a means of safeguarding against the possibility of seizure orders given by civil or ecclesiastic authorities.

Because of Chile's known poverty, due in part to the lack of important silver or gold mines and due also to the constant attacks on Spanish villages by Indians, few Portuguese dared travel to the region. For this reason, even in Santiago, the Chilean territory's principal city, there were only about three thousand settlers of Spanish origin around the year 1630. This number had risen to nearly six thousand by 1642 when a full sixth of the population was lost in a great earthquake that completely devastated the city. For the next few decades, the residents of Santiago lived in the most alarming misery, which prompted Bishop Gaspar de Villaroel's urgent request for aid from Lima. It is therefore understandable that very few Judaizers risked settling in Chile, and when they did, it was due to the immediate need to escape orders for their capture given by the tribunal of the Holy Office in Spain or to escape the denouncements of its commissioners in Buenos Aires.

This was apparently the case of Doctor Rodrigo Henríquez de Fonseca (whose parents were imprisoned in Spain for being Judaizers), his wife, and Luis Rivero, his brother-in-law.[9] These three had fled to Santiago, changing their surnames to Sotelo before setting sail for the New

World. The arrival of Doctor Henríquez de Fonseca and his wife, Leonor de Andrade, is of special interest in the history of Jews in Chile because they were the first Jewish couple to settle there. In addition, their daughter, who was born in Santiago in late 1665, was the first known child of both a Jewish father and mother in Chile. When Doctor Henríquez de Fonseca committed the indiscretion of signing a document with his real name, the Holy Office's commissioner identified him, having already received the orders for his arrest from Lima. Their trial lasted a number of years, and after being tortured, the doctor and his wife admitted to having practiced various Jewish customs in both Spain and the New World. Once the brother-in-law, Luis Rivero, had confessed to being "a follower of Moses' Law, he killed himself by bloodletting," as the Inquisitors of Lima so concisely state in a letter.

Of special importance here is the last known Inquisition trial in Chile, that of Leonel Gómez Pereyra, who was born to Jewish parents in Viana, Portugal, around 1636.[10] To avoid being identified, he adopted the name León Gómez de Oliva. Owing to the length of his trial, which began in July 1679 and continued until May 1683, and the extensive personal data that he himself provided, we are able to reconstruct the biography of one of the many Portuguese who settled in Chile during the seventeenth century. Within many important social circles in the country it was common knowledge that he was a New Christian, but this did not prevent León Gómez from marrying an Old Christian gentlewoman and attaining important positions, such as that of councilman. Although he was sentenced by the tribunal of the Holy Office to suffer "the confiscation of his goods ... for formal guilt of Judaism," he became "an Established brother of Saint Peter's guild in the cathedral of this city [Santiago]"; received the "Letter of benefactor in the Society of JHS [Jesus]"; and obtained the "Letter of brotherhood in the Religion of my father, Saint Augustine." León Gómez de Oliva must have had many powerful friends. Because this "penitent" had made important donations to the "Main Church" and the Monastery of Santa Clara, I suspect that he had befriended a number of influential members of the clergy. This being so, we can understand that, in 1708, upon signing his last will and testament, he dared request a "burial in the Church of our Lady of Mercy in this city," and that his body be accompanied to the sepulcher "by the priest and sacristan of my parish with the cross held high."

Peru's highlands, with their important silver mines, indisputably attracted more Portuguese in the sixteenth century than did any other region. The Inquisitors Verdugo and Gaytan, from the tribunal in Lima, call our attention to this fact in a report sent to Madrid in May 1622: "The village of Potosí is full of Portuguese ... and generally speaking they are all from the Hebrew nation, and our experience shows that those who have been imprisoned by the Inquisition all Judaize" and that "they now live very cautiously and they are no longer as easily identifiable as before."[11]

Portuguese miners and merchants were not the only settlers of Potosí and the Peruvian highlands, however. Many clergymen and men of letters also took up residence there as well. In 1629, the chronicler Vázquez de Espinosa estimated this region's Spanish population to be about four thousand, whereas Lima's Spanish inhabitants numbered only ten thousand. In a Royal Bull from the end of October 1603, specific reference was made to the potential harm done by Portuguese clergy with Hebrew origins. One such clergyman was the bishop of Tucumán, Friar Francisco de Vitoria, who "is kin to the Piedras Santas family from Granada, known Jews, and whose brother, Diego Pérez de Acosta … of Jewish class and lineage" was found guilty of adhering to "Moses' Law" in 1602.[12]

Just as illuminating is the case of the Portuguese clergyman, Diego López de Lisboa, who was burned to death for being a Judaizer. Although they were known to be Jewish in Spain as well as in Lima, both he and his wife falsely claimed to be Old Christians. In Lima, Diego López de Lisboa came to be the chaplain to Archbishop Fernando Arias de Ugarte. In 1635, documents from the tribunal of the Holy Inquisition in Lima name him as they tell how "many people came to this archbishop's windows, saying, 'Cast that Jew from Your Majesty's house.'"[13]

Two of López de Lisboa's four children occupied important posts in Peru. The first, Diego, changed his surname to León Pinelo and in 1647 was awarded the cathedra of *Prima Cánones* (ecclesiastic theology) in the University of San Marcos. Yet a number of Inquisitors believed that it was "very dangerous to entrust the interpretation of the sacred Canons, the ecclesiastic material, and the sacraments to a person so foul and suspect as he." Despite these doubts, Diego León Pinelo was later appointed rector of the University of San Marcos and General Protector of the Indians of Peru.[14]

Even more famous than Diego de León Pinelo was his brother, Antonio, who had used the same surname as Diego since 1636 and who was considered an illustrious writer and bibliographer and a legal expert. After moving to Madrid, Antonio published a number of works, among them the *Sumarios de la recopilación general de las leyes* on the laws of the Indies. As a result of his important publications, he is rightly known as the father of American bibliography.

If Potosí became the third most populous city in Hispanic America, relying on Vásquez de Espinosa's *Compendio y descripción de las Indias Occidentales*, we see that Lima was the second most important city in the New World (after Mexico City) in 1630. During the second half of the seventeenth century, Lima was also the favorite South American city of New Christians and crypto-Jews. In fact, we have a picturesque description of Peru and Chile provided by an anonymous Portuguese Jew in the first decade of the seventeenth century. This author also spoke favorably of neighboring regions as he considered the possibilities for commercial exchange with the Netherlands. His *General Description* gives many details, among them important data concerning Spanish fortifications in the different ports and cities of the region. This information was of special use to the Dutch West India Company, which would soon begin its colonizing expeditions into new American territories.

It is important to note that the author of the *Description* was a Jew and that, after his formal baptism, he was able to live in the viceroyalty of Peru without complications and without being bothered by the tribunal of the Inquisition. After having lived, for the most part, in Lima for some ten years, this Jew left Peru around the year 1615. Sadly, his *General Description* is the only source of information that issues directly from a Jewish resident of those territories.[15]

The number of Portuguese Judaizers must have risen considerably in the 1630s, judging by the increasing number of public trials occurring in Lima, as well as the large quantity of Portuguese accused in the "Great Complicity" or "Conspiracy" proceedings that ended in the trials of 1639.[16] In this process, no fewer than fifty-seven of the total sixty-three accused were Portuguese or sons of Portuguese.[17] Of the six remaining, four were from Seville, a city with a high concentration of *conversos*, many of whom set sail for the New World during the unification of Iberian kingdoms.

The most important of the massive detentions of Portuguese occurred in Lima in 1635, when a third of the city's Judaizing population was captured. According to a document sent to Madrid by the Inquisitors on 18 May 1635, this event plunged the city into bankruptcy and brought about the ruin of the major part of its commerce.[18] What is more, it alarmed the commissioner in Chile, who then ordered a census of the Portuguese living in that territory. A total of twenty-eight people were counted, but this prompted no Inquisitorial proceedings since there were no denunciations of them as being Judaizers.

The aforementioned Inquisitorial report of May 1635 also provides us with other details concerning the Portuguese presence in Lima. For example, the majority were single and had arrived in Lima between 1628 and 1630. An important sector of commerce rested in their hands, and the Inquisitors wrote, "the Spaniard who does not have a Portuguese for a business partner fears he will not be successful." What is more, "all merchandise, from brocade to sackcloth, from diamonds to trinkets, all passed through their hands." The Inquisitors knew full well that these Portuguese developed both business and family ties with other New Christian countrymen throughout the countries of the Old World and the New. The Inquisitors also knew of the double religious lives led by many of these Portuguese, as demonstrated in a document that attests, "generally none is caught without their rosary, reliquary, icons ... and other devotions.... They know the catechism, pray the rosary and, when asked ... why they pray, they reply that they never forget their prayers in times of need, as in prison, and they appear devout in order to deceive, so that they will be taken for good Christians."

The arrests that took place during the "Great Complicity" proceedings came about because of the indiscretion of a single *converso*, Antonio

Cordero, who in August 1634 was accused by the Holy Office of practicing Jewish customs.[19] He and the others who were detained were tortured and forced to reveal the names of still others who were involved. These prisoners also provided details concerning Jewish practices, rites, and customs as well as the places where Judaizers met to pray. As a result, Manuel Bautista Perez's name appeared as the spiritual leader or "Great Captain."[20] He was

> A man of good reputation and was deemed the oracle of the Hebrew nation, always considered to be the principal observer of Moses' Law. He presided over the meetings concerning this law, which were held in his house. He had many spiritual books and dealt with Theologians of Portuguese descent.... On the outside, he seemed a good Christian, celebrating the Holy Sacrament, hearing especially those masses and sermons which told the stories of the Old Testament.... Although he tried, he could not foil the astute members of the Holy Office of the Inquisition who eagerly collected proof of his deceit in performing these acts. He was captured for being a Judaist ... and listened to his sentence with grave dignity. He died unrepentant, telling the executioner to do his job.

Although the Inquisitors do not give a reason, the bachelor Francisco Maldonado de Silva was implicated in the trials of 1639 and taken prisoner by the tribunal of the Holy Office in Chile. Along with ten other accused, he was sentenced to *"relajado en persona,"* whereas Manuel de Paz, who killed himself in prison, was condemned to *"relajado en estatua."* In my 1984 book, *Historia de los Judíos en Chile*, I make known all of the existing biographical information and documentation concerning Maldonado de Silva. It is notable that this distinguished figure, martyred for his faith, had no problem traveling to, and establishing himself in, Chile, although both his father and older brother had been brought before the tribunal of the Holy Office in Lima in March 1605. Nor was this background a professional obstacle, since he was given work as a doctor in Santiago's Hospital of San Juan de Dios in 1619. Yet because he had openly confessed his Judaism to his younger sister Isabel in 1625, he was arrested, taken to the secret prisons of the tribunal of the Holy Office in Lima, and burned at the stake at an auto-da-fé on 23 January 1639 (Fig 10.2).

After the massive trials of 1639, the activities of the tribunal of the Holy Office in Lima abated. A significant number of Judaists left the city, surely, or ceased their practice of Jewish rites. After 1666, no one is mentioned as having been accused of Judaizing in the Acts of the Holy Office. In 1736, María Ana de Castro, an almost legendary figure who had love affairs with many of Lima's aristocrats, was the last person to be sentenced and burned alive at the stake.[21]

Although no more cases of "Judaizers" are known to exist in the available documents of the tribunal of the Holy Office in Lima during the colonial period, the interpretation of the information we do have continues.

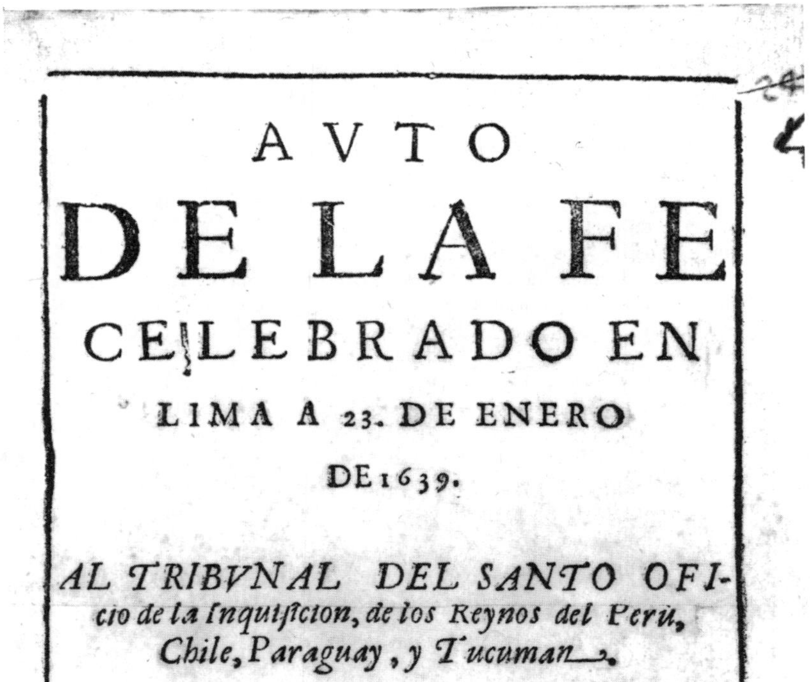

A V T O

DE LA FE

CE₁LEBRADO EN

LIMA A 23. DE ENERO

DE 1639.

AL TRIBVNAL DEL SANTO OFI-
cio de la Inquuficion, de los Reynos del Perú,
Chile, Paraguay, y Tucuman⸳

POR EL LICENCIADO D. FER-
nando de Montefinos Presbitero, natural
de Offuna.

CON LICENCIA

DE SV EXCELENCIA, DEL ORDI-
nario, y del fanto Oficio. Impreffo en Lima,
por Pedro de Cabrera; Año de 1639.

Vendenfe en la tienda de Simon Chirinos, Mercader de Libros.

FIGURE 10.2   Title page of a pamphlet relating to the auto-da-fé in Lima, 23 January 1639.

Notes

Translated from the Spanish by Carrie C. Chorba.

1. Günter Böhm, *Los Judíos en Chile durante la Colonia* (Santiago, 1948).
2. Ibid., 5–9.
3. Carlos Larrain de Castro, "Los Judíos en Chile Colonial," *Judaica* 133–134 (July–August 1944):27–28.
4. José Armando de Ramón Folch, *Descrubrimiento de Chile y compañeros de Almagro* (Santiago, 1953), 167–68.
5. Larrain de Castro, "Los Judíos," 34.
6. Antonio R. Rodriguez Moñino, "Pedro Mexia de Ovando, cronista de linajes coloniales. Andanzas Inquisitoriales de 'La Ovandina,'" *Tierra Firme*, no. 3–4 (1936):413.
7. Günter Böhm, "Luis Noble: La Historia de un soldado judío en Chile," *Sefardica* 7 (1989):50.
8. Günter Böhm, *Historia de los Judíos en Chile*, vol. 1 (Santiago, 1984), 21–23.
9. Günter Böhm, "Criptojudaismo en América Latina," *Sefardica* 10 (1993):52–53.
10. Ibid., 53–57.
11. Letter written by the Inquisitors Francisco Verdugo and Andrés Juan Gaytan, 4 May 1622. Archivo Histórico Nacional, Madrid (Inquisición Libro 1038, fls. 417v–418v).
12. Günter Böhm, "Algunos Clérigos 'portugueses' en América del sur colonial," *Sefardica*, no. 3 (1985):33.
13. Ibid., 36–37.
14. Ibid., 39.
15. Günter Böhm, "Una descripción del reino de Chile por un judio 'portugués,' a comienzos del siglo XVIII," *Maguen-Escudo* 100 (1966):20–24.
16. Mentioned by the Inquisitors as "*complicidad granda*."
17. Böhm, *Historia de los Judios en Chile*, vol. 1, 141, 399–426.
18. Ibid., 345–67.
19. Ibid., 329, 345–49.
20. Ibid., 420–21.
21. José Toribio Medina, *Historia del tribunal del Santo Oficio de la Inquisición en Lima*, vol. 2 (Santiago, 1956), 273–74.

PART III

THE LUSO-BRAZILIAN EXPERIENCE: JEWS IN PORTUGUESE LATIN AMERICA

– Chapter 11 –

MARRANOS AND THE INQUISITION: ON THE GOLD ROUTE IN MINAS GERAIS, BRAZIL

Anita Novinsky

O NE OF THE LEAST KNOWN FACTS in the history of Jewish involvement in the expansion of Europe is the role of marranos in Brazil at the beginning of the modern era. New Christians, descendants of Jews who converted to Catholicism, tried to take advantage of the opportunities opened up by the Atlantic sea routes to the west to begin new lives—lives that in many cases had been suspended by the persecutions of the Holy Office of the Inquisition.

This essay will focus on the region of Minas Gerais during the first half of the eighteenth century, a period in which the Portuguese Inquisition waged its most rigorous attacks against descendants of Jews. My research is based entirely upon as yet unpublished documents, primarily fifty-seven transcripts of trials concerning prisoners from Minas Gerais, all of whom were incarcerated in Portugal. These documents reveal the involvement of New Christians in expeditions in search of gold, in the construction of early settlements and villages, in mineral extraction, and in commercial, political, administrative, and cultural spheres, along with the persecutions they suffered in a new world molded upon old prejudices.

The discovery of gold deposits at the turn of the century produced a veritable rush toward the mines, both from Portugal, where entire villages were emptied, and from São Paulo, Rio de Janeiro, Bahia, and Pernambuco. Approximately 300,000 Portuguese set off in search of the mining regions of Brazil in the eighteenth century, a considerable number of whom were New Christians.

Before discussing the history of New Christians in the gold region, however, I want to turn to some more general considerations concerning the Jewish role in European expansion. Alfredo Margarido, an eminent professor from the University of Paris, has written that had the Jewish community not existed, European expansion would have been slower and the Portuguese would not have achieved their worldwide presence.[1] A well-known essayist on Portuguese culture, Margarido credits the techniques, experiences, and wealth of the Jews (or New Christians) with imposing a well-defined path for European expansion, which led to the enlargement of the known world. The dissemination of Portuguese and Spanish Jews created a network of relations between far-flung outposts of the empire, which in turn stimulated commerce during an age when communications were extremely difficult.[2]

The introduction of the Inquisition tribunal in Portugal was a reaction to the development of a competitive and upwardly mobile mercantile middle class that inserted itself into the spheres of power, thereby threatening the aristocracy's political and financial hegemony. The tribunal covered itself in a mantle of "holiness" and extended its control over the entire empire. Religion and all of its symbolic trappings served a practical end: to prevent the ascension of a new class with new demands and new values that directly contradicted the beliefs held by leading conservative groups in Portugal. A desire to appropriate the material goods accumulated by the New Christian mercantile bourgeoisie was also a factor in bringing the Inquisition to the recently discovered, gold-producing regions of Brazil.[3]

Professor Jonathan I. Israel, like Professor Margarido, has also called attention to the Jewish contribution to economic life in the early modern period. He states that the preeminence of Sephardic Jews in the world economy has been one of the most remarkable phenomenons in history.[4] Scattered to the four corners of the earth, the Sephardic Jews maintained a central role in the Western European market over the course of three centuries, as well as in the economic interactions between the Middle East, West Africa, India, the Caribbean, and Brazil.

According to Professor Israel, the reasons for this success lie in the social, religious, cultural, and economic ties that these Sephardic Jews established between commercial communities that were enormously distant from each other. At a time when communications in Europe were slow and difficult, the Sephardic Jews were able to maintain contact with their brethren in the most distant regions in the world.[5] Although he includes Brazil in this economic web, Professor Israel does not investigate closely the extensive commercial network created by Brazilian New Christians, nor its relevance within a global economic context.

A third, rather bold thesis, which has been widely contested by traditional historians, is that of Ellis Rivkin. Rivkin's argument seems to me to be extremely pertinent to the Brazilian phenomenon.[6] He stresses the importance of Portuguese Jews in unleashing a "process of modernization and westernization that transformed Europe's destiny." Whereas Spanish Jews were mired in the diaspora, Portuguese crypto-Jews were involved in large-scale enterprises overseas. Rivkin also calls attention to an important and original fact in Jewish history that has given rise to polemical debate: the Portuguese New Christians' "option" to remain New Christians. Even when these New Christians found themselves living in regions of Europe that afforded them relative tolerance, they would often choose to return to Portugal or to live in lands belonging to the Portuguese crown, where they would suffer from legal discrimination yet also benefit from great opportunities for social and economic advancement. In Rivkin's opinion, the religious identity of the New Christians was "negotiable," and they chose their unique role as entrepreneurs over their Jewish religious identity. Portuguese New Christians were neither sincere New Christians nor crypto-Jews, but rather "crypto-individualists."[7] In large part, this description corresponds to the situation in Brazil, especially with regard to wealthy businessmen and contractors, although one must be careful not to generalize, since Rivkin's argument does not apply well to the complexity and dynamics of the Brazilian marrano phenomenon in its entirety.

* * * *

A NEW ERA IN THE ECONOMIC HISTORY of Portuguese New Christians began in the eighteenth century with the discovery of gold deposits in Brazil. Accounts of the economic activities and daily social life of New Christians in Minas Gerais are essentially absent from Brazilian historiography, with the exception of the work of J. Gonçalves Salvador. Prominent Brazilian historians have minimized or ignored the role of Jewish descendants in the colonization of Brazil, from an economic as well as a social and cultural standpoint. In his classic work on Minas Gerais, Augusto Lima Júnior calls attention to the large New Christian population, yet states that "rarely one finds in Minas Gerais proceedings against New Christians for practicing Judaism."[8] Caio Boschi, a specialist in colonial Minas history, wrote in one of his articles that "there are no decidedly pronounced traces of Jewish religious life in colonial Minas."[9] The abundant documentation I examined in the archives of the extinct Inquisition tribunal, referring to Minas Gerais and the New Christians, reveals a quite different scenario, however. Professor José Gonçalves Salvador, using genealogical research, has reconstructed the Jewish origins of a large portion of the *mineiro* population (i.e., those living in Minas Gerais), and furnished us with important data for understanding the "quality" of the people who made up Minas society.[10] Yet it is the detailed study of the trials of those New Christians who were condemned that offers us a fuller picture of the daily life and the manner of thinking of the first *mineiros*; this type of analysis has not been attempted until now.

The New Christians who migrated to Brazil—who forged through virgin territory, captured Indians, and came into conflict with the Jesuits—were men of a radically different mindset from the Ashkenazim Jews or the Sephardic Christian converts who spread across the Netherlands, France, and Italy. Highly assimilated and distanced for over a century from Jewish culture, their adventurous and violent lifestyle was markedly different from that of Jews in other parts of the world. The degree of assimilation and integration of New Christians in the social and political context of colonial Brazil may be understood by looking at three men of Jewish origin who distinguished themselves in the political and administrative life of Minas Gerais: Garcia Rodrigues Pais, Miguel Teles da Costa, and Manuel Nunes Viana.

Garcia Rodrigues Pais, the son of Fernão Dias Pais, a well-known "emerald hunter," organized the first pioneering and founding expedition in Minas Gerais, building a route to Minas called *Caminho Novo* (the New Road), which also became known as *Caminho do Comércio* (the Commercial Road). This road considerably shortened the journey from Rio de Janeiro, the port from which basic goods flowed between Portugal and Ouro Preto. In 1702, in recompense for his services to the crown, Garcia Rodrigues Pais was appointed Inspector General of the Mines, a position of such prestige that it encouraged him to request entry into the renowned Order of Christ. Entry was refused because he was "dishonored as a New Christian by the part of his maternal grandmother."[11] Legislative action and prejudice against Jewish descendants managed to affect New Christians up to the fifth or sixth generation. While the struggle for survival in America eased the barriers between Old Christians and New Christians, the latter, primarily merchants, were still regarded with suspicion by the Portuguese government. Yet the decisive factor in the inclusion of New Christians in the local elite was their level of wealth, which in Brazil could both "whiten the skin" and "erase the stain" of Jewish blood.

Nothing is known of Garcia Rodrigues Pais's Jewish practices or feelings, if any, since the chief sources we have for uncovering the daily lives of Portuguese people of Jewish origin in America are the records of the Inquisition, by which Garcia was never condemned.

Another figure featured in the early history of Minas Gerais, and one who assumed an important administrative post, is Head-Captain Miguel Teles da Costa, of whom there are several reports because he was arrested by the Inquisition and accused of Judaism in 1713.[12] Miguel Teles da Costa was named Head-Captain of the villages of Itanhaen, Ilha Grande, and Parati by the Portuguese king. A landowner in Nossa Senhora do Carmo, he was one of the first settlers of the region and belonged to a secret society of New Christians formed by a group of merchants and mining businessmen residing in Rio das Mortes.

Miguel Teles da Costa was arrested in Rio de Janeiro along with other New Christians accused of following the "law of Moses." As a merchant, he would send colonial products to his associates in Lisbon, one of whom was his brother Francisco Mendes de Castro. From Rio de Janeiro he would also order shipments of goods for Minas Gerais, aided by his nephew Diogo Lopes Flores. In 1704 he forwarded more than twenty shipments of goods to Rio das Mortes, an abundant gold-producing region. He grew corn and beans, and owned slaves, horses, weapons, and various other worldly possessions, as listed in his personal inventory.[13] He built a permanent residence in Rio das Mortes, which he later converted into lodgings to house friends who would travel to Minas Gerais on business.[14] Miguel Teles da Costa was the chief authority in the region, responsible for the defense and supervision of the border around Minas Gerais, to which entry was granted only with "special permission." The charge leveled against him was that he allowed entry to certain people, probably New Christians, "without permission." In spite of his prestige and jurisdiction over considerable territories in Minas Gerais, he was unable to escape the deputies of the Inquisition who roamed the region. He was arrested, taken to the dungeons of the Inquisition, and tortured, and all of his possessions were confiscated. He died destitute and insane.[15]

A third figure, also a New Christian and one of the most interesting personalities in colonial history, was Manuel Nunes Viana.[16] There is detailed information concerning his violent, unusual, and contradictory personality, as well as his involvement in a civil war with the *paulistas* (i.e., those from São Paulo) for the possession of *mineiro* land (land rich in gold). We know little about his Judaism. Of Jewish origin, he was a close friend of Miguel Mendonça Valladolid, a businessman who traveled the commercial routes between São Paulo, Rio de Janeiro, Minas Gerais, Bahia, and Colônia do Sacramento, and with whom he learned Jewish prayers.[17] Manuel Nunes Viana was born in Viana do Castelo, Portugal, and made his fortune in Bahia and Minas Gerais dealing in slaves and gold. In 1710, he owned several profitable gold mines in Caeté and other regions, and maintained a monopoly on the supply of meat to Minas Gerais. He was a leader in the *mineiro* division of the bloody "War of the Emboabas" in 1708, participating in a veritable massacre in Capão da Traição, in which numerous *paulistas*, both New and Old Christians, were killed. He became known in Brazilian history as the "King of the Emboabas," and was proclaimed provisional governor of the entire Minas region. Despite his disagreements with the viceroy, he received a letter of commendation from the king of Portugal for "services rendered." Remarkably, he was accepted into the elite and prestigious Order of Christ despite his Jewish origin, which demonstrates the arbitrariness of those who exercised the "purity of blood" laws.

Although Manuel Nunes Viana was barely literate, he harbored cultural ambitions. In 1728, he financed the publication of a book by Nuno Marques Pereira, *Compêndio do peregrino da América* (Compendium by a Traveler from America), a work that achieved enormous success. It is reported that he owned a library and that he also financed the printing of the third volume of *Décadas* (Decades) by Diogo do Couto.[18] Manuel Nunes Viana lived as many other New Christians—divided between two worlds. In one he uttered Jewish prayers, in the other he delivered his two daughters to a Lisbon convent.

Occupation of land in Minas Gerais took a different form than in other parts of America. Opportunities for quick wealth and rapid upward social mobility were more abundant than in regions dominated by the sugar economy. Scattered throughout Brazil, New Christians maintained a vast network of communications amongst themselves, and the fact that they were dispersed throughout America, and the world as well, made possible a network of economic transactions with which Old Christians could scarcely compete. While Portugal attempted to maintain strict control over the region, especially because of frequent smuggling at Brazilian ports and the mass of foreign adventurers who attempted to gain entry without permission, it appears that New Christians received secret information that made it easier for their fellows to arrive in Minas Gerais.[19]

New Christians in the Minas region were involved in a variety of activities: they bought and sold slaves and necessary items for residents, and as cattle-breeders supplied meat to the entire region. They participated in the extraction of gold and were artisans, doctors, and lawyers. They acquired books and wrote poetry.[20]

According to a study by Ida Levkovitch, based on a tabulation of goods confiscated by the Inquisition from New Christians of Minas Gerais, only 23 percent of those sentenced were involved in mining; 64 percent were merchants, and 6 percent were agriculturists.[21] New Christians who combined mining with farming and the trading of slaves with other merchandise achieved the highest economic gains. In Ouro Preto in 1740, for example, the greatest fortunes were in the hands of those New or Old Christians who combined several occupations at once. Thus, Ignacio Dias Cardoso appears as a farmer, merchant, miner, corn and bean plantation owner, and master of two sugar mills, as well as the owner of lands devoted to mineral extraction. His fortune totaled 26,295,311 reis. Yet very few New Christians can be compared to powerful tycoons such as the New Christian Manuel de Albuquerque e Aguilar, who was perhaps the wealthiest of all, with 57,330,000 reis, and not even to Francisco Ferreira Izidro (or Isidoro), whose fortune reached 10,709,000 reis.[22]

Flavio Mendes de Carvalho, who tragically disappeared, was a diligent researcher on the Inquisition and New Christians[23] and was responsible for a pioneering survey based on 129 inventories regarding the approximate value of goods confiscated from convicted New Christians in various regions of Brazil.[24] His results shed some light on the financial status of the marranos: 78 percent of the 129 sentenced belonged to the middle class, and only 5.4 percent were powerful magnates who alone contributed 52 percent of all confiscated goods, with almost half the total derived from sugar mill owners.

Based on the 129 cases studied by Carvalho, the following list provides the distribution of the patrimony confiscated by each captaincy between 1704 and 1761, measured in gold (in terms of present-day values in grams):[25]

Rio de Janeiro	3,144,917 gr.
Bahia	976,915 gr.
Minas Gerais	752,846 gr.
Goiás	68,476 gr.
Parahiba	23,811 gr.
Pernambuco	16,452 gr.
São Paulo	2,106 gr.
Sergripe	1,044 gr.
Total	4,986,567 gr.[26]

During his reign, King João V received in revenue from Brazil 107 million cruzados (379 tons) of gold.[27]

* * * *

THE SLAVE TRADE WAS THE DRIVING FORCE in the economy of the Atlantic, and slave trafficking became one of the most profitable commercial enterprises in Brazil. Slave trade contractors authorized by the Portuguese crown brought Africans to waiting New Christian merchants at the ports of Rio de Janeiro and Bahia, who transported the slaves to Minas Gerais where they were resold, usually on credit. José Gonçalves Salvador asserted that the "slave-trafficking lords" were primarily New Christians. Yet when he listed the names of the traffickers, he did not provide any empirical proof; his conclusions are thus based merely on names that were most common among New Christians.[28]

Taking as a source the property inventories of 130 New Christians who were arrested in Brazil in the first half of the eighteenth century, I found twenty-five who were residents of, or at least regularly present in, Minas Gerais.[29] None of these twenty-five New Christians identified himself as a slave trader; rather, they described themselves as buyers, sellers, and transporters of merchandise from one region to another in Brazil. These merchants were entirely distinct from international slave trade contractors who journeyed to Africa in search of slaves, often using their own ships.

I also did not find among the seventy-one New Christians from Rio de Janeiro mentioned in the inventories any who claimed to have received slave shipments from overseas. It is a slightly different story in Bahia, where three out of twenty-one registered prisoners were slave traders to Africa: José da Costa, who went to Angola and Sudan in search of slaves; Antônio Cardoso Porto, also called Belchior Mendes Correa, who brought slaves from Sudan; and Tomás Pinto Corrêa, who brought shipments of slaves from Angola that had been ordered by several individuals.[30]

Family ties were of fundamental importance in commercial transactions enacted by New Christians in Minas. Davi de Miranda, Damião Rodrigues Moeda, Francisco Nunes de Miranda, and João de Moraes Montesinhos, among many others, worked in connection with their relatives.

There was tremendous mobility among New Christians in the colony. Francisco Nunes de Miranda, for example, had residences in Bahia, Rio de Janeiro, and Rio das Mortes. He did business with the tycoon Francisco Pinheiro and with his relative José da Costa, who transported slaves from the Ivory Coast and Angola to Brazil.

Smuggling, fraud, and theft were daily occurrences in Minas Gerais. By 1725 smuggling was occurring at an alarming rate. The governor himself, D. Lourenço de Almeida, participated actively in diamond smuggling. Old Christians and New Christians both participated in illegal trade, which at the time was not viewed as an ethical or moral violation of legal commercial practices; rather, it was regarded as an essential part of trade under an imperial and colonial regime.[31] Contraband goods were a part of daily life in the eighteenth-century colony, as well as in the court, on the seas, and in the markets. Church and state officials, merchants, mine owners, masters of sugar mills, professionals, and artisans observed that being exposed to the realities and ramifications of contraband activities was inevitable.[32] Yet the controlling influence of the Portuguese crown was intensely felt. In connection with an accusation involving illegal minting, the name of the New Christian Manuel de Albuquerque e Aguilar appears.

On the basis of current findings in studies that focus on New Christians in Minas Gerais, we can affirm that a relatively high percentage of the population was of Jewish origin—if one includes also those who resided in Rio de Janeiro and Bahia but regularly spent long periods of time in Minas Gerais. One hundred fifty New Christians who were either permanent or part-time residents in Minas Gerais appear on the "Guilty List," an inventory compiled by the Inquisition containing names of New Christians from all over the world who were either under suspicion, accused, or imprisoned.[33] It is a striking fact that the number of New Christians residing in several Brazilian cities exceeded the total number of Jews living in Amsterdam when the Sephardic community there reached its height. The total number will always remain unknown, given that we can obtain demographic data only about New Christians who were arrested or accused as Judaizers before the Inquisition. Most New Christians who went to Brazil were not arrested and were widely dispersed within the Brazilian population. Currently, we can list approximately five hundred New Christians in Minas Gerais who were either accused or imprisoned.

The following information is based on an analysis of the fifty-seven New Christians who were convicted in Minas Gerais (see the Appendix at the end of this chapter). The greatest number of New Christians were arrested during the period of highest gold production in 1728, 1729, 1730, 1732, and 1734, with the highest numbers recorded in 1728 and 1729, when eight people were imprisoned each year. Twenty-one New Christians were burned at the stake in Brazil (two "in effigy" and nineteen "in person"). Among those consigned to the flames "in person," eight resided in Minas Gerais (permanently or part-time), that is, approximately 42.11 percent. (Among prisoners in Brazil, only those accused of Judaism received the death sentence).

These individuals were burned "in person" in Minas Gerais in the years indicated: Miguel de Mendonça Valladolid, 1731; Diogo Correa do Valle, 1732; Luis Miguel Correa, 1732; Domingos Nunes, 1732; Manoel da Costa Ribeiro, 1737; Luis Mendes de Sá, 1739; Martinho da Cunha Oliveira, 1747; João Henriques, 1748. Not included in this list, nor among the fifty-seven New Christian prisoners previously mentioned, is the alleged Judaizer and cabalist Pedro Rates Henequim—who was burned at the stake in 1748 after having lived twenty years in Minas Gerais— because investigations about his origin, based on insufficient evidence, mistook him initially for an Old Christian.[34]

The Portuguese authoritarian regime was extended to the Brazilian colony, where control of the behavior, beliefs, and ideas of the population was implemented by means of two systems: investigations (so-called "visits") within a diocese, conducted by bishops with the assistance of local clergy; and Inquisitorial investigations (also "visits") ordered by Portugal and conducted by visiting officials or commissioners, who acted as religious agents working on behalf of the Inquisition, or even by laymen, the so-called "Familiars" of the Holy Office, assigned to spy on and apprehend suspects. The hearings organized for the diocesan investigations have been widely researched and analyzed in recent years,[34a] resulting in the discovery of a clear distinction between the social classes of those accused. It becomes apparent from this research that the poorer, more destitute portion of the population, consisting primarily of Old Christians, blacks, slaves, and *pardos* (like mulattos, *pardos* are racially mixed) came under the jurisdiction of the bishop, while the New Christians, the middle-class, businessmen, influential merchants, liberal professionals, and even self-employed artisans fell under the responsibility of Inquisitorial agents.

In the episcopal inquiries, the crimes—particularly those committed by Old Christians—consisted of witchcraft, blasphemy, usury, apostasy, bigamy, slander, soliciting, and offenses against customs. The infractions were tried in the locale, and the punishments were minor, consisting of a few admonitions by the bishop and donations to be made to the Church. In the inquiries performed by Inquisitorial officials, however, Judaism was the most frequent crime. The accused were New Christians who were brought to trial in Portugal and whose possessions were confiscated when they were sent to prison. These two systems of control did not have definite boundaries, but they may be distinguished by the social class at which each system was aimed.

Although Judaizing New Christians were the prime target of the Inquisition in Minas Gerais, others suspected of practicing witchcraft,[35] of soliciting (the seduction of women by priests in the confessional),[36] of sodomy,[37] and of sexual crimes[38] were also included and arrested. According to Caio Boschi, the diocesan investigations complemented the Inquisitorial institution and could be thought of as veritable itinerant tribunals.[39] The "visitor" would go from village to village questioning the population. When the crimes were considered "minor," the sentence was given *in loco*; when a crime was considered "major," the case was transferred to the ecclesiastical tribunal established in the town of Mariana. In very rare cases, the question was sent to the Inquisition in Lisbon. My research, however, did not unearth any evidence to support the claim that there was direct participation by the agents of the Holy Office in these diocesan "visits." The greatest number of episcopal investigations occurred during the decade of the 1730s, the period in which the Inquisition maintained the largest number of prisons in the colony.

The majority of New Christians brought before the Inquisition in Minas Gerais were accused of the same crime: Judaizing. The actual guilt or innocence of the accused continues to be an essential question among scholars of the Inquisition. To what extent were the prisoners practicing Judaism, if at all, and to what degree did the system rely on the blameworthy for the preservation and legitimization of the Inquisitorial institution, thus virtually manufacturing Judaizers through the use of tricks and strategies? Faced with differences of opinion among historians, it seems of the utmost importance to consider the views of contemporaries of the period who had the courage to express their criticisms of the Inquisitorial system, and, whenever possible, to listen to the voices of the accused. There is a considerable amount of information on this subject that has surfaced from intersecting sources and serves to illuminate the issues raised by historians, such as José Antônio Saraiva and Israel Révah, among others.[40]

The marranos themselves knew how the tribunal "operated" and what methods were used to incriminate New Christians. The Jesuit Father Antônio Vieira left one of the most powerful testimonies of unjust persecutions against the New Christians, and his affidavit is cogent, given that it was spoken from "inside" the Church. In a famous letter addressed to Pope Innocent XI, Father Antônio Vieira exposed the material interests and the unjust rulings of the Portuguese tribunal.[41] Ironic references by the condemned themselves, regarding the reasons for the persecutions they endured, also reveal the fact that at the time there was widespread consciousness of the Church's material interests.

To be spared from death, the New Christians had to confess to practicing Judaism. The tribunal needed criminals in order to survive as an institution that derived its main financial support from confiscations. If the accused insisted upon their innocence, they were deemed contrary and obstinate, suspected of hiding accomplices, and subjected to capital punishment. The following anecdote illustrates that New Christians understood how to escape the death penalty. Upon leaving prison, one New Christian encounters a friend who asks him, "So, how did you escape death?" And he responds, "As all others do, by telling them I was a Jew."[42]

From the fifty-seven Inquisition cases in Minas Gerais, I have chosen a few examples that demonstrate the marranos' conflicted behavior, their double identity, their freethinking, their "Judaism." The case of Diogo Corrêa do Vale and his son Luiz Corrêa confirms Father Antônio Vieira's observations about the tribunal's methods. Born in Seville, Diogo Corrêa do Vale was a widower who lived in Oporto. He was a graduate of the school of medicine at the University of Coimbra. After several members of his family were arrested by the Inquisition in Portugal, he escaped to Brazil with his son, settling in Vila Rica de Ouro Preto. On 12 September 1730, he was arrested along with his son, Luiz Miguel Corrêa.[43] In a letter to the Inquisition tribunal by Dr. Lourenço de Valadares Freire, an agent of the Holy Office, sent from Vila Rica in 1730, we are privy to the words Luiz Miguel Corrêa spoke to Lieutenant Martinho Alvarez, the officer who arrested him: "They say that the Holy Office is just, yet I see now that it is not, for it indicts innocent men."[44]

Accusations of Judaizing aimed at both Diogo Corrêa do Vale and his son were derived entirely from their lives spent in Oporto twenty years before, when Luiz was a child. The Inquisitors were not able to compile evidence from their time in Minas Gerais. Diogo's imprisonment was apparently founded upon old professional rivalries among Oporto's physicians based on the different treatments given their patients. His friends in Oporto tried to intervene on his behalf, attesting to his honorable conduct and to his sense of charity both as a Christian and a doctor in that he "cared for the ailing poor free of charge." Despite Diogo's efforts to defend himself, asserting to the end that all the accusations against him were false, the Inquisitors did not alter his death sentence. Diogo insisted that he had always lived under Christ's law and that he wanted to die under it, but his Jewish origins sealed his fate.[45]

The case of his son, Luiz Miguel Corrêa, is even more tragic because the latter's adherence to the Christian faith is evident throughout his trial. Having experienced a strong penchant for the religious life and wishing to become a clergyman, he sought the help of the bishop of Rio de Janeiro. The bishop immediately dissuaded him by citing the improbability of his ambitions, given that he was a New Christian and that many members of his family had been condemned by the Holy Office. In a last, desperate attempt, Luiz informed the bishop of his willingness to sell off all his slaves and worldly goods in order to buy the "proof of the purity of his blood, as many others were doing." It was hopeless. On the last day of his trial before the Inquisitors he pleaded that even if they declared him innocent, they should sentence him to life imprisonment so that he could deal with his salvation, "since he could not become a priest because of the impurity of his blood." He also claimed that the fear of death had placed him in a state of "desperation," and thus he had falsely denounced himself and had wrongly accused others of practicing the "law of Moses." He stood steadfast in his innocence of the crime of Judaizing until the end. He was burned to death at the stake on the same afternoon as his father.[46]

"Purity of blood" statutes were applied less rigorously in Brazil than in Portugal. A great number of New Christians who had "infected blood" were received into the bosom of the Church when it was to the Church's advantage, or when New Christians offered money in exchange. In Portugal, the Inquisitor Martins Mascarenhas had sold "Certificates of Purity" at a fixed price.

Marranism was a multifaceted phenomenon. As I have suggested several times, there was not one but many marranisms in Minas Gerais, as in the rest of Brazil. The phenomenon includes various types of behavior and should not be understood only in the narrow sense of crypto-Judaism. Marranism must be considered in a broad context, as in the manner suggested by the French philosopher Edgard Morin.[47] The marrano represents the universal, often unconscious, condition of men who are removed from the societies in which they live. The marrano is a man who lives in a world without belonging to it. In this sense, we find in Minas Gerais, as in the rest of Brazil, behavior that cannot be defined as merely actions in compliance with specific Jewish dietary laws, fastings, or abstention from working on Saturdays, among other principles. Marranism among the Portuguese in Brazil was primarily a mental attitude, a sentiment, an outlook on life, rather than a religious observance.[48] If a substantial portion of New Christians managed to overcome ethnic, social, and religious barriers to become part of a larger community, another portion remained loyal to the traditions inherited from their ancestors. Paradoxically, historical memories of centuries of suffering, in addition to the direct experience of social and legal exclusion, increasingly reinforced resistance to adopting official religious ideas. The New Christians' greatest contribution to eighteenth-century enlightened thinking in Brazil was a critical approach to religion.[49]

Diogo Nunes Henriques, a wealthy businessman who was arrested in Minas Gerais in 1728 for having declared that "each person should live and die according to the Law which best suits him,"[50] had a different experience from that of Luiz Miguel Corrêa. The crime that led him to Lisbon's prisons was his support of freethinking, a position inconceivable to the majority of his Portuguese contemporaries. As soon as they received the accusation against him, the Inquisitors set out to investigate his life in minute detail: "from which country he originated," his "way" of life, "in which part" of Minas Gerais he lived, and his "ethnic background." New information was collected, including the fact that his house in Ouro Preto was the headquarters of a secret society of New Christians at which congregated the

Minas elite: David Mendes, Domingos Nunes (Diogo Nunes Henriques's nephew), the sugar mill owner Domingos Rodrigues Ramires who had lived in Rio de Janeiro, João da Cruz, the fabrics merchant David de Miranda, Francisco Nunes, Duarte Rodrigues, Manuel Nunes de Paz (Diogo Henriques's son), Manuel Nunes Sanches, among many others, all of whom were neighbors.[51]

Diogo Nunes Henriques is portrayed as a learned man, given that one of the accusations against him was that he "was inclined to read numerous books." Old Christians who testified against him claimed that they had never seen him pray or teach his slaves the doctrines of the Christian faith, as was the custom in rural areas. A tailor declared to the investigative agents that he had never seen Diogo with rosary beads and that he disregarded the rules of Lent, teaching heresies to his slaves. According to his Old Christian neighbors, Diogo also called attention to himself whenever he was tired, by sighing "Oh God!" without ever uttering the name of Jesus. And he committed what was considered a serious crime: he would gather various members of the Miranda family and friends "in order to read books."[52]

One of Diogo Nunes Henriques's nephews, Domingos Nunes, also provides interesting information concerning the daily affairs of this secret society in Minas Gerais. The Inquisition had been pursuing him since 1726. An order for his arrest had been issued in 1728, though he was not captured until two years and seven months later, after which he was turned over to the Lisbon Inquisition on 12 October 1730.[53] Seventeen business associates, with whom he had traded in Brazil and who were subsequently imprisoned, denounced him: Gaspar Fernandez Ferreira (or Pereira), a businessman in Ouro Preto; Miguel da Cruz, a businessman who also resided in Rio de Janeiro; Manuel Nunes da Pax, a businessman and resident of Minas Gerais; Gaspar Henriques, a *mineiro* resident in Bahia; Manoel Nunes Bernal, a ship's captain and resident of Rio de Janeiro; Jeronimo Rodrigues, a dealer and resident of Bahia; Joseph da Cruz Henriques, head tithe-collector and resident of Ribeirão do Carmo; Joseph Rodrigues Cardoso, no occupation listed, who was originally from Bahia and a resident of Ribeirão do Carmo; Domingos's uncle, Diogo Nunes Henriques, a businessman and resident of Ouro Preto; Antônio da Fonseca Rego, a sugar cane worker originally from Pernambuco, and a resident of Paracatú; Antônio Rodrigues Campos, a manioc worker and resident of Bahia; Diogo Dias Corrêa, no occupation listed, who was a resident of Santos; Luiz Vaz de Oliveira, originally from Spain and a resident of Ribeirão do Carmo; David Mendes da Silva, a resident of Ouro Preto; and Miguel Henriques, a dealer and merchant in Ribeirão do Carmo.[54] New Christians' domestic transactions required that they travel to far-flung regions and that they establish true commercial networks for their trade. These secret New Christian associates offered support, security, and credit to each other despite the knowledge that, if arrested, all members would denounce one another.

Several doubts and questions emerge concerning the nature of Domingos Nunes's Judaism. It seems that since childhood he had been instructed in the Jewish faith. He set up house in Minas Gerais and brought in shipments of assorted merchandise. Traveling throughout the colony, he came into contact with all of the major merchants. When submitted to torture, he denounced all of his associates who lived in the regions of Caeté, Cachoeira, Paraopeba, Congonhas, Vila Pitangui, village of Antônio Pereira, Fanado Mines, Serro Frio, and Rio das Mortes, in addition to many others from Rio de Janeiro, Bahia, and Santos. Domingos tried to save his life in any way possible. The "watchmen" who guarded his cell twenty-four hours a day accused him of "fasting in a Judaizing way," of having "looked up at the sky," of having made "Jewish gestures," of having written something "secretive" on the headboard of his bed, and then immediately erasing what he had written so no one could read it. After having used all possible arguments, including that he had fasted in his cell because he had wanted to kill himself, Domingos Nunes wound up like all the other accused—confessing his complicity in Judaism. Moreover, he repeated a prayer praising a single God, creator of the universe, soliciting His forgiveness and help:[55]

> You are the ruler of this damned world
> Hear Lord our Prayer
> Receive our Adoration
> Do not make us walk in sadness
> For the Soul you have given us
> Infinite you Holy Father
> Who has created light and day
> With great wisdom you have made it grow night
> Great are our sins
> Greater is your Holy Power
> We have already
> Confessed Lord
> From All the truth
> Deliver us from all the darkness
> May our souls be saved
> Before Your Holy Power
> Lord
> Amen.

> Great Lord Creator of the Universe
> As a Great Sinner
> I confess to you O Lord
> As such I recognize myself
> And ask you for forgiveness
> I am not worthy of such lofty pardon
> Witness Lord my anguish
> That which I deserve
> Witness what I endure

Give me strength
Almighty Powerful
Great Lord
Amen.[56]

Domingos was burned at the stake in 1732.

* * * *

THE SECRET SOCIETIES THAT WERE CREATED in Minas Gerais followed the gold route. Secret meetings were immediately organized in each town or village founded in gold-producing regions, for instance, in some of the houses in Ouro Preto, Tijuco (a diamond-mining region), Rio das Mortes, and Ribeirão do Carmo. During the course of these meetings, business transactions occurred, trust was established, and at the same time resistance was formed, as well as a particular "feeling" for the world: marranism.[57] Among the participants in these groups were crypto-Jews, nonbelievers, agnostics, and others identified as Jews not only because of their conduct or beliefs but also because of their origin. The secret societies of Minas Gerais formed by crypto-Jews and heretics were not a new phenomenon; rather, they were the product of a long process that had matured over the course of two centuries as an inheritance from their forebears. In Brazil, this process began during the formation of the first settlements in São Vicente, São Paulo, Bahia, and Pernambuco soon after the discovery of Brazil. The New Christians spread throughout the colony as the land was explored and as new settlers, adventurers, and fugitives escaping Inquisitorial persecutions arrived.

Once the gold route was established, Inquisitors ordered that control over the population of Jewish origin be intensified. The main areas targeted were also the wealthiest: Rio de Janeiro and Minas Gerais. The New Christians of Paraíba, who were also intensely pursued during this period (approximately forty-nine sentenced), consisted of a community of laborers with little property but who possessed some goods including slaves.

The persecution of New Christians in Minas Gerais followed the same pattern of the two previous centuries. It affected those New Christians whose parents, grandparents, and siblings had already experienced the prisons of Lisbon, including those belonging to the oldest families in the colony.

We can divide the behavior of the marrano in Brazil in general and in Minas Gerais into two major groups: crypto-Jews, who actively performed some Judaic ceremonies, and skeptics, for whom religion was a problem rather than a source of comfort. Secrecy was also part of the world of marrano skeptics and nonbelievers, for they shared a common ancestral identity with the crypto-Jews.

Jewish practices in Minas Gerais were cloaked in symbolism; secret communications were often made in code. In general, these crypto-Jewish customs and ceremonies were similar to those practiced by New Christians or *conversos* in Portugal and Spanish America, as well as in other regions of Brazil. A few omissions from orthodox practices and some syncretisms exist, with observances primarily concentrated on the fastings of Yom Kippur, the observance of the Sabbath, the celebration of Passover, and the holiday in honor of Queen Esther, as well as some dietary restrictions. To complete the picture of marrano religion, there was belief in a single God, the creator of the universe; the rejection of salvation through Christ; and an aversion to religious imagery and confession. Yet the principal dividing factor between crypto-Jewish New Christians and Old Christians was the issue of the Messiah.

The overall content of crypto-Jewish prayers associated with the marranos of Minas Gerais expressed characteristic concerns of "guilt and redemption." Life's vicissitudes were regarded as stages in the process of redemption. Marrano religion thus fulfilled a social function: deliverance from economic and social oppression. It was inexorably linked to the idea of salvation through the "law of Moses," which compensated for the marranos' condition as "other" or "outsider." A message was thus clandestinely passed on from one generation to the next that encouraged persecuted New Christians who could not find a "response" in the official religion to make sense of their lives. "Daily" and "covert" activities supplied the marranos in the gold region with comfort and meaning. In the words of Max Weber, we can say that the religious demands of the marranos were demands for compensation, typical of those who are disadvantaged. Memory of the historic origins of the Jews had a primarily symbolic effect upon the New Christians, in that it offered them a system for justifying their existence. Their beliefs represented hope, while the ties bonding marrano nonbelievers and agnostics with crypto-Jews granted all a sense of "belonging." With its various regional subtleties, marranism in Brazil was a long-standing phenomenon featuring traits that defy generalization. Brazilian marranism must be understood in the context of the formation of Brazilian culture, a culture that the marranos unwittingly helped to create.

APPENDIX

New Christians—Minas Gerais—Prisoners*

Name Inquisition Process No.	Born In	Residence	Profession	Marital Status	Age Approx.	Prison Year	Name of Father Birth, Profession	Notes
Ana do Vale 6989	Rio de Janeiro	Minas de Cachoeira		Single	25	1734	Domingos Rodrigues Ramires Sugar Mill Landlord	Family imprisoned
Antonio Carvalho de Oliveira 10474	Santalhão (Miranda Bishopric)	Minas Gerais	Businessman	Single	37	1731	Francisco de Gamboa Businessman	Family imprisoned
Antonio de Sá de Almeida 8025	Vila de Almeida (Lamego Bishopric)	Minas do Serro Frio	Miner	Single	28	1734	Manuel Henriques de Leão Merchant Residence: Almeida	Family imprisoned
Antonio Fernandes Pereira 10481	Mogadouro (Braga Arch-diocese)	Minas Novas de Arasauay	Miner	Single	30	1730	Manoel Francisco Fernandes Shopkeeper	Family imprisoned
Antonio José Cogominho	Évora	Minas and Portugal	Inspector (Minas de Sabará)	Married		1743		
Antonio Ribeiro Furtado 2801	Bragança	Minas do Serro Frio	Businessman Weaver	Single	32	1751	José Ribeiro Weaver Born in: Bragança	Family imprisoned
Antonio Ribeiro Sanches 11603	Monforte (Guarda Bishopric)	Minas do Paracatú	Doctor	Single	37	1747	Manuel Nunes Ribeiro Farmer Born in/Residence: Monforte	Family imprisoned
David de Miranda 7489	Almeida (Lamego Bishopric)	Carmo Minas	Businessman	Single	43	1714 and 1728	Francisco Rodrigues Businessman	Family imprisoned

*This list is not a definitive one. Other prisoners lived simultaneously in other regions of Brazil.

(Continued)

Name Inquisition Process No.	Born In	Residence	Profession	Marital Status	Age Approx.	Prison Year	Name of Father Birth, Profession	Notes
David Mendes da Silva 2134	Vila Nova de Foscoa (Lamego Bishopric)	Minas do Serro Frio	Businessman	Single	40	1730	Gregório da Silva Residence: Bahia Businessman	Family imprisoned
Diogo Correa do Vale 821	Sevilha Castela Kingdom	Minas de Ouro Preto	Doctor	Widower	58	1730 1732— Burned at the stake	Luis Correa Businessman Residence: Vila Real	Family imprisoned
Diogo Dias Correa 2646	Freixo de Nemão (Lamego Bishopric)	Minas and Madeira Islands	No profession	Single	18	1728	Antonio Dias Fernandes Merchant Born in: Castela Residence: Lisboa	Family imprisoned
Diogo Nunes 7488	São Vicente da Beira (Lamego Bishopric)	Curralinho Minas de Ouro Preto	Businessman	Widower	53	1729	Diogo Henriques Residence: Proença Merchant	
Diogo Nunes Henriques 4895	São Vicente da Beira (Guarda Bishopric)	Minas de Ouro Preto	Tax collector	Married	53	1718		Family imprisoned
Diogo Nunes Henriques or Francisco Rodrigues Pereira 7487	Freixadas (Vizeu Bishopric)	Minas de Ouro Preto	Businessman	Married	62	1728	Manuel Fernandes Residence: Freixadas Tanner (silk)	Family imprisoned
Domingos Nunes 1779	Freixadas (Vizeu Bishopric)	Minas Gerais	Businessman	Single	38	1730 1732— Burned at the stake	Antonio Rodrigues Born in: Freixadas Businessman	Family imprisoned
Domingos Rodrigues Ramires 6517	Rio de Janeiro	Rio de Janeiro and Minas	Sugar mill landlord	Married	30	1710	Duarte Róis de Andrade Residence: Rio de Janeiro Sugar mill landlord	Family imprisoned

Name	Birthplace	Location	Occupation	Status	Age	Year	Notes	Family
Duarte da Costa Fonseca 6759	Chaves (Braga Archdiocese)	Serro Frio Minas Novas	Miner Businessman	Married	35	1735	Agostinho de Fonseca Chaves Lives from his income	Family imprisoned
Elena do Vale 4220	Rio de Janeiro	Vila Rica de Ouro Preto		Single	26	1734	Domingos Rodrigues Ramires Sugar mill landlord	Family imprisoned Sister of Ana do Vale
Fernando Gomes Nunes 4058	Manteigas (Guarda Bishopric)	Vila Rica de Ouro Preto	Businessman	Single	44	1739	Francisco Gomes Born in: Cáceres (Castela) or Belmonte Residence: Almeida Merchant	Family imprisoned
Francisco Correa Denounced		Rio de Janeiro and Minas Gerais	Tenant			1728	Diogo Correa do Vale Doctor Burned at the stake	Family imprisoned
Francisco de Lucena Montarroyo 1340	Rio de Janeiro	Rio de Janeiro and Minas Gerais	Miner	Married	26	1712	Diogo de Montarroyo de Lucena Born in/Residence: Rio de Janeiro	Family imprisoned
Francisco de Siqueira Machado 1892	Rio de Janeiro	Rio de Janeiro Minas Gerais	Doctor	Married	42	1708	José Fernandes de Miranda Born in: Mirandinha Residence: Rio de Janeiro Merchant	Family imprisoned
Francisco Ferreira Izidro or Izidoro 11965	Freixo do Nemão (Lamego Bishopric)	Vila do Carmo (Minas Gerais)	Miner	Single	41	1726	Luiz Vaz de Oliveira Born in: Torre do Moncorvo Residence: Rio de Janeiro Merchant	Family imprisoned
Francisco Nunes de Miranda	Beja-Portugal	Guarapirang in 1723 and Ribeirão do Carmo		Married		1732 order of prison		Family imprisoned

(Continued)

Name Inquisition Process No.	Born In	Residence	Profession	Marital Status	Age Approx.	Prison Year	Name of Father Birth, Profession	Notes
Henrique Froes or Muniz 426	Covilhã (Lamego Bishopric)	Ouro Preto Sumidouro	Miner Businessman	Single	37	1734	Manuel Frois Residence: Covilhã Farmer	Family imprisoned
Ignácio Cardoso de Azevedo 5447	Rio de Janeiro	Vila Rica de Ouro Preto and Rio de Janeiro	Lawyer	Married	35	1712	Agostinho de Paredes Born in/Residence: Rio de Janeiro Sugar mill landlord	Family imprisoned
Isabel Palhana 4953	Rio de Janeiro	Minas	—	Married	27	1715	Antonio Farto Divino	Auto-da-fé in 1716 Family imprisoned
Jerônimo Rodrigues 10003	Escalião (Lamego Bishopric)	Bahia and (Minas)	Businessman	Married	50	1729	José Cardoso Born in/Residence: Escalião Merchant	Family imprisoned
João da Cruz 9089	Almeida	Bahia and Minas	Tanner	Single	24	1710	Francisco Rodrigues de Almeida Residence: Bahia Tanner	Family imprisoned
João da Cruz Henriques 10004	Almeida or Pinhel	Ribeirão do Carmo	Bill collector	Single	26	1728	Antonio Rodrigues Born in: Almeida Merchant	Nickname: "o carregado"
João de Matos Henriques 3752	Maçal do Chão	Guarapiranga	Merchant	Single	30	1729	Francisco da Cruz Henriques New Christian Born in: Almeida Residence: Maçal do Chão Lived from his income	
João Henriques 8378	São Vicente da Beira	Minas de Paracatu	Pharmacist	Single	27	1747 1748— Burned at the stake	João Henriques Born in: São Vicente da Beira= Residence: Castelo Branco Pharmacist	

Name	Birthplace	Residence	Occupation	Status	Age	Year	Relative	Notes
João Morais Montesinhos 11769	Bahia	Minas de Ouro Preto	Businessman	Single	27	1729	Luiz Mendes de Morais Born in: Almeida Residence: Bahia	Family imprisoned
João Nunes Vizeu 1195	Idanha, a Nova	Rio das Mortes and Rio de Janeiro	Doctor	Married	40	1710	Manuel Nunes Vizeu Born in: Castelo Branco Residence: Rio de Janeiro Farmer	Family imprisoned
João Róis de Mesquita 8018	Vinhaes	Ribeirão do Carmo	Bill collector	Single	26	1733	Manuel Róis de Mesquita Grocer	
José Nunes 430	Freixo de Espada a Cinta	Serro Frio	Grocer	Single	38	1734	Francisco Nunes Born in: Freixo de Espada a Cinta Twister (silk)	
Joseph Rodrigues Cardoso 19	Bahia	Curralinho		Single	21	1729	Jerônimo Rodrigues Cardoso Residence: Bahia Businessman	Family imprisoned
Luis Alves or Álvares Montarroyo 695	Rio de Janeiro	Minas	Farmer Lived from his income	Single	32	1712	Diogo de Montarroyo Born in/Residence: Rio de Janeiro Sugar mill landlord	Family imprisoned
Luis Mendes de Sá 8015	Coimbra	Rio das Contas	Camboeiro	Single	37	1738 1739— Burned at the stake	Salvador Mendes de Sá Born in: Bragança Residence: Lisboa and Holland Merchant	Family imprisoned Luis Mendes de Sá born in the prison of Coimbra
Luis Miguel Correa 9249	Pinhel (Vizeu Bishopric)	Vila Rica de Ouro Preto	Farmer	Single	26	1730 1732— Burned at the stake together with his father	Diogo Correa do Vale Born in: Pinhel Residence: Vila Rica Doctor Burned at the stake	Family imprisoned

(Continued)

Name Inquisition Process No.	Born In	Residence	Profession	Marital Status	Age Approx.	Prison Year	Name of Father Birth, Profession	Notes
Luiz Vaz de Oliveira 9969	Castela Kingdom	Minas do Ribeirão do Carmo	Businessman	Single	23	1730	João Sanchez Maioral Born in: Castela Residence: Freixo da Espada a Cinta Pharmacist	His mother was burned at the stake. Family imprisoned
Manoel Nunes da Paz 9542	Castela Kingdom	Curralinho Ranch (Minas)	Businessman	Married	35	1727	Diogo Nunes Henriques Born: Pinhel Residence: Minas Farmer	Family imprisoned
Manoel Nunes Sanchez or Mendes 11824	Idanha Nova (Guarda Bishopric)	Minas dos Fanados	Businessman Miner	Single	30	1730	Manuel Nunes Sanches Born in/Residence: Idanha Nova Doctor	Family imprisoned
Manuel da Costa Espadilha 1831	Panamacor (Guarda Bishopric)	Guara-piranga Minas de Ouro Preto	Shopkeeper	Married	40	1729	Antonio Gomes Nunes Born in/Residence: Panamacor Merchant	Family imprisoned
Manuel da Costa Ribeiro 1361	Celorico (Guarda Bishopric)	Vila Rica de Ouro Preto	Farmer Businessman	Single	24	1734 1737— Burned at the stake	José Carvalho Almeida Born in/Residence: Celorico Merchant (silk)	Family imprisoned
Manuel de Albuquerque e Aguilar 4407	Castelo Rodrigo (Lamego Bishopric)	Vila Rica de Ouro Preto	Businessman	Single	38	1732	Antonio Siqueira Cabral Residence: Castelo Rodrigo Lived from his income	He doesn't know if his family was imprisoned.
Manuel de Meza	Portugal	Assistant in Minas	Lawyer	Single		1732	José Pesso Businessman	
Manuel Gomes de Carvalho	Celorico	Vila Rica de Ouro Preto	Miner	Single	45	1734	Gaspar Carvalho	

Name	Birthplace	Location	Occupation	Marital status	Age at imprisonment	Year	Relative	Family
Martinho Cunha de Oliveira 8106	Idanha Nova (Guarda Bishopric)	Minas de Ouro Preto and Vila Fundão (Guarda Bishopric)	Businessman	Single	20 (1st imprisonment) 52 (2nd imprisonment)	1712—1st 1746—2nd 1746—Burned at the stake	Manuel da Cunha Born in: Montemor Residence: Fundão	Family imprisoned
Marcos Mendes Sanches 2141	Idanha Nova (Guarda Bishopric)	Rio das Mortes (Minas)	Miner	Single		1730	Manuel Nunes Sanches Doctor	Family imprisoned
Miguel da Cruz 11330	Maçal do Chão (Portugal)	Ribeirão do Carmo and Rio de Janeiro	Businessman	Single	27	1727	Francisco da Cruz Henriques Born in: Almeida Residence: Marçal do Chão Farmer	Family imprisoned
Miguel Mendonça Valladolid 9973	Valladolid (Castela Kingdom)	Assistant in Minas	Businessman	Married	33	1729 1731—Burned at the stake	João Castro Mendonça Born in/Residence: Valladolid Merchant	Family imprisoned
Miguel Nunes de Almeida 9248	Bahia	Curralinho (Minas) and Bahia	Merchant	Single	24	1729	Félix Nunes de Miranda Born in : Almeida Businessman Burned at the stake	Family imprisoned
Miguel Nunes Sanches 8112	Idanha Nova (Guarda Bishopric)	Paracatu	Businessman	Married	39	1747	Manuel Nunes Sanches Born in/Residence: Idanha Nova Doctor	Family imprisoned
Miguel Teles da Costa 6515	Trancoso (Vizeu Bishopric)	Rio das Mortes	Capitão—Mor	Single	55	1710	Diogo Mendes de Castro Born in: Trancoso Residence: Lisboa Lived from his income	Family imprisoned
Pedro Nunes de Miranda 9001	Castelo Rodrigo (Castela Kingdom)	Bahia and Rio das Mortes	Farmer	Single	30 (1st imprisonment) 50 (2nd imprisonment)	1714—1st 1731—2nd	Francisco Nunes de Miranda Born in: Almeida Residence: Bahia and Minas Doctor	Family imprisoned

(Continued)

Name Inquisition Process No.	Born In	Residence	Profession	Marital Status	Age Approx.	Prison Year	Name of Father Birth, Profession	Notes
Salvador Rodrigues de Faria 9395	Rio de Janeiro	Rio das Mortes (Minas Gerais)	Miner	Single	37	1734	Simão Farto Deniz Born in/Residence: Rio de Janeiro Merchant	Family imprisoned

Source: Lisbon Inquisition. Arquivo Nacional da Torre do Tombo. Portugal. Manuscripts.

Notes

Translated from the Portuguese by Marguerite I. Harrison

1. Alfredo Margarido, "Le Rôle des Juifs dans l'Expansion Europeéne," *Andorra* (1984): 218–29.
2. Ibid.
3. About the goods confiscated from the New Christians arrested in Brazil in the eighteenth century, see Anita Novinsky, *Inquisição, Inventários de Bens Confiscados a Cristãos-Novos, Brasil, Século XVIII, Fontes para a História de Portugal e do Brasil* (Lisbon, 1978).
4. Jonathan I. Israel, "The Sephardi Contribution to Economic Life and Colonization in Europe and the New World (16th–18th centuries)," in *Sephardi Legacy*, ed. Haim Beinart, vol. 2 (Jerusalem, 1992), 365–98.
5. Ibid.
6. Ellis Rivkin, "How Jewish Were the New Christians?" in *Hispania Judaica*, vol. 1: History (Barcelona, 1980), 105–15, and idem "Uma História de Duas Diasporas," in *Iberia Judaica*, ed. Anita Novinsky and Diana Kuperman (São Paulo and Rio de Janeiro, 1992), 267–75.
7. Rivkin, "Uma História," 274.
8. Augusto Lima Junior, *A capitania das Minas Gerais* (Belo Horizonte, 1978).
9. Caio Boschi, "As Visitas Diocesanas e a Inquisição na Colônia," in *Inquisição, Anais do Primeiro Congresso Luso Brasileiro sobre a Inquisição*, vol. 2 (Lisbon, 1989), 965–96, esp. 968.
10. José Gonçalves Salvador, *Os Cristãos Novos em Minas Gerais durante o Ciclo do Ouro* (São Paulo, 1992).
11. For information on Garcia Rodrigues Pais, see ibid., 117.
12. Trial against Miguel Teles da Costa, Inquisition of Lisbon, #6515, Arquivo Nacional da Torre do Tombo, Lisbon. See also Rachel Mizrahi Bromberg, *A Inquisição no Brasil: Um Capitão-Mór Judaisante* (São Paulo, 1984).
13. About the goods confiscated from Miguel Teles da Costa, see Anita Novinsky, *Inquisição, Inventários de Bens Confiscados*, 223–24.
14. Trial against Miguel Teles da Costa, #6515, op. cit.
15. Ibid.
16. In reference to Manuel Nunes Viana, see Salvador, *Os Cristãos-Novos*, 11.
17. Trial against Miguel de Mendonça Valladolid, Inquisition of Lisbon, #9972, Arquivo Nacional da Torre do Tombo, Lisbon.
18. Charles R. Boxer, *A Idade do Ouro no Brasil* (São Paulo, 1963), 320.
19. A book entitled *Itinerário Geográfico*, written by Francisco Tavares de Brito and printed in 1732 by the press belonging to Antonio da Silva, was distributed in secret; it gave directions for traveling to Minas Gerais. The John Carter Brown Library owns a copy of this document.
20. The first poet to surface in the eighteenth century in the mine region of Goias was Antonio Ferreira Dourado, also a businessman, arrested by the Inquisition in Vila Boa de Goiás in 1760 and sentenced to life imprisonment (Trial against Antonio Ferreira Dourado, Inquisition of Lisbon, #6268). The Inquisition confiscated 23.469 kg. of gold from him, according to Flavio Mendes de Carvalho's evaluation in his work *Inquisição: Uma avaliação de Bens Confiscados a Judeus Brasileiros. Século XVIII* (manuscript belonging to Anita Novinsky). Three more New Christians accused of Judaism were arrested in Goias: Thomas Pinto Ferreira, a farmer, in the year 1760 (Inquisition of Lisbon, #8659), and his brother Dr. Jose Pinto Ferreira, a graduate in law at the University of Coimbra, also in 1760 (Inquisition of Lisbon, #8912); and Fernando Gomes Nunes (or Belmonte), a merchant, in 1739 (Inquisition of Lisbon, #4058). In the mine region of Paracatu, near Minas Gerais, we found three other New Christians condemned for Judaism: Miguel Nunes Sanches, businessman (Inquisition of Lisbon, #8112); Dr. Antonio Ribeiro Sanches, graduated in medicine at the University of Coimbra (Inquisition

of Lisbon, #11603); and João Henriques, pharmacist (Inquisition of Lisbon, #8378). All trial proceedings can be found in the Archivo Nacional Torre do Tombo.

21. Ida Lewkowicz, "Confiscos do Santo Ofício e formas de riquezas nas Minas Gerais no século XVIII," in *Inquisição, Ensaios sobre Mentalidade, Heresias e Arte*, ed. Anita Novinsky and Maria Luiza Tucci Carneiro (São Paulo, 1992), 208–24.

22. Ibid.

23. Carvalho, *Inquisição: Uma avaliação de Bens Confiscados*.

24. Novinsky, *Inquisição, Inventário de Bens Confiscados*.

25. Carvalho, *Inquisicão: Uma avaliação de Bens Confiscados*.

26. Ibid.

27. The evaluation of the equivalent of 379 tons of gold was made by Carvalho, *Inquisição: Uma avaliação de Bens Confiscados*, 15.

28. J. Gonçalves Salvador, *Os Magnatas do Tráfico Negreiro* (São Paulo, 1981).

29. Novinsky, *Inquisição, Inventário de Bens Confiscados*. With reference to New Christians, the issue of residency is a complicated one, given that they frequently lived in one region but were also regularly present in another; they were also not very precise when submitting statements to this effect. Among those mentioned I included Miguel de Mendonça Valladolid, who lived in both São Paulo and Minas Gerais.

30. Ibid., 157, 168, 247.

31. Ernest Pijning, "Controlling Contraband: Mentality, Economy and Society in Eighteenth Century Rio de Janeiro" (Ph.D. diss., Johns Hopkins University, 1997).

32. Ibid.

33. Anita Novinsky, *Rol dos Culpados* (São Paulo, 1992).

34. About Pedro Rates Henequim, see Anita Novinsky, "The Inquisition and the Mythic World of a Portuguese Cabalist in the 18th Century," in *Proceedings of the Eleventh World Congress of Jewish Studies* (1994), 115–22.

34a. For studies about Minas Gerais based on the diocesan investigations, see Laura de Mello e Souza, *Os Desclassificados do Ouro. A Pobresa mineira no século XVIII* (Rio de Janeiro, 1982); Luciano Raposo de Figueiredo, *Barrocas Famílias* (São Paulo, 1997), and idem, *O Avesso da Memória* (Rio de Janeiro, 1993); Francisco Vidal Luna and Iraci del Nero, "Devassa nas Minas Gerais; observações sobre casos de concubinato," *Anais do Museu Paulista*, vol. 31 (São Paulo, 1982); Caio Boschi, "As Visitas Diocesanas e a Inquisição na Colônia," in *Inquisição, Anais do Primeiro Congresso Luso Brasileiro sobre a Inquisição*, vol. 2 (Lisbon, 1989), 965–96.

35. Laura de Mello Souza, *O Diabo e a Terra de Santa Cruz* (São Paulo, 1986).

36. Lana Lage da Gama Lima, "Guardiães da Penitência: O Santo Ofício português e a punição dos Solicitantes," in *Inquisição, Ensaios sobre Mentalidade, Heresias e Arte*, ed. Anita Novinsky and Maria Luiza Tucci Carneiro (São Paulo, 1992), 703–38.

37. Luiz Mott, "Justícia e Misericórdia: a Inquisição portuguesa e a repressão ao nefando pecado da sodomia," in *Inquisição, Ensaios*, ed. Novinsky and Carneiro, 703, 738.

38. Ronaldo Vainfas, *Trópico dos Pecados* (Rio de Janeiro, 1989).

39. Caio Boschi, "As visitas Diocesanas," 991.

40. With reference to the debate concerning the interpretation of sources, see the discussion between I. S. Révah and António José Saraiva, "Polêmica acerca da Inquisição e Cristãos-Novos," in António José Saraiva, *Inquisição e Cristãos-Novos* (Lisbon, 1985), 211–91.

41. *Carta do Padre António Vieira sobre a causa do Santo Ofício escrita ão Santíssimo Pde. Inocêncio XI*, manuscript #49/IV/23, Biblioteca da Ajuda Lisbon. See also Anita Novinsky, "Padre António Vieira, a Inquisição e os Judeus," *Novos Estudos*, CEBRAP 29 (March 1991):172–81; published in English in *The Frank Talmage Memorial*, vol. 2, *Jewish History*, vol. 6, no. 1–2 (Haifa, 1992), 151–62. See also Novinsky, "Sebastianismo Vieira e o Messianismo Judaico," in *Sobre as naus da Iniciação, Estudas Portugueses de Literatura e Historia*, ed. Carlos A. Iannone and Renata S. Junqueira (São Paulo-Araraquara, 1998), 65–79.

42. *Cadernos do Promotor de Lisboa* no. 23, Arquivo Nacional da Torre do Tombo, Lisbon; Anita Novinsky, *Cristãos-Novos na Bahia*, 2nd ed. (São Paulo, 1992), 142.

43. Anita Novinsky, "A Inquisição no Brasil. Judaisantes ex-alunos da Universidade de Coimbra," in *Universidade, História, Memória, Perspectivas*, Actas do Quarto Congresso História da Universidade, 7th Centenary (Coimbra, 1991), 315–27.

44. Trial against Luís Miguel Corrêa, Inquisition of Lisbon, #9249, Arquivo Nacional da Torre do Tombo, Lisbon.

45. Trial against Diogo Corrêa do Valle, Inquisition of Lisbon, #821, Arquivo Nacional da Torre do Tombo, Lisbon.

46. Trial against Luís Miguel Corrêa, op. cit.

47. Edgar Morin, *Mes Démons* (Paris, 1994), 138–84.

48. See Anita Novinsky, "Cristãos-Novos no Brasil, Uma Nova Visão do Mundo," in *Arquivos do Centro Cultural Calouste Gulbenkian, Mélanges offerts a Fréderic Mauro*, ed. Centro Cultural Calouste Gulbenkian, vol. 34 (Lisbon and Paris, 1995), 387–97.

49. With reference to the Brazilian experience in terms of a critical approach to religion, see Anita Novinsky, "Estudantes brasileiros afrancesados da Universidade de Coimbra. A Perseguição de Antonio Morais Silva," in *A Revolução Francesa e seu impacto na América Latina*, ed. Osvaldo Coggiola (São Paulo, 1990), 337–71.

50. Trial against Diogo Nunes Henriques, Inquisition of Lisbon, #7487, Arquivo Nacional da Torre do Tombo, Lisbon.

51. Ibid.

52. Ibid.

53. Trial against Domingos Nunes, Inquisition of Lisbon, #1779, Arquivo Nacional da Torre do Tombo, Lisbon.

54. Ibid.

55. Ibid.

56. Prayers uttered during the session of 12 October 1730, Trial #1779, op. cit.

57. With reference to marranism in Brazil, see Anita Novinsky, "Jewish Heresy in Colonial Brazil," *Proceedings of the Sixth World Congress of Jewish Studies*, vol. 2 (Jerusalem, 1975), 111–21, and Novinsky, "A Critical Approach to the Historiography of Marranos in the Light of New Documents," in *Studies on the History of Portuguese Jews from Their Expulsion in 1497 through Their Dispersion*, ed. Israel Katz and M. Mitchell Serels (New York, 2000).

– Chapter 12 –

OUTCASTS FROM THE KINGDOM: THE INQUISITION AND THE BANISHMENT OF NEW CHRISTIANS TO BRAZIL

Geraldo Pieroni

Lisbon, 1581. It's the beginning of the united period of the two Iberian crowns. At a reception given in honor of the new King of Portugal, Phillip II, the colony of Brazil was symbolically represented by a feminine figure holding a sprig of sugar cane in her hand with a caption that read: "*I have been the place of banishment for the condemned.*"[1]

ONE OF THE MAJOR PREOCCUPATIONS of the judges of the "Tribunals of Faith" was the preservation of religious order through the quelling of heterodoxies. The Inquisition was granted authorization to function in Portugal on 23 May 1536, and the first auto-da-fé[2] ceremony occurred in Lisbon in 1540. Because of diplomatic disagreements between the Portuguese monarchy and the papal court, however, the tribunal was only definitively established on 16 June 1547, by order of an edict of Pope Paul III, the "Meditatio Cordis." The hunt for Judaizers had officially begun. What was the motive behind this repressive legal action?

At that time, the main justification for the punishment of those who violated Divine law was the salvation of their souls, even if accomplishing this goal made it necessary to exclude them from society, much as weeds are separated from healthy stalks of wheat. In order to reunite a dissident minority to Christian society, the Inquisition, in an extremely vigilant way, resorted to punishment and to catechization (pedagogical means of social and religious reintegration). The primary reason for legalizing a "Tribunal of Faith" on Portuguese soil was the battle against the lapsing or backsliding of New Christians who, according to the crown and the Church, continued to practice Hebrew beliefs after their "conversions"—the mandatory baptisms that began to be enforced late in 1496.

From that moment on, Jews were no longer "Jews of the synagogues" who lived in their districts or ghettos, private communities in which they freely practiced their religion. Prior to the 1496 edict, these communities had existed all over Portugal: in Lisbon, Santarém, Évora, Porto, Faro, Setúbal, and Portalegre. With the establishment of mandatory baptism and the institution of the Holy Office, the new minority no longer enjoyed the juridical, ethnic, or religious legitimacy that had previously been granted by the Afonsin Ordinances. Henceforth this minority became "Christian"—or rather, "New Christian"—and was stigmatized and viciously persecuted.

As its title reflects, this chapter focuses on social exclusion, the Inquisition in Portugal, and the exile of New Christians to Brazil. The core of my discussion concerns the seventeenth century, although a seventeenth century deliberately extended so that we can better confirm transformations evident only in the long run. My purpose is to analyze the apparatus that promoted the establishment and practice of deportation to Brazil as a punishment meted out by the Portuguese Inquisition's judicial system.

Banishment

The cross, the olive branch, and the sword—the symbols of the Inquisition—represent the weapons that the institution used in order to integrate a dissident minority into a Catholic majority. Severity and forgiveness, vigilance, castigation, and catechizing—these were the Inquisitorial *compellere intrare*[3] during an era when fear was institutionalized. Everyone feared the king and the Inquisitors. Sons feared fathers, women feared husbands, everyone feared God—His chastisements during life on earth and His eternal punishments thereafter.[4]

Banishment was one of the Holy Office's preferred punishments. This type of disciplinary action, implemented within a broad penal system, had been widely practiced in Portugal since the early Middle Ages. By examining the Portuguese legal system, we can confirm that the practice of exile was a convention employed by both ecclesiastical and secular judges. Secular tribunals and the tribunals of the Inquisition therefore operated similar types of correctional systems that functioned in parallel ways. Although jurisdictions, prisons, and judges were naturally different once a sentence of exile overseas had been levied, all those condemned by secular or Inquisitorial tribunals were united in a common location in Lisbon, the Limoeiro prison, where criminals and sinners would fearfully await their embarkation date.

As a result of the maritime expansion that occurred during the fifteenth and sixteenth centuries, the kingdom's undesirables could, for the first time, be deported to territories overseas. In the case of Brazil, as it happens, the first Portuguese inhabitants were two convicts abandoned on the beach by Pedro Álvares Cabral in 1500. These deportees became future symbols strongly rooted in the ideals of the Brazilian people. Would Brazil be, therefore, a land of exile?

The king was the representative of the Portuguese judiciary, and the Inquisition tribunals were extensions of royal power. In theory, at least, intervention in and discipline of Catholic heterodoxies was a means of reinforcing the notion that the king, as God's representative, had power over the territories he controlled. The Church was united with the crown against social, religious, and moral threats. In the mind of the king, the supreme judge, as well as in those of the legislators, the existence of evil necessitated a judicial system with laws and principles aimed at protecting society. The twin notions of sin/reform and of crime/punishment are manifested in its ordinances. Reform through penitence and punishment through legal sentencing allowed order to be restored to a world knocked off balance by sin and crime. Royal and ecclesiastical authorities perceived their "holy mission" to be the administering of justice, given that sin and crime injured God in heaven and His representatives on earth. Within this judicial system, secular, Inquisitorial, and ecclesiastical tribunals were able to work unanimously.

For the Inquisition, exile provided a double function: on one hand, it operated as a defense of social and religious order, and on the other, as a purification process for sins committed. One cannot, therefore, examine exile imposed by the Inquisition in Portugal without taking into account the penitential dimension embedded in each sentence.

New Christians and the Inquisition

New Christians accused of crypto-Judaism were those who appeared most frequently on the lists of autos-da-fé. Appearing far less often were those who had violated Catholic morals and were also sentenced to exile: bigamists, sodomites, and seductive priests, along with other sources of disorder, including sorcerers, visionaries, and blasphemers. All were perceived to represent a threat to the consolidation of the kingdom's social, political, and religious unity and to its support of Roman Catholicism.

The daily lives of New Christians were strictly scrutinized. All were suspected of Judaism. "In small countries, where not one door is opened, nor one word uttered, that the rest of the world does not learn of it,"[5] nothing escaped the eyes of the informers. From the cradle to the coffin, everything pertaining to private, domestic life or to social life could be denounced. All those who did not participate in confession during Christmas, Easter, and Pentacost fell under suspicion of heresy. Catholic laymen could only possess in their homes the Bible, the Psalms with the Breviary, and Our Lady's Book of Hours, though never the vernacular version.[6] New Christians were accused of behaving in public as "good Mass-going Catholics" while secretly, in the privacy of their homes, continuing to observe the "Sabbath and fastings prescribed by Judaism." A large number of New Christians, particularly those of generations who had converted prior to mandatory baptisms, had thoroughly absorbed Catholicism, assimilating the principle and the practices of the Catholic Church; but they also may have bequeathed to their descendants a diluted version of the "law of Moses." Both crypto-Judaizing New Christians and New Christians fully loyal to Catholicism were seized by the Holy Office, and many were condemned to exile on Brazilian soil. Any minor gesture that could be construed as suspicious was reason enough to be thrown into the Inquisition prisons of Lisbon, Coimbra, and Évora. Francisco Bethencourt affirms that extensive and intensive searches for Judaizing New Christians were typical of the "style" of the Portuguese Holy Office, which had no equivalent either in relation to the Roman Inquisition, which considered Judaism a residual fault, or to the Spanish tribunals, which had ended massive persecution of Judaizers at the beginning of the sixteenth century and from then on had treated Judaism as a minor crime.[7]

In order to eradicate Judaizers from Portuguese soil, the Inquisitors established a general practice of denunciation. The condemning doctrine was based on the amount of Jewish blood that each person had in his veins. There frequently appear in the Inquisition records meticulous categorizations based on the purity of one's blood, as the following examples demonstrate: Brites Maria, "completely XN"; Maria Gomes, "part XN"; Diogo Dias, "three-fourths XN"; Alexandre Tavares, "one-half XN"; Simão Roiz, "one-third XN"; Margarida de Souza, "one-fourth XN"; João Fernandes, "one-eighth XN."[8]

The Jesuit António Vieira severely criticized the Portuguese Inquisition's actions, testifying to the great difficulty he had in comprehending the abuses it committed in the mass persecution of New Christians. He accused the Holy Office of apprehending "many people who did not have much of what one might there call the Jewish Nation, more than an eighth, or a sixteenth.... Such subtleties have never been seen in the world, to divide into eight parts, to find in them their sixteenths, their thirtieth parts and their thirty-second parts." Father Vieira would ask the Inquisitors: "Does Portugal's air create Jews?"[9]

Thousands of men and women accused of Judaism passed through hundreds of auto-da-fé ceremonies of the Holy Office. As we have already mentioned, many New Christians were exiled to Brazil. Those charged with Judaizing represented more than half of all the criminals banished to the Brazilian colony, that is, 52.7 percent; of these, women constituted the majority (65 percent). Male New Christians exiled to Brazil represented a smaller percentage because many of them were sentenced to forced labor in the galleys, a punishment reserved exclusively for men.

TABLE 12.1 Banishment to Brazil

	Numbers	Percentage
Judaism	311	52.7
Bigamy	88	14.9
Deceit	55	9.3
Witchcraft	43	7.3
Sodomy	25	4.2
Revelation of secrets	18	3.1
Visions	14	2.4
Blasphemy	10	1.7
Solicitation	7	1.2
Other	19	3.2

Note: Number of cases analyzed: 590

Source: ANTT, General Council of the Holy Office, Books 433 (Coimbra), 434 (Évora), 435 (Lisbon).

TABLE 12.2 Exile to Brazil by Century (sixteenth, seventeenth, eighteenth)

	16th			17th			18th			Total		
	W	M	T	W	M	T	W	M	T	W	M	T
Judaism	1	3	4	180	88	268	20	19	39	201	110	311
Bigamy	7	7	14	43	16	59	10	5	15	60	28	88
Deceit	16	4	20	9	22	31	3	1	4	28	27	55
Witchcraft	1	1	2	21	12	33	4	4	8	26	17	43
Sodomy	0	1	1	1	23	24	0	0	0	1	24	25
Revelation of secrets	0	7	7	3	7	10	1	0	1	4	14	18
Visions	1	0	1	10	1	11	2	0	2	13	1	14
Blasphemy	0	0	0	1	8	9	0	1	1	1	9	10
Solicitation	0	0	0	0	5	5	0	2	2	0	7	7
Other	0	1	1	3	12	15	0	3	3	3	16	19
Total	26	24	50	271	194	465	40	35	75	337	253	590

Notes: Number of cases analyzed: 590; W=Women, M=Men, T=Total

Source: ANTT, General Council of the Holy Office, Books 433 (Coimbra), 434 (Évora), 435 (Lisbon).

To be exiled overseas, especially to Brazil, meant crossing the ocean and living for three, five, or ten years in a different and peripheral world. The Inquisitors seemed to have assumed that for Europeans life in Brazil was a veritable purgatory, since the Inquisition considered exile to a colony as a sentence justified only for the most serious offenders. As viewed by the Inquisition, banishment, like purgatory, was a strict but transitory sentence. It remains to be seen if the deportees were able to make use of the imposed purgatorial exile.

New Christians Banished to Brazil

Each New Christian has his or her own story, and it is by way of these personal histories that we can understand how the Inquisition condemned the accused to prison sentences, confiscation of goods, forced labor in galleys, banishment, and death by fire. The following examples refer exclusively to New Christians exiled to Brazil.

"O, Almighty God of Israel, Lord of Abraham, having heard Daniel, hear, Lord, my prayer." This was the prayer uttered in an Inquisition's prison by Baltazar Soares, a thirty-year-old medical doctor. Son of Diogo Dias Caldeirão, also a doctor, and Inês Soares, he was accused of praying the Psalms of David without the Gloria Patris. Baltazar, married to Andresa Gomes, was in a prison of the Holy Office for five years before being condemned to an additional five-year exile to Brazil in an auto-da-fé on 9 September 1708.[10]

Whereas New Christians were not necessarily Judaizers, the special logic of the Portuguese Inquisition resulted in Baltazar Soares's condemnation for crypto-Judaism. The Inquisition saw a potential heretic in every New Christian, and the Holy Office's methods did not allow any New Christian to escape the tribunal unscathed. Denunciations, often without substantiation, were enough to convict an accused.

The Évora Inquisition imprisoned several members of the Almeida family, all New Christians. Among them was Maria, who had been denounced by her father Pedro, her brother António, and her sisters Helena and Inês, all themselves incarcerated by the Holy Office. Twenty-seven-year-old Maria de Almeida was married to a shoemaker, Luís Vieira, and on 7 July 1644 was *relaxada*[11] for not declaring all her offenses and for not supplying the Inquisitors with the names of those people with whom she was acquainted. Aware of the fact that she would die on a pyre, Maria de Almeida requested another hearing in which she "confessed all her sins." In the auto-da-fé of 21 October 1644, she was condemned to life in prison and to the penitential garment, a *sambenito* with "emblems of fire." The Inquisitors further sentenced her to six years of exile in Brazil. Before departing, she signed the term of secrecy and went to the outcasts' prison to await a ship that would transport her overseas.[12]

In Portugal, the number of individuals suspected of Judaism kept rising steadily. It was not enough to punish New Christians once; as time went on, the Inquisition continued to search for renegades who had been condemned before. Once the first generation had been punished, then it was the second and the third. The source continued its fervent flow. As António Vieira asserted in a letter written during the first years of the Restoration, the methods of the Inquisition actually perpetuated the existence of Judaism in Portugal.[13] Backsliding charges against those supposedly reconciled with and accepted back into the bosom of the Church increased the ranks of prisoners accused of Judaism. Accused and accusers alike were now children, nephews, nieces, and grandchildren who, as prisoners, when reprehended, tortured, and threatened with death, would accuse their parents, uncles, and grandparents who were well familiar with the prisons and techniques of the Inquisition, for they had previously experienced these same forms of torture.

New Christian Maria Gomes was seventeen when she was sentenced by the Holy Office on 1 April 1629. She received the well-known *sambenito* as punishment and departed for Monte-mor-o-Novo, her hometown, to fulfill her spiritual penance. She was again imprisoned on 21 April 1630 for refusing to wear the penitential garment in her local church. After being reprimanded, she promised to obey the Inquisitors. Forty-four years later, precisely on 6 September 1674, Maria Gomes, now a widow, was again imprisoned. Among her many accusers was her nephew José Mendes, a soldier in the town of Estremoz, who was also confined by the same Inquisition. In the auto-da-fé that took place on 28 March 1683, Maria Gomes was sentenced to two years of banishment in Brazil for "reverting to Judaism." In addition to exile, this transgressor received "spiritual penances and teachings on matters of the faith."[14]

In the minds of the Inquisitors, the fact that New Christians behaved outwardly as "good Catholics" was merely proof of their cunning in masking their true identities. Without question, crypto-Judaizers existed in Portuguese society during the Inquisitorial repression and were punished for practicing the "law of Moses" and for preserving the customs and traditions of their ancestors. The fact that they were sentenced a second time for "reverting to Judaism" would seem to indicate that many New Christians continued to practice principles found in the "ancient law." Nevertheless, the majority of Inquisitorial cases involving New Christians exiled to Brazil clearly reveals that the practice of Catholicism was soundly present in their prayers, confessions of faith, and daily rituals. Following are two such instances.

Ana Rodrigues was accused of Judaism; according to the Inquisitors' calculations, she was "three-fourths New Christian." She was married to a soldier named António Coelho and was twenty-three years old when the authorities of the Lisbon Inquisition sentenced her to three years of exile in Brazil. After the auto-da-fé, she was sent to Limoeiro prison where she endured many hardships, "suffering great affliction in her soul for not being able to receive the communion sacrament." She begged permission to receive the "most holy sacraments" by invoking the "five tribulations of Christ Our Lord." During Lent, in 1655, the Inquisitors allowed her to go to confession and to partake of the Holy Communion. Ana Rodrigues was accused of "observing the Sabbath and of not eating pork," even though she continued to uphold her Catholic faith by professing with great devotion that she believed in everything that the Catholic Church teaches its followers.[15]

Fernando de Morales Penso, a twenty-five-year-old New Christian, single, born in Lisbon, was imprisoned by the Holy Office and sentenced to five years of exile in Brazil. The Inquisitors demanded that as soon as he touched Brazilian soil he would send a certificate to the Holy Office Board in Lisbon confirming his arrival and his pledge that "he would not leave Brazil before the end of his sentence." Fernando left Portugal on board the ship *Diligente* and while on the high seas sent a letter to the Lisbon Inquisitors, dated 29 October 1683, stating: "It is absolutely necessary to relieve my conscience by telling Your Excellencies that since the day I was baptized until today I have never ceased being a true Catholic, never did a single thought allow me to stray from the Laws of Our Lord Jesus Christ under which I was well instructed, and therefore I declare to Your Excellencies that everything that I claimed in my confessions to the Holy Office, concerning me, and against those close to me, was false, and I confessed what I did not do for fear of death and to save my life."[16]

If we determine the traits of those New Christians who were banished to Brazil by analyzing Inquisitorial cases, then at first glance we can assert that they were predominantly Catholic, both in practice and in belief. It is very difficult to ascertain, however, to what extent the confessions made to the tribunal were sincere. It is evident that during brutal interrogations the prisoners' judgments were completely impaired by the Inquisitors' methods: after numerous sessions of inquests and torture, their ability to think or speak critically would have been diminished. The belief that they had betrayed their religion, the desire to save themselves and the lives of family members, the remorse over having accused relatives and friends, the discomfort of the prisons, the exhaustion—everything closed their minds. Anita Novinsky states that "If many generations of Catholicism had not turned New Christians into good Catholics, it neither, for the most part, turned them into Jews.... He is considered a Jew by Christians and a Christian by the Jews.... The New Christian creates his own defenses against a world in which he does not belong. He is, above all, a New Christian."[17]

Our last case is an example of how New Christians were put aboard ships and delivered to the authorities in Brazil. Escolástica de São Bento and her mother Maria Cordeira were imprisoned and sentenced by the Coimbra Inquisition. Taken to the Holy Office by Manuel de Abreu Bacelar, Escolástica arrived in jail elegantly dressed. She had brought with her "a gold trinket, silver buckles, black lace gloves with silver fringe, cultured pearls around her neck, and two silver pins." After several warnings in prison, she admitted she was a follower of the "law of Moses," along with several other people whom she named one by one. The Inquisitors decided that Escolástica de São Bento was a Judaizer and, thus, a "heretic and an enemy of the holy Catholic faith," deserving of the highest sentence of excommunication, in addition, significantly, to the confiscation of all her possessions by the treasury office. Following advice to confess all her sins with signs of remorse and begging forgiveness of the Inquisitorial judges, the defendant was received in the "Sanctity and Union of the Holy Mother Church." She declared herself guilty, renouncing her "heretical faults."[18]

Maria Cordeira, Escolástica's fifty-three-year-old mother, was given the same sentence, and both departed for Brazil to carry out their exile. Mother and daughter had been accused by their nephew and cousin António da Gama, a tailor residing in Aviz. António was thirty when the Holy Office imprisoned him on 2 September 1714. Accused of Judaism, he accepted the offenses with which the Inquisitors charged him, but soon thereafter went completely mad, and it became impossible to force him to repeat his confessions.

Upon embarking and after having crossed "the great ocean waters," mother and daughter arrived in São Salvador da Bahia de Todos os Santos and were handed over to João Calmon, commissioner of the Holy Office. On 3 July 1719, he wrote to the Portuguese Inquisitors confirming the arrival of the Judaizing offenders: "From the Holy Office Tribunal of the Coimbra Inquisition were sent by way of the Porto ships that docked here, to this city in Bahia, Escolástica de São Bento, daughter of Francisco Rodrigues, weaver, native of Aviz and resident of the city of Coimbra, with three years of banishment in Brazil.... Maria Cordeira also arrived, widow of Francisco Rodrigues, nicknamed the Sapé, weaver, native of Aviz and resident of Coimbra." Maria Cordeira was also sentenced to "another three years of banishment in Brazil." The two women had embarked on the ship *Nossa Senhora do Vale e São Lourenço*, whose captain was Manuel Cardoso Meirelles.[19]

To have access to and to analyze an Inquisitorial trial account is to have the opportunity to bring the domestic and social life of a person of the seventeenth century into the present day. It is like being presented with an open safe that reveals the secrets and afflictions of Holy Office offenders. If a first reading of these documents unearths statements obviously inspired by the Inquisitorial authorities that provoked them, a more careful reading exposes the hidden feelings of those condemned. All of this documentation allows us to understand the lives of the men and women of this period; it permits us to penetrate the daily routines and the fragmented families of these New Christians. Dominated by fear, they were subjected to severe degradation in their personal lives, which for many ended in exile to a distant land, a punishment aimed at both social exclusion and purification of souls. The exclusion of undesirable elements from the community was used by the ancien régime as a means of achieving social normalization. The practice of banishment was an obvious form of social vengeance against transgressors of royal laws. For the Inquisition, banishment functioned as what was believed to be a necessary religious and social defense against heterodox infection, while at the same time, serving as a mystical procedure for the purification of sins.

Notes

1. Gil de Methodio Maranhão (explicação de), *Documentos para a História do Açucar*, vol. 1 (Rio de Janeiro, 1954), xv.
2. Public penitential ceremony used by the Holy Office.
3. Means of forced entrance.
4. Maria José Pimenta Ferro Tavares, *Judaísmo e Inquisição* (Lisbon, 1987), 186.
5. ANTT (Arquivo Nacional da Torre do Tombo), Inquisition, General Council, Loose Documents, Group 2645, 114.
6. BNL (Biblioteca Nacional de Lisboa), Periodicals Room, reference J. 5543B: "Monitório de D. Diogo da Silva," in Mendes dos Remédios, "Os Judeus portugueses perante a legislação inquisitorial," *BIBLOS – Boletim da Biblioteca da Faculdade de Letras da Universidade de Coimbra*, vol. 1, nos. 10 and 11 (October/November 1925).
7. Francisco Bethencourt, "A Inquisição," in Yvette Kace Centeno, comp., *Portugal: Mitos Revisitados* (Lisbon, 1993), 104.
8. "XN" is the abbreviation for New Christian, notation used by the Holy Office notaries.
9. ANTT, Inquisition, General Council, Loose Documents, Group 2645, 114.
10. ANTT, Évora Inquisition, trial account 4002: Baltazar Soares. All prayers that did not include "glory to the Father, the Son, and the Holy Ghost"—the well-known Gloria Patris—were proof of heterodoxy: the rejection of the second person in the Trinity, Christ, God and Messiah.
11. *Relaxada:* a term used by the Inquisition, meaning the accused was to be relinquished to a civil court to be executed under the death penalty.
12. ANTT, Évora Inquisition, trial account 9172: Maria de Almeida.
13. ANTT, Inquisition, Council General, Loose Documents, Group 7, no. 2645, 145.
14. ANTT, Évora Inquisition, trial account 4586: Maria Gomes.
15. ANTT, Lisbon Inquisition, trial account 11019: Ana Rodrigues.
16. Ibid., trial account 6307: Fernando de Morales Penso.
17. Anita Novinsky, *Cristãos-Novos na Bahia* (São Paulo, 1972), 160–61.
18. ANTT, Coimbra Inquisition, trial account 1725: Escolástica de São Bento.
19. Ibid.

PART IV

FROM TOLERATION TO EXPULSION: IDENTITY, TRADE, AND STRUGGLE FOR SURVIVAL IN FRANCE AND CARIBBEAN FRENCH AMERICA

– Chapter 13 –

THE PORTUGUESE JEWISH NATION OF SAINT-ESPRIT-LÈS-BAYONNE: THE AMERICAN DIMENSION

Gérard Nahon

THE JEWISH NATION OF SAINT-ESPRIT-LÈS-BAYONNE was established on the Atlantic coast of France, at the westernmost point of the diaspora, by Portuguese New Christians originating from the forced conversions of 1497. Like the Jewish Nation of Bordeaux, it owed its existence to the *Lettres patentes* granted in 1550 by Henri II to the New Christians or Portuguese merchants. Consequently, the status of these groups, who were not recognized as Jews, was an ambiguous one up until the French Revolution. Bayonne was the Jewish community that was closest to the Iberian Peninsula. Along with its sister communities of Bidache, Peyrehorade, and Labastide-Clairence, it received emigrants from the Peninsula beginning in the sixteenth century. Some of these emigrants went on to the New World.[1]

In the seventeenth century, Jews who had left Bidache for Brazil and others from Peyrehorade living in Mexico were put on trial by the Inquisition. It is thanks, in part, to these trials that we have records of the private lives and regular religious practices of Jews from Peyrehorade.[2] The primary wave of migration, however, was toward the French Antilles, Martinique, and Guadeloupe, which opened a Portuguese connection with the Americas. The conquest of Cayenne—previously a Dutch territory—by the French on 15 May 1664 caused Portuguese Jews to move from French Guyana to Suriname, and established lasting ties between the Portuguese in France and those in Suriname. Curiously, this exodus of Jews toward Dutch-held Guyana, or Suriname, was in a sense counterbalanced by fresh arrivals of Christian and Jewish immigrants from La Rochelle. In 1725, King Louis XV refused to allow the Suriname Jews to return to Cayenne. Under pressure from the Jesuits, Louis XIV had on 28 April 1684 issued a decree expelling the Jews everywhere from Martinique to Bayonne. Subsequently, the Black Code (Versailles, March 1724) prohibited the establishment of any Jewish settlement in the French colonies, especially Louisiana, from which Louis XV expelled "all the Jews who may have settled there ... as avowed enemies of the Christian name."[3] Though only partially enforced, this expulsion jeopardized the continued presence of Jews in the French colonies. In fact, it scattered Jewish families native to the Bayonne region throughout the Dutch, English, and Danish colonies, where they enjoyed a higher status.[4] The American lands touched by the Jews of Bayonne thus extended from Suriname to Newfoundland and Labrador, along with Curaçao, Martinique, Jamaica, Barbados, Saint Eustatius, Saint-Domingue, Saint Thomas, Louisiana, and L'Isle Royale, previously known as Cape Breton and now as Nova Scotia.[5]

This chapter aims to define a French model—exemplified in the case of Bayonne—of relations between a Portuguese Jewish Nation and colonial America. Certainly the Portuguese Jews from Bordeaux played a far greater role in Atlantic trade than did those from Bayonne. But the bulk of research has concentrated on the Bordelais model, leaving Bayonne virtually unexplored. For this reason I will concern myself almost exclusively with the Portuguese Jewish Nation of Bayonne. For my sources I have relied primarily upon notarial deeds from Bayonne in the seventeenth and eighteenth centuries preserved in the Archives des Pyrénées Atlantiques in Pau.

Economic, Familial, and National Connections

One of the seven principal ports of the French kingdom, Bayonne was oriented mainly toward the Atlantic Ocean and the Americas for its commercial activities. The Jews of Bayonne participated in the maritime enterprise as well as in the colonization and exploitation of the French Antilles, where some of them settled with their families.

On 11 March 1715, Jacob Henriques de Castro and Samuel Teilles fitted out the fishing ship *Le Prude*, which caught and dried cod in Labrador. According to Anne Zink, at the end of the eighteenth century "nearly all the Jews, like the true Bayonnais they were, chose to invest in cod fishing." The following day, Moïze Pereira-Mendes equipped another ship, the *Marianne*, for the same purpose. Others fitted out vessels to hunt and render whales in Newfoundland. The Jewish merchants of Bayonne invested in maritime ventures lasting several months, and thus became acquainted with the hazards of long-distance navigation on the Atlantic.[6]

They imported colonial products such as cacao and animal pelts, and were in a position to appreciate the difference in quality between cacao from Caracas and cacao from the Antilles. They exported manufactured products including cloth, various trades goods, and notions. Some of their ships bore Jewish names, perhaps following the example of the Jewish "fleets" of Curaçao. Thus on 25 May 1695 Georges Mendes and Jean Gomes Sampayo planned to send the ship *Le Roy David* to Newfoundland under the Spanish flag, and on 27 February 1720 Gabriel Rodriguez Silva fitted out and provisioned the *Sara* for fishing off Ile Royale. On 5 June 1706, Antoine Alvares engaged the frigate the *Sainte Anne* to transport cloth from Brittany for sale in the islands. A meeting of the Commerce Bureau on 17 November 1729 examined a request by Jacob Silva, a Bayonne apothecary, who was seeking to ship "chests filled with drugs and medicines ... on vessels bound for the French islands in America." The Jewish merchants of Bayonne also insured ships, as Isaac Léon did on 15 January 1726 for the *Saint Jean de Bayonne*, sailing for Martinique. On 17 September 1750, Izaac Delcampo sold manufactured goods bound for Louisiana on *La Gracieuse.*[7]

A number of Jews from Bayonne, and even more from Bordeaux, acquired land and slaves in Martinique, where they settled in the seventeenth century and planted new crops, particularly cacao. In a petition to Louis XIV on 17 July 1689, Benjamin da Costa d'Andrade, a "Portuguese of the Hebrew Nation," explained "that he went to live on the island of Martinique and transported a large quantity of merchandise to trade there and to attract commerce from several places in order to profit and please Your Majesty, and built several houses there as well as a brewery on which he spent a large sum of money." Some of these Jews were to establish themselves in North America. Isaac Monsanto of New Orleans conducted business with Bayonne firms between 1758 and 1769.[8]

In the eighteenth century, Jews from Bayonne also lived in Jamaica, Curaçao, and Suriname. Aron de Castro Solar, whose father lived in Bayonne, settled in Port-au-Prince in Saint-Domingue. Léogane was where Michel Lopez de Paz, physician to the king, had his practice. Despite the changing politics of the French government, a Jewish community took root in Martinique. On 4 July 1764, it presented the Comte d'Estaing, "representing the person of His Majesty in the Leeward Islands of America," with a request on behalf of the "Community of merchants of the Hebrew Nation living both in this Island and in its dependent islands and being subject to the domination of His most Christian Majesty."[9]

The intellectual contribution of the Jews in colonial America was admittedly very modest. Still, an author born in the southwest of France was the first to introduce biblical poetry to the New World. Daniel-Israël Lopez-Laguna spent his youth in Peyrehorade. In 1691, he offered a sonnet to his rabbi Yshak de Acosta, the author of *Historia Sacra Real*, on the book of Esther. He then moved to Spain and went on to settle in Jamaica, where he wrote his masterpiece, *Espejo fiel de Vidas que contiene los Psalmos de David in verso*, published in London in 1720. He returned to Jamaica, and on 11 August 1721, in the presence of two witnesses, Moses Gutierez and Isaac Rodrigues de Leon, he made out his will, requesting that his body be buried in the Kingston cemetery beneath a gravestone worth 10 pounds that was imported from London. The exact year of his death (Marcus puts it at 1722) and his tomb—although marked in the Kingston cemetery—do not figure in the recent publication of Jewish inscriptions in Jamaica. He was survived by three sons named David, Jacob, and Isaac.[10]

Temporary Residence versus Permanent Settlement: Familial and National Strategies

The eighteenth century was for the Jews the century of the emigrant. At the bottom of the socioeconomic ladder, did Bayonne, like Amsterdam, export its poor to the colonies? In the summer of 1746, Ishac de Selomoh Abarbanel Souza wrote to the Portuguese Jewish Nation of Amsterdam to request financing for the voyage to Suriname of a vagabond, Abraham Lopes Rephael, and his family.[11]

Wealthy merchants also set up trading posts in the colonies and acquired properties there, a practice exemplified by Josias Gabay Ferro. Born in Spain in 1653, he passed through Bayonnne only briefly on his way to Amsterdam, finally settling in Curaçao where he was among the island's richest Jews. In 1709, he made a will mentioning a brother in Amsterdam, Abraham Gavay, and another brother in Bordeaux, Isaac Gavay. He also had five sisters, one of whom was still living in Spain with her son, Manuel Ferro. The four other sisters lived in Bayonne. Josias Gabay Ferro died on 14 August 1723 in Curaçao.[12] On 23 March 1720, Jacob Henriques de Soza, living in Jamaica, received power of attorney by associates in Bayonne following the death of Isacq Rodriguez Soza in Jamaica. At Le Cap, on 18 February 1785, Faxardo granted power of attorney to the older son of Brandam in Bayonne. David Nones-Lopes, residing in Saint-Domingue, on 2 February 1790 loaded the vessel *La Bayonnaise* with 315 pelts. On 12 March 1775, Aron Robles the younger, a merchant in Port-au-Prince, received a transfer of 150 livres from a bailiff at the headquarters of the Bayonne admiralty. One Izaac Victoire, a trader at Cap-Français, was granted power of attorney on 6 December 1785 by Salomon Levy in Bayonne. Rachel Carvaillo Frois was most unhappy on 20 February 1705, because she had long since received no support from her absent husband, Isaac Nunes Carvallo, who had gone to Jamaica about six years earlier. On 21 July 1789, Abraham Suarès conferred power of attorney upon his uncle, who was "about to return home to the English island of Jamaica." There were also Jewish companies in the colonies, such as Pereira-Souares Frères et Compagnie, mentioned at Le Cap on 20 October 1785, which sent trade goods on the ship *Les Quatre amis* to a Bayonnais by the name of Destandeau.[13]

Lasting settlement was also concretized by marriages contracted in the colonies. "Jewish Atlantic endogamy," to use Anne Zink's expression, was embodied in numerous marriages between young people from Bayonne living in Curaçao in the eighteenth century. Isaac Mendès de Sola, born in Bayonne, married Esther de Mezas, born in London, in Curaçao on 2 June 1734. Abraham Flores, another native of Bayonne, married Esther de Jacob Athias de Neyra y Chaves in Curaçao on 12 August 1742. In 5504 (1743–1744), the synagogue Mikveh Israel honored Abraham Flores by naming him *Hatan Tora*, or "Bridegroom of the Torah," that is, the first reader of the law. He died before 1764, followed by his widow in 1770. He must have had a tidy fortune since, according to a list made up between 1 July 1764 and 1 July 1765, his widow owned three slaves. Moyses Oliveyra Isidro from Bayonne married Rachel, daughter of Jacob Campos de Leon, in Curaçao on 10 September 1771. Moïse Prois d'Andrade, born in Bayonne, married Rachel, daughter of Isaac de Sola and his wife, a Nuñes da Costa, in Curaçao on 8 August 1781. David de Jacob Nunes-Tavarez, from Bayonne, married Zipporah de Leon in Curaçao on 21 January 1787. Mozes Gomes de Fonseca from Bayonne married Sara de David Rodriguez da Costa on 28 January 1787 in Saint Eustatius. Jacob de Abraham Rodriguez, born in Bayonne, married Ribca, daughter of Abraham Flores and Athias de Neyra, in Curaçao on 17 April 1791.[14] Jacob Baiz, born in Bayonne in 1779, married Lea Oliveira Isidro in Curaçao in approximately 1806. He was to die in the Danish island of Saint Thomas in 1857.[15]

At the end of a life rich in travel and adventure, those who succeeded in America made wills. As their final resting place they chose the cemeteries of the English or Dutch Antilles, since Jews were rarely allowed Jewish burial in French territory. I am indebted to my friend Mordechai Arbell for an epitaph in French that he found in the Charlotte Amalie cemetery in Saint Thomas: "Here lies the body of Abraham Gomez Vaez born in Bourg Saint-Esprit in the city of Bayonne on 24 March in the year 1759 and deceased in Saint-Thomas on 17 March in the year 1810 at the age of 51 years minus seven days." David Cardozo Pereira, born in Peyrehorade, was buried in Curaçao on 22 October 1786. In his will he bequeathed one hundred florins of his property to his sister Sara Cardoze living in Bayonne, and he also prohibited the sale of his house on Breedestraat. Moses Jussurun Cardosso made his will on 9 December 1725 at Port Royal in Jamaica. Though we have no proof that he was from Bayonne, there is no doubt that he maintained relations with the French community; indeed, he bequeathed ten pounds to the poor of Bayonne.[16]

The Jews of Bayonne who settled in America took part in familial strategies. On 19 September 1776, Jacob d'Isaac Delvaille registered a notarial deed to arrange his sister Debora's marriage in Bayonne to Jacob de Joseph Valery on 23 December y 1776. His brother Moïse had stipulated in his will, dated 2 November 1773, that the marriage of his sister Lea "can be accomplished only with the approval of my brother Jacob d'Isaac Delvaille, now in Cap Saint-Domingue," and had appointed Jacob his general and universal heir. On 17 June 1785, Abraham Pessoa, living in

Curaçao, was named the universal heir of his brother Moïse, a Hebrew teacher in Bayonne.[17]

Some expatriated natives of Bayonne, however, planned to return to their country of origin after making a fortune. Abraham Péreira Mesquita of Jamaica instructed his father, living in Bayonne, to purchase for him a country property "in that land where he wished to return to make his home." He therefore bought "the house and possessions of Sanguina" for the sum of twenty-five thousand livres. In this paradigmatic case, the period spent in America enabled him to build up wealth in the form of real estate in France, where Portuguese Jews had the right to own land. Abraham Péreira Mesquita died before entering into possession of his property, as attested by a deed dated 5 February 1755. Since he still owned property in Suriname, his father and heir chose Abraham Pardo, "a merchant in the colony of Suriname in Holland," to manage it. Mardochée Mendès-France, who paid three thousand livres' worth of taxes in Port-au-Prince on 22 October 1764, returned to Bayonne with all of his overseas properties intact. In 1794, his fortune was estimated at 150 thousand francs, "not counting his property in America."[18]

American Spaces Internalized

The Jews of Bayonne thus had property, commodities, ships, and families in America. What place did America hold in their conversations, their thoughts, their plans and dreams? In his library, Aron Colaso had copies of Cesar de Rochefort's *Histoire naturelle et morale des îles Antilles de l'Amérique ... avec un vocabulaire caraïbe* (Rotterdam, 1658) and Richard Blome's *L'Amérique angloise ou Description des isles et terres du roi d'Angleterre dans l'Amérique avec de nouvelles cartes de chaque isle et terres* (Amsterdam, 1688). This last title was "written in English by Richard Blome, primarily to encourage those who wish to settle in America under the dominion of the King of England, to make their way there." These books include discussions of the Jewish settlements, even on the Jewish origins of the indigenous inhabitants, and contain some quite striking passages, such as the following:

> As for their [the indigenous inhabitants'] origins, I am not disinclined to believe that they are of the Jewish race, and I think for the following reasons that they are descended from the ten tribes: Because they had to go to a land that was neither cultivated nor known, which must certainly be Asia or Africa, for it was not Europe. And the one who imposed this severe law upon them could easily have smoothed the way for them; and it is not impossible to go from the easternmost points of Asia to the westernmost points of America. To me their faces resemble Jewish faces, and their children especially, and so closely that when you see their children you would almost think you were in London in the Duckeplat or Berrystraet where most of the Jews live, and not only that, but their ceremonies are similar, they count by moons, they

offer up first-fruits, they have a sort of festival of the Tabernacle; it is said that their altar is placed on twelve stones; mourning lasts a year for them; the customs of their women, along with several other things, which do not come to mind right now, coincide with Jewish customs.[19]

Jacob Rodriguez Péreire, the Portuguese Jewish Nation's agent in Paris, defended the rights of Jews in the French colonies and demonstrated a perfect understanding of their situation. In 1779, he presented a long treatise on the subject to the minister of the navy. For their part, in Le Cap on 22 June 1782, the Jews of the French Antilles registered the *Lettres patentes* obtained in 1776. Curiously enough, the same agent of the Jewish Nation in Paris wrote a treatise on improving navigation at sea. He thus carried over to the scientific realm the maritime experience of the Portuguese outfitters of Bordeaux and Bayonne.[20]

America, land of settlement and commerce, was part of the political activity of the Jewish Nation, which claimed the rights enjoyed by the Jewish Nation in Suriname. Were its members also inspired by the example of the Jewish plantations of Suriname, bearing names of places in the Holy Land—Carmel, Hebron, Succoth, Beersheva? Albert Bernal gave the names Jerusalem, Hebron, and Moriah to properties acquired in the vicinity of Bayonne.[21] The American dream certainly pervaded conversations and thoughts. In 1738, a Jewish girl named Esther Brandeau donned a disguise and, under the name of Jacques Lafarge, embarked as a cabin boy on a vessel bound for Canada.[22] After lengthy consultations, the administration decided to send her back to France; the sequel to her adventure is not known.

On a graver note, a Jew leaving Bayonne would make his will upon sailing overseas: every departure was an act of daring, and those who set off were conscious that one phase of life was coming to an end. Jacob d'Isaac Delvaille, a merchant of the Jewish Nation, wrote on 29 October 1769, before embarking on the *Neptune de Bayonne* bound for Cap-Français: "[B]eing on the verge of leaving for America and fearing death and the uncertainty of its time, in order to forestall untoward consequences, I declare this to be my last will and testament."[23]

Was there still nostalgia for the lost America, that is, Brazil, where the first official Jewish community of the New World had known a brief existence during the period of Dutch occupation? As of 23 April 1725, Isaac Henriques Julian from Bayonne still owned a house in Amsterdam named "Le Recife en Brésil." Located on the Lange Houtgracht, the house with its warehouses and dependencies had been bequeathed to him by his father.[24] In a letter written in Bayonne on 24 March 1789 to Joseph Brandon, who lived in Paris, Abraham Silveyra describes a share in a house that was to go "to your *American* uncle Joseph." This was Jacob Rodrigues Bernal, who was nicknamed "the American." Had he made a fortune in the New World? It is difficult to know, for many young men had set off for the colonies in order to make a life for themselves. In April

1772, one Isaac Sossa, twenty years old, embarked on the ship *La Mindroc* and sailed for Le Cap and afterward Jamaica, "where he had personal business." By 9 September 1772, the same Isaac Souza had already returned to Bayonne on the ship *Les deux Joseph.* Izaac Goutiérez, aged thirty, and Abraham Delvalles, aged twenty, both of the Jewish Nation, boarded the brigantine *La Fillou,* bound for Port-au-Prince; on 1 June 1772, they arrived in Curaçao. On 15 March 1777, Jacob Gomes the younger, of the Jewish faith, thirty-one years old, embarked on the vessel *L'Actif* to sail to Saint Eustatius, "where he has settled." If nothing else, Jacob Rodrigues Bernal acquired revolutionary tendencies in America: he was to become the secretary of the Jean-Jacques Rousseau Revolutionary Committee, which governed the region of Bayonne during the Reign of Terror. Moïse Suarez invested the fortune he had amassed overseas in a chateau and was dubbed *"le Milord."* Jacob Mendes Capotte, *écrivain public,* was "about to sail on the ship named *La Société,* bound for Port-au-Prince" "where he must remain to carry on trade" on 12 and 14 March 1775.[25]

After her husband's death, Sara Oxeda, whose husband Abraham Gabay Isidro had been a rabbi in Barbados, returned to her family in Bayonne—perhaps somewhat the richer. She brought to fruition her ambitious plan to publish her husband's Hebrew work entitled *Yad Abraham.* She wrote a foreword in Portuguese and had this book printed in Amsterdam in 1758.[26]

Conclusion

The American dimension of the Jewish community in Bayonne was manifested in the commercial, maritime, and colonial enterprises carried out during the eighteenth century in the New World territories of the European powers. This dimension strengthened the political and economic roots of Portuguese Jews in France itself, as they acquired real estate and launched major industrial enterprises in the nineteenth century, such as the construction of railroads and the development of navigation by steam. Was the impact of the Bayonne Jews on America in general as negligible as Marcus has claimed it to be in his discussion of English colonies? Indeed, Marcus wrote, "Though the Jews of the French Islands had traded intensively with their coreligionists in England's North American colonies, their influence on the emergent Anglo-Jewish communities in the North Atlantic appears religiously and culturally to have been nil."[27] It should be pointed out that the only self-study produced by a Jewish Nation in colonial America was a French work published in 1788 in Paramaribo under the title *Essai historique sur la colonie de Suriname ... avec l'histoire de la Nation Juive Portugaise & Allemande y etablie, leurs privilèges immunités & franchises....* The connection between Bayonne and Suriname explains in part such a surprising linguistic choice, whereby French supplanted the Spanish of the *Nacion* as the language of culture.[28]

The influence of the French connection was to make itself felt in North America as well. Benjamin Nones, born in Bordeaux, became president of the Jewish Community of Philadelphia in the nineteenth century. Henri de Castro, alias Moïse Henriquez Castro, born in Bayonne on 17 July 1786, transported five thousand Alsatians on twenty-seven ships and invested $150,000 in order to colonize the western part of Medina. He gave his name to a county south of Amarillo and to the town Castroville, Texas.[29] Alongside the American dimension of Bayonne we must not forget the Bayonnaise dimension of American Judaism.

Notes

Translated from the French by Jennifer Curtiss Gage.

1. On Bayonne, see Pierre Hourmat, *Histoire de Bayonne des origines à la Révolution française* (Bayonne, 1986). The *Lettres patentes* of 1550 and those that followed through the end of the eighteenth century are published in Gérard Nahon, *Les "Nations" juives portugaises du Sud-Ouest de la France (1684–1791)* (Paris, 1981), 21–46. On the subject of these "Nations," the reader is referred to the classic work by Louis Francia de Beaufleury, *Histoire de l'établissement des Juifs à Bordeaux et à Bayonne depuis 1550* (Paris and Bordeaux, year VIII [1800]); new ed. with a preface by Jean Cavignac, *L'établissement des Juifs à Bordeaux et à Bayonne* (Bayonne, 1985); A. Detcheverry, *Histoire des Israélites de Bordeaux* (Bordeaux, 1850); T. Malvezin, *Histoire des juifs à Bordeaux* (Bordeaux, 1875; repr. Marseille, 1976); H. Léon, *Histoire des Juifs de Bayonne* (Paris, 1893; repr. Marseille, 1976); G. Cirot, *Recherches sur les Juifs espagnols et portugais à Bordeaux* (Bordeaux, 1908); G. Cirot, *Les Juifs de Bordeaux, leur situation morale et sociale de 1550 à la Révolution* (Bordeaux, 1920), of which only the first volume was published; and especially Frances Malino, *The Sephardic Jews of Bordeaux: Assimilation and Emancipation in Revolutionary and Napoleonic France* (Alabama, 1978). To these works may be added my own synthetic research: "Les sefarades dans la France moderne (XVIe–XVIIIe siècles)," *Les Nouveaux Cahiers*, no. 62 (1980):16–25; idem, "The *Conversos* in France in the 16th to the 18th Centuries," in *Culture and History, Ino Sciaky Memorial Volume*, ed. Joseph Dan (Jerusalem, 1987), 185–203 [in Hebrew; summary in English, xvii]; idem, "The Sephardim of France," in *The Western Sephardim: The History of Some of the Communities Formed in Europe, the Mediterranean and the New World after the Expulsion of 1492*, ed. R. D. Barnett and W. M. Schwab (Grendon, Northants, 1989), 2:46–74; idem, with Jean Cavignac, "Les communautés israélites du Sud-Ouest," in Gildas Bernard, *Les familles juives en France XVIème siècle–1815. Guide des recherches biographiques et généalogiques* (Paris, 1990), 39–49; idem, "Communautés espagnoles et portugaises de France (1492–1992)," in *Les Juifs d'Espagne, histoire d'une diaspora 1492–1992*, ed. Henry Méchoulan (Paris, 1992), 111–44; idem, "Le modèle français du marranisme: perspectives nouvelles," in *Inquisição. Ensaios sobre Mentalidade, Heresias e Arte*, ed. Anita Novinsky and Maria Luiza Tucci Carneiro (Rio de Janeiro, 1992), 227–65; idem, "Des Nouveaux Chrétiens à la Nation juive portugaise," in *Moreshet Sepharad: The Sephardi Legacy*, ed. Haim Beinart (Jerusalem,1992), 640–63 (in Hebrew), English translation, "From New Christians to the Portuguese Jewish Nation in France," *Moreshet Sepharad: The Sephardi Legacy*, ed. Haim Beinart (Jerusalem, 1992), 2:336–64; idem, "La 'Nation juive' de Saint-Esprit-lès-Bayonne du XVIe au XVIIIe siècle: escale ou havre de grâce?," in *1492/1992. L'Exode des juifs d'Espagne vers Bayonne: Des rives de l'Ebre et du Tage à celles de l'Adour. Colloque international,*

Faculté pluridisciplinaire de Bayonne–Anglet-Biarritz, 7, 8, 9 avril 1992, ed. Maïté Lafourcade (Bayonne, 1993), 1–30; idem, "Yshak de Acosta et David Silveyra: mémoire rabbinique, mémoire politique de l'Espagne, Bayonne 1722–1790," in *Mémoires juives d'Espagne et du Portugal,* ed. Esther Benbassa (Paris, 1996), 145–69. Also useful is the catalogue of the Musée Basque, *Les Juifs de Bayonne 1492–1992: Exposition présentée à la Salle Ducéré de la Bibliothèque Municipale de Bayonne* (Scénographie: Dominique Berthomé, curator: Olivier Ribeton) (Ville de Bayonne, 1992); as well as G. Nahon, "La Nation juive portugaise en France XVIeme–XVIIIème siecle: Espaces et pouvoirs," *Revue des études juives* 153 (1994):353–82. An additional source is Antonio-João Simoes Serra, *Subsidios para a Historia dos Judeus Portugueses em França, I. A Comunidade de Baiona* (Lisbon, 1963), which I was unable to consult for the present work.

2. Claudine Laborde-Sabarots, "Fernando de Médina, Juif de Peyrehorade face à l'Inquisition de Mexico au XVIIe siècle," *Bulletin de la Société de Borda,* Dax, 116th year, no. 422 (1991):207–41; Haïm Beinart, "The Trial of Moshe and Ya'acov Gomez, Jewish Inhabitants of Peñaorada (Near Bordeaux)," *Jewish History* 6, no. 1–2 (1992):xi–xxii (in Hebrew).

3. The first version of the Black Code issued in Versailles in March 1685 applied to the islands in general. The first article stipulated: "We wish and intend for the Edict issued by the late King of glorious memory, our Lord and Father, on 23 April 1615, to be executed in our Islands; in so doing, we enjoin all of our officers to expel from our islands all the Jews who have established residence there, who, as the declared enemies of the Christian name, are ordered to leave within three months from the day of publication of the present notice, on pain of confiscation of body and property," Jean-Baptiste Labat, *Voyage du chevalier des Marchais en Guinée isles voisines et à Cayenne fait en 1725, 1726, 1727 contenant une description très exacte & très étendue de ces païs et du commerce qui s'y fait* (Amsterdam, 1731), 3:155, according to records dated 6 May 1687, Saint-Domingue. The tenor of the 1724 text is quite similar: "The Edict issued on 23 April 1615 by the late Louis XIII of glorious memory will be executed in our province and colony of Louisiana, in so doing, we enjoin the Directors General of the said company and all of our officers to expel from the said country all the Jews who may have established residence there, who, as the declared enemies of the Christian name, are ordered to leave within three months from the day of publication of the present notice, on pain of confiscation of body and property," ibid., 177–78; separately printed copy, *Le Code Noir ou Edit du Roy, servant de règlement pour le gouvernement & l'administration de la justice, police, discipline & le commerce des esclaves nègres, dans la province & colonie de la Louisiane, donné à Versailles au mois de mars 1724*(Paris, 1727).

4. On the Danish possessions, see Jens Larsen, *Virgin Island Story: A History of The Lutheran State Church, Other Churches, Slavery, Education, and Culture in the Danish West Indies, now the Virgin Islands* (Philadelphia, 1950), 96–97; list of religious buildings in Sainte-Croix in 1784: 1 Jewish, 152: "In 1685 Denmark had Proclaimed religious tolerance to the Jews on St. Thomas, allowing them, as well as the Roman Catholics, to hold private religious services. There is no information of such religious services being held by the Jews until after 1781, when, after the sacking of St Eustatius, the greater part of the Jews there came to St. Thomas. In 1796 the Jews formed a congregation and built a synagogue under the appellation of Blessing of Peace."

5. On the Jews in the French colonies, see the series of articles by Abraham Cahen, "Les Juifs de La Martinique au XVIIe siècle," *Revue des Etudes Juives* 2 (1881):93–122; also indispensable is "Les Juifs dans les colonies françaises au XVIIIe siècle," *REJ* 4 (1882):127–45 and 236–48; *REJ* 5 (1882):68–92 and 258–72. The question is raised again by J. Petitjean-Roget in "Les juifs à La Martinique sous l'Ancien Régime," *Revue d'histoire coloniale* 43 (1956):138–58. On Jamaica, see Jacob A. P. M. Andrade, *A Record of the Jews in Jamaica from the English Conquest to the Present Time* (Kingston, 1941). I am indebted to M. Mordechai Arbell for providing me with a photocopy of this extremely rare work. Some information on the Jews in Barbados are to be found in Robert H. Schomburck, *The History of Barbados comprising a geographical and statistical description of the*

Island, a sketch of the Historical events since the settlement and an account of its geology and natural productions (London, 1848), 97–98, 107, and 432. Their first settlement dates from 1628, and the first Jewish grave from 1658. The community opened five cemeteries, and its synagogue, whose denomination was *Kaal Kadosh Nidhe Israel,* was destroyed by a hurricane in 1831. On Saint Eustatius, see Jacob R. Marcus, *The Colonial American Jew 1492–1776* (Detroit, 1970), 1:141–43.

6. See Anne Zink, "L'activité des juifs de Bayonne dans la seconde moitié du XVIIe siècle," in Lafourcade, *1492/1992,* 85–107, 97. The following deeds are cited: 11 March 1715, Archives des Pyrénées Atlantiques III E 4439, Grosse: Jacob Henriques de Castro and Samuel Teilles for five thousand pounds at 25 percent on *La Prude* fishing and drying cod in Labrador. Cod fishing and drying on Ile Royale or Cape Breton—today the part of Canada known as Nova Scotia—benefited from various tax exemptions. See, for example, *l'Arrest du Conseil d'Estat du Roy concernant le commerce qui se fait aux Isles Françaises de l'Amérique, des morues séches et des huiles provenant de la pesche des sujets de Sa Majesté à l'Isle Royale du 20 may 1718.*

7. Deed of 23 May 1695, Leonor Gomes de Sampayo and Catherine Mendes de Medine: agreement with Jean Drouillet on the ship *Le Roy David,* III 3175; 27 February 1720, contract of grosse: Samuel Gradis and Samuel Alexandre the younger to Gabriel Rodriguez-Silva, *La Sara,* fishing at L'Isle Royale, III E 4630; deed of 5 June 1705 certifying the quality of cacao transported on the *Saint Jean Baptiste,* III E 4428; deed of 5 June 1706, contract on the sale of cloth shipped from Bretagne to the islands on the *Sainte Anne,* III E 4428. On Jacob Silva, see *Séances du Bureau du Commerce, année 1729,* Paris, Archives Nationales F 12 * 76, 649. On Isaac Leon, see III E 4156; on Izaac Delcampo, III E 4655. On Jewish maritime credit at Bayonne, see the important article by Anne Zink, "Les Juifs de Saint-Esprit-lès-Bayonne et le prêt à la grosse aventure," in *Archives juives* 29(2) (1996):20–35.

8. Benjamin da Costa d'Andrade's petition is in the Archives du Ministère des Affaires Etrangères. I am especially grateful to Hugues de Dianoux de la Perrotine for a photocopy of this document. On Isaac Monsanto, see Bertram-Wallace Korn, *The Early Jews of New Orleans* (Waltham, 1969), 161–62.

9. On Aron de Castro Solar, see G. Nahon, *Les Nations juives portugaises,* doc. 8, 18–20. On Lopez de Paz, a relative of David Gradis of Bordeaux, see Abraham Cahen, "Les juifs dans les colonies françaises au XVIIIe siècle," *REJ* 4 (1882):132–33. For the 1764 petition, see Archives de la Marine, Collection Moreau de Saint-Méry, Colonies, vol. 15, art. juif, Cahen, "Les juifs dans les colonies françaises," 237–38.

10. See Cecil Roth, Laguna, Daniel Lopez (c. 1653–c. 1730), *Enc. Jud.* 10, col. 1361–62; Marcus, *The Colonial American Jew,* vol. 1, 127–28; C. Cabezas-Alguacil, "Un acercamento a la obra de Daniel López Laguna Espejo fiel de Vidas," *Miscelanea de Estudos arabes y hebraicas* (1988–89):37–38 and 151–62. For the sonnet, see G. Nahon, *Les Nations,* doc. 110, 357–58. Regarding the year of his death, see Marcus, *The Colonial American Jew,* vol. 1, 128. Testament Island Record Office, Spanish Town, Jamaica, Liber XVI f° 32, excerpts; the grave is mentioned in Andrade, *A Record of the Jews in Jamaica,* 130 and 225. On the subject of funerary inscriptions in Jamaica, see Richard D. Barnett and Philip Wright, *The Jews of Jamaica: Tombstone Inscriptions 1663–1880,* ed. Oron Yoffe (Jerusalem, 1997).

11. For the expression "the century of the immigrant," see Marcus, *The Colonial American Jew,* vol. 1, 255. Letter of 15 *menahem* 5506, 1 August 1746, Amsterdam, Gemeente Archief PA 334 92, published in G. Nahon, *Les nations juives,* doc. 86, 289.

12. The Hague, Rijksarchief, Oud Archief van Curaçao [1708–1845] 1545 no. 221; see Isaac S. Emmanuel and Suzanne A. Emmanuel, *History of the Jews of the Netherlands Antilles* (Cincinnati, 1970), vol. 2, 750–51; epitaph in I. S. Emmanuel, *Precious Stones of the Jews of Curaçao* (Assen, 1957), 250.

13. Deeds of 23 March 1720, III E 4630; 18 February 1785, III E 4234; 2 February 1790, III E 4239; 12 March 1775, III E 4576; 6 December 1785, III E 3958; 20 February 1705, III E 4206; 21 June 1789, III E 4516; 20 October 1785, III E 3958.

14. For the expression "l'endogamie juive atlantique," see Zink, "L'activité des juifs des Bayonne," 101. On marriages, see Emmanuel and Emmanuel, *History*, 1001 (Isaac Mendès Sola). Regarding Abraham Flores: marriage, see Emmanuel and Emmanuel, *History*, 690; mention of the title *Hatan Tora*, 788. In the inventory after the death of Esther Flores were gold amulets, Inv. OAC 983 n° 112, Emmanuel and Emmanuel, *History*, 1046. A complete list of slave owners on the island appears in OAC 907, no. 66, littera a, Emmanuel and Emmanuel, *History*, 1036–45; Abraham Flores's widow is mentioned on page 1043. For the other marriages, see Emmanuel and Emmanuel, *History*, 914 (Moyse Oliveira Isidro); 893 (Moïse Frois d'Andrade); 1050 (David de Jacob Nunes-Tavarez and Moyse Gomez de Fonseca); 985 (Jacob de Abraham Rodrigues; 849 (Jacob Baiz).
15. See Emmanuel and Emmanuel, *History*, 849.
16. List of four Jewish houses on Breedstraat in Willemstead or Punda in 1715, The Hague, Rijksarchief, West India Company 206, 35–41; see Emmanuel and Emmanuel, *History*, 770. Jews from Bayonne made wills that are preserved in the Island Record Office, Spanish Town, Jamaica, filed under the following code: liber XXI 76 (1737), XXXVII, 367 (1768); cf. Marcus, *The American Colonial Jew*, vol. 3, 1403n. 6. Excerpt from the will of Moses Jussurun Cardosso from the Island Record Office, Jamaica, liber XVII, fol. 104, in Andrade, *A Record of the Jews in Jamaica*, 180.
17. Deeds of 19 September and 23 December 1776, Archives des Pyrénées Atlantiques, III E 4577. Will of 2 November 1773, III E 4574, no. 206. List of ship-owners, The Hague, Rijksarchief, Oud Archief van Curaçao [1708–1845] 837, see Emmanuel and Emmanuel, *History*, 699; list of brokers in Curaçao, The Hague, Rijksarchief, Oud Archief van Curaçao [1708–1845] 911 no. 169, *Naamlijst van ... der Regeeringe en Gequalificeerde Persoonen ... op 't Eyland Curaçao* (Amsterdam, n.d); see Emmanuel and Emmanuel, *History*, 759. Abraham Pessoa appears among the members of the community in Curaçao beginning in 1769; see Emmanuel and Emmanuel, *History*, 1030. Will of 17 June 1785 and inventory after the death of Moïse Pessoa on 22 June 1785, Archives des Pyrénées Atlantiques in Pau, III E 4586.
18. Declaration by Jacob Péreira-Mesquita of 5 February 1755, III E 4181, on the purchase of this property. Jacob-Péreira-Mesquitta's power of attorney to Abraham Pardo, 11 April 1752, III E 4656. I have not identified Abraham Péreira Mesquita's property on the list of "Names of plantations on the Surinam river, from its source to the fortress of Amsterdam," which contains the names of Jewish plots but not—with a few exceptions—those of their owners, in Philippe Fermin, *Description générale, historique, géographique et physique de la colonie de Surinam* (Amsterdam, 1769), vol. 1, xv–xvi. Concerning the river, see also page 10: "But going further up, one comes upon a little village, named Torrarica, located on the left bank, which is inhabited only by a few Jewish planters. Eight leagues from here is another Jewish village, in which there is a very large and lovely synagogue"; on the Jewish synagogues, see page 28: "the Jews, of whom there were a considerable number, both Portuguese and German, also have two synagogues. That of the former is quite beautiful; but that of the Germans is far less attractive." On the map in volume 1 can be read: *Village de Juifs* and *Savane des juifs*. On Alexander Lavaux's color map figures a 288-acre plot numbered 82 in the name of Adam Pardo; is this an erroneous transcription of the name of Ab[raha]m Pardo, Abraham Péreira Mesquita's proxy? For the tax paid by Mendès-France's in Port-au-Prince, see Abraham Cahen, *REJ* 4 (1882): 245; for his fortune in Bayonn, see "Tableau des citoyens dont la fortune s'élève au-delà de 40.000 francs," Léon, *Histoire*, 167; Ernest Ginsburger, *Le Comité de surveillance Jean-Jacques Rousseau. Saint-Esprit-lès-Bayonne, Procès-verbaux et correspondance 11 octobre 1793–30 fructidor an II* (Bayonne, 1989, 2nd ed.), 165.
19. List of Aron Colace's books, Amsterdam, Gemeente Archief, Archief Weeskamer, K 18, published in G. Nahon, *Les Nations*, doc. CLI, 442–49, nos. 16 and 154. For the reference, see Richard Blome, *L'Amérique angloise ou Description des isles et terres du roi d'Angleterre dans l'Amérique avec de nouvelles cartes de chaque isle et terres* (Amsterdam, 1688), 156–57.

20. The treatise by Jacob Rodrigue Péreyre is published in Abraham Cahen, "Les juifs dans les colonies françaises," *REJ* 5 (1882):81–85. On Péreyre, see Renée Neher-Bernheim, "Un savant juif engagé: Jacob Rodrigue Péreire (1715–1780)," *REJ* 142 (1983):313–451.
21. Henry Léon also lists "Jérusalem, Hébron et Moriah, isolate houses, surrounded by land, occupied by small farmers and built by M. Albert Bernal, who gave them these names in memory of the history of the Hebrew People"; in Léon, *Histoire*, 413.
22. On Esther Brandeau, see Archives Nationales (Paris), Colonies B 68 f° 29 v° (290 v°), B 71 f° 8, 1739–40; Joseph R. Rosenbloom, *A Biographical Dictionary of Early American Jews: Colonial Times through 1800* (Lexington, 1960), 13; and Benjamin G. Sack, *History of the Jews in Canada* (Montreal, 1965), 6–9. See also my review in *REJ* 125 (1966):458; Gaston Tisdel, article on "Brandeau, Esther," *Dictionary of Canadian Biography* (Toronto, 1966); and Marcus, *The Colonial American Jew*, vol. 1, 377–78. I have been able to locate only a few of the documents relating to this affair that are cited by the late Benjamin Sack, and unable to trace the young girl's subsequent adventures. On the place of this episode in Canadian historiography, see Richard Menkis, "Antisemitism and Anti-Judaism in Pre-Confederation Canada," in *Antisemitism in Canada: History and Interpretation*, ed. Alan T. Davies (Waterloo, Ontario, 1992). See also Laurence F. Tapper, *Sources d'Archives sur les juifs canadiens*, 2nd ed., revised and augmented (Ottawa, 1987).
23. Departure of the *Neptune*, Arch. Nat. Colonies F 5 B 30; testament, Arch. Pyr. Atlant. III E 4570 n° 151.
24. Arch. Pyr. Atlant. III E 3726.
25. On Jacob Rodrigues Bernal, see Léon, *Histoire*, 162 and 385; the letter is published in G. Nahon, *Les Nations juives portugaises*, doc. 158, 436–37. Passengers on board Arch. Nat. Colonies F 5 B 38: Isaac Sossa (162 and 167), Izaac Goutiérez (162), Abraham Delvaille (id.); F 5 B 30: Jacob Gomes (193). For Moïse Suarez, see Léon, *History*, 161 and 467. On Jacob Mendes Capotte, Arch. Pyr. Atlant. III E 4576.
26. Cf. Cecil Roth, "The Remarkable Career of Haham Abraham Gabay Izidro," *Transactions of the Jewish Historical Society of England* 24 (1974):211–13, of which the late R. D. Barnett provided me with proofs prior to publication. Notary Bertrand Forgues, Arch. Pyr. Atlant. III E 4566, n° 38. Reg. des Décès, Registre des naissances, Arch. Bayonne, GG Suppl. Israélites 15 (3) 292. On the sometimes stormy career of this rabbi in Suriname, see G. Nahon, "Recherches sur les relations intercommunautaires: Amsterdam et la diaspora sefarade," *Ecole Pratique des Hautes Etudes, Ve section: Sciences religieuses. Annuaire*, vol. 87 (1981–82/1978–79):247–50.
27. Jacob R. Marcus, "Jews in the French Indies 1654–1800," in Marcus, *The Colonial American Jew*, vol. 1, 85–94 and 95.
28. In their preface, on page vii, the regents of the offer the following explanation: "Privés des connoissances nécessaires, forcés en quelque façon d'écrire dans une langue qui n'étant point la nôtre [en note: elle est la Portuguaise & l'Espagnole] *nous* fut apprise moins par des principes que *par une routine*, peut-être même vicieuse."
29. On Henry Castro, see Henry Cohen, "Henry Castro, Pioneer and Colonist," *Publications of the American Jewish Historical Society* 5 (1896):1–5; Audrey Goldthorp, "Castro's Colony" (Master's thesis, University of Texas, 1928); Bernard Postal, art titled *Texas*, in *Encyclopaedia Judaica*, 15 col. 1035; Julia Nott Waugh, *Castroville and Henry Castro, Empresario* (San Antonio, 1934); Bobby Weaver, *Castro's Colony: Empresario Development in Texas 1842–1856* (Texas University Press, c. 1985). For Castro's *état civil*—his biography prior to his voyage to America has been very little studied—see Registre des naissances de la Nation juive, Arch. Bayonne, GG Suppl. Israélites 15(3) 104.

– Chapter 14 –

ATLANTIC TRADE AND SEPHARDIM MERCHANTS IN EIGHTEENTH-CENTURY FRANCE: THE CASE OF BORDEAUX

Silvia Marzagalli

URING THE EIGHTEENTH CENTURY, French foreign commerce grew remarkably. Since exports and imports essentially took maritime routes, the Atlantic port cities—Bordeaux in particular—played a major role in French economic expansion to the New World. By the middle of the eighteenth century, Bordeaux was the major French port. The city's success was mainly due to a boom in the Atlantic and colonial trade, although its Asian trade also increased in the decade prior to the French Revolution. Until the loss of Canada in 1763, Bordeaux also traded with New France, but the core of the city's commercial expansion was in the Caribbean. From the early 1720s up until the Revolution in 1789, Bordeaux merchants imported increasing quantities of sugar, coffee, and indigo from the three French colonies of Martinique, Guadeloupe, and, in particular, Saint-Domingue. The value of Bordeaux's colonial trade in 1789 was more than ten times higher than it had been in the 1720s. Since the domestic French market could absorb only a limited portion of these huge amounts of colonial goods, merchants re-exported the vast majority of them to Northern Europe, together with more traditional regional products, such as French wine, brandy, and dried fruits.[1]

Colonial trade was strictly governed by France through an array of legislation known as the *Exclusif*, or the "exclusive system." According to this mercantilist rule, only French merchants could trade with the French colonies. Although colonial planters repeatedly ignored this legislation and sold a great deal of their produce to foreigners, the exclusive system nevertheless had a major effect upon the Bordeaux merchant community. Whereas French merchants concentrated on colonial trade, their foreign colleagues living in the city specialized in European trade. French authorities deplored the fact that French merchants left most of the freights and profits from the re-export trade to German, Dutch, and British ship-owners, but this division of labor proved highly functional. Foreign merchants in Bordeaux were therefore numerous.

Scholars have done a considerable amount of research on the cosmopolitan Bordeaux merchant community of the late seventeenth and eighteenth centuries.[2] Existing studies generally tend to classify the merchants according to their religious belief. Historians have highlighted that, although the city's population was almost entirely Catholic, Protestants and Jews were remarkably numerous within the merchant elite.[3] In the international trade of late eighteenth-century Bordeaux, for example, one merchant out of every four or five was a Jew.[4]

Despite the considerable interest that historians have taken in the Bordeaux merchant community, the importance of the Jews in the city's economic expansion still needs investigation. It is not that scholars have neglected Bordeaux's Jews; the first history of this community was published at the end of the eighteenth century, and other works were published in the nineteenth and early twentieth centuries.[5] More recently, France Malino has brilliantly dealt with the question of their political and institutional status in Bordeaux, and Jean Cavignac has studied the demographic and social structure of the Bordeaux Jewish community.[6]

However, all of these scholars were concerned mainly with the problems of Jewish integration and assimilation within French society. The specifically economic role of the Bordeaux Jewish community is therefore largely marginal in existing literature. Apart from case studies of single Jewish merchant houses,[7] some evidence of the importance of the Jewish merchants for French expansion to the west can also be found in works on religious minorities in the French colonies.[8] These studies tend to concentrate upon the legislation, which first authorized, then forbade, Jewish settlement in the French colonies, but they also underline that, despite all the difficulties, Jewish planters and merchants were in fact tacitly admitted into most of the French Caribbean islands. Many questions, however, still remain unanswered. Jews certainly contributed to the prosperity of French colonial trade, but was their role of decisive importance? And did their commercial organization have any special characteristics?

Despite the substantial bibliography concerning both Bordeaux and its colonial trade, we know remarkably little about the importance of Bordeaux Jews in French commercial expansion in the New World. The question as such has not been raised before. Even if they provide a valuable framework within which to analyze this specific problem, French historians on Bordeaux are above all interested in the commercial successes of the city. They might study Jewish merchants, but their primary aim is to explain the life of Bordeaux, not the Jewish role in transatlantic expansion.

One might expect to find something with regard to this problem in debates for or against Jewish integration that occurred in eighteenth- and nineteenth-century France, since the economic utility of the Jews was one of the main arguments used in favor of their emancipation.[9] However, the analyses were mainly confined to France, rather than to her colonies. If French colonial governors and intendants[10] occasionally underlined the utility of Jewish settlers in the Caribbean, their remarks were solely confined to administrative correspondence and found no echo in public debate. Also, the arguments were highly ideological—a defense of Jews might, for example, be used as a pretext to attack the Jesuits—so that it becomes difficult to use these sources to assess the real economic importance of the Jews in the French colonies.

In order to put forward a tentative evaluation of this subject, it is first necessary to assemble the evidence, which is quite scant and dispersed throughout the extensive literature on eighteenth-century Bordeaux. The aim of this essay is to demonstrate the possible value of such research. What was the place and importance of Jewish merchants in eighteenth-century Bordeaux, and how exactly did they participate in the Atlantic trade? What legal opportunities were available to them to live in and to trade with the French colonies? We will concentrate here on Bordeaux colonial trade, rather than on the intercolonial trade in which Jews were also active, but which did not directly benefit the city's economy. Did Jewish commercial strategies in the Atlantic trade differ from those of non-Jewish Bordeaux merchants? This question raises the more general question of the comparative advantage that Jews might still have had in the later phase of European expansion to the west.

I want first to review the legal situation of Jewish merchants both in Bordeaux and in the colonies, and then to concentrate on the activities of some of those Jewish merchants of Bordeaux who participated in French colonial trade. Finally, I want to assess the Jewish merchants' indirect contribution to this trade through their involvement in the finance and insurance businesses.

The Jews in Bordeaux: Origins, Evolution, Occupations

The literature on the Bordeaux Jewish community is, as has been mentioned, abundant. The demographic evolution and the geographical origins of these immigrants are relatively well known. Jews had been expelled from France at the end of the fourteenth century. The Jewish community of eighteenth-century Bordeaux was, therefore, the result of Jewish emigration in modern times, mainly from the Iberian Peninsula.

The first New Christians arrived in southwest France at the end of the fifteenth century, both from Spain and from Portugal. This emigration continued during the seventeenth and eighteenth centuries, especially from Portugal. By then, Jews were officially tolerated in Bordeaux and had formed their own community. Sources are therefore more abundant. During the eighteenth century, the Jewish population of the city increased from five hundred to fifteen hundred inhabitants, that is, from 1 to 1.5 percent of the city's total population. Whereas earlier immigration was due to religious intolerance in the Iberian Peninsula, Jean Cavignac explains the large number of arrivals in the eighteenth century by reference to Bordeaux's economic prosperity and to the existence of an already well-established Jewish community in this town.[11] According to the 1808 Napoleonic census, there were 2,063 Jews in Bordeaux, over three-fourths of whom were designated as "Portuguese."[12]

The Jewish community of Bordeaux was one of the most important, both demographically and economically speaking, in eighteenth-century France. The southwest region of France was one of the few major areas of Jewish settlements in France.[13] There were also important Jewish communities in both Lorraine and Alsace, where twenty thousand Jews lived in 1784, and in the territories of Avignon and the Comtat Venaissin, belonging to the Pope. The Jewish community in Paris was formed by immigrants from all of these areas.

The political situation of these communities varied greatly, since France was far from being, at that time, a centralized or homogeneous nation. A great ambiguity characterizes the political status of these Portuguese immigrants in Bordeaux during the sixteenth and seventeenth centuries. In 1550, the French king had granted large privileges to the "merchants and other Portuguese, called the New Christians" who had settled in southwest France. In fact, they essentially enjoyed the same rights as native Frenchmen. They could also obtain French naturalization, as well as the title of *bourgeois de Bordeaux*,[14] which implied several further commercial privileges.

These measures pertained, however, only to those Portuguese immigrants considered New Christians, that is to say, Catholics. This distinction explains why, until the eighteenth century, there was apparently no contradiction between, on the one hand, the various orders expelling Jews from Bordeaux, and on the other, the ordinances protecting Portuguese merchants: French authorities pretended or assumed that the latter were in fact Christians.

Most of these New Christians had escaped from religious persecution carried out against the Jews. If some of them had converted to Christianity, the majority remained secretly attached to their religion. It is, of course, truly difficult to apprehend the actual religious practice and beliefs of these early immigrants, since they publicly conformed to the Catholic religion: they let their children be baptized, they married in front of a Catholic priest, and they were buried in Christian cemeteries.

The fundamental ambiguity in the French legislation affecting Portuguese immigrants disappeared in 1723, when a royal act confirmed once again the privileges that had been accorded to the Portuguese New Christians of Bordeaux in 1550. Now for the first time, the Portuguese were officially recognized as Jews. This might seem surprising, especially if one considers that from the 1680s Louis XIV had adopted a severe policy against religious minorities, both Protestant and Jewish. Certainly, as Frances Malino points out, the conjunction of economic and financial crises at the beginning of the eighteenth century had proved the economic utility of Jewish capital and had led to the official recognition of this religious minority in 1723. However, a change had also taken place within the Portuguese community of Bordeaux itself, which had begun to emerge as a well-organized "nation."[15]

After the turn of the century, Jewish families abandoned the fiction of Catholicism and no longer let their children be baptized. A few years later, they acquired land in order to provide for their own cemetery, and, in addition, although they still married in front of a Catholic priest—this was the only legal way of getting married in modern France—the ceremony took place outside of the church. From 1699, there was also a *sedaca* in Bordeaux—a charitable organization that later became synonymous with the Portuguese Jewish nation. The decisive impulse toward these changes had come from the new wave of immigrants who had arrived in Bordeaux after 1683 as a result of the persecutions of Don Pedro in Portugal. These families were possibly more attached to their Judaism than those who had previously settled in Bordeaux, and were definitely less disposed to live there as Christians. They sought recognition by the king as one of the organized communities (*corps*) that traditionally provided the structure of French society. As such, they would have the right to rule their own community and to levy money for its functioning. This approach proved successful, and some well-known Portuguese merchants of eighteenth-century Bordeaux were able to benefit from the commercial expansion of the city, not as New Christians—now an uncertain condition—but as members of a recognized Jewish community, which afforded more protection.

Historians have often underlined the contribution made by the Jews to the economy of modern Europe. In France, scholars have repeatedly stressed the strong presence of Jews, as well as of Protestants, in finance and trade.[16] These studies, however, have tended to concentrate upon a number of prominent bankers or merchants, neglecting to point out that in early modern Europe the vast majority of the Jewish population, along with the Christian inhabitants of the city, lived in a very precarious economic situation. Most of the Jews in eighteenth-century Bordeaux were in fact shopkeepers and retail dealers, and they hardly contributed, even indirectly, to the city's Atlantic trade.

However, within the Jewish community, a few individuals came to prominence because of their fortune and prestige. According to a 1734 report by the intendant of Bordeaux, there were at that time five or six Jewish ship-owners trading with the American colonies and, in addition, a few others who were involved in banking. Each of these Jews was responsible for a "very considerable business."[17] In 1747, David Gradis,

Jacob Peixotto, Jacob Raphaël, Gabriel Da Silva, and Salomon Francia were the five most taxed Jewish merchants in Bordeaux,[18] and their names were well known in international trade. In the second half of the century, other Jews, such as the Rabas or the Lopès-Dubecs, contributed through trade and banking to Bordeaux's commercial success.

The Bordeaux Jewish merchants concentrated mainly on three sectors: trade to Spain, colonial trade, and banking. As we will see, all of these activities contributed directly or indirectly to Bordeaux's expansion to the New World.

The Jews in the French Colonies: A Precarious Status

Most Bordeaux merchants involved in colonial trade had a family member in the Caribbean who kept them informed about prices and production, who sold their cargo, who organized the return voyage of the ship with the shortest possible delay, and who made sure that the colonial planters paid off their debts. The correspondence of Jacob Azavedo in the early 1770s shows that the Bordeaux Jewish merchants were perfectly conscious of the importance of relying upon a commercial partner in the colonies.[19] However, were these Jewish merchants allowed to operate with the same freedom as their Catholic colleagues?

Whereas the Jewish merchants' situation in Bordeaux was relatively safe, thanks to the protection granted them in the sixteenth century, this was not the case in the French colonies, where Jews did not enjoy the same degree of security and where their position was, in fact, most precarious. An analysis of the evolution of the legal status of Jews in the French colonies is therefore necessary in order to better understand the delicate situation in which the Bordeaux Jewish merchants found themselves and to better appreciate their initiative under such difficult circumstances.

Compared to other European countries, France was relatively late in undertaking occupation of territories in the New World. The expulsion order issued against Jews on 23 April 1615 was to be applied both in France and in the French colonies.[20] At that time, however, the colonial expansion of France was still extremely limited, and the effects of this decision were largely insignificant.

It is uncertain whether the French would have found Jews in Martinique when they took possession of this island from the Dutch in 1635. The Dutch, unlike the French, had largely protected Jews,[21] and when France later acquired Remire (Cayenne) in 1664, two paragraphs of the treaty explicitly granted protection and religious freedom to Jewish colonists, who had settled there under Holland's favorable legislation.

In the seventeenth century, Jewish capital proved in fact to be useful to the French colonial administrators, who were consequently to underline, in their reports to Paris, the economic value of these settlers and were to defend them from the attacks of the missionaries, in particular, those of the Jesuits. Besides providing capital and banking services, Jews may also have transferred technology to the French colonies. The introduction of the new techniques used in sugar cane and cacao production is commonly attributed to Benjamin Dacosta, a Jew who had settled in the French Fort St. Pierre after the Portuguese conquest of Recife (1654).[22]

At the beginning of French colonization of the Caribbean, Jewish colonists were mainly engaged in trade and offered useful credit to other settlers, as well as to the authorities. Thanks to the Sephardim diaspora, they had contacts with Amsterdam and were thus able to provide information on world markets directly from the most important European port. Isaac Pereira possibly obtained his naturalization in 1676 as a reward for the information from Curaçao that he gave to the French authorities during the war against Holland.[23]

In the second half of the seventeenth century, some Jews started to acquire land in the French colonies and became planters. By 1680, there were sixteen Jewish proprietors in Martinique, and at least four of them owned slave-run sugar plantations. This was also the case for a Jew in Granada.[24] New problems then arose for the French authorities. One of the main arguments used to legitimize slavery had been religious: slaves were offered the opportunity of getting to know the Christian gospel and thus to save their souls. Missionaries regularly visited and catechized slaves in the plantations of the French Caribbean. How could they possibly tolerate that nominally Catholic slaves lived under the rule of a Jewish master in a colony that belonged to the "very Christian" king of France?

By 1680, Jesuit protests on this problem found an attentive listener in Louis XIV, who sought religious unity in his kingdom. In 1685, the Edict of Nantes of 1598, which had conferred religious rights to Protestants, was revoked. In that same year, the *Code Noir*, or "Black Code," standardized the legislation for French colonies. The first article of the code banned non-Catholics from living in the territories belonging to the king of France, thus condemning both Jews and Protestants to expulsion within three months. This code was henceforth used to govern all French colonies and was systematically applied to new conquests, for example to Saint-Domingue—present-day Haiti—which was officially acquired by France in 1697. It was on the basis of the *Code Noir* that Jews were expelled from Louisiana in the 1720s and were never really able to settle in New France.[25]

A change in government attitude toward the Jews was already perceptible in 1683, when an order was issued that proscribed Jews from settling in French colonies. The fact that the *Code Noir* had to repeat this expulsion order two years later proves that the earlier edict had not been rapidly executed; nevertheless, the change in policy was clear. France was closing her colonies to religious minorities in the 1680s, whereas other European powers were explicitly granting protection to Jews in order to promote the economic development of their own possessions in the New World. Britain had in fact authorized Jewish settlement in Barbados in 1661, and Holland had granted equality of rights to Jews in Guyana in 1667.[26]

After their expulsion, Martinique Jews left for Curaçao, St. Eustatius, and Barbados before eventually trying to come back to this French colony with the complicity of the French colonial authorities, who found their presence and their credit facilities extremely useful.[27] The same happened in Saint-Domingue. Even if the *Code Noir* officially forbade Jewish settlement, the local governor and intendant generally sought to protect those Jewish colonists already on this island or who wished to settle there.[28] The Jews, however, had no legally recognized status in the French colonies. Being considered foreigners (Portuguese), the king of France could, for instance, confiscate their property at their death (*droit d'aubaine*). Their security depended entirely upon the benevolent protection of the local authorities, and thus in 1765, when the new governor of Saint-Domingue arrived with a negative attitude, the Jews were first heavily taxed and then threatened with expulsion.[29] This did not, however, prevent Abraham Gradis from acquiring a sugar mill on the island in the following year.

In the late 1770s, the crown once again changed its policy. In 1776, Jews were unofficially granted the right to live in Martinique provided that they did not profess their religion publicly. It was the same year in which the French king confirmed the privileges of the Portuguese Jews of Bordeaux. This act was officially registered in Cap-Français in 1782, thus definitively solving the problems of inheritance for those Bordeaux Jews dying in the colonies.[30] In the 1780s, Jews must in fact have been quite numerous in Saint-Domingue: twenty-two Bordeaux Jews were to ask for indemnities after the slave revolt and the independence of Haiti.[31]

All in all, French legislation concerning Jews in the colonies remained restrictive throughout most of the eighteenth century. The actuality, however, was quite different from the laws, and Jews could in fact live in the islands, as long as they acted as Christians. Despite all the difficulties, some Jewish colonists were thus able to make their fortune in the French islands. A study of Bordeaux's Jewish merchants may clarify how.

The Activities of Some of Bordeaux's Jewish Merchants Participating in French Colonial Trade

Compared to other French ports, such as Rouen for instance, Bordeaux entered into colonial trade relatively late. The Rouen Sephardim merchants were already participating in overseas colonial trade during the first half of the seventeenth century. This was not the case in Bordeaux, where in the same period the merchants essentially confined their trade to Europe.[32]

Bordeaux New Christians were not pioneers in the American trade venture. In fact, in the 1670s and 1680s, they were mainly shopkeepers.

The few wealthy Portuguese merchants at Bordeaux were involved in local and regional trade rather than in international commerce.[33] As the city turned toward colonial trade, however, especially once the *Lettres patentes* of 1717 had granted to Bordeaux's merchants the right to trade with the colonies, its Sephardim merchants immediately recognized the commercial opportunities of this branch of trade. In fact, as we have seen, the expansion of Bordeaux into the colonial market attracted an increasing number of Jewish merchants, who settled in this French town throughout the eighteenth century.

Zvi Loker underlines three factors that might have favored Jewish success in the French Atlantic trade: their family networks, the geographic mobility necessitated by their persecution, and their knowledge of foreign languages, such as Spanish or Portuguese, which proved useful in trade.[34] In order to judge whether these factors still gave any comparative advantage to Jewish merchants over non-Jewish merchants in Bordeaux's eighteenth-century colonial trade, it might be useful to have a glance at the trade patterns that they used.

Bordeaux Jews, throughout the eighteenth century, seem to have been able to settle their relatives in the French Caribbean without any major problems. As we have seen, Jews were tolerated in French colonies, provided that they did not publicly exercise their religious beliefs. In fact, many of them lived in the colonies under the pretense of being Christian. The Raba brothers, for instance, wealthy merchants of late eighteenth-century Bordeaux, settled in the city in 1763 from their native Bragança in Portugal. Shortly after their arrival in France, they were circumcised. However, when François (Benjamin) and Antoine (Moise) Raba went to Saint-Domingue in 1779, they managed to obtain a certificate from a Capuchin affirming that they were Catholics before obtaining a letter of naturalization and thus becoming French subjects.[35]

The Rabas are probably the best example of the fortune that Jewish merchants of Bordeaux could make in the French colonies. At their deaths, all of the brothers were able to leave substantial fortunes to their heirs: Moise left 300,000 francs in 1806, Aaron 270,000 francs (1810), Abraham 369,000 francs (1810), Jacob 316,000 francs (1817). Finally, Salomon "the American," the Portuguese consul at Bordeaux, left 580,000 francs (1820). Although Jacob was associated with his brothers' firm, he was in fact a doctor. His brothers, however, were all merchants. With the exception of Aaron, who directed the business in Bordeaux, all of the others had spent at least a part of their lives in Saint-Domingue.

Like the Rabas, many other Jewish immigrants of eighteenth-century Bordeaux sent a member of their family to the Caribbean shortly after their arrival in this French town. Jean Cavignac lists some fourteen Jewish families who had arrived in Bordeaux after 1748 and who later settled a son or a brother in Saint-Domingue.[36] As Bordeaux's colonial trade rapidly expanded during the second half of the eighteenth century, Bordeaux's Jews increased their activities in the Caribbean.[37] However, some Bordeaux Jews had already adopted the strategy of sending a relative to the colonies in the early eighteenth century. David Gradis, for instance, had established his nephews in both Saint-Domingue and Martinique in the 1720s.

The Rabas were not the only successful Jewish merchants from Bordeaux involved in colonial trade. There were also others, for example Gradis, Dias-Pereyra, Lopès-Dubec, Pimentel, Sasportas, Sequeyra, and Totta, who made their fortunes in this trade. Most of them had arrived in Bordeaux during the second half of the eighteenth century,[38] but some, like David Gradis, had already traded with the colonies during the early 1720s.

The Gradises, the Lopès-Dubecs, and the Rabas created a solid family tradition in trade, and they stand out among the twenty-five most prominent Bordeaux families who dominated Bordeaux's political and social life in the 1830s.[39] Salomon Lopès-Dubec made his fortune through colonial trade with Saint-Domingue. In 1783, he sent his fourteen-year-old son to Cap-Français, and in the same year he entered into partnership with his cousins, who had settled in the island a number of years before.[40] This pattern seems to have been common for all the major colonial merchants, both Jewish and Christian.

Not every Bordeaux Jew who left for the colonies became a successful sugar planter or a rich merchant, however. Isaac-Henry Mendès-Furtado, for example, arrived with his father at Bordeaux in 1748, at the age of eighteen. He left this city for Saint-Domingue, where he was to become a retail dealer before returning to Bordeaux and dying there in 1791.[41] Like many of the young Catholics leaving Bordeaux for the colonies, Mendès-Furtado did not succeed in making a considerable fortune. Possibly he lacked experience, or perhaps he lacked relatives and partners upon whom he could rely.

The example of Isaac Mendès-France proves that success could be relatively easily obtained, provided that one belonged to the right network. Isaac Mendès-France was born in 1720 in Bordeaux, where his father was a merchant. At the age of twelve, Isaac was sent to Amsterdam for his commercial education. In 1743, he married Judith Da Costa, the daughter of a rich Jewish merchant of Bordeaux. This enabled him to become a colonial merchant and a ship-owner. Having sustained heavy losses in the early 1750s, he left for Saint-Domingue at the end of the Seven Years' War. He settled in Petit Goave where he cultivated and traded in coffee and cotton, and he succeeded in making a fortune within a few years. In fact, he possessed all that was required to become successful: both capital and a trade network, in Bordeaux as well as in the French colonies. In 1775, he came back to France, leaving his two sons in the colony. He acquired several houses and landed properties in Bordeaux, and he became a *bourgeois* in 1779. The same Isaac Mendès-France was involved in a famous lawsuit as a result of having brought two slaves back with him from Saint-Domingue. Under French legislation, a slave became free as soon as he or she arrived in France. The trial brought by these two slaves against their master was to become the pretext for violent anti-Semitic attacks during the 1770s.[42] But Mendès-France's behavior did not differ from that of many Catholic planters coming back to France from the West Indies.

Slavery in the French colonies, as well as the slave trade itself, was not the prerogative of a specific religious group: Catholic, Protestant, and Jewish merchants of Bordeaux were all involved in this trade. With ten slave ship voyages, the Gradises were among the seven largest Bordeaux slave traders in the eighteenth century. If one considers, however, that Jews made up 20 to 25 percent of local merchants, the direct participation of Bordeaux Jewish shippers in the slave trade from 1685 to 1826 was quite limited: four Jewish houses out of a total of 186 (2.2 percent), and twenty expeditions out of 460 (4.3 percent). Even for David Gradis & Sons—the most important Jewish firm at Bordeaux that was involved in the slave trade—this form of trade played only a minor part in its activities: from 1718 to 1789 the firm sent 221 ships to the colonies, only ten of which (4.5 percent) carried slaves.[43]

It is possible that the modest participation of Bordeaux Jews in the slave trade was due to their lack of connections or relatives in Africa. In African trade, French ship-owners had to rely entirely upon their captain, and French captains were all Catholic. For direct colonial trade, on the other hand, Jewish merchants had a relative in Saint-Domingue or Martinique to whom they could consign the cargo. This could not have been the case for the slave trade. David Gradis & Sons was an exception in that the firm had close links to government circles. Immediately after the Seven Years' War, Abraham Gradis was able to enter into a partnership with the French governor of Gorée and rely on him for the purchase of slaves on site.[44]

The Gradises, together with the Rabas, were probably the most famous Jewish merchants of eighteenth-century Bordeaux. The Rabas had settled in Bordeaux after the Seven Years' War, and their success coincides with the most glorious phase of eighteenth-century Bordeaux trade. The Gradises illustrate, on the other hand, the ascension of a Jewish family in the first half of the century. They were also to make a fortune in the colonial trade, but they were involved with royal officials and with the slave trade as well.

The Gradises had begun to outfit ships for the Caribbean in 1717, when the king's *Lettres patentes* had authorized Bordeaux merchants to equip ships for the colonies and had granted them exemption from fees. At that time, David Gradis was already a well-known merchant who had specialized in the textile trade. Through the marriages of his daughters, he became linked to a number of important Jewish merchants and bankers: his sons-in-law were Louis Lopès-Depas, whose brother had good connections in Saint-Domingue; Jacob Peixotto, the son of a Bordeaux Jewish banker with relatives in Amsterdam; and Samuel Alexandre, whose father was a wealthy shipper and banker in Bayonne.[45] Like Mendès-France, David Gradis belonged to a Jewish network that could support him and ensure his commercial success. In 1724, he sent two of his nephews, Jacob Mendès and Miranda, to Saint-Domingue. From then on, David Gradis was to consign at least four ships to them every year. In 1726, he placed another nephew, Abraham Gradis, in Martinique;[46] Abraham Gradis eventually entered into partnership with David Mendès, the younger brother of Jacob. David Gradis could therefore rely on relatives in both Martinique and Saint-Domingue to sell his cargoes and to assume responsibility for the return cargo for Bordeaux.

One peculiarity of the Gradises in eighteenth-century Bordeaux was their important connection to the crown. When war broke out in 1744, the Gradises diversified their investments and chartered some of their ships to the king.[47] This experience gained them contacts among the Canadian authorities, and as the peace returned in 1748, the Gradis firm developed its associations with François Bigot, intendant of New France, and Jacques-Michel Bréard, controller of the marine in Quebec City. From 1749 to 1755, Gradis sent annually, on behalf of the Société du Canada, a ship to Bigot and Bréard. These two officials systematically conflated private and public interest and used their influence to favor Gradis's ships and cargoes. When the partnership was finally dissolved, the firm David Gradis & Sons had made 451,152 livres profit.[48] In the same period, Gradis also chartered some of his ships to the crown for the French Caribbean. This paid well, provided that one could wait for the notoriously protracted repayment of state debts. Only a solid firm with the requisite contacts with members of the government could invest in such expeditions. During the Seven Years' War, Gradis was again involved in the chartering of ships for the king, and he profited from the increasing royal expenditures in New France.[49] His familiarity with governmental circles permitted Gradis to obtain, in 1779, an exemption from the *droit d'aubaine* in the colonies. Because of his link to the French court, Bordeaux's Jewish community also called upon him to occasionally defend the interest of the Portuguese merchants of Bordeaux in Paris.[50]

Gradis's business was highly diversified. From 1753, he had financed the activities of Lavalette, the superior of the Jesuits in Martinique, whose bankruptcy during the Seven Years' War was made the pretext for the suppression of the Company of Jesus in France in 1764. Gradis had also lent money to Prunes, a magistrate of the Parliament of Bordeaux, and from whom he was eventually to acquire a sugar plantation in Martinique when Prunes was no longer able to pay off his debts. Finally, the Gradises owned vineyards around Bordeaux.

Richard Menkis has underlined that, although the ties with their co-religionists were necessary and largely used, the Gradises' success depended also upon their ability to enter into good relationships with non-Jews: the government, ship captains, and a number of Catholic merchants, magistrates, and even clergymen looking for their financial support.[51]

Bordeaux Jews certainly had extensive connections. However, nothing in these brief profiles of prominent Jewish merchants from eighteenth-century Bordeaux seems to give to them a comparative advantage over their Christian colleagues. The precarious situation in which they were placed as Jews in the French Caribbean would suggest that they were in fact rather disadvantaged.

The activities of the Gradis family, and particularly its link to the crown, were possible because of the financial solidity of this firm, and one could argue that it was precisely their strength in finance and banking that permitted Bordeaux Jews to acquire some relevance in the Atlantic trade. Since finance could also contribute indirectly to Bordeaux's expansion to the New World, it is necessary to examine briefly these activities, before summing up the role of the Jews in the colonial trade of this city.

The Indirect Participation of Bordeaux's Jewish Merchants in the Atlantic Trade: Investment, Finance, and Insurance Businesses

Even if they did not send a ship on their own account to the colonies, Bordeaux's Jews could contribute to the city's commercial expansion by financial participation in these maritime ventures. The brothers Louis and François Lopès-Depas, for example, together lent 5,000 livres to Jacques Perreire in 1727, who sent his ship *Jacob* to Martinique.[52] In this case, they financed a Jewish ship-owner, but Jews were also, in some cases, shareholders in ships belonging to Catholic merchants. Lopès-Dubec, for instance, while sending his own ships to the islands, also acquired shares in a great number of colonial expeditions organized by other Bordeaux merchants.[53] The diversification of investments in several shipping ventures was a common way of reducing risk and was a strategy used both by Jewish and Christian merchants.

Beside this participation in the financing of ships to the colonies, Bordeaux Jews also indirectly assisted the commercial expansion of eighteenth-century Bordeaux through their prominent position in the sectors of banking, finance, and insurance. Planters in the colonies could, for instance, draw on a Bordeaux Jewish banker in order to make their payments,[54] thus facilitating financial exchanges between the colonies and France. There were only a few prominent bankers in eighteenth-century Bordeaux, and most of them were Jews. Bordeaux Jews did have a comparative advantage in the city's banking, since they could benefit from the Sephardim diaspora: they often had relatives in London and Amsterdam, the two major financial centers of the time.[55]

Bordeaux's merchants certainly received precious financial assistance from Jews living in other cities. Jacob Azavedo was just a modest commissioner and insurance merchant when he arrived in Bordeaux in 1746.

He had a close relative in Bayonne, however, and was therefore able to provide Bordeaux merchants with Spanish and Portuguese specie, which they used for their colonial trade.[56] The Bayonne connection was particularly valuable for getting specie to Bordeaux because of its proximity to Spain and therefore to the silver coming from its American colonies. French merchants could buy colonial produce at lower prices in the French Caribbean if they paid cash. There was consequently a constant demand for specie in French ports. Thanks to their relations with Spain, Portugal, and Bayonne, Bordeaux's Jews enjoyed an enviable situation in this particular branch of trade.[57]

Bordeaux's Jewish merchants were also able to benefit French trade to the New World by their insurance services. The proceedings of a trial against Joseph David Gabriel Da Silva,[58] a Jewish merchant based in Bordeaux who went bankrupt, reveal that he had insured a ship owned by Journu *frères* of Marseilles for 32 thousand livres, a considerable amount, as merchants rarely risked more that two thousand or three thousand livres on a single ship. This was the practice, for instance, of Jacob Azavedo, who carefully collected information on the captain, the vessel, and the ship-owners before insuring part of a ship's value for her voyage to the colonies.[59]

In general, however, it is extremely difficult to quantify the indirect contribution made by the Jews to Bordeaux's expansion to the New World, since we have no means of reconstructing a complete picture of the complex network of finance, insurance, and banking services. The few examples above serve to show simply that Jews were involved at all levels of colonial trade, and it is possible that through their involvement in banking and insurance they provided the most useful services of all for the colonial trade of Bordeaux. This point certainly needs to be further investigated.

Conclusion

Bordeaux's Jews contributed, both directly and indirectly, to the economic expansion of France into the New World in the eighteenth century. According to Jean Cavignac, eighteenth-century Bordeaux was a *havre de tolérance*, a "harbor of tolerance" that offered Jews and Protestants the opportunity to trade and to make their fortune.[60] The condition of Jews in southwest France was in fact more favorable than anywhere else in the kingdom; this situation certainly explains the importance of Bordeaux's Jewish community. Some of its prominent members participated, as we have seen, in the colonial venture. Far from being representative of the role played by the Jews in eighteenth-century French maritime trade, the case of Bordeaux is therefore unique, both because of its specific legislation concerning the Jews and because of the importance of this maritime city in French trade.

If a comparison has to be made, Bordeaux's Jewish merchants should be compared to their colleagues in England or in Holland, as they were all to engage in colonial and Iberian trade, as well as in banking and insurance.[61] However, the position of the Bordeaux Jews in the French colonies was much more precarious than that of the English and Dutch Jews. On ideological and religious grounds, the king of France was to refuse throughout the eighteenth century to grant to all Jews the right to settle in the colonies, whereas the English and the Dutch colonies were much more open to Jewish participation.[62]

If Bordeaux Jews engaged, despite all the difficulties, in American trade, it was because they understood that the economic context was extremely favorable and because their expectation of profits was not deceived. It cannot be claimed, however, that they had a comparative advantage over their Christian colleagues in the Caribbean colonial trade.

Christians and Jews adopted the same strategies of establishing a relative in the colonies, and often of acquiring plantations. It has been difficult to identify any facet of the Jewish trade in the French colonies that was specific to it. In addition, if the Gradises or the Rabas were among the richest merchants of Bordeaux, they were far from being the only ones, and many Christian merchants also had a great deal of success in colonial commerce, such as Bonnaffé and Nairac, both of whom were Protestant.

If family links resulting from the Sephardim diaspora gave any advantage to Bordeaux's Jews, this would have been in the banking and insurance sectors. The connection with Spain and Portugal was particularly valuable for the trade in specie. Bordeaux colonial merchants needed silver and gold for its extra European trade, and the Jews provided an essential service in this regard. The diaspora to London and Amsterdam, and to Hamburg and other city ports, provided Bordeaux's Jews with a solid network for conducting financial operations.

Family and co-religionist networks were certainly fundamental factors in explaining the Jewish success in eighteenth-century Bordeaux, but they do not explain everything. Gradis's success in New France was due, as we have seen, to his links with the crown and to his dealings with Catholic ministers and colonial officials. It was thanks to their family relations in London and Amsterdam, where Jewish capital was largely available, that Bordeaux's Jews could certainly find underwriters in these two major insurance centers. However, Gradis was also to rely on Nairac, a Bordeaux Protestant based in Amsterdam (which invites a consideration of another diaspora—that of the Huguenots).[63] The Jewish contribution to Bordeaux's expansion to the west is incontestable, but it was not confined to a circle of co-religionists.

Notes

1. For an analysis of Bordeaux trade and merchants in the eighteenth century, see François Crouzet, "La croissance économique; le commerce de Bordeaux; la conjoncture bordelaise," in *Bordeaux au 18e siècle*, ed. François-Georges Pariset, vol. 5 of the *Historie de Bordeaux* (Bordeaux, 1968), 191–323; Paul Butel, *Les négociants bordelais, l'Europe et les Iles au XVIIIe siècle* (Paris, 1974). This is a shorter version of Paul Butel, "La croissance commerciale bordelaise dans la seconde moitié du XVIIIe siècle" (Ph.D. diss., Université de Paris I, 1973).
2. Among others, Perry Viles, "The Shipping Interests of Bordeaux, 1774–1793" (Ph.D. diss., Harvard University, 1965); Butel, *Les négociants bordelais*; Peter Voss, "Bordeaux et les villes hanséatiques, 1672–1715. Contribution à l'histoire maritime de l'Europe du Nord-Ouest" (Ph.D. diss., Université de Bordeaux III, 1995).
3. In underlining the importance of non-Catholic houses in Bordeaux, these studies are probably influenced by the echoes of Max Weber, Werner Sombart, and other scholars of early capitalism. The quantitative relevance of Jews and Protestants possibly justifies a classification based on ethnic and religious factors; however, Bordeaux's scholars have rarely tried to analyze the nature of the relation between religious belief and economic success.
4. Jean Cavignac, *Les Israélites bordelais de 1780 à 1850. Autour de l'émancipation* (Paris, 1991), 101–4. As we will see, the presence of Jews in Bordeaux was officially admitted in 1723. In the seventeenth century, authorities referred to them as New Christians or Portuguese merchants. They lived within the frame of Catholicism, but they abandoned this façade and emerged as an organized Jewish community at the turn of the century. In this essay we will eventually refer to Portuguese New Christian merchants of Bordeaux as "Jews," even before 1723, like the historians of Bordeaux used to do.
5. Salomon Francia De Beaufleury, *L'établissement des juifs à Bordeaux et à Bayonne* (Paris, an VIII [1799]; reprint Bayonne, 1985, with intro. by J. Cavignac); Armand Detcheverry, *Histoire des Israélites de Bordeaux* (Bordeaux, 1850); Théophile Malvezin, *Histoire des Juifs de Bordeaux* (Bordeaux, 1875); Georges Cirot, *Les Juifs de Bordeaux, leur situation morale et sociale de 1550 à la Révolution* (Bordeaux, 1920).
6. Frances Malino, *The Sephardic Jews of Bordeaux: Assimilation and Emancipation in Revolutionary and Napoleonic France* (University, Ala., 1978); Cavignac, *Les Israélites bordelais*. See also Jean Cavignac, *Dictionnaire du Judaisme bordelais aux XVIIIe et XIXe siècles: biographies, généalogies, professions, institutions* (Bordeaux, 1987). For a detailed bibliography on Bordeaux's Jews, see Gérard Nahon, "Théophile Malvezin et l'histoire des Juifs à Bordeaux; biographie et mise à jour bibliographique," *Bulletin de l'Institut aquitain d'études sociales (I.A.E.S.)* 30 (1977):7–26, and the introduction of the 1985 reprint of Francia De Beaufleury, *L'établissement des juifs.*
7. Richard Menkis, "The Gradis Family of Eighteenth-Century Bordeaux: A Social and Economic Study" (Ph.D. diss., Brandeis University, 1988). The author analyzes the various activities of this Jewish merchant family in eighteenth-century Bordeaux in order to assess the importance of the Jewish network for the success of this firm. See also Jose do Nascimento Raposo, "Don Gabriel de Silva, a Portuguese-Jewish Banker in Eighteenth-Century Bordeaux" (Ph. D. diss., York University, Toronto, 1989). Gabriel da (or de) Silva (1683?–1763) was a private banker and was not directly involved with colonial trade.
8. On religious minorities in the French colonies, see Abraham Cahen, "Les Juifs de la Martinique au 17e siècle," *Revue des Etudes Juives* 2 (1881):93–122, and idem, "Les Juifs dans les colonies françaises au 18e siècle," *Revue des Etudes Juives* 4 (1882): 127–45, 236–48; 5 (1882):68–92, 258–72; I. S. Emmanuel, "Les Juifs de la Martinique et leurs coreligionnaires d'Amsterdam," *Revue des Etudes Juives* 123 (1964):511–16; Zvi Loker, "Une famille juive au Cap: membres de la famille Depas (ou De Paz) à Saint-Domingue," *Conjonction. Revue franco-haïtienne* 133 (March–April 1977):126–31,

and Zvi Loker, "Colonies juives aux Antilles," *Les nouveaux Cahiers* 86 (1986):57–61; G. Lafleur, "Minorités religieuses aux Antilles françaises du Vent sous l'ancien régime" (Ph.D. diss., Université de Paris IV, 1984).

9. This argument is in fact common throughout most of Europe: see Todd Endelman, "L'activité économique des Juifs anglais," *Dix-huitième siècle* 13 (1981), special issue *Juifs et Judaisme*:113–26; Menkis, "The Gradis Family," 58–87.

10. The intendant was a revocable representative of the king sent to the provinces to supervise the local administration.

11. Jean Cavignac, "L'immigration des Juifs portugais à Bordeaux au XVIIIe siècle," *Actes du 38e Congrès de la Fédération Historique du Sud-Ouest* (Pau, 1985), 125–38, esp. 127–28.

12. The other Jews in Bordeaux were from Avignon (7.5 percent) and from Alsace (14.5 percent). The Jews from Avignon did not enjoy the privileges of the Portuguese Jews until the second half of the eighteenth century.

13. Beside Bordeaux, there was an important Jewish settlement in Saint-Esprit, in the outskirts of Bayonne. The Saint-Esprit community was in fact demographically more important than that of Bordeaux. On Bayonne Jews, see Gérard Nahon, "Les communautés judéo-portugaises du Sud-Ouest de la France (Bayonne et sa région), 1684–1791" (Ph.D. diss., Université de Paris, 1969); see also Nahon's contribution to this volume.

14. This title was hereditary and was granted to propertied citizens already resident in Bordeaux for a number of years. Only a small minority of Bordeaux's inhabitants enjoyed this status. In order to become a *bourgeois*, one had to be Catholic. Many New Christians acquired this title before 1679, after which date hardly any Sephardim became a *bourgeois de Bordeaux*. Between 1722 and 1752, out of a total of 350 new *bourgeois*, there were only three Jews, all of them merchants. Many prominent Jewish merchants were, however, already *bourgeois*, having inherited this title from their New Christian fathers. See Cirot, *Les Juifs de Bordeaux*, 16–37.

15. Malino, *The Sephardic Jews*.

16. Endelman, "L'activité économique," has analyzed the ideological framework of these early analyses as far as England is concerned.

17. Reported by Malvezin, *Histoire des Juifs*, 179.

18. Unpaged preface by Jean Cavignac to Francia De Beaufleury, *L'établissement des juifs*.

19. Cited in Paul Butel, "Contribution à l'étude des négociants juifs portugais de Bordeaux et de Bayonne: le cas de la maison Azavedo," in *Actes du 35e Congrès de la Fédération historique du Sud-Ouest* (Bayonne, 1981), 219–41.

20. Zosa Szajkowski, "Jewish Emigration from Bordeaux in the 18th and 19th Centuries," *Jewish Social Studies* 18 (1956):118–24.

21. Whereas Cahen, "Les Juifs dans les colonies," states that there were some Jews in Martinique in 1635, Lafleur, "Minorités religieuses," has found no positive evidence. By 1654, however, there was a significant Jewish settlement in Martinique, which in his view should be attributed to immigration from Brazil.

22. Jean Petitjean-Roget, "Les Juifs à la Maritinique sous l'ancien régime," *Revue d'histoire des colonies* 43:2, no. 151 (1956):138–58, sees this as a legend, but other scholars still credit this event. See, for instance, Loker, "Colonies juives," 58. If the evidence is scarce, it is, however, likely that the Jewish diaspora from Brazil greatly facilitated a technological transfer from the more developed Dutch colonies to the French islands. Portuguese Jews had also introduced techniques of chocolate production in Bayonne: Henry Léon, *Histoire des Juifs de Bayonne* (Paris, 1893; rep., 1976), 69. On the role of the Dutch Jewry in Brazil in the seventeenth-century Atlantic trade, see Jonathan I. Israel, *European Jewry in the Age of Mercantilism, 1550–1750* (2nd ed., Oxford, 1989), 106–7.

23. Lafleur, "Minorités religieuses," 328–29.

24. Cahen, "Les Juifs de la Martinique"; Loker, "Colonies juives"; Lafleur, "Minorités religieuses," 322–36. According to Lafleur, Guadeloupe seems to have had fewer Jewish settlers.

25. See Bernhard Blumenkranz, ed., *Histoire des Juifs de France* (Toulouse, 1982), chap. 4; Menkis, "The Gradis Family," 34–37. Compared to Huguenots, Jews seem to have played a minor role in the French trade to New France: see John Bosher, *The Canada Merchants, 1713–1763* (Oxford, 1987).

26. England had granted equal rights in Barbados and Jamaica in 1740; Elie Barnavi, *Histoire universelle des Juifs: de la genèse à la fin du XXe siècle* (Paris, 1992).

27. On these aspects, see Lafleur, "Minorités religieuses," 435–39.

28. They also tried to influence a change in Paris by stressing the losses the colonies had incurred on account of the departure of the Jews, and by underlining the positive role that the Jews played in non-French colonies. For some excerpts of this correspondence, see Petitjean-Roget, "Les Juifs à la Maritinique." See also Cahen, "Les Juifs de la Martinique" and Cahen, "Les Juifs dans les colonies."

29. On the situation of the Jews in Saint-Domingue, see Pierre Pluchon, *Nègres et Juifs au XVIIIe siècle* (Paris, 1984), 91–115. See also Yvan Debbash, "Privilège réél ou privilège personnel? Le statut des Juifs portugais aux Iles," in *Religion, société et politique. Melanges en hommage à Jacques Ellul* (Paris, 1983), 213–29.

30. Malvezin, *Histoire des Juifs*, 225–28.

31. See Cavignac, *Les Israélites bordelais*, sources: I.

32. Prominent Bordeaux merchants in the seventeenth century were mainly the Dutch and the Germans. See Bertrand Gautier, "Les marchands étrangers à Bordeaux et à Rouen dans la première moitié du XVIIe siècle," *Bulletin du Centre d'histoire des Espaces Atlantiques* 7 (1995):9–32; Voss, "Bordeaux et les villes hanséatiques."

33. Malino, *The Sephardic Jews*, 8.

34. Loker, "Colonies juives."

35. Cavignac, "L'immigration des Juifs," 137.

36. Cavignac, "L'immigration des Juifs."

37. Jean Cavignac has found more than thirty different Bordeaux Jews subscribing to a notary act in Cap in the years preceding the French Revolution: Jean Cavignac, "Un exemplaire 'marchand portugais,' Salomon Lopès-Dubec (1743–1835)," *Archives juives* 18:4 (1982):67–72. A short biographical sketch of those Bordeaux Jewish merchants (*négociants*) listed in the 1808 census shows that many of them still had a relative in the French colonies (Cavignac, *Les Israélites bordelais*, 119–32).

38. Cavignac, "L'immigration des Juifs."

39. Jean Cavignac, *Les vingt-cinq familles. Les négociants bordelais sous Louis-Philippe* (Bordeaux, 1985), 151–69.

40. The autobiography of Salomon Lopès-Dubec, containing many details on his trade activities, has been published by Zosa Szajkowski, "Notes autobiographiques d'un armateur bordelais, Salomon Lopès-Dubec," *Revue historique de Bordeaux* n.s. 19 (1970): 93–110, and by Jean Cavignac, "L'autobiographie de Salomon Lopès-Dubec (1743–1835)," *Archives juives* 19:1–2 (1983):11–28.

41. Cavignac, "L'immigration des Juifs," 131, and Cavignac, *Les Israélites bordelais*, 339. Like the Rabas, he left in his will some of his money to the Jewish as well as to the Catholic poor people of Bordeaux.

42. Pluchon, *Nègres et Juifs*.

43. Eric Saugera, *Bordeaux, port négrier, XVIIe–XIXe siècles* (Paris and Biarritz, 1995), 229–34.

44. Menkis, "The Gradis Family," 157, 166–67.

45. Ibid., 104–5.

46. Abraham Gradis died in Martinique in 1738. On Gradis, see Jean de Maupassant, *Un grand armateur de Bordeaux, Abraham Gradis, 1699?–1780* (Bordeaux, 1931); Jean Schwob d'Hericourt, *La maison Gradis et ses chefs* (Argenteuil, 1975); and Menkis, "The Gradis Family."

47. David Gradis died in 1751, at the age of 86. For a number of years prior to his death, his son Abraham had directed the family firm. Abraham had gained his commercial education in Holland and in London.

48. See Menkis, "The Gradis Family," 178–245.

49. On the modifications in the trading patterns to New France in the last twenty years of French rule, see J. S. Pritchard, "The Pattern of French Colonial Shipping to Canada before 1760," *Revue française d'histoire d'Outre-mer* 64, no. 231 (1976):189–210.
50. Menkis, "The Gradis Family," 143–45.
51. Menkis, "The Gradis Family."
52. Petitjean-Roget, "Les Juifs à la Maritinique."
53. A list of his participation in the expeditions of other Bordeaux merchants appears in Jean Cavignac, "L'autobiographie de Salomon Lopès-Dubec."
54. Lafleur, "Minorités religieuses."
55. G. Nahon has underlined the strong dependence of the Bordeaux Jewish community upon the Sephardim community of Amsterdam: Gérard Nahon, *Métropoles et périphéries sefarades d'Occident. Kairouan, Amsterdam, Bayonne, Bordeaux, Jérusalem* (Paris, 1993), 95–183.
56. On Azavedo, see Butel, "Contribution à l'étude des négociants juifs."
57. On this particular matter, see Paul Butel, "Contribution à l'étude de la circulation de l'argent en Aquitaine au XVIIIe siècle," *Revue d'histoire économique et sociale* 52 (1974):83–109.
58. Zosa Szajkowski, *Franco-Juidaica, an Analytical Bibliography of Books, Pamphlets, Decrees, Briefs and Other Printed Documents, Pertaining to the Jews in France, 1500–1788* (New York, 1962), 99.
59. Butel, "Contribution à l'étude des négociants juifs."
60. Cavignac, "L'immigration des Juifs."
61. Endelman, "L'activité économique."
62. A. N. Newman, "The Sephardim of the Caribbean," in *The Western Sephardim: The History of Some of the Communities Formed in Europe, the Mediterranean and the New World After the Expulsions of 1492*, ed. R. D. Barnett and W.M. Schwab (Grendon, 1989), 445–73.
63. Menkis, "The Gradis Family," 168.

– Chapter 15 –

Jewish Settlements in the French Colonies in the Caribbean (Martinique, Guadeloupe, Haiti, Cayenne) and the "Black Code"

Mordechai Arbell

THE DUTCH AND THE ENGLISH competed in attracting Spanish-Portuguese Jewish settlers to their colonies at the end of the seventeenth century, especially those Jews who were forced to leave Dutch Brazil in 1654 and had experience with tropical agriculture. Such people were considered an excellent colonizing element for the Wild Coast of the Guianas—British Suriname and Dutch Berbice, Demerara, Essequibo, Pomeroon, and Cayenne. The colonial authorities offered the Jewish settlers what they needed most: rights and privileges that they could not obtain in other parts of the world. The settlers' knowledge of Spanish and Portuguese also made the Jews attractive in the Caribbean area, for they could facilitate illicit trade with the Spanish and Portuguese colonies in South America.

In French America the case was different. The French, being Catholic, saw the Iberian New Christians' reversion to Judaism as a sin. The Catholic orders, especially the Jesuits, were opposed to any Jewish settlement, and they were particularly in opposition to the semi-private landowners who for a time ruled the colonies in the name of France. These landowners felt that a Jewish presence would be helpful in the development of the French colonies and also hoped that it would boost their personal wealth.

Such conflicting positions made Jewish life in French America quite insecure; Jewish well-being depended upon the arbitrary stances of the different administrators of those territories. Each side tried to exert influence in Paris and in the royal court. The chief ministers tended to side with the colonial governors, whereas the Catholic orders acted through their colleagues in the royal court in their quest to bring about the expulsion of the Jews from the French colonies.

Strong Jesuit pressure resulted in the signing of the *Code Noir* ("Black Code") in 1683 by Louis XIV (put into effect in 1685), which led to the exile of most of the Jews from the French possessions in the Caribbean and the Guianas.

The Jews of Martinique and Guadeloupe

The Jewish history of Martinique and Guadeloupe is relatively short, spanning only about sixty years. It opened with the arrival of the first Jews from Amsterdam—who came in the 1620s to manage Dutch interests in the commercial outposts established on the islands—and closed with the expulsion of the Jews in 1685. Although short lived, the Jewish presence had significant impact on life in Martinique and Guadeloupe. It brought important changes in their economic structures while at the same time creating strains in the relations between the islands' lay rulers and the Catholic establishment.

In 1635, Armand Jean du Plessis Cardinal Richelieu founded the Compagnie des Isles d'Amerique (The Company of the Islands of America) with the intention of developing the production of and commerce in tropical plants. He saw in the West Indies a source of income for the French crown and state. The establishment of the Company encountered fierce opposition from the settlers and planters already there, however. Company regulations dictated the collection of commissions and taxes at the rate of 20 percent of sales and the levying of an import tax on goods entering France, with general preference being given to trade with France exclusively.

The Company's establishment coincided with the 1635 occupation of Martinique on behalf of France by Pierre Belain d'Esmanbuc. D'Esmanbuc had invaded and occupied St. Christopher (St. Kitts) ten years earlier in 1625 and had agreed to divide possession of the island in half with the British. At St. Kitts, he initiated the development of tobacco growing and indigo production. The subsequent capture of Guadeloupe by Jean du Plessis, Sieur d'Ossenville, in 1635 raised hopes in France that large-scale development and steady income from its American island possessions were possible.

Those hopes did not materialize. The principal product, tobacco, was usually sold in non-French markets, thus depriving France of taxes. When tobacco prices in the world markets dropped lower and lower, the Company of the Islands of America in 1649 was forced to sell its rights to private owners—seigneurs—who would rule the islands in a French version of Dutch patroonships and English royal patents. In 1649, the islands of Guadeloupe and Marie Galante were purchased by the Houel family, and Martinique, St. Lucia, Grenada, and the Grenadines by Monsieur Dyel du Parquet, a nephew of d'Esmanbuc.

When the French first occupied Martinique in 1635, they found there a number of Jews who had arrived earlier from Amsterdam to serve as agents and managers for Dutch enterprises in the islands. The Dominican monk Jean Baptiste du Tertre, who arrived in Martinique in 1640 and remained there for sixteen years, described a fire in which sixty Dutch warehouses were consumed,[1] a fact affirming that the Dutch presence on the island had been considerable.

The French did not at this time disturb the resident Dutch Jews, whose numbers were not significant. Moreover, the Jews were dispersed among warehouses, plantations, and stores all over the island and, so far as is known, did not form a community. The Jews were able to work and prosper under twenty years of French rule, tolerated and protected by the French governors who needed their commercial and financial acumen and whose services they made use of. Gradually, however, the success of the Jews aroused the jealousy of the French settlers and merchants. At the same time, the growing number of Catholic monks and priests arriving in the colony could not bear to see Jews residing in French-ruled territory.

The situation of the Jews in Martinique changed dramatically with the Portuguese reoccupation of Dutch Brazil in 1654. Ships loaded with Jews, Dutch refugees from Brazil, and other Protestants roamed the Caribbean Sea seeking possibilities for settlement. The monk du Tertre described the arrival of refugees from Brazil as follows:

> A ship of 1400 tons sailed toward our islands and reached Martinique at the beginning of 1654. Its leaders disembarked and came to present their homage to M. du Parquet, and to ask him to agree to their settling in his island, on the same terms and conditions as the French settlers. M. du Parquet was well disposed and made some promises, but the reverend Jesuit fathers declared to him that this was against the intention of the King, and that the introduction of these people into the island, the majority of whom were Jews and the others heretics, would introduce heresy and Judaism, and they managed to convince him. He decided with regret to reject them, in the politest way possible.[2]

When the governor of Guadeloupe, M. Houel, learned of the refugees being refused entry into Martinique, he hoped they would come to Guadeloupe—as they did. Tertre details for us the refugees' arrival:

> A big ship full of inhabitants of the island of Tamarica (Brazil), and their slaves, anchored at the island, and four leaders from the vessel came to ask his permission to reside in his island with their families, [and] their slaves, on the same conditions as the other inhabitants. M. Houel received them well, and accepted their request with great joy.

Other ships came the next night. One Dutch frigate, the same day, two other big ships arrived with inhabitants of Paraiba (Brazil), and the next Wednesday, a big ship with the garrison of Tamarica and Paraiba.[3]

In his description, du Tertre informs us that the refugees from Brazil— whose number he set at about 900, including slaves—came with a great deal of property. The expectation in Guadeloupe was that once they had landed, these refugees from Brazil would spend great sums of gold and silver locally in order to establish themselves.

The governor of Martinique, du Parquet, observing that he was losing a rare opportunity to make profits and that all the settlers from Brazil were landing in Guadeloupe, expressed his anger to the Jesuit fathers. This prompted the Jesuit *Supérieur* to travel to Guadeloupe to convince Houel to expel the new arrivals, but without success. Du Tertre says that Houel told the *Supérieur* to mind his own business. Thus, the Jews and the Dutch settled in Guadeloupe. Shortly thereafter, another ship of refugees arrived in Martinique with three hundred Dutchmen and Jews. This time M. du Parquet received them with open arms.[4] From various sources and documents, it is quite clear that according to the terms of surrender between the Dutch and the Portuguese in Brazil, the Dutch and the Jews could leave Brazil with their movable property, their money, and their slaves. This meant that the Jews arriving in Martinique and Guadeloupe did in fact have property with them.

As for the slaves, du Tertre[5] comments that the Dutch and the Jews brought with them two kinds of "Brazilian savages"—one group consisted of Christians, and they were slaves; the other group consisted of pagans, and they were freemen. The term "savages" was generally used in those times to refer to Indians. As far as we can unravel the history of the Jewish settlements in the Caribbean and the Guianas, it seems that in many places the authorities—British, Dutch, or French—would generally not permit Jews to have servants or slaves who were Christians. In some instances, the Jews were accused of opposing the baptism of those in their service. Therefore, it can be deduced that the pagans were Indian servants of the Jews, not Africans, and were treated as freemen, but were undoubtedly in bondage. They were free to work on the Sabbath, Saturdays, for their own income and received plots of land from their masters on which they cultivated potatoes and manioc. They then sold their produce on the free market, thus generating personal income.[6]

The permission given to Jews to settle in Martinique and Guadeloupe also attracted some French Jews of Spanish-Portuguese origin who were living in Bayonne and Bordeaux. These people were often relatives of those who had come from Brazil, a development that increased the number of Jews in the French islands. It is difficult to evaluate the exact number of Jews on Martinique and Guadeloupe in 1658. A conservative estimate might be about three hundred out of a population of about five thousand whites.

The Jesuit fathers, who saw the settlement of Jews as a battle they had lost, did not rest, making incessant efforts to rid the islands of Jews. On 2 April 1658, the Sovereign Council of Martinique issued a decree "prohibiting the Jews from dealing with commerce on the islands," but due to the intervention of the governor—Seigneur du Parquet—a new decree several months later "reestablished the privileges given to the Jews to engage in commerce," canceling the previous decree.[7] The Jesuit fathers based their fight for expulsion of the Jews on Article 4 of the charter of the Company of the Islands of America, approved by the French king, which stated "No one who is not a citizen and does not follow the Roman, Apostolic Catholic religion will be permitted to settle in the islands, colonies or settlements." Furthermore, Article 6 of the Company's contract with d'Olive and du Plessis, who captured Guadeloupe, stated, "only French and Catholics can settle."[8]

The Portuguese, Dutch, and Brazilian Jews, immediately after settling, began to establish commercial houses, sugar cane fields, and sugar mills on a large scale. This brought a period of prosperity to the impoverished islands and profits to their owners, Houel and du Parquet. Antoine Biet, a Catholic priest stationed in Cayenne, in French Guyana, described his dismay upon his visit to Martinique in 1662:

> Since the Jews owned the main stores and the best choice of merchandise, but were not allowed to observe their Sabbath which fell on the market day, they managed to transfer the market day to Friday. This was agreed to by the governor.... So the Jews who are not tolerated in France, have been able on a French island to practice Judaism, and from Friday sunset until Saturday at the same hour they rest and do not sell any merchandise to anyone. On the other hand, they easily profane holy Sunday and church holidays, selling to many people what they need, and Catholics assemble in their stores.... The Jews, the biggest and most cruel enemies of Jesus Christ, whom they crucified, publicly exercise their religion and keep their Sabbath. The Jews have storehouses in Fort St. Pierre, and in the city where vessels anchor. They are the main merchants and have the good graces of M. du Parquet (the governor-owner) and his wife. Therefore, all the inhabitants who have prepared sugar, tobacco, ginger, and indigo and others do not use Saturday for public weighing.[9]

The main Jewish contribution to Martinique and Guadeloupe was what we today call agro-industry. The French islands were relatively late in developing sugar production. It was only after the settlement of the Jews from Brazil, who were experienced sugar refiners and merchants, that the sugar industry picked up. In 1661, there were seventy-one sugar mills in Guadeloupe, with Martinique lagging behind. Ten years later, however, in 1671, Martinique had 111 sugar mills with 6,582 workers and slaves laboring in them. By 1685, the number had reached 172 mills. This success led many planters to switch from tobacco culture to sugar cane.[10] One of the most prominent sugar producers was Benjamin d'Acosta de Andrade, a Jew born as a *converso* in Portugal, who had settled in Dutch

Brazil and came to Martinique in 1654. He was the owner of two of the largest sugar mills in Martinique (the site is still shown to tourists visiting the island). D'Acosta de Andrade is also known and remembered for establishing the first cacao processing plant in French territory.

Cacao processing for chocolate began in the Spanish colonies in America, but processing in Martinique advanced quickly. At first, chocolate was not well received by the French public, and the custom duties on it were high. Its popularity grew over the years, however, and by 1684 more and more cacao processing plants were built in Martinique. Sugar and chocolate being highly complementary foods, chocolate became Martinique's most important export. D'Acosta de Andrade, however, could not benefit from its development. In 1664, in response to the growing profits of the Caribbean colonies, Jean Baptiste Colbert (1619–1683), the chief minister of Louis XIV, formed the Compagnie des Indes Occidentales (The Company of the West Indies), which was intended to centralize authority over the colonies, transferring their administration from the seigneur-owners to the direct control of the French crown. According to the new company's rules, all commerce had to go through French hands and had to be conducted only with France. Thus d'Acosta de Andrade had to abandon his enterprises,[11] which passed into the hands of his French partners.

These restrictions hampered the flourishing trade between Martinique and Amsterdam, carried out mainly by Jews on both sides of the ocean. The new rules stemmed mainly from the fact that the Company of the West Indies regarded the Jews as competitors. The Jews' close contacts with Amsterdam and the Dutch island of Curaçao had led to the diversion of a large part of Martinique's produce to non-French ports, causing a loss to the French treasury. At the same time, Jewish prosperity was the object of envy by a large section of the French planters in Martinique and Guadeloupe. The Brazilian Jews had not only the expertise but also the financing for their sugar mills, which required a considerable initial investment. The majority of the French planters continued planting tobacco and gradually became more and more impoverished. Their need for cash indebted them to Jewish moneylenders. The Jews were also accused of investing their profits outside of Martinique, therefore depriving the islands of cash liquidity. Thus, a coalition formed by the Jesuit fathers and French planters and merchants went into action to put constraints on Jewish life and to bring about the expulsion of the Jews.

The coalition managed to force Governor Prouville de Tracy to issue, in 1664, an act in which a paragraph is included saying that "those of the Jewish Nation must purchase and sell on the day of Sabbath, unless otherwise ordered by his Majesty."[12] The unhappy de Tracy sought help by asking for clearer instructions from France. He received ambiguous ones, namely "The King does not want to alter what has been practiced till now towards the Huguenots and the Jews."[13] De Tracy's only recourse was to close his eyes to transgressions against his own act. The Jews continued keeping the Sabbath.

The appointment, in 1667, of De Baas as governor led to a positive attitude toward the Jews. In a short time, De Baas, a person of culture, tolerance, and liberal ideas, became convinced that the Jewish presence was necessary for the welfare of the islands, especially their plantations and industries. His naming as governor encouraged the Jews to make a direct appeal to Louis XIV—conducted by three relatives of Martinique Jews in Amsterdam[14]—for the right to engage in commerce equal to those of the other inhabitants of the islands.[15] Undoubtedly the petitioners[16] had coordinated the petition with Governor de Baas, who gave it a positive recommendation. This resulted in the letter of 23 May 1671 to de Baas signed by Louis XIV and co-signed by the chief minister, Colbert, as follows:

> M. de Baas has informed us that the Jews established in Martinique and other islands have invested considerably in the tilling of the land and in fortifying their establishments, for the public utility. By this letter I inform you that my intention is that you take care, that they have the same privileges as the other inhabitants of the said islands, and you allow them complete liberty of conscience, but taking the necessary precautions, so that the exercise of their religion will not scandalize the Catholics.[17]

From this letter the Jews deduced that they could continue to practice their religion, on the condition that they not do so openly. This encouraged them to ask the Amsterdam Portuguese Jewish community for a Bible scroll (Torah), which was received in 1676 by Benjamin d'Acosta de Andrade.

The Jews of Martinique read the king's letter well. Further proof of its meaning appears in the diary for 1671 of the French king's emissary to the French colony of Cayenne, Le Febvre de la Barre, in which he writes:

> The sole religion permitted to be practiced in the islands is the Catholic one. Although there are some inhabitants of the region claiming to be Reformist and also some declared Jews in Martinique, they are not permitted to make any public manifestation of their religion.[18]

It has been theorized that a synagogue was built in Martinique, and several possible sites have been suggested. However, services were supposedly conducted in a private house, transformed for the occasion into a prayer house, which gradually became an improvised synagogue.

The happy and quiet Jewish existence of the Martinique Jews continued until the death of Governor de Baas in 1677. His replacement, Charles de Courbon, Count de Blenac, a devotee of the Jesuits, had served as confessor of Louis XIV. His main aim was the expulsion of the Jews from Martinique, and he constantly appealed to the court to take measures against the Jews. His efforts had varying results. His own intendant on the island, Sieur Begon, and some of his functionaries opposed him. Contradictory reports about the Jews reached Versailles, and Colbert himself did not want to change the status quo.

A petition instigated by de Blenac was presented to Colbert by the Jesuit fathers of the island in 1681. In the petition, the Jews were accused of having Christian slaves, of blaspheming the name of Jesus, of killing the babies born to their Christian slaves so they could not be baptized, of openly observing the Sabbath, Passover, and other Jewish holidays, of circumcising their newborn males, of preparing their meat according to Jewish laws, and so on. The petition recommended that Jews be tolerated only for commercial purposes, that they be distinguished from others by a special outward sign, that no Jew be permitted to arrive in Martinique with the intention of settling, that no permission be given to Jews to own slaves, and that no Jews who had once been baptized and since returned to Judaism be permitted to stay on the island.[19] In light of the mounting campaign against them, the Jews of Martinique began gradually to abandon the island. Guadeloupe, its history replete with upheavals, also saw its Jewish population sharply diminishing.

When Count de Blenac was on leave in France in 1683, he found Colbert in bad health, and using his personal contacts in the French court he managed to obtain the king's signature on an order for the Jews' expulsion from the islands, with a letter confirming the receipt of the Jesuits' petition. To be certain that the order would be executed without delay, the king included this decree in the first article of the "Black Code" (*Code Noir*) in 1685, which reads:

> We wish and intend that the edict of the late king, of glorious memory ... of April 23, 1615, be implemented in our Islands, which enjoins our officers to expel from the Islands all of the Jews who have established residence there, who as declared enemies of Christianity, we order them to depart within three months from the day of publication of the present decree, on pain of confiscation of their person and goods.[20]

There are differing estimates of how many Jews were in Martinique at the time of the *Code Noir* and the expulsion. They probably numbered less than one hundred, including the families Pereira, Franco Athias, Molina, Letov, Barjuda, Pinheiro, d'Andrade, Louis, da Gama, Bueno, Cohen, Lopez, Gabay, Israel, d'Acosta de Andrade, Vaz, and Nunez.[21] Most of the Jews left Martinique for Curaçao. The historian of Curaçao and its chief *Haham* (rabbi), Isaac Emmanuel, has identified the families Vaz, Andrade, de Molina, da Gama, Franco Athias, Pinheiro, Pereira, da Acosta, de Andrade as residing in Curaçao.[22] The Torah scroll, together with the ornaments of the improvised synagogue, were carried from the island by those expelled.[23]

There remain today some sites related to the Jewish presence in seventeenth-century Martinique—ruins of sugar mills, mansions, and so on, particularly in the so-called Old Brazilian quarter. A Guadeloupe legend still tells of a Jewish fisherman named Pietrz who, after arriving from Brazil, started a fishing business on a point on the coast. Under the British occupation in 1759, a city was founded named Point-au-Pitre, on the same spot, the point of Pietrz, where the fisherman had settled.[24]

The "Black Code" was subject to various interpretations. Some maintained that it concerned not all the Jews—only those who were not French citizens,. In other instances it was inferred that Jews could travel to the islands but not reside in them. Based on the *Lettres patentes* signed by the French kings, the question arose whether the Portuguese Jews already residing in France could be denied residence in the French colonies. Most of these questions remained subject to the different interpretations and decisions of local magistrates. We can cite two cases concerning Martinique.

The Dominican father Jean Baptiste Labat describes the arrival in Martinique in 1699 of a member of the Benjamin d'Acosta de Andrade family who had come from Curaçao to arrange for the collection of debts owed to a relative who had died. The family's industries there had been taken over by d'Acosta de Andrade's Christian partners. The visit yielded no results; payment was refused.[25] But from this visit itself, as well as from others we are aware of, we may conclude that visits were possible.

As for residence, it depended on one's connections to the authorities. David Gradis, a Portuguese Jew living in Bordeaux, founded one of the big companies trading with the French colonies, and had obtained permission to have his two nephews, Mendes and Miranda, reside in Martinique as trading partners. The company was an important one, with about six of the company's ships arriving in Martinique every year. In one of those ships came the son of David Gradis, Samuel, who died in Martinique in January 1732. He was buried in a monastery, Frères de la Charité, with all the appropriate Jewish prayers, but without a tombstone marking his grave. From this event we can deduce that in 1732 there were at least ten Jews residing in Martinique, enough to form a minyan (the prayer quorum of ten Jewish males) for a Jewish burial.[26] By the time of the French Revolution, however, there was, for all practical purposes, no significant Jewish presence in Martinique or Guadeloupe.

Cayenne (Today French Guiana)

Of the various European nations with colonial ambitions, the French made the greatest effort to settle the island of Cayenne. In 1631, an early group of French settlers made the mistake of getting involved in the internal quarrels of the local Indians, which led to the dissolution of the settlement. In 1643, a French company was established in Rouen under the name Cape North Company, and Charles Ponces, Sieur de Bretigny, sailed to Cayenne with about three hundred persons. As was the case in the first attempt, the French colonists quarreled with the Indians and among themselves (Bretigny being very dictatorial, cruel, and contentious). In 1645, Bretigny was killed by the Indians, and the colony dispersed. Still another French effort met with a similar fate, and the French were driven out of Cayenne.[27]

The Dutch commander Guerin Spranger, finding Cayenne abandoned by the French, received a grant from the Dutch States General and formed a Dutch colony in Cayenne in 1656. This colony passed over to the control of the Dutch West India Company, whose aim was to attract suitable colonists to settle in Cayenne. One of their more specific objectives was to draw Jewish settlers experienced in dealing with tropical products. One of the refugees from Dutch Brazil, David Nassy, negotiated with the Amsterdam Chamber of the West India Company a grant of liberties and exemptions, dated 12 September 1659, for a Jewish colony on the island of Cayenne.[28] The grant states (in Paragraph I) that David Nassy and his partners are to be patroon and patroons of a "Colony in the island of Cayenne ... provided they do not extend so far from the Colony of Cayenne as to interfere with other settlers." We understand from this section of the text that the company's intention was to have an exclusively Jewish settlement that was to be distant from the lands tilled by non-Jewish settlers around the city of Cayenne. The grant given to David Nassy provided for freedom of conscience, the building of a synagogue, and the opening of a school—on condition that these same rights also be given to non-Jews wishing to reside in the colony.

Notwithstanding this, when the group of Jewish colonists, composed mainly of Jewish refugees from Brazil and a number of Jews from Amsterdam, arrived in September 1660, the Dutch governor, Jan Classen Langendijk, prevented them from disembarking. The only alternative he offered the Jews was the privilege of establishing a colony not on the island of Cayenne but on the mainland. The governor, however, came under political pressure: his own people, about thirty-five in number, believing the Jews would bring prosperity to the island, declared that they would not remain beyond their term of service if the governor refused land to the Portuguese Jews. The peaceful Indians, too, welcomed the Jews.[29] Apparently, the governor finally gave in and permitted the Jews to land and settle on the island of Cayenne in accordance with the grant of privileges they had in hand. The Jews situated themselves on the western side of the island of Cayenne in a place called Remire or Irmire. Remire was described by Jacques Bellin as "the most smiling and the most fertile region of the island from which the French, in 1634, chased away the Arikorets and other Indian nations."[30]

The Jews planted sugar cane, erected a sugar mill, produced dyes from indigo and roucou, and experimented with various undeveloped tropical products. The township was protected by a fort, and presumably there was also a synagogue, since we know that the community had an orderly life with its own rules and regulations. There exists an acknowledgment for a gift of a Torah scroll donated in 1659 by the Amsterdam community for use in Cayenne; it was signed by David Diaz Antunes and

Abraham Enriquez Flores. Normally, a Torah scroll was used and kept only in a prayer house.[31] In contrast to the French who had preceded them, the Jews remained on good terms with the local Indians.[32]

Not everybody looked upon the success of the Jewish settlement with admiration, however. The French priest and historian du Tertre, after describing Remire, explains that "since the island of Cayenne was abandoned by the French, some Dutch people and Jews expelled from Brazil by the Portuguese arrived and found there well-planned gardens and a good fort with its cannons, so that it was not difficult to settle there."[33]

The French priest Father Labat, a colleague of du Tertre and his successor in several duties, mocks the foregoing account and its assumptions. He presents a contrary view, adding that the reason for the success of the Remire Jewish settlement was the gradually improving relations with the Indians, as opposed to the actions of the French. He also describes the thriving sugar plantations and the cultivation of cotton, indigo and roucou, and states that "a successful commerce ... was carried on with those of their nation and others. They lived there in peace till the subsequent French occupation."[34]

One of the specialties of the Jews who settled on the Wild Coast was the preparation of vanilla extract. In the narrative of Labat,[35] who resided in Martinique, there is a description of the arrival on the island of one of the heirs of Benjamin d'Acosta de Andrade, who had been in Cayenne, and of the effort Labat made to induce him to reveal the method for the preparation of vanilla. The importance of vanilla and the Jewish control of its preparation can also be seen in the reports of the Dutch governor of Pomeroon (today the Republic of Guyana), where another group of Jews had settled on the Wild Coast. The historian Ternaux-Compans's description of Remire tells us that

> David Nassy ... obtained the title of Patroon-Master and in 1659 went with a large number of his compatriots to Cayenne. In the following year, these were joined by the persons of the same religion who had quit Leghorn, and these likewise devoted [themselves] to the cultivation of the earth. The prosperity which this colony enjoyed during its short existence is proof that the Jews are not so unfit, as has been believed, for agricultural enterprises.[36]

It is quite clear that the leaders of the Jewish settlers in Cayenne were David Nassy and his group, exiles from Dutch Brazil. They were joined, however, by Jews from Leghorn (Livorno), mostly of North African origin, who had lived as marranos in Spanish-held parts of Algiers (Oran, Mers el Kebir). After emigrating to Leghorn, these marranos reverted to Judaism.[37] They remained among the poorest people in overcrowded Leghorn, and hence were good prospects for the Dutch West India Company to resettle on the Wild Coast. It is difficult to estimate how many boatloads of Leghorn Jews reached Remire. Documents mention at least two: one went directly to Cayenne, and one, on board the *Monte de Cisne*, reached the island of Tobago, from where, after a disastrous period, a group finally made their way to Cayenne.

Details on the everyday life of the Jews in Remire are also very scarce. It is not easy even to estimate their number. The best documents are those describing the exodus of the Jews from Cayenne after the French occupation, at which time there were between three hundred and four hundred Jews. From different sources chronicling the history of what is now French Guiana, it is clear that the settlement of the Jews in Remire was far more successful economically and agriculturally than the larger settlement of the capital—the city of Cayenne.

In Cayenne, as in Martinique and Guadeloupe, we find differences in the colonization methods of the French and the Jews. Success in tropical agriculture required very thorough preparation of the land, adaptation to the climate, experience, and perseverance—all of which together necessitated a substantial initial investment. The Jewish exiles from Brazil had the experience, could easily adapt to similar tropical conditions, and were ready to invest. The French colonizing companies were quite reluctant to make even the initial outlays required, which was one of the causes of their failure.

In October 1663, M. Le Febvre de la Barre and Sieur Bouchardeau persuaded Colbert to form the French Equinoctial Company for the settling of the Wild Coast. De la Barre was appointed governor of the island of Cayenne, and Alexandre Prouville de Tracy was charged with the duty of driving out "by force of arms any person established there, which the French considered their territory."[38] The Dutch commander of the colonies in Cayenne—Querin Spranger (himself a refugee from Dutch Brazil)—was surprised to see on 26 February 1664, a fleet of five vessels, with twelve hundred French colonists accompanied by two warships, arriving in Cayenne during a period of peace between France and Holland. He felt compelled to give in without a fight, so as to obtain more advantageous terms in the surrender agreement.

We find in the agreement, annotated and signed by de Tracy as the representative of the king of France and by de la Barre acting for the Equinoctial Company and as its new director, the following concessions made to the Dutch:

Paragraph 4— ... be it enacted that there shall be given us the free and most public exercise of religion; and the undersigned lords shall protect us in it [referring to de la Barre; signed by de Tracy]

Paragraph 5—The Jews demand also the free exercise of their religion as in the preceding article. [referring to de la Barre; signed by de Tracy]

Paragraph 9—That the expenses incurred by the Patroon and individuals of the Hebrew colony shall be repaid. [It was de la Barre who had to decide on this article][39]

The acceptance of Paragraphs 4 and 5 are quite exceptional in the relations of French colonies with the Jews.

Du Tertre's description of the ceremony celebrating the French victory shows that colonial wars in that period still had strong religious overtones:

> De Tracy, seeing de la Barre well established in the island of Cayenne, sent Father Beaumont of the Dominican Order to erect the Cross in his name as a sign of his piety. The priests and lay[men] were joyous when they saw the sign of our Redemption, erected again in the place from where it was torn out by the Jews and the heretics."[40]

As for the rights of the Jews under the French, the situation remained ambiguous. The Dutch historian Hartsinck asserts that after the agreement was made, the French captured six Dutch vessels that had come to trade, plundered the inhabitants, "and finally shipped both Christian and Jews to Rochelle leaving them to find their way to their fatherland as best they could."[41] Hartsinck's account was widely criticized by a series of historians[42] who saw it as far-fetched to think that Christians and Jews were transported to La Rochelle in France and then sent off to trek all the way to Holland. For persons well acquainted with the geography of Suriname, it is clear that the people were transported to the outpost La Rochelle on the border of French Guiana and Suriname. (See the map prepared by the Dutch army officer in Suriname, John Gabriel Stedman, who fought there from 1772 to 1777. Stedman mentions La Rochelle of Suriname several times in his narrative.)[43] France was not mentioned in the original.

From the above, it is clear that some of the Cayenne Jews and Protestants had been taken to La Rochelle in Suriname and that the Jews found their way to Suriname's Jewish Savanna, with its recently founded settlement. In Jewish Savanna there is a region called Cajane (Cayenne in Dutch). The old cemetery of the Jewish Savanna contains graves of Jews born in Leghorn, who undoubtedly had been among those who had settled in Remire[44] and were then evacuated to Suriname. Not all Jews left Remire. It was in the interest of the French company to keep the promised liberty of conscience. The Jesuit fathers had not yet reached Cayenne, so the economic motivation to keep the Jews prevailed. It is Le Febvre de la Barre himself who gives a description of the situation in Remire after the French occupation: "There is another town, Armire, occupied by Jews, who number sixty whites and eighty-five blacks. Further up, there is a chapel and a water-powered mill, and about sixty French and twenty-five blacks."[45] This description helps us understand that a portion of the Jews of Remire had left, that the water-powered sugar mill, in which Jews specialized, was no longer in their hands, and from a minimum of three hundred to four hundred Jews, only sixty remained. The abandoned houses were occupied by French newcomers.

In 1667, following the orders of British General Henry Willoughby, whose base was Barbados, Captain Sir John Harman invaded Cayenne. The only strong resistance to the British was in Remire. The British orders were to burn the town and destroy it. The French commander de Lezy fled with two hundred of his soldiers to Suriname. Taking as much plunder as the vessels could carry, Harman proceeded to demolish the sugar works and the plantations and to set fire to the houses.

The British ships being quite full, it was impossible to carry off all of the French prisoners, many of them sick and diseased. Willoughby's orders were to take on board only the Jews. These orders caused resentment among the British officers, who were "aggrieved that any of the French should be left behind, being Christian, and the Jews numbering fifty to sixty should be carried off." In a most unusual act, they dared to ask for clearer instructions from Lt. General Willoughby and Captain Harman. An officer boarded the commander's ship, *The Swan*, and submitted a document with the officers' questions, which was returned to the officers with remarks[46] as follows:

Queries	*Remarks*
Whether all the French Prisoners, men, women, and children can with convenience be transported to the Barbados or not; if not the whole number, whether such thought fit to exchange?	To take as many as fit for exchange.
May the remaining part be provided for with homes, baking stones, iron pots, and working tools?	Willoughby agreed to this.
That the fort be, as far as possible, demolished along with all the strong buildings on the island, only some cottages preserved to provide shelter for women and children.	Agreed to.
Whether any or all of the Jews do concern his Majesty's interest, or the parties designated for transport, or hence be left behind.	It is necessary for the Jews to be transported for the several reasons fit to be given to his Majesty.

There was obviously a clear interest in having the Jews in British territory. The French prisoners were exchanged in Martinique. As for the Jews, they sailed with the fleet proceeding to Suriname and may have landed there. The fleet's next station was the home base of Barbados. Jews were needed there, too. For the British, the development of the sugar industry was a national objective, and they felt they could achieve it through the Jews.

Sometime later, the Suriname Jews petitioned to return to Cayenne. Abraham Cahen found in the archives of the French Ministry of the Marine a letter by Secretary of State M. de Phélipeaux responding to a petition dated 1725:[47] "I have reported to the King the request of the Jews of Suriname for permission to settle in Cayenne. His Majesty does not see it convenient to support it." This sealed the short episode of Cayenne in Jewish history until 1994, when in January of that year I received an official fax from Mrs. Abchee of Cayenne announcing the establishment of a Jewish community there after a hiatus of almost 330 years.

Haiti

In the second half of the seventeenth century, the French gained control of the western part of the island of Hispaniola (or Saint-Domingue, or Haiti). By the treaty of Ryswick in 1697, Spain officially ceded western Hispaniola to France. French buccaneers already had a foothold there, and French planters had begun to settle there before the signing of the treaty. Individual Jews who left Brazil in 1654 had reached Haiti and, using their expertise in sugar growing, either worked on French plantations as specialists or had small plantations of their own. Their small number, scattered in all parts of the relatively large "half island," was never sufficient for the formation of a congregation. The "Black Code" of 1685 ordering the expulsion of the Jews from the French islands caused most of that meager number of Jews to leave the island.

In spite of the "Black Code," a few Jews remained on French islands; some were "tolerated" by the local authorities either as a special favor or owing to an interest on the part of the French government. Portuguese Jews from Bordeaux and Bayonne could in some cases arrange with the local authorities for special permission to reside in the French islands, and *lettres de naturalité* were obtained. With more liberal interpretations of the "Black Code," more explicit permissions—*Lettres patentes*—were given to Jews, particularly those representing big companies that the government wished to see prosper. As noted earlier, one of the most prominent examples was the Gradis family of Bordeaux, which had commercial interests in the French colonies. Jews such as these had the influence and ability to obtain permission for relatives and friends to reside in the French colonies. In 1717, David Gradis, founder of the company David Gradis & Sons, began producing arms, which required him to have strong commercial and maritime relations with the colonies. By 1722, he had opened offices in Martinique and in different locations in Haiti—Cap-Français (Cap-Haitien of today), Saint Louis, Fonds-de-l'Isle à Vaches, and Leogan. He placed in those offices his Jewish friends and relatives.

Certainly by 1739 there was a tendency to interpret the "Black Code" in such a way as to permit some Jews to reside in the islands without voiding the force of the code. In a letter of 12 August 1739, the Messrs Champigny and de La Croix, administrators of the French Windward Islands, offered the following interpretation to the minister of state, M. Phélipaux, Comte de Maurepas:

> not as in the case of France, in the Islands and in the French colonies, according to the first article of the Black code, His Majesty orders all his officers to expel all the Jews from those islands, where they reside, as enemies of the Christian Name …
>
> This law is very strict. But it seems that it should be applied only to Jews coming here on their own and without permission. All those who obtain such permission must not be identified with those whom His Majesty declared enemies of the Christian Name.[48]

Such interpretations were common at several levels of authority, thus permitting the issuance of *Lettres patentes*. The privileges of Portuguese Jews were based on the rulings of the French kings, starting in 1550 when Henry II made an exception of "Marchands et autres Portugais, appelés Nouveaux Chrétiens" (merchants and other Portuguese, called New Christians), and these privileges were reconfirmed by the French kings who reigned after him. In the following example, the merchant house David Gradis & Sons requests *Lettres patentes* to reside in Haiti.

> The Messrs David Gradis & Sons, Portuguese Jews, ask His Majesty for "Lettres Patentes" on the basis of which they could use their residences for their business, which they will need to acquire in the colonies.…
>
> For more than forty years the House of Gradis has been in charge of supplying goods to the colonies in America and Africa, and of other important operations in the service of His Majesty. It has always, in peace or war, executed the multiple functions given to them with exactitude and energy. The House has been very useful also to the city of Bordeaux and its citizens with the income generated.
>
> In the colonies in America they have lent funds to important colonists that were paid for by acquiring several residences in St.-Domingue [Haiti] and in Martinique.
>
> According to the State laws, Portuguese Jews have in all the territory of the Kingdom, Country, Lands under His Majesty, the same rights and privileges as the other subjects, for commerce, possession of houses, and testaments. Those rights and privileges were given to Portuguese Jews by Henry II, and reconfirmed by the subsequent kings.
>
> As these reconfirmations were not registered by the tribunals of the Colonies, Messrs Gradis ask His Majesty to show his satisfaction with the large number of expeditions carried out in the service of the State, by approving the "Lettres Patentes"…
>
> The privileges that the constitution of the Colonies permit to be given to Portuguese Jews, are not yet legally determined, but it is to be thought that Messrs Gradis, naturalized from father to son, for two centuries, in the

kingdom, and their armaments and their commerce, often very useful to the service of His Majesty, make them especially worthy of the "Lettres Patentes" they ask for.[49]

The *Lettres patentes* requested were approved. In them, however, it was made clear that the "Black Code" was still in force.

> In a report made by the Minister of State, having the Department of the Marine, the Conseil des Dépêches [Cabinet], on which basis the Lettres Patentes have been awarded to Messrs Gradis, Portuguese Jews, French-born, residents of Bordeaux, and given the rights of French citizens on the Island of St.-Dominigue [Haiti] and all other French colonies, taking into account that Royal Edict of 15 April 1615 [Edict signed by Louis XIII but never enforced], and article 1 of the Edict of March 1685 [the "Black Code"], where the King's officials are expressly ordered to expel all the Jews from the colonies."[50]

Among the other benefits of this confirmation of rights was that it helped to overcome one of the disabilities of the Jews in the French colonies: in case of death, their wills were not respected by the courts of law and were declared null and void. Therefore, property in the estate was declared vacant and reverted to the authorities (*droit d'aubaine*). In such decisions, the courts based their reasoning on the *Code Noir*, Article 1. In one case in which the deceased was born Christian but was of Jewish origin, the disability was ruled still to exist, since "the mere fact of changing the Jewish religion by conversion to Christianity does not remove the Jewishness of the *converso*, not even in the second generation, nor does it curtail the disabilities."[51]

When the minister of state Phélipaux expressed his worry over Jews from Bordeaux asking daily for permission to settle in the islands, a query was sent to the administrators of Haiti about the number of Jews residing there. In a letter dated 4 July 1743 by Larnager, governor, and Maillart, intendant, it was reported:

> The businessmen Miranda and Mendes, residents of Fonds de l'Isle à Vaches for fifteen to twenty years, have large-scale commerce and are very honest; bachelors.

> In Cap Français, Jacob Suares, a businessman of very good reputation, has been resident for many years; bachelor.

> In St. Louis, M. de Paz has had several male and female children from a black woman to whom he is very loving. She was liberated from slavery years ago, but he has not married her. To the children he is very tender and has sent them to his parents in Bordeaux to be educated.[52]

To which the Minister answered on 3 September 1743,

> Since there are only three, forming two houses, not married, and they are engaged in commerce, you can tell them that there is no inconvenience in

tolerating them in the colony. As the King sees it, they can remain as long as their conduct remains as it is till now. His Majesty, however, does not wish to see this nation multiply in St.-Domingue.[53]

Because the report was not decisive about the Jewishness of M. de Paz, only three Jews were counted.

Notwithstanding the restrictions, the number of Jews increased, attracted by the now flourishing Haiti, often called *La perle des Antilles* (The Pearl of the Antilles). The growing number of Jews can be deduced from several documents in different French archives under the names de Pas,[54] Lopes,[55] Mendes France,[56] Sordis, Cordova,[57] Ravel, Nathan, Pereyra.[58]

Usually, non-Catholics were buried in plots reserved for Protestants, Jews, Muslims, and non-baptized slaves, or in private graves on the ground of their property. In November 1984, Dr. William Hodges and Miss Jennifer Hamilton discovered a Jewish cemetery in Cap-Haitien, in which three gravestones were found intact.[59] The inscriptions were solely in French, but their content makes clear that the deceased were Jewish. On the gravestone of Abraham Molina it is written, "Le bien heureux," which is a translation of the Portuguese *benaventurado* found on most Jewish gravestones in the Caribbean. On the same gravestone and on that of Sara Fasto we see the letters *S.A.G.D.E.G.*, which stands for the words *su alma goza de eterna gloria*, written on most Portuguese Jewish graves. This is the only Jewish cemetery that has been found in Haiti. The years written on the gravestones, 1789, 1790, and 1791, show that the burials took place during the period of the French Revolution and at the start of the Haitian revolution. Hodges, versed in Haitian history and founder of the historical museum De Guahaba in Limbé, explains that the preservation of the tombstones was "due to the special admiration the Haitian revolutionary slaves had for the Jews, also victims of blind discrimination."[60]

It is impossible to learn the exact number of Jews residing legally or illegally in Haiti during the eighteenth century. At best, a general idea can be reached through estimates based on different kinds of data. A thorough study has been made by the Archives of the Gironde on the Jewish families in Bordeaux, France, in the eighteenth and nineteenth centuries.[61] It shows that of the 118 Jewish families listed, forty-one of them had members who had lived in Haiti and returned to Bordeaux. The breakdown was: nineteen had lived in Cap-Haitien, sixteen in Port-au-Prince, two in Petit Goave, one in St. Louis, one in Jacmel, one in Cap Tibouron, one in Leogan, and for the others there are no precise details as to place of residence.

We must also remember that families who remained in Haiti after the Haitian revolution, or who emigrated elsewhere, were not taken into account. If we add to them the Jews from Bayonne who had settled in Haiti, and Ashkenazi Jews from Nantes and Nancy, the number is much larger. Bertram Korn mentions at least two families in New Orleans who had arrived there from Haiti (Lopes Pardo and Lopes Dias) and supposes that there were more.[62] The contacts between Jews living in Haiti, New Orleans, and Charleston were quite frequent, and refugee Jews may have settled in those mainland cities.

The other source of Jews in Haiti was Curaçao. Trade between Curaçao and Haiti was very brisk between 1789 and 1795. Curaçao Jews settled mainly in Cap-Français (Cap-Haitien) where, as we noted, the only Jewish cemetery in Haiti was found. Curaçao community archives show that circumcisions were performed there until at least 1783. The number of Jews in Cap-Haitien was such that in 1790 they engaged the services of Dr. Isaac Cardozo as a religious leader. Curaçao Jews also settled in Jacmel, Jeremie, Les Cayes, and in smaller numbers in St. Louis and Port-au-Prince. Small numbers of Jews from Jamaica and St. Thomas also settled in Haiti.

The second largest Jewish concentration after Cap-Français was in Jeremie. Situated on the southern peninsula of Haiti, it was a lively port surrounded by plantations and quite isolated from the main parts of Haiti. When the series of uprisings of mulattos and black slaves started in 1792, it became a convenient refuge for white settlers. On 19 September 1793, these settlers called for English assistance, and the area was occupied by the English for the next five years. In Jeremie, the Jewish presence was economically dynamic, and the Jews attained a stable financial position and relatively high social position. In notarial records studied by Loker for the period 1786 to 1800, at least nineteen Spanish-Portuguese Jewish families resided in Jeremie. Except for one from Curaçao, most of this group came from France—Bordeaux, Bayonne, and Avignon. They earned a living mainly from managing plantations (sugar, coffee, cacao, and indigo) and from retail trade.[63] The number of Jews may have been larger, since there were non-registered, non-practicing ones, and also racially mixed ones—mulattos of Jewish origin having Portuguese Jewish names.

In contrast to Cap-Français, where institutional Jewish life was influenced by Curaçao, in Jeremie there are no indications of organized Jewish life or cemeteries. Most of the Jeremie Jews left with the advent of the first Afro-American state. Many Jewish enterprises were ruined by the Haitian revolution, and commerce came to a standstill. The majority of the Jews left, but not all did so. We still find births and deaths of Jews registered in Haiti until 1850. The majority of members of the Masonic Lodge in Port-au-Prince in 1847 were Jewish,[64] but by the second half of the nineteenth century almost no Jews remained in Haiti.

A particular Haitian phenomenon was the sizable community of officially freed slaves (*affranchis*) who became city dwellers. Some of them were well educated and gradually became the Haitian middle class. They also became the ruling class after the liberation of Haiti. As has been mentioned, Jews occasionally intermarried with them. When I met some of those families, while serving as non-resident ambassador of Israel to Haiti, they knew of their Jewish past and had documents to prove it. An example is the Decastro family, who are descendants of Joseph Henriquez De

Castro and Rachel Felicite Mendes France, who married at the beginning of the nineteenth century. Joseph's sister Abigail Henriquez de Castro married Mardochee Mendes France.[65]

Count d'Estaing and the Jews

In 1764, Jean Baptiste Charles Henri Hector Comte d'Estaing was named governor general of the "French Windward Islands of America." He came to Haiti after serving in India and was known as an energetic reformer. Following his stint in Haiti, he captured the islands of Grenada and St. Vincent for France, served in the French Revolution, and was a rear admiral in the French forces during the American Revolution. In 1792, he was promoted to admiral, commanding the entire French navy, but ultimately he was beheaded by the guillotine for "being sympathetic to the Royal house."[66]

Until d'Estaing's arrival in America, Jewish existence was tolerated, and a semi-legal way was found to permit the residency of Jews, despite the "Black Code." D'Estaing started energetically to better the infrastructure of the colony. He offered the Jews of Saint Louis and Les Cayes his protection and intervened on their behalf, on condition that they contribute money to public projects: fountains, batteries, ships, roads, inns. Knowing that their precarious semi-legal status might worsen if they refused, the Jews stalled. D'Estaing took their silence to mean acceptance.[67]

Receiving information that the Jews were preparing to complain to David Gradis in Bordeaux, who was at that time responsible for the provisioning of the French garrisons in Cayenne, Haiti, Martinique, and Guadeloupe, d'Estaing wrote to the minister of the marine, foreign affairs, and war, the duc de Choiseul, on 8 September 1764:

> I want to report to you that I want to contribute to the public welfare and not to the synagogues of St. Louis and Les Cayes. The Jews, owners of slaves who become Jewish like them, who purchase and own land in a Christian country, must, if they want to be tolerated, bring water to the towns, supply ships to the King, and perform other useful deeds which will give them honor in future centuries. What I asked of them is not much. Mister Gradis may disapprove and shout. I will take into account these small donations when I measure the good or bad conduct of these sons of Moses.[68]

He also enumerated the projects: a water conduit to the city of St. Louis, with a fountain; a battery for four cannons; an inn with space for horses; seven thousand pounds yearly in cash for the supply of five companies of soldiers: fifty thousand pounds in two payments for the purchase of ships, and ten thousand pounds in cash for another big ship.[69] After assessing the financial worth of each Jew and deciding the sum he must pay, d'Estaing nominated the Jew Daguilard (d'Aguilar) to be the leader of the Jews in the colony and responsible for collecting the money.

In the meantime, on the basis of information about d'Estaing's excesses in Haiti, the duc de Choiseul began to lose confidence in him. The duke wrote to the king explaining that some of the governors in the American colonies were "despotic, ignorant and unreasonable," and he added that "one like that is M. d'Estaing, whom I consider to be a man of superior talent, but he is crazy and dangerously insane and his intendant dishonest."[70] Already in the final days of 1764, an act of accusation was issued in Paris against d'Estaing. One paragraph states that:

> Jews of the colony were taxed considerable sums, including the Portuguese Jews who have the privilege of establishing themselves in all the lands under French domination, and in France. The English have one principle, they attract them, this industrious people, giving them sizable privileges, and it can be said that it was the Jews who made Jamaica flourish.[71]

Either because he learned of these accusations or was satisfied that the money for his projects had been collected, d'Estaing had a change of attitude, and in a decree issued on 16 January 1765, Article 5, he says,

> In all cases it was always taken into account that the money given by the Jews will pay an interest of 5 percent.... A plan has been introduced for the return of the above sums in order to have the confidence of the Jews for future loans.

And in Article 9 he states,

> The Jews of the North demand to pay free of charge and not as a loan the sums mentioned, taking into account that the "Lettres Patentes" given to the Jews by his Majesty to the Portuguese Jews insure them in this colony, and it seems these "Lettres Patentes" attract them to this colony.[72]

These paragraphs coincide with the letter from the minister of the marine to d'Estaing on 18 January 1765:

> I have received your letter of Sept. 8, relative to the contributions which have been imposed on Jews of St.-Domingue, in order to finance some projects of public utility in the colony. The King to whom I reported, approved everything you have done on this subject. I believe my duty is to observe that you must use the contributions with the greatest moderation. The Jews, although from a different religion, are free men, very useful to the state and to the colony, for their attachment to culture and their proficiency in commerce, and if they are treated with rigor, they can take elsewhere their fortunes and their capacity.[73]

To this d'Estaing and the intendant Magon wrote on 8 January 1766 to the minister,

> There are two kinds [of Jews], the agriculturist and the tradesmen. They have contributed to the gift for d'Estaing, have given charity to the hospital, to the

people, and to the colony. These industrious people contribute to the growth and wealth of the colony. Religion does not seem to be a sufficient obstacle to deprive the colony of these people.[74]

The Intended Expulsion of the Jews from Cap-Français

On 2 April 1765, a petition was submitted to d'Estaing signed by 152 merchants, captains of ships, and other businessman of Cap-Français that accused the Jews of residing in Cap-Français and in Saint-Domingue, contrary to the "Black Code"; sending sums of money to synagogues elsewhere; damaging the national commerce by maintaining connections in foreign colonies; traveling from country to country and creating fraudulent bankruptcies, causing the state to lose the taxes that would ordinarily be obtained from them; clipping; taking over the interior commerce of the colony; and ruining the French merchants. D'Estaing referred the petition to the judge of Cap-Français, who then issued the following order on 10 April 1765:

> The petition submitted to the Governor-General by 152 merchants, captains of ships and businessman.... We are taking into account [the] above act, [and] order that article 1 of the edict of March 1685 [the *Code Noir*] will be put into force according to its letter and spirit.
>
> Therefore we order all and every one of the Jews which are in our jurisdiction or can establish residence in it, to leave in three months from the day of publication of this order; and if the Jews mentioned fail to leave in three months, we order that they will be persecuted in their bodies, and their holdings confiscated for the King's profit. We also authorize, in accordance with their demand, the merchants, captains, businessmen and others, to make after the above three months, denunciations to the King's prosecutor, of every Jew who remains in our jurisdiction; without prejudicing the privileges, if some were accorded to certain Jews, and those registered by law in this colony.[75]

The group of petitioners expected to receive the approval of the governor general on the basis of his previous attitude toward the Jews, but the petition found a different d'Estaing. Subdued by the letters he had received from the minister of the marine and by the investigation against him, d'Estaing did not enforce the order of the judge of Cap-Français. On 21 June 1765, he gave the Jews "letters of relief of appeal of the sentence of the Judge," and the case was abandoned.[76] Thus, the Jews returned to their semi-protected situation. Daguilard, exhausted by his function of being responsible for the Jews, hated by the Catholic merchants, and ruined financially, embraced the Catholic faith.

In 1779, in a note by the king to the governor and the intendant, we find "His Majesty is willing to allow those [Jews] who are established in [Saint-Domingue] not to be troubled for their creed so long as they abstain from all public exercise of their religion."[77] Until the French Revolution, nothing more changed. The Jews were "tolerated."

Jewish Life in Haiti

Being spread out all over the country, the Jews could not form a real congregation. Jewish marriages, however, were performed, and Jewish holidays observed—especially in Cap-Français. There was no real discrimination in day-to-day life. Dr. Michel Lopes de Pas, resident of Leogane, recommended by the intendant Wilton on 24 December 1714, was appointed *medecin du roy* (king's physician) and, in 1723, a member of the superior council of the colony.[78] Other Jews were named as judges in tribunals and for other public functions.

The Town of Moron Founded by a Jew

Moron is a town of twelve thousand inhabitants, forty kilometers from Jeremie. A Portuguese Jew from Curaçao settled in Jeremie and became a businessman and planter. In 1787, he purchased land in what is today Moron. Undoubtedly, he was the founder of this locality. Moreover, local legends say that the town of Moron was founded by a Jewish rabbi.[79] It may be that in a small house on his property, the Jews would meet to pray.

The Mendes France Family

The late premier of France, Pierre Mendes France, did thorough research on his family roots, and among his ancestors he found Isaac Mendes France. Isaac settled in Haiti in 1763 where his brother David was already established in Port-au-Prince. Together with his son Mardochee (see above), they settled in Petit Goave. In 1779, Isaac returned to Bordeaux.[80] We can get an idea of the property of a typical Jewish family in Haiti from a document in the American Jewish Archives that lists the possessions of the Mendes France family (several houses, stores, plantations, and coffee and cotton mills).[81]

Jews left Haiti gradually. The slave rebellion did not cause a panicky evacuation, but resulted in a gradually diminishing Jewish population. In the next century, in the 1920s, Jews from Syria, joined later by Jews from Germany and Eastern Europe, settled in Haiti. In time, they reached thirty to forty families, but a congregation was not formed. With the unstable political and economic situation in Haiti in the 1990s, only five or six Jewish families remain there. Haiti is an example of non-centralized Jewish life in the Caribbean. Jews were a minority in a rather large white population of some twenty thousand to thirty thousand. With the French authorities usually hostile to the Jews, Haiti is not typical of the Jewish life in the Caribbean, but it is part of it anyway.

Notes

1. Jean Baptiste du Tertre, *Histoire generale des Antilles habitées par les Francais* (Paris, 1667), 1123.
2. du Tertre, *Histoire*, 460–61. Translated by the author.
3. Ibid., 463–64.
4. Ibid.
5. Ibid., 492.
6. Ibid., 515.
7. Abraham Cahen, "Les Juifs de la Martinique au XVIIe siècle," *Revue des Etudes Juives* 31 (1895):95–96.
8. du Tertre, *Histoire*, 49 and 68.
9. Antoine Biet, *Voyage de la France equinoxical en l'isle de Cayenne* (Paris, 1664), 303–4. Translated by the author.
10. Pierre Pinchon, ed., *Histoire des Antilles et de la Guyanne* (Toulouse, 1982), 93–94.
11. Jean Baptiste Labat, *Nouveau voyage aux isles de l'Amérique*, vol. 6 (Paris, 1722), 3.
12. Cahen, "Les Juifs de la Martinique," 96.
13. Ibid.
14. Jacob Pereira da Silva, David da Acosta d'Andrade, and David Lopez Henriques.
15. Isaac Emmanuel, "Les Juifs de la Martinique et leurs coreligionaires d'Amsterdam au XVIIe siècle," *Revue des Etudes Juives* 123 (1964):511–16.
16. Cahen, "Les Juifs de la Martinique," 98.
17. Ibid., 99. Translated by the author.
18. Antoine Joseph Le Febvre de la Barre, *Relation de ce qui s'est passé dans les isles de Terre ferme de l'Amérique, pendent la derniere guerre avec l'Angleterre et depuis en execution du traitté de Breda*, vol. 1 (Paris, 1671), 36. Translated by the author.
19. Cahen, "Les Juifs de la Martinique," 116–21.
20. Louis XIV, *Code Noir*, Edit du Roy servent de reglement touchant la police des Isles de l'Amérique Françoise. Signed Louis Roy de France et de Navarre, Colbert, Le Tellier, Versailles, 1685.
21. Archives of Ministère de la Marine (Colonies—Martinique), 1683, Paris.
22. Emmanuel, "Les Juifs," 516.
23. Ibid., 515.
24. Albert Gassman, *Dictionary of the French and Netherlands Antilles* (Metuchen, NJ, 1978). Pieter is hardly a Jewish name. However, we find Salomon Pietrz in New Amsterdam, and a study by Dr. Isaac Prins of Jerusalem showed that his original name was Cardoso (*Old Archief of Amsterdam*, doc. No. 3583) and that he was Jewish.
25. Labat, *Nouveau Voyage*, vol. 4, 106.
26. Abraham Cahen, "Les Juifs dans les colonies françaises au XVIIIe siècle," *Revue des Etudes Juives* 4 (1882):132.
27. James Rodway, *Chronological History of the Discovery and Settlement of Guyana 1493–1668* (Georgetown, 1888), 104, 112, 129, 130.
28. Jan Jakob Hartsinck, *Beschryving van Guiana, of de Wildekust* (Amsterdam, 1770), 940; English trans. in J. Rodway, *Chronological History*, 145.
29. Jac Zwarts, "Een Episode mit de Joodsche kolonisatie an Guyana (1660)," in *West Indische Gids (WIG)* 9 (1928):519–30; Herbert Bloom, "The Dutch Archives with Special Reference to American Jewish History," *Publication of the American Jewish Historical Society* (1931), refers to the document, Notarial Archives, Pieter Padthuysen (1659), vol. 2888, on the deposition of the captain who brought the Jews to Cayenne—"The Commander [Langedijk] did not wish to permit the settlement ... and did not wish that the colonists

remain on the island either as colonists of the company or under him"; see also vol. 2899, fols. 344–55, 10/5/1660.

30. Jacques Bellin, *Description Geographique de la Guyane. Ccontenant les possessions et les establissemens des François, les Espagnols, les Portugais, les Hollandois dans ces vastes pays* (Paris, 1763), 16. Translated by the author.
31. Zvi Loker, "Les Juifs a Cayenne 1660–1667," in *La Grande Encyclopédie de la Caraïbe,* vol. 7 (Samoli, 1990), 22–27; Isaac Emmanuel, "Fortunes and Misfortunes of the Jews in Brazil (1630–1654)," in *American Jewish Archives* (January 1955):21–23.
32. James Rodway, *Guiana, British, Dutch and French* (New York, 1912), 57.
33. R. P. Jean Baptiste du Tertre, *Histoire generale des Antilles habitees par les Francais* vol. 3 (Paris, 1667), 12. Translated by the author.
34. Jean Baptiste Labat, *Voyage du Chevalier de Marchais en Guinée ... et a Cayenne* (Amsterdam, 1731), 99.
35. Jean Baptiste Labat, *Nouveau Voyage aux Isles de l'Amérique,* vol. 3 (Paris, 1772), 106.
36. H. Ternaux-Compans, *Notice Historique sur la Guyane francaise* (Paris, 1843), 66; Samuel Oppenheim, "An Early Jewish Colony in Western Guiana and Its Relation to the Jews in Suriname, Cayenne, and Tobago," in *PAJHS* 16 (1908):123.
37. Daniel Levi de Barrios, "Triumphal carro de la perfecion por el camino de la salvacion," in *El Triumpho del Gobierno Popular* (Amsterdam, 1701), 631–635.
38. Rodway, *Chronological History,* 164–65.
39. du Tertre, *Histoire,* vol. 3, 34.
40. Ibid. Translated by the author.
41. Hartsinck, *Beschryving,* citing "Hollandize Mercurius," of July 1664, page 127: "Zu voeren de Joden en Christen van hun welvaren berooft en ser pover stelt na Rochel on van der tu mosen veotern hun vaderland."
42. Oppenheim, "Early Jewish Colony," 135; Loker, "Les Juifs," 24; Zvi Loker, "Cayenne— a Chapter of Jewish Settlement in the New World in the 18th Century," in *Zion* (Jerusalem), 112n.; Dr. L. L. E. Rens "Analysis of Annals relating to Early Jewish Settlement in Surinam," in *Vox Guyanne* (Paramaribo, 1954), 25, in which Rens further states that about one hundred Jews were shipped to La Rochelle.
43. John Gabriel Stedman, *Narrative of a Five Years Expedition against the Revolted Negroes of Surinam in Guiana, on the Wild Coast of South America from 1772 to 1777, Elucidating the History of That country,* London, 1796, 87: "A Jew soldier of the society past La Rochelle accompanied him"; and 241, "During all this time strong patrols cruised between Magdeburg, La Rochelle, and the Jew Savannah...."
44. Fred Oudschans Dentz, "Wat er Overbleef van het Kerkhoff en de Synagoge var der Joden Savanne in Suriname," in *WIG* 29 (1948):210–34. "The Grave of Abraham Mendes Vaez born in Livorno died in 1697 at the age of 64."
45. Le Febvre de la Barre, *Description de la France Equinoctiale cy devant appellée Guyanne et par les Espagnols "El Dorado"* (Paris, 1688), 52.
46. V. T. Harlow, ed., *Colonizing Expeditions to the West Indies and Guiana* (London, 1924), 241.
47. Cahen, "Les Juifs dans les colonies françaises," 130.
48. Archives du Ministère de la Marine—Correspondence générale—Colonies—1739, cited in Cahen, " Les Juifs dans les colonies françaises," 136.
49. Archives Nationales de France (Colonies), Paris, E210 folio 13, published in Zvi Loker, *Jews in the Caribbean* (Jerusalem, 1991), 242–43.
50. Archives Nationales de France (Colonies), E210, folio 106, published in Loker, *Jews in the Caribbean,* 248.
51. Loker, *Jews in the Caribbean,* 268.

52. Archives du Ministère de la Marine—Collection Moreau St. Mery (Colonies) + XV art.; Cahen, "Les Juifs dans les colonies françaises," 141.
53. Ibid., 142. Translated by the author.
54. Archives Nationales de France (Colonies), F5 B39.
55. Ibid., F5 B42
56. Ibid.
57. Loker, *Jews in the Caribbean*, 222.
58. Archives Nationales de France (Colonies), F5 B53 and Loker, *Jews in the Caribbean*, 222–26.
59. William H. Hodges, *Les Juifs au Cap—evidence d'une communauté Juive au Cap Français* (Limbe, Haiti, 1983), 3.
60. Hodges, *Les Juifs au Cap*, 4.
61. Jean Cavignac, *Dictionaire du Judaisme Bordelais aux XVIIe et XX e Siècles* (Bordeaux 1987), 9–125.
62. Bertram Wallace Korn, *The Early Jews of New Orleans* (Waltham, 1969), 72.
63. Zvi Loker, "Jews in the Grand'Anse Colony of Saint-Dominigue," in *American Jewish Archives* 34:1 (1982). Families mentioned are: Alvares, Cardoze, D'Almeyda, Da Sylva, Lange, Lopez de Paz, de Lima, Maduro, Montes, Moron, Penha, Petit, Rodrigue, Seixas, Vidal.
64. Archives Israélites (Paris, 1847), 861–63.
65. Laurore St. Juste, "Ancêtres de Pierre Mendes-France originaire d'Haiti," in *Créations Haitiano-Françaises*, 12–13 July 1971. On the Mendes France family, see notes 80 and 81 below.
66. Albert Gastman, *Historical Dictionary of the French and Netherlands Antilles* (Metuchen, N.J., 1978), item 22.
67. Cahen, "Les Juifs dans les colonies françaises," 239.
68. There is no mention anywhere else of the existence of such synagogues. It was supposed that a ruin in Jeremie might have been a synagogue, but there is no proof.
69. Archives Nationales—Ministère de la Marine (Colonies), Saint-Domingue—Correspondance Générale (1764).
70. Giraud, "Memoire de M. Choisel remis au Roi en 1765," in *Journal de Savants* (April 1881):255, cited in Cahen, "Les Juifs dans les colonies françaises," 237n.
71. Archives Nationales de France, Ministère de la Marine—Correspondance Générale, Colonies, Saint-Domingue, 1764, cited in Cahen, "Les Juifs dans les colonies françaises," 248.
72. Collection Moreau St. Mery—Ministère de la Marine—Archives Générales de France, Colonies t. XV Juifs, cited in Cahen, "Les Juifs dans les colonies françaises," 244.
73. Archives Nationales de France (Colonies)—Ministère de la Marine—Correspondance Générale—Saint-Domingue, 1765, in Cahen, "Les Juifs dans les colonies françaises," 78.
74. Archives Nationales de France C9 A127 Of 1 vol. 5, copy in American Jewish Archives, Cincinnati, SC 8047.
75. Moreau de Saint-Mery, *Lois et constitutions des colonies françaises d'Amérique sous le Vent*, vol. 4 (Paris 1787):850.
76. Ibid., 853.
77. Archives Nationales de France C9 B21 file 1479, copy in the American Jewish Archives SC. 8047.
78. Loker, *Jews in the Caribbean*, 218. See also Zvi Loker "Dr. Michel Lopes de Pas—Médecin et Savant de Saint-Domingue," *Revue d'Histoire de la Médécine Hebraique* 37 (1980):55–57.

79. Zvi Loker, "Simon Isaac Henriquez Moron—Homme d'Affaires de la Grand Anse," *Revue de la Société Haitienne d'Histoire, de Géographie et de Géologie* 125 (1979):56–59; and Zvi Loker, "Un Juif Portugais Fondateur de Moron," *Conjonction, revue Franco Haitienne* 139 (1978):87–88.

80. Jean Lacouture, *Pierre Mendes France* (New York, 1984), 18.

81. List of properties situated in Saint-Domingue, having belonged to the Mendes France family, Manuscript, in American Jewish Archives SC 8042, based on file A 114 II Cote 30 in Archives Nationales de France.

– Chapter 16 –

NEW CHRISTIANS/"NEW WHITES": SEPHARDIC JEWS, FREE PEOPLE OF COLOR, AND CITIZENSHIP IN FRENCH SAINT-DOMINGUE, 1760–1789

John D. Garrigus

THE CASE OF SAINT-DOMINGUE'S SEPHARDIM illustrates that the story of Jews in Europe's expansion westward is about more than the survival or mutation of deeply rooted family traditions. Old World questions about Jewish political identity did not disappear in the Americas. Rather, these persistent issues forced colonists and their children born in the New World to reconcile European philosophies with American conditions. In the case of the largest slave colony in the Caribbean, Saint-Domingue's Jews helped translate emerging French nationalism into an attack on racial prejudice that eventually produced the Haitian revolution. By raising complex issues of national identity and citizenship in French America after 1763, Sephardic merchants and planters provided a model for another group whose place in colonial society was equally ambiguous: Saint-Domingue's free people of color.

In the mid-1780s, the self-proclaimed leaders of the colony's "mulattos"[1] adopted many of the techniques that colonial Jews used to fight for legal rights. Their challenge to a racial hierarchy that had only recently acquired full legitimacy threatened the ideological basis of plantation society. By 1791 political and military struggles between colonial "whites" and "mulattos" had become so vicious that a great slave rebellion was possible.

The civil positions of colonial Jews and free people of mixed European and African parentage were parallel because elites in France began to construct new definitions of French citizenship in the mid-eighteenth

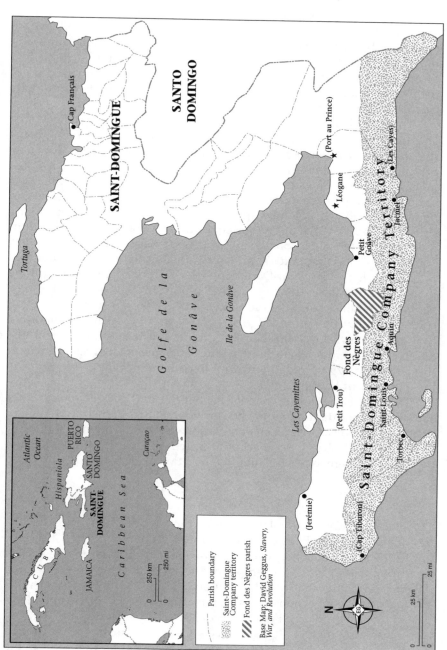

MAP 8 Lands of the Saint-Domingue Company, 1698–1720

century. In Paris and elsewhere, Jansenist judges and Protestant leaders pushed royal administrators to recognize that property, loyalty, and civic utility, not orthodox Catholicism, defined French identity.[2] At the same time, royal bureaucrats eager to open France to wealthy families born outside its borders began to free these influential immigrants from traditional legal disabilities. By 1789, therefore, the continuum of rights and disabilities separating non-French residents and native-born subjects of the French monarchy was increasingly simplified into two mutually exclusive categories: citizen and foreigner.[3]

These gradual but important changes in the way France defined civil and national identity had a profound impact on the kingdom's most dynamic overseas possession. Dominguan elites were quick to adopt new French ideas, including a greater sympathy for the loyalty of resident Jews. At the same time, however, social and political tensions in this slave society after the Seven Years' War produced newly scientific definitions of racial identity that colonists applied to free people with unprecedented rigor.[4] Equipped with a more "objective" racial ideology, colonial authorities labeled a few old colonial families as *gens de couleur* and insisted such "quadroons" and "mulattos" were not authentically French. At the very same time, however, Saint-Domingue's Jews were successfully fighting much older prejudices, to the point that administrators were freeing some Sephardic families from the old discriminatory laws. I hypothesize that colonial Sephardim provided free people of color with an important example of how to reclaim their French identity. It was no accident that Julien Raimond, the "quadroon" planter and free colored spokesman in the 1780s and 1790s, traded with and lived next to some of the colony's most important Jewish families.

The civil struggles of colonial Sephardim and *gens de couleur* after 1763 were important steps in the development of French and Haitian national identities. Out of a shared marginality and a common footing in Caribbean contraband, Sephardim and free people of color challenged the laws and stereotypes defining them as non-French.

* * * *

THE FRENCH CROWN had allowed Sephardic Jews fleeing Portugal to settle in southwestern France from the 1550s. Known as New Christians until 1723, after which they could acknowledge their Judaism openly, this small population was an example of the ways in which the emerging Atlantic economy challenged traditional ideas about French identity. Through their connections to the Sephardic diaspora, Bordeaux's Jews helped the city grow into France's most important Atlantic port. This network was also invaluable to France's Caribbean possessions, though questions about Jewish loyalty and identity were harder to resolve in the islands. In the 1650s, Sephardim fleeing the collapse of Dutch Brazil introduced cacao and sugar processing to Martinique, but colonial authorities forced the Jews out in 1683. The crown wanted to protect French merchants and planters from the Dutch competition and the religious diversity associated with these enterprising colonists. Two years later, the first article of France's new collection of slave laws, the *Code Noir*, ordered governors to expel all Jews from the French Caribbean.

Saint-Domingue was still a frontier society in 1685. Ten times larger in area than Martinique and Guadeloupe put together, it had no strong religious institutions and was still dependent on illegal foreign trade. Despite regulations, Dominguan authorities did not closely monitor the Jewish population, let alone expel it. Sometime before 1710, Michel Lopez Depas, a thirty-year-old doctor from an important Bordeaux Sephardic family, arrived in the colony. Energetic and respected, he was appointed royal physician in Petit Goâve, at that time the colonial capital. Lopez Depas apparently converted to Christianity, and went on to serve as a judge on the colony's Superior Council in 1723. In the 1730s he presented a large and inexpert painting of the archangel Michael to the nearby parish of Fond des Nègres, where he owned property. The parish promptly named Saint Michael as its patron saint.[5]

Whether or not such conversions were sincere, royal officials in Saint-Domingue may have considered Jewish commercial contacts too valuable to lose.[6] Sixty years earlier, Sephardic expertise, capital, and connections had helped to establish valuable cacao and sugar plantations in Martinique, and Versailles wanted a similar transformation in Saint-Domingue. When Michel Lopez Depas first arrived in Saint-Domingue, much of the colony's southern peninsula was under the control of a royal monopoly company. Versailles hoped this unsettled coast would serve as an entrepôt for smuggling goods into Spanish America, but its monopoly company collapsed in 1720.[7] English and Dutch merchants outmaneuvered the French in Spanish colonial markets, and even bought the tobacco, cacao, and indigo produced in this frontier region of Saint-Domingue. Indeed, by 1713 a thriving community of free black farmers had taken root in the fertile hollow thereafter known as Fond des Nègres, growing cacao and presumably trading it to the merchants of Jamaica and Curaçao.[8] A substantial portion of this contraband cacao was carried by Sephardic merchants.[9] The Spanish traveler Gregorio de Robles visited Jews in Jamaica at the end of the seventeenth century, who told him they used the smaller Spanish coins they earned in contraband to "trade with the Indians, mulattos and mestizos, carrying off their goods at the same time, a commerce that yielded them much profit." The free black cacao growers of Fond des Nègres probably sold their crops to traders like these or to other Jamaican or Curaçaoan merchants, at least until 1715 and 1716, when a blight eliminated Saint-Domingue's cacao groves forever.[10]

It is likely that Michel Lopez Depas was aware of this commerce, though there is no direct evidence that contraband cacao drew him to Fond des Nègres.[11] His brother Louis had married into the Gradis family of Bordeaux, modest textile merchants until 1718. The Gradises switched

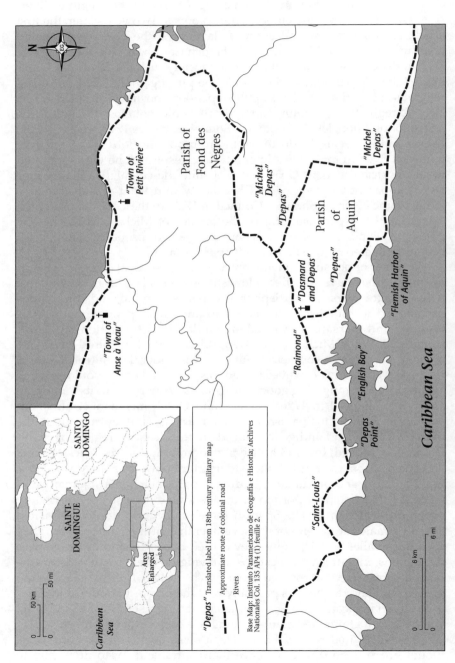

MAP 9 Depas Family Properties, Saint-Domingue

to colonial commerce about the time Michel arrived in Saint-Domingue. By 1728 they had increased their trading capital from roughly 5,000 livres tournois to 162,000 and were sending three ships a year to Saint-Domingue's southern peninsula.[12] Twenty years later they had become such important shippers that in 1751 they received letters of nobility for their role in supplying Quebec in wartime.[13] This service to Versailles continued through the Seven Years' War and the War of American Independence, during which they furnished at least two million livres tournois in specie to pay colonial troops.[14]

Along with these official contacts, the Gradises in Bordeaux and Michel Lopez Depas's family in southern Saint-Domingue were heavily involved in smuggling. From before 1720 until the end of the century, contraband dominated the economy of this peninsula. French commercial restrictions were greatly resented throughout the colony, and contemporaries reported that the indigo and sugar plantations of the southern peninsula were almost entirely dependent on merchants from Jamaica and Curaçao. Trade with France was especially limited during periods of war, when famine forced royal officials to legalize foreign shipping.

This situation further explains why colonial officials did not expel, or even identify, Jewish families. In 1741, Saint-Domingue's administrators told Versailles that there were only three Jews in the colony. They mentioned Michel Lopez Depas, but did not count him as Jewish because of his conversion.[15] Christian or not, the doctor sent to France for his brothers, who became wealthy planters and merchants in this part of the colony, maintaining close relations with the Gradis house of Bordeaux through intermarriage.[16] The growing colonial branch of the Lopez Depas family also participated in contraband trade with Curaçao, where Lopez Depas was a common name in the Jewish community.[17] These profitable connections allowed Michel's brother François, a merchant, to raise nine legitimate children in Aquin parish, just south of Fond des Nègres. In 1763 Philippe Lopez Depas, another brother, owned an Aquin estate with sixty-three slaves valued at 200,000 livres.[18]

Trade with Curaçao and Jamaica was an important resource for another group that had no openly acknowledged place in French colonial society before 1763: free people of color. By mid-century, the slaves and free black farmers of Fond des Nègres and elsewhere had intermarried with European immigrants, producing a second and third generation of free and independent families, many of them of mixed European-African descent.[19] In fact, one of the southern peninsula's wealthiest men of color was Michel Depas, a free "mulatto" who lived in Aquin parish and was probably the illegitimate son of Michel Lopez Depas.[20] In 1743 royal administrators described "M. de Paz" as having several children with a former slave woman to whom he was very devoted. "To the children he is very tender and has sent them to his parents in Bordeaux to be educated."[21] Indeed, a Michel Depas worked in the Gradis merchant house in Bordeaux in the late 1730s and early 1740s.[22] In the 1760s, a hostile colonial governor described the free "mulatto" Michel Depas as "a courtier of Mr. Gradis."[23] This second Michel Depas did considerable business with his father and, at the son's death in 1783, left an estate with sixty-seven slaves, twenty-seven slave huts, an animal pen, and seven different outbuildings. In his dining room the notaries found fourteen silver place settings and other silver tableware, while in his study they discovered an "optical box" and prints for viewing with this device.[24] In the late 1780s, Michel's sons married, forming households as wealthy as those of many members of the white colonial elite.[25]

A number of prominent families of mixed European-African descent in this region had contraband connections to Curaçao, even if they were not related to Sephardim.[26] Julien Raimond, an indigo planter of one-quarter African ancestry who led free colored political efforts after 1782, owned land next to the white and mulatto members of the Depas family and traded with both Bordeaux and Curaçao, as they did. When Raimond deposited an inventory of his commercial papers with a notary in 1785, 40 percent of these documents (60 of 159) included overseas transactions.[27] Forty-four of his receipts were with Bordeaux merchants or captains, but he had six from Curaçao and four from Bruges and Ostend, compared to only two from the important French port of Nantes. Furthermore, Raimond traded with Sephardic merchants in Saint-Domingue. He sold dye to David Henriques and Captain Jacob Mendes Henriques of Curaçao in 1780 and 1781, and later dealt with the Henriques firm when it opened a trading counter in Aquin. He paid a bill to "Levé," a merchant-goldsmith in Jacmel and owed money to one "Paraire," a merchant in Petit Trou. Raimond also dealt with Salomon d'Aguilar, a Jew living in Curaçao who had roots in Port-au-Prince and family in Aquin.[28]

These Jewish families and their neighbors of mixed African-European descent experienced a major social change after the end of the Seven Years' War in 1763. For the first time in the colony's history, planter elites and royal administrators examined the civil status of Jews and free people of color in an attempt to create a new kind of "patriotic" colonial public.

This new attitude was partly inspired by changes in France. The influence of the Enlightenment and a long struggle between the crown and its highest judges were producing greater sympathy for the civil rights of Protestants and of those who held Jansenist views about communion and sin. As Peter Sahlins has pointed out, after 1685 "royal officials and petitioners worked out a set of legal and administrative fictions to mask religious difference."[29] By the end of the eighteenth century, jurists and writers were increasingly collapsing the many corporate identities that had defined the subjects of the king of France into the term "citizen." In 1787, as part of this process, Protestants were granted full civil status.[30] Sahlins's study of the more than seven thousand letters of naturalization issued in France between 1660 and 1789 reveals that the crown readily made wealthy non-Catholic foreigners into French subjects, giving them the right to bequeath French property to their heirs. By the Revolution, says Sahlins, the ease with which a person could be naturalized had effectively simplified the many social identities and corporate statuses separating *aubaines* (foreign-born residents of the kingdom) from *régnicoles* (native-born subjects of the crown). Those living under the French monarchy were increasingly regarded as either "citizen" or "foreigner."[31] France's desire to participate in the expansion of the Atlantic economy accelerated this expanding definition of who was French. Although Ashkenazic Jews in eastern France bore heavy legal disabilities until the Revolution, Sephardic Jews in the southwest were given nearly complete civil and religious rights in 1723, a date that coincides closely with Bordeaux's expansion into the Atlantic trade.[32]

These new ideas about French citizenship arrived in Saint-Domingue in 1763 at the end of the Seven Years' War. The Treaty of Paris brought unprecedented prosperity to planters and merchants. With Quebec under British control and a long wartime blockade over, Saint-Domingue more than ever became the focus of French overseas attention. European emigration boomed, and coffee joined sugar as an important colonial export. The annual volume of the African slave trade tripled from 1763 to 1788, but the war left troubling questions about colonial allegiance to France. During the hostilities, colonists in the supposedly more loyal French islands of Guadeloupe and Martinique had surrendered to the British quickly, even eagerly. Saint-Domingue's inhabitants had long complained about French trade rules and the rigors of militia duty, and the war had expanded both burdens. Before the peace, Versailles, hoping to cement Dominguan loyalty, had offered to abolish the colonial militia when the conflict was over. This was done in 1763, but the following year Versailles sent a new governor to reestablish the militia.

This official, Charles d'Estaing, was deeply smitten with the neoclassical notions of patriotism that many French military reformers adopted after the war.[33] Saint-Domingue was notorious for its planters' individualism and for their complete lack of social attachment to each other. Nevertheless, d'Estaing believed that by artfully reforming the militia, renaming it the National Legion, and creating ranks and medals, he could instill a civic spirit in the colony. As part of achieving this new public-spiritedness, the governor proposed fundamental changes in the civil status of colonial Jews and free people of color. He was shocked to find that Saint-Domingue had nearly fifty Jewish families, instead of three as his predecessors had reported. Describing these individuals as foreigners who needed to earn their toleration, the governor instituted a tax "for the public good." He ordered the Sephardic families of the southern peninsula to pay for bridges, defense batteries, and aqueducts.[34] D'Estaing was particularly troubled by the wealth of Michel Depas, the free "mulatto," whom he described as a "courtier of Gradis" and a

trouble maker [*mauvais sujet*], against whom there are a multitude of complaints by the planters; free mulatto and bastard [*Batard*]. He owns a very sizable plantation at the Grande Colline with 120 slaves; moreover he has another plantation at the Colline à Mangon with 30 slaves. He has rebelled several times against commands which have been given to him in the interest of good public order.[35]

He ordered Depas to pay a 50,000 livres tax, equal to the value of a sizable plantation. Lesser amounts were levied against other families and individuals.

The governor predicted that his anti-Semitic measures would be challenged at court by the powerful Gradis family, and he was right. Versailles was horrified at his orders and reversed them. The minister, Choiseul, called d'Estaing "a fool, a dangerous one."[36]

D'Estaing wanted to define these successful Sephardic colonists as foreigners, but he took the opposite approach with the colony's free people of color. Because he hoped to build the martial, not commercial, spirit of the colony, d'Estaing planned to recognize families of mixed European-African ancestry as "white," to reward them for military service. The governor was impressed with free colored enthusiasm and ability in the ranks, but he also wanted to increase the number of officers' commissions available for French immigrants. He therefore proposed to exclude men of color from leadership positions in their own units. Reasoning that appropriate rewards would sweeten the sting of this reform, he envisioned special medals and pensions for deserving men of color. These awards would culminate in an official recognition of "whiteness" for the greatest heroes of this class.

Although d'Estaing hoped to expand the hitherto informal definition of "white" to include some families of acknowledged mixed ancestry, his efforts inspired a new era of racism in Saint-Domingue. Colonists drew on new biological theories published in Europe for their new, more rigidly genealogical and "scientific" definition of racial difference, but at root their efforts were prompted by anxiety about white society in Saint-Domingue. The colonial elite hoped that the end of the war in 1763 would begin the "rule of law," and eliminate the private "arbitrary" power of military officials like d'Estaing. These planters and merchants wanted more commercial freedom and fewer wars in the Caribbean. They welcomed the new public buildings, promenades, fountains, and theaters the government was planning for Saint-Domingue. The colony's first permanent printing press arrived from France in 1763, and officials began to build new colonial roads and reform the postal service.[37] According to Moreau de Saint-Méry, "finally the light of civilization and politeness appeared after the peace of 1763."[38] A planter wrote in the new colonial newspaper in 1769: "... this colony now has something for every taste: plays, concerts, libraries, sumptuous parties, where gaiety and wit wipe away tiresome boredom. Buccaneers have given way to ballet-masters."[39]

Yet this elite was keenly aware that Saint-Domingue was not France. Commentators worried that the selfishness and hedonism of their fellow colonists—fed by the sexual power masters had over slaves and encouraged by self-interested royal officials—would prevent the flowering of this new French civilization. The many elite colonists who had read Montesquieu's chapters on tropical societies in *Spirit of the Laws* were well aware of the connections he drew between climate, marriage customs, and political forms. For Montesquieu, despotism was a central feature of societies where the seraglio had replaced marriage. *Spirit of the Laws* also warned that tyranny threatened when women ran free, unrestricted by male heads of household.[40] Advocates of a new, virtuous "civilized" community in Saint-Domingue saw both harems and harlots when they described the sexual power that some women of color had over white colonists, and the affection many fathers had for their illegitimate colonial children.[41]

By attempting to increase the power of the military and revise informal racial categories, d'Estaing inadvertently prompted the formation of a new, self-consciously "white" patriotic identity in Saint-Domingue. His attempts to make Saint-Domingue into a tropical Sparta were rejected by the colony's high councils, whose judges were born in the islands but were keenly aware of how metropolitan judges were fighting the crown. Versailles assigned a new governor to reestablish the militia, but this man, the Prince de Rohan-Montbazon, called public assemblies that only inflamed anti-militia sentiment. In 1769 royal troops and pro-militia colonists had to suppress an anti-militia revolt in the southern peninsula and in the hinterland of Port-au-Prince.[42]

This failed uprising only confirmed white elite suspicions about "tyrannical" royal appointees. They proclaimed that true colonial patriotism was seen in commercial success, not martial virtue. In March 1779, as five hundred men of color were enlisting to fight the British in North America, the colonial newspaper ridiculed d'Estaing's outmoded ideals:

> To the honor of humanity, surely one will never again see a ferocious and barbarian mother send her son to his death with a dry eye, without emotion see him again pale and bleeding and believe she owes this horrible sacrifice to the fatherland.... These awful traits, so long admired by our fathers, are unnatural and make any respectable and sensitive soul tremble.[43]

These words were a message to d'Estaing, who was in the colony when they were published, as commander of the North American expedition. The paper urged "humane" colonists to donate their profits, not their blood, to the French cause. It launched a subscription drive to purchase a naval vessel as a gift for Louis XVI.[44]

In constructing a new white identity based not on culture, religion, or class, but on the complete absence of African ancestry, Dominguan elites combined misogynist anti-court rhetoric, partially inspired by Montesquieu, with the new racial science of Buffon and others to cut all persons of any African descent out of respectable colonial society.[45] In 1685 the *Code Noir* had given ex-slaves and their offspring all the privileges of French subjects. Though social and legal distinctions between whites and *gens de couleur* had existed in the colony since the 1720s, a number of established families of mixed descent were legally regarded as "white" up to the middle of the century. Julien Raimond and other neighbors of the Lopez Depas in Fond des Nègres and Aquin parishes were among this number. After 1769, however, officials began to record African descent far more carefully, separating "white" from "colored" families. The colonial councils passed new laws restricting the public activities of these families and other "ex-slaves." Now all persons of any African descent—no matter how remote the ancestor, how wealthy the family, or how European the lifestyle—were to be classed as freedmen or *affranchis*.

To further separate proper French families from these foreigners, in 1773 a new law directed free people of color to take an "African" name so they would not be confused with "respectable" families. Michel Depas, the free mulatto planter, formally asked the governor and intendant to be exempted from this requirement, but on 5 June 1777 he officially became Michel Medina, adopting another name prominent in the Sephardic networks to which his Lopez Depas brothers and cousins belonged.[46]

If the negative reaction to d'Estaing's plan for racial integration helped produce a more far-reaching racism toward people of color, the governor's anti-Semitic measures were followed by colonists' greater acceptance of Sephardim as French. This was in part because colonists now looked to skin color rather than religious belief as the primary determinant of social status, and also because these Jewish families seemed to represent commercial rather than military virtues. Although Versailles had granted Jews full citizenship in Bordeaux in 1723, members of this group officially had no such rights in Saint-Domingue. As *aubaines* or foreign-born residents, Jews outside Bordeaux could not draft a valid testament.[47] Even before the Seven Years' War, however, Dominguan high courts upheld Jewish wills.[48] The failure of d'Estaing's anti-Jewish tax of 1764 seemed to confirm colonial acceptance of Jewish citizenship. Into the 1770s, although Versailles warned against giving colonial Jews full legal rights as a class, colonial judges repeatedly upheld Jewish testaments, negating the most severe disability of *aubaine* status. In 1783 a new colonial minister, the Maréchal de Castries, extended full civil rights to Sephardim in Saint-Domingue's rich north province. Here, where most Jewish commerce fell within the bounds of legal trade and where the Jewish population was the largest, Jews would have the same rights that they enjoyed in Bordeaux.[49] Though Suarez d'Almeyda was a name associated with Jewish contraband traders along the southern coast, in Cap Français Jean-Baptiste Suarez Dalmeïda served as royal attorney in the local court, and then for the Cap Français council.[50]

Despite Castries's reforms, the extent of Jewish rights remained unclear outside the north province. In 1782, the death of the planter Philippe Depas in Aquin parish raised the question of whether his daughter, who had followed a family tradition by marrying one of her Gradis cousins in Bordeaux, could inherit colonial property.[51] Courts validated the Depas testament, partly because of "the services this [Gradis] family has rendered to the state."[52]

Castries himself was probably behind this decision. Though he opposed contraband, the minister recognized its utility. During the War of American Independence, he had opened all Dominguan ports to international shipping, allowing merchants from Curaçao, especially, to supply food during the British blockade.[53] After the war, he permitted limited international commerce along the entire southern coast of Saint-Domingue and in six other French Caribbean ports.[54] In 1781 Castries even suggested that he might be open to redefining the racial, as well as religious, restrictions on citizenship in Saint-Domingue.[55]

Wealthy colonial families of color responded enthusiastically to the possibility of repealing the strict racial laws laid down after d'Estaing's governship. In 1782, elite members of the free population of color, from families that had been mostly considered "white" before 1764, approached colonial administrators with a patriotic proposal that owed far more to the example of their Jewish neighbors than to the martial admonitions of d'Estaing. Julien Raimond asked to be allowed to solicit contributions from free people of color for the colonial gift of a ship for Louis XVI. Apparently following the recommendation of the colonial newspaper that "respectable and sensitive" souls sacrifice their fortunes, not their lives, for France, Raimond collected over 900 livres for the monarch's tribute. The following year Raimond penned the first of four letters to the ministry arguing that light-skinned men like him should be officially reclassified as "new whites."[56] Though he did not explicitly refer to his Dutch commercial contacts or Sephardic neighbors, Raimond made a case for free colored citizenship that was strikingly similar to the situation in Curaçao and among Jews in Saint-Domingue. In the Dutch entrepôt, with its large Jewish and free colored populations and relatively open conception of citizenship, after 1769 prosperous light-skinned mixed families had been allowed to serve with white militia units.[57] In a similar way, admiration for the utility of Jewish commerce in Saint-Domingue had prompted elites to disregard metropolitan laws and recognize important families like the Depas as de facto citizens, on a case-by-case basis.

In essence, Raimond was arguing that the same kinds of administrative euphemisms that had been developed for wealthy foreigners in France be applied to wealthy free men of color like himself. Colonial condemnations of mulatto immorality derided the "vice of their birth." Raimond did not mention it, but the same phrase was used to describe foreigners in France, and royal letters of naturalization could easily erase this obstacle.[58] In the same way, Raimond did not remind the minister that the ancestors of his neighbors the Lopez Depas had been *Nouveaux Chretiens* in France before 1723, and *Cristãos-novos* in Portugal even earlier, but he did ask that wealthy people of color be renamed *nouveaux blancs*.

In 1784 the indigo planter and his wife moved to France. Raimond met with Castries, who had been replaced as colonial minister, and petitioned his successor to adopt the very limited reforms described above, but little happened in this arena before 1789. Instead, full citizenship for men like Raimond came in the early years of the French Revolution, at about the same time as it did for the Gradises and other Bordeaux Sephardim. Both groups used the debates about representation and active versus passive citizenship in 1789 and 1790 to advance their cases. An anonymous pamphleteer in Paris borrowed the language of Jewish petitioners for civil rights when he argued that free men of color were *régnicoles*, free-born Frenchmen.[59] The colonists' club of Bordeaux, whose president was David Gradis, supported free colored demands for representation in the National Assembly at the end of the summer of 1789, even though the delegates would not recognize the active citizenship of Bordeaux Jews until January 1790.[60]

The movement for Jewish citizenship provided even greater support for free colored recognition in the person of Abbé Grégoire. Known in the Assembly as "the protector of the Jews," Grégoire knew little about France's colonies until he met Raimond in Paris in 1789. By early 1790 he had become a noted voice in debates on this issue, and had adapted his pro-Jewish arguments for the free colored cause as well.[61] Though Raimond himself never published any explicit comparisons between free people of color and Jews, in his first pre-Revolutionary manuscript he pointed out that prejudice kept wealthy men of color from even so minor a post as parish sexton.[62] Grégoire, who drew heavily on Raimond's papers for his own publications, noted in an 1789 manuscript in favor of free colored citizenship that the wealthy Jewish doctor Depas had been a member of the colony's highest court and that his grandnephew had served as sexton of the Aquin parish church.[63] If the crown allowed Jews such honors, why were mulatto planters excluded? The Abbé de Cournand, another Parisian supporter of free colored citizenship, compared the situation of free colonial people of color to that of Jews in Europe in a 1790 pamphlet deeply informed by Raimond.[64]

In May 1791, the National Assembly, spurred by the power of these arguments, did extend civil rights to the wealthiest and oldest free families of color in the French Caribbean. It was white colonial resistance to even this limited reform that plunged Saint-Domingue into civil war, which in turn helped produce the great slave uprising of August 1791.

* * * *

THE MANY SIMILARITIES between the pre-Revolutionary situation of Saint-Domingue's Sephardim and prominent free families of color are more than coincidental. Simultaneously enriching France and themselves, Jewish merchants and planters offered Versailles the best reason to replace old corporate labels with new secular, individualistic categories in the colonies. If French-born colonists like Michel Lopez Depas or his brother Philippe were useful and loyal to France; why couldn't they be French? But this enlightened vision of civic community, while discounting old religious classifications, installed new corporate groupings in their place. Scientific theories about the superiority of European over African blood reinforced a profitable system of plantation slave labor and required increasing vigilance in free colonial society against persons of mixed ancestry. After 1763 these "mulattos" could not be fully French, no matter their birthplace, religion, wealth, education, or civic service.

Contact between Sephardim and free families of color prospering along a forgotten coast near the edges of the French, English, Dutch, and Spanish empires revealed the contradiction between these two trends. The money Julien Raimond earned selling indigo to merchants from Curaçao helped him finance five years in Revolutionary Paris, dismantling colonial racism, but contact with Jewish colonists also helped Raimond see how to argue for French citizenship. The support of the Gradises and other Bordeaux Sephardim for free colored citizenship in 1789 and the conversion of Grégoire from advocate of Jewish integration to supporter of French citizenship for free and enslaved people of color further illustrate the connections between these political struggles.[65]

In the colonies, on the very edge of what was considered "France," Jews and people of mixed African and European descent tested and helped explode the narrow definition of who might be a French citizen. The heirs of their struggle discovered that the new ideas of race and identity were too difficult to reverse, especially when fused with the profits generated by slavery. Rather than fight Europe endlessly over who could be French, in 1804 these revolutionaries created Haiti, a new American nation with a racial identity all its own.

Notes

1. I use quotation marks around "mulatto" and other racial terms for two reasons. First, contemporaries applied the term to the entire free population of color, though some of these people were of full African descent and many others were, technically, some mixture of African and European other than "mulatto." Secondly, I use quotation marks because this chapter is about the social construction of these racial terms. Until recently, historians of Saint-Domingue have treated racial categories as objective descriptors, ascribing the dramatic increase in the colony's free colored population on the eve of the French Revolution to demographic factors or to increasing manumissions, rather than to new definitions of the line between "white" and "colored." See, for example, Jean Meyer et al., *Histoire de la France coloniale des origines à 1914* (Paris, 1991), 165.
2. Jeffrey Merrick, "Conscience and Citizenship in Eighteenth-Century France," *Eighteenth-Century Studies* 21 (1987):48–70; Gary Kates, "Jews into Frenchmen: Nationality and Representation in Revolutionary France," *Social Research* 56 (spring 1989):223, 232.

3. Peter Sahlins, "Fictions of a Catholic France: The Naturalization of Foreigners, 1685–1787," *Representations* 47 (summer 1994):85–110.

4. John D. Garrigus, "'Sons of the Same Father': Gender, Race, and Citizenship in Saint-Domingue, 1760–1792," *Visions and Revisions of Eighteenth-Century France*, ed. Christine Adams, Jack R. Censer, and Lisa Jane Graham (University Park, 1997), 137–53. The rise of racism in 1760s France is treated in Pierre Boulle, "In Defense of Slavery: Eighteenth-Century Opposition to Abolition and the Origins of Racist Ideology in France," *History from Below*, ed. Frederick Krantz (Oxford, 1988), 219–46, and, most notably, in Sue Peabody, *"There Are No Slaves in France": The Political Culture of Race and Slavery in the Ancien Régime* (Oxford, 1997), which are important additions to the earlier survey of the topic by William B. Cohen, *The French Encounter with Africans 1530–1880* (Bloomington, 1980).

5. Méderic Louis Elie Moreau de Saint-Méry, *Description topographique, physique, civile, politique et historique de la partie française de l'isle Saint Domingue* (Paris, 1984), 1196. Frances Malino, *The Sephardic Jews of Bordeaux: Assimilation and Emancipation in Revolutionary and Napoleonic France* (University, Ala., 1978), 10, reports that in Bordeaux a number of Jews converted to Catholicism in order to practice medicine.

6. Pierre Pluchon, *Nègres et juifs aux XVIIIe siècle: Le racisme au siècle des lumières* (Paris, 1984), 102, 109.

7. Charles Frostin, "Les Pontchartrain et la pénétration commercial française en Amérique espagnole," *Revue historique* (April–June 1971):307–36.

8. Pierre de Vassière, *Saint Domingue (1629–1789): La société et la vie créole sous l'ancien régime* (Paris, 1909), 40–41, notes 2 and 4, 43–44, note 2; Jean-Baptiste Labat, *Nouveau voyage aux isles de l'Amérique* (Fort-de-France, 1972), 114–15.

9. On Jews in the Caracas cacao trade, see Celestino Andres Arauz Monfante, *El contrabando holandes en el Caribe durante la primera mitad del siglo XVIII* , vol. 1 (1984), 47–59. Curaçaoan smuggling of cacao and other commodities from French and Spanish territories began in earnest during the War of Spanish Succession (1701–13), according to Cornelis Goslinga, *The Dutch in the Caribbean and in the Guianas, 1680–1791* (Assen, 1985), 190, 196, 225. Goslinga, 106, 196, 202, reports that the increase in Curaçao's eighteenth-century smuggling trade coincided with the growth of the Sephardic Jewish population at Willemstad.

10. Gregorio de Robles, *America a fines del siglo xvii: Noticia de los lugares de contrabando* (Valladolid, 1980), 32–36. On the disastrous cacao fungus and the series of insect plagues that blighted the early agricultural promise of Fond des Nègres, see Pierre François Xavier de Charlevoix, *Histoire de l'isle espagnole ou de S. Domingue; écrite particulièrement sur les mémoires manuscrits de P. Jean-Baptiste le Pers*, vol. 2 (Paris, 1730–1731), 360, 390 and Moreau de Saint-Méry, *Description*, 1197–99.

11. Chocolate-making was a specialty trade of Sephardic Jews in Bordeaux and Bayonne; Jean Cavignac, *Les israélites bordelais de 1780 à 1850: Autour de l'émancipation* (Paris, 1991), 154.

12. Paul Butel, *Les négociants bordelais: l'Europe et les îles au xviii siècle* (Paris, 1974), 317; Richard Menkis, "The Gradis Family of Eighteenth-Century Bordeaux: A Social and Economic Study," (Ph.D. diss., Brandeis University, 1988), 104–5.

13. Pluchon, *Nègres et juifs*, 58.

14. Malino, *Sephardic Jews of Bordeaux*, 14; Menkis, "The Gradis Family," 156; Jean Tarrade, *Le commerce colonial de la France à la fin de l'ancien régime: L'évolution du régime de 'l'Exclusif' de 1763–1789* (Paris, 1972), 309, 475; Zvi Loker, *Jews in the Caribbean: Evidence on the History of the Jews in the Caribbean Zone in Colonial Times* (Jerusalem, 1991), 255.

15. Pluchon, *Nègres et juifs*, 93–94, 102; Zvi Loker, "Were There Jewish Communities in Saint Domingue (Haiti)?" *Jewish Social Studies* 45 (1983); Zvi Loker, "Docteur Michel Lopez de Paz: médecin et savant de Saint-Domingue," *Revue d'histoire de la médecine hébraïque* 33, no. 134 (1980):55–57.

16. These close connections with the family in Bordeaux do not provide strong evidence about Michel Lopez Depas's religion. In 1763 one of his nieces in Bordeaux was a nun

in a convent where another family member was a pensioner. Nevertheless, they still received property in testaments of Jewish family members; Butel, *Négociants bordelais,* 337; Moreau de Saint-Méry, *Description,* 1196, 1236, 1251, 1518, 1519; Pierre Pluchon, *Nègres et juifs,* 59; one of Michel Lopez Depas's nieces married into the Gradis family and another into the Mendès family at Bordeaux. Register 430 of the notary Daudin de Belair, 3 June 1762, vente, French National Archives, Overseas Section (henceforth ANSOM); register 431 of the notary Daudin de Belair, 16 January 1764, affranchisse-ment, ANSOM. In Bordeaux in 1753 Henriette Lopès Depas married David Da Silva of Amsterdam; Louis Lopès Depas was married to Ricka Gradis. Butel, *Négociants borde-lais,* 336–37.

17. Isaac S. and Suzanne A. Emmanuel, *History of the Jews of the Netherlands Antilles* (Cincinnati, 1970), 828–30, 964–66; register 102 of the notary Belin Duressort, 15 November 1768, procuration, ANSOM; Zvi Locker [sic], "Une famille juive au Cap: Membres de la famille Depas (ou de Paz) à St-Domingue," *Conjonction: Revue franco-haïtienne,* no. 133 (1977), 130, note 4, found a "Depas" and several "Lopez Depaz" in Martinique. He describes a "de Pas" tombstone in a cemetery in Spanish Town, Jamaica, citing *Caribbean Quarterly* 3 (1967):56.

18. Loker, "Were There Jewish Communities?" 138; register 360 of the notary Casamajor, 3 December 1754, vente, ANSOM; register 430 of the notary Daudin de Belair, [il-legible] February 1763, vente, ANSOM; the median price for the sale of rural land in the Saint Louis *quartier* of which Aquin formed a part was 6,750 livres in the period 1760–69. The average price was 23,846 livres. There were a number of other Jewish families in the southern peninsula, especially by the 1780s. In 1787 in Aquin, for example, the trader David Daguilar of Bayonne married Rachel "Pinet" of Amster-dam, whose father Raphael "Pina" was also a merchant at Aquin. Their guests included Antoine Robert Suarès Dalmeida, Jacob Castro, Fernandes ainé, Elias and Fonseco; register 1594 of the notary Scovaud, 25 September 1787, marriage, ANSOM; Jean Cavignac, *Les israélites bordelais,* 123, shows a Jacob Dalmeyda in Bordeaux iden-tifying himself as a "merchant in Tiburon," in Torbec parish, farther down the coast. In Anse à Veau on the northern coast of the peninsula, a member of the Astruc fam-ily, of Avignon and Bordeaux, was militia commander in 1785. Register 745 of the notary Gaudin, 24 November 1787, marriage, ANSOM; register 743 of the notary Gaudin, 5 September 1785, marriage, ANSOM; Cavignac, *Les israélites bordelais,* 170–71, 271.

19. Though many free people of color were illegitimate, "intermarriage" is not just a euphemism. Jacques Houdaille, "Trois paroisses de Saint-Domingue au 18Ie siècle," *Population* 18 (1963):93–110, uses church registers from the neighboring parishes of Jacmel, Cayes de Jacmel, and Fond des Nègres. He finds that 17 percent of all recorded church marriages there before 1730 were between whites and people of color. Further-more, these numbers remained fairly consistent after this date: 8 percent in the 1730s, 17 percent in the 1740s, 17 percent again in the 1750s, 20 percent in the 1760s, 13 per-cent in the 1770s and 17 percent again in the 1780s.

20. In Garrigus, "Blue and Brown: Contraband Indigo and the Rise of a Free Colored Planter Class in French Saint-Domingue," *Americas* 50 (1993):251, I mistakenly described Michel Depas as the nephew of Michel Lopez Depas and the son of Philippe Lopez Depas. Although Philippe did have several free children of color, the papers left by the younger Michel Depas at his death indicate that this man of color had done much business with "M. Michel Depas his father" and owed his estate nearly 3,000 livres in 1760. Register 1451 of the notary Paillou, 15 October 1783, inventaire, ANSOM.

21. Mordechai Arbell, "Jewish Settlements in the French Colonies in the Caribbean," in this volume, above, cites Abraham Cahen, "Les juifs dans les colonies françaises au 18I siècle" *Revue des études juives* 4 (1882):141.

22. Menkis, "The Gradis Family," 110, 174.

23. This was Governor Charles d'Estaing, whose contempt for Depas and Jews in general is noted below.

24. Register 1451 of the notary Paillou, 15 October 1783, inventaire, ANSOM.
25. Their three marriage contracts assembled property worth 143,200, 61,372 and 60,838 livres, while the white daughter of an indigo planter had a dowry of 93,700 livres and a royal attorney in the same region had 70,000 livres in property at marriage. Register 1415 of the notary Monneront, 14 January 1789, marriage, ANSOM; register 1452 of the notary Paillou, 10 January 1785, marriage, ANSOM; register 1452 of the notary Paillou, 11 April 1785, marriage, ANSOM; register 739 of the notary Gaudin, 15 October 1782, marriage, ANSOM; register 1588 of the notary Scovaud, 16 January 1781, marriage, ANSOM.
   The wealth of this strata of the free colored elite was comparable to that of Bordeaux's wholesale merchants (négociants). Paul Butel found that nearly half the marriage contracts in this French commercial milieu in the years 1787–89 listed property that would have been worth between 17,600 and 68,267 livres in the colonies. Butel, Négociants bordelais, 294.
26. Nevertheless, at least a few other families were. Like the Lopez Depas of Aquin, the Pinet and Dulièpvre of Torbec parish had both "white" and "colored" branches and close relations with other prominent free colored families at Torbec. See register 1587 of the notary Scovaud, 30 October 1780, marriage, ANSOM; register 1588 of the notary Scovaud, 7 May 1781, marriage, ANSOM.
27. Register 1452 of the notary Paillou, 5 April 1785, dépôt des papiers, ANSOM.
28. In 1780 one Louis Daguilard was collecting bills for a French ship in Aquin; register 1587 of the notary Scovaud, 19 November 1780, ANSOM. That same year, however, he bought a schooner (goelette) from a Curaçao captain in the harbor at Les Cayes and resold it to wholesale merchants in the same town. Daguilard was the attorney for the widow of Philippe Lopez Depas and her son-in-law Jacob Gradis in Aquin. Register 1403 of the notary Monneront, 10 October 1781, procuration, ANSOM.
29. Sahlins, "Fictions," 102.
30. Merrick, "Conscience and Citizenship," 69–70.
31. Sahlins, "Fictions," 86–95.
32. Silvia Marzagalli, "Atlantic Trade and Sephardim Merchants in Eighteenth-Century France: The Case of Bordeaux," in this volume, above. The treatment of Bordeaux's Jews was not a simple question of "progress" toward citizenship, however. Louis XVI refused to expand the territory in France in which Bordeaux Jews could enjoy full rights, and in the 1780s there was new intolerance and expropriations against Jews. Sahlins, "Fictions," 99.
33. André Corvisier, Armies and Societies in Europe, 1494–1789 (Bloomington, 1979), 103. In 1791 d'Estaing published a neoclassical tragedy in verse entitled Les thermopyles, according to Alexander Lawrence, Storm over Savannah: The Story of Count d'Estaing and the Siege of the Town in 1779 (Athens, Ga., 1951), 13.
34. Loker, Jews in the Caribbean, 227, cites Col. C9A120, Archives Nationales, d'Estaing's "Nottes sur les Juifs de St. Louis, et des Cayes qui ont offert par requêtes et pour être tolérés de contribuer au bien publique"; Pluchon, Nègres et juifs, 91, 105–6.
35. Loker, Jews in the Caribbean, 230, cites Col. C9A 120, Archives Nationales.
36. Loker, Jews in the Caribbean, 227; Pluchon, Nègres et juifs, 96.
37. See James E. McClellan, Colonialism and Science: Saint Domingue in the Old Regime (Baltimore, 1992), 44, 80, 82, 94, 99.
38. Col. F376, 151, Archives Nationales.
39. Jean Fouchard, Plaisirs de Saint-Domingue: Notes sur sa vie sociale, littéraire et artistique (Port-au-Prince, 1955), 53.
40. Joan Landes, Women and the Public Sphere in the Age of the French Revolution (Ithaca, New York, 1988), 36: cites Spirit of the Laws, Book 7, Chapter 9. On the degree to which Montesquieu's writings were invoked by d'Estaing's opponents, see the unsigned, "Reflexions sur la position actuelle de Saint-Domingue," in Col. F3192, Archives Nationales. In 1776 Hilliard d'Auberteuil attempted to supply "what is lacking from the perfection

of Montesquieu's immortal book" in his controversial *Considérations sur l'état présent de la colonie française de Saint Domingue*, vol. 1 (Paris, 1776), 18–19.

41. On the combination of sexual and political imagery in colonial writings about race, see Garrigus, "Sons of the Same Father," 137–53.

42. See Charles Frostin, *Les révoltes blanches à Saint-Domingue aux XVII et XVIIIe siècles* (Paris, 1975).

43. *Affiches Américaines*, Tuesday, 30 March 1779 no 13; Bibliothèque Nationale 4, lc 12 20/22.

44. Garrigus, "Catalyst or Catastrophe? Saint-Domingue's Free Men of Color and the Battle of Savannah, 1779–1782," *Revista/Review Interamericana* 22 (1/2) (1992):116.

45. See Garrigus, "Sons of the Same Father," for more on this theme.

46. Register 1451 of the notary Paillou, 15 October 1783, inventaire, ANSOM. The Medinas were prominent in Bordeaux and in Curaçao. Pluchon, *Nègres et juifs*, 59; Isaac S. and Suzanne A. Emmanuel, *History of the Jews of the Netherlands Antilles* (Cincinnati, 1970), 691, 695, 697, 700, 1034. Some of the new laws against people of color can be found in Moreau de Saint-Méry, *Loix et constitutions des colonies françaises de l'Amérique sous le vent* (Paris, 1785–1790):4:225, 229, 342, 412, 466, 495; 5:384–85, 823; Col. F3243, p341, Archives Nationales; Col. F3273, 119, Archives Nationales; Col. F391, 115, Archives Nationales; Col. F3189, decree of 2 June 1780, Archives Nationales.

47. Pierre Pluchon, *Histoire de la colonisation française: Le premier empire colonial* (Paris, 1991), 106.

48. In 1751, the Léogane council, the colonial equivalent of a French *parlement*, ordered that the property of David Cardoze be returned to his brother and heir, Emmanuel Cardoze of Bordeaux. In 1759 the council of Port-au-Prince quashed a judicial order against the estate of Moïse Aguilard, and its decision was upheld by the council of Cap Français. Pluchon, *Nègres et juifs*, 110–11.

49. Pluchon, *Nègres et juifs*, 113–15.

50. Moreau de Saint-Méry, *Description*, 373, notes that Jean-Baptiste Suarez d'Almeïda gave a six foot by four foot portrait of Louis XVI to hang in the hall of the local court. Antoine Robert Suarés Dalmeida was at the marriage of David Daguilar and Rachel Pina in Aquin in 1787. Register 1594 of the notary Scovaud, 25 September 1787, marriage, ANSOM.

51. In addition to their political, kin, and commercial connections in Saint-Domingue, the Gradises had already acquired considerable colonial property by collecting on planters' bad debts. This meant that the inheritance problem had already risen once. In 1752 Esther Gradis, married to a Bordeaux gentile, had contested the will of her brother Abraham. She argued that since Jews had no legal status in the French Antilles they could not transfer colonial property in such a document. A colonial court upheld Abraham's Gradis's testament, nevertheless. Pluchon, *Nègres et juifs*, 111; Menkis, "The Gradis Family," 157; Debbasch, "Privilège réal ou privilège personnel? Le statut des 'Juifs portugais' aux îles" in *Religion, société et politique: Mélanges en hommage à Jacques Ellul* (Paris, 1983), 217.

52. Loker, *Jews in the Caribbean*, 238–39.

53. Charles Frostin, "Saint-Domingue et la révolution américaine," *Bulletin de la société d'histoire de la Guadeloupe* 22 (1974):101–2.

54. Pluchon, *Histoire*, 754; Jean Tarrade, *Le commerce colonial de la France à la fin de l'ancien régime: L'évolution du régime de 'l'Exclusif' de 1763–1789*, vol. 2 (Paris, 1972):629.

55. Yvan Debbasch, *Couleur et liberté: Le jeu du critère ethnique dans un ordre esclavagiste* (Paris, 1967), 126; Bailey Stone, *The Genesis of the French Revolution: A Global-Historical Interpretation* (Cambridge, 1994), 125–27.

56. Col. F391, 177–95, Archives Nationales.

57. Wim Klooster, "Subordinate but Proud: Curaçao's Free Blacks and Mulattos in the Eighteenth Century," *New West Indian Guide/Nieuwe West-Indische Gids* 68 (3/4) (1994):294.

58. Sahlins, "Fictions," 86–87.

59. "Précis des gémissemens des sang-mêlés dans les colonies françaises. Par J.M.C. Américain, Sang-mêlé" (Paris, 1789).

60. Gabriel Debien, "Gens de couleur libres et colons de Saint-Domingue devant la constituante, 1789–Mars 1790," *Notes d'histoire coloniale* 18 (Montréal, 1951):26.

61. David Geggus, "Racial Equality, Slavery, and Colonial Secession during the Constituent Assembly," *American Historical Review* 94 (1989):1290–308. A comparison of Grégoire's arguments for Jewish and free colored citizenship is not possible here, but his similar use of gender imagery and other tropes in both causes is striking. See Jean Tild, *L'Abbé Grégoire, d'après ses mémoires* (Paris, 1946), 21; Pluchon, *Nègres et juifs*, 82–87; and Grégoire's free colored writings, for example: Henri Grégoire, "Mémoire en faveur des gens de couleur ou sang-mêlés de St.-Domingue, et des autres Isles françoises de l'Amérique, adressé à l'Assemblée Nationale. Par M. Grégoire, curé d'Embermenil, Député de Lorraine" (Paris, 1789).

62. Col. F391, 183, Archives Nationales.

63. Loker, "Dr. Michel Lopez Depas," cites Séries AD VII "Inventaire des pièces non-imprimées déposées au Comité Colonial de l'Assemblée Générale, liasse A, dossier 2, page 49, note 6, Archives Nationales.

64. Abbé de Cournand, "Requête présentée à nosseigneurs de l'assemblée nationale en faveur des gens de couleur de l'île de Saint Domingue" (Paris, 1790).

65. These connections continued in the Haitian revolution. Free people of color in the southern peninsula were sustained in their struggle against whites in 1792, as in earlier wars, by smugglers from Curaçao. In 1797, Julien Raimond, by then a prominent figure in the government of Toussaint Louverture, chose Philippe Depas the younger, presumably the son of his neighbor, as one of four men "worthy of confidence" in the southern peninsula, including him on a list with his own brother, another close free mulatto friend, and a respected white moderate. He described Depas as a "white colonist, respected for his knowledge and his character." Julien Raimond, *Rapport de Julien Raimond, commissaire délégué par le gouvernement français aux Isles-sous-le-vent, au Ministre de la Marine* (Cap Français, an V), 6. In 1799 the failed attempt of the Sephardic merchant Isaac Sasportas to raise black and free colored rebels in Curaçao and then Jamaica for Toussaint Louverture again shows the use of Jewish commercial connections during the revolution. Zvi Loker, "An Eighteenth-Century Plan to Invade Jamaica: Isaac Yeshuron Sasportas, French Patriot or Jewish Radical Idealist?" *Transactions, Jewish Historical Society of England* 28 (1984):132–44.

PART V

BLOSSOMING IN ANOTHER WORLD: THE JEWS AND THE JEWISH COMMUNITIES IN DUTCH AMERICA

– Chapter 17 –

THE JEWS OF DUTCH AMERICA

Jonathan I. Israel

T HE FIRST HALF OF THE EIGHTEENTH CENTURY undoubtedly represents
the most flourishing period of Dutch America in practically every
respect and also the most flourishing phase by far of the Jewish communities in Dutch America. At that time, the Sephardic congregations of
Curaçao and Suriname were the largest and commercially most important Jewish communities to be found anywhere in the Western Hemisphere, and it was during the eighteenth century that the Jews of the
Dutch American colonies exerted their greatest impact on the economic,
political, and cultural life of the New World as a whole.

The two principal Jewish communities in the Dutch American
colonies were, as has often been remarked, very different in character.
Curaçao, the larger and more prosperous of the two, was essentially a
maritime commercial and financial center with links all over the
Caribbean and South and North America, as well as with Amsterdam
and the rest of the United Provinces. It could, with some justification, be
called the "Amsterdam of the Caribbean." As a consequence of its geographical position and economic role, Curaçao Jewry always maintained close religious, social, and cultural ties—to an extent and in ways
that the Jews of Suriname and the small communities of western
Guyana could not—with all the other Jewish communities of the
Caribbean and North America, in the latter case principally New York
and Rhode Island. Whereas Suriname had little direct contact with the
Jewish communities in the Americas outside the Guyanas, except for
Curaçao, Curaçao was the hub around which the communities on St.
Eustatius, St. Maarten, and, to an extent, all the other Jewish communi-
ties in the New World revolved.

Suriname Jewry, by contrast, together with the small communities in western Guyana, was in the main, until the 1760s, a plantation society. The bulk of its members were planters (or belonged to the families of planters, or those who worked for, or with, the planters) engaged in tropical agriculture. From the origins of Suriname Jewry in the middle of the seventeenth century until the beginning of the eighteenth century, the Suriname plantations were overwhelmingly geared toward production of sugar cane. Later, coffee also developed into a major cash crop. During the second half of the eighteenth century, however, Suriname's plantation economy—most of all, the Jewish sector of it—rapidly declined. Whereas in 1730 Jews still owned 115 out of 440 sugar and coffee plantations in Suriname, by 1788 this figure had dropped to only forty-six.[1] Two substantial synagogues were to be seen in Suriname: one, built in 1685, was inland, among the plantations, situated on the Suriname River; the other, of considerably later construction (1735), was on the coast, in the port of Paramaribo.[2] An exceptionally grand occasion in the history of Suriname Jewry occurred in 1785 at the time of the celebrations to mark the centenary of the inauguration of the synagogue of Jodensavanne, as the inland synagogue and the Jewish village around it were called. The governor of the colony and other colonial dignitaries attended, as did all the leading figures of the Jewish community of Paramaribo. It was a glittering event: the magnificent banquet offered to the guests was illuminated by over a thousand Chinese lanterns. But it was also a deeply melancholy event, for by that time only a handful of Jews, some twenty impoverished families, still resided at Jodensavanne.[3] The Jewish planter elite and their society had virtually disintegrated. The great bulk of Suriname Jewry had drifted to Paramaribo and had been transformed into a maritime trading community. If, by 1791, the total population of Paramaribo was estimated at nearly 13,000, no fewer than 1,050 of these were Jews (620 Sephardim and 430 Ashkenazim).[4] Besides these, there were only another 200 or so Jews, mostly Sephardim, scattered among the plantations and at Jodensavanne. Thus, by the end of the eighteenth century, Curaçao and Suriname Jewry, formerly each so different from the other, had come to resemble each other: both dwelt in sizable harbor towns economically and culturally tied to commerce, shipping, and the sea.

Meanwhile, at Curaçao, the synagogue Mikveh Israel, which had been constructed in the years 1730–32 to replace an earlier, smaller structure, was both the largest synagogue in the Dutch American colonies and the largest to be found in the Western Hemisphere. It remains today one of the prime tourist sites of the Caribbean in the midst of a well-preserved Dutch colonial town, which retains much of its eighteenth-century character and profile. Curaçao can indeed be said to have been the "mother" community of the Jewish Caribbean ever since the 1660s.[5]

In 1702, there were 126 Jewish families (the great majority Sephardic) living on Curaçao, totaling together with a number of widows and other single people over 600 souls, a figure that, by 1789, had risen to over

1,500.[6] Of these, 1,495 were reported as living in the island's main town, Willemstad, with just two or three dozen living on the island's estates and on the neighboring island of Aruba. Meanwhile, what was originally a small Sephardi community—in 1722 there were only 21 Jews out of a total population of 204—on the island of St. Eustatius, little more than a large rock in the sea near Puerto Rico, grew into an extremely vigorous trading community of middling size by the third quarter of the century.[7] The original synagogue of St. Eustatius was built in the years 1737–38. After this structure was demolished by a hurricane, a second and larger synagogue was constructed in 1772.

Compared with all the other Jewish communities in the New World, the commercial and cultural connections of the Jews of Curaçao and St. Eustatius were exceptionally extensive and widespread. While commerce and the sea were fundamental to all the Jewish and Portuguese New Christian congregations in the New World, Edmund Burke's remark in reference to the Jews of St. Eustatius, which describes them as the "links of communication in the mercantile chain," applies more comprehensively and impressively to these two communities than to any others.[8] It is true that the Jewish communities of Barbados and Jamaica in the eighteenth century were relatively large: that of Barbados has been estimated at over four hundred by 1750,[9] and that of Jamaica at around nine hundred by 1770. But, in large part, this was due to both islands being major plantation economies with much larger total populations than Curaçao or St. Eustatius and to the fact that Jews played a significant role in retailing. With regard to Jewish involvement in inter-American trade, however, neither of their Jewish communities can be said to have rivaled Curaçao or St. Eustatius in the mid-eighteenth century.

There were continual shifts in the pattern of Curaçao's inter-American commerce, and the table, which appears at the end of this chapter, listing fifty-nine ships arriving at Curaçao during the six-month period from July to December 1714 probably overstates the intensity for the eighteenth century as a whole of the island's links with the North American colonies, and certainly underestimates the intensity of Curaçao's links with La Guaira and other ports of central Venezuela, near Caracas. What is entirely typical is Curaçao's unique role as a bridge between Spanish America, English America, and French America, as well as with the Danish island of St. Thomas, and its function as a conduit linking all these with the Dutch global maritime trading system centered in Amsterdam.[10]

The largest category of vessels arriving in the port of Willemstad in the second half of 1714 had sailed via St. Thomas, an island in the northern Caribbean near Puerto Rico which though officially Danish had a community of planters and merchants most of whom were Dutch and which, with the liberal trading policy upheld by the Danish crown, functioned, for all practical purposes, as part of the Dutch New World maritime trading system.[11] As always in Curaçao's maritime history, numerous vessels arrived from Venezuela and other parts of Spanish America, particularly Hispaniola and Puerto Rico. At the same time, many ships arrived from the English colonies. Curaçao's thriving commerce with North America, illegal in the eyes of the British crown and Parliament, was in no small measure an extension of the trade with Spanish America, which, since being opened up in the 1660s, was the foundation of the island's prosperity. The traffic to the Venezuela coast and Spanish islands was conducted in small vessels—sloops and barques—since the northern coast of Spanish South America had very few harbors that were safe for larger vessels and, from these, foreign vessels were largely excluded by the Spanish crown. At the height of its prosperity, Curaçao had a fleet of some eighty barques and sloops, a considerable proportion owned by Jews.[12] On the outward voyage to Venezuelan ports, these barques carried textiles and other manufactured goods shipped out from Amsterdam, as well as slaves. On their return to Willemstad they brought a constant stream of silver, dyewoods, cacao, and high-quality tobaccos. But to service Curaçao's large traffic, fit out the ships, and feed the island's population, garrison and seamen—the island then as now was rather barren, had few trees and low rainfall—large quantities of provisions and ships' stores were needed. These supplies were often obtained from New York, which retained its predominantly Dutch character at least until the middle of the eighteenth century, and also from Boston, Rhode Island, and Virginia. In exchange for these supplies, the North American colonists—illegally in British eyes—imported Dutch manufactures and East India commodities.

The importance of Venezuela in the Dutch Atlantic trading system as a whole derived partly from its large output of cacao and the good quality of its tobaccos, and partly also from its trade with other parts of Spanish South America, which generated a constant flow of silver along the Andean passes to Caracas. A valuable part of Curaçao's traffic with the mainland involved the western Venezuelan ports of Coro, Rio de la Hacha, and Maracaibo which stood opposite the entrance to the main passes running southwest between the two principal spines of the Andean sierra all the way to Popayán, Quito, and the viceroyalty of Peru.[13] In this way, Curaçao also formed a commercial link between the Spanish American Pacific and the Atlantic.

It was in order to tap into this thriving transit traffic along the north coast of South America and to purchase cacao that Dutch and Dutch Jewish colonists established the settlement at Tucacas, facing Aruba, on the northwest coast of the peninsula of Paraguana, in western Venezuela, in or around 1693.[14] Despite several attacks by Spanish troops and Indians sent from Coro, the Jewish community at Tucacas maintained its existence and a substantial trade at least until well into the 1720s. The locality was inaccessible yet close to major trade routes. The merchandise was mostly stored in warehouses on a small offshore island, which on at least one occasion was successfully defended by fire from four armed Dutch vessels. Reportedly, most of the Jews' houses and a small synagogue were located on the mainland.

Of course, the merchants on Curaçao and St. Eustatius, or at Paramaribo, St. Thomas, or for that matter, Tucacas, were by no means all Jewish—far from it. On Curaçao, as in Jamaica and Barbados, there were groups of wealthy and influential Protestant merchants who had no particular liking for the Jews and, on occasion, sought to use political and legal means to prejudice or obstruct Jewish involvement in trade. Analysis of Curaçao's trade with Amsterdam in the early eighteenth century shows that a majority of the merchants participating in importing and exporting from, and to, the United Provinces—booking space on the large West India Company vessels used to carry much of the traffic—were in fact Sephardic Jews. Nevertheless, the largest and wealthiest participants in the commerce were Dutch Protestants and several German Lutherans.[15] Overall, it would seem that the Jews accounted for considerably less than half of the total traffic between Amsterdam and the Caribbean, but their role was, even so, very substantial. When the marine insurance consortium, or society of underwriters, maintained by the Curaçao merchants was reorganized in 1759, Jews owned 123—slightly under one-third—of the total of four hundred shares.[16] It is probable that this sort of proportion, roughly one-third, characterizes the Jewish role in Curaçao's trade as a whole.

The fact that the largest and most flourishing Jewish communities in the Americas in the seventeenth and eighteenth centuries were those in the Dutch colonies might well appear, at first glance, to be a direct result of the fact that in the seventeenth century the Dutch Republic was—and enjoyed the reputation of being—the most tolerant of European societies. If the Jews in Curaçao, Suriname, western Guyana, St. Eustatius, and New York possessed a greater degree of economic, legal, and religious freedom than Jews did in other parts of the Americas, one might well suppose that it is the Dutch context in Europe that explains this. And yet it is arguable that the relative tolerance of the United Provinces compared to other European societies in the seventeenth and eighteenth centuries is not a sufficient explanation of why the Jewish communities in Dutch America presided over Jewish life in the New World until the end of the eighteenth century to the extent that they did. In the first place, the Dutch colonial context was often noticeably less tolerant in religious matters than was society in the Dutch homeland itself, especially as compared to the province of Holland. This is evident not only in the example of the territories under the rule of the Dutch East India Company (VOC), including Dutch South Africa, which was notoriously intolerant until the beginning of the nineteenth century,[17] but also in the social context established in New Netherland, which until the late 1650s was likewise characterized more by Calvinist intolerance than by any tendency to promote religious and social freedom.[18] In the second place, it is undeniable that after the Glorious Revolution of 1688–91, society in Britain and the British colonies in the Americas was at least as flexible and accommodating toward religious dissenters and minorities as the Dutch Republic, and arguably more so.

Nevertheless, it is as true of the eighteenth century as it is of the seventeenth that Jews in the English colonies in the New World did not play as large a part in inter-American commerce and navigation, and were not as prominent in the trade between the motherland and the Western Hemisphere, as were the Jews of the Dutch American colonies. The most important reason for this striking difference, in my view, lies not in any European factor but rather in the psychological, cultural, and economic consequences of the relatively brief, but profound, Jewish experience in Brazil.[19] The crucial difference between the Jewish trading communities in the English and Dutch colonies is that the latter were much more successful in establishing enduring links with the markets of Ibero-America. This success seemingly had its origins in the strategy adopted by the Dutch early in the seventeenth century in Brazil. After its formation in the years 1621–22, the Dutch West India Company selected as its chief objective in the Americas, and concentrated most of its resources on, the attempt to wrest control of Brazil's sugar production—and with it the entire European market for sugar—from the Portuguese. This strategy, rather than that of capturing islands in the Caribbean to use as trading bases or of colonizing tracts of land in North America, required the West India Company to rely to a quite unprecedented extent on Sephardic Jews as intermediaries and adjuncts to support its trade.

As a newly created organization, the West India Company could not embark on a vast and complex enterprise in Brazil without drawing on skills, expertise, information, and resources acquired previously by others. Ever since the 1590s, Amsterdam and its sugar refineries had been importing growing quantities of Brazilian sugar indirectly, via Lisbon and Oporto, by means of a commercial network largely dominated by Portuguese New Christians collaborating with relatives who had returned to normative Judaism in Amsterdam and Hamburg.[20] A set of links had been created connecting the Jewish community in Amsterdam—whose business life in the early decades of its existence was chiefly geared to the importing of Brazilian produce—with closely related New Christian merchant communities in metropolitan Portugal and in Brazil, as well as other parts of the Portuguese empire, including the Azores and Madeira, which frequently figured in the maritime interactions between Portugal and Brazil. Moreover, though most cargoes of Brazilian produce reaching the Jews of Amsterdam before 1621 came indirectly, via Lisbon and Oporto, having crossed the Atlantic in Portuguese ships, there is no doubt that a certain proportion of consignments were shipped directly from Brazil to Sephardic merchants in Amsterdam and also Hamburg.

Significantly, one of the earliest documents that has survived concerning the direct passage of ships returning from the New World to the Netherlands expressly states that it is "true that on a number of occasions various ships sailing from Brazil and thereabouts, and having loaded there with sugar and brazilwood, have arrived here by-passing Portugal."[21] In July 1603, one of the leading Portuguese merchants in

Amsterdam at that time, Manoel Rodrigues Vega, indicated the name of his factor residing at Bahia in Brazil, Dias Querido, mentioning that he had sent him cargoes of knives and haberdashery. Several of the Jews who settled in Amsterdam early in the seventeenth century had in fact lived in Brazil, under Portuguese rule. One of these men, Diogo Dias Querido, whose name in the synagogue was David Querido—probably the same person who had been Rodrigues Vega's correspondent in Bahia, Dias Querido, who is known to have lived for several years in Brazil and who was a native of Oporto—became a substantial merchant in Amsterdam. In 1604 this Diogo Dias Querido had 1,900 guilders invested in the Dutch East India Company, and in 1611 he was named in a debate in the Consejo de estado, the highest-ranking council of the Spanish monarchy, as one of the principal Dutch interlopers in the Guinea trade. Dias Querido imported sugar to Holland from both Brazil and the West African colony of São Tomé, usually via Lisbon from where he also shipped sugar to Livorno and Venice.[22]

During the early 1630s, the West India Company captured sizable portions of northern Brazil, invested heavily in forts and garrisons to defend its Brazilian conquests, and found itself under intense pressure from investors to develop its newly acquired but half-ruined colony as rapidly as possible. Many of the sugar plantations had been destroyed in the fighting, and it was probably impossible to restore the colony's earlier profitability and prosperity without encouraging the existing Portuguese planters to reinvest in their plantations and sugar mills and to buy fresh slaves and equipment. Such a strategy would have required the West India Company to advance supplies, equipment, slaves, and money on credit, which the Company, with its huge expenditures on military and naval armaments, its ten thousand employees, and its rapidly mounting debts, was in no position to do.[23] There was in fact no alternative but to permit and encourage Portuguese Jewish emigrants from Amsterdam— drawing on the capital of the Amsterdam Sephardic community—to settle in sizable numbers in Dutch Brazil and become the brokers and intermediaries, the links in the chain, that got the Dutch Brazilian economy working again. While the Company retained its monopoly over the importing of slaves, which it shipped in from West Africa, and over the export of brazilwood, a red dyewood important in the European textile industry, it was forced by circumstances to turn over to the Jews most of the business of advancing money, goods, and slaves to the planters, and, in exchange, the business of buying up the raw sugar. From the outset, the Jews were the principal intermediaries between the Dutch West India Company and the Portuguese Catholic planters.[24] A few of the Jews who settled in Dutch Brazil themselves acquired plantations and sugar mills, but the great majority resided in Recife or other fortified places and engaged in trade.

In this way, Sephardic Jews of Portuguese origin, who already knew the language of the country and had a long experience of the trade in

Brazil sugar, became the largest group of white civilians living under Dutch rule in northern Brazil, evidently outnumbering both the Dutch Protestants (other than soldiers), on the one hand, and Portuguese Catholics, on the other. By 1644, at which point the Jewish community of Dutch Brazil was at its zenith, Jews numbered approximately 1,450 out of a total white civilian population in the colony of some three thousand.[25] For a time, the revived sugar economy of New Holland, as the Dutch called northern Brazil, flourished, enabling the West India Company to dominate the European sugar market for some ten to twelve years.[26] The colony's resurgent economy was completely ruined, however, by the uprising of the Portuguese Catholic planters, backed by forces sent from Bahia, against the Dutch and Dutch Jews—the latter being hated both as religious enemies and as creditors—which erupted in 1645. Almost the entire colony outside the walls of Recife was engulfed in fighting. Within months, most of the sugar plantations had been burned and the colony's agriculture, commerce, and financial systems paralyzed. Although the Dutch retained control of Recife and its immediate vicinity and some other localities until 1654, when all the remaining Dutch fortresses in Brazil were surrendered to the Portuguese, and although a substantial core of the Jewish community remained in Recife until the end, half or more of the Jews who had settled there left in the intervening period, as confidence that the Dutch would be able to restore their military control and their rule gradually evaporated. Most of these Jews returned across the Atlantic to the United Provinces but a substantial number remained in the New World or eventually returned there after a period in the Dutch Republic.

The success and vigor of Jewish society in Dutch Brazil had been short-lived, lasting only from around 1633 to 1645, by which date it was effectively undermined. But it was also unprecedented and unique as regards the considerable degree of economic and religious freedom, as well as the secure legal status, that the Jews who emigrated to Dutch Brazil had been able to secure from the West India Company. A new kind of Jewish society had been created, quite different from any previous Jewish society in the Old World, geared to tropical agriculture and based on skills and expertise that the Jews were in an exceptionally strong position to exercise. This created the possibility that the Jews would function as intermediaries between the Dutch and any Ibero-American markets that the Netherlanders might prise open in the future and would powerfully contribute to the development of plantation agriculture.

Why intermediaries between the Dutch and Ibero-America, and not between the English and Ibero-America? It would be wrong to argue that in the middle years of the seventeenth century the Dutch colonies in the New World were in need of the skills, expertise, and resources of Jews forced out of Brazil while the English colonies were not. By the time the last batch of more than six hundred Jews departed from Recife in Dutch ships following the surrender of the colony in 1654, the island of Barbados was already developing under English rule into the most thriving sugar economy in the Caribbean, with the assistance of a number of Dutch and Dutch Jewish entrepreneurs, while it was only one year later, in 1655, that English forces wrested Jamaica from the Spaniards.[27] Furthermore, the new English Parliamentary regime, headed by Oliver Cromwell, showed much more interest in accommodating the Jews within England's expanding mercantile system than the Stuart kings had previously. Consequently, it hardly seems possible to argue that Sephardic Jewish skills and enterprise in the Americas in subsequent decades came to be concentrated in the Dutch rather than the English colonies because the former were more tolerant or accommodating during the crucially formative decades following the collapse of Dutch Brazil.

The true explanation in my view is not that the Dutch were more tolerant than the English in the period from the 1650s onwards, but rather that the wider geo-political context of the New World during the second half of the seventeenth century did not favor an English breakthrough in terms of trade, investment, and maritime contacts into the markets of Spanish America. The chief reason for this, I would argue, is that the Spanish, who were aggressively attacked by Cromwell's England in 1655 and remained at war with England until 1660, were now (in contrast to the first half of the seventeenth century) a good deal more afraid of England's rapidly growing military, naval, and commercial might in the Western Hemisphere than they were of the no longer rapidly expanding Dutch trading system. In fact, it was clear by the 1650s that England had more potential for attacking and dismembering Spain's American empire—and a far more active interest in doing so—than any other European power. After the final peace between Spain and the Dutch was signed at Münster in 1648, the Dutch Republic continued to be considered a commercial threat to Spain's interests in America, but no longer the kind of political and strategic threat that both England and France increasingly showed themselves to be.

During the second half of the 1650s, Spain was at war with both France and England, and its normal transatlantic maritime system was heavily disrupted, causing severe shortages of imports of every kind, including slaves, throughout Spanish America. The result was a sensational upsurge in smuggling in open violation of the Spanish crown's highly restrictive mercantile regulations, with illegal cargoes being shipped to Buenos Aires as well as to numerous ports in the Spanish Caribbean, a traffic heavily dominated by the Dutch.[28] This activity was extensively connived at not only by Spanish officials in the colonies but now also by ministers in Madrid. The feeling was that if Spain's American colonies had to obtain supplies and slaves from somewhere, it was better to obtain them from the Dutch, who were no longer a threat to the physical existence of the Spanish American empire, than from the English and French, who were. In the early 1660s, this new and close interaction between the Dutch colonies and Spanish America was made semi-legal by the decision of the Spanish crown to sign contracts for slave imports to

Spanish America with a group of Genoese factors in Madrid, who were authorized to obtain their slaves from Curaçao.[29] This proved to be the decisive step in making Curaçao the principal link in the direct traffic between the Dutch colonies and Spanish America and in inducing the West India Company to tolerate what soon became a thriving private trade in small barques and sloops between Curaçao and the Spanish American mainland.[30]

The crucial importance of Spanish policy during the second half of the seventeenth century in determining the shape and distribution of Jewish settlement and activity in the New World is, in my view, demonstrated by the reluctance until the late 1650s of the Dutch West India Company to tolerate Jewish private trade outside of Brazil. Even in Dutch Brazil there had been a certain amount of opposition from the predominantly Protestant investors in the West India Company, and from the Zeeland and some other regional chambers of the Company in the Netherlands, to the large measure of private (and especially Jewish) trade that the Company's chief directors had been persuaded to permit. There was a strong feeling among the investors that the Company in which they had invested their money, and which had to shoulder the huge costs of conquering and garrisoning Brazil, ought to reap all the profits.

With the collapse of the economy of Dutch Brazil in 1645–46, both the Company and the Jews began to think seriously about transferring both sugar production and the sugar trade elsewhere. For more than a decade, until the late 1650s, the Company's directors pursued a policy of willingness to put Jewish skills and enterprise to work in developing the agricultural potential of their American colonies (other than Brazil), while at the same time attempting to block Jewish participation in the commerce of these same colonies.

This phenomenon is evident in the case of New Netherland, where the Calvinist town council of New Amsterdam responded to the arrival of several groups of Sephardic Jews, who had left Brazil in 1654, by endeavoring to obstruct their entry into shopkeeping as well as general commerce. In their letter of 26 April 1655 to Peter Stuyvesant, the governor of New Netherland, the West India Company directors remarked that they would have liked to accede to the pressure from the Protestant population to exclude the Jews from the colony entirely, but had decided that this would have been unjust, since the Jews had sustained very heavy losses at the hands of the Portuguese in Brazil, and inadvisable "because of the large amount of capital which they have invested in the shares of this Company."[31] Consequently, the Jews were permitted to settle in New Netherland, but under greater restrictions than they had been subjected to in Brazil as regards both their trade and their religious activity. Later that year, Stuyvesant expressly forbade the Jews to trade up the Hudson River to Fort Orange (i.e., Albany) or on the Delaware River.[32] The Jews complained to the Company directors, and in June 1656, the company wrote instructing the governor that the Jews were to be allowed to trade to Fort Orange and on the Delaware, but, in contrast to Brazil, were to remain excluded from shopkeeping, as they were in Amsterdam itself.[33] In January of 1657, Stuyvesant and the New Netherland colonial council issued measures to ensure Jewish exclusion from all retailing except for religious articles and ritually slaughtered meat for their own community.

Another illustration of the tendency in the aftermath of the Brazilian revolt to try to obstruct Jewish entry into commerce in the other Dutch American colonies is the Company's policy for the three "Curaçao islands"—Curaçao, Bonaire, and Aruba. It is remarkable that in the long period between the Dutch occupation of these islands in 1634 and the late 1650s, the Curaçao islands totally failed to develop into any sort of Caribbean trading entrepôt under Dutch control. Despite the fact that Willemstad was one of the best harbors in the Caribbean, and despite Curaçao's proximity to the Spanish American mainland, the islands attracted practically no trade—to such an extent that on several occasions, including in 1651, the West India Company directors seriously considered abandoning the islands altogether so as to save the expense of garrisoning them.[34] Yet even in these unpromising circumstances, several years after the disruption of the economy of Dutch Brazil, the Company still showed itself unwilling to countenance the establishment of a Jewish trading network based on Curaçao.

The first contract for Jewish settlement on Curaçao, drawn up between the Company and João de Yllão in March 1651, provided for the shipping of fifty Jewish colonists to the island for the purpose of cultivating the land and establishing plantations, but not for Jewish participation in trade. Indeed, the Company directors were suspicious—as they confided to Stuyvesant, at the time governor of Curaçao—that the offer on the part of the Jews to establish plantations was just a pretext to get the Company to agree to Jews being admitted to the islands, and that in reality de Yllão "and his associates have quite another objective in view, namely to trade from there to the West Indies and the Spanish Main."[35] When in the following year the Company directors signed a second contract for Jewish settlement on Curaçao, this time with David Nassi (alias Joseph Nunes da Fonseca), the latter undertook to bring "a large number of people," many of whom were doubtless refugees from Brazil, to cultivate the land, but again there was no permission to trade. "Time will tell whether we shall succeed well with his nation," the directors wrote to Stuyvesant. "They are a crafty and generally treacherous people in whom therefore not too much confidence should be placed."[36] The contract expressly reserved the logwood and salt assets on the three islands—their only valuable resources—for the Company's own use, and also failed to grant Nassi and his associates full freedom of religion, such as they had enjoyed in Brazil. By late 1652 the Company directors had concluded that João de Yllão and the twelve other Jews who had settled on Curaçao with him—there is no evidence that Nassi ever went—were neglecting to "plant tobacco, indigo, cotton and other staples," which is what they had been given permission to do, and were in fact busy cutting logwood and trying to use it to trade with other Caribbean islands, and were also exporting the islands' horses. The directors wrote to Curaçao insisting that "no more horses shall be exported from Buenairo, Curaçao and Aruba but they shall remain there to be used in time in our province of New Netherland."[37] In June 1653 it was again reported that the Jews on Curaçao were not cultivating the land but cutting dyewood and "exporting horses from the islands of Aruba and Bonaires to the Caribbean and other neighbouring isles."[38]

Nor was this restrictive policy applied at this stage only in New Netherland and the Curaçao islands. During the 1650s, the West India Company was interested in developing the island of Tobago—which the Dutch called New Walcheren—as a commercial depot close to the Guyanas, but were reluctant to permit the Jews to engage in Caribbean commerce from there.[39] Even in the case of the (in most respects) extremely liberal privileges conceded in 1657 by the Zeeland towns for Jewish settlement in western Guyana, or Nova Zeelandia as it was then called, the stress was on religious freedom and on encouraging the Jews to acquire land and establish plantations as well as to engage in "hunting and fishing" rather than on the establishment of commerce, though the document does concede that "it shall be lawful to trade with the Indians."[40] Only in 1659 were the Jews on Curaçao granted full freedom to trade.

In conclusion, in the 1640s and during most of the 1650s there was little or no disposition on the part of the Dutch West India Company to encourage the Jews to rebuild in other parts of Dutch America the kind of large-scale transatlantic commerce that they had been able to develop in Brazil in the 1630s and early 1640s. There was, in fact, absolutely no intrinsic reason why the principal Jewish trading and maritime network in the New World of the late seventeenth and eighteenth centuries should have been based in Dutch America rather than in the English Caribbean colonies. That Curaçao became the principal hub of Jewish inter-American trade—along with St. Eustatius, St. Thomas, and several other depots after 1660—seems to be due chiefly to geo-political factors and, in particular, to the marriage of convenience that developed in the New World maritime trade between the Spanish empire and the Dutch Republic from the late 1650s until the end of the Habsburg era in Spain in 1700. It was during those decades that the Jews of Dutch America became what might fairly be described as the preeminent intermediaries and specialists in inter-American trade.

TABLE 17.1 The Inter-American Trade of Curaçao and St. Eustatius

| | Curaçao (July–Dec. 1714) | | St. Eustatius (1773) |
	arriving from	leaving for	arriving from
St. Thomas (Danish)	14	1	0
New York (New Amsterdam)	9	5	3
Venezuela	7	3	0
Hispañola	7	3	0
Jamaica	3	1	1
Antigua	2	2	4
Nevis	2	0	1
Virginia-Maryland, N. Carolina	2	0	3
Rhode Island (Root Eiland)	1	1	13
Barbados	6	2	8
Boston	1	0	5
Bermuda	0	1	3
Guadeloupe	0	0	24
Martinique	0	0	23
Saint Christopher	0	0	9
Saint Maarten	0	0	5
Puerto Rico	1	0	1
Tobago	1	0	0
Monserrat	0	0	2

Notes

1. Robert Cohen, *Jews in Another Environment: Surinam in the Second Half of the Eighteenth Century* (Leiden, 1991), 61–75; see also Cornelis Ch. Goslinga, *The Dutch in the Caribbean and in the Guianas 1680–1791* (Assen, 1985), 353, 362.
2. On the synagogues of Suriname, see Günter Böhm, "The Synagogues of Suriname," *Journal of Jewish Art* 6 (1978):98–104; and the essay by Rachel Frankel in this volume.
3. Goslinga, *The Dutch in the Caribbean*, 363.
4. Cohen, *Jews in Another Environment*, 63–65; Goslinga, *The Dutch in the Caribbean*, 519.
5. Yosef Kaplan, "The Curaçao and Amsterdam Jewish Communities in the 17th and 18th Centuries," *American Jewish History* 72 (1982):197–202; Yosef Hayim Yerushalmi, "Between Amsterdam and New Amsterdam: The Place of Curaçao and the Caribbean in Early Modern Jewish History," *American Jewish History* 72 (1982):191–92.
6. I. S. and S. A. Emmanuel, *History of the Jews of the Netherlands Antilles*, 2 vols. (Cincinnati, 1970), vol. 1, 277, and vol. 2, 763; Goslinga, *The Dutch in the Caribbean*, 263 and 239; J. I. Israel, "The Sephardi Contribution to Economic Life and Colonization in Europe and the New World (16th–18th Centuries)," in *Moreshet Sepharad: The Sephardi Legacy*, ed. Haim Beinart (Jerusalem, 1992), 389–90.
7. Emmanuel, *History*, vol. 1, 519, 522, and 524; see also Günter Böhm, *Los sefardíes en los dominios holandeses de América del sur y del Caribe 1630–1750* (Frankfurt, 1992), 219–22.
8. Emmanuel, *History*, vol. 1, 525.
9. See S. A. Fortune, *Merchants and Jews: The Struggle for British West Indian Commerce, 1650–1750* (Gainesville, Fla., 1984), 48.
10. J. I. Israel, *Dutch Primacy in World Trade, 1585–1740* (Oxford, 1989), 396.
11. On the links between St. Thomas and Curaçao, see Israel, *Dutch Primacy*, 326, 368–69, 374; and W. Westergaard, *The Danish West Indies under Company Rule (1671–1764)* (New York, 1917), 121, 209, 332.
12. Georges Scelle, *La traite négrière aux Indes de Castille: contrats et traites d'Assiento*, 2 vols. (Paris, 1906), vol. 2, 160, 309–10; Israel, *Dutch Primacy*, 369.
13. Israel, *Dutch Primacy*, 323–24, 369.
14. I am greatly indebted to Mordechai Arbell for allowing me to see the typescript of his article on Jewish settlement in Tucacas, forthcoming in *American Jewish Archives*.
15. See the lists of commodity and bullion consignments from Curaçao to Amsterdam in Algemeen Rijksarchief, The Hague, West India Company Archives, vols. 568 and 569. However, the Jewish share of Curaçao's trade with the Spanish American mainland was probably larger than this; see Goslinga, *The Dutch in the Caribbean*, 240.
16. Goslinga, *The Dutch in the Caribbean*, 201.
17. J. I. Israel, *The Dutch Republic: Its Rise, Greatness, and Fall 1477–1806* (Oxford, 1995), 951–56.
18. G. L. Smith, *Religion and Trade in New Netherland* (Ithaca, N.Y., 1973), 190–94, 215–16.
19. Israel, "Sephardi Contribution to Economic Life," 380–84; see also J. I. Israel, "Dutch Sephardi Jewry, Millenarian Politics, and the Struggle for Brazil (1640–1654)," in *Sceptics, Millenarians and Jews*, ed. D. S. Katz and J. I. Israel (Leiden, 1990), 76–97.
20. J. I. Israel, "The Changing Role of the Dutch Sephardim in International Trade, 1595–1715," *Dutch Jewish History* 1 (1984):33–42.
21. See E. M. Koen, ed., "Amsterdam Notarial Deeds Pertaining to the Portuguese Jews in Amsterdam up to 1639," no. 87, in *Studia Rosenthaliana* 2 (1968):257: "verclaert ende geaffirmeert hoe waerachtig is dat tot meermalen diversche scheepen uit Bresilien ende die quartieren commende (ende alder suyckeren ende bresilienhout geladen hebbende) alhier te lande sijn gearriveert ende Portugael verbijgeloopen, alwaer die selve schepen gedestineert waren ..."
22. J. I. Israel, "The Jews of Venice and Their Links with Holland and with Dutch Jewry (1600–1710)," in *Gli ebrei e Venezia secoli XIV–XVIII*, ed. Gaetano Cozzi (Milan, 1987), 101–2.

23. C. R. Boxer, *The Dutch in Brazil 1624–1654* (Hamden, Conn., 1973), 64–66, 75–80.
24. Ibid., 133–44; Arnold Wiznitzer, *The Jews of Colonial Brazil* (New York, 1960), 120–38; Israel, "Dutch Sephardi Jewry, Millenarian Politics, and the Struggle for Brazil," 76–88.
25. Arnold Wiznitzer, "The Number of Jews in Dutch Brazil, 1603–1654," *Jewish Social Studies* 16 (1954):107–14; I. S. Emmanuel, "Seventeenth-Century Brazilian Jewry: A Critical Review," *American Jewish Archives* 14 (1962):32–68; see, however, the dissenting view in Böhm, *Los sefardies*, 67–69.
26. Israel, *Dutch Primacy*, 167–70; Israel, "Sephardi Contribution to Economic Life," 382–83.
27. V. T. Harlow, *A History of Barbados, 1625–1685* (Oxford, 1926), 44, 93–94; J. I. Israel, "Menasseh ben Israel and the Dutch Sephardic Colonization Movement of the Mid-Seventeenth Century (1645–1657)," in *Menasseh ben Israel and His World*, ed. Yosef Kaplan, Henri Méchoulan, and Richard H. Popkin (Leiden, 1989), 144, 148–50.
28. Israel, *Dutch Primacy*, 240–42.
29. Scelle, *Traite négrière*, vol. 1, 484–85; S. van Brakel, "Bescheiden over den slavenhandel der West-Indische Compagnie," *Economisch-Historisch Jaarboek* 4 (1918):61–66; J. M. Postma, *The Dutch in the Atlantic Slave Trade 1600–1815* (Cambridge, 1990), 33–36.
30. In March 1661, the Spanish ambassador at The Hague reported to Madrid that the Dutch on Curaçao had now "established large stores with every kind of merchandise there which they deliver during the night, using long boats, taking back silver bars and other goods," Archivo General de Simancas, Libros de la Haya, vol. 43, fo. 94.
31. Smith, *Religion and Trade in New Netherland*, 214.
32. Ibid., 215.
33. Ibid., 216.
34. Van Brakel, "Bescheiden," 49–50; W. R. Menkman, *De Nederlanders in het Caraibische zeegebied* (Amsterdam, 1942), 44–45.
35. G. H. Cone, "The Jews of Curaçao According to Documents from the Archives of the State of New York," *Publications of the American Jewish Historical Society* 10 (1902):143.
36. G. H. Cone, "The Jews of Curaçao," 147–49; Emmanuel, *History*, vol. 1, 43.
37. Cone, "The Jews of Curaçao," 150.
38. Ibid., 150–51.
39. It is not known exactly why there was no response to the Jewish request of July 1654 to settle Tobago; see Mordechai Arbell, "The Failure of the Jewish Settlement on the Island of Tobago," *Proceedings of the Eleventh World Congress of Jewish Studies* (1994), vol. 3, 304–5.
40. Robert Cohen, "The Edgerton Manuscript," *American Jewish Historical Quarterly* 62 (1973):333–47.

– Chapter 18 –

THE JEWS IN SURINAME AND CURAÇAO

Wim Klooster

I N HIS FAMOUS BOOK OF 1788 on the Jews of Suriname, David de Isaac Cohen Nassy argued that "the Portuguese Jews have settled in Suriname on much happier and more favorable terms than anywhere in the universe: all and sundry were put on a par with the colonists of the Protestant faith: all offices and functions were open to them unconditionally."[1] Both Suriname and the insular Dutch colony of Curaçao were, relatively speaking, models of tolerance in the days of the ancien régime, offering attractive opportunities to Jewish settlers. The Jews, in their turn, made significant contributions to the economic growth of these colonies. In this essay, I will analyze the nature of these contributions.

Suriname: The Vicissitudes of Plantation Agriculture

An English colony since 1651, Suriname numbered no more than a few dozen Jews[2] until a group of about one hundred arrived from Cayenne in 1665 or 1666, after the loss to France of the neighboring Dutch settlement. They were joined by Jews who had originally left the Netherlands and Leghorn for Dutch colonies in Pomeroon, Essequibo, and Tobago. The English authorities granted several privileges to the Jewish population, including freedom of worship, the free exercise of their customs, and exemption from work on Sabbaths and holidays. Likewise, on Sundays they were allowed to work, to have their slaves work, and to visit relatives.[3]

The Dutch government affirmed these rights after a naval squadron from the province of Zeeland had conquered the colony in the last year of the second Anglo-Dutch war (1665–67). Occasionally, Jews had to defend their privileges vis-à-vis the colonial authorities, as for instance when their dispensation from work on the Sabbath and their right to labor on Sundays came under attack. When in 1675 a law was passed forbidding all inhabitants to work on Sundays, the Jews rose in protest, fearful that their slaves would spend the entire weekend in idleness. However, the Society of Suriname, which administered the colony, decided that the regulation did not extend to the Jews or their slaves.[4]

While dozens of Jews took refuge in Jamaica after the Dutch capture of Suriname, those who stayed behind traveled up the Suriname River and settled in an area that came to be called the Jodensavanne ("Jewish Savannah"). The reason for this move seems to have been that all of the high ground in Thorarica, the main settlement in the English period, had already been occupied. Overlooking two deep valleys and rising thirty feet above sea level, the Jodensavanne, which soon boasted eighty houses, developed into the world's largest Jewish agricultural community.[5]

Surinamese agriculture invariably impressed foreign travelers. The low situation of the marshy coastal plain and the large amount of precipitation required massive drainage, irrigation, and architectural ingenuity to sustain the production of sugar, coffee, cotton, and cacao.[6] A French visitor, V. P. Malouet, observed: "When a settler of St. Domingue or Normandy wants to get rich, he just has to work the fertile soil in the usual way; the colonists of Suriname almost have to bring about the miracle of a second creation; they have to put in order the muddled elements, separate the slimy soil from the water, and erect immense buildings on firm ground in the middle of swamps."[7]

Most Jewish plantations were concentrated inland, where the land was less swampy and therefore easier to bring into cultivation. Even so, planting was a tall order. The sugar plantation "De Drie Gebroeders" on the Suriname River was a case in point. The owner, Samuel d'Avilar, successfully added to his estate for over twenty-five years, leaving it in excellent condition at his death in 1769. His heirs, however, could not manage the plantation, and it deteriorated rapidly in the next decades.[8]

The successful operation of Suriname's plantations required a large labor supply that was met by the importation of African slaves. Initially, demand far exceeded supplies. David Nassy's assertion that by 1690 some nine thousand enslaved Africans, spread among forty sugar mills, were already in the service of Jews, therefore seems exaggerated.[9] In 1684, the entire Afro-Surinamese population stood around four thousand, and few ships arrived from Angola or West Africa in the next few years.[10] It was only after the 1730s that large numbers of Africans were disembarked in the colony, resulting in a slave population of almost sixty thousand in 1774.[11] The continuous importation of slaves cannot be explained simply by the expansion of land under cultivation. Other significant factors were the high mortality of the slave population and the ever swelling number of runaways. One planter complained in 1706 that an average plantation lost six slaves a year.[12]

In the second half of the eighteenth century, both Jewish and gentile planters were tied increasingly to mortgage-granting merchant-bankers in the Netherlands. The lack of investment opportunities in the mother country had created a surplus of capital for which Suriname provided an outlet, all the more since coffee prices were constantly rising on the world market. The floating of bonds by metropolitan investors rendered money available for loans to planters. Plantation real estate valuations, however, were often groundless, so that the loans bore no relation to the actual value of the assets. The illusion of a flourishing plantation economy was enhanced by the almost unlimited availability of credit. When the moment came to settle their debts, however, many planters were unable to pay, and their plantations were sold to metropolitan creditors.[13]

Tax lists suggest that the Jews sustained heavier financial losses than did gentiles. While in 1772 the Jews paid more than one-fourth of the property tax (26.1 percent), eight years later their share had fallen to 22.7 percent. The Jews lost more in all quarters than their non-Jewish neighbors, and as a result, two-thirds of the Jews in Suriname were reduced to poverty.[14] Most Jewish estates had to be relinquished, with their owners and families moving en masse from the Jodensavanne to the city of Paramaribo.[15] While 115 out of 401 plantations (28.7 percent) had been in Jewish hands around 1730,[16] in 1788 only forty-six out of 591 remained (7.8 percent). Of these forty-six, thirty produced timber and provisions, and only sixteen were export-oriented coffee and cotton estates. Sugar cultivation had in large part been abandoned during the investment boom. By contrast, only 109 of 545 gentile plantations had abandoned the production of cash crops by 1788.[17]

The debt crisis only partly explains this divergent development. The fortunes of Jewish planters had begun to decline prior to the crisis because of the changing condition of their plantations. Jews had taken up agriculture along the upper reaches of the Suriname and Commewijne rivers at an early stage, and were faced with the depletion of their soils long before their gentile colleagues on the lower reaches of the rivers.[18] Already by mid-century, therefore, the main activity in the Jodensavanne was the cutting of wood for boards and shingles.[19]

The Jewish role in plantation agriculture further declined in the following decades. By the early nineteenth century, no more than twenty-three Jewish plantations were producing export crops; all other so-called "plantations" were in actual fact timber grounds that hardly turned a profit. The Jodensavanne, by then, was all but deserted; the few remaining villagers were septuagenarians. In 1832, shortly after the Dutch agronomist Teenstra had met "oppressive poverty on the ruins of former greatness,"[20] a fire destroyed the place for good.

Curaçao: Smuggling for a Living

At about the same time the first Jews settled in Suriname, another group of Jews took up residence on Curaçao. The West India Company had captured the Caribbean island in 1634 from thirty-two Spaniards, and initially used it as a military base. Invasions of the Spanish Main from Curaçao were carried out almost every year, and death and destruction were spread to Maracaibo, Santa Marta, and Cartagena. With the peace in 1648, Curaçao lost its military function and languished for several years. The Company board even toyed with the idea of giving up the island, together with the neighboring islands of Aruba and Bonaire, but abandoned the thought after careful consideration.

It was unclear at the outset what Curaçao's new destiny was to be, but it soon emerged that cash crop production was not a viable alternative. The poor soil and lack of rainfall wrecked all attempts to grow tobacco, cotton, indigo, and sugar. The island's estates eventually specialized in the production of maize, the staple food of the slaves and, during droughts, of the cattle as well. Since cattle-breeding was more valuable than agriculture, all "plantations" were eventually transformed into dairy-producing mixed farms with oxen, calves, sheep, and poultry.[21] But even then, Curaçao's produce did not meet the needs of its population.

What saved the island, eventually, was the business instinct of its citizens, who soon transformed Curaçao into an American counterpart of Amsterdam—a staple market where numerous European commodities were piled up, awaiting sale to customers in the French, English, and Spanish colonies. Curaçao's remarkable commercial development, which began in the 1660s, was matched by a population increase. The number of free residents of Willemstad rose from 300 in 1675 to 850 in 1715, and by 1789 was up to 6,000; the latter group included 2,469 Protestants and 1,095 Jews. Having first arrived in the 1650s, the Jewish community grew rapidly, through both natural increase and the immigration of new families from the Netherlands and refugees from the French island of Martinique in 1685.[22] By the middle of the eighteenth century, the number of Jewish families was up to about half that of the gentiles,[23] and this ratio remained the same until at least 1789 (Table 18.1).

As in Suriname, the Jews of Curaçao could count on protection by Dutch officials. The West India Company guaranteed them freedom of religion and safeguarded their property rights. Although conflicts between Jews and Christians were even more rare than in Suriname, they did occur. Jewish schooling on Sundays, for instance, irritated Governor Faesch in 1740 so much that he ordered the schools to close on that day of the week. It is likely that this measure did not remain operational for long and soon afterward a compromise was reached, allowing Jewish schools to hold Sunday classes, albeit without choral singing.[24] A more serious conflict erupted in 1682. Spanish sailors, reportedly in accordance with an old custom, hoisted a dummy to the masthead of their vessel on

Maundy Thursday, and put it on fire. The dummy not only represented Judas Iscariot, it was also an effigy of Curaçao's rabbi.[25] The Dutch factor of the slave trade, Balthasar Beck, who apparently greeted the spectacle with approval, was dismissed from the post of captain of the civil guard.[26]

The arrival of the Jews may have been the single most important impetus to Curaçao's rise as a regional entrepôt. Although they did not shun agriculture, the Jews soon found out that it paid to go into commerce. Before long, many merchants and ship-owners were Jews who made full use of their particular advantages: mastery of the Spanish language and family networks across the Atlantic with various relatives acting as business associates.

Since their trades forced the Jews to live close to the commercial center, most settled down in Punda, the old part of Willemstad, staying there even as a growing number of Protestants moved to the new residential areas of Otrabanda, Pietermaai, and Scharloo. In the process, the Old Town underwent a remarkable change. While in 1707, the Protestants had outnumbered the Jews in seven of the eight main streets, even in the Joodestraat,[27] by 1789, 860 Jews and 658 Protestants were living in the old part of Willemstad. Almost seven of every eight urban Jews (84.1 percent) then resided in Punda, compared to only one-third of the urban Protestants (Tables 18.1 and 18.2).

Jewish Trade Networks

The vast majority of the cacao, tobacco, hides, and other shipments sent by Curaçaoan Jews to Amsterdam were consigned to other Jews, quite often a member of the same family who served as the consignor, as is shown in the Appendix at the end of this chapter. When possible, trade between Curaçao and other parts of the New World was also conducted with fellow Jews. Commercial ties between the Sephardim of Curaçao and the Jews of New York were sustained by the bonds of matrimony, which joined the Dovales, Pardos, Naftalis, and Pinheiros of New York to the De Casseres, Idanha de Casseres, Lopez da Fonseca, and Mendes da Gama of Curaçao.[28] Esther Levy from Curaçao was married to Daniel Gomez (1695–1780), a merchant who sent 133 ships to the Dutch island between 1739 and 1772. His thirty-five correspondents on the island were all Sephardic Jews.[29]

While the importation of flour, bread, butter, meat, and other provisions from Manhattan was indispensable to Curaçao, Spanish American produce formed the backbone of Curaçao's trade. For every ship arriving from New York between 1751 and 1752, there were eight coming in from the Spanish colonies, and the average value of their cargoes was many times greater.[30] This trade was certainly not dominated by Jewish networks; the Spanish mainland and the Spanish Caribbean lacked sizable Jewish communities at this juncture. Seymour Liebman's assertion that

TABLE 18.1 Urban Settlement Patterns, Curaçao, 1789

	Protestants	Jews	Servants	F.N.W.	Slaves
Old Town Families	194	219		132	
Old Town Persons	658	860	223	401	2,773
Otrabanda Families	192	14		423	
Otrabanda Persons	593	80	134	1,497	1,598
P & S Families	204	26		250	
P & S Persons	750	83	126	719	1,048
Total Persons	2,001	1,023	483	2,617	5,419

Adapted from: General survey of Curaçao and dependent islands, Appendix no. 16: Report of private houses. Algemeen Rijksarchief (ARA), The Hague, Raad van Coloniën 120. P & S stands for the quarters of Pietermaai and Scharloo. F.N.W. means free non-whites.

TABLE 18.2 Urban Distribution of Social Groups, Curaçao, 1789

	Protestants	Jews	Servants	F.N.W.	Slaves
Old Town	32.9	84.1	46.2	15.3	51.2
Otrabanda	29.6	7.8	27.8	51.2	29.5
P & S	37.5	8.1	26.1	27.5	19.3
Total	100.0	100.0	100.0	100.0	100.0

Adapted from: General survey of Curaçao and dependent islands, Appendix no. 16: Report of private houses. ARA Raad van Coloniën 120. P & S stands for the quarters of Pietermaai and Scharloo. F.N.W. means free non-whites.

branches of the "Mikveh Israel" community were established in Caracas and Coro, thereby laying the foundation of a ramified trade network, is simply not true for the eighteenth century.[31]

Still, the commodity trade with such places was important enough for Mikveh Israel, the Jewish community of Curaçao, to ignore one of the ordinances of its parent community in Amsterdam, the Talmud Torah congregation. Whereas all other ordinances were adopted, members of Mikveh Israel were not banned from staying in "countries of idolatry," a reference to the lands ruled by the Catholic kings of Spain and Portugal. Obeying this ordinance would have left many Jews penniless.[32] Jewish activities were not confined to ship-owning and maritime trade; many chose related professions. By the eighteenth century, there were twice as many Jewish dealers in houses and plantations as Protestant brokers, while the insurance business was practically a Jewish monopoly.[33]

The commodities that the Curaçaoans sold to these "countries of idolatry" had all been shipped in from Dutch ports, which is not to say that all the goods were produced in the Netherlands; most, in fact, were not. Linen, the main item, was mainly from Silesia, Saxony, and Westphalia, with the finer sorts coming from France. Other cloth included woolens, and lace and silk fabrics trimmed with gold and silver.[34] Provisions tended also to be non-Dutch in origin, such as Madeira or Bordeaux wines and Marseilles ham. Cinnamon, pepper, and other Asian spices also found a ready market.

Although Curaçao was a major transit port for African slaves from around 1660 until 1716, allegations about a heavy involvement of the island's Jews in the Atlantic slave trade are generally not true.[35] A few Jews were involved at one time or another,[36] but the local representatives of the West India Company were invariably Protestants. On the other hand, Jewish settlers, like the Protestants, bought slaves from the Company for their personal use.[37] It is telling that the collapse of the island's slave market after the War of the Spanish Succession (1701–13) did not lead to considerable financial loss for the Sephardim of Curaçao.

From the neighboring Spanish provinces, Jews and other Curaçaoans imported a wide array of locally cultivated crops and products. Since the bulk of Curaçao's trade was with Venezuela, the world's leading cacao producer from the mid-seventeenth to the early nineteenth century, cacao became the main import item of the Dutch island. Its exports to the United Provinces came to almost one and a half million guilders in the first half of the eighteenth century, with an estimated value of over 800,000 guilders.[38] Whereas there was only one kind of cacao, tobacco purchased by the Curaçaoans came in all shapes, sizes, and grades. Tobacco from Puerto Rico, Santo Domingo, Martinique, and New Granada was shipped to the Netherlands in the form of leaves, but Venezuelan tobacco was typically processed first and then sent in so-called canisters, that is, baskets containing rolls of spun tobacco. One canister variety, Barinas tobacco, was aimed at connoisseurs. The Venezuelan revolutionary Francisco Miranda found it advertised on signboards in Amsterdam's Jodenbreestraat.[39]

Other than these luxury goods, Curaçaoan imports from Spanish America included hides from Venezuela, Santo Domingo, and Cuba, and logwood and dyewood from Río de la Hacha, Santa Marta, and Campeche.[40] The French Caribbean colonies of Saint-Domingue, Martinique, and Guadeloupe, supplied sugar, coffee, and indigo, all crops of secondary importance to Curaçao's trade. Finally, consignments of flour, bread, and butter reached Curaçao from British North America.

The vessels used for this regional commerce were sloops and, as the eighteenth century advanced, increasing numbers of schooners. Equipped with oars, the fast schooners were well suited to both the coastal and the long-haul trade. The names of some of the vessels leave little doubt about their owners. The archives are full of names such as the *Masaltob*, the *Abraham en Isaac*, the *Bathseba*, and the *Bekeerde Jood* (Converted Jew).[41] A trading voyage normally included several stations. It was generally not remunerative to sail straight back and forth between Curaçao and a

Spanish American port, because the value of the products that were procured was outweighed by the expense of equipping vessels. Added to this financial consideration were the difficulties ship-owners experienced in their efforts to recruit enough crewmen. It was therefore advisable to have the same crew make as many short voyages as possible before dropping anchor again in Curaçao.[42]

An exchange of letters sometimes preceded Curaçaoan deals with Spaniards, and the costs of voyage between Willemstad and the Spanish Main were quite often partially met by Venezuelan merchants. Smugglers also made use of Spanish messengers to arrange transactions, or invited Spanish merchants on board to discuss the kinds of goods that were to be traded. The Dutch side usually made a payment and the Spanish promised to land their merchandise on the beach the next day.[43] Curaçaoans also dealt directly with Spanish or Creole planters inland.

Not much business was conducted in Willemstad, since Spanish merchants and ship-owners tried to avoid seizure by Venezuelan coast guards, fitted out by the Compañía Guipuzcoana, a Basque company founded to combat contraband trade. The ships that did put into the Dutch island were often bound for Veracruz, Santo Domingo, or Puerto Rico with more cocoa on board than had been registered. This surplus cocoa was exchanged at Curaçao for linen goods and other European articles, which were afterward sold at the official destination. The Venezuelan sloops that regularly sailed to the island of Margarita carrying dried and salted goat meat also stopped at Curaçao. The sloops were indeed loaded with meat, but stowed underneath this were large amounts of cocoa and hides, which were to be sold in Curaçao in exchange for textiles.[44]

Such roundabout methods were necessary because of the risks involved in the trade between Spanish subjects and foreigners. The Spanish monarchy considered any such commercial contacts as illegal, a view shared by the Dutch Republic in the bilateral treaties of 1648 and 1650, and once again at the Peace of Utrecht in 1713–14. In reality, however, the West India Company did not thwart the traders in any way. Spanish authorities, on the other hand, were instructed to put up a vigorous fight against smuggling. To deter and curtail this many-headed monster, coast guard vessels patrolled the littoral of various Spanish colonies. Shunning the official ports,[45] Curaçao's vessels mostly sailed to bays, coves, and inlets along the coast, where the large coast guard ships could not navigate.

Even in those places, it was advisable to proceed with caution. Conducting business was particularly risky for some of the less affluent Curaçaoans, among whom there were several Jews, who tried to supplement their slender incomes with retail trade.[46] In the event of capture by a coast guard vessel, all commodities carried on board were lost. Still worse, quite a number of common sailors, including some Jews, were clapped in irons and condemned to serve on the galleys of North Africa, while others ended up in "la Carraca," a prison in Cádiz, Spain, which bore a sinister reputation on Curaçao.[47]

It is no surprise, therefore, that the Jews of Curaçao were resentful of the Compañía Guipuzcoana. A diary kept by a Spaniard who stayed on the Dutch island at the time of an English assault on Venezuela in 1743, reveals the ill will that the company had aroused. One entry describes the reaction to the news that an English squadron of twenty-three ships, known to be preparing an assault on Venezuela, had dropped anchor in the main port of La Guaira.

> This news caused such delight and satisfaction among the inhabitants of this city that they were exalting the English all day long until night fell and the god Bacchus settled them down.... The ones who went most out of their way to celebrate the news were the Jews, who proclaimed in loud voices in the Spanish tongue: citizens and residents, victory is ours, because ... the Great God of Israel has drawn the sword of His justice against these Basque dogs who have inflicted so much damage on us.[48]

It should be emphasized, however, that it was not difficult to bribe land guards with a hunk of cheese or a bottle of brandy. Moreover, chance encounters with *guardacostas* were the hazards of a profitable job. Once the Venezuelan shore was reached, the Curaçaoans were usually received with open arms by local settlers, who appreciated the regular availability, low prices, and assortment of Dutch supplies. The reliability of Dutch merchants contrasted sharply with that of their Spanish colleagues. From Cádiz, the only port in Spain authorized to trade with the Indies, only three ships with goods were sent to Caracas, and three more to Maracaibo during the War of the Spanish Succession. The province of Río de la Hacha, another hotbed of Curaçaoan smuggling, received not a single ship from Cádiz between 1713 and 1763.[49]

If most business between ill-supplied Venezuelans and eager Curaçaoans was originally organized in the central parts of Venezuela's littoral, one place was an exception to this rule: Tucacas, a small village near Coro, located within easy reach of Curaçao via the Yaracuy River, in a sparsely populated area with only a few Indian villages. It did not pay for the authorities in Caracas to have it patrolled continuously, and the Curaçaoans seized the opportunity to establish a settlement of their own there in the late seventeenth century. In fact, a group of Jews seems to have pitched camp in Tucacas after an epidemic had swept through Curaçao.

Tucacas soon became a major Curaçaoan trading place. In 1720 the Spanish examining magistrate Olavarriaga concluded that Tucacas was the place where most deals between the Dutch and the Spanish were carried out. Over a million pounds of cacao were traded there annually, and in addition, tobacco, cows, and mules were sold to Curaçao. The leadership of this thriving colony was first in the hands of Jurriaan Exteen, also known as "Jorge Cristian," a ship's captain in the service of the Jewish merchant Phelipe Henriquez. Exteen styled himself the "Marquis of Tucacas" and, according to some witnesses, lived in splendor.[50] He was later succeeded by Samuel Hebreo, who appropriated the title "Lord of Tucacas" for himself. During his rule, the colony consisted of seventeen houses and a synagogue[51]

The importance of Tucacas in the contraband trade did not go unnoticed, and the Spanish government decided to stamp out the Dutch settlement completely. In 1710, the chief ensign of the town of Coro was sent to Tucacas with 150 Indian archers, who destroyed several houses and killed the cattle the Dutch had left behind.[52] Only a few years went by, however, before another Spanish expedition could report the presence of two hundred armed Dutch males in Tucacas. Time and again, Spanish authorities tried to chase away the intruders. In 1721, they tore down the synagogue,[53] and in 1734, Governor Martín de Lardizábal erected a fort with four cannon at Tucacas. But the soldiers who were assigned to man the fort deserted in protest against their low wages, and in 1740 a joint effort by Curaçaoans and Englishmen from St. Christopher led to the fort's destruction.[54] By then, Tucacas had lost much of its commercial strength. Most of the production and trade of cacao had shifted from coastal Venezuela, which was beginning to show signs of overcultivation, to the banks of the Tuy River.[55]

The Adventures of Phelipe Henriquez

One of Curaçao's Jewish merchants involved in the Tucacas trade was Jacob Senior (ca. 1660–1718), who adopted his grandfather's name Phelipe Henriquez when he took up trade. He came from a family of New Christians that had fled Portugal in the 1590s. Felipe Henriques (1589–1656), alias Juda Senior, became a merchant in Amsterdam, and traded with several places in the Mediterranean.[56] He left a son Mordechay who served Johan Maurits van Nassau-Siegen, the governor of Dutch Brazil. Johan Maurits created a favorable social climate that attracted numerous Amsterdam Sephardim. Mordechay's son Phelipe was born around 1660 in Amsterdam. At the age of twenty-five, he arrived in Curaçao with three of his brothers and built up a merchant fleet. Another brother stayed behind in Amsterdam to secure freight for the outgoing ships. At Curaçao, Henriquez established relationships with traders in numerous Spanish colonies and went on to become a successful merchant and ship's captain.

In general, it was difficult for Jews to profess their faith on board the trading vessels among a majority of gentiles: Protestant Dutchmen, Germans, and Scandinavians, as well as Roman Catholic slaves and free blacks. There are, however, some references in the archives to Jews who made no secret of their conviction. Amanuel Alvares Correa, for instance, was a merchant on a sloop that was seized in 1746 near Caracas by an English ship. At the subsequent trial in Newport, Rhode Island, he swore an oath on the Pentateuch.[57] Phelipe Henriquez was also open about his

Judaism. He claimed he led his crew in Christian prayer in the morning and in the evening, and thereafter had a quiet read in a Hebrew prayer book. When his business took him to Río de la Hacha, he observed the "law of Moses" so unabashedly that the local pastor was scandalized and lodged a complaint in Cartagena de Indias.

Before long, Henriquez landed in the dungeons of the Inquisition in Cartagena. The official reason given was his trade in arms and ammunition. However, in a report he wrote after his release, Henriquez relates that he was accused of slaughtering chickens in a ritual Jewish manner in Santa Marta on the coast of present-day Colombia. During an interrogation, he denied this allegation by saying that he was not qualified to perform that function, and that local Jews had done it in his stead.[58]

His captivity ended after only ten weeks when his freedom was bought by the director of the Portuguese Cacheu Company, which possessed the *asiento*, the monopoly to supply Spanish America with slaves; Henriquez had served this company as the Curaçao factor. A few years later, he was appointed the agent of a French company that had acquired the *asiento*.[59] Such international contacts led to his involvement in diplomacy. During the War of the Spanish Succession, he was in the service of the camp of Archduke Charles, the candidate for the vacant Spanish crown who was supported by an alliance of Great Britain, the Dutch Republic, Austria, and Brandenburg-Prussia. The candidate favored by Spain and France, on the other hand, was the grandson of Louis XIV, later Philip V. The Jews of Amsterdam and Curaçao backed the archduke, fearing that Philip's victory would lead to a pronounced French predominance in the trade with Spanish America.[60]

Charles deployed ambassadors in all quarters of the world to plead his case. One of them was the Italian count de Antería, Charles's ambassador to northern Spanish America, who used Curaçao as an operational base in his attempts to win the people of Venezuela over to the archduke. Antería availed himself of the vessels of Phelipe Henriquez and his excellent contacts with the Venezuelans. As a reward for this help, Phelipe was promised the governorship of Venezuela.[61] Shortly after the outbreak of the war, Phelipe made his way to The Hague, presumably for high-level deliberations that must have also involved Phelipe's brother-in-law, who acted as Charles's consul in Amsterdam. Unfortunately for them, the archduke lost the war.

Phelipe was among Curaçao's men of property. Other Jews in Curaçao could hardly get by on their monthly wages. Yet to all, Curaçao was a safe haven, a place to live their lives in freedom. The departure of many Jews in the early nineteenth century was not the result of any change in the Dutch policy. The commercial prosperity of Curaçao, rather, had come to an end after the French invasion of the Dutch Republic in 1795. Shipping traffic with Amsterdam and Zeeland was frequently interrupted, and the British occupations of 1800–03 and 1807–16 were very prejudicial. The high taxes that were levied prompted the Jews to leave the island. Some came back in later years, but they would never see the return of the golden age of Curaçao.

Conclusion

Their conquests of Curaçao and Suriname left the Dutch in the seventeenth century with dissimilar Caribbean endowments. While Suriname's climate lent itself to the production of tropical crops, Curaçao's excellent natural port was conveniently located to conduct trade with the Spanish Main. Neither place, however, was a land of plenty, and only through perseverance could the potential of each be realized. In this respect, the agricultural and commercial activities of Jewish colonists proved to be indispensable. The Jews prospered in the tolerant social climate that prevailed under the umbrella of the Dutch colonial governments. Despite occasional tensions with the gentiles, they came to form one-third of the white population in both Suriname and Curaçao. This strong presence was truly unique in the history of the European expansion.[62]

APPENDIX

Curaçao's Jewish Merchants and Their Amsterdam Consignees:
The Ship *de Juffrouw Gesina*, 1744[63]

Curaçao Jews	Amsterdam Jews and Gentiles
Aron de Chaves Jr.	Aron de Chaves
Jacob Suares	Joseph da Fonseca Chaves
Abraham Suares Jr.	Joseph da Fonseca Chaves
Abraham de Isaac Senior	David Semah Aboab Jr.
Isaac Henriques Cotinho	Joseph da Fonseca Chaves
Ester de Aron Motta	Joseph da Fonseca Chaves
Abraham Jesurun Sasportas	Joseph da Fonseca Chaves
Abraham & Isaac de Marchena	Christiaan van Eghen*
Abraham Floris & Moses de Castro	Moses de Crasto
Isaac Cardoze	Elias Gomes Suares
Joseph Jesurun Henriques	Salomon Gutierres
Joseph da Costa Gomez	Jacob Temmink Adriaansz*
Joseph da Costa Gomez	Widow of Pieter Root* &
	Joan Willem Bongaard*
Joseph da Costa Gomez	Cornelis de Meij*
Joseph da Costa Gomez	Christiaan G. Frederiks*
Joseph da Costa Gomez	Aron Jesurun
Joseph da Costa Gomez	Dirk Entvogel*
Joseph & Isaac da Costa Gomez	Abraham & Moses de Raphael
	Mendes da Costa
David Lopez Lagunes	Abraham de Moses da Costa Gomez
Abraham Flores & Moses de Castro	Moses & David Mendes da Costa
Moses de Castro	Moses de Crasto
Moses de Abraham de Chaves	Moses de Chaves
Aron de Chaves Jr.	Aron de Chaves
David Jesurun & Mordechay de Crasto	Moses & David Mendes da Costa
David Jesurun & Mordechay de Crasto	David Henriques de Castro
David Jesurun & Mordechay de Crasto	Moses Capadoso
David Jesurun & Mordechay de Crasto	Jacob Machoro
David Jesurun & Mordechay de Crasto	Abraham & Moses de Raphael
	Mendes da Costa
David Jesurun & Mordechay de Crasto	Salomon Gomes
David Jesurun & Mordechay de Crasto	Jacob de Prado & son
David Jesurun & Mordechay de Crasto	Jacob van Ghesel*
David Jesurun	Isaac de Salomon Jesurun
Mordechay de Crasto	Isaac de Salomon Jesurun
Jacob de Mordechay de Crasto	Jacob Jr. & Abraham Semah Ferro Jr.
Abraham Flores & Moses de Castro	Abraham & Moses de Raphael
	Mendes da Costa
Joseph da Costa Gomez	Abraham & Moses de Raphael
	Mendes da Costa
Jacob Fidanque	Herman Beerens & son*
Jacob Fidanque	Adam Bartelsman*

Curaçao Jews	Amsterdam Jews and Gentiles
Widow Ribca Alva	Isaac Dias
Isaac de Jacob Henriques Fereyra	Abraham Henriques Fereyra
Isaac de Jacob Henriques Fereyra	Henrique Vaes de Oliveira & sons
Abraham Bueno Vivas	Joseph da Fonseca Chaves
Moses de Benjamin Jesurun	Joseph da Fonseca Chaves
Rachel Henriques Moron	Aron Jesurun
Cohen Henriques Jr.	Joseph da Fonseca Chaves
Cohen Henriques Jr. & Isaac Juliao	Joseph da Fonseca Chaves
Sara de Mordechay Alvares Correa	Aron Jesurun
Manuel & Daniel da Costa Gomez	Abraham Lopes Lagunes
Abraham Jesurun Sasportas	Aron Jesurun
Aron Henriques Moron	Hobbe Strandwijk*
Isaac Belmonte	Christiaan van Eghen*
Neyra & Widow of Anthony de Neijra & sons	Moses David Mendes da Costa
Moses Penso	Henrique Vaes de Oliveira & sons
Moses Penso & Jacob Lopez Dias	Joseph Rodrigues da Costa
Moses Henriques Cotinho	Christiaan G. Frederiks*
Isaac Juliao	Joseph da Fonseca Chaves
Abraham & Isaac de Marchena	Aron Jesurun
Abraham & Isaac de Marchena	Abraham & Moses de Raphael Mendes da Costa
Joseph & Jacob da Costa Gomez	Isaac Orobio de Castro
David de Mordechay Senior	David Semah Aboab Jr.
Isaac de Abraham Baruch Louzada	Isaac Orobio de Castro
Abraham Baruch Louzada	Isaac Orobio de Castro

*The names of the gentiles are indicated with an asterisk.

Source: ARA, Nieuwe West-Indische Compagnie (NWIC) 591, fols. 231–33.

Notes

1. [David de Isaac Cohen Nassy,] *Geschiedenis der Kolonie van Suriname: Behelzende derzelver opkomst, voortgang, burgerlyke en staatkundige gesteldheid, tegenwoordigen staat van koophandel, en eene volledige en naauwkeurige beschryving van het land, de zeden en gebruiken der ingezetenen. Geheel op nieuw samengesteld door een gezelschap van geleerde joodsche mannen aldaar* (Amsterdam and Harlingen, 1791), 101–2.
2. There is evidence that Jews were living in Suriname as early as 1643: Samuel Oppenheim, "An Early Jewish Colony in Western Guiana, 1658–1666, and Its Relation to the Jews in Surinam, Cayenne and Tobago," *Publications of the American Jewish Historical Society* 16 (1907):97.
3. Günter Böhm, "The Synagogues of Surinam," *Journal of Jewish Art* 6 (1978):99. L. L. E. Rens, "Analysis of Annals Relating to Early Jewish Settlement in Surinam," in *The Jewish Nation in Surinam: Historical Essays*, ed. Robert Cohen (Amsterdam, 1982), 36.
4. Robert Cohen, *Jews in Another Environment: Surinam in the Second Half of the Eighteenth Century* (Leiden, 1991), 125–26. Jewish labor on Sundays was also disputed in Paramaribo. The opening of Jewish shops on that day was bound to invite a negative response from the consistories of the Dutch and French communities. They complained that shopkeepers were putting their wares on the windowsill and selling them on the streets. The government thereupon forbade the Jews to open their shops on Sundays. What also worried the consistories was Jewish women sewing and practicing other handicrafts in their doorways at the Christian church-time. See Placard of 21 November 1718 [no. 279] in *Plakaten, ordonnantien en andere wetten, uitgevaardigd in Suriname, 1667–1816*, ed. J. Th. de Smidt (Amsterdam, 1973), 323–24.
5. F. C. Bubberman et al., *Links with the Past: The History of the Cartography of Suriname 1500–1971* (Amsterdam, 1973), 53. Cf. for the history of the Jews of early Dutch Suriname, Claudia Schnurmann, *Atlantische Welten. Engländer und Niederländer im amerikanisch-atlantischen Raum 1648–1713* (Cologne, Weimar, and Vienna, 1998), 218–20, 229–52.
6. Alex van Stipriaan, *Surinaams contrast. Roofbouw en overleven in een Caraïbische plantagekolonie 1750–1863* (Leiden, 1993), 79.
7. V. P. Malouet, *V.P. Malouet's franz. Seewesens-Administrators's Reisen nach dem Französischen Guiana und nach Surinam* (Weimar, 1805), 150.
8. Van Stipriaan, *Surinaams contrast*, 93–94.
9. The slaves were owned by one hundred families and some fifty bachelors. In all, Nassy lists 92 Sephardic and ten to twelve Ashkenazi families for the year 1690: [Nassy,] *Geschiedenis der Kolonie van Suriname*, 74–75.
10. We have two data for 1684: a poll and land tax list recording 3,226 black slaves (972 of whom employed by 163 Jewish men and women), and a probably more reliable bookkeeper count of 4,237: Victor Enthoven, "Suriname and Zeeland: Fifteen Years of Dutch Misery on the Wild Coast, 1667–1682," in *Shipping, Factories and Colonization*, ed. J. Everaert and J. Parmentier (Brussels, 1997), 255; J. M. van der Linde, *Surinaamse suikerheren en hun kerk. Plantagekolonie en handelskerk ten tijde van Johannes Basseliers, predikant en planter in Suriname, 1667–1689* (Wageningen, 1966), 50. For the slave trade in this period, see Cornelis Ch. Goslinga, *The Dutch in the Caribbean and in the Guianas 1680–1791* (Assen, Maastricht, and Dover, N.H., 1985), 418–20; Johannes Menne Postma, *The Dutch in the Atlantic Slave Trade 1600–1815* (Cambridge, Mass., 1990), 356–57.
11. Van Stipriaan, *Surinaams contrast*, 311 (table 44); Henk den Heijer, *Goud, ivoor en slaven. Scheepvaart en handel van de Tweede West-Indische Compagnie op Afrika, 1674–1740* (Zutphen, 1997), 366.
12. Postma, *Dutch in Atlantic Slave Trade*, 184. Annually in the eighteenth century, three hundred slaves ran away, and one hundred of them were never recovered. Van Stipriaan, *Surinaams contrast*, 386, citing Wim S. M. Hoogbergen, *De Boni-oorlogen, 1757–1860; Marronage en guerrilla in Oost-Suriname* (Utrecht, 1985), 54.
13. Van Stipriaan, *Surinaams contrast*, 207–25.

14. Cohen, *Jews in Another Environment*, 85.
15. As many as 150 families set up retail businesses in Paramaribo, even though there was room for only a few such traders.
16. At least seventy plantations on the Suriname River are indicated as having Jewish owners on the 1737 map of A. de Lavaux, *Algemeene Kaart van de Colonie of Provintie van Suriname.*
17. [Nassy,] *Geschiedenis der Kolonie van Suriname*, second pagination, 5–6.
18. Alex van Stipriaan, "An Unusual Parallel: Jews and Africans in Suriname in the 18th and 19th Centuries," *Studia Rosenthaliana* 31, no. 1/2 (1997):78.
19. Two Diaries or Notebooks of the Artist John Greenwood, fols. 101–2, New York Historical Society.
20. M. D. Teenstra, *De landbouw in de kolonie Suriname voorafgegaan door eene geschied- en natuurkundige beschouwing der kolonie,* vol. 1 (Groningen, 1835), 135.
21. "Consideratien over den toestand van t'eijlant van Curacao," 1695, Algemeen Rijksarchief [The Hague] (ARA) Verspreide West-Indische Stukken 394; Report by W. A. I. van Grovenstein and W. C. Boeij, The Hague, 11 February 1791; ARA Verspreide West-Indische Stukken 972; Justin Girod-Chantrans, *Voyage d'un suisse dans différentes colonies d'Amérique pendant la dernière guerre* (Neuchatel, 1785), 99; Joh. Hartog, *Curaçao. Van kolonie tot autonomie,* vol. 1 (Aruba, 1961):368–69. J. A. Schiltkamp, *Bestuur en rechtspraak in de Nederlandse Antillen ten tijde van de West-Indische Compagnie* (Willemstad, 1972), 30–31; W. E. Renkema, *Het Curaçaose plantagebedrijf in de 19e eeuw* (Zutphen, 1981), 15–16, 252–54.
22. One of them was Benjamin de Casseres, the nephew of Spinoza. I. S. Emmanuel, "Les juifs de la Martinique et leurs coreligionnairs d'Amsterdam au XVIIe siècle," *Revue des Etudes Juives* 123 (1964):516.
23. Goslinga's claim that the Jewish population swelled again at mid-century as a result of migration from St. Thomas and the United Provinces cannot be substantiated. Family tax lists, published by the West India Company in 1746, 1750, and 1755, reveal that the number of Jewish families remained roughly the same in these years, declining even slightly from 156 to 153 to 151. However, the Jewish group gained demographic weight because the gentile population decreased in this period from 349 to 312 families and then dropped to 270. Goslinga, *Dutch in Caribbean*, 114–15. Family tax lists, Curaçao, 1746, 1749, 1755. ARA Nieuwe West-Indische Compagnie (NWIC) 594, fols. 132–39, NWIC 597, fols. 903–20, NWIC 600, fols. 1010–25.
24. Isaac S. Emmanuel and Suzanne A. Emmanuel, *History of the Jews of the Netherlands Antilles,* vol. 1 (Cincinnati, 1970), 152.
25. The spectacle had roots in medieval Europe, where Judas was hanged with a moneybag suspended from his neck to personify avarice. All of the standard forms of Jewish dress were applied to Judas. Lester K. Little, "The Jews in Christian Europe," in *Essential Papers on Judaism and Christianity in Conflict: From Late Antiquity to the Reformation,* ed. Jeremy Cohen (New York and London, 1991), 289, 296n.
26. Governor Nicolaas van Liebergen to the WIC, Chamber of Amsterdam, Curaçao, 25 April 1682; Meeting of the Council of Curaçao, 28 March 1682; Memorandum of "Jan Ignacius" Echeverria, Curaçao, 14 April 1682, ARA NWIC 617, fols. 149–52, 178, 193–94.
27. Bernard R. Buddingh', *Van Punt en Snoa. Ontstaan en groei van Willemstad, Curaçao vanaf 1634, De Willemstad tussen 1700 en 1732 en de bouwgeschiedenis van de synagoge Mikvé Israël-Emanuel 1730–1732* ('s-Hertogenbosch, 1994), 78.
28. Also, the New York merchant Mosseh Hizquiau Lopes da Fonseca, a former Curaçaoan, married Rachel Israel of Curaçao in 1736. Isaac S. Emmanuel, *Precious Stones of the Jews of Curaçao: Curaçao Jewry 1656–1957* (New York, 1957), 261, 316.
29. Daniel Snydacker, "Traders in Exile: Quakers and Jews of New York and Newport in the New World Economy, 1650–1776" (Ph.D. diss., The Johns Hopkins University, 1982), 268–71, 278–79; Jacob R. Marcus, *The Colonial American Jew 1492–1776,* vol. 2 (Detroit, 1970), 596–97, 602, 607, 618; David de Sola Pool, *Portraits Etched in Stone: Early Jewish Settlers 1682–1831* (New York, 1952), 237–38.

30. From 16 October 1751, through 15 October 1752, 149 vessels from Spanish American colonies dropped anchor in Willemstad compared to eighteen from New York. In 1785 and 1786, seventeen ships came into Willemstad from New York. ARA NWIC 598, fols. 947–65, 1210–21, NWIC 599 fols. 22–28, 94–97, 136–39, 258ff, 409ff.

31. This assertion by Liebman is based on a quotation from Melvin H. Jackson. Liebman's discussion of Curaçao's Jews is full of errors. He wrongly argues, for instance, that Jewish enclaves existed in Venezuela before 1693, and identifies Tucacas with Puerto Lopez, Colombia. Seymour B. Liebman, *New World Jewry, 1493–1825: Requiem for the Forgotten* (New York, 1982), 183ff.

32. Yosef Kaplan, "The Curaçao and Amsterdam Jewish Communities in the 17th and 18th Centuries," *American Jewish History* 72 (1982):200–202.

33. In 1734, thirty-nine out of forty-four insurers were Jews, while sixty years later, there were seventeen Jews among twenty-five sworn brokers.

34. Wim Klooster, *Illicit Riches: Dutch Trade in the Caribbean, 1648–1795* (Leiden, 1998), 178–79.

35. The Nation of Islam, the radical movement of black Muslims headed by the well-known activist Louis Farrakhan, has tried to show that the Atlantic slave trade was a kind of Jewish specialty. Its allegations, gathered in Nation of Islam, *The Secret Relationship Between Blacks and Jews* (Chicago, 1991), were answered by Seymour Drescher, "The Role of Jews in the Transatlantic Slave Trade," *Immigrants and Minorities* 12 (July 1993):113–25; David Brion Davis, "The Slave Trade and the Jews," *The New York Review of Books* 41 no. 21 (22 December 1994):14–16; and Eli Faber, *Jews, Slaves, and the Slave Trade: Setting the Record Straight* (New York and London, 1998). See also essays by Drescher and Pieter Emmer in this volume.

36. Other Jews actively involved were Moshe Lopez, a.k.a. Francisco Lopez Henriquez, Manuel de Pina, and Manuel Alvares Correa: Emmanuel and Emmanuel, *History of the Jews*, vol. 1, 76.

37. Ibid., 77–80. For the development of Curaçao's slave trade, see Wim Klooster, "Slavenvaart op Spaanse kusten. De Nederlandse slavenhandel met Spaans Amerika, 1648–1701," *Tijdschrift voor Zeegeschiedenis* 16, no. 2 (1997):121–40.

38. Klooster, *Illicit Riches*, 185.

39. H. K. Roessingh, *Inlandse tabak. Expansie en contractie van een handelsgewas in de 17e en 18e eeuw in Nederland* (Zutphen, 1976), 238–39; Wim Klooster, "De reis van Francisco Miranda door de Republiek in 1788," *De achttiende eeuw. Documentatieblad van de Werkgroep Achttiende Eeuw* 25, no. 1 (1993):79.

40. Agustín Moreno Henríquez to José de Galvez, Amsterdam, 11 February 1778, Archivo General de Indias [Seville] (AGI), Indiferente General 2412.

41. Governor Isaac Faesch to the WIC, Chamber of Amsterdam, Curaçao, 16 May 1753, ARA NWIC 599, fol. 679.

42. Citizens of Curaçao to the West India Company, Chamber of Amsterdam, 1761 or 1762, ARA NWIC 603, fols. 1446–47; Willem Kock, boatswain, to the WIC, Curaçao, 13 July 1753, ARA NWIC 1161 fol. 6; Vicente de Amézaga Aresti, *Vicente Antonio de Icuza. Comandante de corsarios* (Caracas, 1966), 49–50.

43. Interrogation of Pieter Taeijste, Curaçao, 6 February 1766, ARA NWIC 605, fols. 210–11. Testimonies of Joseph Gatardo and Ignacio de la Raza, Curaçao, 7 August 1731, ARA NWIC 580, fol. 483.

44. Agustín Moreno Henríquez to José de Galvez, Amsterdam, 11 February 1778, AGI Indiferente General 2412.

45. Only rarely, Curaçaoans would conduct business in La Guaira or Puerto Cabello, Venezuela's official ports. Around 1720, the Curaçaoan Jew "Coche" Pereira traded for more than eight months in Puerto Cabello, purchasing cacao and tobacco from one estate. He was protected by Captain Diego de Matos Montañés, who, ironically, had plenary power to combat contraband trade. Mario Briceño Perozo, "Estudio Preliminar," in Pedro José de Olavarriaga, *Instrucción general y particular del estado presente de la Provincia de Venezuela en los años de 1720 y 1721* (Caracas, 1965), 11, 30.

46. J. G. Pax and Nathaniel Ellis, delegates of the Council of Curaçao, to Governor Faesch and Council, Curaçao, 24 September 1753, ARA NWIC 599, fols. 912–13. Monthly wages of the sailors are mentioned in ARA Oud Archief Curaçao [OAC] 814, fol. 482.

47. This happened to Jacob and Abraham Henriquez Moron, Ishac de Medina, Jacob Moreno Henriquez, and Abraham de Belmonte (1733), Mosseh de Selomoh Levy Maduro (1734), Jeudah Alva (1748), Abraham Pinedo and Manuel Tabuada (1764), Daniel Martines and Salomon Calvo (late 1760s), and Aron de David Uziel Cardozo (1773). Testimony of Abraham Dias and David Jesurun Henriquez, Curaçao, 6 January 1749, ARA OAC 820, fol. 11; Emmanuel and Emmanuel, *History of the Jews*, vol. 1, 222–26; Zvi Loker, *Jews in the Caribbean: Evidence on the History of the Jews in the Caribbean Zone in Colonial Times* (Jerusalem, 1991), 72–73.

48. Diary of Juan Francisco Navarro, Curaçao, 3 March–3 April 1743, Annex to San Gil to Marqués de Villarias, The Hague, 4 July 1743, Archivo General de Simancas, Estado 6275.

49. Analola Borges, "El inicio del comercio internacional venezolano (siglo XVIII)," *Boletín de la Academia Nacional de Historia* [Caracas] 46, no. 189 (1965):28–29; Geoffrey J. Walker, *Spanish Politics and Imperial Trade, 1700–1789* (Bloomington, 1979), 63; Lance R. Grahn, "An Irresoluble Dilemma: Smuggling in New Granada, 1713–1763," in *Reform and Insurrection in Bourbon New Granada and Peru*, ed. John R. Fisher, Allan J. Kuethe, and Anthony McFarlane (Baton Rouge and London, 1990), 131.

50. Clara Catharina Kerckrinck and David Senior to Interim-Governor Jonathan van Beuningen, Curaçao, 13 October 1716, ARA Staten-Generaal 9489.

51. Borges, "Inicio del comercio internacional," 33. Governor Juan Pedro van Collen later claimed, without a shred of evidence, that the erection of a synagogue had been one of the reasons for the foundation of the Compañía Guipuzcoana. Juan Pedro van Collen to the WIC, Curaçao, 7 June 1737, ARA NWIC 583, fol. 301.

52. Juan Jacobo Montero de Espinosa to King Philip V, Caracas, 9 April 1711, AGI Santo Domingo 697. Statement by Domingo de Arostegui, San Juan de Guaiguaza, 3 February 1718, AGI Santo Domingo 697; Olavarriaga, *Instrucción general y particular*, 247.

53. Four years later, however, a Spanish report again mentioned the existence of a Dutch "church" in Tucacas. Briceño Perozo, "Estudio Preliminar," 149n. "Relacion que el Conde Clavijo hase de lo sucedido con los Navios que apreso olandeses," Cartagena, 17 March 1725, ARA Staten-Generaal 7128.

54. Statement by Martín de Lardizábal, governor of Caracas, Caracas, 15 October 1734, AGI Santo Domingo 710. Marquis de San Gil to the States General, The Hague, 28 December 1741, ARA Staten-Generaal 7138; "Information Collected by Delegates of the Council of Curaçao," 6 September 1743. ARA NWIC 590, fols. 547–52.

55. Robert James Ferry, "Cacao and Kindred: Transformations of Economy and Society in Colonial Caracas," (Ph.D. diss., University of Minnesota, 1980), 189. Dorothy Cairns Tamaro, "A New World Plantation Region in Colonial Venezuela: Eighteenth-Century Cacao Cultivation in the Tuy Valley and Barlovento," (Ph.D. diss., Boston University, 1988), 68.

56. Notice of intended marriage, 13 December 1617, DTB 668/130, Gemeentearchief Amsterdam (GAA). Act of 14 January 1620, GAA Notarieel Archief (NA) 625, fols. 439–41. Acts of 28 August and 12 December 1622, NA 646, fols. 224, 341. I would like to thank Odette Vlessing of the Amsterdam Gemeentearchief for providing reproductions of the index cards.

57. Dorothy S. Towle, *Records of the Vice-Admiralty Court of Rhode Island 1716–1752* (Washington, D.C., 1936), 348.

58. In 1636, the Inquisition arrested twenty "judaizing Portuguese." There are actually indications that a small group of Portuguese Jews in Cartagena was in touch with the Dutch West India Company as early as the 1630s: Nikolaus Böttcher, *Aufstieg und Fall eines atlantischen Handelsimperiums. Portugiesische Kaufleute und Sklavenhändler in Cartagena de Indias von 1580 bis zur Mitte des 17. Jahrhunderts* (Frankfurt am Main, 1995), 90, 106, 116–18.

59. At Utrecht in 1713, following the War of the Spanish Succession, the *asiento* was granted to Britain. The British *asentistas* subsequently very rarely called on the Dutch entrepôt.

60. Jonathan I. Israel, "The Dutch Republic and Its Jews During the Conflict over the Spanish Succession (1699–1715)," in *Dutch Jewish History: Proceedings of the Fourth Symposium on the History of the Jews in the Netherlands 7–10 December, Tel Aviv-Jerusalem, 1986*, ed. Jozeph Michman (Assen and Maastricht, 1989), 118–19.

61. Patent, issued by Governor Jeremias van Collen, Curaçao, 2 June 1702, AGI Santo Domingo 696; J. de Wildt, secretary of the Amsterdam Admiralty, to Pensionary Anthonie Heinsius, Amsterdam, 9 November 1703, in *De briefwisseling van Anthonie Heinsius 1702–1720*, ed. A. J. Veenendaal, Jr., various vols. (The Hague, 1976–), vol. 3, 532; "Concept tot veroveringe en verdelinge van de Spaense Westindien tussen Hollant en Engelant," The Hague, December 1707, ARA Aanwinsten 1906 XLIII 23.

62. In 1787, the number of Surinamese whites was estimated at 3,356, including 1,311 (39.1 percent) Jews, but not counting around one hundred free mulatto Jews. This percentage was higher than that in Dutch Brazil, whose Jewish population has often been overstated. Jews accounted for only one thousand at most, and probably even less than five hundred, out of a total population of 3,400 in 1645. Gonsalves de Mello claims that approximately 350 of Recife's 1,704 inhabitants were Jews: José Antonio Gonsalves de Mello, *Gente de Nação. Cristãos-novos e judeus em Pernambuco 1542–1654* (Recife, 1989), 282.

63. This ship of ca. 90 tons left Curaçao for Amsterdam on 30 April 1744.

– Chapter 19 –

AN ATLANTIC PERSPECTIVE ON THE JEWISH STRUGGLE FOR RIGHTS AND OPPORTUNITIES IN BRAZIL, NEW NETHERLAND, AND NEW YORK

James Homer Williams

IN THE MIDDLE THIRD OF THE SEVENTEENTH CENTURY, Jews experienced a range of treatment within the Dutch Atlantic world. Amsterdam tolerated a sizable Jewish community and became the center of Jewish life in western Europe. Dutch Brazil encouraged Jewish settlement in an ecumenical effort to wrest Brazil from Portuguese control. There, hundreds of Jews flourished, as they did later in other Dutch colonies of South America and the Caribbean. Yet in New Amsterdam, geographical precursor to the center of North American Jewry—New York City—Dutch leaders persecuted a few dozen Jews and succeeded in preventing the creation of a prosperous Jewish community.

The central question to which this essay offers an answer, therefore, is why similar Jews within a seemingly uniform Dutch Atlantic world faced a range of challenges and were welcomed in some places and not in others. An examination of Jewish experiences in Amsterdam, Recife, and New Amsterdam suggests that a complex set of variables were at work in determining the particular situation in which the Jews found themselves. These variables included Dutch leaders' valuation of the Jews' usefulness to the larger community and empire, the number of Jews compared to Christians, the perceived threat that Jewish merchants posed to Christian merchants, and the background and temperament of Dutch officials in each locale.

In recreating an Atlantic context for the Jewish quest for a significant place in the Dutch world of Europe and the Americas, this essay hopes not only to solve the puzzle mentioned above but also to transcend some of the limitations in previous accounts of the Jews in early America. Though it has received a great deal of attention—far beyond the actual number of people involved probably warrants[1]—the history of the Jews of New Amsterdam suffers from narrow interpretations by historians interested in the Jewish experience in relatively small geographic areas, such as a city, colony, or region. From this perspective, the two dozen Jews in New Amsterdam are "pilgrim fathers," the first wave of religious troops who established a "precarious North American beachhead" for Judaism, or they are the first indication of "the reversal of the pendulum of Jewish migration" toward the west.[2]

On the other hand, scholars of Dutch colonization prefer to place the Jews within a broader type of intolerance with New Netherland's director-general Peter Stuyvesant as the exemplar. One could accept Frederick Zwierlein's insistence that Stuyvesant's "persecution of the Jews" was simply a part of the general unadulterated religious bigotry of orthodox Calvinists toward Lutherans, Quakers, Catholics, and other non-Calvinists who attempted to settle and worship in New Netherland[3]—if not for the fact that accepting this simplistic view ignores the strikingly different reception Jews received in Dutch Brazil and in Holland itself.

Early modern historians increasingly speak of an Atlantic world, a concept that tries to transcend political boundaries and reconnect mobile people, goods, and ideas as they moved within and between North and South America, Africa, and Europe.[4] This essay proceeds in sections that follow Jews chronologically through three areas of the early Dutch Atlantic world: Holland, Brazil, and New Netherland. It soon becomes apparent that nowhere in the Dutch world of the early to mid-1600s did Jews achieve perfect equality, but they did not expect to, either. What did Jews demand and reasonably expect to achieve? The rights and privileges granted to them in Amsterdam served always as the model when Jews ventured to the western reaches of the Dutch empire. These rights included the exercise of their religion—officially, only in private households so as not to challenge the public monopoly of the Dutch Reformed Church, but in practice, fairly openly in synagogues. They also expected the opportunity to engage in trade, though they accepted other economic restrictions. In return, Jews invested in the Dutch India companies and contributed in myriad ways to the propulsion of the United Provinces into a golden age in the seventeenth century.

A final, shorter section continues the story into the English period after the Dutch lost New Netherland in 1664. This section contrasts the Jewish experience in Manhattan under Dutch and English rule but also places English policies toward Jews in New York in the larger context of the English imperial world in the late seventeenth century. Ironically, the permanent foothold for Jews in mainland North America came not under the auspices of the Dutch, whom scholars and the public perceive as cosmopolitan and tolerant, but under the English, who are seldom noted for a willing acceptance of cultural differences in the early modern world.

* * * *

MOST JEWS IN HOLLAND, BRAZIL, AND NEW NETHERLAND could trace their lineage to Portugal, even though by the time of Dutch colonization in the Americas in 1624 some of them were Dutch-born. Jews in Portugal, who accounted for 20 percent of the population in 1496, had fared better than those in Spain, at least until 1536 when João III, the Portuguese monarch, received permission from Rome to create a Portuguese Inquisition. Those Jews forcibly converted to Christianity were known as New Christians— *Cristãos novos* in Portuguese, *conversos* in Spanish. Early in the 1500s, New Christians established themselves as the leaders of finance and international trade in Portugal, where they enjoyed a monopoly, and in Portuguese colonies such as Brazil. When the crowns of Spain and Portugal united in 1580, the Portuguese New Christians also assumed major roles in the merchant communities of Spain and its overseas empire. For generations after the original forced conversions, descendants of the original New Christians were still known by that term, even if for scores of years their religious devotion had been orthodox Christian. Within a largely anti-Semitic Europe, they could never escape their ancestry as Jews. Across the globe, "Portuguese," "New Christian," and "crypto-Jew" were often used as synonymous religious terms, though with questionable validity. The Portuguese Jesuit theologian António Vieira noted that "in popular parlance, among most of the European nations, 'Portuguese' is confused with 'Jew.'"[5]

In the Low Countries, Christians had essentially driven Jews out by 1550. When the seven northern provinces rebelled in the 1570s, the political chaos and *politique* philosophy of William of Orange combined to open the door to Portuguese New Christians to settle again in the United Provinces. Many New Christians reverted to Judaism when they arrived in Amsterdam. After the Dutch extended their blockade of Antwerp in 1595, New Christian merchants in Portugal shifted their trade to other ports, most notably Amsterdam. From 1595 to 1620, the eve of Dutch colonization in North America, the Portuguese Jewish community in Amsterdam grew rapidly and with little resistance from the burgomasters of the city, who recognized that the Jews, whether New Christian or observant, opened new trade relationships with Portugal and the Portuguese colonies. The prosperity of the Dutch Sephardim in the first six decades of the seventeenth century rose and fell with the vicissitudes of Spanish-Dutch relations. As the historian Jonathan Israel indicates, progress was "extremely sporadic." Dramatic gains were made only during times of peace between the United Provinces and Spain, that is, during the truce from 1609 to 1621 and the decade after the second Spanish-Dutch war, from 1646 to 1655. "By the mid-seventeenth century," historian Miriam Bodian concludes, the Amsterdam Jewish community "had risen to a position of international importance in the Jewish and commercial spheres," making it "a nerve center for a commercial, ethnic, and religious network of considerable complexity."[6]

Two diasporic Jewish movements created this complex network centered in Amsterdam. The Jewish community there—and it *was* a community, Bodian insists—was part of "two far-flung diasporas": the Jewish people in general who spread across Europe and eventually the globe, and the *conversos* and ex-*conversos* who traced their heritage to Spain and Portugal. In Amsterdam, the Sephardic community constructed a collective identity around the Portuguese phrase *os da nação* (those of the Nation). "It was the term 'nation' that carried the effect," Bodian states, for it "evoked an aura, drama, and historical experience which outsiders could not grasp," and which linked the Amsterdam community to other elements of the "Portuguese" diaspora: in Hamburg, Salonica, Rouen, Livorno, Pisa, Jerusalem, Tunis, Brazil, Suriname, and Curaçao. To the Dutch, however, the Portuguese Jews became known as the *Portugeesche Natie* (Portuguese Nation), a use of the word "nation" that stretched from Roman antiquity through the medieval period to mean "a local community of foreigners (never one's own community)."[7]

Commerce, not religion, largely determined the relationship between the Dutch and the Portuguese communities in Amsterdam, a city that had become in the early and mid-seventeenth century the center of colonial trade in northern Europe. The Jews specialized in the so-called "rich trade" of colonial products such as sugar, tobacco, spices, and diamonds, which they traded almost exclusively with Portugal, Madeira, and the Azores. Their age-old expertise benefited the Dutch as well, as they expanded into Brazil, which will be discussed below. Lest we fall into the stereotype of the rich Jewish merchant, however, it is helpful to point out that the Amsterdam community included not only dominant merchants engaged in international trade but also a large number of "middling" and poor folks. Cultural fissures also developed, for by the late 1630s, the community included some five hundred Ashkenazi refugees from Eastern Europe. These Yiddish speakers were culturally distinct from the Portuguese and were usually poor, and therefore resented. The Portuguese community's population stagnated around one thousand members, with many families recently gone to Brazil or other European cities.[8]

If commerce smoothed the relationship between Portuguese Jews and the Christian merchant elite of Amsterdam (the "regents"), then the Dutch Reformed clergy (*predikants*) threatened that relationship with demands for discriminating regulations against the Jews. The clergy were not of one mind, however, with a conservative majority demanding rigorous bans against any non-conformist worship while clerical minority sought toleration. By necessity, the secular magistrates, drawn mostly from the Calvinist merchant elite, played referee in the push-and-pull struggles over how Calvinist Holland (and the other six provinces) would be. Bodian asserts that the Portuguese Jews sought "maximum opportunity and well-being (including religious freedom)" for their community. The regents' focus was on maintaining civil peace.[9]

The conflict at the core of Dutch society and identity formation, however, was not Christian-Jewish but Protestant-Catholic. During the decades-long struggle against Spain, Dutch Protestants adopted the attitude *liever Turcx dan Paus*, "better Turkish than papist." This focus on Catholics explains why Amsterdam Jews were allowed to build a synagogue in 1612, a full *two centuries* before Amsterdam Catholics could worship publicly. During crises such as flooding, pestilence, and war, the *predikants* blamed backsliding Christians, not Jews. "It was Catholic churches, not synagogues, that suffered damage at the hands of angry mobs," Bodian concludes, "and it was a demonized 'popery' against which Protestant preachers fulminated."[10]

Since the Jews were not those demonized, it was easy and expedient for the magistrates of Amsterdam (particularly the burgomasters) to evade the complaints of the clergy by ignoring them. The result was a gap between official policy and actual practice when it came to the rights and privileges that Jews would enjoy. The burgomasters allowed a Portuguese merchant to buy burghers' rights (*poortersrecht*) in 1597. A resolution passed the next year extended the right to other Portuguese, with two stipulations. First, the purchasers must be Christians and "that before taking the [burgher's] oath they be warned that in this city no religion can or may be practiced other than that practiced publicly in the churches," in other words, Calvinism. While seeming to prohibit Jews and Catholics from purchasing the burghers' rights, in fact the resolution served merely to warn non-Calvinists that their religious rights were restricted. The magistrates tolerated Catholic worship if conducted privately, and they allowed Catholics and Jews to purchase the burghers' rights, although certain restrictions did apply. An ordinance in 1632, for instance, "specifically prohibited Jewish *poorters* from carrying on retail trade or guild trades—that of the brokers' guild excepted." Furthermore, they could not hold public office, nor could their children inherit the burghers' rights as Christian children did from their parents.[11]

So within twenty years of their arrival in Amsterdam, Portuguese Jews had worked under the umbrella of legal disability in terms of economic and religious activity to create in reality a situation of remarkable privileges enjoyed by few Jews elsewhere in Europe. Their skills in adapting to circumstances—and the magistrates' willingness to connive with them against the orthodox Reformed ministers—is illustrated in the building of the first synagogue in 1612. After construction of the building had begun, the city council passed a resolution prohibiting anyone from the Portuguese Nation from living or worshiping in the building, "on penalty of having the said house or building razed." While some Reformed ministers spit vitriol at the Jews and the magistrates followed with a resolution against the synagogue, construction continued. The compromise was to transfer ownership to a Christian (the Catholic Nicolaes van Campen, himself a member of the council in spite of regulations against Catholics holding office), who then rented the building to the Jews. Catholics sometimes followed the same tactic to maintain their secluded houses of worship (*schuilkerken*), but they rented from Protestants.[12]

As long as the Jews of Amsterdam kept a low religious profile in public, they could function normally in Dutch society, suffering only some restrictions on their economic activities (not enough to prevent many from becoming wealthy) and their political rights (though it is not certain that Jews even *wanted* to hold political office). In Amsterdam, Jews and Christians largely lived in separate spheres that intersected only in the economic realm. Neither side wished for social and religious interaction.

What happened in Amsterdam, however, did not necessarily dictate Dutch policies toward Jews in other cities, some of which were less welcoming than Amsterdam, or in the colonies, where the West India Company (WIC) operated autonomously. Neither the province of Holland nor the States General of the United Provinces ever promulgated a uniform Jewish policy. When presented with just such a statute in 1619, the States General declined to take action, thereby leaving regulation of the "Hebrew Nation" (*Hebreeusche Natie*) in the hands of local authorities and leaving intact the ordinances directed at the Jews of Amsterdam passed by the burgomasters in 1616. These ordinances warned the Jews "not to speak or write anything (and to ensure that nothing be spoken or written) that may, in any way, tend to the disparagement of our Christian religion; not to attempt to seduce any Christian person away from our Christian religion or to circumcise one; and not to have any carnal relations, whether in or out of wedlock, with Christian women or girls, not even those of ill repute." Thus, "in characteristically evasive fashion," Bodian remarks, the burgomasters "neither granted nor denied Jews the right to public worship."[13]

Since the magistrates of Amsterdam had created a place for the Portuguese Jews, it should come as no surprise that when plans arose for Dutch activity in Brazil, they included the Jews. By 1621, when the WIC formed and began its plans for colonization of North America, there was already a substantial population of New Christians in Portuguese Brazil and a Portuguese Jewish community of approximately eight hundred in Amsterdam (less than 1 percent of the city's population). From the early 1600s, Amsterdam Jews had been the intermediaries in trade between Holland and Brazil. The historian Daniel M. Swetschinski has suggested that this trade "should really be seen as a triangular Holland-Portugal-Brazil route with as yet no direct traffic between Holland and Brazil." Portuguese Jewish merchants in Amsterdam could not operate independently but rather were partners with kin situated in merchant communities across the Atlantic world. "Considerations of kinship," Swetschinski concludes, "were uppermost in the minds of Amsterdam's Portuguese Jews."[14]

These Portuguese Jews also actively supported Dutch Christians in their struggle against Spain for independence. It was natural in 1623 for Dutch officials to suggest that Jews would help them conquer Brazil, which was still under the united crowns of Spain and Portugal. In his conquest proposal, Jan Andries Moerbeeck surmised that because most of the Portuguese residents of Brazil were Jews, they were inevitably enemies of Spain, and the Dutch could expect no resistance from them. In the conquest of Bahia in 1624, several dozen Jews did join the expedition from Holland, and some New Christians in Brazil collaborated with the Dutch, who immediately proclaimed a policy of religious toleration. Such collaboration was always dangerous, however. When the Portuguese recaptured Bahia a year later, they executed four "men of the Hebrew Nation."[15]

The Dutch returned in 1630 to conquer Pernambuco in northeastern Brazil. In the plans for conquest approved by the States General, the WIC promised that "The liberty of Spaniards, Portuguese, and natives, whether they be Roman Catholics or Jews, will be respected." As at home and in its other colonies, the WIC established the Dutch Reformed Church for public worship, but it left everyone free of molestation "or inquiries in matters of conscience or in their private homes." In Brazil, "no one should dare to disquiet or disturb them [Catholics and Jews] or cause them any hardship—under the penalty of arbitrary punishments or … severe or exemplary reproof." With the Dutch seen as tolerant Protestant liberators from Spanish Inquisitorial oppression, the New Christians of Recife, a historian of Brazilian Jews commented, "rejoiced at the arrival of the Dutch expedition."[16]

A variety of Jews in the Dutch expedition made their way into Brazilian society: soldiers, company interpreters, citizens joining relatives, and perhaps a few German and Polish Jews. There were immediate success stories. The mercenary soldier Moses Navarro, for instance, petitioned to stay on as a free citizen (*vrijluiden*) after his three-year contract, and in 1635 received a broker's license for trading in sugar and tobacco. So many Jews emigrated from Amsterdam in search of the newly opened economic opportunities in Brazil that the three Sephardic congregations in Amsterdam combined into one in 1639. Meanwhile, some New Christians of Pernambuco reverted to Judaism and were circumcised, provoking "a great scandal for the Christian people," according to a contemporary Catholic historian.[17]

The golden age of Dutch Brazil—and the peak of Jewish prosperity there—came under the relatively enlightened governor-generalship of Johan Maurits van Nassau-Siegen (1637–1644). This nobleman, great grandson of King Christian III of Denmark (1503–1559) and great nephew of William I, Prince of Orange and stadholder of Holland (1533–1584), towers over the history of Dutch Brazil and proved a blessing to Jews. The WIC encouraged Jews to emigrate to Brazil, where they proved useful as cultural brokers with the Portuguese. Jews dominated tax farming and the domestic slave trade in Brazil, but they were excluded from public office. They served in the militia with other free citizens, but Johan Maurits exempted them from guard duty on Saturdays in exchange for a fee.[18]

/

Johan Maurits's Calvinist heritage[19] and his early statements about Jews did not foretell his eventual promotion of religious toleration. Soon after his arrival in Brazil, he encouraged Reformed ministers to turn their conversion efforts to Indians, Catholics, and Jews alike. "It is necessary to destroy the deep-rooted pretension of the Jews to observe the Mosaic Law and to wait for the restoration of the Kingdom of Israel," Johan Maurits said. "They must be persuaded that Jesus Christ, the son of Mary, was the promised Messiah, who has already arrived, and to revere and believe in him." Evidently, this puff of Christian bravado was meant for the consumption of the Reformed clergy, for a minister to the French Protestant community in Brazil confirmed that Johan Maurits privately detested the Jews. Yet he succeeded in separating his own feelings from company policy and soon became known as a man of "benevolence, forgiveness, affability and fairness" to Reformed, Catholics, and Jews alike. In the end, no Jews converted, nor were they really expected to. Instead, within months of Johan Maurits's arrival the Jews had established two synagogues in Recife, in violation of the Reformed monopoly on public worship.[20]

Jewish success, in turn, provoked resentment from Portuguese Catholics—the Old Christians. Catholics had fallen from the status of the oppressor to the position of the conquered, and suffered the further humiliation of being mocked by Jews. Even though the Brazilians shared Christianity with the Dutch, theirs was the evil papism so despised by Calvinists in the 1600s.[21]

The economic usefulness of the Jews in the conquest and thereafter tempered Johan Maurits's private bigotry toward Jews. As long as this usefulness lasted, WIC officers allowed the Jews to bend the rules, just as they were accustomed to doing in Amsterdam. In 1638, however, the Reformed clergy asked Johan Maurits to disallow public worship by the Jews, and the synagogues were closed. The government prohibited street processions by Catholics or Jews and warned the Jews to worship "so secretly that they should not be heard." Yet the issue was by no means settled and was not simply a matter of religious policy, for the Dutch also had to consider the colony's future and the place of Catholics and Jews in its success. As more Dutch people acculturated to Brazil, the usefulness of the Jews diminished, while increasing numbers of Dutch colonists interpreted the Jews' success as coming at the expense of Christians.[22]

Johan Maurits's mediation of competing ethnic and religious interests in Brazil produced what historian C. R. Boxer has called a "policy of masterly inactivity," which tried to blunt the complaints of Reformed clergy while balancing the views of the Jews and the Catholics. Jews believed that their unquestioned loyalty to the Dutch Republic and their contributions to the success of the WIC should translate into greater liberties for themselves. Johan Maurits wrote to the Company and concurred that the Jews were loyal, but the Portuguese Catholics, he knew, could not be trusted for a moment.[23]

All in all, however, Portuguese Christians enjoyed greater political rights, in spite of their disloyalty, than Dutch Jews enjoyed. The reality of population proportions undoubtedly shaped Johan Maurits's policies as much as his religious sympathies did, for New Holland, as the Dutch called their part of Brazil, was never a colony where the Dutch themselves settled in great numbers. The twenty thousand Portuguese colonists and six thousand African slaves, not to speak of the local native groups, vastly outnumbered the Dutch civilian population, Christian and Jew, which reached only three thousand in number.[24] Jews, a double minority, were granted political rights equivalent to those given Indians and Africans in Brazil. Many of them succeeded economically, it is true, and they must have found Brazil an attractive opportunity since in 1645 Jews accounted for up to one-half the civilian white population in Dutch Brazil. They also remained steadfastly loyal to the Dutch during the years of rebellion from 1645 to the fall of Recife in 1654.[25]

Their loyalty, however, was never rewarded with religious or political equality in Dutch Brazil. Were the Dutch simply exploiting the Jews, or more charitably, were they unusually tolerant in an intolerant age? Either way, the precise experience of the Jews in Dutch Brazil helps to explain what to modern eyes may seem to be an inconsistent policy toward ethnic and religious groups. At an official level, religious difference mattered, but at the practical level, economic, military, or political utility counted for more. In short, *politique* clashed with religious zeal and bigotry.

When they reconquered Dutch Brazil, the Portuguese offered generous terms, including a pardon in article one for "all nations of whatever quality or religion they may be … although they may have been rebellious against the Crown of Portugal—the same also granted to all Jews.…" Other articles allowed all Dutch subjects retention of their property and future treatment as if they were Portuguese. Regarding religion, the Dutch would be treated like foreign residents of Portugal. Those who did not wish to remain were given three months to arrange a departure.[26]

Nearly all the Dutch chose to leave, but a shortage of ships prevented their departure within three months. As the 26 April deadline approached, Dutch leaders requested an extension from the Portuguese government. General Francisco Barreto de Menezes replied that all Christians and Jews who missed the deadline would continue to receive mild treatment, "except the Jews who had been Christians, these being subject to the Holy Inquisition, wherein I cannot interfere."[27] Given this prospect, it is hardly surprising that all professing Jews, six hundred in all, emigrated to Amsterdam, to other European cities, or to Caribbean colonies. A small group of Jews sailed from Recife in February 1654 on the same ship with a Reformed minister. Outcasts, all were bound for New Netherland. After being blown off course and waiting for several months in the Caribbean for other transportation, the group resumed its journey to New Amsterdam.[28]

The Portuguese Jewish refugees from Dutch Brazil did not start well in New Netherland. The arrival of "23 souls, big as well as little," stirred

up the Dutch community of New Amsterdam, particularly because the
Jews owed more than 1,500 guilders to the captain and crew for their passage. The local court ordered their furniture and other property sold to
satisfy the debt, thus leaving the refugees not only religious outcasts, but
poor ones at that. These mostly Sephardic refugees joined Jacob Barsimson, an Ashkenazi who had arrived a month before as just another immigrant sent with the blessings of the WIC to build the population of the
struggling colony. Only with the arrival of the Brazilian refugees in September did the presence of Jews create a stir.[29]

In a settlement of several thousand, these two dozen Jews faced different circumstances than in Brazil. In New Netherland, they were vastly
outnumbered and of no immediate use to Peter Stuyvesant and his
colony. Moreover, Stuyvesant was no Johan Maurits. The two men shared
a commitment to the WIC, a military career, and a Calvinist zeal from
their upbringing. In the last year of Johan Maurits's rule in Brazil,
Stuyvesant in his capacity as governor of the Caribbean islands of Aruba,
Bonaire, and Curaçao led an expedition to capture St. Martin from the
Spanish. In 1644 with ships borrowed from Dutch Brazil, Stuyvesant laid
siege, endured a shattered right leg, but after a month returned to
Curaçao without victory. His eighteen-month tenure at an end, and his
life miraculously intact, Stuyvesant repaired to the Netherlands.[30]

Two years later in 1647, he arrived in New Netherland with an artifi-
cial leg and an appointment to serve as director-general. He immediately
set about shaping up the colony to match his character: "God-fearing,
honest, hard-working, abstemious," according to one biography. As the
son of a Calvinist minister and as a career official in the WIC since 1632,
Stuyvesant could be expected to serve the company and the Dutch
Reformed Church loyally.[31]

And so he did, but as episodes in New Netherland would show, his
actions were motivated more by religious zeal than by a pragmatic policy
aimed at Company prosperity, such as Johan Maurits's. To be sure, both
Dutch governors strove for peace and prosperity in their respective
domains, but the fundamental difference between Stuyvesant and Johan
Maurits was the path they chose in hopes of achieving their goal. Their
choices mirrored the dichotomy in the debate about religious diversity
and tolerance that had been raging in the Netherlands since the 1570s.
Johan Maurits reflected the pragmatically tolerant end of the spectrum in
the vein of the Amsterdam regents and the Arminian writer Simon Epis-
copius, who believed that the security and happiness of states was best
achieved where citizens enjoyed intellectual and religious freedom.
Stuyvesant sided with the strict Calvinists who continued to insist that
diversity and toleration would undermine social harmony and endanger
the peace and prosperity of the provinces, a belief that impelled them to
suppress public deviation from the Reformed norm.[32]

In spite of these differences in circumstances and leadership, relations
between the Jews and Reformed citizens of New Netherland resembled

those in Amsterdam and Recife. Wherever they went in the Dutch Atlantic world, in fact, Jews found themselves in similar struggles for the economic rights and religious toleration they enjoyed in Amsterdam. Wherever they went, Jews sparked intense reactions and lengthy transatlantic conversations between Reformed clergy, colonial officials, company directors, and Netherland politicians about the place of Jews in an increasingly global Dutch world and an increasingly diverse Dutch culture.[33]

Stuyvesant wished for Jews to have no place in his colony. Within three weeks of the Jews' arrival, he reported to the company directors in Amsterdam that, "for the benefit of this weak and newly developing place," he had "require[d] them in a friendly way to depart." In language reminiscent of Johan Maurits in the 1630s, Stuyvesant called the Jews a "deceitful race" and "hateful enemies and blasphemers of the name of Christ" who should not be allowed "further to infect and trouble this new colony."[34] Immediately, then, it is clear, the magistrates and clergy of New Netherland interpreted Jews not as useful allies in the development of a colony (as in Brazil) but as godless competitors and troublemakers who must be purged. Peace and prosperity demanded it.

When word reached Holland of the Jews' reception in New Amsterdam, the Amsterdam Jewish community mobilized in defense of the rights of Jews to remain in New Amsterdam with the same privileges that Jews enjoyed in Amsterdam. In January 1655, "the merchants of the Portuguese Nation," as they called themselves, petitioned the Amsterdam chamber of the WIC, which administered affairs in New Netherland. The petition reminded the directors of the great influx of Jews from Brazil, all of whom could not stay in Amsterdam. To prevent immigration to New Netherland would damage the Jewish community and hinder the Company, and it was unfair to those Jews who had "at all times been faithful" to the Company in Brazil and had risked their "possessions and their blood." The Jews demonstrated a keen understanding of imperial rivalries in the mid-seventeenth century by suggesting that the Dutch would fall behind the French and the English, who allowed Jews to travel to their Caribbean colonies. Besides, how could the Company restrict the Jews "who reside here [in Amsterdam] and have been settled here well on to about sixty years, many also being born here and confirmed burghers, and this to a land [New Netherland] that needs people for its increase?" Calling upon sentiments of past loyalty and prospects of continued utility to the Company, the Jews asked to "enjoy liberty on condition of contributing like others" to the prosperity of New Netherland.[35]

The lines of debate had been drawn. Stuyvesant and the colonial and Amsterdam clergy would insist on religious purity as a keystone to success for New Netherland. Jews relied on their experience in Holland and Brazil to argue for a uniform application throughout the Dutch Atlantic world of the limited privileges that they had in Amsterdam. Moderating the extremes were the Company directors and occasionally their High Mightinesses in the States General of the United Provinces. Who could disagree with the Amsterdam Jews' assessment that in the colonies land was "extensive and spacious"? With the exception of the Reformed Church, with its focus on God before mammon, everyone could also agree that "the more of loyal people that go to live" in the colonies, "the better it is in regard to the population of the country" and the income to be derived therefrom.[36] This is precisely the bind in which the orthodox Calvinist Stuyvesant found himself: he needed to populate New Netherland with loyal citizens, but he could not stomach tolerating Jews as a means to do so.

The directors sympathized initially with the troubles that Stuyvesant foresaw with the Jews, but they nonetheless agreed with the petition from the Amsterdam Jews and ordered Stuyvesant to be tolerant. Because of the losses Jews suffered in Brazil, and "also because of the large amount of capital which they still have invested in the shares of the company," the directors concluded that it would be "somewhat unreasonable and unfair" to prevent their access to New Netherland. "You will now govern yourself accordingly," they wrote.[37]

Stuyvesant continued to resist. "To give liberty to the Jews will be very detrimental," he warned again. First, they would inevitably snatch business from Christians, a prospect that most Europeans at the time regarded as fact. More to the point for Stuyvesant was the door that toleration would open to other heretics. Once Jews had liberty, "we cannot refuse the Lutherans and Papists."[38]

Meanwhile, the New Amsterdam clergy seconded Stuyvesant's predictions of religious chaos and urged the classis of Amsterdam to pressure the WIC to preserve the Reformed monopoly. In March 1655 the Reverend Johannes Megapolensis wrote his impression of the Jewish refugees. On the one hand, they had been nothing but "godless rascals" and a drain on the Christian poor relief system. On the other, contradictorily, he feared they would soon overwhelm the Christians, take all the trade, and "then build here their synagogue." To him a religious domino effect was a real possibility. New Netherland suffered already from diversity—"Papists, Mennonites and Lutherans among the Dutch," "Puritans or Independents, and many Atheists and various other servants of Baal among the English under this Government, who conceal themselves under the name of Christians." A flood of "obstinate and immovable Jews" from Holland would certainly "create a still greater confusion."[39]

Ordered to let the Jews remain, Stuyvesant and his council did their best to make life for Jews in New Amsterdam more restrictive than for Jews in Amsterdam. In 1655 the council considered three areas of community and economic activity: military service, trade rights, and the ownership of real estate. In each area, Jewish activity was limited. Supposedly at the request of the captains and officers of the militia, who felt an "aversion and disaffection ... to be fellow soldiers ... and to mount guard in the same guardhouse" with Jews, and also because Jews in Netherlands' cities did not serve in the militia, the council exempted Jews from military service in exchange for a monthly fee, as was done in Amsterdam. Jacob Barsimson and Asser Levy, however, petitioned to serve in the militia, since as manual laborers they could not afford the exemption fee. The council denied their request and told them they were free "to depart [the colony] whenever and wherever it may please them."[40]

In November, several Jews petitioned to conduct trade in all parts of New Netherland, as they thought was provided in the company's order early in the year. The council, "for important reasons" that it never specified, denied the request and restricted Jews to trade in the city of New Amsterdam alone. Just before Christmas, Salvador Dandradj, a Jewish merchant, petitioned the council to approve his purchase of a house in New Amsterdam. Again, the council refused "for important reasons" his right to own real estate. When the seller objected, the council ordered him to auction the house again. When the price was nearly 300 guilders (a laborer's annual income) less than Dandradj had bid, Stuyvesant and his council agreed to contribute half the difference, or 148 guilders, to the seller, "a man needed by his family, having a house full of children."[41] In this last instance, the leaders of the colony literally paid for their religious bigotry.

With the Amsterdam Jewish community on the backs of the WIC directors, it proved futile for Stuyvesant to hedge on Jewish rights forever. In March 1656, the directors reminded him that they had granted the Jews "the same liberty that is granted them in this country ... with respect to civil and political liberties," meaning limited but significant privileges. As stated above, Amsterdam Jews by this time had a synagogue, but the directors continued to refuse New Amsterdam Jews "license to exercise and carry on their religion in synagogues or gatherings," a policy that applied to every non-Reformed group, not just Jews. Stuyvesant replied that the Jews had every privilege and freedom to trade as the other inhabitants of New Netherland, but they were still prohibited from "the free and public exercise of their abominable religion." He noted sarcastically that "what they may be able to obtain from your Honors time will tell."[42]

This letter crossed the Atlantic simultaneously with a stern rebuke from the directors that seemed to settle the Jewish matter once and for all. The directors had "learned with displeasure" that the director and council had prohibited Jews in New Netherland from trading outside New Amsterdam, in contradiction to the directors' orders, and from owning real estate, in contradiction to the practice in Holland. "We wish that this had not occurred," wrote the directors, "but that your Honors had obeyed our orders which you must hereafter execute punctually and with more respect." Some restrictions were acceptable, however. "Jews or Portuguese people" should not be allowed to become mechanics (i.e., craftsmen) or to have open retail shops, occupations still closed to Jews in Amsterdam. In every respect, the directors expected the Jews to model themselves after those in Amsterdam, and for Stuyvesant to let them.

Jews should "quietly and peacefully carry on their business" and "exercise in all quietness their religion within their houses." It only seemed natural that they would "build their houses close together in a convenient place on one or the other side of New Amsterdam—at their choice—as they have done here" in Amsterdam.[43]

Did Stuyvesant take this rebuke to heart in 1656? A court case that summer suggests so, and it reveals more about the Jewish refugees' struggle to find a place within the majority culture. In early June, Nicasius de Sille, a law enforcement officer in New Amsterdam, charged David Ferera with removing a chest of goods from the house of the bailiff, contrary to the bailiff's orders. That Ferera used "many hasty words uttered in his language"[44] compounded the offense, for the court felt him "in serious contempt and disregard of justice." New Netherland court records reveal no shortage of similar cases wherein the court zealously punished disrespectful citizens. In this case, however, there were the added elements of Ferera's religion, his inability to speak Dutch, and the court's bigotry toward Jews. Jews were almost always clearly labeled in the records, even when their Judaism had nothing to do with the case. Sille demanded "that the said Jew shall be publicly whipped at a stake" and banished, but the court decided for the moment only to imprison him.[45]

The case dragged into July as Ferera appeared with a translator to answer the charges. The city court fined him 800 guilders. In late July Ferera appealed "with humble reverence" for a reduced penalty to Stuyvesant and his council. From jail Ferera confessed "his ignorance of Dutch laws and customs and lack of knowledge of the language," both of which prevented him from understanding the gravity of his offense. "To prevent costs and so dispatch the suit quickly," the director and council on 26 July appointed arbitrators, including Ferera's interpreter Joseph da Costa, another Jew. Their decision was recorded the same day: a fine of 120 guilders plus 50 guilders in costs. A far cry from whipping and banishment (or an 800-guilder fine), the final arbitrated sentence suggests that not all Dutch officials were out to ruin the Jews and perhaps that the Amsterdam directors' letter of 14 June had arrived in New Amsterdam and encouraged Stuyvesant to blunt the city court's original blow at Ferera.[46]

Lest we conclude that all the Christian residents of New Netherland were unadulterated anti-Semites, it is worth remembering that the Dutch leaders of New Amsterdam and New Netherland always debated the cases before them and usually recorded the range of verdicts and punishments voted by each member of the council and the court. So there was always a range of attitudes within the larger consensus that Jews were unwelcome competitors in the colony. Occasionally, one can even detect a bit of toleration, by any standard, as on 3 June 1658. On that Monday court day, Adriaen Keyser brought a suit against Jacob Barsimson, who failed to appear. Instead of holding Barsimson in contempt, however, and assessing court costs, as was frequently the case when a party to a suit failed to appear, the court was more lenient. "Though deft. is absent," the record states, "yet no default is entered against him, as he was summoned on his Sabbath."[47]

Within another year most Jews would depart for greater opportunities in other colonies. Stuyvesant, in effect, succeeded in making New Netherland unattractive to prospective Jewish immigrants. For those few that stayed, the years of Dutch rule that remained would be more tranquil. An episode in 1657 suggests that Stuyvesant would fight no more, at least about economic privileges. In April, Asser Levy petitioned for the burghers' rights, and Jacob Cohen Hendricus requested permission to bake bread in the city of New Amsterdam. Levy claimed "that such ought not be refused him as he keeps watch and ward like other Burghers," and he showed "a Burgher certificate from the City of Amsterdam that the Jew is Burgher there." The burgomasters refused Levy and referred him to the director and council. As for Hendricus, he also knew his rights should compare to Amsterdam Jews, so he asked for the limited right to sell bread "with closed door." Again, the burgomasters refused, citing orders from the director and council and the "Honorable Lords Majores," perhaps meaning the Amsterdam directors. They erred, of course, since Amsterdam authorities prohibited Jews only from open retailing.[48]

Not to be outdone, the "Jewish Nation" of New Amsterdam reminded Stuyvesant that by denying Jews the burghers' rights the burgomasters had ignored the directors' order of 1655, the one that must be obeyed. With no commentary, the director and council charged the burgomasters to admit Levy, and Jews in general, to the burghers' rights.[49]

If these Jews were not "pilgrim fathers" and their Dutch tormentors were not simply unthinking bigots, then what were they? In addition to migrating within the Dutch Atlantic world, the refugees from Brazil acted out another episode in a drama that had begun thirty years before when the WIC planned New Netherland as an outpost of Dutch culture, including Reformed religion. This colony, at least, would be more narrowly Dutch than Holland, not to mention Amsterdam with its growing diversity. The definition of "Dutchness" created in 1624 and guarded thereafter began with the monopoly on the Reformed religion in terms of public worship, with the guarantee of freedom of conscience otherwise. Company officials in the colony must be Reformed, which created a two-tiered system of political rights. To this core, the directors added layers of meaning, including an insistence that all civil, military, and judicial business be conducted solely in the Dutch language. Colonists were also required to take an oath of allegiance to the States General and to the Company. Legal matters must be conducted according to Dutch practices, and commerce should follow Dutch forms.[50] In short, these regulations, along with the Atlantic itself, screened out those who did not already fit the definition of Dutchness or who were unwilling to conform to it, and they meant that Jews would not enjoy all the privileges they had known in Amsterdam.

By the 1650s, however, it was becoming clear that this zeal for a pure Dutch colony was in effect driving current residents away or potential immigrants toward other colonies that were more hospitable, especially in religious matters. The concerns in Amsterdam of the directors and the Jewish community were realistic: both agreed that loyal Dutch residents were desirable immigrants to New Netherland, which needed more people if it hoped to survive, surrounded as it was by growing English colonies. Rather than open the doors to Dutch Jews, who had proven their loyalty in Brazil, Stuyvesant, backed by the Reformed clergy, clung to the ideal of New Netherland as a Christian colony, even if that meant welcoming foreigners of questionable loyalty. Just as the Dutch fled Brazil and some Jews arrived in New Netherland, England and the United Provinces were completing the first Anglo-Dutch war. Tensions were high in New Amsterdam for fear that the English would pounce on the Dutch colony. Nevertheless, at the same time that Dutch leaders asked two dozen Jewish refugees with a Dutch identity to leave Manhattan, English refugees from New England were forming towns a few miles away on western Long Island. For a decade, the Dutch rightly questioned their loyalty, yet Stuyvesant assumed the best from the English because they were "brothers" in Calvinist religion.[51]

Centuries later, all this may seem foolhardy, nonsensical, or ironic. The question remains as to how two similar colonies, New Holland and New Netherland, starting with essentially the same policies could result in strikingly different characters, in particular for the Jews who tried to settle there. The first variable was the number and time of arrival of the Jews. In Brazil, they arrived with the first Dutch expeditions and in large numbers that continued to grow. In New Netherland, they arrived thirty years after the colony was founded. Another factor was the Jews' usefulness. In Brazil, they were valued initially as vital allies and cultural brokers for the Dutch. In New Netherland, a trade network was already in place when the Jews arrived, so they were seen immediately as dangerous competitors. In Brazil, unlike North America, the Dutch conquered another group of Europeans. This large community of Portuguese Catholic Christians, New and Old, necessitated a more flexible application of the Reformed monopoly that was the official policy in all Dutch colonies.

Finally, we should not overlook the force of personality, for the fate of the Jews in Brazil depended in large measure on Johan Maurits and in New Netherland to the same degree on Peter Stuyvesant. Both began their colonial service as zealous defenders of the Reformed Church, but one became a governor willing to look the other way while the other remained steadfastly opposed to toleration, despite the economic gains that it might bring. The man who left Brazil in 1644 did not share the same temperament with the man who saw New Netherland fall in 1664. In his advice to his successors, Maurits recommended religious toleration. "In ecclesiastical matters or affairs of the Church, toleration or compliance is more necessary in Brazil than with any other people which has been granted religious freedom," Johan Maurits wrote. "If fervour and Christian zeal for the true worship urges you to think otherwise, it is better if you do not manifest it. Every one of you should suppress personal feelings in this matter in order to avoid great inconvenience."[52] It is impossible to imagine Stuyvesant saying these words. He never changed his view of Jews as a "deceitful race." The Jews who sought refuge in New Netherland learned this lesson: Jews within the confines of the Dutch Atlantic world in the mid-seventeenth century, though dealing with similar Dutch leaders, through the peculiarities of time, place, and personality could expect uneven treatment in their struggle for rights, ranging from conditions in Amsterdam, arguably the best place in Europe for Jews, to conditions in New Netherland, certainly the worst.

* * * *

IN THE DECADE BETWEEN 1654, when the Jews arrived in New Netherland, and 1664, when the English conquered the colony, Dutch Jews found more economic, political, and religious hospitality in other colonies. Attention shifted to the Caribbean in the WIC's struggle to compete with English imperialists. In 1657 the Zeeland chamber of the WIC issued a charter for Nova Zeelandia, a new Dutch colony in the Essequibo and Pomeroon river regions of western Guiana. The charter granted Jews "very unusual" privileges, in historian Jacob Marcus's estimation, for it included the free and open exercise of religion, freedom to engage in any occupation, full burghers' rights to trade, and the right to exercise minor judicial functions within their community. Lest the Zeeland chamber look unusually tolerant, it should be noted that the initiative for the colony came from the Jewish community and succeeded in spite of Christian prejudice.[53] It represents a classic case of the Dutch dilemma in the seventeenth century: how to reconcile economic desires, nationalism, and Calvinist zeal.

While several hundred Jews of various stripes—mostly Sephardim from the United Provinces, Brazil, Morocco, and Livorno—ventured to Nova Zeelandia, other Jewish communities soon formed in Suriname[54] and on Curaçao. The latter became the largest Dutch American Jewish community and faced few, if any, disabilities from the Dutch authorities. Historian Wim Klooster argues: "They could practice their religion unhindered and were protected in all possible ways by the West India Company." Unlike Brazil and New Netherland, with its anti-Semitism thinly disguised, if disguised at all, in Curaçao "even unofficial anti-semitism seems to have been a rare phenomenon." Calling upon their expertise in the network of Portuguese Jews, Jews in Curaçao dominated some professions, such as trade, brokerage, and insurance.[55]

Comparisons between Brazil, Curaçao, and New Netherland, though beyond the scope of this essay, would be useful for understanding the Atlantic world, particularly because Jews traded between New Netherland and Curaçao, and Stuyvesant was the director-general of both colonies. The Jewish community of Curaçao emulated the Amsterdam

Jewish community, which was entrusted with the same role as mediator and advocate that it had played for the benefit of the Jews in New Amsterdam. A web of transatlantic conversations occurred among Dutch people in Curaçao and Amsterdam, similar to the conversations about Dutch identity discussed above in reference to New Netherland.[56]

With English rule, the political metropolis for the region shifted from Amsterdam to London. The Atlantic world of English Jewry was limited in comparison to Jews in the Dutch, Spanish, and Portuguese worlds. There were far fewer Jews in England and its colonies. Nevertheless, a Jewish community redeveloped in New York City after 1664, and in all English colonies similar issues of toleration and equality arose in the treatment of the Jewish minority.

There were no Jews in England from 1290 to 1656. When they allowed Jews re-entry in 1656, the English treated them differently than the Inquisitorial Catholic European states. On paper, at least, English Calvinist policies closely resembled the practices of the Dutch Reformed in Holland and in the WIC colonies. In short, nearly everyone was anti-Semitic. Yet the English passed no laws in the seventeenth century that targeted Jews. Rather, Jews suffered the same disabilities in law that affected other non-Anglicans. The English limited the privileges of dissenting Protestants, Catholics, and Jews in a variety of ways: municipal and guild restrictions, the establishment of the Church of England, alien status that limited citizenship rights, the prescription of Anglican sacraments, and the requirement to subscribe to state oaths.[57]

In practice, Jews found life tolerable enough that hundreds soon settled in the English world. By 1689, sixty to eighty Jewish families lived in England. Although the Toleration Act of 1689 did not extend to them, Jews in London continued to worship publicly in a synagogue, as they had done as a privilege (not a right) extended by the king-in-council since 1673. Much like the Dutch had done earlier in the century, the English encouraged Jews to settle in English colonies as a strategy to increase population and develop healthy trade. Legal disabilities still applied, with the exception of religious laws, which did not automatically extend to the colonies. In the West Indian sugar islands, colonial legislatures restricted Jewish rights and privileges the most. Jamaica in the late seventeenth century resembled New Netherland insofar as its residents complained about the competition from Jews and tried to limit the economic and political freedoms of Jews more than the crown charter allowed.[58]

In the mainland colonies, discrimination was less direct. In New York, the Jewish struggle for economic and religious rights was largely anticlimactic. After the nadir of 1664, when only four Jews were known to live in the colony, the Jewish population did not flourish dramatically in the light of English toleration, nor was there much of a struggle for economic opportunities. Instead, Jews gradually spread up the Hudson Valley and made gains in population and wealth in Manhattan. In 1674,

James, duke of York, instructed Governor Edmund Andros to tolerate all dissenters. Four years later, Andros reported "Religions of all sorts" in the colony, including "Quakers and Anabaptists, of severall sects, some Jews, but presbiterians and Independents most numerous and substantiall." Four Jews were listed on a November 1676 tax list. In 1682, Asser Levy, a carryover from Dutch times, died, leaving an estate that symbolized his achievement of "considerable status" as a butcher in Manhattan. According to Leo Hershkowitz, the expert on Levy, he was "a real 'Pilgrim,'" for "he remained while others left"; he was a success, and "he more clearly integrated himself within the host society."[59]

The turn of the century brought growth and stability. An influx of substantial families and individuals led to the creation of a group of wealthy merchant shippers among New York's Jews. In 1730 the community dedicated the first synagogue built specifically for that purpose in British North America. The synagogue of Mikveh Israel, in Willemstad, Curaçao, donated 272 ounces of silver to the New York synagogue, Shearith Israel, to help pay for construction. The receipt recording the donation indicates the continuing presence of the Portuguese Jewish network in the Atlantic world. Written in both English and Portuguese, it was signed by Moses Gomez and Rodrigo Pacheco of Curaçao and by Jacob Franks of New York. By then about 225 Jews coexisted with the city's eight thousand residents.[60]

Like the Dutch in Brazil, the English inherited a community of Jews in New York. Their treatment of the Jews subsequently was a product of the same variables that explain the differences between the Jewish experience in Brazil and in New Netherland. First, the community of Jews in Manhattan was tiny and remained unthreateningly small into the mid-1700s. Second, the political leader of the colony, later to become James II, was himself a Catholic and therefore tended to favor toleration of non-Anglicans in his colony. Finally, the English grew to see the Jews as a valuable resource in the building of an Atlantic empire.

In spite of occasional disputes between Christians and Jews in New York, the Jews experienced a gradual expansion of rights and privileges from 1664 to 1740. The Dutch surrender agreement included a pledge from the English that all residents of New Netherland would be treated as free denizens of New York with full property rights and "the liberty of their consciences in divine worship." The English agreed, therefore, to treat the Jews as they were already inclined to do, that is, with toleration but at the same time enforcing certain disabilities. Over time, the Jews managed to eliminate most of the disabilities in practice, if not officially. One of their momentary defeats came in 1685 when Governor James Dongan, a Catholic, endorsed the Jews' petition to worship publicly. The mayor and aldermen denied the request, however, citing the charter of 1683, which declared that "noe publique worship is tolerated ... but to those that professe faith in Christ."[61] The Dutch policy continued, therefore, well into the English period.

In terms of political rights, Jews remained second-class citizens, like all non-Anglicans, and could not hold high office. They worked toward more liberal naturalization laws after 1700 and succeeded by 1718 in being elected as constables in New York City and in avoiding disqualifying tests and oaths. They apparently voted successfully, too, at least in local elections as long as they met freehold qualifications. The political struggle reached across the colony in an election in 1737. In that year, the legislature voided Jewish votes for a candidate after his opponent argued that English law disqualified Jews from voting. That the challenger clinched his argument against the Jews by resurrecting their alleged guilt for the Crucifixion should lend caution to an overly sanguine picture of the Jewish experience in colonial New York. There was still anti-Semitism aplenty. The greatest shift in English policy toward Jews in the colonies came in 1740 with passage of the Plantation Act. Primarily meant to encourage Jewish traders to populate British America, the act shifted control of naturalization to imperial authorities. In making it easier for Jews and foreign Protestants to become naturalized British citizens, the government hoped to create another competitive edge against its European rivals.[62]

Ironically, if one looked only at the Jewish struggle for rights and opportunities in Manhattan, one would be forced to conclude precisely the opposite of the traditional view of the colonial Dutch as clones of cosmopolitan, tolerant Amsterdam, and of the English as perhaps the most insular and prejudiced toward strangers of any early modern Europeans. This distorted view, based on one local situation in North America, should caution us again to view cultural issues cross-culturally and in the comparative setting of the Atlantic world. Only then can one place the struggle between Stuyvesant and the Jews in its proper context, as part of an ongoing battle to preserve an orthodox Dutch identity in one of the least significant outposts of the Dutch world, New Netherland. And only then can one begin to identify the factors that shaped the reaction of Christian Europeans when Jews wished to settle and trade in their midst. As Amsterdam, Brazil, New Amsterdam, and New York illustrate, the power of personality, the vagaries of time, the sometimes overwhelming desire for profit, the size of the Jewish community in relation to the Christian majority, the perceived usefulness of the Jews in the construction of colonies and empires, the strength or weakness of anti-Semitism among local residents and clergy, and the availability of greater opportunities elsewhere all determined the contours of the Jewish struggle for rights and opportunities at any particular place and time in the Atlantic world.

Notes

An earlier, shorter version of this essay was presented at the annual meeting of the American Historical Association, New York, 5 January 1997. A grant from the Middle Tennessee State University Faculty Summer Research Program assisted the completion of early revisions. Final revisions were made while the author was a National Endowment for the Humanities Fellow at the Newberry Library, Chicago, 1998–99. The author thanks Jane Gerber, Leo Hershkowitz, Milton Klein, Dennis Maika, John Murrin, Ernst Pijning, Susan Pyzynski, Ben Schmidt, David Sheinin, Beth Slinkard, and Walter Renn for their assistance and encouragement.

1. See the bibliography of Chapter 1 in Howard M. Sachar, *A History of the Jews in America* (New York, 1994), 937–40, and the notes and bibliographic essay in Eli Faber, *A Time for Planting: The First Migration, 1654–1820*, The Jewish People in America, vol. 1 (Baltimore, 1992).

2. Arnold Wiznitzer, "The Exodus from Brazil and Arrival in New Amsterdam of the Jewish Pilgrim Fathers, 1654," *American Jewish Historical Society Publications* (hereafter *AJHS Publs.*) 44 (1954):80–97; Sachar, *History of the Jews in America*, 13; Jacob R. Marcus, *The Colonial American Jew, 1492–1776*, 3 vols. (Detroit, 1970), 215.

3. Frederick Zwierlein, *Religion in New Netherland: A History of the Development of the Religious Conditions in the Province of New Netherland, 1623–1664* (New York, 1910). One recent account ignores the persecution of Jews altogether: "In their colonies in both South America and North America (New Amsterdam), the Dutch offered all immigrants the same religious freedom as was offered in Holland itself." *A Historical Atlas of the Jewish People: From the Time of the Patriarchs to the Present*, ed. Eli Barnavi (New York, 1992), 152.

4. Bernard Bailyn, "The Idea of Atlantic History," *Itinerario* 20 (1996):19–44. Bailyn is the leading proponent of Atlantic history in the United States in his role as the director of Harvard University's International Seminar on the History of the Atlantic World, 1500–1800, which has gathered young scholars annually since 1996. The concept has spread recently to historians of the Jewish experience, most notably Eli Faber, whose *A Time for Planting* includes Chapter 2, "The Atlantic World of Colonial Jewry." Since he concentrates on the area that eventually became the United States, his Atlantic world refers mostly to the eighteenth century, when several Jewish communities were well established along the eastern coast of North America.

5. Jonathan I. Israel, *European Jewry in the Age of Mercantilism, 1550–1750* (Oxford, 1985), 104–5; Frédéric Mauro, "Merchant Communities, 1350–1750," in *The Rise of the Merchant Empires: Long-Distance Trade in the Early Modern World, 1350–1750*, ed. James D. Tracy (New York, 1990), 267–68; Robert L. Carothers, "Marking Another Anniversary: The Diaspora of the Sephardic Jews," *Rhode Island Jewish Historical Notes* 11 (1992):113; Arnold Wiznitzer, *Jews in Colonial Brazil* (Morningside Heights, N.Y., 1960), 1; C. R. Boxer, *The Portuguese Seaborne Empire, 1415–1825* (New York, 1969), 11–12, 266–70; Vieira quoted in Miriam Bodian, *Hebrews of the Portuguese Nation: Conversos and Community in Early Modern Amsterdam* (Bloomington, 1997), 13. Bodian's is the most thorough examination of the Amsterdam Jewish community in the seventeenth century. See also Bodian, "'Men of the Nation': The Shaping of *Converso* Identity in Early Modern Europe," *Past and Present* 143 (May 1994):48–76.

6. Israel, *European Jewry*, 38, 50–51, and "Spain and the Dutch Sephardim, 1609–1660," *Studia Rosenthaliana* (hereafter *SR*) 12 (1978):1–61, quot. on 1; A. T. van Deursen, *Plain Lives in a Golden Age: Popular Culture, Religion and Society in Seventeenth-Century Holland*, trans. Maarten Ultee (New York, 1991), 32–33; Bodian, *Hebrews of the Portuguese Nation*, ix.

7. Bodian, *Hebrews of the Portuguese Nation*, ix, 6.

8. Ibid., 4, 50.

9. Ibid., 53, 57.
10. Ibid., 55.
11. Ibid., 58.
12. Ibid., 59.
13. Ibid., 61.
14. Wiznitzer, *Jews in Colonial Brazil*, 43–44; Daniel M. Swetschinski, "Kinship and Commerce: The Foundations of Portuguese Jewish Life in Seventeenth-Century Holland," *SR* 15 (1981):52–74, quots. on 61, 65.
15. Wiznitzer, *Jews in Colonial Brazil*, 45–49, 52, 56. For more on the Jews in Brazil, see Marcus, *Colonial American Jew*, chap. 3, and C. R. Boxer, *The Dutch in Brazil, 1624–1654* (Oxford, 1957), passim.
16. Wiznitzer, *Jews in Colonial Brazil*, 57–58. Toleration quotations are from Article 10 of the conquest plans approved by the States General on 13 October 1629. For Brazilian perspectives on Dutch Brazil and the Jews, see G. Freyre, "Johan Maurits van Nassau-Siegen from a Brazilian Viewpoint," in *Johan Maurits van Nassau-Siegen, 1604–1679: A Humanist Prince in Europe and Brazil*, ed. E. van den Boogaart (The Hague, 1979), 237–46; José Antônio Gonsalves de Mello, *Gente da Nação: Cristãos-novos e judeus em Pernambuco, 1542–1654* (Recife, 1989), part II; Frans Leonard Schalkwijk, *Igreja e Estado No Brasil Holandês, 1630–1654* (Recife, 1986); and José Gonçalves Salvador, *Os Cristãos-Novos: Povamento e Conquista do Solo Brasileiro (1530–1680)* (São Paulo, 1976), 328–68.
17. Wiznitzer, *Jews in Colonial Brazil*, 59–60; R. G. Fuks-Mansfeld, "Bevolkingsproblematiek in Joods Amsterdam in de Zeventiende Eeuw," *SR* 18 (1984):141–42. See also Arnold Wiznitzer, "Jewish Soldiers in Dutch Brazil, 1630–1654," *AJHS Publs.* 46 (1956):40–50, and idem, "The Jews in the Sugar Industry of Colonial Brazil," *Jewish Social Studies* 18 (1959):189–98.
18. Wiznitzer, *Jews in Colonial Brazil*, 64–65, 69, 71–72.
19. See M. E. H. N. Mout, "The Youth of Johan Maurits and Aristocratic Culture in the Early Seventeenth Century," in van den Boogaart, *Johan Maurits van Nassau-Siegen*, 13–38.
20. Wiznitzer, *Jews in Colonial Brazil*, 65–66; Jose Antonio Gonsalves de Mello, "Vincent Joachim Soler in Dutch Brazil," in van den Boogaart, *Johan Maurits van Nassau-Siegen*, 249–51, quot. on 251. See also Arnold Wiznitzer, "The Synagogue and Cemetery of the Jewish Community in Recife, Brazil, 1630–1654," *AJHS Publs.* 43 (1953):127–30.
21. De Mello, "Vincent Joachim Soler," in van den Boogaart, *Johan Maurits van Nassau-Siegen*, 249; Wiznitzer, *Jews in Colonial Brazil*, 73.
22. Wiznitzer, *Jews in Colonial Brazil*, 73–75; José Antônio Gonsalves de Mello, "The Dutch Calvinists and Religious Toleration in Portuguese America," *The Americas* 14 (1957–58): 485–88.
23. Boxer, *Dutch in Brazil*, 122; Wiznitzer, *Jews in Colonial Brazil*, 75.
24. I thank Pieter Emmer for this point. Wim Klooster reminds us that, contrary to some writings on the subject, the Jews of Brazil never outnumbered those in the Netherlands. Wim Klooster, *The Dutch in the Americas, 1600–1800* (Providence, R.I., 1997), 28.
25. Wiznitzer estimates 1,450 Jews in 1645 (*Jews in Colonial Brazil*, 130). Isaac S. Emmanuel has challenged that estimate with his own: no more than 1,000 ["Seventeenth-Century Brazilian Jewry: A Critical Review," *American Jewish Archives* 14 (1962):32–68, on 41]. C. R. Boxer emphasizes the religious and cultural differences between the Dutch and Portuguese that Johan Maurits was never able to bridge and that contributed to the Portuguese revolt ["The Recovery of Pernambuco (1645–1654)," *Atlante* 2 (1954):1–17, on 2].
26. *Accord van Brasilien, Mede van 't Recif, Maurits-Stadt ende de omleggende Forten van Brasil* (Amsterdam, 1654), quoted in Arnold Wiznitzer, "Exodus from Brazil," 81–82.
27. Quoted in ibid., 84.
28. Wiznitzer, *Jews in Colonial Brazil*, 140–41, and "Exodus from Brazil," 80–97; Isaac S. Emmanuel and Suzanne A. Emmanuel, *History of the Jews of the Netherlands Antilles*, 2 vols. (Cincinnati, 1970), 46. For the difficulties of tracing the Jews from Recife to New Amsterdam, see Egon and Frieda Wolff, "The Problem of the First Jewish Settlers in New Amsterdam, 1654," *SR* 15 (1981):169–77.

29. Record from the burgomasters and *schepens* of New Amsterdam, 7 September 1654, transcribed and translated in Arnold Wiznitzer, "Exodus from Brazil," 87, 91–93; Samuel Oppenheim, "More about Jacob Barsimson, the First Jewish Settler in New York," *AJHS Publs.* 29 (1925):39–52. For a convincing analysis of the origins of the 1654 cohort of Jews in New Amsterdam, see Leo Hershkowitz, "New Amsterdam's Twenty-Three Jews—Myth or Reality?" in *Hebrew and the Bible in America: The First Two Centuries,* ed. Shalom Goldman (Hanover, N.H., 1993), 171–83.

30. Henry H. Kessler and Eugene Rachlis, *Peter Stuyvesant and His New York* (New York, 1959), 37, 47–49.

31. Ibid., 37, quot. on 6.

32. Jonathan Israel, "The Intellectual Debate about Toleration in the Dutch Republic," in *The Emergence of Tolerance in the Dutch Republic,* ed. C. Berkvens-Stevelinck, J. Israel, and G. H. M. Posthumus Meyjes, Studies in the History of Christian Thought, vol. 76 (New York, 1997), 10–19. See also M. E. H. N. Mout, "Limits and Debates: A Comparative View of Dutch Toleration in the Sixteenth and Early Seventeenth Centuries," 37–47, and James D. Tracy, "Erasmus, Coornhert and the Acceptance of Religious Disunity in the Body Politic: A Low Countries Tradition?," in *The Emergence of Tolerance in the Dutch Republic,* ed. Berkvens-Stevelink et al., 49–62; and Andrew Pettegree, "The Politics of Toleration in the Free Netherlands, 1572–1620," in *Tolerance and Intolerance in the European Reformation,* ed. Ole Peter Grell and Bob Scribner (New York, 1996), 182–98.

33. The full story of the New Amsterdam Jews is omitted here in favor of using only enough to draw parallels and distinctions between Holland, Brazil, and New Netherland. For reliable accounts, see Marcus, *Colonial American Jew,* chap. 9; George L. Smith, *Religion and Trade in New Netherland: Dutch Origins and American Development* (Ithaca, N.Y., 1973), chap. 13; and Henri and Barbara van der Zee, *A Sweet and Alien Land: The Story of Dutch New York* (New York, 1978), 290–93.

34. Stuyvesant to the Amsterdam chamber (WIC), 22 September 1654, in Samuel Oppenheim, "The Early History of the Jews in New York, 1654–1664: Some New Matter on the Subject," *AJHS Publs.* 18 (1909):4–5. If Stuyvesant had ever had thoughts that Jews could benefit the WIC's colonies and live harmoniously with other colonists, his experience with a group of Jews in Curaçao in the early 1650s may have convinced him otherwise. As the non-resident governor of Curaçao, Stuyvesant knew that Jews admitted onto the island to farm had instead traded with the Spanish, in competition with the WIC (Marcus, *Colonial American Jew,* 176–77).

35. Petition of the Jewish Nation to the Amsterdam chamber (WIC), January 1655, in Oppenheim, "Early History of the Jews," 9–11.

36. Ibid., 10.

37. Amsterdam chamber (WIC) to Stuyvesant, 26 April 1655, in ibid., 8. Estimates of Jewish investment in the WIC vary. C. R. Boxer states: "The part played by the Jews in the formation of the two great India Companies was virtually negligible." In the WIC, eighteen Jews contributed 36,000 of the original 3 million guilders (1.2 percent). In 1658, eleven Jews appeared on a list of the 169 leading shareholders (*Dutch in Brazil,* 10–11). Stephen Alexander Fortune cites Jews as 4 percent of WIC investors in 1656 with an increase to 6.5 percent in 1658 and 10 percent in 1674 [*Merchants and Jews: The Struggle for British West Indian Commerce, 1650–1750,* n. 37 (Gainesville, Fla., 1984): 177–78].

38. Stuyvesant to the Amsterdam chamber (WIC), 30 October 1655, in Oppenheim, "Early History of the Jews," 20.

39. Megapolensis to the classis of Amsterdam, 18 March 1655, in ibid., 74. This is a retranslation of the letter originally translated in *Ecclesiastical Records: State of New York,* ed. Edward T. Corwin, 7 vols. (Albany, N.Y., 1901–16), vol. 1, 334–36.

40. Resolution to exempt Jews from military service, 28 August, Petition, 5 November 1655, in *Council Minutes, 1655–1656,* ed. and trans. Charles T. Gehring, New Netherland Documents Series, vol. 6 (Syracuse, N.Y., 1995), 81, 128.

41. Petition of Salvador Dandradj, 17 December, Decision on the petition, 23 December 1655, Petition of Teunis Craay, March 1656, in Gehring, *Council Minutes*, 149–50, 166–67, 268.
42. Amsterdam chamber (WIC) to Stuyvesant, 13 March, Stuyvesant to Amsterdam chamber (WIC), 10 June 1656, in Oppenheim, "Early History of the Jews," 21.
43. Amsterdam chamber (WIC) to Stuyvesant, 14 June 1656, in ibid., 33.
44. It is most likely that his language was Portuguese, although the court secretary noted at one point that "Frere was always accompanied by a Jew who understood and spoke both Dutch and Hebrew." Berthold Fernow, ed., *The Records of New Amsterdam from 1653 to 1674 Anno Domini*, 7 vols. (New York, 1897), vol. 2, 141.
45. Ibid., 130–31, 141–43.
46. Ibid., 141–47; David Ferera and Joseph D'Acosta to the director general and council, 24 July 1656, in Oppenheim, "Early History of the Jews," 82.
47. Fernow, *Records of New Amsterdam*, vol. 2, 396.
48. Oppenheim, "Early History of the Jews," 35.
49. Ibid., 36.
50. A. J. F. van Laer, ed. and trans., *Documents Relating to New Netherland, 1624–1626, in the Henry E. Huntington Library* (San Marino, Calif., 1924), 2, 5, 6, 8, 93–94, 113–14, 117.
51. Dutch-English relations are recounted in more detail in Chapter 4 of my dissertation, "Cultural Mingling and Religious Diversity among Indians and Europeans in the Early Middle Colonies," (Ph.D. diss., Vanderbilt University, 1993).
52. Quoted in de Mello, "Vincent Joachim Soler," in van den Boogaart, *Johan Maurits van Nassau-Siegen*, 253.
53. Marcus, *Colonial American Jew*, 144–50, quot. on 145; Emmanuel and Emmanuel, *History of the Jews*, 68.
54. "The most notable characteristic of the Suriname Jews was their dedication to agriculture. The colony grew into the largest Jewish agrarian settlement in the world," called the Jodensavanne. A synagogue was built in 1685. Klooster, *The Dutch in the Americas*, 68.
55. Ibid., 75.
56. Marcus, *Colonial American Jew*, chap. 7; Yosef Kaplan, "The Curaçao and Amsterdam Jewish Communities in the 17th and 18th Centuries," 193–211, and Yosef Hayim Yerushalmi, "Between Amsterdam and New Amsterdam: The Place of Curaçao and the Caribbean in Early Modern Jewish History," *American Jewish History* 72 (1982–83): 172–92. "Throughout the seventeenth and eighteenth centuries, the cockpit of Western Hemisphere Jewry remained in the Caribbean ...," concludes Robert P. Swierenga in *The Forerunners: Dutch Jewry in the North Atlantic Diaspora* (Detroit, 1994), 33. He overestimates the "civil and economic rights" gained by the Jews in New Amsterdam and ignores the Essequibo colony (ibid., 38).
57. "Before 1701 the state oaths (oath of allegiance and oath of supremacy) were sworn under the Test Act and required the taking of the Anglican sacrament as a precondition, thus disabling Protestant Dissenters, Jews, and Roman Catholics.... After 1701 the state oaths were no longer sworn under the Test Act but a new oath, the oath of abjuration included the phrase 'upon the true Faith of a Christian,' thus disabling Jews." Sheldon J. Godfrey and Judith C. Godfrey, *Search Out the Land: The Jews and the Growth of Equality in British Colonial America, 1740–1867* (Montreal, 1995), 16, Table 1 on p. 19. For the roots and transplantation of anti-Semitism to the Americas, see Frederic Cople Jaher, *A Scapegoat in the Wilderness: The Origins and Rise of Anti-Semitism in America* (Cambridge, Mass., 1994), esp. chap. 3, and Leonard Dinnerstein, *Antisemitism in America* (New York, 1994), chap. 1.
58. Godfrey and Godfrey, *Search Out the Land*, 16, 23, 40–42; Samuel J. Hurwitz and Edith Hurwitz, "The New World Sets an Example for the Old: The Jews of Jamaica and Political Rights, 1661–1831," *American Jewish Historical Quarterly*, 55 (1965–66):37–56.
59. Answers of inquiries of New Yorke, 16 April 1678, in E. B. O'Callaghan and Berthold Fernow, eds., *Documents Relative to the Colonial History of the State of New York*, 15 vols.

(Albany, N.Y., 1853–87), vol. 3, 262; Leo Hershkowitz, "Asser Levy and the Inventories of Early New York Jews," *American Jewish History* 80 (1990–91):21–55; Hershkowitz, "New Amsterdam's Twenty-Three Jews," in Goldman, *Hebrew and the Bible in America*, 179–81.

60. Marcus, *Colonial American Jew*, 308–9; Richard B. Morris, "Civil Liberties and the Jewish Tradition in Early America," *AJHS Publs.* 46 (1956):20–39; Zvi Loker, *Jews in the Caribbean: Evidence on the History of the Jews in the Caribbean Zone in Colonial Times* (Jerusalem, 1991), 80–81.

61. Quoted in Marcus, *Colonial American Jew*, 397–98, 401.

62. Ibid., 405–8; Godfrey and Godfrey, *Search Out the Land*, 55; Morris, "Civil Liberties and the Jewish Tradition," 32–33. Milton M. Klein, the eminent historian of colonial New York, states: "In general, I am not persuaded that conditions were better for Jews under the English than under the Dutch. The Jews did not have the influential friends in high places in England that they had in Holland" (letter to the author, 6 June 1997). For more on the growth of the early New York Jewish community, see Hershkowitz, "Asser Levy and the Inventories of Early New York Jews," 21–55; idem, "Some Aspects of the New York Jewish Merchant Community, 1654–1820," 10–34, and Doris Groshen Daniels, "Colonial Jewry: Religion, Domestic and Social Relations," *American Jewish Historical Quarterly* 66 (1976–77):375–99.

– Chapter 20 –

ANTECEDENTS AND REMNANTS OF JODENSAVANNE: THE SYNAGOGUES AND CEMETERIES OF THE FIRST PERMANENT PLANTATION SETTLEMENT OF NEW WORLD JEWS

Rachel Frankel

O N 12 OCTOBER 1785 the synagogue Bracha veShalom (Blessing and Peace), in Jodensavanne (Jews' Savannah) of the Dutch colony of Suriname, celebrated its hundredth anniversary. Governor Wichers, the Councils of Police, notable citizens from the capital city of Paramaribo, and some sixteen hundred other people attended. There were tables with over three hundred dishes and one thousand Chinese lanterns. People ate and drank. Speeches were made, Hebrew prayers were delivered, and poems were recited. The concluding celebration, a splendid ball at midnight, lasted until dawn.[1]

Today all that remains of Jodensavanne, the first permanent Jewish plantation settlement in the Americas, is a brick ruin of the formerly grand synagogue (see Fig. 20.1), the first of any architectural significance in the New World. Additionally, there remain two overgrown cemeteries, each with marble and bluestone graves inscribed primarily in Hebrew and Portuguese, some with illustrative imagery. Also, there exists a third weathering cemetery with uniquely and artistically crafted wood and concrete grave markers. Furthermore, it is possible that remains of an earlier and more modest synagogue of the settlement lie buried in the jungle.[2] Jodensavanne is remotely located north of the Amazon River Basin.

Planting primarily sugar, the Jews on the upper reaches of the Suriname River in 1667 (see Fig. 20.2) were predominantly Sephardic. They

FIGURE 20.1 Courtyard entrance gate posts and remains of the east wall of the synagogue, Bracha veShalom, Jodensavanne [Jews' Savannah], Suriname. Built in 1685; last used in 1865. Photograph by Rachel Frankel, 1995.

FIGURE 20.2 Detail from an anonymous manuscript map on vellum, "A Discription of the Coleny of Surranam in Guiana Drawne in the Yeare 1667." The location of the Jewish settlement on the upper reaches of the Suriname River is indicated with the word "Jews," to the upper right of the large lettering "MOR."

came to Suriname from a variety of places. Some came from Amsterdam as well as other cities in Europe. Others came from Brazil, where they had mainly been planters and had been introduced to the practice of slavery.[3] By 1664 roughly two hundred Jews, who had been settled for less than a decade in neighboring Cayenne while it was in Dutch hands, came to Suriname. The Jews from Cayenne originated in such places as Livorno

(Italy), Amsterdam, and Brazil. Jews might also have come to Suriname from the Pomeroon settlement in what was the Dutch colony of Essequibo (today, the Republic of Guyana).[4] Some claim that Jews came to Suriname in the 1650s from Barbados, with the English royalist Willoughby. While the exact demographic make-up of the Jews who settled Suriname may be debated, it is certain that they were not a homogeneous group. Amsterdam's Sephardic community served as the religious authority, but the Jews of Suriname had many other places, references, and experiences from which to draw to form their identities.

Likewise, the Africans enslaved in Suriname on the plantations of the Jews were not a homogeneous group. Although they were, at this time, predominantly from what was referred to as Guiny, on the west coast of Africa in the area of the Congo, they were a mixture of several nations—nations who often were at war with one another on the African continent.[5] Upon the arrival of a shipment of enslaved Africans, planters used a divide-and-rule strategy and are said to have not "put two [of the same ethnic group] in any one lot."[6] While most of the Africans in Suriname were brought directly from Africa, some were brought to Suriname by Jews who emigrated there from other sugar planting colonies in the New World.

Although there were many differences among the religious practices of the Africans in Suriname, they all believed in a supreme power, an omnipotent god on whose supernatural power man is wholly dependent. In addition to the supreme being, there were also earth-spirits and the world of ancestors, the last of which are much closer to man and directly influence his life.[7] The belief in the world of ancestors for the Africans in Suriname meant belief in the transmigration of souls from one body into another. This meant that they would, upon death, return to their own countries where they would be reincarnated. Death for these enslaved, frequently tortured, and sometimes executed Africans on Suriname's plantations, was seen as freedom. Like the Jews, many of the Africans were circumcised.[8]

Suriname became a Dutch colony in 1667. The peace treaty of Breda confirmed the Dutch title to Suriname and ceded New Amsterdam, later New York, to the British. In the 1660s, privileges were accorded to the Jews, first by the English, and then again by the Dutch. These rights granted the Jews exemptions and immunities both as an ethnic minority and as Dutch burghers. Furthermore, the Jews had the opportunity to live their lives as an autonomous religio-cultural enclave. These privileges were the most liberal Jews had ever received in the Christian world, for it had not been since the first century, when Rome made it possible for some privileged Jewish subjects to become citizens of the Roman Empire, that Jews had benefited from such rights.

Prior to the 1685 construction of the synagogue Bracha veShalom, there did not exist in the New World any synagogue of major architectural stature. However, the Jews of Suriname did have European architectural sources from which to draw for inspiring the design of a great synagogue: Jacob Jehudah Leon Templo's model of Solomon's Temple, and the illustration (see Fig. 20.3), first published in 1642 and then again in 1667 in *Biblia Hebraica* by the Amsterdam Jewish printer Joseph Athias, had provided an influential model for the construction of Amsterdam's 1675 united Sephardi congregation's "Esnoga [synagogue]." Nonetheless, a synagogue is not the Temple, for the latter was believed to be instituted by the Lord, whereas a synagogue becomes sacred because God's law is read there by men. In addition to drawing upon the authoritative work on Solomon's Temple by the Jesuit Fathers Geronimo Prado and Juan Baptista Villalpando, Templo contributed some differences. He conceived of a more sober, less baroque, more Dutch vision of the Temple.[9] Templo's model, which he displayed in his home, and the published illustrations undoubtedly provided architectural imagery for the design of Bracha veShalom as well.

The magnificent synagogue of Amsterdam (see Fig. 20.4), built ten years prior to that of Jodensavanne, provided a significant precedent for Jodensavanne's synagogue, for not only were the Jews of Amsterdam closely linked through business, family ties, and historic background to those in Suriname, they also observed the faith identically. The services in Suriname attempted, although not necessarily with success, to duplicate those of Amsterdam. The Jews of Amsterdam and those of Suriname both referred to themselves as "of the Nation," meaning the Portuguese-Hebrew Nation, or as "Portuguese Jews." Both groups of Jews were of the same double diaspora: firstly, from Roman-occupied Palestine, and secondly, fourteen centuries later, from the Iberian Peninsula.

Nonetheless, however much the two communities resembled one another, there were significant differences. Although both communities used outsiders to design and build their synagogues, these outsiders were quite different from each other. In Amsterdam, where Jews were banned from the Dutch guilds, the congregation's leaders selected Elias Bouman, a gentile, as the architect for their new synagogue. Similarly, a gentile, Gillis van der Veen, served as the Amsterdam synagogue's master carpenter. In Suriname, likewise, the Jews presumably depended on others,[10] primarily Africans,[11] to build their synagogue, but it is still unknown who designed Bracha veShalom. Additionally, the two communities existed in different environments. The Jews of Amsterdam lived in an urban and cosmopolitan environment, surrounded and dominated by gentiles. The Jews of Suriname lived in an isolated autonomous colonial agricultural settlement (see Fig. 20.5) with 105 Jewish men, in 1684, outnumbering Jewish women by a ratio of almost two to one. Enslaved Africans constituted 84 percent of the total Jodensavanne population, with 543 males and 429 females. Additionally, there was a small minority of enslaved American Indians as well as those more numerous who maintained their freedom.[12] Furthermore, in Amsterdam there was an Ashkenazic community of Jews who had their own monumental synagogue. In

FIGURE 20.3 Anonymous colored engraving of Solomon's Temple according to Jacob Juda Leon Templo, taken from *Biblia Hebraica* (1667). Courtesy of the Jewish Historical Museum, Amsterdam, from the book *The Esnoga: A Monument to Portuguese-Jewish Culture* (Amsterdam, 1991).

FIGURE 20.4 Southwest view of Amsterdam's Esnoga, inaugurated in 1675. The auxiliary buildings in the foreground fortress the sanctuary building. Photograph by Rachel Frankel, 1996.

FIGURE 20.5 View from the west of the synagogue Bracha veShalom, a detail from the lithograph *Vue de la Savanne des Juifs sur la Rivière de Surinam* (View of the Jews' Savannah on the Surinam River), P. J. Benoit, *Voyage à Surinam* (Bruxelles, 1839). Courtesy of General Research Division, The New York Public Library, Astor, Lenox, and Tilden Foundations.

Jodensavanne, there was no Ashkenazic community, only ten to twelve Ashkenazic Jews who, according to *Essai Historique*, resided at Jodensavanne through the bonds of marriage. Although there were other Europeans and religious minorities living in Suriname at the time of the construction of Bracha veShalom, including the pietest sect of Labadists whose utopian settlement existed further up on the Suriname River, the various European groups lived apart from one another. In 1684 Jews made up 25 percent of the total European population of Suriname.[13]

For all Jews, the most sacred religious act is that of reading the Pentateuch, or Torah, the first five books of the Bible believed to be given to Moses by God. The Torah, considered in its widest sense, is the Lord's will and deed.[14] Objects in which the Torah is stored and the spaces it traverses on its way to being read become sacred. The Torah is kept in the *hekhal* (ark) and read from the *tevah* (reader's platform). Typical of Spanish-Portuguese synagogues as far back as those of Italy of the early seventeenth century (which are thought to have influenced that of Amsterdam) is a bifocal layout with the *hekhal* and *tevah* at opposite ends of the sanctuary. The *hekhal* is always on the side of the sanctuary facing Jerusalem. In the Western world this is the east wall. The *tevah* is opposite it, at the western end of the sanctuary. Also typical of Spanish-Portuguese synagogues is that half the congregation sits on the north side of the sanctuary and the other half on the south side. Each half of the congregation faces both the *hekhal* and the *tevah*. This split-congregation, bifocal layout not only activates the reading of the Torah, as it is walked from one end of the sanctuary to the other—from the *hekhal* to the *tevah*—to be read, but it dynamically demonstrates the focus of the faith. This floor plan configuration perfectly describes that of Amsterdam's synagogue (see Fig. 20.6) and many others.

In traditional orthodox Judaism, Jews must learn Hebrew, study the Torah, and practice its teachings. However, Jewish law exempts women from required attendance in synagogue due to their domestic obligations. The Torah can not be publicly or ritually read unless ten men are present. Subsequently, space must be created for keeping the Torah and for gathering to read it. Jewish men are esteemed if they participate in reading the Torah and are scholars of the literature. Jewish women, quite differently, are responsible for executing the domestic laws and teachings of the Torah. During the centuries of the Inquisition, when Jews were forbidden to gather to study the Torah, Judaism persisted cryptically, primarily in the privacy of the home. In this period, women were often the keepers of the faith, taking over roles formerly held by men. They conducted marriages and performed other rituals of Judaism, which had to be performed in secret, usually within the confines of home.[15] Synagogues are not, typically, the realm of women. In the Amsterdam synagogue, as in most of the Spanish-Portuguese synagogues, women wishing to attend services sat separately in a gallery reserved exclusively for them, elevated and directly above that of the men.[16] In other European synagogues, since

FIGURE 20.6 Interior view, facing east, of Amsterdam's Esnoga. The *tevah* (reader's platform) in the foreground; the *hekhal* (ark) in the background. Photograph courtesy of Sephardic Congregation of Amsterdam.

the fourteenth century, women sat separately from the men, sometimes in an annex elevated above the men and sometimes to the side.[17] The women's gallery at Jodensavanne was, as shall be shown, different from that of Amsterdam.

Although it is not clear where converted male Jews may have sat in the Amsterdam synagogue, it is known that they were never appointed to official posts in the Jewish community and that the Jewish law stipulating that a convert not be given a post with coercive authority was followed. Furthermore, in 1644, the men of the Mahamad (governing body) decreed that "circumcised Negro Jews" were not to be called to the Torah or given any honorary commandments to perform in the synagogue.[18] In Suriname, in the eighteenth century, this lack of full privileges among both the male and female Jews of African descent would lead to unprecedented disruptions and acts in the greater Jewish community.

There are additional dissimilarities between the synagogue of Amsterdam and that of Jodensavanne. In Amsterdam, the synagogue plan is a complex of buildings, at the center of which is the sanctuary building (see Fig. 20.7). An asymmetrical courtyard surrounds the sanctuary building on three sides. Auxiliary buildings, such as the religious school, the library, and the *mikveh* (ritual bath) surround the courtyard. Although there are several entrances to the courtyard, through the wall of auxiliary buildings, and several to the synagogue, the western entrance dominates the plan. Unlike Amsterdam's synagogue, the synagogue in Jodensavanne, including the sanctuary and auxiliary spaces, is all assembled in one building (see Fig. 20.8). Furthermore, the synagogue building existed at the center of a four-sided symmetrical courtyard, and instead of being protected by a perimeter buffer of buildings, the synagogue was surrounded only by a wooden gate with identical gate entrances at each of the four sides. Three of the four gates led directly to the three entrances to the synagogue. The west gate led to the entrance hall and auxiliary spaces of the synagogue. The north and south gates led to the symmetrical entrances to the synagogue sanctuary. The two synagogues are further distinguished from one other stylistically. The exterior of the Amsterdam synagogue expresses Classical symmetrical architecture, whereas that of Jodensavanne recollected Dutch vernacular (see Fig. 20.9) and exhibited asymmetry on its north and south façades.

Just outside of Amsterdam, on the Amstel River, at Ouderkerk, is the cemetery of the Sephardic Jews of Amsterdam. In 1614 the first burial took place. A small gravestone bears the inscription of a Hebrew poem in which the deceased, a child, himself speaks and says that he was the first to be buried in the cemetery. This cemetery is renowned for its illustrated engraved tombstones that some say are in defiance of the second commandment in the Torah (Exod. 20: 4–5) against graven images (a measure against idol worship). The *ohelim* (solid tent or prism) tombstone forms found at Ouderkerk resemble the grave markers in Spanish Muslim cemeteries.[19] More common at Ouderkerk—and also found in the

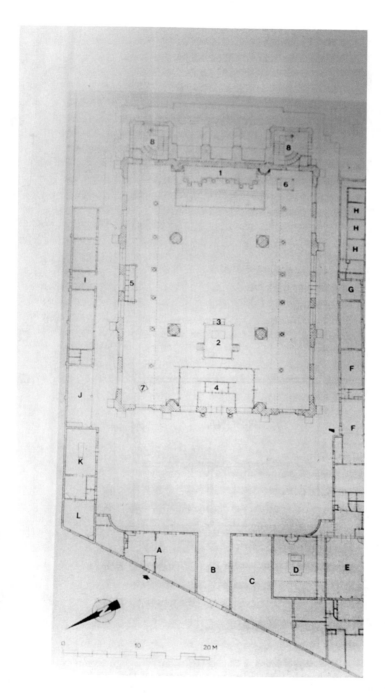

FIGURE 20.7 Plan of the Amsterdam Esnoga complex. Sanctuary building at center; isolated from surrounding buildings housing auxiliary functions. 1= *Hekhal.* 2=*Tevah.* 4=*Tevah.* 8=Women's entrance to sanctuary. 8=Women's entrance to stairs to gallery. B=Main entrance to synagogue complex. Courtesy of Historical Buildings Department, after J. S. Baars and J. W. Kuiper, with additions by D. P. Cohen Paraira, from the book *The Esnoga: A Monument to Portuguese-Jewish Culture* (Amsterdam, 1991).

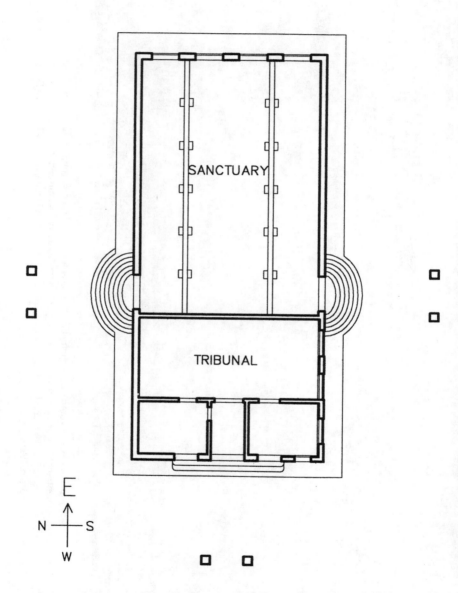

FIGURE 20.8 Plan of the extant remains of Bracha veShalom synagogue complex with building and courtyard, built in 1685, Jodensavanne, Suriname. Drawing by architect Rachel Frankel, based on 1997 field survey by Rachel Frankel and Caribbean Volunteer Expeditions.

FIGURE 20.9 View of Jodensavanne with Bracha veShalom, the tallest building, on the far right, from G. W. C. Voorduin, *Gezigten uit Neerland's West-Indien, naar de natuur geteekend* (Amsterdam, 1860–62).

Sephardic cemeteries in Curaçao, Suriname, and other places—are the flat horizontal slabs with imagery depicting episodes of the biblical name of the deceased. Imagery referring to an individual's life is also common. The sources of the imagery were the illustrated publications, Bibles especially, of the day.[20] According to Joseph Gutmann: "... the stones at Ouderkerk [and Curaçao] differ entirely from the austere tombstones of their Dutch Protestant neighbors and from their Ashkenazim brethren. Such elaborately sculpted horizontal Jewish tombstones were unknown in Medieval Spain. Devoid of figural ornamentation, the medieval Spanish Jewish tombstones followed the practice found in Muslim cemeteries."[21]

Also at the Bet Haim (House of Life, a common term for a Jewish cemetery) at Ouderkerk is the cleansing house or Rodeamentos House (House of Circlings). The first name refers to the house's function as the place where the ritual washing of the dead body takes place. The second name refers to the seven circular walks that are made around the coffin of the deceased male. The house was built in 1705, and although there is no known information about a cleansing house that existed before 1705, it is thought that one did exist.[22]

The cemetery and burial practices at Ouderkerk in some ways foretell what would occur at Jodensavanne. Firstly, Ouderkerk replaced an earlier cemetery in Groet, which was unsatisfactory for the Jews because of its distant location from Amsterdam, and up until 1634, bodies were removed from Groet and reburied at Ouderkerk. Thus, one can conclude that it was permissible among the Sephardim of Amsterdam not only to start new cemeteries, but also to remove and reinter the deceased. Secondly, the original parcel of land of the Ouderkerk cemetery was augmented by subsequent purchases; hence, one can conclude that unlike the Ashkenazim, who were prohibited to add to the land of a cemetery, these Sephardim could. Thirdly, adjacent to the cemetery at Ouderkerk is the so-called del Sotto cemetery. This cemetery resulted from a dispute between the Jewish community and the del Sotto family who, in 1670, purchased their own tract of land for their family burials. In 1691 the dispute was resolved, and three-fourths of the del Sotto family cemetery was merged with that of the Jewish community. One-fourth, however, remained in the hands of the del Sotto family, who continued to be buried there.[23] Thus, there is a precedent for a separate family cemetery. Fourthly, the deceased were transported to the riverside location of the Ouderkerk cemetery by boat, as would have been the case for Jews of Suriname, whose plantations, cemeteries, and synagogues lined the Suriname River and, later, whose town homes were farther downriver in Paramaribo. Fifthly, although the feet of the deceased usually are placed facing east toward Jerusalem,[24] at Ouderkerk, and at Jodensavanne, the graves do not uniformly adhere to this custom. Sixthly, unlike the Ashkenazim, many Jews of Amsterdam, like those before them in Spain, acquired burial places during their lifetime.[25] Jews of Amsterdam, Curaçao, and Suriname were also known to commission their tombs during their lifetime. Lastly, in 1647, it was decided that a separate section of the cemetery at Ouderkerk would be marked off for the burial of all the "Jewish Negroes and mulattos" except for those Negroes and mulattos who had married whites or those who were born of a marriage performed under a bridal canopy with a religious ceremony.[26]

Almost as early as the Jews came to Suriname, they buried their dead with expensive imported tombstones much resembling those at Ouderkerk and on the island of Curaçao in the Caribbean. The first cemetery of the Jewish settlement, referred to as the Cassipora cemetery (because of its proximity to the creek so named that flows into the Suriname River), holds about two hundred tombstones that may date back at least to 1669, if not before. The latest grave is thought to be of 1840.[27] Like Ouderkerk, the graves are inscribed with texts in as many as three languages: Hebrew, Portuguese, and Dutch. There are a few *ohelim* (see Fig. 20.10) and some of the more numerous horizontal graves at Cassipora have illustrative graven images. The tree being axed down by the angel of death (see Fig. 20.11), or the hand of God, is an ancient and popular Jewish symbol, especially in sepulchral art. Its antecedent appears as early as in the mosaic floor at the fifteen-hundred-year-old Bet Alpha synagogue in Israel, where Abraham is shown about to sacrifice the life of his son. This image refers usually to a life taken before its time, typically that of a young person.

The Cassipora cemetery shares another similarity with that of Ouderkerk. According to the rigorous investigative work done in 1995 by Dr. John DeBye and Mr. and Mrs. Arthur Strelick, it appears that the Da Costa family had a separate section of the cemetery and that it was not uncommon for families to group themselves together,[28] as at Ouderkerk. However, unlike Ouderkerk, the majority of tombs at the cemetery at Cassipora are oriented similarly but unusually northeast, rather than east.

The question of a separate section of the Cassipora cemetery for Jews of African descent remains unanswered. According to the late Robert Cohen, the 1754 *hascamoth* (rules) continued a trend of earlier bylaws, containing a full section about the relationship between black and white Jews, which Cohen quotes: "… since experience has taught how prejudicial and improper it would be to admit Mulattos as *Yahidim* [full members], and noting that some of these have concerned themselves in matters of the government of the community [the Jewish community], it is resolved that henceforth they will never be considered or admitted as *Yahidim* and will solely be *Congreganten*, as in other communities."[29] However, based on the reactionary tone of the *hascamoth*, it is likely that in early Suriname, Jews of African descent enjoyed fuller rights than they did in subsequent years and in other places.

In 1682, the Jews of Suriname secured a land grant from Samuel Nassy, a Jewish planter on the Suriname River. This property, a bit down the river, about one mile north, from the Cassipora cemetery (and, it is said, from the location of the earlier synagogue, see Fig. 20.12), according to the *Essai Historique*, existed on fresh ground, on the Savannah.[30] This

FIGURE 20.10 *Ohelim* (prism-shaped) tombstones at Cassipora cemetery. Tomb of David de Meza, inscribed with Hebrew calendar date of death, 5499 (1739). One side of the stone is carved in Hebrew and the other in Portuguese. Photograph by Rachel Frankel, 1997.

FIGURE 20.11 Tomb at Cassipora cemetery with two graven images. Above are crossbones and a skull, a common image, possibly alluding to messianic passages in the book of Ezekiel. The ax cutting down a tree refers to a life ended before its time (see Rochelle Weinstein, *Sepulchral Monuments of the Jews of Amsterdam in the Seventeenth and Eighteenth Centuries* [New York, 1979]). Photograph by Rachel Frankel, 1997.

FIGURE 20.12 [Willem Mogge], "Caerte ofte vertooninge vande Rivieren van Suriname en Commewijne" (Chart or display of the Suriname and Commewine Rivers) (Amsterdam? Anno 1671), which includes the place name "Joodese Synagoge," roughly in the center of the map, above "Morgename," at the approximate location of the first synagogue of Suriname.

location would become the new town center, Joods Dorp (Jews' Village), and the site of the community's second synagogue and cemetery.

In 1684, one year prior to the time of the construction of Bracha veShalom, what would become known as Jodensavanne contained a population of at least 1,158 people, with Africans outnumbering Jews at least six to one.[31] Central to Jodensavanne's culture were its riverside sugar plantations, grand synagogue, and cemeteries, built primarily by African hands. Jodensavanne flourished for a century. In fact, it was profitable enough to have helped to finance the construction of the Congregation Shearith Israel's early synagogue in Manhattan, as remembered twice a year by its present-day congregation.[32]

Despite the absence of any precedent for New World synagogue architecture and the Jews' inexperience in building design and construction concerning edifices of any significance, Bracha veShalom was built. According to *Essai Historique*, the synagogue existed on high ground, thirty to thirty-six feet above the river to which it was adjacent. It sat in the middle of a spacious rectilinear courtyard, met by four cross streets, with large houses built at its corners. This village square measured 450 feet long by 300 feet wide. The houses, reports *Essai Historique*, were "grandes & commodes, quoique d'une Architecture médiocre qui sent encore l'économie de nos ancêtres: il y en a cependant quelques unes passablement belles" (large and commodious, although of a mediocre architecture which as of yet expresses the thrift of our ancestors; however, there are some which are passably attractive).[33] The lithographs of Benoit and Voorduin confirm the synagogue's hilltop location and show it as the tallest building at Jodensavanne's town center.

The choice of site for Bracha veShalom is not unusual. According to Talmudic interpretation, a synagogue should be located on the highest site in a town; also, the synagogue should be taller than other houses in a town. Furthermore, it is convenient to locate a synagogue near water for the ritual bath and other religious observances.

A new cemetery was also established at this time, the community thereby abandoning its first, except for the interment of those members of the old families who wished to be buried near their ancestors.[34] This second cemetery is but a few hundred yards east from Bracha veShalom. It contains about five hundred marble and bluestone tombs. The flat stones rest horizontally and have epitaphs in Hebrew, Portuguese, and/or Dutch and illustrative graven images, much like those at Cassipora and Ouderkerk (see Figs. 20.13 and 20.14). The inscriptions date from the seventeenth, eighteenth, and nineteenth centuries. The arrangement of the graves, as at Cassipora and Ouderkerk, is not regular per cardinal direction. It is yet to be determined if bodies were removed from the Cassipora cemetery and reinterred at the later cemetery.

Like the Cassipora cemetery, the second cemetery does not seem to have had a separate section for Jews of African descent. However, it is known that in 1790 the leader of the black Jews, Joseph de David Cohen Nassy, was given a marginal grave "in a swamp and only one foot deep."[35] Although the cemetery is not distinguished, it may be that the grave of this Jew is at the second cemetery where its south portion has lower ground compared to that of Cassipora and thus where one might encounter swampy shallow earth.

FIGURE 20.13 Tomb at the second Jewish cemetery in Suriname, with the image of a ruler on a throne and a poetic Hebrew text. The text was transcribed and translated by the late Manfred Lehmann during his 1959 visit to Jodensavanne, and was reproduced in *The Jerusalem Post*, 7 April 1978. It reads in part that the deceased was "a man who was always first in every holy enterprise ... who chanted pleasantly the songs of Israel within the congregation named Bracha veShalom in the city of Suriname, the wise and understanding communal leader, the exalted, pious and humble Rabbi David Hezekiah Baruch Louzado ... who departed this life at the will of the Lord of Heaven and earth on the second day of the new moon of Iyyar 1825." Photograph by Rachel Frankel, 1997.

FIGURE 20.14 Tomb at the second Jewish cemetery in Suriname, with Portuguese text and an image indicating that the deceased was taken before his or her time. Photograph by Rachel Frankel, 1995.

What remains of the synagogue, originally built of brick with flat clay tile roofing, sits in the midst of the no longer apparent village square. The ruin of the synagogue measures ninety-four feet along its east-west axis and forty-three feet across its north-south width (see Fig. 20.15).[36] According to Teenstra, who visited Jodensavanne in 1828, the synagogue was thirty-three feet high and had two pointed gables.[37] Teenstra's account concurs with that of *Essai Historique* in that the synagogue had large, brown hardwood columns with a properly constructed wooden vault rising above. In this double-height space, reserved for the men, existed a large ark of beautiful cedar wood, in which the Scrolls of the Law were kept: "... it is of a beautiful architecture, and ornamented with very well-executed sculptures which reflect much honor (considering the infancy of the colony when it was built) upon the one who fashioned it."[38] Opposite the *heckal*, on a kind of raised platform or second story, beyond the main sanctuary, which was the section for the men, was the section for the women, which was situated above the synagogue's auxiliary spaces that were separate from the sanctuary. The extant remains and historical descriptions of the main sanctuary suggest that it duplicates the north-south, split-congregation, bifocal layout, with seating facing both the ark and reader's platform as exists in Amsterdam and is typical in other Sephardic synagogues. However, at Bracha veShalom, the women's seating does not conform to that of the men as it does in Amsterdam and other places. At Jodensavanne the women faced the ark and the whole of the sanctuary, as a conventional audience does a stage. Also, the women's gallery was set back from the men's sanctuary, rather than above it.

At Bracha veShalom, the women's section could have held at least eighty women, about twenty more Jewish females than were inhabitants of Jodensavanne in 1684.[39] Each row (see Fig. 20.16) could have been made up of four five-person benches, and there could have been at least four rows of benches, with leftover room in the rear of the gallery where views to the sanctuary would have been more or less obscured. Seats there would have been deemed unacceptable and undesirable. The men's section had capacity for at least 160 individuals, roughly fifty-five more males than the settlement had in 1684. While it is known that in the eighteenth century male Jews of African descent were relegated to the bench of the *Abelim* (mourners),[40] it is unknown if this was the case in the first years of the synagogue. Naturally, in 1685, at the time of constructing the synagogue, the Jews of Jodensavanne would have built a structure that could support a hoped for expanding population.

Essai Historique provides further descriptions of Bracha veShalom:

> as its other ornaments [the synagogue had] the crowns of silver with which the Scrolls of the Law are decorated, and other necessary furnishings of the same metal, large candlesticks of yellow copper with several branches, and chandeliers of several kinds which cost the individuals who donated them a considerable sum. Below the women's gallery there is a chamber where the

FIGURE 20.15 Courtyard entrance gate posts and remains of the west wall (and twentieth-century reconstructions) of the synagogue Bracha veShalom. Photograph by Rachel Frankel, 1995.

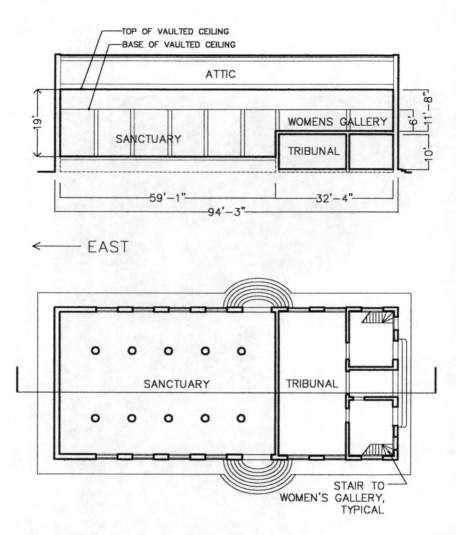

FIGURE 20.16 Preliminary interpretative drawings of the plan and section of the synagogue Bracha veShalom, 1685, Jodensavanne, Suriname. Drawing by architect Rachel Frankel, based on a 1997 field survey by Rachel Frankel and Caribbean Volunteer Expeditions.

regents hold their meetings, having next to it the archives of the Jewish community kept in very good order. Everything there is so properly built and the synagogue has such an indescribable majesty, that although its size is quite ordinary, it elicits the admiration of those who see it for the first time.[41]

The open town plan of Jodensavanne, defined by four streets meeting at right angles forming an orthogonal gated courtyard with entrances at each of its four cardinal points, with the synagogue at the center, is unprecedented in synagogue architecture and synagogue site planning. Nonetheless, it is not unexpected in the context of Jodensavanne, a Jewish haven, where for the first time Jews had the opportunity to design virgin landscape and construct it according to their needs, beliefs, and hopes. Whereas their brethren in Europe lived in cramped and, in some instances, walled cities where permission to build a synagogue was difficult to obtain and Jews were rarely given any choice of the site upon which to build their synagogue, the Jews of Jodensavanne found themselves in a place with almost no man-made environment and at full liberty to site and build their synagogue on the acreage given them by their own Samuel Nassy in 1682.[42] Thus, the Jews had the unique opportunity to model and build their view of the world and how it should be. Therefore, in accordance with Talmudic interpretation, the synagogue was sited upon a hill and was the tallest building in the town. Additionally, the synagogue was adjacent to a river, convenient for access to flowing water for the purification rituals. More unusual and significant, the site plan for Jodensavanne permitted approach to the synagogue courtyard from all sides: from north, south, east, and west. Despite the harsh reality of the threat of slave revolts or of raids from former slaves living independently in their newly established villages in the interior, from European powers, and from native Americans, the town was laid out as if in a perfect world. In an environment in which the river was the medium of transport, the Jews built four roads, in parallel and perpendicular pairs, beside the river front. These came together in idealized geometry to form the synagogue square. The courtyard surrounding the synagogue and defining the square had four gates, each at the midpoint of its four sides. Three of the courtyard gates led directly into the synagogue. Two of these, on the north and south sides, led directly into the sanctuary. It is unlikely that this plan evoked anything but the age-old messianic hope of the Jewish people and echoed the messianic literature and expectations popular in this era.

The novel synagogue and town plan, instead of having buffer auxiliary buildings on its courtyard perimeter, as in Amsterdam and elsewhere, had only railings and gated entrances at each of its four sides. It also had a geometrically idealized village square, which testified to the Jews' hope for the coming of the messianic age, as anticipated daily by their (and all observant Jews') recital of the Amidah:

> Sound on the great Shofar the summons for our freedom; set up the banner to gather our exiles, and bring us together from the four corners of the earth soon unto our own land. Blessed art Thou, Lord, who wilt gather in the dispersed of Thy people Israel.

The town plan of Jodensavanne, an unprecedented place of full Jewish life, symbolically and spatially, if not architecturally, refers most certainly to the ideal of an age of peace—an end of war and of oppression, as stated in Isaiah 43: 5–6:

Fear not for I am with you; I will bring your offspring from the east, and from the west I will gather you. I will say to the north, give up, and to the south, do not withhold; bring my sons from afar and my daughters from the end of the earth, everyone who is called by my name, whom I created for my glory, whom I formed and made.

Although slavery is sanctioned by the Bible, consider the irony of the design intent, in that the majority of Jodensavanne's inhabitants were held in bondage.

Unfortunately, what remains today of Bracha veShalom is not necessarily authentic. There have been two efforts of ruin preservation in this century, both of which have resulted in some misleading effects. The first cleanup of Jodensavanne was conducted in the 1940s. The Dutch colonists used Nazi and German prisoners, formerly held in Indonesia, to perform the labor of cleaning up both the cemetery and the ruins of the synagogue of Jodensavanne. About thirty years later, another cleanup was performed. As a result, the extant remains can not be relied upon to be authentic when judging from a non-invasive field investigation. Archival documents, historical descriptions, and comparative studies are critically necessary to reconstruct the architectural history of the synagogue.

For example, the Voorduin sketch of 1860 of Bracha veShalom shows that windows did not exist at the ground level of the synagogue's east wall (see Fig. 20.17). Yet the extant remains indicate that there were four windows at what would have approximated ground level inside the raised sanctuary. To further confuse matters, the sketch shows that at the upper height of the sanctuary, the synagogue had three windows. Such asymmetric fenestration, with three windows above and four below, would not have existed on even the most common of buildings at the time, let alone the synagogue.

It is quite common, as Voorduin's sketch indicates, to eliminate fenestration on the portion of the east wall where the Torah is kept. The synagogue in Amsterdam exemplifies this. Also, in the Dutch Caribbean colony of St. Eustatius, the synagogue there, initially built in the early 1730s and then rebuilt in 1772, does not have fenestration on the portion of the east wall where the *hekhal* existed. Rather, the eastern façade (exterior) at St. Eustatius employs faux windows on the portion of wall where, on the interior side, the ark is kept, thereby creating the illusion of a façade of full fenestration. Perhaps at Bracha veShalom, the fenestration on the eastern façade was similar. It is easy to conclude that such design was merely architecturally correct—to avoid the monotony of portions of blank wall. However, it may express the persistence of the masking, secrecy, and illusion practiced by crypto-Jews in places where the Inquisition existed. For example, some historians believe that the sand on the floor of the sanctuary at the synagogue in Jodensavanne—as well as at those synagogues built later in the capital of Suriname and on the island of Curaçao—is thought, in part, to recollect the need to muffle the sounds

FIGURE 20.17 Looking west at the cemetery and east façade of the synagogue of Jodensavanne, from G. W. C. Voorduin, *Gezigten uit Neerland's West-Indien, naar de natuur geteekend* (Amsterdam, 1860–62).

of the footsteps of the men who gathered to read the Torah in places where the Inquisition was feared.

Techniques of masking and the making of masks were also common in the rich artistic traditions of the Africans enslaved on the plantations of the Jews. The earth-spirits, previously mentioned, were often presented as masks, whereas the supreme being is never pictured as images in Africa, for the supreme being is so distant and so comprehensive in its nature that it is not to be imagined.[43] (Ironically, this is much in keeping with the Torah's second commandment against graven images, which was less conservatively adhered to by the Jews of Jodensavanne.) Masking is also an important technique for expression among the various secret societies of Africa, which form to govern communal life or comprise a particular guild.[44]

In Suriname, where Africans no longer were among their own kin or ethnic group, they developed new languages, religious rites, and burial practices, many of which persist to this day as practiced by their descendants. The African techniques of masking, secrecy, and illusion persisted in Suriname not only because they were universally familiar to the diverse population of Africans, but also because they provided strategies required for survival under the institution of New World slavery.

Bracha veShalom had a typically Dutch-style profile. The squared-off top parts of the end brick walls served two purposes for building in Holland. They create an architectural detail for chimneys and provide a practical way to finish off masonry; pointed top ends do not typically or practically exist in masonry construction. However, there would have been no need for a chimney at the synagogue in tropical Suriname. Might then the typically Dutch style of the synagogue building express the Jews' patriotism, remembrance of, or deference to the Netherlands—the nation that had given them and their brethren back in Amsterdam religious rights? Or is it the style imposed in absentia by a Dutch architect back in Amsterdam, where Jews were excluded from the building guilds?

Regarding the Bet Haim at Jodensavanne, three critical questions arise. Firstly, did there ever exist a house of seven circuits in which the ritual washing and circlings occurred? If not, how did the burial rites proceed and how did they come to be? Secondly, do the graven images on Jodensavanne's tombstones, which so closely resemble those of contemporaneous Portuguese Jewish cemeteries in Amsterdam and Curaçao, suggest an intended uniformity in the sepulchral art of Portuguese Jews throughout the New World and Europe, or was it simply due to the community's lack of sufficiently skilled craftspeople and of adequate stone? Thirdly, does the irregular layout of the cemetery's tombstones, often in opposition to rabbinical rules on burial placement arrangements, reflect the persistence of individuals who desired unconventional burial adjacencies due to intermarital ties (unusually close among the Sephardim of the time), or might it express a cabalistic idea that cemeteries be labyrinthine? Or, does it reveal special conditions of burial placement for *Congreganten* Jews of African descent?

The discussion of the African antecedents of the architecture and culture of Jodensavanne is enormously important. African and Jewish cultures were in close contact in Suriname and clearly affected one another. Benoit's drawing (see Fig. 20.18) documents or perhaps illustrates such proximity: On the right is the workshop of an African-American tailor, complete with his African name (Koffi is a common West African name, particularly among the Eve people of West Africa) prominently displayed. On the left is a shop of clothes and other ready-made goods. Its proprietor is a merchant of Sephardic stock, with his ethnic name similarly displayed.

From Zimmerman's map of 1877, another example of Jewish and African-American cultural proximity exists. The map shows an enlargement of a section through the Suriname River at the location of Jodensavanne. It depicts the synagogue and, adjacent to it and specifically noted, a Bomax ceiba tree, the formal embodiment of immortal ancestors in West African worship and referenced as such on Zimmerman's map. Does this represent Jewish tolerance of African religion or African adoption of ground considered holy by the Jews? Do the Jewish converts and offspring of Jewish fathers and African, non-Jewish mothers—considered by authoritative Jewish law to be non-Jews—who were raised, educated, and identified as Jews, exemplify the Jews of Jodensavanne's rejection of the usual reluctance of Jews to accept converts,[45] or does it simply imply dominance by the ruling minority? Whichever may be the case, are there parallels to be found in the architecture of the synagogue or in the configuration of the cemeteries? Why at Bracha veShalom is the design of the women's gallery less inclusive compared to its predecessor in Amsterdam? Did it reflect less honor given to Jodensavanne's Jewish women, some of whom, as early as 1685, were of African as well as Ashkenazic descent? Does the consolidation of functions within one building at Bracha veShalom—as opposed to the design of Amsterdam's synagogue and subsequent synagogues in Suriname and the Caribbean with their separate auxiliary buildings—simply express economical use of materials (shared walls, foundations, and roofs), or is it evocative of the freedom and optimism felt by these uniquely privileged New World Jews, anticipating the messianic age with open arms and architecture?

By the mid-eighteenth century, Jodensavanne was in decline. Sugar prices had dropped, many planters found themselves in default on their loans, and raids on the plantations by Bosnegroes (enslaved Africans who escaped the plantations and established their own distinctively ethnic communities farther into the country's interior) threatened all. In 1757, John Greenwood, an American artist visiting Jodensavanne, noted in his diary that the place "is as empty as the church is of Sunday, the Jews being all gone to the plantations, except a few vagabonds who make this place their sanctuary or asylum, when they run from the town for debt or any misdemeanors."[46] At the time of the hundredth anniversary jubilee, in 1785, the synagogue of Bracha veShalom was already a relic of the past,

FIGURE 20.18 "A gauche, la boutique d'un vette warier; à droite, la boutique d'un snerie ou tailleur" (To the left a clothier's shop; to the right that of a tailor), from P. J. Benoit, *Voyage à Surinam* (Bruxelles, 1839). Courtesy of General Research Division, The New York Public Library, Astor, Lenox, and Tilden Foundations.

visited and cherished as a historic monument by Jodensavanne's former inhabitants and their descendants. By 1787, meetings of the Mahamad were no longer held at Jodensavanne, now replaced by Paramaribo. By the 1830s Jodensavanne was all but abandoned. The year 1865 was the last time the synagogue was used, and in 1873 its roof caved in, with no subsequent repairs being made.

By the early eighteenth century some of the Jews of Jodensavanne had already begun to move to Paramaribo, where they constructed new synagogues and cemeteries and established themselves primarily as merchants. Some also emigrated to other places in the Caribbean and North America or returned to Amsterdam. In Paramaribo, there are two synagogues, both of wooden construction. The first, built in 1716, replaced an earlier synagogue that was converted into a house for the sexton of the Spanish-Portuguese synagogue. A new synagogue, Neveh Shalom (House of Peace), was completed in 1723. However, this building was completely rebuilt between 1834 and 1842 (see Figs. 20.19 and 20.20). In 1735 Neveh Shalom was sold to the Ashkenazi Jews, and the Spanish-Portuguese Jews built a new synagogue, Tsedek veShalom (Justice and Peace), that same year. This synagogue, although never completely rebuilt, was significantly altered when its roof was raised to provide gallery space for the women (see Fig. 20.21).[47] It is unclear where the women sat prior to the gallery addition. Despite the grandeur of these buildings, the Portuguese Jews considered their building only a house of prayer, not a synagogue. In their regulations, the Jews stated that there was only one synagogue, the one at Jodensavanne.[48]

At the end of the eighteenth century, a synagogue of the Jews of African descent existed in Paramaribo. Prior to the establishment of their synagogue, these Jews founded their own society, in 1759, which they called Darkhei Yesharim (The Ways of the Righteous). Their synagogue was demolished around 1800.[49] Unfortunately, little is known of the architecture of this latest, now lost, synagogue of Paramaribo. However, the earlier two synagogues exist to this day and manage, against great odds, to survive. Although these two synagogues share architectural features with the one at Jodensavanne and with other Sephardic synagogues, they lack Jodensavanne's unique elements. Absent are the messianic design intent in the plan of the synagogue complex, the Dutch-style building profile, the attached auxiliary spaces, the faux windows (if in fact they did exist at Jodensavanne), the set-back and perpendicularly aligned women's gallery, and, most apparently, the brick construction.

Within walking distance of the Jewish cemetery at Jodensavanne is the so-called "Creole" (in Suriname, meaning descendant of an African slave) cemetery. Those graves still visible date from the nineteenth and twentieth centuries. The heart shape found on some of the graves in this cemetery (see Figs. 20.22 and 20.23) is most likely a *sankofa* (go back to fetch it), a symbol for the important proverb of the Akan people of West Africa, from whom many Surinamers descend, "Se wo were fi na wo sankofa a yenkyi" (it is not a taboo to go back and retrieve if you forget).[50] It may also be an *akoma* (the heart) symbol of love, patience, goodwill, faithfulness, and endurance.[51]

When displayed, the *sankofa* symbolizes the wisdom in learning from the past in building for the future. Elsewhere, in Africa and in African-American cemeteries, the *sankofa* is found. One example, in particular, is that on the remains of an eighteenth-century coffin in the New York African Burial Ground.[52] The shape at the tip of the grave marker in Suriname symbolizes the same, although upside down. The *sankofa* symbol, typical of African symbols, is flexible and can be adapted as required.[53] Descendants of the African diaspora in Jodensavanne, not unlike the Jews, held respect for the belief that wisdom was passed down by the ancestors to future generations. Surinamer-Africans expressed this belief on their tombs, in particular, through this age-old symbol—as did the Jews with their graven images of biblical episodes—for the edification of posterity.

In the nineteenth- and twentieth-century Sephardic cemetery in Paramaribo, the heart-shaped *sankofa* and *akoma* symbols appear (see Fig. 20.24), coinciding with the Star of David (see Fig. 20.25), the Hebrew name of the deceased, and the typical Sephardic flat horizontal tomb. However, gone are the illustrative engraved images. Here, the horizontal stone tombs, European in origin, are joined by sepulchral art of African origin, thereby forming the only uniquely Jewish-African style of tomb known in the New World.

FiGURE 20.19 Exterior view of the south and west façades of the synagogue Neveh Shalom in Paramaribo, Suriname, which was originally built in 1723 and completely rebuilt between 1834 to 1842. The sanctuary was entered at doors on the south façade (under the pediment and columns), from the north (not shown), and at the center door (of three) on the western façade. The second-story women's gallery was accessed by two staircases located to the left and to the right of the center door on the western façade. Photograph by Rachel Frankel, 1997.

FIGURE 20.20 Interior view of the synagogue Neveh Shalom, in Paramaribo, looking east. The *tevah* (reader's platform) is in the foreground, the *hekhal* (ark) in the background. Note the minimal fenestration on the east wall and the sand-covered floor. Photograph by Rachel Frankel, 1997.

FIGURE 20.21 Exterior view of the north and east façades of the synagogue Tsedek veShalom, in Paramaribo, Suriname, built in 1735 and significantly altered over time. Regrettably, the entire interior of this synagogue has been removed from the building and sent to Israel because the local population can no longer afford to maintain it. Photograph by Rachel Frankel, 1995.

Figure 20.22 Tomb with *sankofa* (or *akoma*) on a horizontal gravestone from Jodensavanne's "Creole" cemetery. Photograph by Rachel Frankel, 1995.

FIGURE 20.23 Vertical grave marker with *sankofa*, from Jodensavanne's "Creole" cemetery. Photograph by Rachel Frankel, 1997.

FIGURE 20.24 Tombs with horizontal gravestones, vertical wooden markers with *sankofa* finials, and *akoma* heart symbols attached, Sephardic cemetery, Paramaribo, Suriname. Photograph by Rachel Frankel, 1997.

FIGURE 20.25 Vertical wooden post, fallen down, with *sankofa* finial and Star of David attached, Sephardic cemetery, Paramaribo, Suriname. Photograph by Rachel Frankel, 1997.

Notes

1. Translated by Ir. D. P. Loemban Tobing from the Dutch article by Fred. Oudschans Dentz, "Wat er Overbleef van het Kerkhof en de Synagoge van de Joden-Savanne in Suriname," in *De West-Indische Gids* (Negen en Twintigste Jaargang, 1948), 214.
2. [David Cohen Nassy?], *Essai Historique sur la Colonie de Surinam* (Paramaribo, 1788), refers to the location of Suriname's first synagogue in Torrica (or Thorarica). In 1788, at the time of the writing of the historical essay, as well as in 1672, when this synagogue was built, Torrica was the name of the important harbor town, further downriver from where the Jews had settled by the mid-1660s. Torrica was also the name of one of the five divisions that the Dutch formed in their new colony as early as 1670. The town of Torrica existed in Divisie Thorarica (the Division of Torrica) much like New York City exists in the State of New York. By the mid- to late nineteenth century, the original five divisions had changed and merged, and the once important town of Torrica had long since disappeared. However, the town persisted in memory as the only place bearing this name, and by the turn of the twentieth century this reference, in *Essai Historique*, to the early synagogue being located "in Torrica," served to confuse readers into thinking that this synagogue existed in the town of Torrica. In fact, this synagogue was in the Divisie Thorarica, on the Suriname River, about one mile south of Jodensavanne where exist the remains of the synagogue Bracha veShalom. The fact that no synagogue existed in Torrica, the town, at this time, is further substantiated by the absence of any mention of Jews being there in an otherwise complete and "impartial description" of the place by George Warren in 1667. However, prior to the establishment of the Jewish settlement in the Division of Torrica in the 1660s, it may be possible that a small and short-lived Jewish community existed in the town of Torrica.
3. Alex van Stipriaan, "An Unusual Parallel: Jews and Africans in Suriname in the 18th and 19th Centuries," in *Studia Rosenthaliana* 31 (1/2) (1997):74.
4. Mordechai Arbell, "The Jewish Settlement in Pomeroon/Pauroma (Guyana) 1657–1666," in *Revue des Etudes Juives* (July–December 1995):358–59.
5. George Warren, *An Impartial Description of Surinam* (London, 1667), 19.
6. Richard Price, *The Guiana Maroons: A Historical and Bibliographical Introduction* (Baltimore, 1976), 19.
7. Rene S. Wassing, *African Art: Its Background and Traditions* (Hong Kong, 1968), 192.
8. Warren, *Impartial Description*, 19–20.
9. Judith Belinfante et al., *The Esnoga* (Amsterdam, 1991), 56–58.
10. Victor Enthoven, "Suriname and Zeeland: Fifteen Years of Dutch Misery on The Wild Coast, 1667–1682," in *International Conference on Shipping, Factories and Colonization*, ed. J.Everaert and J. Parmentier (Belgie, 1996), 253–54. It was hard to find personnel, and all kinds of private initiatives were taken to hire a work force. Agents of planters in Holland, from 1669–1679, contracted craftsmen such as carpenters, mill builders, coopers, bricklayers, etc.
11. Enthoven, "Suriname and Zeeland," 255, Table I, from Algemeen Rijksarchief, The Hague (ARA). In 1684, the year prior to the construction of Bracha veShalom, there were 163 Jews in Suriname and 972 Africans enslaved to them.
12. Enthoven, "Suriname and Zeeland," 255, Table I (ARA).
13. Johannes M. Postma, *The Dutch in the Atlantic Slave Trade, 1600–1815* (Cambridge, Mass., 1990), 185.
14. Carol Krinsky, *Synagogues of Europe* (Cambridge, 1985), 6.
15. Israel Broadcasting Authority, "The Crypto-Jews of Portugal," *Out of Spain, 1492: A Journey Through Spain with Yitzhak Navon* (Israel Broadcasting Authority, 1992), Parts 1 and 2.
16. Nonetheless, there are exceptions among the Sephardim of Amsterdam and those of other places. Krinsky, *Synagogues of Europe*, 390, writes: "in the synagogue [of Amsterdam] of

1639, some of the gallery space was reserved for men; at least one of the galleries which ran around three sides of the interior held men." Additionally, according to the Italian Jesuit priest, Pietro della Valle—who in 1626 visited the Great (Old) Synagogue at Aleppo, Syria—men and women sat together, each family having its particular place, with Syrians on the right side and Sephardim on the left (from the photographic exhibit, *The Jews of Syria* by Robert Lyon, co-curated by Professor Samuel Gruber and Dr. Edward Aiken at Yeshiva University Museum, New York, 1997–98).

17. Krinsky, *Synagogues of Europe*, 29.
18. Yosef Kaplan, Henry Méchoulan, and Richard H. Popkin, *Menasseh Ben Israel and His World* (Leiden, 1989), 57–58.
19. Rochelle Weinstein, "Sepulchral Monuments of the Jews of Amsterdam in the Seventeenth and Eighteenth Centuries" (Ph.D. diss., New York University, 1979), 49.
20. Weinstein, "Sepulchral Monuments."
21. Joseph Gutmann, *The Jewish Life Cycle* (Leiden, 1987), 20–21.
22. L. Alvares Vega, *Het Beth Haim van Ouderkerk* (Ouderkerk aan de Amstel, 1994), 23.
23. Alvares Vega, *Het Beth Haim van Ouderkerk*, 15–16.
24. Gutmann, *The Jewish Life Cycle*, 19.
25. H. J. Zimmels, *Ashkenazim and Sephardim* (Hoboken, N.J., 1996), 183.
26. Yosef Kaplan et al., *Menasseh Ben Israel*, 58.
27. John DeBye, *De Joodse begraafplaats te Cassipora* (http://www.cq-link.sr/personal/debye/cassipora/index.ht, 1998), graciously translated by Wim Klooster.
28. Ibid.
29. Robert Cohen, *Jews in Another Environment: Suriname in the Second Half of the Eighteenth Century* (Leiden, 1991), 161.
30. [Nassy?], *Essai Historique*, seconde partie, 23 and 49.
31. These are figures from Enthoven's article, "Suriname and Zeeland," Table 1: 255. However, *Essai Historique* claims that in 1690 there were ninety two Jewish families, ten to twelve German Jews united to the Portuguese there by bonds of marriage and fifty bachelors who did not belong to these families. Of the Black slaves, there were said to be at least nine thousand. In contrast, according to the Johannes Postma (*The Dutch in The Atlantic Slave Trade*, 185) the population of Suriname in 1684 was no more than four thousand people in total, and by 1695, the total population was still less than five thousand people.
32. *Prayer Book for Yom Kippur* [Day of Atonnement] of the Congregation Shearith Israel in The City of New York, 332; four synagogues are named in the customary blessing on Yom Kippur given to those who contributed to it. Thanks to the Rev. Abraham Lopes Cardozo and his wife, Mrs. Irma Carodozo, of Shearith Israel for finding this reference and to Professor Jonathan Sarna for his help with its translation and explanation.
33. [Nassy?], *Essai Historique*, seconde partie, 50.
34. Ibid., 23.
35. Cohen, *Jews in Another Environment*, 163.
36. From the 1997 field survey done by the author and the volunteers of Caribbean Volunteer Expeditions.
37. M. D. Teenstra, *De Landbouw in de Kolonie Suriname* (Groningen, 1835), 137.
38. [Nassy?], *Essai Historique*, 51.
39. Enthoven, "Suriname and Zeeland," Table 1: 255.
40. Cohen, *Jews in Another Environment*, 161.
41. [Nassy?], *Essai Historique*, 51.
42. Ibid., 49.
43. Wassing, *African Art*, 192.
44. Wassing, *African Art*.
45. Yosef Kaplan et al., *Menassah Ben Israel*, 54–55.
46. John Greenwood, *2 Diaries or Notebooks* (Manuscript Department, New York Historical Society), 101–2, transcribed and shared by Wim Klooster.

47. Günter Böhm, "The Synagogues of Surinam," *Journal of Jewish Art* 6 (1978):103.
48. Ibid.
49. Ibid., 104.
50. Kwaku Ofori-Ansa, *Meanings of Symbols in Adinkra Cloth* (1993).
51. Ibid.
52. Kwaku Ofori-Ansa, Associate Professor of African Art History at Howard University, written and oral communications with the author, winter 1997–98.
53. Ibid.

PART VI

"THE BROKERS OF THE WORLD": AMERICAN JEWS, NEW CHRISTIANS, AND INTERNATIONAL TRADE

– Chapter 21 –

JEWS AND NEW CHRISTIANS IN THE ATLANTIC SLAVE TRADE

Seymour Drescher

IN STUDYING THE WESTWARD EXPANSION of Europe after 1500, "the development of an Atlantic economy is impossible to imagine without slavery and the slave trade."[1] During three and a half centuries, up to twelve million Africans were loaded and transported in dreadful conditions to the tropical and subtropical zones of the Americas. This massive coerced transoceanic transportation system was only one element of a still broader process. Probably twice as many Africans were seized within Africa for purposes of domestic enslavement or transportation to purchasers in the Eastern Hemisphere during the same period. The coerced movement of Africans long exceeded the combined voluntary and involuntary migrations of Europeans. By the beginning of the nineteenth century, between two and three Africans had been landed in the Americas for every European who crossed the Atlantic.[2]

This major human migration involved the direct and indirect participation of many individuals and institutions in Europe, Africa, Asia, and the Americas. It required an enormous number of interlocking activities, within and between continents. Although tens of thousands of direct participants involved Muslims, Christians, Jews, and others who could be classified by religion, and scores of groups that could be classified by ethnic affiliation, the history of the slave trade is usually considered in terms of geography and state sponsors. Geographically, the trade is analyzed in terms of a triangular trade in which Europeans provided capital, organization, and the means and manpower of transoceanic transportation; Africans provided the captives and the means of intracontinental movement; and Europeans in the Americas provided the means for redistributing transported captives to productive occupations in various regions.[3]

Politically, the slave trade is usually framed in terms of a succession of national entities drawn into and dominating the trade as suppliers, carriers, and purchasers. Although every European polity bordering the Atlantic attempted to enter into the Atlantic slave trade between 1450 and 1800, a small number of states dominated the European-sponsored enterprises. Chronologically, the trade as a whole is generally broken down into three phases. Each succeeding phase of the slave trade was numerically larger than its predecessor. In the century and a half of the first phase (1500–1640), 788,000 Africans were embarked on the "Middle Passage," or about 5,600 per year. During the course of the second phase (1640–1700), 817,000 left Africa, or about 13,600 per year. In the final phase, between 1700 and British abolition in 1807, 6,686,000 were exported, or about 62,000 per year. Thus, four out of every five Africans transported to the New World between 1500 and 1807 were boarded in the final phase (see Map 10 and Table 21.1).[4]

TABLE 21.1 Coerced African Migrants Leaving for the Americas by National Carrier (in thousands)

1500–1700 (Phases I and II)

Carrier	Before 1580	1580–1640	1640–1700
Spanish	10	100	10
Portuguese	63	590	226
British	1	4	371
Dutch	0	20	160
French	0	0	50
Total	74	714	817

1700–1808 (Phase III)

Carrier	Totals
British	3,120
Portuguese	1,903
French	1,052
Dutch	352
American	208
Danish	51
Total	6,686

Sources: David Eltis, *The Rise of the African Slave Trade in the Americas* (New York, 2000), 9, table I-I; and David Richardson, "Slave Exports from West and West-Central Africa, 1700–1810: New Estimates of Volume and Distribution," *Journal of African History* 30 (1989):1–22, 10, table 4.

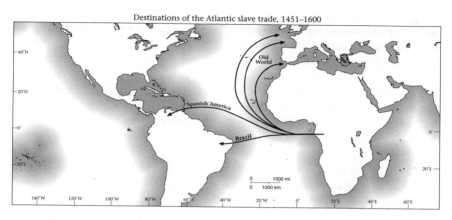

Destinations of the Atlantic slave trade, 1451–1600

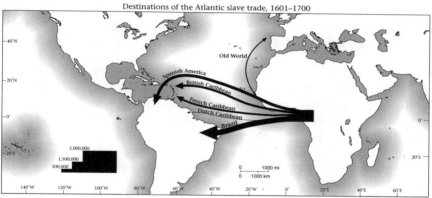

Destinations of the Atlantic slave trade, 1601–1700

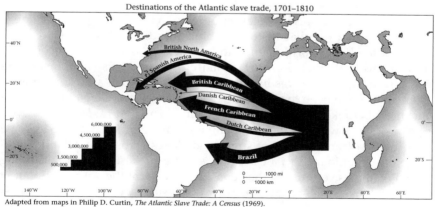

Destinations of the Atlantic slave trade, 1701–1810

Adapted from maps in Philip D. Curtin, *The Atlantic Slave Trade: A Census* (1969).

MAP 10   Growth of the Atlantic Slave Trade

For most scholars of the slave trade, economic, demographic, and political categories are the most significant variables in determining the coerced movement of Africans. Once launched, they look to economics or political economy to explain the flow of people from Europe to the coast of Africa and of captive Africans from the coast of Africa to the Americas. Price, mortality, health, age, sex, provenance, destination, and occupation are the key variables. Economic and demographic conditions, inflected by political attempts to bend those conditions in favor of one nation or another, define the priorities of analysis.[5]

This essay, however, deals with the impact of a particular religious minority upon economic and demographic developments in the Atlantic world over three centuries. Analyzing the role of religious or ethno-religious groups in the African slave trade within the familiar framework of nations and regions presents unusual methodological difficulties. Historians are acutely aware that the trade involved tens of thousands of perpetrators. Among them were pagans, Muslims, Catholics, Protestants, and Jews. Those who were involved may be further divided into scores of groups by ethnic designation, including every major entity ever defined as a "race." Scholars incorporate these entities contingently as they analyze the core processes of the trade itself. Even in regard to the study of slave trading collectivities, it is rare that historians regard the religious affiliation of the European participants as of more than limited significance, compared with economic relationships. The trade flowed easily from one religious and commercial entity to another. Culturally defined identities may have had some impact upon the fundamental choice of viewing Africans as enslavable, but over the whole period of its rise the transatlantic slave trade appears to have been an activity extraordinarily responsive to cost-benefit calculations.[6]

Analyzing the specific relation of Jews to the Atlantic slave trade is warranted by a peculiar historiographical tradition. "Scarcely were the doors of the New World opened to Europeans," declared the economist and historian Werner Sombart, "than crowds of Jews came swarming in.... European Jewry was like an ant-heap into which a stick [expulsion from Spain] had been thrust. Little wonder, therefore, that a great part of this heap betook itself to the New World.... The first traders in America were Jews," as well as "the first plantation owners" in African São Tomé and the first transplanters of sugar and slaves across the Atlantic. Jews were the "dominant social class [*die herrschende Kaste*]" of Brazil. Along with Portuguese criminals, they constituted almost the entire population of that colony, which reached its peak of prosperity only with "the influx of rich Jews from Holland." In support of his interpretation, Sombart drew heavily upon accounts by Jewish historians and encyclopedists. As Jewish migration to the Americas swelled at the end of the nineteenth century, writers sought to establish the earliest possible Jewish presence of their ancestors in the New World and to magnify their role in the grand narrative of European westward expansion. The search for Jewish preeminence in Atlantic development continues to find supporters among authors with dramatically contrasting motives.[7]

Sombart's hyperbolic account was correct in one respect. Three centuries of cumulative expulsions of Jews from Atlantic maritime states reached their climax as Europe's great westward expansion began in the fifteenth and sixteenth centuries. The simultaneous departure of both the Columbian expedition and Jews from Spain in 1492 was merely emblematic of a broader movement in European Jewish history. By 1500, Jews had been expelled from the kingdoms of England, France, Spain, and Portugal. Two generations later they had also been excluded from most of the Habsburg Netherlands, from the Baltic seacoast, and from large parts of Italy. This meant that by the time Africans began to be exported to the Americas in significant numbers (ca. 1570), Europe's rulers had forced the overwhelming mass of European Jewry eastward to Poland, Lithuania, and the Ottoman empire. Neither the rulers nor the merchants (including the Jewish merchants) of those new regions of settlement were involved or interested in the Atlantic slave trade.[8]

Jews could not live openly or securely anywhere along the European Atlantic seaboard during the first century after the Columbian expedition, the century in which the Euro-African coastal supply systems and the Iberian-American slave systems were created. Jews were consequently prohibited from openly participating in co-founding the institutions of the slave trade at any terminus of the triangular trade, or in the transoceanic "Middle Passage." One characteristic of this "religious cleansing" of Europe's Atlantic littoral also carried over into the second phase of the slave trade (1604–1700). African forced migration was dominated by political entities that tried to limit the slave trade to their own sponsored contractors in Europe, Africa, and the Americas. Success in long-distance and long-term voyages, as Europeans discovered, was initially enhanced by access to politically privileged monopolies in Europe, trade enclaves on the African coast, and colonial settlements in the Americas. Until the end of the seventeenth century, governmental agencies or quasi-public trading companies aspired to monopoly positions.

The greater the advantage offered by official patronage in any European polity, the less likely there was to be a Jewish presence. In a confessionally intolerant Europe and its overseas extensions, it was virtually impossible for Jews to hold the principal managerial positions in official slave trading entities. During three centuries, Spanish slave trade licenses and *asientos* (monopoly contracts for the delivery of slaves to the Spanish colonies) were never awarded to Jews. Apparently, this was as true in the Portuguese, Dutch, English, and French trades as it was for the Spanish *asiento*. Jews could, at most, exercise occasional influence at the margins of these official agencies as negotiators and consular intermediaries. Even subcontracting to Jewish merchants for the delivery of slaves contributed to the refusal of the Spanish government to renew the *asiento* to the Portuguese Royal Guinea Company at the beginning of the eighteenth century.[9]

Phase One

The Portuguese Atlantic slave trade to the Americas was an offshoot of their fifteenth-century slave trade from the African mainland to offshore islands and metropolitan Portugal. Historians of this pre-Columbian migration stream always emphasize the high degree of state control over this trade. It was conducted under the auspices of a crusading monarchy that was engaged in almost continuous religious warfare with North African Muslim kingdoms. Those who participated in the African coastal voyages of exploration by supplying capital, ships, or manpower included English, French, Polish, and Italians, as well as Iberians. None of the historical accounts of the Portuguese slave trade during the pre-Colombian period discusses a Jewish slaving dimension. The only accounts of a prominent Jewish presence in this initial process of oceanic exploration and trade are related to the scientific and cartographic experts mobilized by Prince Henry the Navigator to track his African exploratory expeditions.[10]

If Jews could play no role in the initial political and legal foundations of the European transatlantic slave trade, the elimination of Jewry from the Iberian Peninsula created a major economic niche for some genetic descendants of the Jews. In 1497, the forced mass conversion of one hundred thousand Iberian Jews residing in Portugal created a novel situation. As Christians, ex-Jews were free to take full advantage of the Portuguese seaborne empire, the first fully global network of its kind in human history. The Portuguese trading network expanded explosively along the coasts of Africa, into South Asia and to the east coast of South America. For nearly a century after the 1490s, the Portuguese held a virtual monopoly in the trades to Europe from these areas.

In one respect, Portugal's post-conversion legislation tended to enhance and prolong the commercial orientation of these legally designated "New Christians" in a society dominated by a traditional system of values and institutions. At the same time, however, Portugal's stigmatization of New Christians as members of a legally separate and inherited status also rendered its members subject to endless genealogical scrutiny, humiliation, confiscation, and violence from generation to generation. The volatile nature of the New Christian position was symbolized by the first mass deportation of European children to the tropics. Following the flight of Jews to Portugal after the Spanish expulsion of 1492, the Portuguese monarch had two thousand children abducted from their Jewish families. They were baptized and deported to Saõ Tomé, an island off the coast of Africa at the latitude of the equator. In a few years, only six hundred children remained alive. The continent that was soon to be called "the white man's grave" was first a "white child's grave." This first cohort of New Christians in Africa was mated at maturity with Africans. Their descendants, along with New and Old Christian Portuguese immigrants who arrived both involuntarily and voluntarily, became Saõ Tomé's principal inhabitants and traders.[11]

New Christians were, of course, legally denied the opportunity to openly profess or transmit Jewish culture and ritual. The Inquisition's premise of "impure blood" and the alleged collective propensity to heresy and "Judaization" transformed descent and kinship linkages into socially explosive material. However, these descendants of Jews were far from being frozen within a rigid endogenous caste system. The idea that New Christians overwhelmingly maintained religious, cultural, or even genealogical continuity with fifteenth-century Iberian Jewry into the eighteenth century was a racial myth. Most of those who remained within the Iberian orbit in fact attempted to assimilate as rapidly as possible. Intergenerational studies of Portuguese and overseas New Christians have concluded that each generation became culturally and religiously more able to live among, practice with, and marry Old Christians. For more than two centuries, however, this trajectory toward assimilation was intercepted by waves of official and popular coercion. Of an estimated one hundred thousand Jews at the time of conversion in 1497 (one-tenth of Portugal's population), no more than sixty thousand New Christians remained in 1542, and perhaps half that number in 1604 (or 2 percent of the population) at the height of their influence in the Portuguese slave trade.[12]

This marginalizing and volatile environment has serious implications for anyone wishing to analyze the economic behavior of New Christians both in general and as slave traders in particular. Their reaction to stigmatization punctuated by purges was a complex pattern of social organization and behavior. Denied full legitimacy in the community of the faithful, New Christians tended to develop trading networks that, as a means of survival, were based above all on family connections, and also tended to narrow their loyalties only to kinsmen or, at the most, to other New Christians who were similarly marginalized. Their ties to a geographically and culturally distant Jewry were often as fragile as those to the more proximate Old Christians among whom they lived in uncomfortable conformity. Unpredictable purges created periodic crises of identity. Those with sufficient resources and anxiety sometimes exited from the Iberian orbit altogether. Small waves of individuals periodically fled to areas where they could escape the Inquisition's procedures.

Not all of those who left Iberia rejoined Jewish communities. Many fled under threat of Inquisitorial persecution to the domains of more tolerant Catholic princes, an indication of a propensity toward Christianization. Economic opportunities frequently took precedence over genealogical vulnerability, even among those who lived beyond the power of the Iberian Inquisitions. A considerable number of those arrested as crypto-Jews in Mexico between 1620 and 1650, for example, had lived unmolested in Catholic Italy and France before risking immigration to the Spanish empire. Moreover, the documented phenomenon of New Christians returning to Iberia from Africa, Asia, or the Americas after having made their fortunes indicates that most wealthy merchants and mercantile families were not necessarily inclined to resettle where they could openly practice Judaism or even practice syncretic brands of family religiosity.[13]

The exercise of caution in lumping together Jews and New Christians in Europe or America is further warranted by developments in Africa. During the late sixteenth century, at the height of their participation in the Atlantic slave trade, a number of New Christians were living as defectors, beyond the Portuguese zone of control in Africa. These New Christian *lançados*, notes John Thornton, established a whole chain of settlements "with posts in Kongo (and often positions in the church and administration of Kongo) and its eastern neighbors as well as in states in the Ndembu region and Ndongo." Thornton, however, makes no mention of the reestablishment of Jewish communities among these New Christian defectors living there or anywhere else beyond the power of the Inquisition and the exclusivist definition of Christianity prevalent in Portugal. On the American side of the Iberian empires, New Christian merchants in the seventeenth-century New World "could social-climb almost as well as Old Christian merchants; it simply took them another generation or two to reach their goal." That goal was "the foundation of an entailed estate and a patent of nobility as a *fidalgo da casa real*." We have no evidence that the Dutch, English, or French Caribbean islands constituted important places of refuge for New World New Christians who might possibly have wished to flee Inquisitorial threats in the nearby Spanish American mainland colonies.[14]

Neither in their social orientation nor in their approach to economic activity, can one differentiate significantly between New and Old Christians in the slave trade. The latter certainly did not shun that economic activity because of its association with crypto-Jews in the popular mentality. Especially in discussing economic activity in the early modern Iberian empire, there is no heuristic value in generically identifying New Christians more closely with Jewish merchants among whom they did not live, than with Old Christian merchants among whom they did live. To conflate two distinct social entities (Jews and New Christians) when attempting to assess the potential roles of religious formations simply begs the question of affiliation.[15]

In comparative terms, however, the early modern Iberian empires allowed New Christians to play a role in the Atlantic slave trade that was never to be matched by Jews in any part of the Atlantic world. When the first global trade network in the world formed at the beginning of the sixteenth century, the New Christians were positioned to become its first trade diaspora. If their quasi-pariah religious status kept them at least once removed from institutional power, that same status tended to make them most effective in a world in which opportunities for long-term credit were dependent upon kinship and trust.

The African slave trade depended upon a complex series of exchanges —from Europe to Africa to America to Europe—in which trustworthy interlocking agents and trained apprentices offered enormous advantages to competing traders. As Joseph Miller notes, slave traders always operated at the margins of the rapidly expanding Atlantic system: "To the extent that merchants from the metropole involved themselves at all in this early trade in slaves, they tended to come from New Christian circles then coming under heavy pressure from the Inquisition at home and seeking respite from persecution in flight to the remote corners of the empire or to Protestant Northern Europe."[16]

The slave trade, therefore, opened up transoceanic niches of entrée and refuge that gave New Christians an initial advantage in human capital over other merchants. Slaving was so valuable an activity in the eyes of rulers that its New Christian practitioners might hope to be specifically exempted from periodic group expulsions. In one purge, New Christians were allowed to remain in Angola only if they were merchants. As commodities, slaves themselves opened niches into the American empires at times when other types of goods were restricted or excluded. Slaving was long a privileged means of gaining a foothold in Spanish as well as Portuguese America, even though there was a tendency for slavers, once established, to switch to other economic activities.[17]

Given this balance of negative institutional, social, and legal coercion and their positive technical and familial advantages, New Christian merchants managed to gain control of a sizable, perhaps major, share of all segments of the Portuguese Atlantic slave trade during the Iberian-dominated phase of the Atlantic system. I have come across no description of the Portuguese slave trade that estimates the relative shares of the various participants in the slave trade by this racial-religious designation, but New Christian families certainly oversaw the movement of a vast number of slaves from Africa to Brazil during its first-century period. James Boyajian identifies one New Christian whose network was responsible for transporting more than 10,200 "pieces" to the New World.[18] Another individual, António Fernandes de Elvas, operated the Angola and Cape Verde contracts between 1615 and 1623. This was also the peak period for general attacks on the crypto-Jewish monopoly of Portuguese trade.

Phase Two

During the "second Atlantic system," about 1640 to 1700, the Iberian near-monopoly was definitively broken. The focus of the slave trade expanded northward from Portuguese Brazil to the Caribbean region. Most northern Atlantic and Baltic Sea states attempted to enter the transatlantic slave system: the Netherlands, England, France, Denmark, Sweden, Brandenburg, and Courland. In the second half of the seventeenth century, the sheer number of state-sponsored companies engaged in the transportation of African slave-laborers reached its peak. For the first time, Jews participated substantially in this more open and competitive environment (Map 11) and played their most tangible role in the slave trade.[19]

By the end of the sixteenth century, a small stream of New Christians had already moved northward from Iberia, settling (either as Christians or as Jews) along a string of Atlantic and North Sea ports from southern France to northwestern Germany (and, eventually, England).[20] Before full-scale Dutch entry, Jewish Sephardim residing in Amsterdam used their comparative advantage in Iberian contacts to begin the first African slaving voyages conducted by professing Jews. Before the founding of the Dutch West India company, Amsterdam Jewish merchants chartered several vessels specifically for the slave trade from West Africa to Brazil and the Spanish Caribbean. The interest of Jewish merchants in the slave trade constituted a small part of their larger interest in the African and Brazilian trades to Europe.[21] Jews operating out of (or migrating from) the Netherlands still did not make a major contribution to the slave trade in most of the geographic segments of the system: fitting slave ships in Europe; managing slave factories, i.e., trading outposts, in Africa; or transporting slaves to the Americas.

During most of the seventeenth century, the Dutch transatlantic trade was conducted primarily by means of a chartered slaving monopoly given to the Dutch West India Company. That Company held on to the slaving monopoly long after it lost its exclusive rights over all other commodities. As they were unable to operate freely outside the Company and were excluded on grounds of religion from serving on its directorate, Jewish merchants could enter the Dutch slave trade in only two ways: as passive investors in the Company itself, or as illegal private traders (interlopers). In the first case, Jewish investment in the West India Company was remarkably small. It amounted to only a 1.3 percent share of the founding capital. At the peak of Dutch influence in the Atlantic slave trade between the early 1640s and the early 1670s, Jews appear to have constituted between 4 and 7 percent of the membership in the West India Company.[22] Jews were a much smaller segment in the Dutch overseas trade than were New Christians in the Portuguese global trade. Dutch society was comparatively much better endowed with capital, commercial skills, and entrepreneurial expertise. There remains, however, the possibilities of illegal, or interloper, trade. It is the one branch of the Dutch slave trade for which I have seen no quantitative estimate of Jewish mercantile participation. However, according to Johannes Postma's comprehensive quantitative estimate of the Dutch slave trade, interlopers accounted for no more than 5 percent of the total transatlantic trade.[23]

In terms of company-sanctioned slaving, Jews were hardly involved in the "Middle Passage." Throughout the period of the West India Company's slave trade monopoly, from 1630 to 1730, only a handful of Jewish merchants are recorded as having been given permission to sail on their own account directly to the African coast. In Africa itself, the rise of the Dutch empire seems to have contributed equally little to the establishment

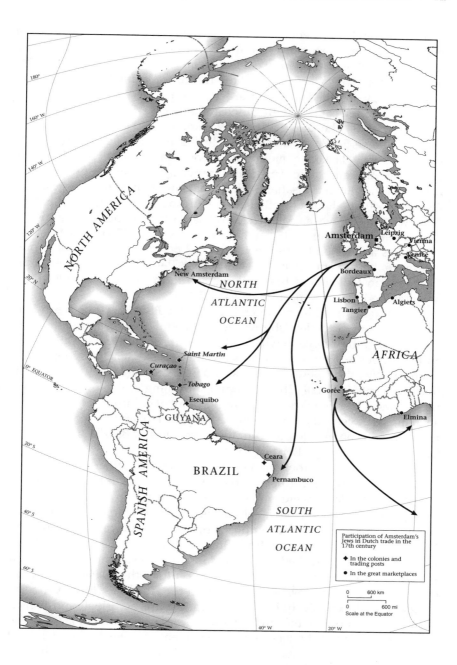

MAP 11 Participation of Amsterdam's Jews in Dutch Trade in the Seventeenth Century

of a strong Jewish presence. The Dutch seizure in the 1630s and 1640s of many important Portuguese trading centers and possessions in Africa resulted in neither a great influx of European Jews nor in a sudden relapsing of resident New Christians (whose ranks, according to contemporary polemicists, were filled with crypto-Jews) into professing Jews.

The main Jewish link with Dutch and other slaving came at the New World terminus. The Dutch were fully launched as a slaving power after their conquests in Brazil and Africa during the 1630s and early 1640s. However, they lacked a metropolitan population eager or desperate enough to relocate to the American frontiers. It was at the first western margin of the Dutch transatlantic trade that Jews played their largest role. Around 1640, the Dutch briefly became Europe's principal slave traders. They welcomed Jews as colonizers and as onshore middlemen in newly conquered Brazil. During the eight years between 1637 and 1644, Jewish merchants accounted for between 8 and 63 percent of first onshore purchasers of the twenty-five thousand slaves landed by the West India Company in Dutch-held Brazil. Perhaps a third of these captives must have reached planters through Jewish traders.

The progressive loss of Dutch Brazil to the Portuguese between 1645 and 1654 brought the Jewish presence to an end. The recapture of Brazil also revealed the degree to which religious affinities between Dutch Jews and Portuguese New Christians were limited by overriding economic interests. It was the New Christians who financed the Portuguese expedition to recapture Brazil. The ritual public burning of one of Brazil's captured Jews in Lisbon marked a definitive point of cultural and commercial alienation between the Jewish community in Holland (which also suffered heavy economic losses from the reconquest of Brazil) and the New Christian merchants in Portugal.[24]

Jewish merchants took up a similar activity at another margin of the Dutch empire, in the Caribbean colonies. Even in the relatively tolerant Dutch empire, Jews were initially more welcome in tropical areas of polyglot European and slave colonization than in temperate zone areas originally designed to be outposts of Dutch culture, including the Reformed religion. Refugees from Brazil and Europe were resettled primarily in Dutch-controlled islands and in Suriname on the coast of South America. By the end of the seventeenth century, the island of Curaçao contained the largest Jewish settlement in the Americas. From Curaçao, Jews engaged extensively in a transit trade with the British and French islands, and, more significantly, with the Spanish mainland. Over the course of the century between its establishment as a Dutch colony in 1630 and the virtual end of its transit slave trade in the 1760s, Jewish merchants settled or handled a considerable (but not yet precisely defined) portion of the eighty-five thousand slaves who landed in Curaçao, about one-sixth of the total Dutch slave trade (see Table 21.2).

As in other sectors of the slave trade, the West India Company's local agents were invariably Christians, and the island's commercial life was

TABLE 21.2 Estimated Traffic and Destination of Slaves Delivered by the Dutch to Curaçao, 1658–1732

Period	Number of Slaves
1658–1674	24,555
1675–1699	25,399
1700–1730	23,716
1731–1795	15,587

Source: Johannes Menne Postma, *The Dutch in the Atlantic Slave Trade 1600– 1815*, 35, 45, 48, 223.

Note: Isaac S. Emmanuel and Suzanne A. Emmanuel affirm that Jewish participation in the slave trade was large in the twenty-five years between 1686 and 1710 (*History of the Jews of the Netherlands Antilles*, vol. 1 [Cincinnati, 1970], 78), a period during which Postma records 26,364 slaves having landed in Curaçao (*The Dutch*, 45, 48). Comparing the Emmanuels' figures for 1700–1705 (1,108 slaves purchased by Jews) with Postma's total of 6,348 slaves delivered to Curaçao in the same period, Jews accounted for 18 percent of the large batch purchases of slaves landed. The Emmanuels listed only purchases of obvious "trade" slaves (ten or more) in their individualized list. However, like other islanders, "almost every Jew bought from one to nine slaves for his personal use" (*History of the Jews*, 78). Since Jews were "the second most important element" of Curaçao's population after the Protestants, amounting to 40 percent of the population of Punda about 1715 (ibid., vol. 1, 115), they may have accounted for nearly half of the slaves purchased in Curaçao from the West India Company in the twenty-five years between 1686 and 1710. By 1765, Jews held only 867 (or 16 percent) of the 5,534 slaves on Curaçao.

dominated by the Protestant majority. Just when Curaçao's participation in the transit slave trade was reaching its zenith at the end of the seventeenth century, wealthier Jews in the Netherlands were forging strong business ties with the island. Sephardic Jewish investors were involved in shipments of slaves from West Africa and in Dutch participation in the Spanish *asiento*. One Jewish family acted as Amsterdam factors for the Portuguese Guinea Company and as its delegates to the Dutch West India Company. Jewish mercantile influence in the politics of the Atlantic slave trade probably reached its peak in the opening years of the eighteenth century. During the War of Spanish Succession (1702–13), the whole trade of Spanish America seemed open to the Dutch. Both the political and the economic prospects of Dutch Sephardic capitalists rapidly faded, however, when the English emerged with the *asiento* at the Peace of Utrecht in 1713.[25]

Less discussion is necessary regarding the Jews in the other colonies of the seventeenth-century Caribbean region. Jewish mercantile activity in the British colonies was a more modest replication of the pattern in the Dutch Antilles. As in the Dutch case, metropolitan Jews played a minor role as passive investors in the seventeenth-century chartered slaving monopolies. Jewish merchants did not invest in the first such company, the Royal Adventurers Trading into Africa, which lasted from 1660 to 1672. Nor did they initially invest in its successor, the Royal African Company (RAC), until the 1690s. Eli Faber's assiduously researched study of Jewish participation in British imperial slavery shows that the peak of Jewish mercantile investment in the Royal African Company lasted from the mid-1690s to the second decade of the eighteenth century. Owning about 10 percent of the RAC's shares during the period when the company accounted for about 20 percent of the English slave trade, Jewish merchants accounted for about 2 percent of metropolitan slaving capital. With the removal of charter restrictions on the Anglo-African trade in 1712 the Jewish metropolitan role declined still further.

During the third quarter of the seventeenth century, Jewish merchants also established a presence in some of the English West Indies, especially Barbados and Jamaica. In neither island did they acquire a large proportion of the island's slaves as planters. However, like non-Jews who resided in the urban areas, they bought a small percentage of less desired slaves, often known as "refuse slaves" for resale and redistribution in the Caribbean transit trade. Eli Faber calculates that Jews purchased 7.1 percent of the slaves landed by the Royal African Company in Jamaica between 1674 and 1700. A corroborating study by Trevor Burnard calculates the Jewish share at 6.5 percent for the slightly longer period of 1674–1708. As in the Dutch Caribbean, Jews were most prominent in the intra-Caribbean branch of the slave trade. Jewish merchants in the English islands never attained the significance of the Curaçao merchants in the Dutch Caribbean. Nowhere in the English Atlantic colonies did Jews own much more than 1 percent of the slaves.[26]

Jewish participation in the French slave trade was more evanescent. In the French Caribbean colonies, a Jewish presence established in the 1660s and 1670s was virtually eliminated by expulsions in the mid-1680s. As slave traders in the French colonies, Jews never approached the significance of their counterparts in the Dutch Antilles. Jews also played marginal roles in the efforts of smaller Northern European maritime states to become players in the Atlantic economy. At a moment when access to this second Atlantic system seemed open, the rulers of Denmark, Sweden, Courland, and Brandenburg all attempted to enter it. Jews of Hamburg and Amsterdam were sought out for advice or expertise. Again, one must note the relatively modest role of even the most prominent of Europe's mercantile Jews in the formation of Atlantic trading enterprises. When the Brandenburg African Company was formed, late in the seventeenth century, its subscribers were principally the elector of Brandenburg, the elector of Cologne, and Benjamin Raule (Zeelander and director-general of the Brandenburg navy). Smaller sums were offered by several of the elector's privy councilors. Raule's own share was underwritten by Dutch investors, presumably including Jews. As in the Dutch case, Jewish participation was auxiliary and nonmanagerial. Jews played an even more marginal role in another slave trade project. In 1669, the count of Hanau wished to found a slave-labor colony within the Dutch West India Company's colonial sphere in South America. His agent made contact with the Company's executive in Amsterdam through a Jewish intermediary. Neither the German prince nor the West India merchants thereafter required the Jew's services.[27]

During the same period, however, other Jews occasionally had more important roles as agents and intermediaries. "The Nunes da Costa, in Amsterdam and Hamburg, were leading participants in setting up of the Portuguese Brazil Company. They also aided the colonial schemes of Duke James of Courland. The Belmontes were closely connected with Dutch bids for the Spanish slaving *asientos*." This flurry of activity coincided with the peak of Jewish entrepreneurial activity in the last third of the seventeenth century.[28] At the height of this second phase of the Atlantic slave trade, the Jewish mercantile influence on its development in Europe, in Africa, and on the Atlantic remained modest. The real importance of the sojourn of Jews in Brazil was that it gave some of them an initial technological advantage in their movement into the Caribbean. Elsewhere, Jewish capital and organization never approached the level of significance attained by that of New Christians in the Americas during the previous century and a half of Jewish exclusion.

Phase Three

The long eighteenth century (1700–1807) witnessed the absolute peak of the Atlantic slave trade in terms of annual slave departures and arrivals. With some local exceptions, the Jewish presence in the slave trade declined rapidly. Intensive research into each of the national trades has failed to turn up more than a handful of Jewish individuals or mercantile families in any of the great slaving systems of the eighteenth century. Research on the French trade has turned up detailed records of a few Jewish families in a trade dominated by merchants of other religious groups. In Bordeaux, the center of Jewish activity in the French colonial trade, Jewish traders accounted for only 4.3 percent of the slaves exported to the New World by the merchants of that city. One Jewish family, the Gradis, ranked among the seven major slavers in eighteenth-century Bordeaux. The prominence of the Gradis family was yet one more demonstration that special political influence was a significant comparative advantage for dealers in slaves. The Gradis family had greater access to institutional centers of power, both on the African coast and in France, than other Jewish mercantile families in the port.[29]

Concerning Britain, Faber shows that the Jewish share of Britain's African trade declined from its minor role in the Royal African Company. Jewish shareholders accounted for less than 1.6 percent of the original capital of the South Sea Company in 1714. As independent investors and ship-owners, the metropolitan Jewish capitalists never accounted for more than 1 percent of Britain's African trade during the last fifty years before slave trade abolition. Eighteenth-century Jews were equally marginal as receivers of consignments of slaves in the colonies. Only an occasional Jewish factor can be identified in any of the islands. Jewish merchants continued to occupy their traditional niche as purchasers of slaves for resale. According to British Naval Office records, 5.9 percent of the twenty-four thousand slaves reexported from Jamaica between 1742 and 1769 were carried on Jewish-owned vessels. Only in two British colonies did Jewish participation rise above the 6 to 7 percent share level of seventeenth-century traders. During the third quarter of the eighteenth century, the combined African slaving voyages of the Rivera and Lopez families of Newport, Rhode Island, accounted for 9 percent of that colony's slaving activity. During the century before Anglo-American abolition in 1807, Jews accounted for about 2 percent of Newport's transatlantic slave trade.

In Jamaica, the Jewish role was more volatile. The revival of the slave trade after the war of the American Revolution was accompanied by a rise of Jewish mercantile participation in the reexport trade. During the mid-1760s, as in the metropolis, fewer than 1 percent of the ships in Jamaica's ports belonged to Jews. Twenty years later their ownership share had increased to 4.3 percent. In the late 1780s, an unprecedented 26.7 percent of reexported slaves were carried in their vessels. Thereafter, their share fell to the seventeenth-century level of 6 percent before British slave trade abolition. The post–American Revolution recovery also stimulated a dramatic increase in the role of Jamaican Jewish merchants as slave factors. From the mid-1790s until 1802, the Jewish-Christian partnership of Alexandre Lindo and Richard Lake was responsible for between 22 and 37 percent of Africans advertised for sale in Kingston, Jamaica.[30]

The eighteenth-century Iberian slave trade is equally notable for the declining significance of its New Christians. They seem to have rapidly disappeared from the discourse of the South Atlantic slave trade. At the beginning of the seventeenth century, Portuguese polemicists inveighed against the New Christian monopoly of the Portuguese trade. By the 1680s, however, the most serious petition against African slavery and the slave trade ever to be laid before the Roman *curia* failed to evoke the old charge of New Christian preponderance. The anti-slavery petitioner had no qualms about invoking Iberian racial prejudice toward the descendants of Jews in support of his case against African enslavement. It was scandalous that impure crypto-Jewish masters held black Christians of pure blood in bondage. The petitioner, however, remarkably failed to assail the predominance or to mention the function of contemporary New Christians in the African slave trade.[31]

Flights of New Christians from the Iberian orbit dwindled in proportion to the decline of Inquisitorial persecutions. The last century and a half of the Portuguese-Brazilian slave trade is a period in which New Christians simply faded into obscurity. When the Iberian Inquisitorial

period came to an end and freedom of religion was introduce
America after the wars of independence, former New Christian
reemerge as Jews, Protestants, or marranists. Roman Catho
remained the overwhelming locus of communal religious identity, w
ever the genealogical composition of the inhabitants. Except in some is
lated villages in Portugal and the Americas, crypto-Jewry had to be
rediscovered or reinvented in the late twentieth century.

Conclusion

During the first three centuries of Atlantic slaving, Europeans landed
eight million African captives in the Americas. By 1800, three million
African-American slaves toiled in houses, shops, farms, and plantations
from the Hudson River Valley to the Rio de la Plata. If it is impossible to
imagine the expansion of the early Atlantic economy without the slave
trade, can the same be said about the role of Jewish merchants in that
trade? Had the return of the Jews to Europe's Atlantic ports been post-
poned until the 1790s instead of the 1590s, the volume of enslavement or
distribution of Africans in the Atlantic system would hardly have been
altered. The "Jewish presence" in the slave trade was too ephemeral, too
localized, and too limited to have made an appreciable difference.

The economic, social, legal, and racial pattern of the Atlantic slave
trade was in place before Jews made their way back to the Atlantic ports
of northwestern Europe, to the coasts and islands of Africa, or to European colonies in the Americas. They were marginal collective actors in
most places and during most periods of the Atlantic system: its political
and legal foundations; its capital formation; its maritime organization;
and its distribution of coerced migrants from Europe and Africa. Only in
the Americas—momentarily in Brazil, more durably in the Caribbean—
can the role of Jewish traders be described as significant. If we consider
the whole complex of major class actors in the transatlantic slave trade,
the share of Jews in this vast network is extremely modest.

Considering the number of African captives who passed into and
through the hands of captors and dealers from capture in Africa until sale
in America, it is unlikely that more than a fraction of 1 percent of the
twelve million enslaved and relayed Africans were purchased or sold by
Jewish merchants even once. If one expands the classes of participants to
include all those in Europe, Africa, Asia, and the Americas who produced
goods for the trade or who processed goods produced by the slaves, and
all those who ultimately produced goods with slave labor and consumed
slave-produced commodities, the conclusion remains the same. At no
point along the continuum of the slave trade were Jews numerous
enough, rich enough, and powerful enough to affect significantly the
structure and flow of the slave trade or to diminish the suffering of its
African victims.[32]

does not hold true for the New Christian mer-
⸍ the trade. The foundations of the Atlantic slave
ı place before New Christians began to appear
sixteenth-century Portuguese Afro-European
idly diminished in significance by the eigh-
⸍ role in the development of the slave trade to
ts full weight. When Portuguese merchants
⸍ global trading diaspora in the history of the world,
⸍ian merchants were prominent in the growth of the Atlantic
economy.[33] Distrusted by Old Christian political and religious elites, New
Christians found a precarious niche in the Atlantic system. Less as a religious group than as a loose network of trading families, they were pioneers in the formation of the European-Asian-African-American complex
that supported the New World's first African-based slave economies.

I lack the basis for a quantitative breakdown of New Christians in the
Atlantic system. However, they seem to have had a more significant function in the operations of the slave trade than would be indicated by their
numerical proportion of the Portuguese or Ibero-American populations.
During the period when Portugal dominated the slave trade to the Americas (1570–1630), New Christians dominated important segments of Portuguese long-distance trade. The majority of these New Christians
successfully effected their own disappearance into African, Iberian, or
Ibero-American identities. A minority worked their way northward or
eastward into various forms of Christianity, Judaism, or a syncretistic
amalgam of both religious systems. In assessing the economic links
between African slaves, New Christians, and Jews in the Americas, one
must bear in mind that although Jews and New Christians shared some
common ancestors, the differences between them became progressively
deeper.[34] Economically speaking, in any given area of the Iberian orbit,
New and Old Christian slave traders constituted denser networks of
interaction than those that remained between Jews and New Christians
across great geographical distances.

Viewing the Atlantic system over the whole period from 1500 to the
age of the American revolutions, it is clear that merchant families of Jewish ancestry possessed their greatest comparative economic advantage at
the beginning of the transatlantic slave trade. In 1500 they found themselves trapped and forcibly converted in a poor country where mercantile skills and capital were at a premium. They also found themselves at
the center of a trading network that circled the globe in a single generation. The network deepened and broadened when the Portuguese and
Spanish empires were ruled by a single monarch between 1580 and 1640.
New Christian families were represented in all zones of the early Atlantic
trade—in Europe, Africa, and Latin America.

During the second phase of the Atlantic slave trade, when observant
Jews first entered the system, they found that their relative advantages
and significance were both sharply reduced in comparison to those of

New Christians within the Iberian orbit. They played minor roles in the European, African, and transoceanic branches of the Northern European trade. Their mercantile communities were far smaller in proportion to Christian networks in Northern Europe than were those of New Christians to Old Christians in Iberia. Their working capital was correspondingly less significant. Finally, any technical advantages that Jewish traders enjoyed over their Dutch, English, or French Christian competitors was far more restricted than had been those of the New Christians in sixteenth-century Iberia.[35]

Only in the Dutch orbit did Jews play a durable, if modest, role. In part, their brief prominence depended as much upon their availability as refugee "risk-takers" in tropical frontier colonies as upon their experience as merchant entrepreneurs in Europe. They were, as the English essayist Joseph Addison correctly noted, "pegs and nails" rather than architects and master builders in the second Atlantic system after 1640. During the third phase of the trade, the significance of Jewish capitalists declined further. When the Afro-American slave trade reached its absolute peak toward the end of the eighteenth century, both Jews and New Christians had nearly disappeared from the records of the transatlantic slave trade.

There is one final indicator of the Jews' eighteenth-century marginality. At two important flashpoints, one in the history of British Jewry, the other in the history of the British slave trade, the empirical insignificance of the relationship between Jews and the Atlantic slave trade was matched by its insignificance in contemporary discourse. In 1753 a bitter debate erupted over a bill to naturalize foreign-born Jews residing in England. A friendly pamphleteer cited as many Jewish contributions to the welfare of the British nation as he could, pointedly including Britain's overseas trades with East India, Jamaica, and Spanish America. There was no mention of Africa or the transatlantic slave trade.[36]

Thirty-five years later, the first European abolitionist crusade began in Great Britain. By the end of the American Revolutionary and Napoleonic wars, its target had expanded to include the entire Atlantic slave trade, symbolized by a declaration against the trade at the Congress of Vienna in 1815. Yet, steeped as they were in the Christian tradition, European abolitionists never sought to add a specifically "Jewish" dimension to their rhetorical attack on the slave traders. Nor did they shift religious responsibility for the traffic from the overwhelming majority of Christian traders toward the few Jewish traders in their midst. Still more significantly, British and French abolitionists never responded to the temptation offered by the mentality of the Iberian Inquisitions. They did not attempt to rewrite the history of the Atlantic slave trade within an antisemitic framework, or to construct a Jewish or crypto-Jewish creation myth. Sombart's later variant of this myth did not draw nourishment from the main current of European antislavery sentiment.

I have not touched upon another large historiographic question—the relation of the eighteenth-century slave trade to the British Industrial

Revolution. Suffice it to say that if the Jewish role in the slave trade was meager, the slave trade's role in generating capital for the British Industrial Revolution (or for the prior Dutch "Golden Age") was equally modest. The Jewish merchants' share of the slave trade's share in accounting for European economic expansion and industrialization was a small fraction of a small fraction. Here again, Iberian New Christian merchants presumably played a much larger role in a trade that probably made them much more important to Portuguese commerce than Jews had been to any early modern European economy. To conclude from this, however, that the slave trade "helped" Portugal to achieve sustained economic progress would be absurd. After three hundred years of sponsoring colonial slavery, neither the Portuguese nor their observers could detect much in the way of economic development in Portugal.[37]

Thus far I have considered what Jewish and New Christian merchants did to expand the flow of Africans within the Atlantic system. But what did the slave trade do for the expansion of European Jewry to the Americas? I noted the important function of the slave trade as an escape hatch for New Christians in Africa and in Latin America, and for Jews in the Caribbean region. One common historiographic inference is that the settlement and liberty of Jews in the New World (albeit on a far smaller scale and less completely than that of other European migrants) was aided by the forced migration of enslaved Africans. The most significant point, from this perspective, is not that a few Jewish slave dealers changed the course of Atlantic history, but that Jews in general found their "threshold of liberation" in regions newly dependent upon black slavery. In this scenario, Sephardic Jews and New Christians who engaged in the European slave trade were pioneers of Jewish resettlement in the early modern world, blazing a path for the liberation of their co-religionists.[38]

A still more intriguing historical question has begun to emerge in scholarly discourse on the role of Jews in the African slave trade. If the empirical record makes it relatively easy for historians of the trade to verify empirically that Jews did not dominate this segment of the Atlantic economy, historians of Jewry have begun to ask why Jews were not more involved than they were in the trade. If there was no special religious inhibition against buying and selling human beings among early modern Jews, why didn't Jewish merchants maximize their presumed advantages: a transoceanic ethno-religious network, and a facility with the important trading languages of the early Atlantic world? From the perspective of a historian of the slave trade, the response might be that these putative advantages were not the significant ingredients for success in the transatlantic slave business. In ethno-religious terms, there was no Jewish communal network on the coasts of Africa. Nor did Jewish multilingualism extend to any special competence in the languages of Africa, although it probably helped in the Caribbean transit trade, where they did find a niche. Success in the African trade depended far more on up-to-date intelligence about the changing tastes of Africans, translatable into rapid business decisions about the optimum assortment of goods for slaving voyages.

Even in most of the Americas, there is ample evidence that the Jewish mercantile network probably counted for little in Atlantic slaving. The evidence of Jewish involvement in the eighteenth-century slave trade presents us with a trail of inter-religious networks as keys to success. In case after case, Jewish merchants who participated in multiple slaving voyages or similar long-term activities linked themselves to Christian agents or partners. In Newport, Barbados, Jamaica, New York, Philadelphia, and Charleston, the pattern was replicated throughout the century before British abolition. A close study of Jews in the slave trade seems to confirm the main focus of slave trade historiography during the past half-century. Economic and demographic variables, inflected by political conditions, remain the decisive elements. It was not as Jews but as merchants that Jewish traders ventured into one of the significant enterprises of the early modern world.[39]

In light of the above analysis, we need to reconsider older assessments of New Christian and Jewish participation in European expansion to the Americas. Tens of thousands of Portuguese New Christians emigrated from Portugal after 1500. If we suppose that they departed from the metropolis at least proportionately to their estimated share of the Portuguese population (10 percent), then seventy thousand of the seven hundred thousand who left Portugal between 1500 and 1700 were New Christians. The movement of Spanish *conversos* would only add to this total. From a cultural perspective, however, three centuries of New Christian migration to the Ibero-Americas and to Ibero-Africa resulted only in the disappearance of New Christians, almost always in favor of fusion with other Catholics. There is no evidence of a rapid reappearance of distinctive marrano (still less of a "New Jewish") religiosity when Ibero-American citizens were finally allowed freedom of worship after their successful wars of independence. At best, New Christian crypto-Jews remained as a smattering of isolated families in the Americas, with a secretive "culture of difference," rather than a web of Jewish or marrano cultural formations. The migratory wave of seventy thousand New Christians to the New World left less of a cultural or communal trace in the Atlantic world of 1800 than a Jewish migration one-tenth as large.[40]

Professing Jews, by contrast, did gain a foothold in the Americas by 1800. Their largest and most successful communities were located in non-Iberian colonies dominated by slave agriculture. Even with the assumption that the Sephardic archipelago was indebted to the Atlantic slave trade for its expansion, it would be truly hyperbolic to say that European Jewry had gained much demographic or cultural advantage from their economic involvement. Nowhere in the Atlantic world did Jews collectively identify themselves in terms of some of their co-religionists' presence in the slave trade. Nor did their economic activities depend more

TABLE 21.3 Jewish Population Centers in the Western Hemisphere, 1500–1800

Area	Census Date	Population (est.)
Recife (Brazil)	1645	1,450
Barbados	1699	250
Martinique	1685	96
Curaçao	1745	1,500
Jamaica	1770	900
Nevis	1678	25
Saint-Domingue	1765	120
New Amsterdam	1654	100
Rhode Island	1774	120
Savannah, Georgia	1733	41
Charleston, S.C.	1800	600
Suriname	1787	1,292

Sources: Malcolm H. Stern, "Portuguese Sephardim in the Americas," *American Jewish Archives* 44 (1992):141–78; R. van Lier, *Samenleving in een grensgebied. Een sociaal-historische studie van Suriname* (Deventer, 1972), 24; cited in Jan Lucassen, "The Netherlands, the Dutch, and Long-Distance Migration in the Late Sixteenth to Early Nineteenth Centuries," in *Europeans on the Move: Studies on European Migration, 1500–1800* (Oxford, 1994), 153–91.

heavily upon that trade than those of other European or African ethnic groups. Even in Curaçao, "it was textiles and hardware which were the real backbone" of the trade of Jewish merchants with Spanish America. Demographically, of the nearly two million Europeans migrating across the Atlantic from 1500 to 1800, far less than 1 percent could conceivably have been Jews. In 1800, the fraction of world Jewry and wealth on the western shores of the Atlantic was smaller still. No Jewish settlement in the Americas had yet gained repute among European Jewry as a vital center of religious or cultural eminence. The appeal of the transatlantic world to the European Jewish imagination before 1800 seems to have been limited.[41] (See Table 21.3.)

Even before the onset of revolutions for independence in the Americas, the largest Caribbean Jewish communities were in decline. Curaçao and Suriname were already stagnant colonies in a minor empire. In the latter case, the late eighteenth-century movement of Jews into the tropical Atlantic eerily echoed the coerced migration with which it had begun from Portugal three centuries before. After 1750, Jewish arrivals in Suriname only barely exceeded departures because of a semicoerced migration from Amsterdam.[42]

As the volume of the transatlantic slave trade moved toward its peak on the eve of the Saint-Domingue revolution of 1791, the Jewish presence in that trade had long since shrunk even from its modest dimensions of the previous century. Above all, no Jewish community in the Americas had emerged as a magnet for the Jewish populations living in the heartland of

Jewry—Eastern and Mediterranean Europe. When a second and far greater wave of Jewish migration flowed to the New World a century after 1800, it owed nothing to the slave trade or to plantation slavery. It began after the demise of the Atlantic slave trade, and it largely avoided the great arc of the Caribbean basin that had once been the center of Sephardic settlement. When the mass Jewish and mass African migrations finally converged in the late nineteenth-century Americas, they were the voluntary migrations of two peoples, among many, yearning to breathe free.

Notes

This essay is revised from a paper delivered at The John Carter Brown Library, 15–18 June 1997. For their helpful comments and generous suggestions, I would like to thank Reid Andrews, Ralph A. Austen, Harold Brackman, Pieter Emmer, Stanley Engerman, Frederic Jaher, Wim Klooster, John McCusker, Robert Paquette, Ernst Pijning, Jonathan Schorsch, Matilde Zimmermann, Norman Fiering, and the participants in the conference (hereafter, JCB Conference) on "The Jews and the Expansion of Europe to the West."

1. P. K. O'Brien and S. L. Engerman, "Exports and the Growth of the British Economy from the Glorious Revolution to the Peace of Amiens," in *Slavery and the Rise of the Atlantic System*, ed. Barbara L. Solow (Cambridge, 1991), 177–209, esp. 207.
2. For estimates, see Philip Curtin, *The Atlantic Slave Trade: A Census* (Madison, 1969); Paul E. Lovejoy, "Volume of the Atlantic Slave Trade: A Synthesis," *Journal of African History* 23 (1982):473–501; David Eltis, "Free and Coerced Transatlantic Migrations: Some Comparisons," *American Historical Review* 88 (1983):251–80; David Richardson, "Slave Exports from West and West-Central Africa, 1700–1810: New Estimates of Volume and Distribution," *Journal of African History* 30 (1989):1–22; Richardson, review essay, "Across the Desert and the Sea: Trans-Saharan and Atlantic Slavery, 1500–1900," *The Historical Journal* 38(1) (1995):195–204; and David Eltis et al., *The Trans-Atlantic Slave Trade*, a data base on CD-ROM (Cambridge, 1999).
3. See Henry A. Gemery and Jan S. Hogendorn, eds., *The Uncommon Market: Essays in the Economic History of the Atlantic Slave Trade* (New York, 1979); Barbara L. Solow, ed., *British Capitalism and Caribbean Slavery* (Cambridge, 1991); J. I. Inikori and S. L. Engerman, eds., *The Atlantic Slave Trade: Effects on Economics, Societies and Peoples in Africa, the Americas, and Europe* (Durham, N.C., 1992); and John Thornton, *Africa and the Africans in the Making of the Atlantic World, 1400–1680* (Cambridge, 1992), 152–82, 206–53. On the Asian dimension of the Atlantic trade, see Sandra Lee Evenson, "A History of Indian Madras Manufacture and Trade Shifting Patterns of Exchange" (Ph.D. diss., University of Minnesota, 1994). Evenson maintains that Indian madras was a "currency that financed two major global trade networks," including the slave trade.
4. For estimates, I have relied upon David Eltis, *The Rise of African Slavery in the Americas* (Cambridge, 2000), 9, table 1; Eltis, "Free and Coerced Transatlantic Migrations," 251–80; and David Richardson, "Slave Exports from West and West-Central Africa: New Estimates of Volume and Distribution," *Journal of African History* 30 (1989):1–22, 10, table 4.
5. See essays in Gemery and Hogendorn, *The Uncommon Market*; Herbert Klein, *The Middle Passage: Comparative Studies in the Atlantic Slave Trade* (Princeton, 1978); Julian Gwyn "The Economics of the Transatlantic Slave Trade: A Review," *Social History* 25 (1992):

151–62. For examples of systematic analysis, see Robert W. Fogel et al., *Without Consent or Contract: The Rise and Fall of American Slavery*, 4 vols. (New York, 1989–92); David Eltis, *Economic Growth and the Ending of the Transatlantic Slave Trade* (New York, 1987). For the cultural context of the selection of Africans as the primary labor force in the plantation Americas between the sixteenth and the early nineteenth centuries, see Eltis, *Rise of African Slavery*, chaps. 1, 3.

6. William A. Darity, "A General Equilibrium Model of the Eighteenth-Century Atlantic Slave Trade: A Least-Likely Test for the Caribbean School," *Research in Economic History* 7 (1982):287–326; Hilary McD. Beckles, "The Economic Origins of Black Slavery in the British West Indies, 1640–1680: A Tentative Analysis of the Barbados Model," *Journal of Caribbean History* 16 (1982):35–56; Raymond L. Cohn and Richard A. Jensen, "The Determinants of Slave Mortality Rates on the Middle Passage," *Explorations in Economic History* 10(2) (1982):173–76; David W. Galenson, "The Atlantic Slave Trade and the Barbados Market, 1673–1723," *Journal of Economic History* 42(3) (1982):491–511; Gemery and Hogendorn, *The Uncommon Market*; Klein, *The Middle Passage*; Julian Gwyn "The Economics of the Transatlantic Slave Trade: A Review," *Social History* 25 (1992):151–62; and Inikori and Engerman, *Atlantic Slave Trade*, passim.

7. Werner Sombart, *The Jews and Modern Capitalism*, trans. M. Epstein, with an American edition by Bert F. Hoselitz (Glencoe, Ill., 1951), 32–33, 363, notes 61–70. For more recent scholarly assertions of Jewish dominance in the early Atlantic slave system, see note 12 below. For polemical accounts of Jewish dominance, see *The Secret Relationship Between Blacks and Jews* (Chicago, 1991), and the commentary of Harold Brackman, *Ministry of Lies: The Truth Behind the Nation of Islam's "The Secret Relationship Between Blacks and Jews"* (New York, London, 1994), esp. 15–17. In scholarly perspective, David Brion Davis notes "the negative but legitimating review" of *The Secret Relationship* by Winthrop D. Jordan in *Atlantic Monthly* (September 1995):109–14; see David Brion Davis, "Constructing Race: A Reflection," in *William and Mary Quarterly*, 3rd series, 54(1) (January 1997):7–18, esp. 11 and note: and the letters of commentary and reply in the January 1996 issue of the *Atlantic Monthly*, 14–15. For a survey of ascriptions of Jewish domination of the slave trade, see Saul S. Friedman, *Jews and the American Slave Trade* (New Brunswick, London, 1998), esp. 1–15, 235–52. Early Jewish historiography on the Americas affirmed the active participation of Jews in transatlantic slavery: "The Jews settled in the American colonies were as actively identified with the institution as any other class of settlers." Max Kohler, "The Jews and the American Anti-Slavery Movement," *Publications of the American Jewish Historical Society* 5 (1897):137–155. Jewish slave traders in Brazil were also the focus of historical scholarship. See Herbert I. Bloom, "A Study of Brazilian Jewish History, 1623–1654," *Publications of the American Jewish Historical Society* 33 (1934):43–125. Jews, while subjected to civil and political disabilities, were always considered to be non-enslavable "Europeans," rather than enslavable Africans. See Eltis, *Rise of African Slavery*, 60. Ironically, the tradition of "Jewish difference" was sometimes exaggerated by Jewish historians to explain the lack of early Jewish opposition to transatlantic slavery. Max Kohler, no less "Orientalist" than his non-Jewish contemporaries, attributed Jewish acceptance of slavery during the colonial period to "oriental customs," which did not tend "to make the Jew an enemy of slavery." See Kohler, "Jews and the American Anti-Slavery Movement," 145. Jews were rather less distinct from their European, American, and African contemporaries than Kohler imagined. See, inter alia, Eltis, *Rise of African Slavery*, chaps. 1 and 3.

8. Jonathan I. Israel, *European Jewry in the Age of Mercantilism 1550–1750*, 2nd ed. (Oxford, 1989), 5–34. In Polish Lithuania, Jews settled away from the Baltic seaboard provinces (ibid., 27).

9. On the establishment of a transoceanic slaving network well before the end of the fifteenth century, see John Vogt, "The Lisbon Slave House and African Trade 1486–1520," *Proceedings of the American Philosophical Society* 117(1) (1973):1–17. For a brief period, from 1698 to 1701, the bulk of Dutch investments in the Spanish slave trade *asiento* also came from Portuguese Jews in the United Provinces. See Wim Klooster, "Contraband

Trade by Curaçao's Jews with Countries of Idolatry, 1660–1800," *Studia Rosenthalia* 31 (1977):58–73.

10. Charles Verlinden, who magnified the role of Jews in the early medieval slave trade, no longer treated them as significant actors in the late medieval period and the transition to the Atlantic system. See Charles Verlinden, *L'Esclavage dans l'Europe Médiévale*, 2 vols. (Brugge and Ghent 1955–77), and idem, *The Beginnings of Modern Colonization: Eleven Essays with an Introduction*, trans. Y. Freccero (Ithaca, N.Y., 1970). On the Genoese as the principal financiers of the Spanish slave trade of the sixteenth century, see Ruth Pike, *Enterprise and Adventure: The Genoese in Seville and the Opening of the New World* (Ithaca N.Y., 1966). The only reference to Jewish involvement in the African trade prior to 1500 that I have come across is a Portuguese license for trading to Guinea in precious minerals and animals from 1469 to 1474. Complaints against a Jewish presence in the Portuguese empire before the expansion to the Americas were directed toward their participation in the sugar trade. See Bailey W. Diffie and George D. Winius, *Foundations of the Portuguese Empire, 1415–1580* (Minneapolis, 1977), 307.

11. Timothy Joel Coates, "Exiles and Orphans: Forced and State-Sponsored Colonizers in the Portuguese Empire, 1550–1720" (Ph.D. diss., University of Minnesota, 1993). On the rapid intermixing of Africans and Europeans, see *Omanuscrito Valentim Fernandes* ed. Joaquim Bensaúde and António Baião (Lisbon, 1940), 122. Robert Garfield concludes that by 1530 most of the surviving original children were probably Christian in fact. At the peak of São Tomé's role in the New World slave trade, it had "a thoroughly Portuguese mulatto population." A. H. de Oliveira Marques, *History of Portugal*, 2 vols. (New York, 1972), vol. 1, 374–75.

12. On the New Christian population of Portugal, see Oliveira Marques, *History of Portugal*, vol. 1, 287. On the complexity of New Christian identity over three centuries, see Anita Novinsky, "Sephardim in Brazil: The New Christians," in *The Sephardi Heritage*, ed. R. D. Barnett and W. M. Schwab, 2 vols. (Grindon, Eng., 1989), vol. 2, 431–44; Martin A. Cohen, "The Sephardic Phenomenon: A Reappraisal," *American Jewish Archives* 44 (1992):1–80; and B. Netanyahu, *The Origins of the Inquisition in Fifteenth-Century Spain* (New York, 1995), xix, 1041–42. One historiographic tradition, represented by José Goncalves Salvador, *Os Magnatas do Tráfico Negreiro XVI e XVII* (Sao Paulo, 1981), 6, is very similar to Gilberto Freyre's earlier portrayals of Jewish merchants as essentially running the Portuguese economy. The state was merely "an obligatory client of the Portuguese Sephardim." Salvador, in an extensive series of racial-cultural categories, places Jews, Semites, ethnic Hebrews, Sephardim, New Christians, and the Jewish race in opposition to Aryans and Old Christians. In this perspective, Salvador claims that by 1600 most of Brazil's churches were run by New Christian Hebrews (Salvador, *Os Magnatas*, 86), and sees the "Jewish" presence as pervasive in Iberian and Ibero-American commercial institutions. Indeed, Spain's "tolerance" for Jews in the seventeenth century is offered as a major reason for Portugal's reassertion of independence in 1640. Compare Salvador's perspective with those of C. R. Boxer, *The Portuguese Seaborne Empire 1415–1825* (New York, 1969), 269–72; and Anita Novinsky, "Padre Antonio Vieira, The Inquisition, and the Jews," *Jewish History* 6(1–2) (1992):151–62. Novinsky found that Brazilian New Christians integrated more fully into the local society than those who went east or north from Iberia. See Anita Novinsky, "A Posição dos Cristãos Novos na Sociedade Bainana," in *Cristãos Novos na Bahia* (Sao Paulo, 1972), 57–103, esp. 57–58. Novinsky and Günter Böhm both deem it significant that when a Jewish community formed in Bahia during the period of Dutch occupation, New Christians did not hasten en masse to join the Dutch Jewish community. See Günter Böhm, *Los sefardies en los domenios holandeses de America del Sur y del Caribe, 1630–1750* (Seville, 1977), 21. On the refusal of many *conversos* to be circumcised so that they could return to Iberia, see Yosef Kaplan, "Wayward New Christians and Stubborn Jews: The Shaping of a Jewish Identity," *Jewish History* 8 (1994):27–41. On the return of many wealthy New Christians from Brazil to Iberia in the 1600s, see Vitorino Magalhães Godhino, "Portuguese Emigration from the Fifteenth to the Twentieth-Century:

Constants and Changes," in *European Expansion and Migration: Essays on the Intercontinental Migration from Africa, Asia and Europe*, ed. P. C. Emmer and M. Mörner (New York, Oxford, 1992), 17. On hasty ascriptions of "Judaization" elsewhere in Europe, see Rose-Blanche Escoupérie, "Sur quelque 'Marchands Portugais' établis a Toulouse à la fin du XVII siècle," *Annales du Midi* 106(205) (1994):57–71. David M. Gitlitz, *Secrecy and Deceit: The Religion of the Crypto-Jews* (Philadelphia, 1996), 76, also concludes that those who assimilated substantially outnumbered those who identified as Jews. It must be emphasized that Jewish historiography in the United States sometimes fused "Marranos, New Christians, or Secret Jews," "whose astonishing tenacity, nay admirable obstinacy" for centuries was verified by the record of Inquisitional confessions, processions, and executions. See M. Kayserling, "The Colonization of America by the Jews," *Publications of the American Jewish Historical Society* 2 (1894):73–76. Kayserling was a major authority for Sombart. The casual conflation of Jews and New Christians occasionally continues in otherwise well-researched histories of slavery.

13. See Jonathan I. Israel, *Empires and Entrepots: The Dutch, the Spanish Monarchy and the Jews 1585–1713* (London, 1990), 328. In economic, as in religious, assessments, the conflation of New Christian and Jewish traders relies on elusive combinations of expansive metaphors and fragmentary "for example" evidence. Among the most notorious and entrepreneurial Portuguese Sephardic families, the Nunes da Costa, one prominent slave trading member (Diogo Peres da Costa) ended his days in Safed having eluded the Inquisition. Another slave trader (Francisco de Victoria), however, remained a sincere Christian, the only New Christian to become a bishop in sixteenth-century America. See Jonathan I. Israel, "Duarte Nunes da Costa (Jacob Curiel) of Hamburg, Sephardi Nobleman and Communal Leader 1585–1664," *Studia Rosenthalia* 21 (1987):14–34. Daniel M. Swetschinski, "Kinship and Commerce: The Foundations of Portuguese Jewish Life in Seventeenth-Century Holland," *Studia Rosenthalia* 15 (1981):52–74: "We can no longer take the proverbial interdependence of the Sephardic diaspora for granted. If and when such interdependence existed, it had little to do with shared 'Sephardichood' *per se*, but derived more precisely from an intricate network of personal kin relations ..." (67). In the economic sphere: "Commercial interests of separate families were paramount ..." (74n.). Chains of commercial-familial links, like chains of Inquisitorial-familial associations, present quite similar conceptual temptations to envision the presence of Portuguese traders as the tip of a "Jewish" or "crypto-Jewish" iceberg: "The problem thus becomes one of trying to imagine from a view of the proverbial tip of the iceberg the contours and size of its invisible larger part." Daniel M. Swetschinski, "Conflict and Opportunity in 'Europe's Other Sea': The Adventure of Caribbean Jewish Settlement," *American Jewish History* 72 (1982):212–40, esp. 215. The iceberg does not travel too well in those tropical waters where we have more precise records of the role of Jews in the slave trade.

14. See Thornton, *Africa and the Africans*, 61–62; idem, "The Development of an African Catholic Church in the Kingdom of Kongo, 1491–1750," *Journal of African History* 25 (1984):146–67; David Grant Smith, "Old Christian Merchants and the Foundation of the Brazil Company, 1649," *Hispanic American Historical Review* 54(2) (1974):233–59. Some New Christians in Spanish America confessed to being introduced to the "law of Moses" in Angola, or going to Angola out of fear of the Inquisition because they belonged to the "Jewish Nation." See Boleslao Lewin, *Singular Proceso de Salomón Machorro* [Juan de León]: *Israelita liornés condenado por la Inquisición* [Mexico 1650] (Buenos Aires, 1977), xii–xviii; and Manuel Tejado Fernandez, *Aspectos de la vida social en Cartegna de Indias durante el seiscientos* (Seville, 1954), 186. These works were kindly brought to my attention by Jonathan Schorsch.

15. See David Grant Smith, "The Mercantile Class of Portugal and Brazil in the Seventeenth Century: A Socio-economic Study of the Merchants of Lisbon and Bahia, 1620–1690" (Ph.D. diss., University of Texas, 1975), 103: "... the distinction between New and Old Christian is quite irrelevant to their functions as merchants and merchant bankers ... engaged in precisely the same kinds of operations, as often as not in

partnership with each other." David Grant Smith and Rae Flory, "Bahian Merchants and Planters in the Seventeenth and Early Eighteenth Centuries," *Hispanic American Historical Review* 58(4) (1978):571–94; James C. Boyajian, *Portuguese Bankers at the Court of Spain 1626–1650* (Rutgers, 1983), esp. chaps. 1–3; idem, "New Christians Reconsidered: Evidence from Lisbon's Portuguese Bankers, 1497–1647," *Studia Rosenthalia* 8 (1978): 129–56; and Oliveira Marques, *History of Portugal*, vol. 1, 287–88. On the insignificance of the migratory flow of New Christians from Latin America to the Northern European-controlled Caribbean, see Swetschinski, "Conflict and Opportunity," 212–40. On Africa, see Robert Garfield, "Public Christians, Secret Jews: Religion and Political Conflict on São Tomé Island in the Sixteenth and Seventeenth Centuries," *Sixteenth-Century Journal* 21(4) (1990):645–54. Garfield concludes that Jews had vanished from the community a century before the outburst of conflict between Old and New Christians. Even in northwestern Europe, "the cultivation of Iberian cultural habits and aristocratic pretensions became a strong distinguishing feature of their Jewish communities." *Conversos* within the peninsula were often regarded "as practicing Catholicism out of prudence, conviction, or inertia." See Miriam Bodian, "'Men of the Nation': The Shaping of *Converso* Identity in Early Modern Europe," *Past and Present* 143 (1994):48–76; esp. 66, 74; and idem, *Hebrews of the Portuguese Nation: Conversos and Community in Early Modern Amsterdam* (Bloomington, 1977), 30–52. Dutch suspicion of Catholics may have encouraged Amsterdam's original Sephardic settlers to hasten conversion to Judaism, even when its practices were still largely unfamiliar to them. Kaspar von Greyerz finds that sixteenth-century New Christians who settled in the Upper Rhine show evidence of an Iberian subculture, but evidence of a "deviant" religious subculture is lacking. "Judaizing" by *conversos* in that region was, as in many other cases, a projection of the Inquisitorial imagination. See Kaspar von Greyerz, "Portuguese Conversos on the Upper Rhine and the Converso Community of Sixteenth-Century Europe," *Social History* 14(1) (1988):59–82. In Brazil, the concept of hidden "Jewish characteristics" could paradoxically subvert all distinctions between "Christian" and "Jewish" practices. The Inquisition's assumptions rendered all religiosity suspect, conformist as well as deviant. In Bahia, the more ostentatiously one wore rosaries and effigies, the greater might be the suspicion of crypto-Judaism. See Pierre Vergier, *Trade Relations between the Bight of Benin and Bahia from the Seventeenth to Nineteenth Century*, trans. Evelyn Crawford (Ibadan, 1976), 69n. On the often unsuccessful attempt to enforce the "congruence of legally defined ethnic and racial categories with social realities," see Stuart B. Schwartz, "Spaniards, *Pardos*, and the Missing Mestizos: Identities and Racial Categories in the Early Hispanic Caribbean," *New West Indian Guide* 71(1/2) (1997):5–19.

16. Joseph C. Miller, "A Marginal Institution on the Margin of the Atlantic System: The Portuguese Southern Atlantic Slave Trade in the Eighteenth Century," in Solow, *Atlantic System*, 120–50, esp. 122–23, 126. See also James C. Boyajian, *Portuguese Trade in Asia under the Habsburgs, 1580–1640* (Baltimore, 1993).

17. Felipe de Alencastro, "The Apprenticeship of Colonization," in Solow, *Atlantic System*, 151–76, esp. 162–63. On the utility of slave trading as an entrée to Mexican residency, see Israel, *Empires and Entrepots*, 322–23; and Boyajian, *Portuguese Bankers*, 13, 33. "Only the Portuguese, who controlled the principal slave stations of West Africa could satisfy the escalating demands of both Brazil and the Spanish colonies for black slaves," and draw Asian commodities into the economic expansion of the Americas (Boyajian, *Portuguese Trade*, 15). On the Atlantic network to Spanish America, see Enriqueta Vila Vilar, "Aspectos Maritimos del commercio de esclavos con Hispanoamerica en el siglo XVII," *Revista de Historia Naval* 5(19) (1987):113–31. Within Europe, Jews also entered trades not blocked by guilds, including newly imported commodities (Israel, *European Jewry*, 62).

18. Boyajian, *Portuguese Bankers*, 32, 233n; Oliveira Marques, *History of Portugal*, vol. 1, 363, 373; Boxer, *Portuguese Seaborne Empire*, 331, 333.

19. See P. C. Emmer, "The Dutch and the Making of the Second Atlantic System," in Solow, *Atlantic System*, 75–96.

20. See Israel, *European Jewry*, chap. 2.
21. Israel, *Empires and Entrepots*, 438–40. Herbert Bloom, whose richly documented study seeks to maximize the Jewish role in Dutch economic activity, does not list slave trading as an occupation of Jews of Amsterdam during the "Golden Age." Herbert Bloom, *The Economic Activities of the Jews of Amsterdam in the Seventeenth and Eighteenth Centuries* (Williamsport, Penn., 1937), chap. 1. In all ambiguous cases, Bloom favors a Jewish identity (see, for example, p. 133, note 52). It is worth noting that of the dozen early seventeenth-century Dutch Sephardim described by Jonathan Israel as traders "on any scale" with the Iberian Peninsula, only Diogo Nunes Belmonte (Ya'akov Israel Belmonte) is identified as a slave trader. See also Jonathan Israel, "Spain and the Dutch Sephardim, 1609–1660," *Studia Rosenthalia* 12 (1978):1–61; esp. 5–6. Although the Portuguese imperium was central to the commercial activities of New Amsterdam's Portuguese Jews, slaving seems to have been peripheral to those activities. (See also Swetschinski, "Kinship and Commerce," 52–74.) Jews entered the slave trade primarily as intermediaries in the distribution process once slaves were landed in the Americas.
22. See Jonathan I. Israel, *The Dutch Republic and the Hispanic World, 1606–1661* (Oxford, 1982), 127; José António Gonsalves de Mello, *Gente da nação* (Recife, 1987), 208; and Stephen Alexander Fortune, *Merchants and Jews: The Struggle for British West Indian Commerce, 1650–1750* (Gainesville, Fla., 1984), 178n. 34.
23. See Johannes Menne Postma, *The Dutch in the Atlantic Slave Trade 1600–1815* (Cambridge, 1990). Some who have argued for a larger Jewish role in Dutch African slaving than is indicated by Jewish investment in the Dutch West India Company invoke private trading as an alternative activity. Postma, however, estimates the entire Dutch interloper trade in slaves at only 14,000 out of 286,000 Africans delivered to America by Dutch ships between 1600 and 1738, or about 5 percent of the total (ibid., 110). Even if one were to discover that Jews were heavily represented in the private Atlantic trade, the vast majority of the Dutch interlopers on the African coast were interested in the Euro-African commodity trade and not the slave trade (ibid., 80). Odette Vlessing asserts that Portuguese Jews had an enormous influence on the development of the Dutch "Golden Age." See Odette Vlessing, "New Light on the Earliest History of the Amsterdam Portuguese Jews," in *Dutch Jewish History*, ed. Joseph Michman (Jerusalem, Assen, Maastricht, 1993), 43–76, esp. 64. Vlessing makes no reference to the magnitude of the Portuguese-Jewish share in the Dutch slave trade. Herbert Bloom indicates that some Jews, in partnership with a Spanish national, financed private slavers to the Spanish colonies (Bloom, *Jews of Amsterdam*, 147 and note). In Bloom's example, however, the slaver's itinerary included Curaçao, where the ship's slaves would have been recorded in the island's imports and in Postma's estimate of interloper traders. See also note 12 above.
24. See Arnold Wiznitzer, *Jews in Colonial Brazil* (New York, 1960); Gonsalves de Mello, *Gente da nação*, 233; and Jonathan Israel, "Dutch Sephardi Jewry, Millenarian Politics, and the Struggle for Brazil, 1640–1654," in *Skeptics, Millenarians and Jews*, ed. David S. Katz and Jonathan I. Israel (Leiden, New York, 1990), 76–97. See also Günter Böhm, *Los Sefardies en los dominios holandeses del Sur y del Caribe, 1630–1750* (Seville, 1977), 75. The Dutch occupied part of northeastern Brazil from 1630 to 1654. Jews clearly played a dominant role as wholesale purchasers of slaves from the Dutch West India Company during five of those years. Egon Wolff and Frieda Wolff, *Dictionário Biográfico:Judaizantes e Judeus no Brazil 1500–1808* (Rio de Janeiro, 1986), show that virtually all Jewish purchases of slaves were clustered between 1641 and 1645. On the dearth of the Jewish merchant involvement in the transatlantic slave trade to the Caribbean, see also Zvi Loker, *Jews in the Caribbean: Evidence on the History of Jews in the Caribbean Zone in Colonial Times* (Jerusalem, 1991), 48–49.
25. The landing in the Americas usually marked the end of the worst horrors of the slaves' coerced migration, but the captives had to endure long and repeated physical inspections by prospective buyers. The healthiest and strongest slaves went first. The remaining ("refuse") slaves were sometimes taken on to other ports for resale. Those

whose family and kinship contacts had survived the "Middle Passage" might be sub-ject to a final separation at this point. See Seymour Drescher, "The Atlantic Slave Trade and the Holocaust: A Comparative Analysis," in *From Slavery to Freedom: Comparative Studies in the Rise and Fall of Atlantic Slavery* (New York, 1999), 312–338. On Jewish mer-chants in Curaçao's slave trade, see especially Klooster, "Contraband Trade," 61–63. The heyday of Curaçao's transit trade occurred later in the eighteenth century, when it was decreasingly dependent on slaves. See P. C. Emmer, "'Jesus Christ Was Good, but Trade Was Better': An Overview of the Transit Trade of the Dutch Antilles, 1634–1795," in *The Lesser Antilles in the Age of European Expansion*, ed. Robert L. Paquette and Stanley L. Engerman (Gainesville, Fla., 1996), 206–22; and Postma, *The Dutch*, 26–55, 197–200, 268–72. Compare these modest assessments of Curaçao's role with Yosef Hayim Yerushalmi's, "Between Amsterdam and New Amsterdam: The Place of Curaçao and the Caribbean in Early Modern Jewish History," *American Jewish History* 7(2) (1982):172–92. Yerushalmi maximizes the value of Curaçao to European expan-sion from the perspective of a historian of Jewry. On the reception of Jewish refugees in New Amsterdam, see James H. Williams, "An Atlantic Perspective on the Jewish Struggle for Rights and Opportunities in Brazil, New Netherland, and New York," in this volume, Chap. 19. On Jewish involvement in European diplomacy and the poli-tics of the slave trade, see Jonathan I. Israel, *Conflicts of Empires: Spain, the Low Coun-tries and the Struggle for World Supremacy 1585–1713* (London, 1997), 392–401. For the latest calculations on the role of Sephardic capital in the Dutch West India Company, see Klooster, "Contraband Trade," 63. By the 1650s, the share of Jews investing in the West India Company had risen to around 4 percent, sufficient perhaps for the Com-pany to protect Brazilian refugees in New Amsterdam from Governor Peter Stuyvesant's expulsion orders. By 1674 Jews owned about 5 percent of the Dutch West India Company's stock.

26. On Jewish merchants in the early English slave trade, see, above all, Eli Faber, *Jews, Slaves, and the Slave Trade: Setting the Record Straight* (New York, 1998), esp. 11–56; and Trevor Burnard, "Who Bought Slaves in Early America? Purchasers of Slaves from the Royal African Company in Jamaica, 1674–1708," *Slavery and Abolition* 17(2) (August 1996):68–92. See also Fortune, *Merchants and Jews*, 48.

27. See Israel, *European Jewry*, 139; Adam Jones, *Brandenburg Sources for West African History 1680–1700* (Stuttgart, 1985); and Pamela Smith, *The Business of Alchemy: Science and Cul-ture in the Holy Roman Empire* (Princeton, 1994), 151. On Portuguese Jewish participa-tion in various African voyages from Baltic ports in the seventeenth century, see Georg Nørregard, *Danish Settlements in West Africa, 1658–1850* (Boston, 1966), 11, 12, 53, 54, 57.

28. Israel, *European Jewry*, 139. Jeronimo Nunes da Costa (1620–1697) seems to have been unusually active among Jews of Northern Europe in his ability to direct mercantile capital toward the Guinea trade of Baltic states at the end of the seventeenth century. He was frequently involved in slaving expeditions from Brandenburg, Glückstadt, and Copenhagen. See Jonathan I. Israel, "An Amsterdam Jewish Merchant of the Golden Age: Jeronimo Nunes da Costa (1620–1697), Agent of Portugal in the Dutch Republic," *Studia Rosenthalia* 18 (1984):21–40, esp. 35–37.

29. On the French slave trade, see Robert Louis Stein, *The French Slave Trade in the Eigh-teenth Century: An Old Regime Business* (Madison, 1979). In Bordeaux, "only two Jewish families, Gradis and Mendez, fitted out more than one slave ship each during the entire eighteenth-century ..." (ibid., 159). See also Silvia Marzagalli, "Atlantic Trade and Sephardim Merchants in Eighteenth-Century France: The Case of Bordeaux" (pre-sented at JCB Conference, "The Jews and the Expansion of Europe to the West," 16 June 1997, and chap. 14 in this volume); Eric Saugera, *Bordeaux, Port Négrier XVIIe–XIXe siècles* (Biarritz, 1995), 229–34; Richard Menkis, "The Gradis Family of Eighteenth-Century Bordeaux: A Social and Economic Study" (Ph.D. diss., Brandeis University, 1988). Silvia Marzagalli kindly brought these last two studies to my atten-tion. Across the Atlantic, Jews of Saint-Domingue constituted about 1 percent of the colony's white population in the late eighteenth century. See Pierre Pluchon, *Nègres et*

Juifs au XVIII siècle: Le racisme au siècle des Lumières (Paris, 1984), 19–93. As with the Gradis family in France, one should note the similarly atypical involvement of Amsterdam's Jeronimo Nunes da Costa in the slave trade of the previous century. His access to the Saõ Tomé and Guinea trades probably depended upon his status as the agent of the Portuguese crown in the Dutch Republic and on his personal link to Portugal's Brazil Company. Thus privileged, Jeronimo seems to have been far more involved in the sugar trade than in the slave trade of Saõ Tomé and the African coast. Jonathan Israel regards this African extension of Jeronimo's economic activity as exceptional (see Israel, "An Amsterdam Jewish Merchant," 30–37).

30. See Faber, *Jews, Slaves, and the Slave Trade*, 73–82, 113–23.
31. See Richard Gray, "The Papacy and the Atlantic Slave Trade: Lourenço da Silva, The Capuchins and the Decisions of the Holy Office," *Past and Present* 115 (May 1987): 52–68. Joseph Miller, a historian of the eighteenth-century Luso-Brazilian slave trade, observes that New Christians were no longer a subject of discussion in this period. (mail communication of 14 June 1996). In Miller's monumental *Way of Death: Merchant Capitalism and the Angolan Slave Trade 1730–1830* (Madison, Wis., 1988), "New Christians" is not an indexed term. Martin Klein, a historian of Africa, has never seen a reference to Jewish slave traders on the African coast in the final period of the Atlantic slave trade (e-mail communication, 22 December 1995). On the general reduction of New Christian influence in the metropolitan Portuguese economy during the second half of the seventeenth century, see Carl A. Hanson, *Economy and Society in Baroque Portugal 1668–1703* (Minneapolis, 1981), 218.
32. Of the fifty to sixty million working Europeans during the peak of the slave trade in the 1780s, up to two million might have been implicated in the trade in one way or another, or in the importation of slave-grown products. In the Americas, a still larger proportion of the descendants of Europeans must have been similarly involved in the same range of economic activities. Given the far larger numbers of those who were enslaved in Africa compared to those who were deported, a large proportion of the active West African population (perhaps twenty-eight million in 1820) must also have been direct participants in the slave trade and its collateral activities along the coast of Africa. For these estimates, see Olivier Pétré-Grenouilleau, *La Traite des Noirs* (Paris, 1997), 42–50; and Eltis, *Economic Growth*, 67, and notes.
33. Boyajian, *Portuguese Trade*, 17. For those who view New Christians interchangeably with Jews, it may indeed be impossible to imagine the Atlantic system without Jewish slave traders: "So we see therefore that if it were not for the high percentage of ships in the hands of men of the Hebrew nation, commerce in the South Atlantic would be almost impossible and therefore likewise the sugar industry and African slavery" (Salvador, *Os Magnatas*, 96). For Salvador, Jews were the proverbial nail for want of which American sugar, African slavery, and the entire black Atlantic diaspora would never have existed.
34. Germán Peralta Rivera, *Los Mecanismos del comercio negrero* (Lima, 1990), 280. For recent attempts to rediscover a vanished Jewish presence in Africa, see Yossi Halevi, "Looking for Jews off Africa's Coast," *Central African Zionist Digest* (April 1995). The recent revival of interest in Jews hidden during the Holocaust seems to find an echo in a rekindled interest in marrano ancestry. Recently, a society for crypto-Judaic studies was formed by people seeking to reclaim a Jewish heritage. See Mary Rourke, "In Search of Hidden Jews," *Los Angeles Times*, 8 February 1997.
35. Greater degrees of human diversity in Africa than on other continents meant that market breakdowns, costly violence, and trade customs varied greatly from region to region. Divergent trading rules had to be learned in Africa, which put a premium on local factors. The Euro-African trade "had to get by without the cross-cultural diasporic merchant communities that [Philip] Curtin describes for other parts of the globe" (Eltis, *Rise of African Slavery*, 154, 164–92).
36. See Faber, *Jews, Slaves, and the Slave Trade*, 35–36 and 271n.
37. See Eltis, *Rise of African Slavery*, 265–66; and Kenneth Maxwell, *Pombal: Paradox of the Enlightenment* (Cambridge, 1995), 17. Jonathan Israel notes that apart from the trade in

diamonds and coral and the Spanish Caribbean trade via Cadiz, Jewish activity in general counted for relatively little in England's eighteenth-century rise to commercial dominance (Israel, *European Jewry*, 242). That characterization equally applies to Jewish activity in the British slave trade. Stephen Alexander Fortune claims "a striking discovery" in finding "a close business relationship between the South Sea Company and Jamaican Jews. He also notes that Jews were stockholders of the company in England and had contacts in the Caribbean (Fortune, *Merchants and Jews*, 137–38). Fortune does not offer any estimate of the amount or proportion of capital so invested by English Jews, or their relative importance as agents or factors in the transoceanic chain of commerce. John G. Sperling, *The South Sea Company: An Historical Essay* (Boston, 1962), is silent on any Jewish role, as is Colin Palmer, *Human Cargoes: The British Slave Trade to Spanish America, 1700–1739* (Urbana, Ill., 1981). As for the Netherlands, by the late eighteenth century, its "Portuguese" Jewry was recognized as having abandoned trading in favor of stock-brokering. See Charles Wilson, *Anglo-Dutch Commerce and Finance* (Cambridge, 1966), 14–15.

38. See, above all, David Brion Davis, *Slavery and Human Progress* (New York, 1984), 101; Seymour Drescher, "The Role of Jews in Transatlantic Slave Trade," *Immigrants and Minorities* 12(2) (July 1993):113–125; David Brion Davis, "The Slave Trade and the Jews," *New York Review of Books*, 22 December 1994, 14–17; and Yosef Hiam Yerushalmi, "Between Amsterdam and New Amsterdam," 177.

39. Gleaned from Faber's accounts of slave traders in *Jews, Slaves, and the Slave Trade*, passim. I have discovered no evidence of a link between metropolitan religious movements and any documented unease about Jewish transatlantic slaving. See Seymour Drescher, "The Long Goodbye: Dutch Capitalism and Antislavery in Comparative Perspective," in *Fifty Years Later: Antislavery, Capitalism and Modernity in the Dutch Orbit*, ed. Gert Oostindie (Leiden, Pittsburgh, 1995, 1996), 25–66, esp. 35n. 22. For a detailed study of Jewish and black interaction during the initial period of European overseas expansion, see Jonathan Schorsch, "Jews and Blacks in the Early Colonial World, 1450–1800" (Ph.D. diss., University of California, Berkeley, 2000).

40. For an estimate of overall Portuguese emigration after 1500, see Stanley L. Engerman and João César das Neves, *The Bricks of an Empire 1415–1999: 585 Years of Portuguese Empire* (Lisbon, 1996), WP22–96, 12. The estimate is based upon data in V. M. Godinho, "L'Emigration Portugaise (XV–XX siècles)—une constante structurale et les réponses aux changements du monde," *Revista de História Económica e Social* 1 (1978). They estimate the total outflow from Portugal for the years 1500 to 1760 at about 1.3 million. Magnus Mörner and Harold Sims, *Adventurers and Proletarians: The Story of Migrants in Latin America* (Pittsburgh, 1985), 10 (also citing Godhino), estimate the total net emigration from Portugal to Brazil between 1500 and 1760 (the limits of Inquisitorial concern with New Christians) at 790,000. A much smaller flow of *conversos* may have emigrated from Spain to the New World. I follow Boyajian in assuming that New Christian emigration from Portugal was at least proportionate to their share of the Portuguese population in 1500 (10 percent). Anita Novinsky finds that at one point New Christians represented 10 to 20 percent of the population of Bahia (see Novinsky, "A Posição dos Cristãos Novos," 57–103, esp. 65).

41. For an estimate of early modern European migration to the Americas, see Eltis, "Free and Coerced Transatlantic Migrations," 255. Based upon Robert Swierenga's estimates, the Jewish population of the New World in about 1800 could not have exceeded 10,000, and no more than that number migrated from Europe to the Americas between 1500 and 1800. He estimates that the Jewish population of the Caribbean was five times its counterpart in the United States in 1790. See Robert P. Swierenga, *The Forerunners: Dutch Jewry in the North American Diaspora* (Detroit, 1994), 36. In a study of Dutch emigration, Jan Lucassen estimates that as many as fifteen thousand Netherlanders may have emigrated "to the colonies in South Africa, the Caribbean, and West Africa" before 1800. Only one quarter of that total would have landed before 1750 (the high tide of Jewish migration). See Jan Lucassen, "The Netherlands, the Dutch, and Long-Distance Migration, in

the Late Sixteenth to Early Nineteenth Centuries," in *Europeans on the Move: Studies on European Migration, 1500–1800*, ed. Nicholas Canny (Oxford, 1994), 153–91, esp. 175–78. Regarding New Christians, the destruction of the genealogical records by the Portuguese government in 1773 completed the official fusion of Old and New Christians and "the disappearance of the Jews and their descendants from Portugal and Brazil." In 1797 the Portuguese government explicitly invited Suriname's Portuguese Jews back "where you would enjoy the greatest security and peace. For presently ... none of the reasons which occasioned your expatriation exists any longer" (quoted in Swetschinski, "Conflict and Opportunity," 212). Swetschinski does not mention any Jewish migration in response to the belated invitation. Nor does he indicate any "internal immigration" by descendants of the New Christians within Portugal or Brazil into the Jewish fold. See also Oliveira Marques, *History of Portugal*, vol. 1, 380. There is no evidence to indicate that any large group of Latin Americans rejoined the Jewish community when a continuous Jewish migration to Ibero-America resumed early in the nineteenth century. See Judith Laikin Elkin, *Jews of the Latin American Republics* (Chapel Hill, N.C., 1980), 14–20. The deeper Jewish and African relationship began, of course, where the transoceanic slave trade finally deposited its victims. Whatever its attractions for seventeenth-century Sephardim, the transatlantic world seems to have appealed much less to the literary imagination of Ashkenazi Jewry. In her biographical sketch of Glikl bas Judah Leib, a merchant of Metz, Natalie Zemon Davis notes that Glikl's autobiography was written "at a time when ... Jews were among the new owners of sugar plantations and of African and Indian slaves in Suriname ...," and when Menasseh ben Israel, of Amsterdam, played with the idea "that the Amerindians were the descendants of the Lost Tribes of Israel." See Natalie Zemon Davis, *Women on the Margins: Three Seventeenth-Century Lives* (Cambridge, Mass, 1995), 41. Yet when she chose to weave an exotic tale about the seafaring quest of a wise Talmudist, Glikl had her hero board a boat bound for the East Indies.

42. See Wim Klooster, "The Jews in Suriname and Curaçao," presented at the JCB conference "The Jews and the Expansion of Europe to the West," and chap. 18 in this volume. On Suriname, see Robert Cohen, *Jews in Another Environment: Surinam in the Second Half of the Eighteenth Century* (Leiden, New York, 1991), 18–20, 175–80.

– Chapter 22 –

NEW CHRISTIANS AND JEWS IN THE SUGAR TRADE, 1550–1750: TWO CENTURIES OF DEVELOPMENT OF THE ATLANTIC ECONOMY

James C. Boyajian

S CHOLARS HAVE LONG BEEN AWARE of the salient role New Christians of Portugal and their Sephardi relatives in Holland, England, France, and the Baltic region played in the development of the Atlantic sugar trade in the sixteenth and seventeenth centuries.[1] For New Christian merchants of the Iberian Peninsula, the Americas, and the Far East, however, sugar was but one element in a global trading network. To be sure, from the early sixteenth century, sugar and sugar trading were important elements in the complex trade. Indeed, many of the leading merchant families of Lisbon, Oporto, and other Portuguese seaports achieved their fortunes through sugar plantation and mill development in Pernambuco, Bahia, and the southern captaincies of Brazil, as well as through the introduction of slaves into Brazil and Spanish America. In the latter half of the sixteenth century, sugar became the springboard to greater commercial activities and wealth. The wealthier New Christians invested in Asian trading to augment their fortunes. In turn, the Asian trade yielded goods marketable primarily in western Africa and the American tropics.[2] Finally, by the early seventeenth century, fortunes amassed initially in sugar trading had propelled a limited number of New Christians into the role of financiers of the Spanish Habsburgs and had thus enabled them to play a major part in European exchange.[3]

Underlying these developments and the ebb and flow of family fortunes was the emerging Atlantic economy. Fueled by the Cape trade to India and the transatlantic slave and commodities trade with the bullion-rich

Spanish American colonies, the commerce of Europe's Atlantic ports eventually overshadowed the ancient Mediterranean trade that had been the center of European economic life since antiquity. New Christians of Lisbon, Seville, Madrid, and Antwerp and their Sephardic cousins in Amsterdam, Hamburg, the Baltic ports, Venice and other northern Italian cities, and the French Atlantic and Channel ports played a prominent role in the elaboration of the Atlantic economy precisely because of their connections to overseas trade in Asia and the South Atlantic.[4] Dutch, French, and English merchants might have enjoyed the advantages of being at or near the source of Baltic grain and timber and of the production of hardware, woolens, and other artisan-crafted goods in Northern Europe, but New Christians, who settled in all corners of the Spanish imperium, were in a unique position to penetrate Spain's bullion-producing transatlantic colonies. In exchange for African slaves, Italian and Northern European goods, and Asian cotton and silk cloth, the New Christians extracted silver and gold bullion and coin from Mexico and Peru. Access to silver bullion enabled New Christians to expand Asian commerce, on the one hand, and to pay for the copper implements and hardware that went into the sugar mills of Brazil, on the other.[5]

* * * *

THE ASIAN TRADE WAS A LUXURY TRADE in speculative goods of high unit value consumed by the relatively small number of persons comprising the wealthiest echelons of society. The trade produced large profits for a handful of very wealthy merchants who could afford the risks and delays involved in the long and hazard-plagued Cape voyages to and from India (*carreira da Índia*) or the Mexican galleon circuit between Acapulco and Manila. Certainly, many smaller investors were tempted to invest in Asian cotton and silk cloth, diamonds, spices, and drugs, and they did so primarily by consigning their capital to the larger players who earned handsome commissions and shares of profits from the joint ventures.[6]

Sugar, too, was a luxury in the sixteenth and early seventeenth centuries, but the ease of the transatlantic voyage to the sugar-producing islands of Madeira and São Tomé and later to Brazil combined with the rather brief turnaround time (a couple of months compared to up to two years for the Cape trade to and from India) enabled many modest investors to participate in sugar cargoes.[7]

Sugar founded the fortunes of many New Christian commercial families in the period from 1550 to 1650, and was absolutely essential to the viability of the small and much less wealthy Sephardi communities that took root in Holland, the French ports, and the Baltic during the final decades of the sixteenth century. With few exceptions, the founders of the Amsterdam, Rotterdam, Hamburg, Rouen, and Bordeaux Sephardic communities were New Christians who had returned to Judaism. They were merchants of rather modest means whose commercial ventures depended on connections to family and associates among the merchants of Antwerp, Seville, Lisbon, Oporto, and the lesser ports of Portugal. The first Jewish merchants of Amsterdam naturally survived by shipping grain, cloth, hardware, and naval stores to Iberian ports. They consigned these goods to New Christian merchants (often their relatives) who loaded return shipments of dried fruit, olive oil, dyes, and wines produced in Portugal and Spain.[8] Yet it is doubtful that the Sephardic community could have thrived and grown as it did were it not for the opportunity to invest in sugar. In most of their trading ventures of the late sixteenth and early seventeenth centuries, the Sephardim acted primarily on commission from their wealthier New Christian kinsmen, who owned the merchandise and earned most of the profits. The Brazilian circuit along with the trade to Barbary were two sectors of Iberian trade in which Sephardi merchants acted as principals, owning a major share in the sugar and other shipments.

For example, Manuel Dias Henriques was among the Sephardi merchants arriving in Amsterdam during the early seventeenth century. Both Manuel and his cousin Miguel Dias de Santiago,[9] who had settled in Antwerp just prior to 1620, had had personal experience in the sugar trade of Brazil between 1595 and 1619. Miguel in Antwerp and Manuel in Amsterdam were able to deal directly with many kinsmen still in Brazil and arrange for shipments of sugar from Brazilian ports directly to Amsterdam. Manuel Dias Henriques was far from alone. Francisco Mendes de Medeiros (alias Isaac Franco Mendes) and Jeronimo Rodrigues de Souza (alias Samuel Abrabanel) were also among the many Sephardi merchants of Amsterdam dealing in sugar in the early seventeenth century with relatives in Brazilian and Portuguese ports.[10]

* * * *

THE SIGNIFICANCE OF JEWISH AND NEW CHRISTIAN INVOLVEMENT in the sugar trade must be gauged by the economic importance of the sugar trade as a whole. The Portuguese introduced sugar culture in Madeira prior to 1497—before the forcible conversion of Iberian Jews in Portugal created the New Christian community—and it spread from there to São Tomé, an island off Africa's western coast. In Madeira, sugar production was on a small scale, characterized by individual landowners working their land. In São Tomé and Brazil, however, the sugar cultivators, or *lavradores*, introduced slave labor to work large tracts. It was only with the development of Brazil's sugar industry and of the slave economy that sugar became a significant element in Atlantic trade and a major new source of wealth.[11]

Perhaps the earliest usable measure of the development of the Brazilian sugar industry is the number of sugar mills. A Brazilian sugar mill typically was built on a large tract of land owned by a *senhor de engenho* who leased out the land to the *lavradores*, who actually cleared the land and cultivated the cane. The *lavradores* delivered the harvested cane to the mill for processing into crude sugar. The *senhor de engenho* exacted a portion of the sugar production in return for the milling and as land rent. Each mill thus served as a complete unit of production, some more successful and productive than others, of course.[12]

By 1570 there already were seventy sugar mills in Brazil, most of them concentrated in Pernambuco and secondarily in Bahia's hinterland. By 1581, little more than ten years later, the number had increased to 131 and twenty years later (ca. 1600) to 230; finally, by 1629 Brazil boasted 346 mills.[13] In less than sixty years the number of mills had increased nearly fivefold. The area of sugar cultivation had expanded, as well, beyond Pernambuco and Bahia in the north. São Vicente, Espirito Santo, and Rio de Janeiro in the south had also become important sugar-producing regions.[14]

What makes this growth all the more remarkable is the fact that each mill represented a fixed investment of at least 6,000 cruzados in costs for construction, materials, copper implements, and many slaves for labor.[15] It is probable that by 1629 the total investment in the sugar industry exceeded 2 and perhaps 3 million cruzados. By 1710, the number of mills grew substantially again, representing an investment of 5 to 6 million cruzados. In addition to the sums expended on mills, *lavradores* had to invest thousands of cruzados in slaves to produce the cane.

The value of the annual sugar production directly reflected the increase in the number of mills and in the investment in production. The tithes (*dízimos*) that the king collected on Brazil's produce are an excellent indicator of the value and growth of sugar production, since sugar comprised over 90 percent of the total value of all Brazilian products. In 1618 the contracts for the collection of the *dízimos*, which prominent New Christian merchants usually held, produced the following revenues (in cruzados):[16]

Pernambuco	75,000
Bahia	62,500
Southern captaincies (Rio, São Vicente, Espirito Santo)	75,500
Total	213,000

Even if we ignore the fact that in order to profit from the venture the contractors had to collect more tithes from the sugar producers than they paid to the crown, Brazil's annual sugar production certainly exceeded 2 million cruzados' worth in Brazilian ports and probably 4 million cruzados delivered in Portugal.[17] During the 1630s and 1640s, when the Dutch temporarily occupied Pernambuco and disrupted sugar production and the trade between Portugal and Brazil, Portuguese sugar production nevertheless increased overall, as sugar cultivation shifted to the south. The tithes for the southern captaincies alone had increased to 100,000 cruzados from 1639 to 1640, to 142,000 from 1648 to 1649, and to 155,000 cruzados in 1651, representing annual production valued at 2 million, 2.8 million, and 3.1 million cruzados in Portugal respectively.[18]

To better appreciate what these numbers mean, by way of comparison, the Dutch capitalized their United East India Company in 1602 with a total of 2.3 million cruzados. In 1640, after almost forty years of operation, the Dutch Company's total capital in Asia was about 4.5 million cruzados, and its annual trade in Asia did not exceed 600,000 cruzados.[19] The Dutch East India Company, which historians often cite as the most successful commercial enterprise of the seventeenth century, returned cargoes of spices and other Asian goods to Amsterdam that were less valuable than Brazil's annual sugar production in the 1630s and 1640s, and the East India Company enjoyed a strict monopoly of Dutch trade with Asia.[20]

* * * *

WHAT PART DID NEW CHRISTIANS and their Sephardic relatives play in this extraordinary commercial development? We have mostly anecdotal evidence of New Christian and Jewish participation in sugar production and trade. Although many New Christians were prominent in the initial development of sugar mills and cultivation in Pernambuco and Bahia during the early decades of the sixteenth century, few of them have left accounts books or other direct evidence of their trade. Employing Inquisition records, Arnold Wiznitzer's pioneering study of "Jews" in Brazil first revealed the exploits of Diogo Fernandes Santiago, who, among others, developed his own sugar mill at Olinda in Pernambuco captaincy. After Indians destroyed the mill, Diogo managed the mills his in-law Bento Dias de Santiago developed and owned near Camaragibe, also in Pernambuco captaincy.[21] Diogo's several daughters married into families (mostly New Christian) that owned a number of sugar mills.[22] By the 1580s João Nunes Correia and his kinsmen also owned up to four sugar mills near Olinda.[23] Meanwhile, in the Bahia region the several members of the large Lopes d'Ulhoa clan developed perhaps a half-dozen sugar mills.[24] In the southern captaincies Duarte Fernandes Vitória, his sons Diogo Fernandes Vitória and Henrique Rodrigues de Barcelos, and their cousin Manuel de Medeiros owned one and possibly several mills in the São Vicente captaincy during the final decades of the sixteenth century.[25] The sum of such evidence supports New Christians developing, owning, and operating fifty-nine mills by the 1630s. A further nine mills belonged to Sephardic owners in Brazil around 1645, after the Dutch invasion and occupation.[26]

Many of these investments were short-lived. In the process of reconquering northern Brazil from the Dutch, the victorious Portuguese seized the Sephardi-owned mills from their owners. Some New Christians sold their mills to Old Christians. Other mills were destroyed in Indian wars or in the struggle with the Dutch, or were confiscated by the Inquisition. Yet each generation produced more New Christian investors in sugar mills in Brazil, suggesting a sustained New Christian investment in sugar production.[27]

From these sparse data alone we can glean that New Christians and Sephardic Jews appear to have played a direct role in developing at least 20 percent of Brazil's sugar productive capacity. Substantial as that was, their role was greater still when we consider the New Christians' financing of sugar cultivation through the slave trade. Slaves and slave labor were indispensable to the colony's economy. Slaves not only cleared the land and planted, harvested, cultivated, and processed the sugar cane, but were also ubiquitous as domestic labor and were even represented in certain positions of skilled labor. In the early seventeenth century, Brazil's merchants and sugar cultivators imported up to four thousand slaves annually.[28] New Christians provided the bulk of these slaves. They contracted with the Portuguese king to administer the slave licensing regime in Portuguese slave stations in Guinea and the Cape Verde islands, and in Angola. The contractor paid the Portuguese king a flat sum for the right to sell the licenses. Although New Christians certainly were not the only slave traders among the Portuguese, the evidence is conclusive that the contractors reserved the bulk of the licenses—and therefore the bulk of the slave trade—for their relatives and other New Christian associates.[29]

At an average of 70 cruzados a head delivered in Brazilian ports, the four thousand slaves were worth 280,000 cruzados annually.[30] Most would have been sold to *lavradores* and mill owners on credit. The parties typically drew up a bill of exchange or other evidence of debt providing for payment of the debt in Brazil at a certain future date when the year's sugar production would have been available. Such financing enabled planters to expand cultivation and yet maintain the lavish lifestyles many were pursuing in the tropical colony.

It is noteworthy that there is little evidence that the Sephardim (that is, observant Jews) participated in the slave trade of their New Christian relatives and associates, or did so on their own—at least not prior to the development of Dutch Brazil in the late 1630s and 1640s.[31] This apparent lack of participation in the slave trade is puzzling, since the New Christian role in the slave trade was so important and the Sephardim's cooperation with New Christian merchants in trade was so intimate. This is particularly true when we consider that family ties were the only reliable vehicle for extended commercial operations and the only guarantee of reasonable transaction costs.

Take, once again, the example of Miguel Dias de Santiago and his cousin Manuel Dias Henriques. Both lived for a period in Brazil as New Christians.[32] Miguel resided in Bahia and traded with Portugal and Northern Europe between 1595 and 1615. Miguel's account books from that period demonstrate his interest in the exchange of all manner of European and Asian commodities for sugar, but there is not one entry recording the exchange of slaves for sugar. When Miguel departed from

Brazil, he settled in Antwerp and continued trading with Brazil in association with Manuel Dias Henriques, who was established by the 1620s in Amsterdam and had assumed the name Matathias Aboab after he reverted to Judaism.[33]

While still a New Christian, Manuel Dias Henriques had shuttled slaves between Angola and Brazil and had finally delivered slaves to Mexico and Guatemala in the early 1620s. He certainly acquired slaves under licenses obtained through another New Christian cousin, Duarte Dias Henriques, who held the slave contract for Angola from 1607 to 1614.[34] Manuel departed from the New World suddenly in 1621, when the Mexican Inquisition initiated a manhunt for him in Guatemala.[35] Manuel arrived in Amsterdam by 1626 (following his late cousin Duarte Fernandes, alias Josua Habilho, another associate in Atlantic sugar trading who had preceded him there by more than a decade).[36] Once established in Amsterdam, it would have been natural for Manuel (now an observant of the "law of Moses") to continue the slave trade he obviously knew from his earlier days and to combine it with his cousin Miguel Dias's sugar trading (now from Antwerp).

Why did Manuel cease slave trafficking when he arrived in Amsterdam? A personal moral aversion to slavery and the slave trade, after his experience in Atlantic slave trading, is possible in Manuel's case. But why did other Sephardic merchants who had similar family commercial connections in Portugal, Spain, Brazil, and the Americas not participate in the slave trade? If the reversion to the Jewish faith was a factor in the Sephardi avoiding the very profitable trade in human cargo, why did many of the Sephardim become slave owners and some Sephardic Jews become slave merchants later, beginning with the development of the sugar industry in Dutch Brazil? Did the licensing regime for the introduction of slaves into Brazil preclude Jews from the trade? If New Christians in Portugal and Brazil could include Jewish relatives in shares of sugar cargoes surreptitiously, why not include them in licenses and cargoes for slave trading? Or did they obscure Jewish participation in this profitable trade so well that today no evidence has survived? We shall probably never have entirely satisfactory answers.

In addition to slaves, Brazilian planters demanded many luxury items and necessities. Many of the luxuries originated in Asia.[37] Cotton and silk cloths from Asia were especially well suited in weight to the tropics, and their high quality appealed to the taste for ostentation that was evident in colonial life. India and the Far East also produced quantities of carved, inlaid, and gilded chests, serving trays, writing boxes, and bedframes. New Christians were well represented in the Asian trades that brought such goods from India annually to Lisbon via the Cape of Good Hope,[38] and we have ample evidence that the Sephardim and New Christians provided many of the luxuries, as well as necessities, to Brazilian markets. As return cargo for these luxuries, of course, New Christian and Sephardi merchants carried off still more sugar.

In terms of value, the Portuguese Asian trade probably topped sugar, at least through the 1620s, and the crown derived more revenue still from the *carreira da Índia* than from Brazil.[39] We know that in the early seventeenth century, Brazil's *dízimos* (tithes) yielded the crown approximately 200,000 cruzados per year, and the brazilwood contract another 60,000 cruzados.[40] At the same time, however, the crown derived as much as 137,500 cruzados in customs from the cargo of a single Indian carrack delivered in Lisbon, and the total revenue from the annual fleet of two or three carracks from India was not far below 300,000 cruzados.[41] This much we know with relative certainty; however, much controversy surrounds the estimated value of an annual *carreira* cargo in Lisbon. A considerable body of evidence supports annual values in the range of 4 to 5 million cruzados delivered in Lisbon between 1580 and 1620, or somewhat more than Frederick Mauro's estimated value of sugar trade of 4 million cruzados during roughly the same period.[42]

Given the importance of both the Brazilian sugar and Asian trades throughout much of the century (1550–1650), it is not surprising that many of the leading merchants of the New Christian and Sephardic communities who began dealing in Atlantic sugar and African slaves were attracted to investing in the *carreira da Índia*'s more risky but equally rewarding trade, once they had accumulated excess capital. In the early seventeenth century, the most successful New Christian merchants of Lisbon, Oporto, Antwerp, and Seville all included Brazilian sugar; Indian diamonds, cottons, and silks; southeast Asian rubies; African slaves; and Asian spices in their merchandise inventories.[43] Similarly, Amsterdam's and Hamburg's more successful Sephardim (including Bento Osorio, Manuel Dias Henriques, Diogo Dias Queirido, João de Paz, André d'Azevedo, and Duarte Nunes da Costa) invested in the Portuguese Asian trade, especially in diamonds and other precious stones.[44] The connection went further, for the Portuguese imported an entire range of cotton cloth—guinea cloth or *panos pretos*—from India exclusively to trade for West African slaves, while every shipment of cottons included quantities of *dotins*, or loin cloth, for the slaves' clothing. New Christian merchants then introduced slaves (as well as the highest quality Indian cottons) into Brazil and exchanged both for sugar.[45]

Manuel de Paz and his half-brother Fernando Tinoco, who headed one of the largest and wealthiest groups of New Christian merchants during the first half of the seventeenth century, illustrate sugar's role as a commercial steppingstone to greater wealth. Indeed, de Paz and Tinoco epitomized the interconnection of the several enterprises. In the mid-sixteenth century their father, Diogo Fernandes do Brasil, managed sugar mills in Pernambuco for absentee mill owners. Prior to marrying Ana de Paz (ca. 1580), daughter of the above-mentioned Diogo Fernandes Santiago, Diogo Fernandes do Brasil and his brothers Duarte Fernandes and Simão Rodrigues do Brasil were developing their own sugar mills near Camaragibe.

Manuel de Paz himself was born in Brazil around 1581, but grew up in Lisbon with his younger half-brother Tinoco. During the first two decades of the seventeenth century, Manuel lived and traded in Goa, investing his father's sugar fortune in diamonds and cotton and silk cloth from India. Manuel's far-flung enterprise eventually involved cousin Francisco Tinoco de Carvalho in Goa as well as another half-brother, Francisco Duarte Tinoco, in Bahia and a cousin, Manuel Rodrigues do Porto, in Olinda.[46] At the same time cousin Diogo Fernandes Tinoco resided in Angola, whence he shipped slave cargoes to Brazil and Spanish America.[47] Still other kinsmen—most notably Duarte Dias Henriques—held slave contracts and were prominent in the slave trade to Brazil and Spanish America. The complex commercial and familial relations among these individuals and members of the Lopes Pinto and Ribeiro, Ulhoa, Nunes de Mattos, Vaaz de Paiva, and Dias Henriques families who dealt in brazilwood and developed their own sugar plantations and mills are too numerous to mention here.[48]

During the 1630s and 1640s, sugar wealth finally brought Manuel de Paz and Fernando Tinoco to Madrid, among the dozen or so New Christian and Genoese merchant-financiers of sufficient wealth to serve as financiers of the vast Spanish monarchy. The network of relatives living in Antwerp as New Christians and in Rouen, Paris, Amsterdam, Hamburg, and Venice privately or publicly as Jews assisted Manuel de Paz and Fernando Tinoco and their associates in Seville and Lisbon in establishing an international payments network that they directed from Madrid.[49]

At least through the early 1600s, the Iberian empires could claim near exclusive sovereignty over Europe's overseas commerce, and even into the 1650s they enjoyed distinct advantages over their rivals in sugar, slave, and diamond trades. The Jewish communities of Amsterdam, Hamburg, and the French ports most of all, and to a lesser extent those of Venice and other Italian cities, depended upon the connection to wealthier Iberian kinsmen, such as Manuel de Paz in Spain and many others overseas. Commercial opportunities in the sixteenth and much of the seventeenth century thus tied Sephardic fortunes to Spain and Portugal.

In the period from 1650 to 1750, however, circumstances had changed for New Christians as well as for Jews. As fortune turned against Spain's and Portugal's rulers, wealthy New Christians, as well as their more modest cousins in Sephardic communities across Europe, suffered significant commercial and financial losses. In the 1630s both Brazilian sugar and the Portuguese Asian trades suffered first from Dutch aggression and secondarily from Dutch competition. Dutch occupation of Brazil's richest sugar-producing captaincies from the early 1630s, of El Mina on the Guinea coast in 1637, and of Angola in 1641, and the privateering activity of the Dutch West India Company (founded in 1621) robbed New Christians of much trade and capital invested in sugar and slaves.[50] The development of sugar production in Rio de Janeiro and other southern captaincies of Brazil and more thoroughgoing New Christian penetration of Spanish American markets largely offset these losses. Rio de Janeiro's sugar industry expanded into the 1640s, only to be depressed in turn during the period from 1650 to 1670 as the Dutch developed sugar culture on a large scale in the West Indies.[51]

Over the long term, the Brazilian sugar trade and the merchants associated with it proved themselves more resilient than their counterparts in the Asian trade. The eclipse of the Portuguese empire and its trade in Asia were pronounced; *carreira* cargoes dwindled to values barely above 1 million cruzados by the 1640s and never recovered. Only a significant diamond trade survived, as New Christian merchants transferred shipments of Indian diamonds (formerly carried in Portuguese carracks via the Cape of Good Hope to Lisbon) to Manila galleons in the Pacific and English shipping via the Cape route, both relatively secure from Dutch attacks.[52]

The separation of the Portuguese from the Spanish crown (the union lasted from 1580 to 1640) also damaged the New Christians' fortunes. In 1640 many prominent New Christians were residing in Spain and Spain's overseas colonies. The new Braganza monarchy in Lisbon, desperately short of funds to finance the protracted struggle with Spain that was necessary to maintain its independence, was only too glad to declare the absentees traitors and confiscate their goods, including sugar mills and plantations in Brazil. The heirs of Duarte Dias Henriques, who owned at least one mill in Pernambuco, and Marcos Fernandes Monsanto, who owned a total of four mills in Espirito Santo, were among the losers.[53] The final blow to the wealthiest New Christian families, however, was the 1648 Spanish bankruptcy that left New Christian financiers (including the heirs of Manuel de Paz and Fernando Tinoco) crippled with millions of ducats of uncollectible loans to the Spanish Habsburgs.[54]

In the century from 1650 to 1750, in the aftermath of New Christian commercial losses, Jews of Holland, England, and France (many of them the direct heirs and commercial successors of New Christians in Portugal, Spain, Brazil, Spanish America, and Portuguese Asia) appeared prominently in the sugar trade of the West Indies (Curaçao, Jamaica, and Barbados in particular), but the Atlantic trade had changed. In the hundred years prior to 1650, colonial trade passed through the Iberian metropolis without stimulating the economy, as the produce—precious metals above all—immediately left the peninsula for the northern markets in exchange for Baltic grain, timber and naval stores, and manufactures. These were the products that the Iberian economies needed for their own populace or to sustain the colonial economies, and which Spain and Portugal did not produce. Additional precious metal flowed out of Spain to finance the imperial burden of defending the Southern Netherlands, Milan, and the Habsburg hegemony in Central Europe. In the period from 1650 to 1750 sugar was but one of several products—including raw cotton, coffee, timber, indigo, cacao, tobacco, and vanilla—that were now the objects of wider consumption. They were no longer viewed as luxuries to be consumed by the few, but rather as staples that had become necessities to a wider urban populace.[55] While the consumption of luxuries and the pursuit of imperial ambitions dominated the Iberian economies, trade and commerce dominated the English economy.[56] The colonial trades thus necessarily had a powerful impact on the metropolitan economy in the seventeenth and eighteenth centuries, especially in England.[57]

At the same time, other conditions of trade had not changed. Having connections in Iberian colonial markets, which produced much silver to exchange for the manufactures the colonial economies could not produce, still carried distinct advantages. Thus, Jews in the West Indies were prominent among smugglers to Spanish America and as staple merchants because they enjoyed the advantages of connections to the Iberian economies.

In the period from 1650 to 1750, the Jewish and New Christian merchants of the sugar and staple trades, many of whom had West Indian representatives, were providing the cheap transaction costs that were necessary to accumulate wealth and induce industrialization in Europe. Their successes, as in the earlier period, were due in part perhaps to religious traditions, but certainly to experience and to family representation throughout the Iberian overseas empires. The family networks expanded, of course, to include new posts in North America, such as New York and Newport in the early eighteenth century.[58] For example, Isaac Henriques of Jamaica had relatives in New York around 1700, and about the same time Moses Lucena and Joseph Mendes of Barbados traded with Joseph's brother Menasses Mendes in London. Earlier in 1685, the Navarro brothers (Moseh of Brazil, Aaron of Amsterdam, and Jacob of London) were prominent in the Atlantic sugar and staple trades.[59]

Jews were unwelcome competitors to the creole merchants of the West Indies, as they had been to Old Christians in the Iberian Peninsula. In Iberian society, the identification of "Jew" with "merchant" in the course of the sixteenth and seventeenth centuries brought even those of partial New Christian ancestry under suspicion, and resulted in their being subjected to the Inquisition's violent persecution. The result of this persecution on the Iberian Peninsula and in the Iberian overseas colonies was to reduce the survivors to a popularly despised caste, distinct from an Old Christian majority who did not (in theory at least) openly follow the commercial profession. To be sure, there was friction between Jews and creoles in the West Indies, too, but there was no comparable institution like the Inquisition. The involvement of the English aristocracy in commerce was such that the social and political elite could not disparage the merchant's work and thus stigmatize the Jew who earned his livelihood from commerce.[60]

Notes

1. See, among other early works, J. Lúcio d'Azevedo, *História dos cristãos-novos portugueses* (Lisbon, 1921), and Jean Denucé, *L'Afrique au XVIe siècle et le commerce anversois* (Antwerp, 1937). I use the term "New Christian" (*Cristão novo*) to refer exclusively to *Portuguese* Jews in the early sixteenth century who adopted the Christian religion, without consideration of the sincerity, depth, or permanence of that conversion, and as distinct from Spanish *conversos*. I use the term "Sephardic" (Sephardi, Sephardim) to refer to practicing or observant Jews, who were, of course, descended from Iberian Jews.
2. See James C. Boyajian, *Portuguese Trade in Asia under the Habsburgs, 1580–1640* (Baltimore, London, 1993), esp. 33–38.
3. See James C. Boyajian, *Portuguese Bankers at the Court of Spain, 1626–1650* (New Brunswick, 1983), esp. 25–35.
4. The classic statement of the shift to Atlantic preponderance in Europe's economic life is Fernand Braudel, *La Méditerranée et le monde méditerranéen à l'époque de Philippe II* (Paris, 1966). See also Frédéric Mauro, *Le portugal et l'Atlantique au XVIIe siècle, 1570–1670; Étude économique* (Paris, 1960). On the New Christians and the Atlantic economy, see Boyajian, *Portuguese Bankers*, 1–16.
5. Boyajian, *Portuguese Trade in Asia*, 29–52.
6. Ibid., 33, 38.
7. Mauro, *Le portugal et l'Atlantique*, 526, and Frédéric Mauro, "L'Atlantique portugais et les esclaves (1570–1670)," *Revista da Faculdade de Letras, Universidade de Lisboa*, 2nd ser., 22 (1956):5–55.
8. The shipments are extensively documented in E. M. Koen et al., "Notarial Records in Amsterdam Relating to the Portuguese Jews in That Town up to 1639," *Studia Rosenthaliana* 1 (1967):109–15; 4 (1970):115–26, 243–61; 5 (1971):211–25; 10(1976):212–30; and 13 (1979):220–43.
9. Public Records Office (PRO), State Papers Miscellaneous (SP), 9/104, "Account Books of a Portuguese Merchant, Miguel Dias de Santiago, 1595–1615," unfoliated; for the family history of Manuel Dias Henriques and his clan, see I. S. Révah, "Pour l'histoire des Nouveaux-Chrétiens portugais. La relation généalogique de I. de M. Aboab," *Boletim Internacional de Bibliografia Luso-Brasileira* 2 (1961):276–312.
10. Koen et al., "Notarial Records," III, no. 1 (1969):123; notarial deed no. 150, 7 September 1604, Francisco Mendes de Medeiros.
11. Mauro, *Le portugal et l'Atlantique*, 1–142
12. Ibid.
13. Ibid.
14. José Gonçalves Salvador, *Os cristãos-novos e o comércio no Atlântico meridional (Com enfoque nas Capitanias do Sul 1530–1680)* (São Paulo, 1978), 39–52.
15. Data for the cost of an *engenho* are scarce, and the value given here is tentative, though I believe it to be a rather low estimate. We know that by the early eighteenth century Manuel do Valle da Silveira, a New Christian merchant of Rio de Janeiro, reported paying 4,000 cruzados for a "share" in an *engenho*. If we assume that his share was one half, then this *engenho* was worth at least 8,000 cruzados. The 4,000 cruzado "price" or valuation may have actually exceeded or fallen below the *engenho*'s original cost, however, depending on its condition and the current market for sugar. The source is Gonçalves Salvador, *Os cristãos-novos*, 143.
16. Data for the table are drawn from Mauro, *Le portugal et l'Atlantique*, 220.
17. Noel Deerr, *The History of Sugar*, vol. 1 (London, 1949–50), 105.
18. Gonçalves Salvador, *Os cristãos-novos*, 181–82.
19. F. S. Gaastra, "The Shifting Balance of Trade of the Dutch East India Company," in *Companies and Trade: Essays on Overseas Trading Companies during the Ancien Regime*, ed. L. Blussé and F. S. Gaastra (Leiden, 1981), 47–69, esp. 60.
20. Gaastra, "The Shifting Balance of Trade," 60.

21. Arnold Wiznitzer, *The Jews in Colonial Brazil* (New York, 1960), 14–23.
22. Arquivo Nacional da Torre do Tombo (ANTT), Inquisição de Lisboa, proceso 6321, Andresa Jorge; proceso 4580, Beatriz Fernandes; proceso 4273, Beatriz de Souza; proceso 9417, Briolangia Fernandes; proceso 11116, Ana da Costa do Brasil.
23. ANTT, Inquisição de Lisboa, proceso 12464, João Nunes Correia; see also Gonçalves Salvador, *Os cristãos-novos*, 166.
24. Charles de Vos, "Limal, ses seigneurs et seigneuries: Don Thomás López de Ulloa, premier Baron de Limal (1621–1655)," *Wavriensia—Bulletin du cercle historique e archéologique de Wavre et de la région* 13 (1964):33–87; ANTT, Inquisição de Lisboa, proceso 5391, André Lopes d'Ulhoa; *Primeira visitação do Santo Ofício ás partes do Brasil, pelo licenciado Heitor Furtado de Mendonça. Denunciações do Bahia, 1591–1593. Serie Eduardo Prado, para melhor se conhecer o Brasil* (São Paulo, 1925), 280.
25. Gonçalves Salvador, *Os cristãos-novos*, 51.
26. Herbert I. Bloom, "A Study of Brazilian Jewish History, 1623–54, Based Chiefly upon the Findings of the Late Samuel Oppenheim," *Publications of the American Jewish Historical Society* 33 (1934):43–125.
27. Wiznitzer, *Jews in Colonial Brazil*, 10, 14–23, 55–56.
28. I have based my estimate of the volume of slave trade to Brazil on the work of Enrique Otte and Conchita Ruiz-Barruecos, "Los portugueses en la trata de esclavos negros de las postrimerías del siglo XVI," *Moneda y crédito* 85 (1963):3–40.
29. Archivo General de Indias, Sevilla (AGI), Contratación, legajo 5763, "Libros de asientos de licencias y despachos de esclavos"; legajo 5766, "Libros de asientos de comisiones y contratos y de despachos de naos."
30. The selling price of slaves in Brazil is based on fragments of the Ximenes d'Aragão family's accounts published in Denucé, *L'Afrique au XVIᵉ siècle*, 52–53.
31. Koen et al., "Notarial Records," 1 (1967):109–15; 4 (1970):115–26, 243–61; 5 (1971): 211–25; 10 (1976):212–30; and 13 (1979):220–43.
32. I. S. Révah, "Pour l'histoire des Nouveaux-Chrétiens portugais," 276–312; PRO, SP, 9/104, "Account Books of a Portuguese Merchant, Miguel Dias de Santiago, 1595–1615," unfoliated.
33. PRO, SP, 9/104, "Account Books of a Portuguese Merchant, Miguel Dias de Santiago, 1595–1615," unfoliated.
34. Mauro, "L'Atlantique portugais et les esclaves," 5–55; AGI, Contratación, "Libros de asientos," no. 2, no. 3.
35. Archivo General de la Nación, México (AGN), tomo 331, "Manuel Díaz Henríquez y Pedro de Silva Saucedo, portugueses, por judaisantes," Guatemala, no. 7.
36. Koen et al. "Notarial Records," II, no. 2 (1968):264–65; Miguel Dias de Santiago's accounts include numerous entries of sugar shipments to Duarte Fernandes and to his several sons (PRO, SP, 4/109, "Account Books of a Portuguese Merchant, Miguel Dias de Santiago, 1595–1615," unfoliated).
37. PRO, SP, 9/104, "Account Books of a Portuguese Merchant, Miguel Dias de Santiago, 1595–1615," unfoliated.
38. For example, the cargo of the galleon *Santo António* from India, arriving in Lisbon in 1616 (Arquivo Histórico Ultramarino, Lisboa [AHU], Caixas da Índia, caixa 326 [1616–17], no. 25, "Caderno das fazendas que leva esta naveta Santo António").
39. Boyajian, *Portuguese Trade in Asia*, 39–42, 247–53.
40. Mauro, *Le portugal et l'Atlantique*, 220; Gonçalves Salvador, *Os cristãos-novos*, 181–82.
41. AHU, Caixas da Índia, caixa 323 (1509–1611), no. 57; caixa 324 (1612–14), no. 140; caixa 330 (1624–25), no. 47; AHU, Caixas do Reino, caixa 1 (1568–1615), no. 85; caixa 2 (1616–18), no. 119.
42. Boyajian, *Portuguese Trade in Asia*, 29–52. The comparison of the Portuguese king's revenues from Brazil and those from the Cape trade to India do not take into account the crown's expenditures in those regions.
43. Boyajian, *Portuguese Trade in Asia*, 29–52.

484 | *James C. Boyajian*

44. Koen et al., "Notarial Records," *Studia Rosenthaliana* 19 (1985):88, no. 2440, 25 June 1621.
45. Boyajian, *Portuguese Trade in Asia*, 141.
46. Boyajian, *Portuguese Bankers*, 26–28, and idem, *Portuguese Trade in Asia*, 109, 119, 133, 136, 163–64.
47. Gonçalves Salvador, *Os cristãos-novos*, 310.
48. Boyajian, *Portuguese Bankers*, 26–29, 74–75, 184–204, 207–09.
49. Ibid.
50. Boyajian, *Portuguese Trade in Asia*, 185–201.
51. Mauro, *Le portugal et l'Atlantique*, 488–95; Gonçalves Salvador, *Os cristãos-novos*, 182.
52. Boyajian, *Portuguese Trade in Asia*, 202–40.
53. Gonçalves Salvador, *Os cristãos-novos*, 52.
54. Boyajian, *Portuguese Bankers*, 154–80.
55. Stephen Fortune, *Merchants and Jews: The Struggle for British West Indian Commerce, 1650–1750* (Gainesville, Fla., 1984), 78–98.
56. Boyajian, *Portuguese Trade in Asia*, 166–84.
57. Fortune, *Merchants and Jews*, 78–98.
58. Ibid., 130–50.
59. Ibid., 133.
60. Ibid., 99–129, 130–50; Boyajian, *Portuguese Trade in Asia*, 166–84.

– Chapter 23 –

NEW CHRISTIANS AS SUGAR CULTIVATORS AND TRADERS IN THE PORTUGUESE ATLANTIC, 1450–1800

Ernst Pijning

S UGAR SHAPED NEW WORLD SOCIETY in the Portuguese, British, French, Dutch, and Danish colonies of South America and the Caribbean. Between 1400 and 1800, sugar, slavery, and plantations were the three key factors in the Atlantic economy in which Europeans, Americans, Africans, and Asians of different religious backgrounds entered. Settlers of Jewish descent, called New Christians, were among the participants who cultivated and traded this sweet cash crop (see Fig. 23.1).[1] This chapter will demonstrate that New Christians found in sugar cultivation and trade new opportunities to gain upward social mobility, but that in order to prosper from their newly acquired status and to avoid Inquisitorial prosecution, New Christians accommodated socially and religiously to local society and its mores.

Jews occupied a precarious position in the Iberian Peninsula. In 1492 the Spanish king and queen, Ferdinand and Isabella, ordered the expulsion of all practicing Jews from their territories. Those who remained had to convert to Christianity and were designated as "New Christians." New Christians were barred from public office and could not receive any royal favors and privileges, and were therefore viewed as second-class inhabitants of the peninsula. Many practicing Jews fled to Portugal, but in 1497 king Manuel followed suit and expelled all unconverted Jews from the Portuguese territories. These measures were enforced through the establishment of the Inquisition, and the first Portuguese auto-da-fé (Inquisitorial punishment in the form of a public procession) was held in 1540.[2]

Both Sephardic Jews, who had fled from the Iberian Peninsula to Northern Europe, and New Christians in Portugal and its overseas territories found attractive opportunities in the trade and cultivation of sugar. Their international network of connections and strategic position in core areas of the sugar market in the commerce of Northern Europe and the Iberian Peninsula gave Sephardic Jews and New Christians an edge over their competitors. Thus, ironically, the expulsion of the Sephardim had given them an economic advantage—one which was, however, checked by the Portuguese Inquisition's activities.

Before addressing the issues of social mobility and accommodation, it is necessary to clarify some terms describing a person's Jewish background. "New Christians," "Old Christians," "Sephardim," "marranos," "Jews," and "crypto-Jews" need explanation, for they are confusing and are used interchangeably in the literature. Before 1492 in Spain and 1497 in Portugal, Jews were allowed to live and worship in the Iberian territories and the Atlantic islands of the Azores, Cape Verdes, Madeira, and São Tomé. Like the authorities in Spain and Portugal before the expulsion, Dutch authorities allowed the practice of Judaism in most of their European and overseas territories throughout the early modern period. Thus, when writing about "Jews" or "Sephardim," I am referring either to Portugal and its territories before 1497 or to the period when the Dutch occupied the northeastern part of Brazil (1630–1654). New Christians are all persons of Jewish descent, in this case Sephardim, living in Portuguese or Spanish territories who were forced to convert to Catholicism and were liable to suffer prosecution by the Church or the Inquisition if found professing their old faith. "New Christian" was a juridical term and does not mean per se that a person so designated was a crypto-Jew or marrano, that is, one secretly professing the Jewish faith and not a sincere Christian. Whether New Christians were crypto-Jews or not falls beyond the scope of this chapter. Rather, I am concerned with the economic and social strategies of all persons of Sephardic origin in the Portuguese Atlantic, whatever their religious practices or beliefs.

Sugar was an international commodity the cultivation of which had spread geographically throughout the early modern period. Sugar originated in Asia, probably in New Guinea, and spread from there through the Far and Middle East to the Mediterranean.[3] Portuguese and Italian merchants first introduced it in the Atlantic from the south of Portugal, the Algarve, in the early fifteenth century.[4] The crop spread to the Madeiras around 1430, and then to other Atlantic islands, such as São Tomé and the Cape Verdes.

The two main areas of cultivation were Madeira and São Tomé, each with its own peculiarities. Madeira's residents were small-scale sugar farmers, whereas São Tomé's cane growers worked on a larger scale, using African slavery in a system that became the model for that of the New World plantations. The difference between the islands can be attributed to climatic conditions. Madeira had a moderate and healthy climate, which attracted many Portuguese and foreign settlers; labor was there-fore less difficult to obtain. In contrast, settling on tropical and unhealthy São Tomé meant almost certain death, and this island consequently charmed fewer planters. Portugal profited most of all from enterprising Genoese merchants, who had introduced the crop from the Mediter-ranean to Portugal and the Atlantic islands. The Italian presence was widely felt in Madeira, but it declined as Portuguese settlers became more attracted to this island.[5]

The New Christian presence on Madeira continued until the early seventeenth century. Jews and later New Christians who settled on the island in the fifteenth and sixteenth centuries were primarily engaged in the sugar trade, but only a few were sugar mill owners.[6] Subsequently, Madeira's New Christian population declined rapidly, particularly fol-lowing the Inquisition's three visits to the island (in 1591, 1612, and 1620), in conjunction with the effects of declining sugar cultivation.[7] Most New Christians left for Brazil and Northern Europe.

The São Tomé case demonstrates that the New Christian presence was not always voluntary. The island served as a dumping ground for the children of Jewish emigrants who were expelled from Spain in 1492 and forcibly converted to Catholicism in Portugal. The Portuguese king ban-ished to São Tomé all Spanish Sephardic children who had not paid a tax for entering the country.[8] Banishment was part of a royal policy to settle the island. Although exile to São Tomé was virtually a death sentence, some New Christian children did survive, but given their young age upon arrival, it is unlikely that they had continued to adhere to their for-mer religion.[9] Their role was important, since all trade became dependent on the local population, who were immune to tropical diseases.

In São Tomé, New Christians became integrated into local society. Given the island's small white population, New Christian status pre-sented no obstacle to marriage; similarly, persons of Jewish descent did not hesitate to marry Old Christians. Thus, men of Jewish descent ended up becoming sugar cane growers, officials, and traders.

In Brazil, New Christians felt much safer. Unlike the situation in Spanish America and Portuguese India, the Portuguese king never per-mitted the Inquisition to gain a firm foothold in Brazil.[10] Nevertheless, through a system of visits and denunciations, almost two thousand Brazilian New Christians were sent to Portugal and found guilty by the Lisbon Inquisition in the eighteenth century alone.[11]

As in the Atlantic islands, New Christians in Brazil found in sugar a quick means for upward social mobility. Recognition of their status, how-ever, depended on their adoption of metropolitan and local norms and values. Therefore, New Christians had to prove their "purity of blood" (*pureza de sangue*) in order to assume their elite status in colonial society. Thus, only through accepting Portuguese ideas of social ascendance could New Christians become part of the colonial elite and diminish their chances of being denounced by the Inquisition.

Portuguese elite status was recognized through one's "purity of blood," which was enhanced by one's ancestors' religion, race, and profession. One had to be of Old Christian origin and be free of any African or American Indian blood, and one's forefathers may not have engaged in any mechanical trade or have worked with their hands. Thus, in order to be accepted to the elite and to display one's wealth and standing—by means of assuming social responsibilities, by donations, by entering a Catholic brotherhood or a third order of a religious congregation, by holding office, or by becoming a member of a military order or an informant of the Inquisition (*familiar*)—one's purity of blood had to be attested to and recognized by a Portuguese council.

Official acceptance of New Christians' elite status depended on their denial of their own ancestry. New Christian elites publicly ignored their Jewish background by seeking to hold offices or honorary functions that were open only to Old Christians. Royal and local acceptance of New Christians in these functions thus allowed the new elites to free themselves from their New Christian ancestry.

Before New Christians could remove the "stain" of their ancestry, they had to avoid engaging in any manual labor and become landowners. In 1803, an anonymous Brazilian complained, "Even the most humble European emigrant, once he has left the shores of Portugal, is never again to use the plough or hoe."[12] Such was the essence of Portuguese society in the tropics: performing manual labor violated Portuguese concepts of status. The very fact of having an ancestor who had been employed in a "mechanical trade" sufficed to disqualify one for elite membership. Hence, even artisans employed slaves, acted as overseers, and left their trade whenever possible. The Portuguese, like every other European country, had a similar bias against merchants: commercial activities were seen as suspect and thus could not increase status.[13] Many Brazilians preferred to leave trade after earning enough profits and credit in the marketplace, and the same was true for the New Christian population. Though they may have been previously engaged in the commercial sector, New and Old Christians alike chose to leave trade for agriculture—which in colonial Brazil meant sugar plantations—upon arrival in the New World, whenever circumstances allowed them to do so.

New Christians followed a career pattern similar to other new Iberian immigrants to the New World colonies—most arrived as bachelors and first engaged in commercial activities.[14] Portuguese emigrants were hired by mercantile houses, which profited from their recent knowledge of the Portuguese market and their connections with the other side of the Atlantic. As David Grant Smith and Rae Flory's study on merchants in Salvador (Bahia) has demonstrated, about 90 percent of all merchants in the late seventeenth and early eighteenth centuries were born in Portugal or the Atlantic islands.[15] Between one-third and one-fourth of the traders were married to merchants' daughters, but the rest married daughters of landowners, professionals, and artisans.[16]

For a newly arrived bachelor, a position in commerce was only temporary. What was most important for his rise in social status was landownership. If he did well in commerce, he could obtain the honorific title of *homem de negócio*, in other words, a long-distance trader, especially in sugar, tobacco, and brazilwood to Europe and slaves from Africa. A newly arrived bachelor would start out humbly as an office clerk for a merchant, with some side dealing of his own. He would subsequently gamble by investing in one or two slave voyages, which were highly profitable, but also highly risky.[17] If he did well, he could either establish his own shop (*mercador de loja*) or become a small trader (*tratante*), or, even better, make a good match and marry the daughter of a *homem de negócio*.

After gaining profits and establishing credit through commercial activities, the merchant or his offspring would turn to agriculture, the military, the clergy, or officialdom to display his wealth and status. Social ascendancy counted for more than monetary profits, but it needed a substantial investment. Sugar cultivation, the most noble of all professions, was less profitable than trade in the commodity, even though building a sugar mill and acquiring slaves required substantial capital and credit.[18]

The highest position to which a Brazilian could rise was a sugar mill owner (*senhor do engenho*). A *senhor do engenho* was a sugar cultivator who possessed his own sugar mill to grind the cane into molasses. Ennobled by landownership, a *senhor do engenho* was far more than a sugar mill owner. He was part of the elite of colonial society, and he could enhance his status by becoming a government representative, either as a member of a nearby municipal council or as a military officer in the backcountry. Even today, large landowners bear the semi-military title of *coronel* and have nearly absolute power over their fellow citizens in the hinterlands of northeast Brazil.

The *senhor do engenho* rented out pieces of his land to other sugar farmers called *lavradores da cana*, who did not possess their own mill, and had to bring the cane to the *senhor do engenho*. These *lavradores de cana* had thus a far lesser social status, but some might amass enough capital or marry well enough to become a *senhor do engenho* themselves. Apart from the *senhor do engenho* or *lavrador da cana* and his family, the only other white persons on a sugar plantation were either an overseer or an engineer (*feitor*), although sometimes even these positions were filled by trusted and skilled slaves or freedmen (see Fig. 23.1)

Farmers (*lavradores*) of other crops, such as tobacco, and manioc were considered to be of a lesser social status. However, Bahian tobacco gained an excellent reputation and became an essential product in the slave trade. Some tobacco farmers did own quite large plantations and could therefore rise in social status, but none of these *lavradores* could approximate the elevated position of a *senhor do engenho*.

The ability of New Christians to reach and maintain a position in the higher social strata of colonial Brazilian society differed among areas and eras. Sugar was first cultivated in Pernambuco, the northeast of Brazil,

FIGURE 23.1 "Brasilise Suyker Werken." The different stages of sugar production in Brazil, from Simon de Vries, *Curieuse aenmerckingen der bysonderste Oost en West-Indische verwonderens-waerdige dingen* (Utrecht, 1682).

where settlers were in high demand and the crown and private owners of captaincies (*donatórios*) appreciated any investment or colonization. The Bahian region was also rich in sugar mills, and became the most important sugar region after the Dutch invasions had destroyed many sugar plantations in Pernambuco. Rio de Janeiro was a minor but not unimportant region for sugar cultivation. In this area, New Christians had many possibilities to establish themselves.

In late sixteenth-century Pernambuco, participation in the Brazilian sugar trade by colonists of Jewish descent was significant, but not dominant. New Christian merchants had invested much in the trade of Pernambuco, the most important Brazilian sugar area before the Dutch invasion of 1630.[19] They used their personal commercial connections in Portugal, Amsterdam, Antwerp, and Hamburg to move sugar from farmer to consumer, but this network was not necessarily ethnically determined, for Old Christians also participated in these commercial transactions.[20] Moreover, the Amsterdam Sephardim did not try to integrate the complete industry, for they rarely invested in the final stage of production, the sugar refineries in the Netherlands.[21]

The situation in Pernambuco changed dramatically when the Dutch occupied the area from 1630 to 1654. During that time, persons of Jewish descent could be divided into two groups: those arriving with the Dutch invaders who previously had lived as openly practicing Sephardic Jews in the Low Countries, and those who had settled in the area as New Christians before the Dutch conquest.[22] Both groups actively participated in the cultivation and trade of sugar, but in different ways.[23]

The Jewish population of Recife was quite large, and principally engaged in trade. About 1,450 Sephardim settled there, making up half of the total white population; they were engaged mainly in the commercial sector.[24] Their expertise in trade may be explained by the specific advantages that the Sephardim possessed. Speaking both Dutch and Portuguese, they could use their linguistic skills to mediate between the two populations. The newly arrived Dutch urban Jewish community had a large stake in the sugar trade, but less so in the crop's cultivation. In some instances, up to one-third of the cargo of homeward-bound sugar vessels was owned by Sephardim.[25]

The number of the newly arrived Dutch Sephardim involved in sugar cultivation, however, was smaller (see Table 23.1). This limited participation contrasts sharply with that of the Portuguese New Christians, who had already been settled for several decades in Pernambuco. The participation of New Christians as *senhores do engenho* in Pernambuco was more substantial.[26] There was a fairly even distribution of New Christians among the agricultural (which included sugar cultivation) and commercial sectors (including the sugar trade) of the Pernambucan economy.

As the Bahian case demonstrated, regional differences played an important role regarding New Christian participation in the sugar trade. In this Brazilian captaincy, New Christian involvement in the sugar trade

TABLE 23.1 New Christians' Professions, According to the Pernambuco Visit of the Inquisition, 1593–1595

Profession	Number of People	Percentage
Agriculture (total)	14	42
Sugar mill owner	3	9
Sugar cane grower	2	6
Sugar mill employee	2	6
Farmer (general)	7	21
Commerce (total)	12	37
Trader	11	34
Commercial (general)	1	3
Professional (total)	7	21
Official	1	3
Artisan	3	9
Other urban professions	3	9
Total	33	100

Source: Heitor Furtado de Mendoça, *Primeira Visitação do Santo Officio as Partes do Brasil: Denunciações e Confissões de Pernambuco, 1593–1595*, 2nd ed. (Recife, 1984).

was more significant than in Pernambuco. David Grant Smith has shown that about 45 percent of the merchants of Salvador in the late seventeenth century were of New Christian origin. This proportion was, however, substantially lower than his finding for Lisbon, where in the same period 70 percent of the merchants were New Christians.[27] More than in the Old World, the New World provided New Christians a better opportunity to involve themselves in more prestigious agricultural activities

New opportunities for enterprising farmers of any denomination were promoted in the early colonization efforts. One of the striking elements of the royal instructions that Tomé de Souza, the first governor-general of Brazil, received in 1548 while settling the new capital, São Salvador da Bahia de Todos os Santos, addressed the distribution of land.[28] It read that land should be liberally granted to any person who possessed the capital to build a sugar mill and a fortified tower. In Bahia, as in Pernambuco, all colonists were welcomed enthusiastically, and their efforts to populate the New World were compensated with free land grants. These colonists included people of diverse backgrounds, even foreigners of English, Flemish, and Italian origin, as well as New Christians. No prosecution of crypto-Jews in Brazil and the Atlantic islands occurred until the 1590s, under the Spanish regime of Philip II (Philip I of Portugal) and his successors, with the exception of one Inquisitorial visit in 1570 to the Azores. In this initially favorable climate, New Christians settled freely in Brazil and engaged in sugar cultivation and trade. As a consequence, by the end of the sixteenth century, no less than 30 percent of the Bahian sugar mills were owned by New Christians.[29]

Recently arrived New Christians quickly integrated into the sugar economy, and some even made the rapid advance to become sugar mill owners as first-generation immigrants. Whereas in the early seventeenth century most New Christians in Bahia were predominantly Portuguese born and active in the commercial sector, by the mid-seventeenth to the early eighteenth century their most successful descendants had entered the socially more elevated profession of sugar mill owner (see Tables 23.2 and 23.3).[30] The absolute number of New Christians involved in trade as opposed to agriculture remained very high, as the number of New Christian immigrants from Portugal had increased in the early eighteenth century. However, the possibilities for promotion from commerce to agriculture became more limited in the eighteenth century when the profits from sugar diminished as a consequence of the lower sugar prices.

The surprisingly large involvement of New Christians in sugar cultivation in Rio de Janeiro stands in stark contrast to the cases of Bahia and Pernambuco. Rio de Janeiro had a different economic make-up than the other two captaincies.[31] Unlike Bahia, Rio de Janeiro was not a major source of sugar exports; rather, the town concentrated on trade with Rio de la Plata (for silver), Minas Gerais (for gold), and Angola (for slaves).

In the early eighteenth century, a surprising number of Carioca New Christians were engaged in sugar cultivation (see Table 23.4). Thus, New Christians were more firmly established in this captaincy than in Pernambuco or Bahia. Agriculture, rather than commerce, was the main

TABLE 23.2 Professions of New Christians in Salvador, Bahia, 1618, According to Inquisition Records

Profession	Number of People	Percentage
Agriculture (total)	16	30
Sugar mill owner	8	15
Sugar cane grower	4	7.5
Farmer (general)	4	7.5
Commerce (total)	26	48
Trader	17	31
Commercial (general)	9	17
Professional (total)	12	22
Official	2	4
Artisan	5	9
Other urban professions	5	9
Total	54	100

Sources: "Livro das Denunciações que se fizerão na Visitação do Santo Officio á Cidade do Salvador da Bahia de Todos os Santos do Estado do Brasil, no anno de 1618," *Anais da Biblioteca Nacional* 49 (1927):76–198; Eduardo d'Oliveira França and Sonia A. Siqueira, "Segunda Visitação do Santo Officio às Partes do Brasil pelo Inquisidor e Visitador o Licenciado Marcos Texeira. Livro das Confissões e Ratificações da Bahia: 1618-1620," *Anais do Museu Paulista* 17 (1967):351–526.

TABLE 23.3 Professions of Male New Christians Found Guilty by the Inquisition, Bahia, 1700–1749 (According to Place of Birth)

Profession	No. of People	Place of Birth Brazil	Other	Unknown
Agriculture (total)	12 (13%)	7	2	3
Sugar mill owner	8	4	1	3
Sugar cane grower	1	1	0	0
Farmer (general)	3	2	1	0
Commerce (total)	55 (60%)	7	39	9
Merchant	18	0	15	3
Trader	31	4	21	6
Commercial (general):	6	3	3	0
Professional (total)	24 (27%)	7	12	5
Artisan:	5	0	3	2
Other urban professions:	19	7	9	3
Total	91 (100%)	21	53	17

Source: Anita Novinsky, *Inquisição, Rol dos Culpados, Fontes para a História do Brasil (Século XVIII)* (Rio de Janeiro, 1992).

TABLE 23.4 Professions and Places of Birth of Male New Christians Prosecuted by the Inquisition, Rio de Janeiro, 1700–1749

Profession	No. of People	Place of Birth Brazil	Other	Unknown
Agriculture (total)	101 (35%)	56	24	21
Sugar mill owner	35	17	9	9
Sugar cane Grower	30	15	10	5
Sugar mill employee	3	3	0	0
Farmer (general)	33	21	5	7
Commerce (total)	79 (27%)	29	35	15
Merchants	9	2	6	1
Traders	44	12	22	10
Commercial (general)	26	15	7	4
Professional (total)	111 (38%)	69	18	24
Official	6	3	2	1
Artisan	11	6	3	2
Other urban profession	94	60	13	21
Total	291 (100%)	154	77	60

Source: Anita Novinsky, *Inquisição, Rol dos Culpados.*

occupation of New Christians in Rio de Janeiro, and they had become a substantial part of the city's elite, which was closely intermarried (see Table 23.5). Especially interesting is the large number of New Christian sugar mill owners; in about twenty years between a third and a fourth of all *senhores do engenho* were prosecuted by the Inquisition.[32]

The number of New Christian sugar mill owners was even higher than that of the less prestigious sugar cane growers. In contrast, only a few Carioca New Christians were established under the most prestigious commercial title of *homens de negócio*. As in Bahia and Pernambuco, newly arrived, Portuguese-born New Christians still preferred commerce. Those who had already settled engaged in agriculture, preferably sugar cultivation, or in major urban professions.

Rio de Janeiro was exceptional. Even though the region was a minor sugar center, its agriculture was stronger than its commerce. The relative weakness of the Carioca commercial sector has been noted before. Many historians have cited the Marquis of Lavradio, a viceroy of the 1770s, who complained that the merchants from Salvador had more capital than those of Rio de Janeiro.[33] Recently, the Brazilian historian João Fragoso documented this discontinuity of the Carioca mercantile enterprise.[34]

In sum, persons of Jewish descent were well represented among the sugar growers on the Atlantic islands and in Brazil. They helped to spread sugar cultivation and its techniques. In Brazil, New Christians shared many norms and values with Old Christians. They moved away from commercial activities as soon as possible in order to climb the social ladder through the more prestigious agricultural activities. However, different

TABLE 23.5 Professions of Partners of Carioca Female New Christians Prosecuted by the Inquisition, 1700–1749

Profession	Number of People	Percentage
Agriculture (total)	89	51
Sugar mill owner	25	14
Sugar cane grower	31	18
Sugar mill employee	2	1
Farmer (general)	31	18
Commerce (total)	41	23
Merchant	2	1
Trader	22	12
Commercial (general)	17	10
Professional (total)	46	26
Official	3	2
Artisan	6	3
Other urban professions	37	21
Total	176	100

Source: Anita Novinsky, *Inquisição, Rol dos Culpados.*

areas and eras reveal different patterns. In sixteenth- and seventeenth-century Pernambuco and Bahia, there was a high degree of mobility. Most of the New Christian sugar mill owners of Bahia were Portuguese born; these immigrants appear to have entered quickly into the local elites. In contrast, New Christians born in Brazil owned a substantial number of the sugar mills in Rio de Janeiro. Moreover, they seemed to have created an exclusive elite through intermarriage within a closed circle. However, even though New Christians successfully achieved social mobility and accommodated to Old Christian norms and values, this did not completely free them from prosecution.

The prosecution of New Christians was strongly motivated by political and economic factors. New Christians' adaptation to local society was therefore no guarantee against Inquisitorial arrests. New Christians had to obscure their Sephardic ancestry by seeking offices, through membership in religious and military orders, and even as informants for the Inquisition. These were all positions that could only be obtained by Old Christians.

Inquisitorial prosecutions were clustered in specific areas and eras. Most Inquisition visits to Brazil and the Atlantic islands took place when Portugal was ruled by Spanish kings, the so-called "Babylonian Captivity" (1580–1640), especially in the 1590s and 1610s. The same occurred in Pernambuco, but hardly any New Christians were prosecuted in this area during the eighteenth century, even though the Inquisition did bring many New Christians from the neighboring captaincy of Paraíba to Lisbon for interrogation.[35] In Bahia, the waves of prosecution were more political than religious in nature, depending on circumstances such as the Dutch invasion of northeast Brazil. One historian has even suggested that they were used to whitewash the clergy's failure to oppose the Dutch invasion after the Dutch were on the defensive in the 1640s.[36]

Political circumstances were most obviously a background to the prosecutions in Rio de Janeiro. Most of the New Christians were incarcerated in the 1710s. Indeed, the Inquisitorial activities were so strongly felt that the French consul to Lisbon remarked in 1714 that the amount of sugar from the Rio de Janeiro fleet had declined dramatically as a consequence of their zealous activities.[37] In the 1710s, a turbulent political decade from both a local and international point of view, Rio de Janeiro survived two invasions by the French, during the second of which the city was effectively ransacked. By that time, the Portuguese king, fearing foreign infiltration of the mining districts, had instituted a policy calling for expulsion of all foreigners from Brazil.[38] Moreover, the first two decades of the eighteenth century displayed constant bickering between ecclesiastical and civil authorities, leading to murders, arrests, suspensions, judicial inquiries, and numerous complaints.[39] The government of Rio de Janeiro, a city strongly influenced by the gold rush, was unstable and seriously challenged, a situation that lasted until Gomes Freire de Andrade's governorship in the 1730s. Although New Christians were officially banned from holding any administrative position, in practice they did. Manoel Correa Vasques, a New Christian, was the judge of the customs, a powerful position in the Carioca administration; he had to sail to Lisbon in order to clear himself of any suspicion of Judaizing.[40] In 1709, one member of the Municipal Council was dismissed for professing the Jewish faith.[41] The presence of New Christians on the Municipal Council was to be expected. They made up a major part of the landed elites in Rio de Janeiro and were therefore identified with the office that promoted the interests of sugar planters.[42]

Local accusations against New Christians were more economically based. Stephen Fortune has argued that British merchants on Barbados and Jamaica petitioned against the presence of Jewish colleagues as soon as they became competitors.[43] In an initial stage, Jews were seen as a powerful stimulus to the economy and invited to the territories. Later, they were persecuted so that British traders might reap economic rewards. Portuguese policies against Jews and New Christians showed similar ambivalence. New Christians were accepted insofar as they could contribute substantially to the Portuguese and Brazilian economies. Thus, Spanish Jews were allowed to settle in the Portuguese territories in 1492 (as well as in the Atlantic islands) and to contribute to the Brazilian Commercial Company in 1649, aiding the Portuguese in their fight against the Dutch. Despite this degree of tolerance, however, New Christians remained suspect to the Portuguese: former Jews were not to be trusted. If economic competition became tense, New Christians were often denounced for secretly professing the Jewish faith, as the cases of Cape Verde, São Tomé, and Dutch Brazil have already shown.[44] In contrast, when politicians sought to stimulate commerce, they raised voices to welcome Jews back with a grant of religious freedom.[45]

As a consequence of this persecution, settlers of Jewish descent sought, and often managed, to become integrated into local society. Social status—the display of wealth rather than wealth itself—brought the greatest personal advantages for New and Old Christians alike. New Christians' involvement in the cultivation of sugar was substantial, but their success was enduring when they not only accommodated to the Luso-Brazilian norms, but also denied their Jewish background. As the Brazilian historian Evaldo Cabral de Mello has demonstrated in the case of Pernambuco, this was exactly what the sugar elites did.[46] It is telling that after 1771, when the Portuguese crown formally abolished the legal distinction between New and Old Christians, the number of Inquisition informants (*familiares*) in Brazil remained quite substantial.[47] Brazilian society was flexible and incorporated New Christians if they had acquired enough status and publicly denied their Jewish background. Even though Portuguese authorities went to great lengths to prove that a person was really pure of blood, Brazilian families were able to manipulate their genealogies, thereby officially changing a New Christian into an Old Christian upon entering the ranks of the elite.[48]

Acquisition of social status, accommodation to local society, and denial of Jewish ancestry were the three steps that New Christians had to take to avoid Inquisitorial prosecution. Portuguese inhabitants of the tropics accepted this integration because they still retained the power to co-opt powerful New Christians once they had complied with their unwritten standards. Conveniently, legal concepts such as "race" and "Jewishness" were negotiable. Thus, for "mulatto" we can read "New Christian" in the following famous words spoken by a Pernambucan man of color to an English settler (about a mulatto sea captain): "He used to be a mulatto, but he isn't any more. How can a member of the elite be a mulatto?"[49] Members of the elite were by definition Old Christians— even if they weren't.

Notes

I would like to thank Norman Fiering, John J. McCusker, Dirk Bönker, and Natalie Zacek for their comments, and Jennifer Curtis Gage for her help with my English.

1. See Philip D. Curtin, *The Rise and Fall of the Plantation Complex: Essays in Atlantic History* (Cambridge, 1990).
2. António José Saraiva, *Inquisição e Cristãos-Novos* (Lisbon, 1969), 68–71.
3. On the spread of sugar cultivation, see Noel Deerr, *The History of Sugar*, vol. 1 (London, 1949).
4. Virginia Rau and Jorge Borges de Macedo, *O Açucar da Madeira nos Fins do Século XV. Problemas de Produção e Comércio* (Funchal, 1962), 11.
5. José Manuel Azevedo e Silva, *A Madeira e a Construcção do Mundo Atlântico (Séculos XV–XVII)*, vol. 1 (Funchal, 1995), 404–6.
6. Rau and Macedo, *O Açucar da Madeira*, 23.
7. Azevedo e Silva, *A Madeira e a Construcção*, vol. 2, 998–991; for the Inquisition in the Atlantic islands, see José Gonçalves Salvador, *Os Cristãos-Novos e o Comércio no Atlântico Meridorial (Com Enfoque nas Capitanias do Sul 1530–1680)* (São Paulo, 1978), 246–51.
8. On sugar in São Tomé, see Robert Garfield, *A History of São Tomé Island 1470–1655: The Key to Guinea* (San Francisco, 1992), chap. 4.
9. Robert Garfield, "A Forgotten Fragment of the Diaspora: The Jews of the São Tomé Island," in *The Expulsion of the Jews, 1492 and After*, ed. Raymond B. Waddington and Arthur H. Williamson (New York, 1994), 73–87.
10. There was some debate about the establishment of the Inquisition. See Royal Letters to Inquisitor General, 22 July 1621 and 8 June 1623, in *A Inquisição em Portugal. Séculos XVI–XVII—Período Filipino*, ed. Isaías Rosa Pereira (Lisbon, 1993), 117, 129–30.
11. Anita Novinsky, *Inquisição, Rol dos Culpados, Fontes para a História do Brasil (Século XVIII)* (Rio de Janeiro, 1992).
12. Memorandum, 1803, Arquivo Histórico Ultramarino [A.H.U.] (Lisbon), Rio de Janeiro, papeis avulsos não catalogados [p.a.n.c.], caixa 204, doc. 9. "Que o Emigrado Europeo da mais humilde classe, depois que sahe do Reino, nunca mais pega no Arado, nem na Enchada."
13. Charles R. Boxer, *The Portuguese Seaborne Empire 1415–1825* (London, 1969), 318–19. For the British case, see, David Hancock, *Citizens of the World: London Merchants and the Integration of the British Atlantic Community, 1735–1785* (Cambridge, 1995), chap. 9.

14. See Catherine Lugar, "Merchants," in *Cities and Society in Colonial Latin America*, ed. Louisa S. Hoberman and Susan M. Socolow (Albuquerque, N.M., 1986), 47–76; Rae Flory and David Grant Smith, "Bahian Merchants and Planters in the Seventeenth and Early Eighteenth Centuries," *Hispanic American Historical Review* 58(4) (1978): 571–94; Susan M. Socolow, *The Merchants of Buenos Aires: Family and Commerce* (Cambridge, 1978).
15. Flory and Smith, "Bahian Merchants and Planters," 575; Catharine Lugar gave an estimate of 80 percent for late eighteenth-century Salvador in "The Merchant Community of Salvador, Bahia, 1780–1830," (Ph.D. diss., State University of New York at Stony Brook, 1980), 55.
16. Flory and Smith, "Bahian Merchants and Planters," 578.
17. João L. R. Fragoso, *Homens da Grossa Ventura: Acumulação e Hierarchia na Praça Mercantil do Rio de Janeiro (1790–1830)* (Rio de Janeiro, 1992), 179–98.
18. Stuart B. Schwartz, *Sugar Plantations in the Formation of Brazilian Society, Bahia 1550–1835* (Cambridge, 1985), 218–41.
19. José António Gonsalves de Mello, *Gente da Nação: Cristão Novos e Judeus em Pernambuco, 1542–1654* (Recife, 1989), chap. 2.
20. Daniel M. Swetschinski, "The Portuguese Jewish Merchants of Seventeenth-Century Amsterdam: A Social Profile," (Ph.D. diss., Brandeis University, 1980), 219–23.
21. J. J. Reesse, *De Suikerhandel van Amsterdam van het Begin der 17de Eeuw tot 1813* (Haarlem, 1908), chap. 6.
22. The major work in English on this topic is still Charles R. Boxer, *The Dutch in Brazil, 1624–1654* (Oxford, 1957). For an overview of Jews in Brazil until 1654, see Arnold Wiznitzer, *Jews in Colonial Brazil* (New York, 1960).
23. Gonsalves de Mello, *Gente da Nação*, chaps. 1 and 2.
24. Frans Leonard Schalkwijk, *Igreja e Estado no Brasil Holandês 1630–1654* (Recife, 1986), 369.
25. Gonsalves de Mello, *Gente da Nação*, 232.
26. Ibid., 7–9.
27. David G. Smith, "The Mercantile Class of Portugal and Brazil in the Seventeenth Century: A Socioeconomic Study of the Merchants of Lisbon and Bahia," (Ph.D. diss., University of Texas at Austin, 1975), 280–81.
28. Regimento of Tomé de Souza in Ignacio Accioli de Cerqueira e Silva, *Memórias Históricas e Políticas da Provincia da Bahia*, ed. Braz do Amaral, vol. 1, 2nd ed. (Salvador, Bahia, 1919), 266, § 11.
29. Schwartz, *Sugar Plantations*, 265.
30. Novinsky, *Cristãos Novos na Bahia*, 176; Flory, "Bahian Society," 97.
31. For a comparison between Salvador and Rio de Janeiro, see A. J. R. Russell-Wood, "Ports of Colonial Brazil," in *Atlantic Port Cities: Economy, Culture and Society in the Atlantic World, 1650–1850*, ed. Franklin W. Knight and Peggy K. Liss (Knoxville, Tenn., 1991), 196–239. For an estimate of the New Christians in seventeenth-century Rio de Janeiro, see José Gonçalves Salvador, *Os Cristãos-Novos, Povoamento e Conquista do Solo Brasileiro (1530–1680)* (São Paulo, 1976), 62–64.
32. According to Antonil (1711), there were 136 sugar mills, while Rocha Pitta (1730) mentioned the number of 101. André João Antonil, *Cultura e Opulência das Drogas e Minas*, ed. Andrée Mansuy (Paris, 1965), 274 and 274n. 1. For the activities of the Inquisition in Rio de Janeiro, see Alberto Dines, *Vínculos do Fogo, António José da Silva, o Judeu e Outras Histórias da Inquisição em Portugal e no Brasil* (São Paulo, 1992); Lina Gorenstein Ferreira da Silva, *Heréticos e Impuros, a Inquisição e os Cristãos-Novos no Rio de Janeiro— Século XVIII* (Rio de Janeiro, 1995).
33. See, for instance, Larissa V. Brown, "Internal Commerce in a Colonial Economy: Rio de Janeiro and Its Hinterland, 1790–1822," (Ph.D. diss., University of Virginia, 1986), 577; Dauril Alden, *Royal Government in Colonial Brazil: With a Special Reference to the Administration of the Marquis of Lavradio, Viceroy, 1769–1779* (Berkeley and Los Angeles, 1968), 381–82. For a description of Luso-Brazilian slave traders, see Joseph C. Miller, "A Marginal Institution on the Margin of the Atlantic System: The Portuguese Southern

Atlantic Slave Trade in the Eighteenth Century," in *Slavery and the Rise of the Atlantic System*, ed. Barbara L. Solow (Cambridge, 1991), 120–51.

34. Fragoso, *Homens da Grossa Ventura*, 179–98.

35. Novinsky, *Inquisição. Rol dos Culpados*.

36. Stuart B. Schwartz, "The Voyage of the Vassals: Royal Power, Noble Obligations, and Merchant Capital before the Portuguese Restoration of Independence, 1624–1640," *American Historical Review* 96(3) (1991):735–62. For the Bahia prosecutions, see Novinsky, *Cristãos Novos na Bahia*; see also Sonia A. Siqueira, *A Inquisição Portuguesa e a Sociedade Colonial* (São Paulo, 1978), 191–93.

37. Dispatch Du Verger to French secretary of state, 22 October 1714, Archives Nationales Paris, Affaires Étrangeres, B/I/653, fl.178r–181v.

38. Manoel S. Cardozo, "The Brazilian Gold Rush," *The Americas* 3 (1946):137–60; Ernst Pijning, "Passive Resistance: Portuguese Diplomacy of Contraband Trade During King John V's Reign (1706–1750)," *Arquipélago-História*, 2nd series, 2 (1997):171–91.

39. See, for instance, dispatch Juiz de Fora to king, 19 December 1707, A.H.U., Rio de Janeiro, papeis avulsos catalogados [p.a.c.] 3051; idem to idem, 2 February 1708, A.H.U., Rio de Janeiro, p.a.c., 3164–3197; Consultation Overseas Council, 2 February 1709, A.H.U., Rio de Janeiro, p.a.c., 3145; idem, 4 November 1715, A.H.U., Rio de Janeiro, p.a.c., 3434–3436; idem. 27 August 1716, A.H.U., códice 233, fl.103r–105r.

40. Dispatch Manoel Correa Vasques to king, 24 November 1722, A.H.U., Rio de Janeiro, p.a.n.c., caixa 13, doc. 22.

41. Representation Municipal Council to king, 26 June 1709, A.H.U., Rio de Janeiro, p.a.n.c., caixa 8, doc. 39.

42. See, for instance, Representation of Municipal Council to king, 6 November 1766, A.H.U., Rio de Janeiro, p.a.n.c., caixa 86, doc. 37. Anita Novinsky observed the same for seventeenth-century Salvador, where quite a few New Christians condemned by the Inquisition had served in the Municipal Council (Novinsky, *Cristãos Novos na Bahia*, 84–87).

43. Stephen A. Fortune, *Merchants and Jews: The Struggle for British West Indian Commerce, 1650–1750* (Gainesville, Fla., 1984).

44. Luís de Albuquêrque and Maria Emília Madeira Santos, eds., *História Geral de Cabo Verde*, vol. 1 (Lisbon, 1991), 169; Gonsalves de Mello, *Gente da Nação*, chap. 3; Schalkwijk, *A Igreja*, 376–77; Garfield, "A Forgotten Fragment."

45. See, for example, Dom Luís da Cunha, *Instrucções Inéditas de Dom Luís da Cunha a Marco António de Azevedo Coutinho*, ed. Pedro de Azevedo (Coimbra, 1929), 98–99; Letter A. Castres to Mr. Amayrant, 26 June 1753, Public Record Office, State Papers Portugal 89, vol. 48, fl.149r–152v; "Plano Geral de Comércio para o Reyno de Portugal," [1767], British Library, Egerton 528, fl.137r–223r; Domingos Vandelli, "Memória sobre a Entrada dos Judeus em Portugal," and "Memória II sobre os Judeus," in *Aritmética Política, Economia e Finanças*, ed. José Vicente Serrão (Lisbon, 1994), 235–40; Daniel M. Swetschinski, "Conflict and Opportunity in 'Europe's Other Sea': The Adventure of Caribbean Jewish Settlement," *American Jewish History* 72 (1982):212–13.

46. Evaldo Cabral de Mello, *O Nome e o Sangue. Uma Fraude Genealógica no Pernambuco Colonial* (São Paulo, 1989).

47. Francisco Bethencourt, *História das Inquisições, Portugal, Espanha e Itália* (Lisbon, 1994), 129.

48. Cabral de Mello, *O Nome e o Sangue*, passim.

49. Henry Koster, *Travels in Brazil in the Years from 1809 to 1815*, vol. 2 (Philadelphia, 1817), 175–76.

– Chapter 24 –

THE JEWISH MOMENT AND THE TWO EXPANSION SYSTEM S IN THE ATLANTIC, 1580–1650

Pieter Emmer

Introduction

WHY DID EUROPE EXPAND? Was it because the smallest of the continents had developed so many dynamic and innovative elements
that it had to spill over? Or was it the other way around—that the process
of rapid innovation and competition pushed out those who could not
keep pace with the developments at home, and who by moving overseas
hoped to re-create the world they had lost in Europe?[1]

To my mind there are many reasons to support the view that the
European expansion contained both progressive and regressive elements.
In fact, it is possible to argue that there came to exist two expansion systems, one dominated by the Iberians and one dominated by Northwest
Europeans, mainly the British, French, and Dutch. In the Iberian, or first,
expansion system, the conservative elements dominated the process,
while in the second expansion system, the innovative elements gained
the upper hand.

I want to consider here various factors that were part of both expansion systems, and to stress that neither of the two expansion systems could
have grown had it not been for the activities of Jews, crypto-Jews and New
Christians, who played a distinct role in both systems. This group constituted the innovative element in the Iberian system of overseas expansion, and after 1580 they were instrumental in transferring the know-how
and the techniques of innovation—indeed, the positive attitude toward

discovery—to the second system. However, after around 1650 the Jewish moment in the expansion of Europe had passed. The Jews had been expelled or had moved from the Iberian world and thus could not oppose the conservative tendencies of the first expansion system. Exactly the opposite development ended the role of the Jews as founding innovators of the second expansion system. In Northwest Europe the innovative participation of Jewish intercontinental settlers, traders, and investors was quickly dwarfed by that of their gentile counterparts. The Jews remained relatively important as traders and planters in the West Indies, but their family networks could no longer compete with the rapidly increasing number of non-Jewish merchants, private firms, and companies operating outside Europe.

In the first section of this chapter, the two expansion systems are described. In the second section, the special link between the Jews and the system of Iberian commerce and colonization is examined. In the third section, the construction of the second expansion system is considered, as well as the vital role of Jews in the various transfers between the two systems. In the last paragraphs, we look at the aftermath of the Jewish moment in the expansion of Europe.

The Two Expansion Systems

The Iberians created a system of overseas trade and settlements that was novel at the beginning, but which soon turned out to be predominantly conservative, i.e. characterized by stagnant economic growth and relatively few geo-political and demographic changes. In Africa and Asia, the first expansion system only established trading forts. Yet, the global web of trading positions was in itself an innovation, which offered wealthy European consumers a vast array of new Asian and African goods. Neither Spain nor Portugal, however, was able to exert much influence on the production of these products. They could not alter the production process, nor were they able to create important industries at home to process semi-finished products from overseas. With the end of the virtual Iberian monopoly on interoceanic trade, which had been in force for more than a century after 1500, the second expansion system developed. The new system saw the installation of a similar network of trading posts in Africa and Asia. This competition brought stagnation and decline to the Iberians. Part of that stagnation, no doubt, could be blamed on the papal treaty that divided the non-European world between the Spanish and Portuguese, precluding competition between them, for competition became the driving force behind the growth of the second expansion system.

A similar division of spheres of influence occurred in the New World, where most conquests were Spanish and only Brazil was in the hands of the Portuguese. In the Americas, the Iberians went far beyond establishing trading posts, creating settlements soon after initial contacts; however, few of these settlements in Spanish America were dynamic. Their agricultural sector was geared to subsistence farming, and production for export was limited. The main export commodity of Spanish America was precious metal, and even that sector of the economy did not show continued growth, for over time, the silver and gold deposits in the New World became more expensive to mine.[2]

That leaves us with the only truly dynamic sector of the colonial New World in this period: the plantation belt of Brazil, which produced sugar for the world market. It was not difficult to increase the amount of land available for the production of sugar since the owners, the Amerindians, could be removed either by treaty or by war at no great cost. Moreover, the importation of machinery and "labor in the cane" could take place in increasing quantities without much restraint. All this suggested that Brazil would become a booming producer of plantation cash crops in ever increasing quantities. In fact, that is what happened—at least until the middle of the seventeenth century. It must be noted that the early growth of the Brazilian plantation economy could not have taken place without the contribution of New Christians who had emigrated from the Iberian Peninsula and without the aid of investors, traders, and shipping firms from Northwest Europe.[3]

The overseas expansion of the British, French, and Dutch got under way a century after the Iberians had started the process. They may have been late, but as soon as their ships crossed the oceans, the impact of the second wave of discoveries, conquests, and settlements was dramatic. True, in Africa and Asia the Northwest Europeans could do little more than create trading establishments, for their immunity from tropical disease was perhaps even less than that of the Iberians. In the New World, however, the Northwest Europeans were able to duplicate the Iberian policy of founding settlement colonies. As in Spanish America, the settlers in British, French, and Dutch North America were mainly interested in subsistence farming and interregional trade—with the exception of New England, which was able to develop transoceanic trading to an extent that surpassed the volume of overseas trading generated by the merchant communities of Buenos Aires and Rio de Janeiro. In addition to trade and settlement, the Northwest Europeans also developed a plantation zone, situated in the southeast of North America and in the Caribbean. At first glance, the Northwest Europeans might seem only to have replicated the first expansion system.[4]

That conclusion, however, would be wrong. On the surface, the trading networks of the first and second systems in Africa and Asia were similar, but in reality there was a great quantitative difference, for the British, the French, and the Dutch sent many more ships and traded in much larger quantities than the Iberians. Great differences—social, economic, and religious—can also be observed between the two systems with regard to the settlement of colonies. In many of the Iberian colonies the Roman Catholic Church had more political power and influence than it possessed even in Spain and Portugal. This also applied to French North America, but much less so to the French Caribbean. In the settlement colonies of the second expansion system, on the other hand, the competing influence of both official and dissenting Churches of Northwest Europe prevented an analogous situation in which a single religious group would virtually exclude all others. Consequently, British and Dutch North America became a haven for a variety of religious refugees from Europe. In the same fashion, the economic and social make-up of the settlers in North America did not stimulate the creation of large *haciendas* with their web of semi-feudal relations, incorporating a substantial Amerindian element. In North America, differences in income, status, and wealth were smaller than in colonial South America, which explains why economic growth in the settlement colonies of the second system was more rapid than in those of the first system. Particular attention should be paid, also, to the different ways in which immigration was organized. In the case of economic expansion, the employers of colonial North America drew labor from the market of mobile proletarian labor in Northwest Europe. Neither Spain nor Portugal had such a labor market.[5]

The economic differences between the first and second expansion systems can best be observed in the distinct plantation belts of Brazil and the Caribbean. From the beginning to the middle of the nineteenth century, when slavery was abolished, the Caribbean and North American cash crop plantations showed unrivaled economic growth. These plantations can be compared with the oil-exporting states of the Middle East today. In comparison, the growth of the Brazilian cash crop sector was much slower and certainly much more uneven. The same discrepancy is evident between the export sectors of the Spanish and North American economies. In both the Portuguese and Spanish cases, non-Iberian investors, merchants, and shipping firms played an important if not a dominant role. At times, it even seemed as if the export sector of the first expansion system had become a function of the second one.[6]

The origins of this massive commercial hemorrhaging of the first expansion system go back to the emigration of the Jews and New Christians from the Iberian Peninsula. In order to survive, these exiles and emigrants took their commercial know-how, their connections and family ties, and their international language skills to the port cities of the second system, to commercial centers such as Bayonne, Bordeaux, Amsterdam, London, and Hamburg. By alienating the Jews, crypto-Jews, and New Christians, the trading sector of Spain and Portugal appears to have hurt itself badly, much more so than the French mercantile and professional sectors were damaged after the expulsion of the Huguenots a century later.[7]

The Jews and the First Expansion System

An Iberian venture into the exploration of the world might have followed naturally from the *reconquista* of the peninsula. Because Spain and Portugal were not among the premier trading nations in Europe, this development did not take place. The Italian city-states, not Spain and Portugal, were the dominant shippers of inter-European trade. After 1492, they continued their commercial ventures behind Spanish and Portuguese fronts. In fact, the Spanish and Portuguese nobility seemed to be interested only in the power and politics of the expansion movement, not in its commercial opportunities.[8]

In the course of the fifteenth century, the Genoese lost their commercial dominance as the bulk of European trade shifted from the Mediterranean to the Atlantic, yet Spain itself was unable to fill the gap. Surely, many port cities stimulated the rise of a group of Spanish merchants and entrepreneurs, but their number and their abilities always fell short of what was required. Throughout the history of Spain, non-Spanish merchants dominated the most dynamic sectors of its trade, commerce, and finance, both inside and outside Europe. The actual development of commercial and financial connections with Spanish America is a case in point. On paper, the Spanish merchants had everything under control. Once or twice a year, a convoy of ships (*flotas*) would sail to the New World carrying products as ordered by the colonists, while on the return voyage the Spanish ships would carry precious metals and some other high-value products. Every effort was made to exclude competition. Unfortunately for the Spanish merchants, the export sector of their New World economy was far more dynamic than the *flota* system allowed for.

The production of the silver mines, for example, could be increased only when more labor became available. Since the Spanish were unable to import more mobile labor from the metropolis by instituting a system of indentured labor, the only alternative was the importation of African slaves. The Spanish commercial community, however, never succeeded in developing a slave trade of its own. As a result, the central agency in charge of the commercial connections between Spain and Spanish America (the *Casa de Contratación* in Seville) had to arrange for foreigners to provide their colonies with slaves, but these contracts were based on the demand for slaves as recorded in past years and could not be continually adjusted when suddenly more slaves were needed. As a result, large numbers of slaves were smuggled in by non-Spanish slave suppliers.[9]

Similarly, major quantities of Spanish American exports "leaked" away to non-Spanish destinations in exchange for these very imports that Spanish manufacturers could not provide. It seems that neither the Spanish government nor the Spanish mercantile elite invested the profits from its American colonies in ways that would boost the productive capacities of the metropolis. Most of the gold and silver from America was consumed in an attempt to prevent the decline of Spain's military position in Europe, notably in Italy and Flanders.[10]

Portugal, on the other hand, seems to have reacted much more adequately to the commercial challenges of its overseas expansion, at least until 1600. The monarchy and nobility in Portugal were no less unsympathetic to trade and commerce than was Spain. However, unlike Spain, Portugal had not expelled its Jews as early as 1492, and during the sixteenth century the Portuguese Jews (now converted to Christianity, at least nominally) together with merchants from Italy were the driving force behind the foundation of a worldwide Portuguese trading network. Of course, we should keep in mind that this trading network was rather limited in scope and volume. The Portuguese had only a few strongholds in Asia and Africa, and much of their "trade" consisted of looting the ships of Arabs, Chinese, and Indian traders. Moreover, the initial phase of Portuguese exploitation of Brazil was also very modest and did not require much investment in labor and equipment—until the beginning of sugar cultivation after the middle of the sixteenth century.[11]

Yet there was a Portuguese trade empire in the making, and the Jews and New Christians played an important if not dominant role in it. Some historians even claim that all merchants in Portugal were of Jewish origin since the contemporary sources use *homens de negócio* synonymously with *Cristãos novos* and *conversos*. Others estimate that about one-third of all merchants in Portugal were of Jewish descent. Even the king of Spain at the time seemed to have equated Portuguese merchants and financiers with New Christians, since he hesitated to ask them for help in financing his wars.[12]

The dominant New Christian and crypto-Jewish presence in Portuguese commerce came to an abrupt end toward the latter part of the sixteenth century when Portugal began to persecute its baptized Jews and recent converts from Judaism. The Inquisition had been active in Portugal since 1547, but its actions became more severe once the king of Spain, Philip II, also became the king of Portugal. The results of this religious cleansing were disastrous: "The main change between the mid-sixteenth century and the mid-eighteenth century was that the Portuguese merchants had disappeared as a commercial force."[13] The Portuguese New Christians took up residence first in the colonies such as Angola and Brazil and, when that became difficult or impossible, in the port cities of Italy, France, the Low Countries, England, and in some Hanseatic cities. The dispersion of New Christian families to Madeira, São Tomé, Angola, Brazil, and the trading cities of Northwest Europe turned out to be a commercial blessing in disguise. The diaspora of the New Christians coincided with the development of the second Atlantic system of trade and settlement, and the New Christians (in some cases returning to Judaism) were the first to exploit the new economic opportunities by transferring an important percentage of the trade in goods and slaves between Portugal and West Africa and Angola; the production, transport, and sale of cash crops from Brazil and the slave trade between Africa and the New World to the second system.[14]

Why did Portugal deliberately shoot itself in the foot by virtually expelling its commercial class? The answer is that Portugal during the ancien régime was a very religious country, and the king and the nobility could do little to stop the policies of the Catholic Church. The Church in Portugal controlled about a third of all economic activities. In Lisbon alone there were five thousand to six thousand begging friars. Within the Catholic Church, the Inquisition had a large degree of autonomy. Its victims had to surrender all their assets, which the Inquisition used to find more victims. Many Portuguese merchants disappeared without a trace into this vortex, because the Inquisition knew that there were many crypto-Jews among the New Christian mercantile groups and that they usually possessed considerable wealth. The Inquisition tended to stifle *all* trade, not only that of vulnerable merchants. Credit extended to Portuguese merchants could not be retrieved if the debtor had been put in prison by the Inquisition. Hence non-Portuguese merchants became reluctant to do business with their Portuguese counterparts.[15]

Of course, there is debate about the causes of Portugal's decline, not all of which were directly related to the persecution of New Christians. It has been pointed out that the profits Portugal derived from non-European trade were bound to decline as soon as the Dutch, the French, and the British ended the Iberian monopoly. It has also been suggested that the Portuguese traders would have lost ground even had the New Christians remained because these merchants had only family networks to rely on, which were not capable of reaching the same level of achievement as that of the overseas trading companies of Northwest Europe.[16]

Despite these explanations, there can be no doubt that the root cause of Portugal's economic decline was the emigration of its merchant class, the intimidation of those merchants who remained, and the absence of an established class of manufacturers. Many of these same causes also apply to Spain. Both countries were monolithically Catholic and, after the departure of the Jews and their descendants, did not even have the advantage of a "Huguenot challenge," as had France. No wonder that later, during the seventeenth century, some Portuguese pamphleteers pleaded for the return of the expelled *Cristãos novos*, but it was too late. "Portugal, awash in gold, knew itself to be poor because it had to pay out that same gold to England and other industrial nations in order to feed and cloth its own inhabitants with foreign products, traded by foreign merchants and conveyed in foreign ships."[17]

The Jews and the Second Expansion System

In view of the disastrously anti-commercial policies of the Spanish and the Portuguese governments, it seems strange that it took the countries of

Northwest Europe so long to break the monopoly of trade and colonization in the overseas world; however, neither France nor England had its
own house in order. It was the Dutch who took the lead in the first global
war to break the Iberian hold on Asia, Africa, and the Americas.

How did the Dutch become a world power (albeit for only half a
century) between 1600 and 1650? It was as though the whole country
turned into one gigantic shipyard. Merchants abounded, sending ships
everywhere in order to buy and sell. Industries abounded, although at
that time there was only small-scale manufacturing rather than the
large-scale factories we have known since the Industrial Revolution.
How were the Dutch able to become the center of the world? Surely,
Great Britain, with more space and double the population, or France,
with six times the population of Holland, both had a greater chance of
becoming world powers before that small, swampy area on the shores of
the North Sea.

There are several reasons why the Netherlands gained ascendancy,
but the three most important factors are: (1) the Dutch internal political
structure, (2) the Dutch position in international politics at the time,
and (3) the superior skills of the Dutch in shipbuilding, manufacturing,
and management.

Although these advantages did help the Dutch to become the world's
most important traders, they were not enough to keep the Dutch in
ascendancy for long. After the middle of the seventeenth century, both
France and England overtook the Netherlands; they simply had more
people, more money, and a much larger internal market. It is remarkable,
in fact, that the Dutch were able to become the leading commercial nation
in the world, even for a relatively brief period.

England and France should have taken the lead in the fight against the
Iberians for mastery of the oceans. England, however, first turned west
toward Ireland, and later had to contend with civil war and regional conflicts as parts of Scotland and Ireland were incorporated into the United
Kingdom. Similarly, religious and regional problems absorbed much of
the energy of the French central government in Paris. That is when the
Dutch saw their chance. They declared themselves to be no longer sub-
servient to the king of Spain, and in so doing they became champions of
local government. Actually, a central Dutch state did not exist; the constituent components—seven independent Dutch states—were the real
powers. Among these states, Holland was the most influential. Within the
state of Holland the cities decided what had to be done. The cities in Holland were all heavily involved in commercial expansion, and the city governments were mainly elected by and composed of merchants.

In addition to their political structure, the organizational talents of
the Dutch should be stressed. The shipping firms were able to offer
freight rates cheaper than their foreign competitors. Dutch merchants
were able to provide an assortment of goods (cloth, spices, grain, and timber, just to name a few) at unbeatable prices. Unlike Spain and Portugal,

and long before they had started to trade globally, the Dutch had worked hard to become the transit market of Europe, in which goods from southern Europe were exchanged against goods from the Baltic. Last, but not least, the Dutch managed to create an environment in which innovations not only could be introduced, but also applied. The decentralized political structure of the Dutch Republic made it very difficult to restrict religious and other freedoms, which was exactly the environment that innovators, many arriving from abroad, needed: a society in which they were able to read and write what they wanted to and where new designs could be tried out for such diverse items as ships, fire extinguishers, limited companies, insurance, drainage pumps (for reclaiming land), cartography, and optical instruments.[18]

A decentralized government made up of merchants, the availability of cheap goods and services, and an innovative environment were the three most important factors that enabled the Netherlands to take the lead in world trade. However, it should be stressed again that none of these factors provided the Dutch with a structural advantage over their competitors. Political decentralization might work wonders for the development of private commerce, but not for the development of empire. In the long run, a strong, central government backed by an efficient tax system would be better able to protect an overseas empire by providing sufficient military and naval power. Between 1620 and 1670 the Dutch merchants were interested in one-time investments and in conquest, but they were not willing to keep paying the large overhead costs necessary to secure their overseas colonies. A diverse market with low prices and cheap freightage was not a great advantage when the number of naval guns and the size of armies decided the fate of overseas colonies.

It was the Portuguese immigrants who taught the Dutch to make money without possessing a large overseas empire. After the immigrants had moved from Portugal, they still profited from the Portuguese empire by developing direct trade with Africa and Brazil, in addition to the triangular trade from their new hometowns. After the Portuguese Jews fled the crumbling Dutch colony in Brazil, they developed an illegal but profitable trade with Spanish America as well as the equally illegal intercolonial trade in the Caribbean. Having imitated the Sephardic example in siphoning off the trade to and from Brazil, the Dutch between 1620 and 1660 temporarily deviated from the Jewish example of trade without empire by conquering part of Brazil, which cost them dearly. After the loss of Brazil, the Dutch once again specialized in trade without empire, and did very well.

Let us return to the first period between 1580 and 1620, when the Dutch started to explore the world beyond Europe and when the New Christians were looking for another foothold in Western Europe after their emigration from the Iberian empire. Amsterdam was an attractive alternative, since the New Christians were granted the right to conduct trade on an equal footing with Dutch merchants and to practice Judaism freely there. However, Portuguese emigrants were well aware of the fact that many other cities were offering similar conditions. Every time the Dutch navy confiscated the ships arriving from Spanish and Portuguese harbors (considered enemy territory), the Portuguese Jews threatened to leave Holland and go elsewhere. Usually, these ships and their cargoes were handed back to the Sephardic merchants of Amsterdam. From the relevant documents it is possible to see that the Amsterdam Sephardic community specialized in the sugar trade. Recent research further allows us to conclude that the Portuguese Jews controlled about 4 to 8 percent of all Dutch trade and about 8 to 16 percent of all Amsterdam trade. The Amsterdam department of the famous Dutch East India Company did not contribute as much trade to the economy of the city as did the Sephardim![19]

The advantage of the Sephardic community in the sugar trade can be explained by the fact that many had first moved to the Atlantic islands and Brazil after their departure from Portugal. The production and trade of sugar were the principal economic activities of the Portuguese colonies. As a case in point, one of the founding members of the Portuguese community in Amsterdam, Jacob Lopes da Costa, should be mentioned. He obtained his wealth during his residence in Brazil as a tax farmer and as the owner of a sugar mill. Another member of the Sephardic community, Duarte Saraiva (1572–1650), was a member of a well-to-do Pernambuco family. He married in Amsterdam in 1598, returned to Brazil in 1612, and went again to Amsterdam during the Dutch occupation of Recife (1630–1654). Some members of the Sephardic community in Amsterdam had resided previously in Hamburg, Portugal, and Venice.[20]

The contracts in the archives of some of the notaries public in Amsterdam show how the Sephardic family network operated. In one such contract between the owner of a ship and an Amsterdam Sephardic merchant, the latter is identified as the charterer of the ship. According to this contract, the chartered ship would leave the port of Dantzig with grain and sail to the southern coast of Spain or to the northern coast of Morocco, where the grain was to be unloaded. From there, the ship would proceed to Tenerife or Cadiz and take in wine, which was to be brought to Bahia in Brazil. From Brazil the ship would sail to Lisbon loaded with sugar. In most of the ports mentioned, a family member of the Amsterdam merchant, or at least a common representative shared by several Sephardic families, would be residing. In the sugar trade, family networks were indispensable, which explains why the Sephardim were able to remain the dominant importers of sugar in Amsterdam until the Dutch conquest of part of Brazil.[21]

The founders of the Dutch West India Company wanted to include the profitable sugar trade with Brazil as part of its monopoly.[22] Of course, the Amsterdam Jews resisted and pleaded to keep their position in the sugar trade to Brazil an exclusive privilege. The cities in North Holland that specialized in the salt trade to the Caribbean were similarly opposed to the inclusion of their trade in the Company's monopoly. In the period before the foundation of the Dutch West India Company, there had been a truce for twelve years (1609–21) between Iberia and Holland. During that time the trade between Brazil and Amsterdam had prospered as never before, so much so that the South American colony seemed to have provided more commercial profits to the Dutch than to its imperial rulers, the Portuguese. Clearly, the incorporation of the trade to Brazil in the West India Company's monopoly could endanger the position of the Sephardic Jews in this trade. In a document dated 1622, the Sephardim of Amsterdam put in a passionate plea to be allowed to retain their particular trade niche. The document begins with a quotation from the 1600 safeguard allowing the Portuguese Jews in the Netherlands to trade with Brazil by way of Portugal. The Jews write that they had conducted trade with Brazil for about forty years, mainly through the Portuguese harbors of Viana and Oporto, as well as Lisbon. This trade had prospered especially during the period of the truce.

> During these 12 years of peace shipping and commerce increased so considerably that more than 10, 12 and even 15 ships were built in this country each year. Those ships brought here by way of Portugal 40, 50 thousands of cases of sugar each year, as well as Brazil wood, ginger, cotton, hides and other goods. We were so successful that during that 12-year period we drove from these waters all the Portuguese caravels that used to carry the sugar. This was caused by the capacity of our ships, so that we could attract half, even two-thirds of this trade to ourselves.[23]

Next the Sephardim described the "profits this province enjoy from this shipping and commerce."

> Building the ships stimulated employment in shipbuilding and shipping through the import of trunks for masts, which were not available in the Netherlands. The Brazil trade also stimulated the export of Dutch merchandise. But most important was the sugar trade itself. It caused the number of sugar refineries in Amsterdam to increase from three to twenty-five in 50 years. Some of the refineries processed 1,500 cases of sugar each year, and the refined product was exported to other countries. At the end of this document the Sephardim emphasized that the Brazil trade was their main domain, not commerce with the East Indies or other areas.[24]

The Jewish share in the export of sugar from Portuguese Brazil to the Netherlands amounted to more than 50 percent. Two-thirds of this trade was in the hands of only twenty-seven Jewish merchants, and their trade niche was severely threatened when the Dutch West India Company launched a series of massive attacks on Portuguese Brazil beginning in 1624. The unobtrusive Jewish penetration of the Brazil sugar trade was replaced by a policy of power politics. The results were disastrous. During the occupation of Pernambuco, the Dutch West India Company was indeed able to obtain sugar from its own colony, but only for a couple of years. The overhead expenses turned the profits of the Brazil trade into a bottomless deficit, and as a result the Dutch West India Company lost its Brazilian possessions again to the Portuguese—without the restoration of the old informal trading networks. In 1674 the Dutch West India Company went bankrupt, which confirmed the wisdom of the Sephardic attempt to steer clear of the Company and preserve its own carefully developed links with Brazil. No wonder relatively few Jewish merchants in Amsterdam invested in the Dutch West India Company.[25]

The conquest of Brazil by the Dutch did offer some new opportunities to the Sephardic community. Large numbers of Portuguese planters and owners of sugar mills fled to the south of Brazil, which remained in Portuguese hands. That abandonment enabled the Dutch as well as Sephardic Jews from Holland to take over Portuguese plantations and sugar mills. Their profits, however, must have been limited, since they lost everything once the Dutch had to surrender the colony in 1654.[26]

The diaspora of about 1,500 Sephardic Jews from Dutch Brazil at the time of the reconquest by Portugal was instrumental in developing a "second Brazil" in the Caribbean. After an initial period during which the European settlers in the Caribbean grew tobacco for export, there was room for change when competition from tobacco growers in Virginia became more intense. Sometime after 1640, the technique of producing sugar was introduced in Barbados, and over time most Caribbean colonies took up producing sugar cane, since the conditions in the region were very favorable. The nucleus of each community of sugar planters in the region was made up of sugar planters from Dutch Brazil, among them an unknown percentage of Sephardim. Other Sephardim settled in the Caribbean to specialize in trade, and the same can be said of those Sephardic exiles who moved from Dutch Brazil to North America. After 1650, however, the Sephardic Jews' contribution to the Atlantic economy was small because their privileged position in the illegal trade to and from Portuguese Brazil had been destroyed.[27]

The End of the Jewish Moment in the Atlantic

After the middle of the seventeenth century, the strategic position of the Sephardim in Atlantic commerce had come to an end. The volume and the complexity of the Atlantic trade began to grow so rapidly that the Jewish share in it was dwarfed. The motor behind this rapid growth in trade was situated in the second expansion system. The plantation belts in North America and in the Caribbean expanded unlike any other region in the Atlantic, as is illustrated by the dramatic increase in the number of slaves exported from Africa to the New World. Between 1600 and 1650, each year on average 7,500 slaves were imported into the New World; between 1650 and 1700, the annual figure averaged 19,400. Jews and

Cristãos novos had played a role in the slave trade before 1650. Their impact was probably at its peak when Sephardic Jews from Portugal moved to Amsterdam and continued their participation in the sugar and slave trades from there. By so doing they taught Dutch merchants how to conduct this trade. However, only non-Jewish Dutch merchants were responsible for the dramatic increase of the slave trade after 1635.[28]

The rapid growth of the Atlantic trade called for new forms of organization. The single Jewish merchant had become a thing of the past, even when he could rely on a network of relations in strategic places. After 1650, the most risky and capital-intensive trades in the Atlantic were executed by trading companies such as the Royal African Company, the Compagnie du Sénégal, and the first and second Dutch West India companies.

Hebrew, Ladino, and Portuguese were no longer required as the linguae francae of the Atlantic, and that advantage of the Sephardic community diminished in value. It was not that another generally accepted language had made the linguistic skill of the Jewish merchant redundant. Exactly the opposite had happened. The creation of multiple trading empires and the commercial compartmentalization of the Atlantic as the result of growth and the policies of mercantilism diminished the need for a lingua franca. After the middle of the seventeenth century, most ships trading in the Atlantic would no longer visit several European ports in order to assemble its cargo. The coast of Africa had been divided into several spheres of influence in which Dutch, French, and English were spoken in addition to pidgin Portuguese. The same applied to the colonies in the New World.

Jewish specialization in finance had also diminished in value. The need for capital in plantation economies in particular had grown so rapidly that most metropolitan firms trading with the plantation belt in the New World were now providing credit and investment capital to the planters. In addition, special investment funds were created allowing metropolitan investors to put their capital into the booming New World ventures.

A good example of the diminishing role of the Jews in the Atlantic economy is provided by the Dutch colony of Suriname. In that colony, the Jews made up a quarter of the planter population. In fact, no country in modern history before the foundation of the state of Israel counted such a high percentage of Jews as Suriname did among its citizens during the plantation period (if one excludes from the total population the black enslaved majority). The Jews were among the first plantation owners in Suriname, and they also constituted the only segment of the white population who remained in Suriname generation after generation and who did not aim to make a fortune solely to return to Europe, as most other whites aspired to do. Over time, however, the Jews became the least successful and indeed the poorest section of the Suriname planter class because they could not keep pace with the growth of the plantation sector in which the number of acres under cultivation, the number of slaves, and the investment in equipment all increased rapidly. At the end of the eighteenth century, the Jewish planters in Suriname were considered to be old-fashioned, backward, and out of step with the new demands and new opportunities (industrialization) of sugar cane production.[29]

The Jews who stayed in the Caribbean and specialized in trade rather than in agriculture, on the other hand, seemed to have fared better. Again, a Dutch colony stands out—the island of Curaçao, which housed one of the oldest Sephardic communities in the West Indies. Curaçao prospered by becoming one of the main exchange centers between the various Caribbean colonies as well as the coastal regions of the Spanish main. Yet it must be stressed again that the majority of the merchants in the Dutch Antilles were not Jewish and that the increase in trade and in the number of merchants over time diminished the relative share of the Sephardim.[30]

* * * *

WHAT SIGNIFICANCE SHOULD BE GIVEN to the Jewish moment in the Atlantic? It seems obvious that the large majority of settlers and slaves moved across the Atlantic only after the Jews had lost their numerically marginal but strategically important position. The Jews were the midwives of the second European expansion system, and that second system in turn was the midwife of the Industrial Revolution (albeit the link is of a qualitative and not a quantitative nature). Around 1750, the American colonies might have been the most rapidly growing market for European goods, but most European goods and services were still consumed in Europe itself. The profits of the plantations and of the Atlantic economy at large could have provided only a minor share of the investments in the nascent industry in Britain; nonetheless, the Atlantic system certainly contributed to the commercial and technological environment in which rapid economic expansion and technical innovation could take place. Seen in this perspective, the Jewish moment in the Atlantic was a steppingstone to the modernization of the world insofar as the Jews mediated the transfer of the innovative elements of the Iberian expansion system to that of Northwest Europe. Jews and Protestants were both religious minorities, but their impact on the making of the modern world was far larger then their numbers would suggest. Max Weber pointed this out regarding the Protestants of nineteenth-century Germany. He could have done the same for the Sephardim of seventeenth-century Western Europe.

Notes

1. G. V. Scammell, *The First Imperial Age: European Overseas Expansion c. 1400–1715* (London, New York, 1989), 51–71.
2. James Lockhart and Stuart B. Schwartz, *Early Latin America and Brazil* (Cambridge, 1983), 151.
3. Stuart B. Schwartz, *Sugar Plantations in the Formation of Brazilian Society, Bahia, 1550–1835* (Cambridge, 1985), 204.
4. John J. McCusker and Russell R. Menard, *The Economy of British America, 1607–1789* (Chapel Hill, N.C., London 1985), 32.
5. Russell R. Menard, "Migration, Ethnicity, and the Rise of an Atlantic Economy: The Re-Peopling of British America, 1600–1790," in *A Century of European Migrations, 1830–1930,* ed. Rudolf J. Vecoli and Suzanne M. Sinke (Urbana, Ill., Chicago, 1991), 58–77; and B. H. Slicher van Bath, "The Absence of White Contract Labour in Spanish America during the Colonial Period," in *Colonialism and Migration: Indentured Labour Before and After Slavery,* ed. P. C. Emmer (Dordrecht, 1986), 19–32.
6. For gaps in the monopoly system of Spanish America, see James Lang, *Conquest and Commerce: Spain and England in the Americas* (New York, 1975), 55–60; and G. V. Scammell, *The World Encompassed: The First European Maritime Empires, c. 800–1600* (London, 1981), 343, 344, 365, 367.
7. James C. Boyajian, *Portuguese Trade in Asia under the Habsburgs, 1580–1640* (Baltimore, London, 1993), 243.
8. Scammell, *The World Encompassed,* 180–83.
9. James A. Rawley, *The Transatlantic Slave Trade* (New York, London, 1981), 51–77.
10. J. H. Elliott, *Imperial Spain, 1469–1716* (Harmondsworth, 1970), 283–91.
11. Scammell, *The World Encompassed,* 240.
12. Maurits Ebben, *Zilver, brood en kogels voor de koning. Kredietverlening door Portugese bankiers aan de Spaanse kroon, 1621–1665* (Leiden, 1996), 110, 111.
13. L. M. E. Shaw, "The Inquisition and the Portuguese Economy," in *Journal of European Economic History* 18(2) (1989):416.
14. Ebben, *Zilver, brood en kogels,* 111–13.
15. Shaw, "The Inquisition," 423.
16. Pieter Emmer and Femme Gaastra, eds., *The Organization of Interoceanic Trade in European Expansion, 1450–1800* (Aldershot, 1996), xvi–xxii.
17. Shaw, "The Inquisition," 416.
18. Jonathan I. Israel, *Dutch Primacy in World Trade, 1585–1740* (Oxford, 1989), 12–37.
19. Odette Vlessing, "The Portuguese-Jewish Merchant Community in Seventeenth-Century Amsterdam," in *Entrepreneurs and Entrepreneurship in Early Modern Times: Merchants and Industrialists within the Orbit of the Dutch Staple Market,* ed. C. Lesger and L. Noordegraaf (The Hague, 1995), 229.
20. Eddy Stols, "Convivências e conivências luso-flamengas na rota do açúcar brasileiro," in *Ler Historia* 32 (1997):119–47; Ernst van den Boogaart, "Los Neerlandeses en el Mundo Commercial Atlántico de la Doble Monarquia Ibérica, 1590–1621," in Ernst van den Boogaart et al., *La Expansion Hollandesa en al Atlántico* (Madrid, 1992), 76–78.
21. Vlessing, "The Portuguese-Jewish Merchant Community," 225, 231–33.
22. Cornelis Ch. Goslinga, *The Dutch in the Caribbean and on the Wild Coast, 1580–1680* (Gainesville, Fla., 1971), 88–93.
23. Vlessing, "The Portuguese-Jewish Merchant Community," 231.
24. Ibid., 231, 232.
25. Jonathan I. Israel, *Empires and Entrepots: The Dutch, the Spanish Monarchy and the Jews, 1585–1713* (London, 1990), 338.
26. José Alexandre Ribemboim, *Senhores de Engenho em Pernambuco Colonial, 1542–1654* (Recife, 1995), 338.

27. Israel, *Empires and Entrepots*, 437–440.
28. Seymour Drescher, "The Role of the Jews in the Transatlantic Slave Trade," in *Immigrants and Minorities* 12(2) (1993):113–25.
29. R. A. J. van Lier, "The Jewish Community in Surinam: A Historical Survey," in *The Jewish Nation in Surinam*, ed. R. Cohen (Amsterdam, 1982), 19–27.
30. Willem Wubbo Klooster, *Illicit Riches: The Dutch Trade in the Caribbean, 1648–1795* (Ph.D. diss., University of Leiden, 1995), 42–44.

PART VII

THE JEWS IN COLONIAL BRITISH AMERICA

– Chapter 25 –

THE JEWS IN BRITISH AMERICA

Jonathan D. Sarna

T HE JEWS IN BRITISH AMERICA" is a topic that could easily consume
many more pages than are available here. To do the topic full justice,
one would need to look not only at the British North American colonies
but also at English Suriname, Barbados, Nevis, and Jamaica, all of which
already had at least some kind of Jewish presence in the second half of
the seventeenth century. In addition to the usual topics—political rights,
economic structure, social and intergroup relations, cultural life, and so
on—one would also want to undertake a detailed comparison between
the condition of Jews in the English colonies and the condition of Jews
back home in the English mother country. Jews were readmitted into
England only in 1655, and began worshipping in public only in 1657. As
a result—and in contrast to what we find in the Dutch colonies—Jews in
British colonies could not look back to the mother country as a model for
how Jews should be treated. Instead, we find Jewish life on both sides of
the Atlantic developing more or less simultaneously. This had important
and relatively unexplored implications both for the Jews and for those
who sought to govern and regulate them.

The more limited topic that I will focus on in this chapter is Jewish
religious life in British America. This is appropriate given the setting in
which this essay was originally presented as a public lecture—the historic
Touro Synagogue in Newport, Rhode Island—and the topic also serves as
something of a corrective to the economic emphasis of so much of the literature concerning this period. Unfortunately, the available data is somewhat skewed, since we know more about Jewish religious life in colonial
New York than anywhere else in British America. Some broader comparisons are possible, however, and there is in any case no reason to believe
that Judaism in New York was sui generis. To the contrary, throughout

British America during our period, Judaism was becoming increasingly distinctive from its European counterpart. This distinctiveness, rooted in the peculiarities of colonial life, set the stage for the better known and more significant transformation of Judaism in the United States that took place following the American Revolution.

From the beginning, religion served as a motivation for Jews who settled in the New World colonies. Following Menasseh ben Israel, many fervently believed that the dispersion of the Jews to all corners of the world was "the hope of Israel," a harbinger of the messianic age. The presumed religious implications of New World settlement are reflected in the revealingly messianic names that many New World synagogues bear: Mikveh (Hope of) Israel (Curaçao and Philadelphia); Shearith (Remnant of) Israel (New York); Nidhe (Dispersed of) Israel (Barbados); Jeshuat (Salvation of) Israel (Newport). Nor should we assume that this is mere lip service to messianic ideas. We know that the Messiah was fervently anticipated by some North American Jews in 1768 and in 1783 on the basis of religious calculations that paralleled Protestant calculations of the same kind. In 1769 we have a remarkable account from the Reverend Ezra Stiles in Newport that during a thunderstorm Jews in his city threw open doors and windows while "singing and repeating prayers ... for meeting Messias." This exotic practice, apparently inspired by the mystical belief that Jews were to be spirited away upon a cloud to Jerusalem, is mentioned by Gershom Scholem, and reflects a custom found in some places in Europe as well at that time.[1]

The defining Jewish symbol of communal religious life and culture in British North America, as elsewhere, was the Torah scroll. Historians generally have not paid sufficient attention to this ritual object; for the most part, they have defined community in terms of institutions, such as when a cemetery was acquired or when a synagogue was established. I would argue, however, that the presence of a Torah scroll is a much more reliable marker of an ongoing Jewish presence, for it created a sense of sacred space, elevating a temporary habitation into a cherished place of holiness and a private home into a hallowed house of prayer. The arrival of a Torah scroll in New Amsterdam in 1655 (brought over from Holland) was a defining moment in the life of the first Jews in that community, while the return of that Torah in 1663 demonstrates that the city's Jewish community had by then scattered. The subsequent reappearance of Torah scrolls in New York under the British signaled that Jewish communal life had been reestablished, and private group worship resumed. Wherever Jews later created communities in British America, as in Savannah, they also brought Torah scrolls with them, or, as was the case in Newport in 1760, they borrowed a Torah from a larger congregation. In smaller eighteenth-century colonial Jewish settlements such as Lancaster and Reading, where Judaism was maintained for years by dedicated laymen without a salaried officiant or a formal synagogue, the Torah scroll functioned similarly as something of a Jewish icon. It embodied the holy presence around which Jewish religious life revolved.[2]

Public worship became available to North American Jews around the turn of the eighteenth century, just about the time that New York's first Quaker Meeting House was erected, and before the Baptists and Catholics had opened churches in the city.[3] For the next 125 years, Shearith Israel dominated Jewish religious life in New York. Indeed, the synagogue and organized Jewish community became one and the same—a synagogue-community—and as such it assumed primary responsibility for preserving and maintaining local Jewish life.

The synagogue-community descended from the *kehillah*, the distinctive form of communal self-government that characterized Jewish life in the Middle Ages. With the advent of modernity, as states consolidated their power over their citizens and individual rights gradually triumphed over corporate or group rights, Jewish communities as corporate political entities came to an end, and in seventeenth-century Western Europe the synagogue became the locus for Jewish self-government. Where multiple synagogues existed, this resulted in communal fragmentation, and in response the Sephardic Jews of Amsterdam in 1638 to 1639 merged their city's synagogues into one, "Kahal Kadosh Talmud Torah." It governed its members much like a church governed its parish, thereby promoting discipline while avoiding the appearance of a Jewish "state within a state." This synagogue-community model, akin to the prevailing Protestant model of the established church, spread quickly and widely, taking hold in Recife, Hamburg, London, the West Indies—and then New York.[4]

The synagogue established in New York, Shearith Israel, was located in a small rented house on Mill Street, today South William Street, but then popularly known as Jews' Alley. The synagogue closely resembled its Old and New World counterparts in assuming responsibility for, and monopolizing, all aspects of Jewish religious life: communal worship, dietary laws, life cycle events, education, philanthropy, ties to Jews around the world, oversight of the cemetery and the ritual bath, even the baking of matzah and the distribution of Passover *haroset* (used as part of the Seder ritual). The synagogue saw itself and was seen by others as *the* representative body of the Jewish community; it acted in the name of all area Jews. In addition, it served as a meeting and gathering place for local Jews, a venue for exchanging "news and tatle."[5]

The advantages of this all-encompassing institution were, from a Jewish point of view, considerable: the synagogue-community proved an efficient means of meeting the needs of an outpost Jewish community. It promoted group solidarity and discipline, evoked a sense of tradition as well as a feeling of kinship toward similarly organized synagogue-communities throughout the Jewish world, and enhanced the chances that even small clusters of Jews, remote from the wellsprings of Jewish learning, could survive from one generation to the next.

Looming large among the values espoused by the synagogue-community throughout British America (and beyond) were tradition and deference. These values had stood Sephardic Jews in good stead for generations and were considered essential to Jewish survival itself. At Shearith Israel, various prayers, including part of the prayer for the government, continued to be recited in Portuguese, and the congregation's original minutes were likewise written in Portuguese (with an English translation), even though only a minority of the members understood that language and most spoke English on a regular basis. Still, Portuguese represented tradition; it was the language of the community's founders and of the Portuguese Jewish "Nation" scattered around the world. (Ladino, or Judeo-Spanish, written in Hebrew letters, was spoken only by the Sephardim of the Ottoman Empire.)[6] In matters of worship, too, Shearith Israel closely conformed to the traditional *minhag* (ritual) as practiced by Portuguese Jews in Europe and the West Indies. Innovations were prohibited; "our duty," Sephardic Jews in England (writing in Portuguese) once explained, is "to imitate our forefathers." On a deeper level, Sephardic Jews believed, as did the Catholics among whom they had for so long lived, that ritual could unite those whom life had dispersed. They wanted a member of their "Nation," the term commonly used to characterize Sephardic Jewry, to feel at home in any Sephardic synagogue anywhere in the world: the same liturgy, the same customs, even the same tunes.[7]

Deference formed part of Sephardic tradition as well. Worshippers expected to submit to the officers and elders of their congregation, which, then and later, were entirely lay dominated. *Yehidim*, generally men of status who materially supported the congregation and subscribed to its rules, made most of the important decisions; they were the equivalent of "communicants" in colonial Protestant churches. The rest of the worshippers, including all of the women, occupied seats but held no authority whatsoever. Within the congregation, as in most religious and political institutions of the day, power was vested in men of means.

Even those without power agreed that disobedience to authority should be punished. In 1760, for example, the congregation severely punished Judah Hays for disobeying the *parnas* (president), although he himself was a significant member.[8] In enforcing discipline through such edicts, Jews were following both the teachings of their ancestors and the practices of their non-Jewish neighbors. Indeed, deference to those in authority and to those who held the largest "stake in society" was accepted by "the bulk of Americans" in the mid-eighteenth century.[9] By contrast, the right to dissent, the right to challenge the leadership in a free election, the right to secede and establish a competing congregation, the right to practice Judaism independently—these were unknown in colonial synagogues. Jews of that time would have viewed such revolutionary ideas as dangerous to Judaism and to the welfare of the Jewish community as a whole—which, of course, helps to explain why the impact of the American Revolution on American Judaism proved so profound.

No Jewish religious authority of any kind in colonial North America possessed sufficient status to challenge the authority of the laity. Neither Shearith Israel nor any of the synagogues subsequently established prior to the Revolution ever hired a *haham* (the Sephardic equivalent of an ordained rabbi), nor did rabbis grace any American pulpit until 1840. London's Sephardic synagogue, by contrast, considered it "necessary and imperative ... to have a Haham," and appointed one in 1664, just seven years after that congregation's founding, to "instruct us and teach the observance of the most Holy Law." In the New World, the Jewish communities of Recife, Curaçao, Suriname, Barbados, and Jamaica all enjoyed the religious leadership of a *haham* at various times in the seventeenth and eighteenth centuries.[10] New York, the "mother" congregation of North American Jews, was the exception; indeed, so far as we know no *haham* was ever employed by any North American colonial congregation. Lack of members and funds partly explain why, but the practice of local Christian churches was probably more important. Only about a fourth of the congregations in the province of New York enjoyed full-time pastors in 1750, and even the Anglicans failed to appoint a bishop to oversee their flock.[11] Jews, therefore, felt no pressure to import a religious authority from abroad. The absence of a professional religious authority did not embarrass them in the eyes of their neighbors. Moreover, the diversity of the North American Jewish community, which by the mid-eighteenth century embraced Sephardim and Ashkenazim from many different locales and was much more diverse Jewishly than Jamaica and Barbados, would have made the task of finding an appropriate *haham* difficult, if not impossible. To compensate, the officiating *hazan* (cantor), in addition to chanting the liturgy, assumed many of the ceremonial functions that a *haham* might otherwise have performed, including, on rare occasions, public speaking.[12]

Colonial mainland American synagogues also differed from their European and West Indies counterparts in their relationship to the state. In Sephardic communities as diverse as those at Bayonne, France, Curaçao and the Virgin Islands, synagogue leaders looked to government to buttress their authority. The leaders of Curaçao's congregation, for example, were constitutionally empowered under various circumstances to seek "the intermediation of the Honorable Governor should all other means fail."[13] In other communities, fear of the state justified extraordinary extensions of Jewish communal power. Concern for "our preservation" led synagogue leaders in London, for example, to demand the right to have "revised and emended" any book written or printed by any local Jew in any language.[14] No such clauses, however, appear in any known American synagogue constitution. In the religiously pluralistic colonial cities where Jews principally settled, local governments (at least in the eighteenth century) extended a great deal of autonomy to churches and synagogues and rarely intervened in their internal affairs. As a result, synagogue leaders, like their church counterparts, found it necessary to fall back upon their own authority. Under ordinary circumstances, they knew, local officials would not step in to help them.

The ultimate authority available to the synagogue-community was the power of the *herem* (excommunication), "the principal means of defining social deviance and of removing from the community wayward members whose actions and behavior offended its values."[15] In the North American colonies, as in eighteenth-century Amsterdam, this punishment was threatened far more often than it was actually invoked, for its effectiveness in a society where Jews were not solely dependent upon one another and where compliance could not be overseen was doubtful. There was, moreover, always the danger that excommunication would backfire and bring the whole Jewish community into disrepute. More commonly, therefore, punishments consisted of fines, denial of synagogue honors, and, most effective of all, threatened exclusion from the Jewish cemetery—punishments limited to the religious sphere and thus parallel to church forms of discipline.

Even these punishments required some degree of communal consensus. The leaders of Shearith Israel found this out the hard way in 1757 when they attempted to crack down on outlying members of the congregation who were known to "dayly violate the principles [of] our holy religion, such as Trading on the Sabbath, Eating of forbidden Meats & other Henious Crimes." Citing Biblical passages, the *adjunta* darkly threatened these wayward members with loss of membership and benefits, including that "when Dead [they] will not be buried according to the manner of our brethren." But six months later, in the face of opposition, they decided to "reconsider." Relying on Isaiah's call to "open the gates" (Isa. 26:2), they welcomed everybody back into the congregation's good graces.[16] Synagogue-communities thus may be said to have patroled "the edges" of irreligious behavior, much as Jon Butler shows New England congregational parishes of the time did. They punished some, a few severely, but let many violations pass without comment. It was more important, they knew, to blazon the possibility of censure than to pursue every accusation.[17]

What really sustained the colonial synagogue-community was not so much discipline as a shared consensus concerning the importance of maintaining Judaism and its central values. Shearith Israel's new Mill Street synagogue, consecrated in 1730, reflected this consensus in its very architecture and design. Never before had North American Jews built (or even owned) a synagogue, so this was their first opportunity to shape the urban landscape. Since the completion of Trinity Church by the Anglicans in 1696, a slew of competing churches had been built in New York City, including a French church, a Dutch church, a Lutheran church, and a Presbyterian church. These opulently designed buildings, with their large spires and towers, had transformed and sacralized the city's religious skyline, displaying the colonists' burgeoning material success for all to see.[18] Jews had likewise achieved material success (the house of Lewis M. Gomez, for example, was assessed at nearly ten times the value of the

Jews' rented house of worship), but the new synagogue building as finally constructed favored tradition over external display. The principal investment was in the interior of the synagogue, designed in classical Sephardic fashion, while keeping the exterior comparatively simple, on the scale of the modest New York churches built by the persecuted Baptists and Quakers. In this, local Jews emulated the pattern of the English Sephardic synagogue Bevis Marks (completed in 1701), and anticipated what the Jews would do in Newport when they built their synagogue in 1763.[19] The architectural message in all three cases was the same—that Jews should practice discretion on the outside by not drawing excessive attention to themselves, while glorying in their faith on the inside, where tradition reigned supreme.

Seating arrangements in the New York and Newport synagogues underscored the power of deference. They mirrored social and gender inequalities within the community and reinforced religious discipline. The congregation assigned a "proper" place to every worshipper, and each seat was assessed a certain membership tax in advance. In New York, members of the wealthy Gomez family thus enjoyed the most prestigious seats and paid the highest assessments. Others paid less and sat much further away from the holy ark. Women, in accordance with Jewish tradition, worshipped apart from men; they sat upstairs in the gallery, far removed from the center of ritual action below. Few women attended synagogue services in Amsterdam, Recife, and London, so there they were free to take any available gallery seat; none was assigned. By contrast, in New York and probably also in Newport, where Jewish women, like their Protestant counterparts, attended public worship much more punctiliously, seats had to be assigned to them on the same basis as for the men. Since the women's section was small, disputes over status and deference abounded—so much so that in New York a special area was eventually reserved just for the elite women of the Gomez clan.[20]

An additional source of tension at Shearith Israel and throughout colonial Judaism—more in North America, as I indicated, than in the Caribbean—stemmed from the ever-growing number of Ashkenazic Jews, immigrants from Central and Eastern Europe whose traditions, background, and world-view diverged markedly from those of the founding Sephardim. In Amsterdam, London, Hamburg, Bordeaux, Suriname, and many other places where Jews lived, Sephardim and Ashkenazim worshipped apart. They formed two Jewish communities, married among themselves, and co-existed uneasily. North American Jews, by contrast, worshipped together, as had also been the case in Recife, with the Sephardim exercising religious and cultural hegemony. This continued to be true in New York, despite the fact that by 1720 Ashkenazim formed a majority of the Jewish population.[21] The fact that the Sephardim came first and enjoyed higher status than the Ashkenazim partly explains this arrangement, but the threat on the part of Curaçao's wealthy Sephardic congregation to stop assisting the New Yorkers unless they agreed not to allow the German Jews "any More Votes nor Authority than they have had hitherto"[22] probably explains more. Nevertheless, Ashkenazim did come to exercise considerable authority within Shearith Israel's new synagogue, serving as officers slightly more often, according to Eli Faber's calculation, than the Sephardim. Jacob Franks, an Ashkenazic Jew, was a perennial leader of the congregation, and Gershom Seixas, its most important and beloved colonial-era *hazan*, was the product of mixed Sephardic-Ashkenazic parentage—as were a growing number of other colonial Jews.[23] Sephardic traditions still held firm, but increasingly it was not Iberian blood ties among kindred members of the "Nation" that buttressed them. Instead, religious ties had become the dominant force among the Jews of diverse origins who worshipped together in New York, and power was slowly shifting to the Ashkenazim.

Synagogue-communities, as they developed in the major cities where Jews lived, bespoke the growing compartmentalization of eighteenth-century Jewish life in British America into Jewish and worldly domains—a distinction unknown to medieval Jews or, for that matter to most European Jews of the day, but characteristic of American Judaism almost from the very beginning. Colonial synagogue-communities did not tax commercial transactions, as synagogues in Amsterdam, London, and Recife did. They did not censor what Jews wrote on the outside, and they did not punish members for deviant personal beliefs or for lapses in individual or business morality. Instead, akin to neighboring churches, they confined their activities to their own sphere, disciplining some religiously wayward congregants with fines and loss of religious privileges, but leaving commercial and civil disputes, even those that pitted one Jew against another, to the general authorities. Some Sephardic Jews went so far as to employ different names in each realm, recalling their former multiple identities as crypto-Jews. The renowned Newport merchant Aaron Lopez, for example, inscribed his business ledgers with his Portuguese baptismal name, Duarte. In the synagogue, he was always known as Aaron.[24]

The problem for early American Jews was that central Jewish observances—maintaining the Sabbath on Saturday, celebrating Jewish holidays in the fall and the spring, and observing the Jewish dietary laws—infringed upon the boundaries that the separation of realms sought so scrupulously to maintain. This engendered painful conflicts between the demands of Jewish law and the norms of the larger secular or Christian society in which Jews moved. Refusing to work on the Jewish Sabbath effectively meant working five days instead of six, since local "blue" laws prohibited work on Sunday, the Christian Sabbath. Jewish holidays similarly conflicted with the workaday world of early America. As for Jewish dietary laws, they made both travel away from home and social interactions outside of Jewish homes both difficult and embarrassing.

Early British American Jews found no easy solutions to these dilemmas. Religious laxity was plentiful, just as Todd Endelman found among English Jews of the time,[25] but there were also those who managed to weave Judaism into the fabric of their daily existence. Indeed, the most striking feature of Jewish ritual life in the colonial period was its diversity—a feature that continued to characterize American Judaism long after the uniformity of colonial synagogue life was forgotten. Within every community, even within many individual families, a full gamut of religious observances and attitudes could be found, a spectrum ranging all the way from deep piety to total indifference.

When it came to the Sabbath, for example, the wealthy Aaron Lopez "rigidly observed ... Saturday as holy time," closing from Friday afternoon to Monday morning. Over a three-year period for which we have records, none of his ships left port on a Saturday.[26] Many surviving colonial Jewish letters also reflect strict Sabbath observance, closing abruptly with comments like "Sabbath is coming on so fast"—writing would then be prohibited.[27] Visiting New York in the middle of the eighteenth century, the Swedish naturalist Peter Kalm heard that the city's pious Jews "never boiled any meal for themselves on Saturday, but that they always did it the day before, and that in winter they kept a fire during the whole Saturday."[28] On the other hand, Kalm also heard reports of Jewish ritual laxity. Indeed, evidence abounds that Jews were trading on the Sabbath and traveling in violation of its commandment to rest—so much so that Shearith Israel once threatened with excommunication wayward members who violated the Sabbath in these ways.[29] The most revealing of all accounts of Jewish Sabbath observance in the colonial period, however, comes from a missionary to the Delaware Indians named David McClure. Sometime in 1772, he spent a weekend in Lancaster and went with a business order on Saturday to the home of Joseph Simon, a prominent local Jewish merchant:

> [Simon] said, "Gentlemen, today is my Sabbath, & I do not do business in it; if you will please to call tomorrow, I will wait on you." We observed that the same reasons which prevented his payment of the order on that day would prevent our troubling him the day following [Sunday]. We apologized for our intruding on his Sabbath, & told him we would wait until Monday. He replied, you are on a journey, & it may be inconvenient to you to wait. He went to call in his neighbor, Dr. Boyd, & took from his Desk a bag, laid it on the table & presented the order to the Dr. The Doctor counted out the money and we gave a recipt. The Jew sat looking on, to see that all was rightly transacted, but said nothing, & thus quieted his conscience against the rebuke of a violation of his Sabbath.[30]

Simon's dilemma—torn between his Sabbath, his business, and what he saw as common courtesy—very much reflected what many an observant American Jew of his day experienced. His use of a surrogate to solve the problem failed to impress the missionary: "... he might as well have done the business himself," he groused. But what made Jewish life among the gentiles so difficult was that any solution would likely have been wrong; often Jewish law and American life simply proved irreconcilable. Jewish holidays, of course, posed similar problems.

Dietary laws posed an even greater problem for colonial Jews, for they were supposed to be observed at all times and had as their religious objective the goal of preventing precisely those kinds of social interactions with non-Jews that commerce and good neighborly relations demanded. Accurate statistics on colonial American Jewish observance of the dietary laws are unavailable. Even without them, however, we know that Jews defined themselves religiously through their practice of these laws; they were what they ate. Some labored to uphold the dietary laws wherever they were, while others quickly abandoned them. Still others, probably the majority, struggled somewhere in between. They maintained a double standard—one for home and one for outside—that effectively mirrored the bifurcated world they inhabited.

While private beliefs and practices defined Jews in British America religiously, and distinguished them from their Christian neighbors, social interactions in trade, in the street, and wherever else Jews and Christians gathered inevitably blurred these distinctions. The majority of Jews, especially in North America, resided in religiously pluralistic communities where people of diverse backgrounds and faiths, including many who had themselves experienced religious persecution, lived side by side. Perhaps for this reason, they felt more comfortable interacting with Christians than Jews did in most parts of the world—so much so that we know of Jews and Christians who joined forces in business, witnessed each other's documents, and socialized in each other's homes. Jews certainly faced continuing outbreaks of prejudice and persecution on account of their faith, and, legally speaking, in most colonies they remained second-class citizens. But from the very beginning of Jewish settlement, Jews and Christians also fell in love and married. This was an alarming development from the point of view of the Jewish community, which for religious and social reasons considered intermarriage anathema. It was also, however, a sure sign of the acceptance of Jews—particularly as only a small number of the Jews who intermarried converted to Christianity in order to do so.

Estimates of Jewish intermarriage in the colonial period range from 10 to 15 percent of all marriages, with men intermarrying more frequently than women, and those living far from their fellow Jews more likely to intermarry than those who lived near them. Available statistics leave many questions unanswered, chief among them whether the rate rose or fell over time. Still, the numbers are far lower than for some other religious groups of the day. New York City's French Huguenots, to take an extreme case, married non-Huguenots between 1750 and 1769 at a rate that exceeded 86 percent![31]

Colonial Jews mostly dealt with intermarriages on an ad hoc basis. Thus, when Phila Franks married the wealthy Huguenot merchant Oliver DeLancey in 1742, her pious, grief-stricken mother withdrew from the city and in traditional Jewish fashion resolved never to see her daughter again, "nor Lett none of the Family Goe near her." Her more politic husband, however, demurred: "Wee live in a Small place & he is Related to the best family in the place," he explained, and tried to promote reconciliation.[32] As a rule, intermarried Jews did sooner or later drift away from the Jewish community, but exceptions to this rule were not shunned, as they might well have been elsewhere. David Franks continued to maintain close social and economic ties to Jews. Benjamin Moses Clava was buried as a Jew. Samson Levy and Michael Judah had their non-Jewish children ritually circumcised, and half a dozen intermarried Jews numbered among the twenty original founders of the Shearith Israel Congregation in Montreal.[33] In each of these cases, a Jewish tradition that was uncompromising on the subject of intermarriage clashed with colonial society's more indulgent social norms. Caught between two realms that they strove mightily to keep separate, colonial Jews vacillated. Once again, Jewish law and American life proved difficult to reconcile.

By the time of the American Revolution, the pluralistic character of American religious life had begun to transform not only social relations between Jews and Christians, but also American Judaism itself. Where in so many other diaspora settings, including the Caribbean, Judaism stood all alone in religious dissent, in America it shared its status with many another minority faith. This forced Jews to change the very way that they thought about themselves; religious pluralism demanded that they reimagine who and what they were. While early on they defined themselves, akin to other Sephardim, as members of the Jewish or Portuguese "Nation," by the eve of the Revolution they more commonly spoke of themselves as members of a "religious society," on the model of parallel Christian religious societies, like the "Society of Friends" (Quakers). When Ezekiel Levy was hired in 1774 to serve as ritual slaughterer, reader, and teacher in Philadelphia, his contract was thus with the "Jewish Society" of that city, not as earlier contracts had read with the "Jewish Nation." Later, in 1783, when New York Jews wrote a formal letter of welcome to Governor George Clinton they used the same term. Revealingly, they juxtaposed "the Society, we Belong to" with "other Religious Societies," as if to underscore that Judaism stood on an equal footing with all the rest.[34]

This development, which as we have indicated was also very much influenced by the increasingly diverse and pluralistic character of North American Jewry—the large number of Ashkenazim and mixed Ashkenazi-Sephardi families—pointed to the growing distinctiveness of the North American Jewish community; increasingly, it was marching to the tune of its own drummer. Elsewhere, in Jamaica and Barbados, Judaism developed along British lines, maintaining for as long as possible the traditions that characterized Anglo-Jewry in the eighteenth century. By contrast, in the wake of the American Revolution, Judaism in the United States, heavily influenced by democratization and American Protestantism, developed during the half-century following independence a character all its own—one that had been anticipated in significant respects already in the colonial era.

Notes

1. Jacob R. Marcus, *The Colonial American Jew, 1492–1776* (Detroit, 1970), 954; *Publications of the American Jewish Historical Society* 34 (1934):70; *The Literary Diary of Ezra Stiles*, ed. Franklin B. Dexter, vol. 1 (New York, 1901), 19; Gershom Scholem, *Sabbatai Sevi: The Mystical Messiah* (Princeton, 1973), 594–95. I am grateful to Jonathan Schorsch for this last reference.

2. *American Jewish Archives* 7 (1955):17–23, 56; *American Jewish History* 80 (1990):22; David de Sola Pool, *Portraits Etched in Stone* (New York, 1952), 188; *American Jewish Historical Quarterly* 54 (1965):247; Morris Gutstein, *The Story of the Jews of Newport* (New York, 1936), 94; David Brener, "Lancaster's First Jewish Community 1715–1804: The Era of Joseph Simon," *Journal of the Lancaster County Historical Society* 80 (1976):232; Joshua Trachtenberg, *Consider the Years: The Story of the Jewish Community of Easton, 1752–1942* (Easton, 1944), 31.

3. Marcus, *Colonial American Jew*, 402; Leo Hershkowitz, "The Mill Street Synagogue Reconsidered," *American Jewish Historical Quarterly* 53 (1964):408.

4. Arnold Wiznitzer, "The Merger Agreement and Regulations of Congregation Talmud Torah of Amsterdam (1638–39)," *Historia Judaica* 20 (1958):109–32; Daniel Swetschinski, "The Portuguese Jewish Merchants of 17th-Century Amsterdam," (Ph.D. diss., Brandeis University, 1980), 337–66; Miriam Bodian, "The *Escamot* of the Spanish-Portuguese Jewish Community of London, 1664," *Michael* 9 (1985):12–13. The Ashkenazi community in Amsterdam established its own congregation in 1635; see Yosef Kaplan, "The Portuguese Community in 17th-Century Amsterdam and the Ashkenazi World," *Dutch Jewish History* 2 (1989):29.

5. Marcus, *Colonial American Jew*, 855–1110; Leo Hershkowitz, ed., *Letters of the Franks Family (1733–1748)* (Waltham, 1968), 60.

6. Herman P. Salomon, "K. K. Shearith Israel's First Language: Portuguese," *Tradition* 30 (1995):74–84.

7. Lionel D. Barnett, ed., *El Libro de los Acuerdos* (Oxford, 1931), 3; H. P. Salomon, "Joseph Jesurun Pinto (1729–1782): A Dutch Hazan in Colonial New York," *Studia Rosenthaliana* 13 (1979):18–29.

8. *Publications of the American Jewish Historical Society* [=*PAJHS*] 21 (1913):50–51, 84.

9. John B. Kirby, "Early American Politics—The Search for Ideology: An Historiographical Analysis and Critique of the Concept of Deference," *Journal of Politics* 32 (1970): 808–38; J. A. Pocock, "The Classical Theory of Deference," *American Historical Review* 81 (1976):516–23.

10. Barnett, *El Libro*, 15; Zvi Loker, *Jews in the Caribbean* (Jerusalem, 1991), 41.

11. Richard W. Pointer, *Protestant Pluralism and the New York Experience* (Bloomington, 1988), 13–15.

12. Hyman B. Grinstein, *The Rise of the Jewish Community of New York* (Philadelphia, 1945), 84–87; Marcus, *Colonial American Jew*, 928–34.

13. Isaac S. Emmanuel and Suzanne A. Emmanuel, *History of the Jews of the Netherlands Antilles* (Cincinnati, 1970), 544; Judah Cohen, "Documents Concerning the Jews of the Virgin Islands" (private collection); Gérard Nahon, "From New Christians to the Portuguese Jewish Nation in France," in *Moreshet Sepharad: The Sephardi Legacy*, ed. Haim Beinart, vol. 2 (Jerusalem, 1992), 248.

14. Barnett, *El Libro*, 11.

15. Yosef Kaplan, "Deviance and Excommunication in the Eighteenth Century: A Chapter in the Social History of the Sephardi Community of Amsterdam," *Dutch Jewish History* 3 (1993):103.

16. The minutes are reprinted in *PAJHS* 21 (1913):74–76.

17. Jon Butler, *Awash in a Sea of Faith: Christianizing the American People* (Cambridge, 1990), 173–74.

18. Ibid., 113–16.

19. Rachel Wischnitzer, *Synagogue Architecture in the United States* (Philadelphia, 1955), 11–19; Carol Herselle Krinsky, *Synagogues of Europe: Architecture, History, Meaning* (Cambridge, 1985), 412–15.

20. Jonathan D. Sarna, "Seating and the American Synagogue," in *Belief and Behavior: Essays in the New Religious History*, ed. Philip R. Vandermeer and Robert P. Swierenga (New Brunswick, N.J., 1991), 189–94; Arnold Wiznitzer, *The Records of the Earliest Jewish Community in the New World* (New York, 1954), 17; Barnett, *El Libro*, 4; David and Tamar de Sola Pool, *An Old Faith in the New World: Portrait of Shearith Israel 1654–1954* (New York, 1955), 44.

21. Jacob R. Marcus, *Studies in American Jewish History* (Cincinnati, 1969), 50; Pool, *Portraits*, 169–73.

22. *PAJHS* 27 (1920):4.

23. Eli Faber, *A Time for Planting: The First Migration* (Baltimore, 1992), 64; Malcolm H. Stern and Marc D. Angel, *New York's Early Jews: Some Myths and Misconceptions* (New York, 1976).

24. Stanley F. Chyet, *Lopez of Newport* (Detroit, 1970), 173.

25. Todd Endelman, *The Jews of Georgian England 1714–1830* (Philadelphia, 1979).

26. Gutstein, *Jews of Newport*, 132; Chyet, *Lopez of Newport*, 158.

27. Jacob R. Marcus, *American Jewry: Documents: Eighteenth Century* (Cincinnati, 1969), 265.

28. Reprinted in Oscar Handlin, *This Was America* (New York, 1964), 32.

29. Grinstein, *Jewish Community Life of New York*, 334; Marcus, *Colonial American Jew*, 956–57.

30. "Lancaster in 1772," *Journal of the Lancaster County Historical Society* 5 (1901):108–9.

31. Malcolm H. Stern, "The Function of Genealogy in American Jewish History," in *Essays in American Jewish History* (Cincinnati, 1958), 85; Marcus, *Colonial American Jew*, 1232; Jon Butler, *The Huguenots in America* (Cambridge, 1983), 187.

32. Hershkowitz, *Letters of the Franks Family*, 116–25.

33. Stern, "Function of Genealogy," 94–97; Marcus, *Colonial American Jew*, 1225–35; Sheldon J. Godfrey and Judith C. Godfry, *Search Out the Land: The Jews and the Growth of Equality in British Colonial America, 1740–1867* (Montreal, 1995), 294n. 14.

34. Marcus, *American Jewry*, 104; Morris U. Schappes, *A Documentary History of the Jews of the United States, 1654–1875* (New York, 1971), 67.

NOTES ON CONTRIBUTORS

Solange Alberro, who earned her Doctorat d'Etat from the Sorbonne, is professor and researcher at the Centro de Estudios Históricos de El Colegio de México and director of *Historia Mexicana*. She is the author of several books including *Inquisición y Sociedad en México, 1571–1700* (1988) and *El Aguila y la Cruz. Orígenes religiosos de la Conciencia Criolla* (1999).

Mordechai Arbell, Research Fellow at the Ben Zvi Institute for the Study of Jewish Communities, Hebrew University of Jerusalem, sits on the board of the Museum of the Jewish Diaspora, Tel Aviv, and has served as ambassador or consul from Israel to Panama, Haiti, Colombia, Korea, and Turkey. His publications include *La Nacion, the Spanish-Portuguese Jews of the Caribbean* (1981) and *Spanish and Portuguese Jews in the Caribbean and the Guianas: A Bibliography* (1999).

Paolo Bernardini earned a doctoral degree from the European University Institute in Florence, Italy, and has held academic and research positions in Germany, England, France, Israel, and the United States, including fellowships at the John Carter Brown Library and the Institute for Advanced Study in Princeton, New Jersey. The author of six books, he is presently teaching at the Institute for International Studies, University of Technology, in Sydney, Australia. Among Dr. Bernardini's publications are: *La questione ebraica nel tardo illuminismo tedesco* (1992) and *La sfida dell'uguaglianza. Gli ebrei a Mantova nell'età della rivoluzione francese* (1996).

Günter Böhm is Professor of History and co-founder and director of the Center for Jewish Studies at the Universidad de Chile, Santiago. In addition to some two hundred articles, he has published nine books, including *Los Sefardíes en los dominios holandeses de América del Sur y del Caribe, 1630–1750* (1992); *Historia de los Judíos en Chile: El Bachiller Francisco Maldonado de Silva* (1984); and *Los Judíos en Chile durante la Colonia* (1948).

James C. Boyajian earned a Ph.D. from the University of California at Berkeley. The recipient of several grants, including two from the National Endowment for the Humanities, he has published numerous articles and two monographs: *Portuguese Trade in Asia under the Habsburgs, 1580–1640* (1993) and *Portuguese Bankers at the Court of Spain* (1983). He is currently engaged in a study of family and economic history of New Christians and Sephardim from 1500 to 1700.

Seymour Drescher is University Professor of History and Professor of Sociology at the University of Pittsburgh and a past secretary of the Woodrow Wilson Center for Scholars in Washington, D.C. He is the author of *Econocide: British Slavery in the Era of Abolition* (1977), *Capitalism and Antislavery: British Mobilization in Comparative Perspective* (1986), and *From Slavery to Freedom: Comparative Studies in the Rise and Fall of Atlantic Slavery* (1999). He has also co-edited several works, including *A Historical Guide to World Slavery* (with Stanley L. Engerman, 1998).

Noah J. Efron founded and heads the Program for the History and Philosophy of Science and Ideas at Bar Ilan University. He recently edited a special volume of *Science in Context* about Jews and science in early modern Europe and is at present completing a book about Jews, Christians, and natural philosophy in Rudolfine Prague. Efron is also a contributing writer for the *Boston Book Review*.

Pieter Emmer is a professor at the University of Leiden, The Netherlands, specializing in the history of European expansion. He has published extensively on the history of the Dutch slave trade, slavery, and migration. His latest book is *The Dutch in the Atlantic Economy, 1580–1880: Trade, Slavery, and Emancipation* (1998).

Norman Fiering has been Director and Librarian of the John Carter Brown Library since 1983. For eleven years he was editor of publications at the Omohundro Institute of Early American History and Culture in Williamsburg, Virginia. He is the author of *Moral Philosophy at Seventeenth-Century Harvard: A Discipline in Transition* and *Jonathan Edwards's Moral Thought and Its British Context*, both published in 1981.

Rachel Frankel, a former Peace Corps volunteer in Togo, West Africa, with a master's degree in architecture from Harvard University's Graduate School of Design, opened her own architectural office in New York in 1996. Since 1994, she has been researching, documenting, and preserving the architectural remains and history of the Jodensavanne settlement in Suriname. The winner of numerous design competitions, she has exhibited throughout the United States and published extensively.

John D. Garrigus is Professor of History at Jacksonville University in Jacksonville, Florida. He has published a number of articles on pre-revolutionary Haiti and is working on a book manuscript about conditions leading to the Haitian revolution.

Jonathan I. Israel is a permanent member of the School of Historical Studies at the Institute for Advanced Study in Princeton, N.J. His *Race, Class, and Politics in Colonial Mexico, 1610–1670*, based on his Ph.D. thesis at Oxford and the Colegio de México, appeared in 1975. Subsequently, he has written mainly on Dutch-Spanish topics as well as on Jewish history. His *European Jewry in the Age of Mercantilism, 1550–1750*, first appeared in 1985 and won the Wolfson Literary Prize for history the following year. He is a member of the British Academy and a Corresponding Member of the Royal Netherlands Academy of Sciences.

David S. Katz is Abraham Horodisch Professor for the History of Books at Tel-Aviv University in Israel. His publications include *The Jews in the History of England, 1485–1850* (1994) and (with Richard H. Popkin) *Messianic Revolution* (1999). His research has concentrated on the boundaries between Christianity and Judaism, and he is now working on a history of the English Bible and a study of the occult tradition between the Renaissance and Fundamentalism.

Wim Klooster, Assistant Professor of History at the University of Southern Maine, earned his doctorate at the University of Leiden. He was a Fulbright Fellow and an Alexander O. Vietor Memorial Research Fellow at the John Carter Brown Library in 1995–96 and a Charles Warren Fellow at Harvard University in 1997–98. He is the author of *The Dutch in the Americas, 1600–1800* (1997) and *Illicit Riches: Dutch Trade in the Caribbean, 1648–1795* (1998).

Silvia Marzagalli holds a Ph.D. from the European University Institute in Florence and is *maître de conférences* at the University "Michel de Montaigne" in Bordeaux, France. She has published a number of articles on the commercial and maritime history of the eighteenth and early nineteenth centuries and is the author of *"Les boulevards de la fraude." Le négoce maritime et le Blocus continental, 1806–1813. Bordeaux, Hambourg, Livourne* (1999).

Gérard Nahon is Directeur d'Etudes in the area of medieval and modern Judaism at the Ecole Pratique des Hautes Etudes, Paris. A former president of the Société des Etudes Juives, he served from 1980 to 1996 as editor of the *Revue des Etudes Juives*. He is the author, co-author, or editor of numerous books, including *Rashi et la culture juive en France du Nord au moyen âge* (1997), *La Terre sainte au temps des Kabbalistes, 1492–1592* (1997), *Métropoles et périphéries sefarades d'Occident. Kairouan, Amsterdam, Bayonne, Bordeaux, Jérusalem* (1993), and *Inscriptions hébraïques et juives de France médiévale* (1986).

Anita Novinsky is an Associate Professor in Brazilian history at the University of São Paulo. The author of numerous articles in books, journals, and encyclopedias, she has also published several monographs, including

A Inquisição (1995), *Cristãos-Novos na Bahia* (1972), *Rol dos Culpados* (1992), and *Inquisição. Bens confiscados a Cristãos-Novos no Brasil, século XVIII* (1978). In 1987–88 she was a research fellow at the John Carter Brown Library.

Geraldo Pieroni holds a doctorate in history from the Sorbonne. A member of the history department at the University of Brasilia, he is currently engaged in research on the Portuguese Inquisition and the Brazil colony. He is the author of *Les exclus du Royaume: l'inquisition portugaise et le bannissement au Brésil, XVIIe siècle* (1996) and *Purgatório colonial: inquisição portuguesa e degredo no Brasil* (1994).

Ernst Pijning, an Assistant Professor at Minot State University in North Dakota, earned his Ph.D. in history from the Johns Hopkins University with a dissertation entitled "Controlling Contraband: Mentality, Economy and Society in Eighteenth-Century Rio de Janeiro." He has recently begun a study of the diamond trade between Brazil and Amsterdam during the eighteenth century.

James Romm, who has taught at Cornell University and Fordham University, is a Professor of Classics at Bard College. In 1993 he held a National Endowment for the Humanities Fellowship at the John Carter Brown Library. Since the publication of his first book, *The Edges of the Earth in Ancient Thought* (1992), he has completed a monograph on Herodotus as well as a series of articles on the Renaissance debate over Greco-Roman discoveries of the Americas. He is currently researching ancient Greek ideas about India and their influence on the European view of the New World.

Robert Rowland, Professor of Anthropology at ISCTE in Lisbon, previously held the Chair of European Social History at the European University Institute, Florence, and served as director of the Historical Sociology Unit at the Gulbenkian Institute of Science in Oeiras, Portugal. He has published widely in the fields of historical anthropology and social history, with particular reference to South European demography and family history, the history of the Portuguese Inquisition, and the methodology of research computing. His latest book is *População, Família, Sociedade (Portugal, Séculos XIX–XX)* (1997).

Jonathan D. Sarna is the Joseph H. and Belle R. Braun Professor of American Jewish History and Chair of the Department of Near Eastern and Judaic Studies at Brandeis University. He has held fellowships from the American Council of Learned Societies and the National Endowment for the Humanities. He is the author, editor, or co-editor of sixteen books, including *Minority Faiths and the American Protestant Mainstream* (1997), *Religion and State in the American Jewish Experience* (with David Dalin, 1997), *JPS: The Americanization of Jewish Culture* (1989), and *Jacksonian Jew: The Two Worlds of Mordecai Noah* (1981).

Benjamin Schmidt is an Assistant Professor of History at the University of Washington in Seattle. His publications include *Innocence Abroad: The Dutch Imagination and the Representation of the New World* (forthcoming) and numerous articles pertaining to early modern cultural history and the development of geography in the Renaissance. He has held fellowships from the National Endowment for the Humanities and from the Ahmanson and Getty Foundations.

Patricia Seed, Professor of History at Rice University, is the author of *Ceremonies of Possession in Europe's Conquest of the New World, 1492–1640* (1995) and of a web site on virtual cartography and the history of navigation.

Eva Alexandra Uchmany, professor and researcher at the Universidad Nacional Autónoma de México, was awarded the 1992 Fernando Jeno International Prize for her book *Life between Judaism and Christianity in New Spain, 1580–1606* (1992). She was a Fulbright Scholar in 1982, and in 1997 a Center for New World Comparative Studies Fellow at the John Carter Brown Library. Her most recent book is *Mexico—India: Similarities and Encounters throughout History* (1998).

Nathan Wachtel is Professor at the Collège de France and Directeur d'Etudes at the Ecole des Hautes Etudes en Sciences Sociales, Paris. The founder and director of the Centre de recherches sur les Mondes américains at the French Centre National de Recherche Scientifique, he has since 1998 served as director of the CNRS Laboratory of Social Anthropology. Of his numerous publications, those translated into English include *Dieux et vampires. Retour à Chipaya* (1992; English translation, 1994); *Le retour des ancêtres. Les Indiens Urus de Bolivie, XXè–XVIè siècle. Essai d'histoire régressive* (1990); *Mémoires juives* (with Lucette Valensi, 1986; English translation, 1993); and *La vision des vaincus. Les Indiens du Pérou devant la Conquête espagnole (1530–1570)* (1971; English translation, 1977).

James Homer Williams, who earned his doctorate at Vanderbilt University, is an Associate Professor of History at Middle Tennessee State University. In 1998–99 he was a National Endowment for the Humanities Fellow at the Newberry Library. He is completing a book, to be entitled *The Cultural Struggle for the Early Mid-Atlantic Colonies*, and has published several articles about the colony of New Netherland. He is a member of the executive committee of the Forum on European Expansion and Global Interaction.

Name Index

Boxer, C. R., 102n, 239n, 349n, 376, 389n, 390n, 463n, 498n, 499n
Boyajian, James C., 17, 23n, 66n, 465n, 468n, 482n, 484n, 515n
Bozio, Thomas, 43, 44, 45n
Brackman, Harold, 461n, 462n
Brahe, Tycho, 61
Brakel, S. van, 349n
Brandeau, Esther, 261, 267n
Brandon, Joseph, 261
Brasil, Ana da Costa do, 482n
Brasil, Diogo Fernandes do, 478
Brasil, Simão Rodrigues do, 478
Braude, Benjamin, 45n
Braudel, Fernand, 11, 482n
Bréard, Jacques-Michel, 279
Brites, Maria, 245
Brito, Francisco Tavares de, 239n
Brochado, Costa, 85n
Brodie, Fawn M., 120n
Bromley, J. S., 103n
Brooke, J. L., 120n
Brooke, Nathaniel, 434n
Brouwer, Hendrick, 94, 95
Brown, Larissa V., 499n
Brunner, Otto, 9
Bruno, Giordano, 3
Bruyn, J., 101n
Bubberman, F. C., 364n
Buddingh, Bernard R., 365n
Bueno (family), 294
Buffon, Georges Louis Leclerc Comte de, 12, 323
Burgos, Baltazar de, 159
Burnard, Trevor, 452, 467n
Buron, Edmond, 44n
Butel, Paul, 283n, 284n, 286n, 328n, 329n, 330n
Butler, Jon, 524, 530n
Butler, Richard Grint, 116, 118
Butterfield, Herbert, 85n

C
Caballería, Marina de la, 191
Cabot, Sebastian, 71n
Cabral, Pedro Alvares, 80, 244
Cáceres y Osorio, Isabel, 205
Caceres, Antonio Diaz de, 151
Cáceres, Diego García de, 205
Caceres, Leonor de, 151
Cahen, Abraham, 264n, 265n, 267n, 283n, 284n, 301, 310n, 329n
Caldeirâo, Diogo Dias, 247
Calmon, Joâo, 250
Calvo, Salomon, 367n

Cameron, Don Allen, 45n
Camões, Luís de, 85n
Campbell, Mary, 45n
Campen, Nicolaes van, 373
Campos (family), 177
Campos, Antônio Rodrigues, 227
Campos, Maria de, 163, 170n
Canny, Nicholas, 470n
Capotte, Jacob Mendes, 262, 267n
Capsali, Eliahu, 67n
Caraci Luzzana, Ilaria, 68n
Caravallo, Antonio de, 166n
Cardado, Antonio Fernandez, 151, 152, 155f, 166n
Cardoso Porto, Antônio (Melchior Mendes Correa), 221
Cardoso, Ignacio Dias, 220
Cardoso, Joseph Rodrigues, 227
Cardosso, Jussurun Moses, 259, 266n
Cardoze, David, 331n
Cardoze, Sara, 259
Cardozo, Abraham Lopes, 435n
Cardozo, Aron de David Uziel, 367n
Cardozo, Irma, 435n
Cardozo, Isaac, 305
Cardozo, Manuel S., 500n
Carena, Cesare, 146n
Carothers, Robert L., 389n
Carpenter, Rhys, 44n
Carrera, José Miguel, 205
Carvaillo Frois, Rachel, 258
Carvajal (family), 177, 180, 193
Carvajal, Luis de (El Mozo), 151, 157, 196
Carvalho, Flavio Mendes de, 220, 221, 239n
Carvalho, Francisco Tinoco de, 479
Carvallo, Isaac Nunes, 258
Casseres, de (family), 354
Casseres, Benjamin de, 365n
Casteloblanco, Antonio Vaez, 155, 162f, 167n, 170n
Castillo, Francisco Fernández del, 201n
Castres, A., 500n
Castries (Marechal of), 324
Castro y Tosi, Norberto, 201n
Castro, Abigail Henriquez de, 306
Castro, Carlos Larrain de, 203, 212n
Castro, Francisco Mendes de, 219
Castro, Henri de, 263
Castro, Jacob Henriques de, 256, 265n
Castro, Jacob, 329n
Castro, João de, 81, 83
Castro, Joseph Henriquez de, 305
Castro, María Ana de, 210
Castro, Moïse Henriquez, 263
Cato, 34

Seixas, Gershom, 526
Selim I (Ottoman Emperor), 55
Seneca, 29, 32
Senior, David, 367n
Sequeyra (family), 277
Sergio, Antonio, 240n
Serra, Antonio-João Simoes, 264n
Serrano y Sanz, Manuel, 200n
Serrão, José Vicente, 500n
Sestieri, Lea, 147n
Sevilla, Simon Vaez, 152f, 155, 158, 162f,
  168n, 169n, 179, 180, 181, 195, 199.
  See also Vaez
Shapin, Steven, 85n
Shaw, L. M. E., 515n
Sheinin, David, 389n
Shelford, April, 67n, 45n
Shem, 27, 34, 36, 107
Shupe, A., 122n
Sibyl (prophet), 36
Silber, Mendel, 66n
Siliceo, Juan Martinez, 165
Sille, Nicasius de, 382
Silva, Antonio da, 239n
Silva, António José da, 142
Silva, David da, 329n
Silva, David Mendes da, 227
Silva, Diego Núñez de, 206
Silva, Francisco Maldonado de.
  See Maldonado
Silva, Gabriel da, 273, 283n
Silva, Gabriel Rodriguez, 257
Silva, Jacob Pereira da. *See* Pereira da Silva.
Silva, Jacob, 257, 265n
Silva, Joseph David Gabriel da, 281
Silva, Juan Rodríguez de, 193
Silva, Lina Gorenstein Ferreira da.
  See Ferreira da Silva
Silva, Pedro Maldonado de. *See* Maldonado
  de Silva
Silveira, Manuel do Valle da, 482n
Silveyra, Abraham, 261
Simoes. *See* Serra
Simon, Joseph, 527
Simon, Richard, 3
Sims, Harold, 469n
Sinke, Suzanne M., 515n
Siqueira, Sonia A., 493, 500n
Siraisi, Nancy, 45n, 67n
Slinkard, Beth, 389n
Smidt, J. Th., 364n
Smith, David Grant, 464n, 465n, 488,
  492, 499n
Smith, Gerald L. K., 116, 348n
Smith, Joseph, 110, 111, 120n

Smith, Pamela, 467n
Smith, Roger C., 85n
Smolowe, J., 121n
Soares, Baltasar, 247, 251n
Soares, Inês, 247
Sobel, Dava, 85n
Sobremonte, Thomas Treviño Martínez de.
  See Treviño
Socolow, Susan M., 499n
Soeiro (family), 104n
Sola, Isaac Mendès de, 259
Solar, Aron de Castro, 257, 265n
Solomon (king), 4, 27–29, 31, 37, 40–42, 45n,
  60f, 64, 398
Solow, Barbara L. 461n, 500n
Sombart, Werner, 10, 283n, 439f, 462n, 464n
Sordis, 304
Sossa, Isaac (Souza, Izaac), 262, 267n
Sousa-Leão, Joaquim de, 101n
Souza, Beatriz de, 482n
Souza, Ishac de Selomoh Abarbanel, 258
Souza, Jeronimo Rodrigues de (Samuel
  Abrabanel), 473
Souza, Margarida de, 245
Souza, Tomé de, 492, 499n
Soza, Isacq Rodriquez, 258
Soza, Jacob Henriques, 258
Sperling, John G., 469n
Spinoza, Baruch, 100, 365n
Spranger, Querin, 296f
St. Juste, Laurore, 312n
Stedman, John Gabriel, 299, 311n
Stein, Robert Louis, 467n
Stern, Malcolm H., 460, 531n
Stiles, Ezra, 520
Stillman, Yedida K., 202n
Stipriaan, Alex van, 364n, 434n
Stols, Eddy, 515n
Stow, Kenneth R., 146n
Strauss, Walter, 101n
Strelick, Arthur, 409
Stuarts (Kings of England), 343
Stuyvesant, Peter, 15, 344s, 370, 378f, 383f,
  388, 391n, 392n, 467n
Suarès, Abraham, 258
Suarez, Moïse, 262, 267n
Suliman (Ottoman Emperor), 55
Sweet, Leonard I., 70n
Swetschinski, Daniel M., 103n, 374,
  390n, 464n, 465n, 466n, 470n, 499n,
  530n
Swierenga, Robert P., 392n, 531n, 469n
Swift, Lesley A., 121n
Swift, Wesley, 116
Szajkowski, Zosa, 284n, 285n, 286n

PLACE INDEX

351; and the slave trade, 454, 457; and the sugar trade, 480
Jeremie, 305
Jerusalem, 30, 33, 37, 110f, 113, 261, 372, 402
Jodensavanne, 336, 351f

K
Kingston, 454

L
La Guaira, 337, 358, 366n
La Mancha, 151
La Rochelle (Suriname), 256, 299
Labastide-Clairance, 255
Labrador, 256
Lamego, 134
Lancaster (U.S.A.), 520, 527
Leogan, 301, 304
Les Cayes, 305, 306
Lima, 146n, 153, 161, 167n, 193, 198, 202n, 203, 205–11
Limbé, 304
Limoeiro, 243
Lisbon, 73, 153, 218; Church control in, 507; Inquisition in, 134f, 161, 226f, 242–48 *passim*, 487, 496; navigation studies in, 77; New Christians in, 142; persecutions of Jews in, 53, 132; and the sugar trade, 471ff; trade with, 340f, 477–80, 511. *See also* Portugal
Lithuania, 443
Liverpool (England), 120n
Livorno (Leghorn), 158, 184, 195, 297, 341, 359, 372, 385, 396
Llerena, 146n
Logroño, 146n
London, 15, 110, 113, 116, 138, 148n, 257f, 280, 282, 481, 505, 521, 523, 525f
Long Island, 384
Lorraine, 271
Los Angeles, 115f
Louisiana, 256, 274
Low Countries, 92, 172, 198, 371, 506

M
Macao, 195
Madeira, 81, 96, 104n, 340, 356, 372, 472f, 486f, 506
Madrid, 153, 167n, 181, 185n, 194, 207ff, 212n, 343f, 479
Maghreb, 172
Majorca, 77, 143, 146n
Malacca, 195
Manhattan, 370, 384, 386ff, 413
Manila, 472, 480

Mantova (Mantua), 19, 48, 59
Maracaibo, 338, 353, 358
Margarita, 357
Mariana, 223
Marie Galante, 289
Marseilles, 281, 356
Martinique, 12, 255ff, 268, 273–78, 280, 287f, 306, 316f, 353, 356
Medellin, 91
Medina, 263
Melaku (island), 80
Mers el Kebir, 297
Metz, 470n
Mexico City, 180, 190, 193f, 199, 202n, 208
Mexico. *See* New Spain
Michoacán, 188
Milano (Milan), 480
Minas Gerais, 10, 215, 217, 219f, 222f, 226f, 229f, 240n, 493
Missouri, 111
Montana, 121n
Monte-mor-o-Novo, 248
Montreal, 529
Moral, 151
Moriah, 261
Morocco, 385, 510
Moron, 309
Münster, 343
Murcia, 146n, 187

N
Nancy, 304
Nantes, 304, 320
Nassau, 88, 94
Ndembu (region), 446
Netherlands, The (Holland), 4, 16, 21, 86–101 *passim*, 105n, 208, 218, 282, 365n, 393n, 462n; colonies of, in America, 350–60 *passim*; colonies of, and Spanish policy, 344; Jews in colonies of, 273ff, 298; rise to world power of, 508–12; synagogues in, 422; and the slave trade, 443, 447f, 450; and the sugar trade, 471f, 480, 491; tolerance of Jews in colonies of, 339–41, 370–88 *passim*. *See also* Low Countries
Nevis, 519
New Amsterdam (New York), 15, 344, 369, 388, 520
New England, 384, 503
New France, 268, 278
New Granada, 91, 97, 174f, 356
New Guinea, 486
New Holland, 342
New Jersey, 116

Subject Index

A

Adamites, 118. *See also* pre-Adamitic people
affranchis, 305. *See also* slaves
agriculture, 291; abolition of slavery and, 504; agro-industry and, 291; Brazilian plantation economy and, 503; cacao and sugar plantations, 317; Catholic planters and, 342; Jewish role in the Caribbean and, 352, 513f; Dutch sugar refineries and, 491; evolution of, in Suriname, 336, 350ff, 423; involvement of New Christians in, 493; slave operated, 459f; and cultivation of sugar cane, 291, 336; and sugar growing in Haiti, 301; and sugar mills in Brazil, 473; tobacco production and, 288; and tropical products, 287, 296
American dream, 260ff
American Judaism, 21
Antiqua Iudaeorum Improbitas, 128
anti-Semitism, 21. *See also* toleration, race, racism
Aristotelianism, 77
art and representations of the New World, 88f
Aryan race, 119
Ashkenazim, 525
asientos. See slave trade
assimilation, 186, 269f; Catholicism and, 245; rejection of, by Portuguese Jews, 192; in Brazil, 218
astrolabe, 77, 79
astronomical techniques, 79f
Atlantis (myth of), 35
aubaines, 321
auto-da-fé, 137, 198; in Lima, 209–11; in Portugal, 242, 247. *See also* exile, Inquisition

B

banishment, 84, 172f; of New Christians, 10; from Cap-Français, 308; from Spain and Portugal, 53, 465, 242f. *See also* exile, Inquisition

Baptists, 525. *See also* Protestantism, Protestants
baroque poetry, 5
bezerrinha de prata, 143
Bible: division of the world according to, 107f; exegesis of, 3; geography in, 28f; landscape painting and, 86f; Latin translation of, 28f; Mormons attitude toward, 111; narratives, 88; Polyglot, 37. *See also* messianism, millennialism, prophecy, Ophir, Solomon's travels
Bible Society, 114
bigamists, 244
Black Code. *See Code noir*
blacks, conversion to Judaism of, 404
blasphemy, 157
book of nature, 81
bosnegroes, 423
British Israelite movement: and anti-Semitism, 116; Aryan Nations and, 119; origins of, 115
British merchants, 19
burial, 259. *See also* cemeteries

C

Calvinism, 15, 373, 385. *See also* Protestantism, Protestants, West India Company
Caminho novo, 218
Cape North Company, 295
carreira da Índia, 478
castas, 175
cemeteries: at Cassipora, 409; Suriname and rabbinical rules regarding, 422; in Jodensavanne, 394ff; Ouderkerk, 409. *See also* burial
Children of Satan, 117f
Christian Aryanism, 119. *See also* British Israelite movement
Christianization, 175, 187
Christology, 153
citizenship, 314, 322ff, 386. *See also* French Revolution, toleration

marranism, 142; agnosticism and, 10; in Brazil, 229f; Christian majority and, 182; definition of, 150f; divisions among family members and, 151; evolution of, 182f; fasting and, 160f; features of, 183f; forms of prayers of, 228f; lack of religious authorities for, 173; learning and, 227; Messianism and, 161f; as multifaceted phenomenon, 226; origins of, in New Spain, 172; and reconversion to Christianity, 297; relativism and, 165; reversion to Judaism and, 297; and religiosity, 150, 157f; rituals of, 178; skepticism in, 230; syncretic aspects of, 164. *See also* crypto-Jews, crypto-Judaism, dual identity, identity, Inquisition, marranos, New Christians

marranos: in Brazil, 215f; their knowledge of Inquisitorial practices, 225. *See also* crypto-Jews, crypto-Judaism, dual identity, identity, Inquisition, marranism, marrano religiosity, New Christians

martyrdom, and Jews in Europe, 55

massacres of Jews, 130f; at Capão da Traição, 219; at Lisbon, 1506, 133

"Meditatio Cordis," 242

merchants: in Bordeaux, 269; Jewish, in the Caribbean colonies, 450; Jewish, in the English West Indies, 452; in the Caribbean, 338. *See also* economy, merchant community, New Christians, trade, West India Company

messianism: among Mexican New Christians, 161; architecture and, 423; chronology and, 163; as redemption in history, 193; and millennialism, 5; Dutch culture and, 94; the New Messiah and, 196; in Eastern Europe, 99; Farissol's accounts of, 53. *See also* Bible, messianism, prophecy

minhag, 522

mixed marriage, 133, 135. *See also* intermarriage

modernity, emergence of, in the Western Hemisphere, 164

modernization, the role of New Christians in, 216f

Mohammedanism, 130. *See also* Inquisition, Muslims

monotheism, diffusion of, 36

Mormons, 9, 110f. *See also* Bible, Protestantism, Protestants

mulattos, 315

Muslims: and science, 74f; fight of, against the Jews, 50; and scientific competition with the Jews, 83. *See also* Mohammedanism

N

nation: concept of, 372; Hebrew, in Holland, 374; Jewish, 1; meaning of, as referred to the Jews, 522; Portuguese, 92; Portuguese-Jewish, 92; Sephardim of Amsterdam as, 100. *See also Hebreeusche Natie*

National Legion, 321

Native Americans: Columbus's views on, 33. *See also* Indians

natural philosophy, 60

navigation, 41; and early modern instruments, 74. *See also* science, trade

New Christians: and agnosticism, 11; Asian trade of, 471, 477; Atlantic system and, 456; beliefs of, 88f, 155; in Brazil, 220, 223f; and Catholicism, 150, 249, 272f; classification of, 135ff; at the time of the Conquest, 189f; commercial networks of, 186f, 473, 506; crypto-Judaism, 1, 145; defense strategies of, 138, 224f; economic impact of, 479; in France, 270f; in French colonies, 287; and the gold rush in Brazil, 215; and the Great Plot, 163; and identity, 8, 165, 190; Inquisition and, 126f; and intermarriage, 133; Judaism and, 244; and literature, 193; in Madeira, 487; and New Whites, 314; and Old Christians, 149, 191ff, 495ff; persecution of, 143, 496; in Peru, 203ff; in Portugal, 135, 444f; and the Sabbath, 178; and the slave trade, 17; and social status, 18, 486ff; in Spain, 145; and sugar cultivation, 465; women among, 177. *See also* agriculture, crypto-Jews, crypto-Judaism, Inquisition, identity, marranism, marranos, trade

New Spain, society in, 176

"New Whites," 13, 323–27. *See also* race, racism

O

Ophir, 38ff; political significance of, 41. *See also* Bible, Solomon's travels

P

Padrón de Conversos, 187

panos pretos, 478

Paradise: discovery of, 33; location of, 50. *See also* Bible, geography

pardos, 223

W

West India Company (WIC), 93, 95, 99, 342, 380, 510; and Brazil, 99, 341; and Jewish private trade, 344f; and toleration, 377; New Netherlands and, 383f; policies of, in New Amsterdam, 379; and relations with the Jewish community of Amsterdam, 381; and slaving monopoly in the Atlantic, 448. *See also* slave trade, toleration, trade

witchcraft, 127. *See also* Inquisition

X

Xuetes, 143

Y

Yehidim, 522
Yom Hakkipurim, 196